The User's Guide to College Writing
Reading, Analyzing, and Writing

Nancy M. Kreml
Diane Rose Carr
Douglas Capps
Janice Jake
Sharon May

Midlands Technical College

Longman

New York   San Francisco   Boston
London   Toronto   Sydney   Tokyo   Singapore   Madrid
Mexico City   Munich   Paris   Cape Town   Hong Kong   Montreal

EDITOR-IN-CHIEF	Joseph Opiela
SENIOR ACQUISITIONS EDITOR	Steven Rigolosi
DEVELOPMENT EDITOR	Katharine Glynn
MARKETING MANAGER	Melanie Goulet
SUPPLEMENTS EDITOR	Donna Campion
MEDIA SUPPLEMENTS EDITOR	Nancy Garcia
PRODUCTION MANAGER	Donna DeBenedictis
PROJECT COORDINATION, TEXT DESIGN, AND ELECTRONIC PAGE MAKEUP	Pre-Press Company, Inc.
COVER DESIGNER/MANAGER	Wendy Ann Fredericks
COVER ART	*Composition*, 1918 by Barth Anthony van der Leck (1876–1958) Haags Gemeentemuseum, Netherlands. © 2000 Artists Rights Society (ARS), New York/Beeldrecht, Amsterdam
PHOTO RESEARCHER	Julie Tesser
MANUFACTURING BUYER	Al Dorsey
PRINTER AND BINDER	RR Donnelley & Sons Company/Crawfordsville
COVER PRINTER	Coral Graphic Services

For permission to use copyrighted material, grateful acknowledgment is made to the copyright holders on pp. 637–638, which are hereby made part of this copyright page.

Library of Congress Cataloging-in-Publication Data

The user's guide to college writing: reading, analyzing, and writing / Nancy M. Kreml . . . [et al.]
    p. cm
  Includes index.

   1. English language—Rhetoric. 2. Report writing. I. Kreml, Nancy M.
PE1408 .U68 2001
808'.042—dc21

00-046111

Please visit our website at **http://www.ablongman.com/kreml**

ISBN 0-321-05082-7

1 2 3 4 5 6 7 8 9 10—DOC—03 02 01 00

Detailed Contents

Part Three Essay Options   225

14 Writing Essay Exams and Timed Writing   226

15 Writing Narration, Definition, Persuasion, and Other Modes   231

A brief overview of contents appears on the inside front cover.
An overview of Chapter 23, A Handbook for Writing Correct Sentences, appears
on inside rear cover.

Rhetorical Contents

Argumentation and Persuasion

Also see Chapter 25: Essays by Student Writers for additional persuasive readings.

Comparison and Contrast

Cause and Effect

Classification

Definition

Description

Exemplification

Necessity is indeed the mother of invention. The five of us who have written this book have taught composition for a number of years; most recently we have worked together in a large writing program, which includes a committee appointed to train adjunct faculty and to identify materials appropriate for our students. For many years, we have struggled to find a rhetoric that addresses the needs of our students and a reader that is appropriate for adult learners in a composition course. The book representatives for our region finally got tired of showing us textbooks that we would turn down and suggested that we write our own. Many years later, here it is. We hope that this book will help you fill those gaps you may have also identified and help your students become successful academic writers.

Although the five of us do not subscribe to the same philosophical, theoretical, or pedagogical base, we all teach the same students. In writing *The User's Guide to College Writing: Reading, Analyzing, and Writing*, we have been governed by what we have found to be effective in teaching our students. This book represents the conglomeration of what we've learned over the years and how we've explained the writing process and strategies to our students. Happily, the majority of these students succeeded in subsequent courses throughout their academic career, and we wanted to share the materials we've developed with our colleagues across the country.

FEATURES OF THE BOOK

Several key features distinguish *The User's Guide to College Writing: Reading, Analyzing, and Writing.*

Emphasis on Academic Writing and Reading

Some writing textbooks focus only on personal writing tasks, and many of these include readings that are used only as springboards for personal essays. These texts also tend to include writing assignments that do not appeal to adult learners and do not provide students with the thinking, reading, and writing skills necessary to succeed in subsequent college courses. We believe that the best way to prepare students for academic writing is to give them academic writing tasks designed for their reading and thinking level and to move them from less difficult to more difficult academic writing tasks through the course of the academic term.

This is not to say that we do not value personal writing; however, we have developed academic assignments that require students to respond to a reading as well incorporate their own ideas, opinions, experiences, and observations.

With the skills related to personal writing and academic writing, students should be prepared to handle any writing task they encounter.

Modular Organization

There are so many variations and choices for completing each step in the writing process, and so many choices for combining all these possibilities in any one chapter, that we felt that inexperienced writers would be overwhelmed if presented with too many at once. Therefore, we created Part Two, "Using Essential Strategies for Writing Essays," to introduce the basics of the writing process and Part Three, "Essay Options," to begin introducing some of the more advanced skills and alternatives commonly taught in basic composition and the first course in freshman composition. Instructors can choose to teach any or all of these chapters in any order they like, allowing the book to be customized to the needs of any particular classroom.

In-depth Discussion of Each Step in the Writing Process

The User's Guide to College Writing: Reading, Analyzing, and Writing is written for students who do not have an innate sense of written English and therefore need very specific, concrete tools to work with. We have found that many of our inexperienced writers do not have the skills or confidence that would allow them to become creative and inspired writers. We believe that *The User's Guide* can teach these students the reading, writing, and thinking skills to help them become productive and successful.

One Central Reading in Part Two

The introduction to the writing process in Part Two, "Using Essential Strategies for Writing Essays," focuses on one reading, Mark Mathabane's "My Father's Tribal Rule," instead of introducing a new reading for each step in the process, which is the common organizing method for current rhetoric/readers. Our method allows students to see the entire process as it relates to one reading, making it easier to understand how the steps are related and how one moves from step to step. Also, using one reading keeps constant the skill level introduced in each chapter in Part Two.

Flexibility in Selecting Readings for Assignments

Because so many examples and so much instructional material is devoted to the reading used in Part Two, some instructors may prefer to use a different reading when assigning students writing tasks related to a reading. To that end, we have included in Part Six, "Essays and Readings," a wide range of readings appropriate for a variety of reading levels and writing assignments. Any of these readings can be assigned instead of Mathabane's "My Father's

Tribal Rule." This flexibility allows instructors to know that the student is working independently and not relying too heavily on material included in the textbook.

Unique Chapters

We have written chapters to explain the critical thinking steps in writing that are often omitted in basic and freshman composition rhetorics. For example, Chapter 5, "Analyzing the Assignment for an Essay," and the "Evaluating Your Prewriting" sections in Chapter 7 are two thinking steps that students rarely find explained in their textbooks. While we recognize that there are many ways to complete these activities successfully, we describe some of the techniques that our students have found helpful as they've begun their development as critical thinkers and writers.

We've also separated the revision and editing steps from the proofreading and formatting steps. Students often try to do all three activities as one step, and we find that they do little actual deep revision for content and organization.

Plentiful Examples of Student Writing

The User's Guide includes many examples of work in progress by student writers, giving realistic models to the students who will use the book. These examples include journal entries, reading responses, answers to questions, and many drafts of essays as they move through the writing process—from the very rough, early attempts to the finished final product. In addition, Chapter 25 includes several complete student essays written in response to the readings.

A Handbook that Emphasizes Error Correction

The handbook in this text is unique. We do not attempt to provide instruction and exercises on every point of grammar. Instead, we focus on the major errors that interfere with communication and often mark students as illiterate in college and in the workplace. In addition, instead of simply stating grammar rules, we have provided an explanation of each rule so that students can find and correct errors in their writing.

We also recognize that students who successfully complete their first composition have not completely mastered or internalized the skills of editing and proofreading. In fact, as students are given more difficult tasks and critical thinking assignments in subsequent courses, they often make many more grammar and usage errors because they are struggling to articulate more complex ideas. For these reasons, we have included instruction on keeping an editing log. By using this log, students learn their weaknesses in grammar and usage and have a means of reminding themselves of what they need to check when finishing a draft for submission and evaluation.

English as a Second Language Features

 We have included instruction for students for whom English is a second language and have marked these sections with a special ESL icon. We have found that the same techniques for helping ESL students learn grammar and usage also work very well with those native English speakers who are not accustomed to communicating in standard written English. Therefore, we encourage you to consider using some of these techniques with all students, not just those traditionally considered ESL. Moreover, students who speak English as a second language can also assist in explaining complicated grammar and usage rules and applying those rules to writing. This peer assistance improves the confidence of ESL students, while improving the editing and proofreading skills of native speakers. In addition, these interactions provide ESL students opportunities for learning American idioms for both spoken and written English.

Integrated Coverage of Personal Writing, Research, and Documentation

 Rather than having separate chapters on word processing, writing personal essays, research, and MLA documentation, we have included relevant instruction on these skills where they best fit into the writing process. The RES icon indicates material related to research, including MLA documentation. The OWN icon represents instruction related to personal writing or writing that is *not* a response to a reading. We have also created boxes for computer tips as well as summary boxes for steps in the writing process. Each chapter begins with a list of the steps discussed prior to the chapter as well as those addressed in that chapter. This is to assist students in using the text as a reference book.

Plentiful Exercises

The User's Guide offers a wealth of exercises. These exercises appear throughout the book and are designed as material for discussion and in-class practices. They are designed to lead to a discussion of the options available to readers and writers, as well as a discussion of the ways to evaluate the effectiveness of a piece of writing. Finally, the exercises encourage students to apply these exercises to their own writing.

ORGANIZATION: HOW TO USE THIS BOOK

Consider this book a well-stocked filing cabinet of materials for teaching students to write academic discourse. In your filing cabinet, you might file all of your handouts on pre-writing together, your notes on drafting behind that, and your materials on revision next, but you probably don't teach your class from the front of your file drawer to the back. Instead, you choose a few materials that will expose your students to a skill and have them practice using it before you move on to the next skill.

Use this book the same way. We have grouped explanations, examples, and activities related to the same skill together in chapters so they are easy to find. You and your students should pick and choose activities that are helpful, but you shouldn't feel obligated to use all of them.

Also, you should feel free to revisit chapters throughout the course as needed. After all, learning to write is not a linear process; it's more like learning to shoot a lay up. To shoot a lay up, a basketball player must learn several skills—dribbling towards the basket, shifting the ball to the shooting hand, jumping off the appropriate foot, and shooting the ball. However, the player doesn't practice each skill until she has it down perfectly and then add the next skill. Instead, she understands how each skill is to be done, practices each skill to get the feel of it, and spends most of her time practicing the skills together. She may return to an individual skill and practice it alone again, but she must soon return to the entire sequence of skills.

Classroom Flexibility

Not all students need every chapter of this book. Some students already know how to respond to a writing prompt. Other students wrestle with this skill and need to spend substantial time learning to analyze an assignment. Still other students are competent with some assignments but need to practice responding to different types of prompts. Depending on the needs of your students, you have many choices:

- Assign exercises, activities, and explanations for class work and discussion
- Assign exercises, activities, and explanations for students to read independently, then ask questions in class
- Assign exercises, activities, and explanations to individual students who need additional work in specific areas
- Omit those parts of the book in which your students are proficient

Encourage your students to use this book as a tool and a resource. Like a handbook, *The User's Guide* can provide help in specific areas while students are writing on their own. In fact, this book is written with the assumption that no one class and no one student will use all of it. Instead, users of this text should use the parts that are helpful, skipping around as needed.

We have organized the book by dividing the basic skills (Part Two) from the more advanced skills (Part Three). We do not imply that this organization is the only way, or even the best way, to teach writing. We know that writing programs are different, and the students they serve are different. Therefore, we invite you to use the material provided in any order you determine to be best for your students and your program.

THE TEACHING AND LEARNING PACKAGE

An **Instructor's Manual** to accompany *The User's Guide to College Writing: Reading, Writing, and Analyzing* is available from the publisher. This IM provides numerous suggestions and helpful advice for using *The User's Guide to Reading, Analyzing, and Writing,* including how to structure and organize the course and how to approach each chapter. Answers to the in-text exercises are provided. To order the Instructor's Manual, use ISBN 0-321-05083-5.

Also available is a book-specific website to accompany *The User's Guide.* Check us out online at **http://www.ablongman.com/kreml**. The Kreml website includes a wealth of writing resources for developing writers, including additional practice and graded quizzes in grammar and the different components of the writing process.

In addition, a series of other innovative supplements is available for both instructors and students. All of these supplements are available either free or at greatly reduced prices.

For Additional Reading and Reference

The Dictionary Deal. Two dictionaries can be shrinkwrapped with this text for a nominal fee. *The New American Webster Handy College Dictionary* is a paperback reference text with more than 100,000 entries. *Merriam Webster's Collegiate Dictionary,* tenth edition, is a hardback reference with a citation file of more than 14.5 million examples of English words drawn from actual use. For more information on how to shrinkwrap a dictionary with this text, please contact your Longman sales representative.

Penguin Quality Paperback Titles. A series of Penguin paperbacks is available at a significant discount when shrinkwrapped with *The User's Guide.* Some titles available are Toni Morrison's *Beloved,* Julia Alvarez's *How the Garcia Girls Lost Their Accents,* Mark Twain's *Huckleberry Finn, Narrative of the Life of Frederick Douglass,* Harriet Beecher Stowe's *Uncle Tom's Cabin,* Dr. Martin Luther King, Jr.'s *Why We Can't Wait,* and plays by Shakespeare, Miller, and Albee. For a complete list of titles or more information, please contact your Longman sales consultant.

The Pocket Reader, **First Edition.** This inexpensive volume contains 80 brief readings (1–3 pages each) on a variety of themes: writers on writing, nature, women and men, customs and habits, politics, rights and obligations, and coming of age. Also included is an alternate rhetorical table of contents. 0-321-07668-0

100 Things to Write About. This 100-page book contains 100 individual assignments for writing on a variety of topics and in a wide range of formats, from expressive to analytical. Ask your Longman sales representative for a sample copy. 0-673-98239-4

Newsweek Alliance. Instructors may choose to shrinkwrap a 12-week subscription to *Newsweek* with any Longman text. The price of the subscription is 57 cents per issue (a total of $6.84 for the subscription). Available with the subscription is a free "Interactive Guide to *Newsweek*"—a workbook for students who are using the text. In addition, Newsweek provides a wide variety of instructor supplements free to teachers, including maps, Skills Builders, and weekly quizzes. For more information on the Newsweek program, please contact your Longman sales representative.

Electronic and Online Offerings

The Writer's ToolKit Plus CD-ROM. This CD-ROM offers a wealth of tutorial, exercise, and reference material for writers. It is compatible with either a PC or Macintosh platform, and is flexible enough to be used either occasionally for practice or regularly in class lab sessions. For information on how to bundle this CD-ROM FREE with your text, please contact your Longman sales representative.

The Longman English Pages Web Site. Both students and instructors can visit our free content-rich Web site for additional reading selections and writing exercises. From the Longman English pages, visitors can conduct a simulated Web search, learn how to write a resume and cover letter, or try their hand at poetry writing. Stop by and visit us at **http://www.ablongman.com/englishpages.**

The Longman Electronic Newsletter—Twice a month during the spring and fall, instructors who have subscribed receive a free copy of the Longman Developmental English Newsletter in their e-mailbox. Written by experienced classroom instructors, the newsletter offers teaching tips, classroom activities, book reviews, and more. To subscribe, visit the Longman Basic Skills Web site at **http://www.ablongman.com/basicskills**, or send an e-mail to **Basic Skills@ablongman.com**.

Daedalus Online Longman and The Daedalus Group are proud to offer the next generation of the award-winning Daedalus Integrated Writing Environment. Daedalus Online is an Internet-based collaborative writing environment for students. The program offers prewriting strategies and prompts, computer-mediated conferencing, peer collaboration and review, comprehensive writing support, and secure, 24-hour availability.

For educators, Daedalus Online offers a comprehensive suite of online course management tools for managing an online class, dynamically linking assignments, and facilitating a heuristic approach to writing instruction. For more information, visit **http://www.ablongman.com/daedalus**, or contact your Longman sales representative.

Teaching Online: Internet Research, Conversation, and Composition, **Third Edition.** Ideal for instructors who have never surfed the Net, this easy-to-follow guide offers basic definitions, numerous examples, and step-by-step information about finding and using Internet sources. Free to adopters. 0-321-07760-1

For Instructors

Electronic Test Bank for Writing. This electronic test bank features more than 5,000 questions in all areas of writing, from grammar to paragraphing, through essay writing, research, and documentation. With this easy-to-use CD-ROM, instructors simply choose questions from the electronic test bank, then print out the completed test for distribution. 0-321-08117-X

Competency Profile Test Bank, Second Edition. This series of 60 objective tests covers ten general areas of English competency, including fragments; comma splices and run-ons; pronouns; commas; and capitalization. Each test is available in remedial, standard, and advanced versions. Available as reproducible sheets or in computerized versions. Free to instructors. Paper version: 0-321-02224-6. Computerized IBM: 0-321-02633-0. Computerized Mac: 0-321-02632-2.

Diagnostic and Editing Tests, Third Edition. This collection of diagnostic tests helps instructors assess students' competence in Standard Written English for purpose of placement or to gauge progress. Available as reproducible sheets or in computerized versions, and free to instructors. Paper: 0-321-08382-2. Computerized IBM: 0-321-08782-8 Computerized Mac: 0-321-08784-4.

ESL Worksheets, Third Edition. These reproducible worksheets provide ESL students with extra practice in areas they find the most troublesome. A diagnostic test and post-test are provided, along with answer keys and suggested topics for writing. Free to adopters. 0-321-07765-2

80 Practices. A collection of reproducible, ten-item exercises that provide additional practices for specific grammatical usage problems, such as comma splices, capitalization, and pronouns. Includes an answer key, and free to adopters. 0-673-53422-7

CLAST Test Package, Fourth Edition. These two 40-item objective tests evaluate students' readiness for the CLAST exams. Strategies for teaching CLAST preparedness are included. Free with any Longman English title. Reproducible sheets: 0-321-01950-4 Computerized IBM version: 0-321-01982-2 Computerized Mac version: 0-321-01983-0

TASP Test Package, Third Edition. These 12 practice pre-tests and post-tests assess the same reading and writing skills covered in the TASP examination. Free with any Longman English title. Reproducible sheets: 0-321-01959-8 Computerized IBM version: 0-321-01985-7 Computerized Mac version: 0-321-01984-9

Teaching Writing to the Non-Native Speaker. This booklet examines the issues that arise when non-native speakers enter the developmental classroom. Free to instructors, it includes profiles of international and permanent ESL students, factors influencing second-language acquisition, and tips on managing a multicultural classroom. 0-673-97452-9

For Students

***Researching Online*, Fourth Edition.** A perfect companion for a new age, this indispensable new supplement helps students navigate the Internet. Adapted from *Teaching Online*, the instructor's Internet guide, *Researching Online* speaks directly to students, giving them detailed, step-by-step instructions for performing electronic searches. Available free when shrinkwrapped with any Longman text. Ask your Longman sales representative for more information.

Learning Together: An Introduction to Collaborative Theory. This brief guide to the fundamentals of collaborative learning teaches students how to work effectively in groups, how to revise with peer response, and how to co-author a paper or report. Shrinkwrapped free with any Longman Basic Skills text.

***A Guide for Peer Response*, Second Edition.** This guide offers students forms for peer critiques, including general guidelines and specific forms for different stages in the writing process. Also appropriate for freshman-level courses. Free to adopters.

***[For Students in Florida] Thinking Through the Test*, by D.J. Henry.** This special workbook, prepared specially for students in Florida, offers ample skill and practice exercises to help students prep for the Florida State Exit Exam. To shrinkwrap this workbook free with your textbook, please contact your Longman sales representative. Also available: Two laminated grids (one for reading, one for writing) that can serve as handy references for students preparing for the Florida State Exit Exam.

ACKNOWLEDGMENTS

Many thanks to the reviewers who provided us with valuable feedback: Kathy Albertson, Georgia Southern University; Gene Armao, El Camino College; Michel deBenedictis, Miami-Dade Community College, Kendall Campus; Elizabeth

DeVore, Lake Land College; Eileen Eliot, Broward Community College; Dr. Joe B. Fulton, Dalton State College; Mary Alice Hardy, Southwestern Michigan College; Crystal Harris, Sinclair Community College; Lauri Humberson, St. Philip's College; Lee Brewer Jones, Georgia Perimeter College; Jan Little, Laredo Community College; Lilane MacPherson, Hudson County Community College; David Rollison, College of Marin; and Pamela Smith, Pellissippi State Technical Community College.

Every published book reflects the work of hundreds of people, many of whom the authors never meet to thank personally. We'd like to thank those who worked behind the scenes to make this textbook a reality. In particular we would like to thank Steven Rigolosi, our Acquisitions Editor at Longman, for sharing our vision; Katharine Glynn, our Developmental Editor, for guiding us through the process; and Elsa van Bergen, project coordinator at Pre-Press Company, Inc., for her careful editing that, along with the prompts from copy editor Stephanie Magean, dramatically improved our text. We would also like to thank the production manager, Donna DeBenedictis, for her thoughtful care and Wendy Fredericks for the cover design. We would also like to thank all of the book representatives who have worked with Longman and Pearson over the years for convincing us to write this book.

We are most indebted to the students, particularly those enrolled in English 100, at Midlands Technical College in Columbia, South Carolina, who not only taught us what they need to know about composition, but also demanded that we find new ways to explain the writing process. A special thanks to the students who allowed us to print examples of work written for their basic composition course: Keenan Johnson, J. P. Myers, Meg Christmas, Jaime Cox, Larry Evans, Rodell S. Johnson, Benjamin W. Munden, Sr., Lois Johnson, Jane Smith, Brian Murray, Stacey Hawkins, and Ave Givens.

We would also like to thank the faculty and staff at MTC for their support throughout this process. The English Department Chair, Dianne Luce, supported and encouraged our work. The English faculty, particularly the English 100 Committee, provided us the opportunity to develop our teaching philosophy and pedagogy: Laurie Cox, Alice Davis, Jackie Frederick, Stan Frick, Keith Higginbotham, Glenn James, Cindy Rogers, and Linda Smith. The Developmental Studies Department supported the project by allowing us to teach developmental reading courses, and Barbara Armbruster reviewed the manuscript, giving us a boost of confidence when we most needed it. We would also like to thank Dr. Jean Mahaffey, Vice President for Education, and Dr. Ron Drayton, Associate Vice President for Education, for creating a work environment in which experimentation is valued and for supporting the work of the English 100 Committee.

We are also indebted to four special people who have been at various times MTC employees and MTC students: Monica Boucher-Romano, Penny Osborne, Connor Stewart, and Gregory Taylor. Without their work to support our many professional projects, we could not have found the time or energy to complete this project. Thanks for all of the researching, copying, running errands, and just being there over the years.

Our families have tolerated our work on this project for many years. Not only have they supported us emotionally by listening to our joys and frustrations, they spent a weekend together at the beach so we could begin writing the manuscript. Thanks to Raedonna Blair, Curtis Carr, Lena Jake, Theo and Daniel Posselt, Bruce Martin, and Myles Martin for tolerating our many hours at the computer, on the phone, and in meetings, and extra thanks to Bill Kreml and Lisa Jackson for proofreading the manuscript. Thanks to Mary Mace for letting us use the beach house. A special thanks to Pigwig Jackson who is a much better writer than any of us will ever be. We would like also like to pay tribute to our four-legged family members: Carl, Cujo, Fernie, Jake, Nuggett, Sherman, and the late Eunice, all of whom assisted in the writing of this book—often by sleeping on or chewing on the manuscript.

We need to also thank the owners and employees of numerous restaurants in Columbia, South Carolina, who fortunately did not charge us rent as we worked through and sat for long hours after the wonderful meals they served at Applebee's, Basil Pot, Beulah's, Blue Marlin, California Dreaming, Dixie Seafood Company, Fatz, New Orleans Restaurant, Rising High Bakery, Rosewood Market, Ruby Tuesdays, and Tiffany's Bakery.

Nancy Kreml
Diane Carr
Douglas Capps
Jan Jake
Sharon May
—*Columbia, South Carolina*

PART ONE

Introduction

1 The Circle of Reading, Writing, and Critical Thinking

Most of the assignments you'll be receiving in college will ask you to read and to write. You'll be required to read textbooks and write answers to exam questions about them; you'll write **summaries** and **critiques** of articles and chapters in books; and you'll write research papers. You'll be using reading and writing skills in your personal life and work life, too: replying to letters and memos, reading reports and summarizing them, and looking up technical information and writing explanations that inexperienced people can understand. All these different occasions for using reading and writing together may seem to be reason enough to prepare to use the two skills together. In addition, if you look more closely at how your mind works when you're reading and writing, you'll see that the two skills are very closely related, and that using both gives you a little more mental power than using each separately.

HOW WRITING IMPROVES READING

Reading is not just the passive act of photocopying the words from the text onto your mind. It's an active process, one that involves using knowledge you already have to help you understand new concepts, and even more, to decide whether those new ideas are worthwhile. Part of learning to read this way is knowing that you must be a reader who is active—willing to work hard and to consider new ideas.

One of the best ways to develop reading skills and attitudes is through writing. Private or **personal writing**, or notes for yourself, can help you prepare to read by thinking and then writing about a topic: taking notes, and jotting down questions, describing reactions, and making comparisons can help you while you read. Writing can help you *after* you read. It is a way of reviewing and seeing how the ideas in a reading are related to each other and to your own ideas. Later chapters in this book give specific techniques for doing all these things.

However, it is another type of writing—**essay** writing—that will help you to become a wiser reader. When you write an essay about a reading, you will not focus only on your first thoughts and responses to the reading. You'll need to examine your responses carefully and consider exactly how they fit with the reading. You'll then return to the reading to be sure that you've reported the author's ideas accurately and clearly.

HOW READING IMPROVES WRITING

One of the biggest problems for any writer is finding material to write about. All of us have spent some time looking at a blank sheet of paper, trying to come up with something to say, or finally writing some words just to fill up the page. Another problem that writers face is remembering that they are writing to readers. It's hard to imagine how your reader might respond to what you've written if you have no idea who your reader is. The most obvious way that reading will improve your writing is by giving you something to say and by helping you understand or imagine possible readers.

When you write in response to something you've read, you have a clear starting place: you know you're writing to a specific person and you know the idea that you want that person to understand, a clear **audience** and a clear **purpose**. But sometimes when you are writing for school assignments you may lose sight of your audience. Reading can help you to be aware of who your possible readers might be. For example, if you've read one or more essays explaining why distributing birth control in high schools is a bad idea, you have a much more specific idea of how to reply to those writers when you decide to write your own essay in favor of this practice. You know their real reasons for believing as they do, and you know the kinds of experience they have had. You can much more easily decide which reasons you need to discuss and what kind of examples the readers will understand. So reading can help you find material to write about, and it can help form a clear picture of the audience you hope to have as readers.

HOW READING AND WRITING IMPROVE THINKING

But reading and writing actually affect each other in much stronger ways. You really learn to write better by reading, and learn to read better by writing—and both skills work together to improve your ability to think. Look at how you learn other skills: if you want to learn to drive a car, for example, you watch someone drive, then try to drive yourself. If you try to learn how to dance, you learn partly by watching other people dance. And if you want to learn to write, you will read other writers. Sometimes you are able to learn a dance step just by imitation and can't explain exactly how you make the movements that you make—your body has started to "think" as a dancer's does. Learning to write is a similar process. You learn many complicated kinds of words and sentences by observing the ways that other writers put words together. Gradually your understanding of the words changes your ideas, and you become a better thinker.

Now that you're in college, one skill you will be learning by observing and practicing is how to use many new languages: the languages of technical fields, like engineering or computers; the language of specific courses, like history or psychology; and even the language of academic books and papers. It's not just a matter of memorizing a list of vocabulary words, like *archetypal, persist, multitude.* You must also learn to follow long and complicated sentences and paragraphs. You probably will not hear a sentence such as the following in conversation, but it's not unusual in a history book:

> Having seen that the archetypal patterns persist throughout a multitude of cultures, we can assume that the term "universal" has some validity.

You'll acquire the ability to read a sentence like this just as you learned to drive or dance. You'll encounter sentences that use these words and follow these rules—and as you did when you learned to dance or drive, you'll try out parts of the sentences yourself, without necessarily thinking about the fact that you are imitating something. You may also look critically at the sentence you create by imitation and decide that it's not as clear as it should be, and then you may search for other, clearer ways to express your own ideas.

A common type of academic assignment that requires you to go back and forth between reading and writing is the research paper. When you read a passage written by another writer, you can understand it on many different levels. If you simply skim over it, you may be able to remember the general idea; if you underline passages and key words, you will have a much deeper understanding. But if you understand the author's ideas well enough to restate them in your own words, you have truly taken in the ideas and made them a part of your own thinking process. If the material you work with is difficult, you will be extending your thinking processes to fit the demands of the writer's thought.

As you read and write in each subject, you'll begin to learn the language of that field. You'll also learn about bigger things than sentences. If you're assigned to write a research paper for a psychology class, probably the first thing you'll want to do is see an example of a paper written for that class, so you can have an idea of the kind of writing you'll need to do. You may look at papers written by other students as well as professional papers. As you read these examples, you will notice the kind of language the writers use—for example, you'll see terms such as *dependent variable,* which you may have thought you understood when you read the text. Now that you need to make the idea of *dependent variables* a part of your own paper, and must organize your ideas around that central idea, you will have to thoroughly understand what it means. You'll have to look up the words and if necessary talk with your instructor until you have a very clear idea of the meaning of the term. When you try to write your own research paper, you'll go back to your examples and read them again. You will then read your own writing and probably revise it to be more like your model.

As you write this paper, you'll also be using other sources. For example, you may find that one writer says:

Hypnotherapy may become the triggering mechanism for recovery of repressed memories of physical and mental abuse.

You work with reading and understanding this idea and finally restate it in your own words:

A person might forget painful childhood experiences but remember them later if hypnotized by a psychologist.

This has given you a new idea; you've also gained a clear understanding of the meaning of important words (*hypnotherapy, triggering mechanism, repressed memories*) and you've also seen how those words are used in a sentence. You continue to do research and find that another writer says:

Current schema often present the phenomenon of repressed memory as pseudomemory, since reconstructive distortions are frequently the product of patients' response to therapists' own unconscious suggestions.

You are now familiar with the term *repressed memory;* so, with help from a dictionary and your psychology textbook, you work with the rest of this sentence until you can restate it in your own words:

Some theories say that people believe they remember things that did really happen or that happened in a different way. Because they trust and want to please the psychologist, they make up these false memories without realizing that they are doing it.

Now you have another idea, as well as additional vocabulary: *schema, phenomenon, reconstructive distortions.* You also have two different ideas to compare. When you begin to write your paper, you can say:

Psychologists disagree about the recovery of repressed memories. Some believe there are actual memories of real abuse, but others think that patients unconsciously create memories as a result of suggestions from others.

You may go on from here to find some ways to decide which of these ideas you want to accept. You may do this by reading more or talking with your instructor and other students. You may think about your own ideas—maybe you decide that repressed memories are not the same for everyone. Depending on your assignment, you may or may not include your own conclusions in your psychology research paper. However, once you've thought about an idea deeply enough to be able to put it in your own words, you probably won't just drop it. The combination of reading and writing has stretched your mind and it probably won't very quickly shrink back again.

An important thing is happening as you go through this process—you're learning to think about psychology. You learn some of this thinking by listening to the instructor and participating in class discussions, but a good bit of the change in your ability to think results from reading and writing, especially as you work with both processes together. Your ideas become increasingly more complex, and soon you will be able to recognize errors and problems in some of the things you read. At this point, you will finally be able to develop and express your opinions about them. A closer look at these related skills may help you see what you will be learning as you use this book.

WHAT IS READING?

As you begin your life as a college student, you will want to learn how to be successful. You will quickly find out that success depends on writing and reading, and on making sure your skills will take you where you want to go. What are the biggest problems in writing and reading for college students? When college professors are asked this question, many will answer that the biggest problem is that students just don't do the reading—at all. When students are asked why they don't complete reading assignments, many have two answers. One is that they can't understand the readings; the second is that the readings are boring.

Let's start with the idea that those two answers are really the same. Of course, reading may be boring if you already know all the facts and ideas in the reading. But you probably won't be taking many courses that you've already mastered. The chances are great that the reading doesn't interest you because you don't yet know enough about the subject to really be reading the material. You can't really read a book or essay or story unless you can be involved in the subject. A book is not a funnel that lets the author pour knowledge into your brain. It's more like a slot machine, where you get something back only when you put something in. When you read, you get back a lot more than you put in. The best part about reading is that it's not a game of chance.

For example, suppose a student in Wisconsin reads a story about violence in Northern Ireland, a story about a prisoner who becomes friendly with the men who guard him. If this student knows nothing at all about Ireland and does nothing but read the story, it will probably seem distant, confusing, and pointless. But if that same student has read the newspapers even a little, she may have learned something about the long history of conflict there. She may have had a history class, where she learned that Ireland was once a separate country. She may remember some Irish music, or think about her Irish friends. But even if Ireland doesn't ring any bells at all for her, she may be able to think of a time when she found something good in people who were supposed to be her enemies. If she can bring any of this experience to the story, she'll be able to understand it much more, and will find it much more interesting. Because she can invest some of her own knowledge and ideas, she was able to get more meaning and ideas from the reading in return.

The Four Levels of Reading

The Levels of Reading
Breaking the code
Understanding the idea
Reacting emotionally
Thinking critically

In this book, we'll be looking at four different levels of reading. At all these levels, you'll be using what you already know to help you understand something new.

Breaking the Code   Many people still think of reading as matching letters to sounds and figuring out how to pronounce a word. For example, when you see the word *symbiotic*, you recognize that the letter *y* in this word must be pronounced like the letter *i*. But decoding the pronunciation is only one step in reading. Think about how that works: you can match the sound to the letter only if you already know the sound; you can identify the word on paper only if you know the spoken word or have some way of learning it. So there's more to reading than pronouncing words.

Understanding the Idea   If you find a sentence with the word *symbiotic*, you may need to look it up in the dictionary. There you will find that *symbiosis* refers to two very different organisms that live very closely together and benefit each other. You think about animals and plants you know, and remember learning about the birds that live with crocodiles and clean their teeth; the bird benefits by getting food and the crocodile benefits by getting clean teeth. That makes the word understandable. But you couldn't get that just by learning how to decode the letters; you had to use the knowledge you already had, put together in a new way to get a new understanding.

This same process is even more important when we read more than just one word. Suppose you see the following sentence:

The police and the drug dealers developed a symbiotic relationship in that town.

Now you know what *symbiosis* means, you think of what you know about word endings, and you decide that *symbiotic* is a form of *symbiosis*. But police and drug dealers couldn't really live together in the way that birds and crocodiles do. So you need a more complicated way of understanding this. You have learned what the word means; you have some knowledge about police and criminals; and finally, you know that sometimes language is used to make comparisons. You now understand the sentence to mean that the police and the drug dealers in that town help each other out. You don't know the specific details because that information must come from additional reading.

Reacting Emotionally   After you understand an idea, you don't just accept it and file it away; you react to it in some way. Your first reaction may be emotional: you may feel angry to think that police and criminals could work together. You may feel indignant, because you may have worked in law enforcement and you may think police are often misjudged. You may laugh, because you've seen cases where police have accepted bribes. Notice that your emotional reaction depends also on what you already know of the world, and emotional reactions can be very different for different people.

Remember that boredom is a form of emotional response. When your main reaction to something you have read is that it's boring, you're not really thinking about the ideas in the reading, but about your feelings. It's fine to have that feeling, but you can't stop with your feelings. You must move on to thinking about what you read, no matter how you feel.

Thinking Critically   To come to any agreed-on understanding of the sentence above, you will need to read critically. This does not mean necessarily finding fault with everything you read. **Critical reading** involves specific types of thinking:

■ Thinking about what you read, not just reacting emotionally.
■ Thinking about what the author wants you to see and making judgments about that.
■ Thinking about why you react the way you do to what the author says.

To be able to think critically, you will need to ask questions about what you've read. Look again at the sentence *The police and the drug dealers developed a symbiotic relationship in that town.* Here are a few ways to think critically about it.

What town was this?

How did the police and criminals benefit each other?

What facts prove that this took place?

Does this seem similar to things that happen here?

What facts do I know that contradict or support this?

What difference does this make?

The answers to these questions will help you as a reader decide whether to accept the statement or not. Without the answers, you may finally have to decide that the sentence is just an idea and won't really be able to say whether it's accurate or not.

If you apply this critical reading process to much of the written material you encounter, you will see how necessary critical reading is for people who live in a complex and diverse society. This book will ask you to develop your ability to read critically.

EXERCISE 1.1   After reading each of the following numbered sentences, indicate what kind of reading is being used in each of the lettered responses—breaking the code, understanding, reacting emotionally, or thinking critically.

1. Capital punishment represents the final stage in the dehumanization process.

   A. To *dehumanize* means to take away the human qualities of something. Therefore this sentence says that people are made into something less than human when they are legally executed for a crime.

   B. People who oppose capital punishment make me sick.

   C. In what way are criminals dehumanized? What are the other stages? Can a human being really be something not human?

2. Bilingual education will undermine the unity of our country.

   A. In what way will the unity of the country be affected by the language people speak? Is there any evidence for this? Are there many countries in which more than one language is spoken? Is unity more important than the other benefits of teaching children in two languages?

   B. *Bilingual* means speaking two languages. I've heard of programs where children of immigrants are taught math and science classes in Spanish. Maybe that's what this sentence is about.

   C. I'm not an immigrant, and I don't have children. This topic is boring.

EXERCISE 1.2 **Using a dictionary if necessary and your own experience if possible, explain what the following sentences mean. Then give an example of an emotional and a critical response to each.**

A. The digital revolution will soon make VCRs obsolete.

B. Smokers' rights are abrogated by the passage of no-smoking bills in some states.

C. All students must attend an orientation seminar.

The Purposes of Reading

You read for many different purposes. When you read a love letter or an angry editorial, you're mainly reading for the emotional content, but when you read a recipe or a course description, you're looking for information. But other reading that you do requires a more thoughtful reaction that will require you to invest more effort. As a student reading a textbook for your psychology course, your main purpose may be to make a good grade in the course. As a citizen and a consumer, you'll be confronted by advertising asking you to choose products and politicians. In all of these roles, you'll need strong critical reading skills to make intelligent choices.

There will be many purposes for your reading. These are likely to be the most common ones:

■ *Personal reading:* You will read a wide variety of things as a part of your personal life. You may read for information to help you decide which car to buy or you may read horror novels for entertainment. You determine your own purpose in your personal reading. When you read for personal reasons, you may decide not to read something that's difficult or uninteresting unless it's something you really need to know.

■ *Academic reading:* When you are reading in college, you will not have a choice about whether you want to read something or not. Your professors will expect you to learn the material, and often that will mean reading chapters or whole books that may be very difficult for you. The purpose of these assignments is partly to give you an understanding of the specific material in the course and partly to improve your thinking skills. You should expect to follow certain steps with academic reading: (1) reread the material several times, (2) mark the book and make notes, (3) use a dictionary, and (4) think about what you have read. In Chapter 4, we will show you some specific techniques. The goals of academic reading usually involve the following:

Gathering facts and ideas about a topic.

Thinking critically about these facts and ideas.

Relating facts and ideas to other readings, lectures, and discussions.

■ *Professional reading:* Reading at work is often very similar to academic reading. You must read certain things because you need the information or because you must make a judgment about ideas presented by the writer. You may see the purpose more clearly, but sometimes reports written by other workers or customers may be difficult to read because they're not written as clearly as much professional writing. You will find that the same critical reading skills you used in academic reading will be necessary when you read for work.

Improving Your Reading

Ways to Improve Your Reading
Be willing to work
Be willing to see new ideas
Read methodically
Read widely
Prepare to read by increasing your knowledge of the world

Whether you read for personal, academic, or professional reasons, it is definitely possible to improve your reading skills. The list below shows you several ways to work to become a better reader. The most important is simply that you must read.

Be Willing to Work   The most important step in improving your reading is motivation. You must realize though that reading is not just a matter of skimming across the pages of a book. You must be willing to work and to invest both time and energy: using dictionaries, taking notes, reading and rereading difficult passages, answering questions.

Be Willing to See New Ideas   Another important part of improving your reading is letting go of the fear of new things and being willing to try hard to use your mind in new ways. Thinking involves examining ideas, not just memorizing. You must be willing to take time to understand ideas even if they challenge the way you see the world. You don't have to give up your own beliefs, but you must be willing to hear ideas in addition to those that are comfortable to you.

Read Methodically   Learn to use the best techniques for reading carefully and working with what you read. You may have learned some of these in other courses, or they may be new to you, but if you practice them with your academic reading, they will help you understand complex and difficult material.

Read Widely   Form an ongoing habit of reading, like the habit of brushing your teeth or exercising. You have seen how much reading depends on the knowledge and experience you already have. Many of the techniques offered by this book will show you how to use your knowledge and experience even more deeply. One of the best ways to increase your knowledge of the world and your experience in life is to read widely. You should take every opportunity to increase your general and personal reading as well as the reading you do for school. Eventually you will see how much that increased knowledge of the world will pay off. One of your goals as a college student should be to increase your reading by some or all of these experiences.

Some ways to read more widely are:

- Read a newspaper every day.
- Read magazines.
- Subscribe to newspapers or magazines or read them in the library.
- Join a book club.
- Talk with friends about books.
- Print and read articles from the Internet.
- Choose a subject and learn all you can about it.
- Trade books and magazines with friends.
- Visit bookstores and used bookstores.
- Look for books at garage sales.
- Ask teachers for old books and magazines.

Prepare to Read by Increasing Your Knowledge of the World   We've seen how you use the knowledge you already have to understand new ideas in your reading. This means that one way to become a better reader is to have more knowledge. All of us gain some knowledge just by living in the world. By making the choice to go to college, you will be increasing your knowledge through all of your courses, but you will also be increasing your knowledge in other ways: by reading outside the classroom; by talking with classmates, neighbors, friends, and coworkers; by watching informative programs on television; by visiting museums, zoos, churches, and different kinds of stores. Anything you learn or experience will give you a little more material to use when you come to the next difficult reading.

Ways to increase your knowledge and experience include:

- Read widely.
- Watch informative programs on television.
- Watch news programs regularly.
- Read the newspaper.

- ■ Get to know new people and talk with them.
- ■ Go to new parts of town.
- ■ Visit museums, zoos, churches, different kinds of stores.
- ■ Ask questions.

WHAT IS WRITING?

Differences Between Speaking and Writing

Writing is one way to use language, but it is not the first way we learned to express ourselves. We first learned to communicate by speaking and listening and only later by writing and reading. Why is speaking so easy for us, yet writing often so difficult? Even though both involve communicating through language, there are several significant differences between speaking and writing.

First, most of us are more accustomed to spoken language. While some forms of speaking, such as speaking in front of a group, may be less comfortable, most of us are at ease speaking with other people on a casual basis. We have also learned quite naturally how to change our speech depending on whom we are talking to; we talk differently to our friends and to our employers. While we need to make the same adjustments when we write, we don't have as much practice. Furthermore, the standards of correctness in written language—punctuation, paragraphing, etc.—tend to be less familiar to us than those we have to consider when we speak.

Second, we are more motivated to speak than to write. Whether we are ordering a meal, purchasing a product, or telephoning a friend, we find it essential to speak. However, it has often been possible to get by without writing very often or very much (though E-mail is making the written word more important for many people). If we want to participate in the events going on around us in our society—which is based on spoken words (think of television and radio)—we have to communicate and the easiest means of communication is often speaking.

Third, we have a sense that what we write is permanent. What we write and how we write it (mistakes and all) is recorded where it can be read again and again; however, what we speak seems temporary and easily corrected if it doesn't come out the way we want it to.

Finally, the biggest difference between speaking and writing is the relationship with an audience. For a writer, audience refers to the intended readers of the writing. For a speaker, *audience* refers to the listeners who are physically present.

Importance of Audience

When you see your audience or listen to their reactions, you can adjust what you say to them. If they don't understand, you can explain further. If they are getting bored, you can try to make it more interesting. If they are offended by what you are saying, you can change tactics or the tone of what you are saying. When you are writing and the audience is not present, you have to guess how they will react.

Identifying your audience and thinking about their needs helps determine the content of your writing. For instance, if you are writing an **argumentative essay** about censoring sex and violence on television, the wording and specific issues you discuss will depend on characteristics of your audience—perhaps their gender, age, education, and occupation. If your reader is a priest, you might focus more on religious matters, but if your reader is a politician, you might center the discussion around legal issues. What you say and how you say it is determined to a large extent by your audience.

In some situations, you may not know who your audience is. If you are writing a letter to your school paper about the student council, your specific audience might be the members of the student council. If the letter appears in the school paper, friends and others familiar with the issue might read it but so might students, faculty, staff, and parents you don't know. You would need to consider whether they will be familiar with the issue you're addressing and how much background information they will need to understand why you are writing the letter, what your concern is, and what your points are. When your audience consists of people you don't know, you must provide enough information to ensure that they understand you.

THE FIVE LEVELS OF WRITING

The Levels of Writing
Personal
Colloquial
Informal
Formal
Academic

Your audience helps you to decide what kind of language you want to use as well as what information you need to give. You need to think about what kind of writing is appropriate for your reader. One way to think about choosing the language for your audience is to think about the *level* of writing, just as you think about the type of clothing to wear for a particular occasion. If you're going out with friends, you'll probably wear informal clothes, like nice jeans and a T-shirt, but if you're going to a wedding, you'll probably wear very formal, elegant clothes. You'll make similar choices about your writing, which generally falls in one of the following levels.

Personal Writing   Personal writing is intended only for you. It does not have to be correct or organized so that anyone but you can follow it. Here are some typical examples:

> grocery list
>
> class notes
>
> journal
>
> brainstorming or prewriting for future writing
>
> **EXAMPLE:** Mom and Dad's party—2 pm—Jan. 12—Clubhouse

Colloquial Writing   **Colloquial communication** is intended for an audience you know well and who does not expect you to be formal or correct. Because your message will be specific to that audience, you may use abbreviations and references known only by that audience:

>   advertisements
>
>   note or letter to friend
>
>   **EXAMPLE:** Mom and Dad's 50th is coming up on January 12. We're throwing a party for them at 2:00 at the clubhouse. Y'all come.
>
>   Jimmy, BB, and Allie

Informal Writing   **Informal communication** is intended to be read by an audience, usually peers, that will expect a standard form and some amount of correctness but not formal language.

>   signs
>
>   interoffice memo
>
>   newsletter
>
>   **EXAMPLE:** Come help us celebrate our parents' 50th wedding anniversary at 2 p.m. on January 12 at the Forest Lake Country Club.
>
>   James, Bruce, and Alice Kelly

Computer Tip

Remember that using E-mail doesn't change the fact that you must write differently for different audiences. Before you click on "Send," read even a short note once with your reader in mind. Think about the words you've chosen and the information you've included: Is this right for your reader? Is it clear?

Formal Writing   **Formal communication** is intended to be read by an audience who will expect a standard form and error-free grammar and spelling. This audience may be readers you don't know well or who are above you in some chain of command (teachers, employers, etc.).

>   research papers
>
>   job résumés
>
>   cover letters
>
>   formal invitations

EXAMPLE:

James, Bruce, and Alice Kelly
cordially invite you to a reception honoring
Mr. and Mrs. Walter B. Kelly
on the joyous occasion of their fiftieth wedding anniversary
at two o'clock on Saturday, January 12, 2002
at the Forest Lake Country Club

EXERCISE 1.3 Write a paragraph describing a trip you have taken, using each level of writing.

Academic Writing The writing you do in your college classes—**academic writing**, as it is called—will require a type of wording, structure, and adherence to certain rules not required by other forms of writing. A library research paper will require you to use quotes, provide citations, supply a works cited list, and conform to the rules of a formal style guide, such as that issued by the Modern Language Association (MLA) or the American Psychological Association (APA). In later chapters of this book, we will help you learn the special requirements of academic writing, not only in your English class but also in any other class—from history and psychology to business—that requires you to write college-level essays.

When you write in an academic setting, you must be particularly mindful of your audience. You may consider your instructor to be an immediate audience completely familiar with the topic you're discussing, but this can be a dangerous assumption. Listen closely to an instructor's directions when an assignment is given because he or she may identify the audience. However, don't make the mistake of assuming that your instructor knows everything about the subject or reading you are discussing. When you make this assumption, you may leave out important information and create an essay that is vague and too general.

If you are discussing a short story, you can't just say that the main character's actions reveal his lack of self-respect. Even though your instructor will have read the story many times, he or she may not be sure which actions you are referring to, may not understand how these actions reveal the main character's lack of self-respect, or may not even agree with you that these actions show a lack of self-respect. Even when writing for your instructors, assume that they need to be reminded of the issues in the reading you are examining.

One way to define your readers is to assume that they have never read the story or essay you are discussing. Using this strategy will ensure that all readers will understand what you are saying.

Remember that academic writing is an exercise in communication, not merely a performance on which you will be graded. You will want to write to be understood, not just to impress your instructor or earn a high grade.

The Importance of Purpose

Another element that determines the form and wording of your writing is your reason for writing it. The wording and structure of a piece of writing—a note to a coworker, a cover letter for a job application, a letter of complaint to a business, a proposal for funding a new project in your job, an essay for a college class—change when your reason for writing changes.

Often audience and purpose go hand in hand, as we see in the following exercise.

| EXERCISE 1.4 | **Read the following account of an automobile accident.** |

On Monday, September 9, I was driving to work in my 1997 Nissan Sentra, headed north on Devine Street. I was checking my hair in the rearview mirror and turning up the radio because my favorite song was playing. When I looked back at the road, I noticed the car in front of me stopping quickly. I put on my brakes and stopped just before rear-ending the other car. I then felt a bump as the car behind me ran into my car. I got out of the car, but the car that hit me—a large green sedan— drove away. Four other cars were stopped behind it, and the drivers of those cars told me that they had hit each other. A woman walking her dog said she got the license number of the car that left and wrote it down for me.

Now write the story as you would tell it to each of the following audiences:

A. the judge in traffic court

B. your best friend

C. your younger brother who is a careless driver

D. classmates, a college class in criminal justice studying evidence

What differences do you notice between each story? Why did you make those choices? What purposes were you trying to achieve in each account?

The Purposes of Writing

Purposes of Writing

To think (you will create and organize ideas)

To inform (your reader will understand)

To persuade (your reader will agree)

To entertain (your reader will enjoy)

You can look at the purposes of writing in several ways. You can think in general terms about the kind of reaction you want your audience to have or you can think about the specific kind of task you want to accomplish. Is it part of your personal life, your school or academic life, or your work? Let's look at four purposes of writing and how they are combined:

■ *To think on paper and organize thoughts:* You may write things down to help you remember them or to learn new material or to help you think through a problem or issue. Usually the personal writing you do for this purpose—notes, outlines, free writing, journals, memos to yourself—will be meaningful and useful to you rather than to another audience.

■ *To inform:* When you write to inform, you want your audience to understand a concept, procedure, or fact. You may write to teach your audience (such as writing instructions for a friend who will be taking care of your pets while you are on vacation), demonstrate your knowledge (such as writing an exam), or explain how to use a piece of equipment at work.

■ *To persuade:* When you write to **persuade**, you want to convince your audience to act or believe in a certain way; you want them to agree with you. You may write a personal letter urging a friend to move to a new house, or you may write an evaluation of an employee, asking for a higher salary for that person. In college, you may write an essay arguing that one view of history is more valid than another.

■ *To entertain:* You may write to entertain your audience, to make them laugh, to tell them a story. You want your audience to enjoy what you have written. A letter to a friend may describe in an amusing way your problems learning to use a computer.

Often you will use the last three purposes in the same piece of writing. For instance, if you are writing to persuade your audience to vote for a particular issue or candidate, you may have to inform your audience about the issue or the candidate. You may include a paragraph with a suspenseful story to illustrate the need for better safety procedures at work.

| **EXERCISE 1.5** | Write a paragraph on the city or town where you live, using each of the following purposes: |

A. persuade a business to relocate

B. explain the history of the area for a history or sociology class

C. make notes on areas where you might want to consider buying a new house

D. tell a friend about holiday decorations in your neighborhood

Improving Your Writing

How to Improve Your Writing

Be willing to work

Be willing to wrestle with your writing

Use other people's writing as models

Accept constructive criticism

Write often

Sometimes people get the idea that they are bad writers almost as if it is genetic, like red hair. But the truth is that writing ability can be greatly improved, especially the writing you do for academic or professional purposes. Writing is a skill that you learn, and you can learn to become a better writer. Here are some helpful principles to remember.

■ *Be willing to work:* Writing is hard work. To improve your writing, you will need to make a commitment of time and energy. You can't just copy papers over to make them neater—you need to put forth the effort to make serious changes. You will need to realize that all good writing is revised many times.

Computer Tip

For many people, writing and revising on a word processor is easier and quicker than writing by hand.

■ *Be willing to wrestle with your writing:* Don't give up when the writing doesn't come easily. You can think of each writing task as a problem to be solved. If you stop before finding a solution, then you haven't completed the task.

■ *Use other people's writing as models:* When you find techniques that work for other writers, try using them yourself. For example, if you find the details in George Orwell's "A Hanging" (pp. 54–58) very effective, you may want to try to include more details in your own writing.

■ *Accept constructive criticism:* Listen to your instructors, tutors, and classmates when they offer suggestions. They aren't making a final judgment on whether your writing is good or bad, but giving you helpful steps to follow. Respond with your mind, not your feelings, and act on their suggestions.

■ *Write often:* As with any skill, the more you practice it, the better you become. If you've ever played sports, you know the importance of consistently practicing. Not every day will be a good day, but your overall performance will improve.

How to Write More Often

Keep a journal. Record not just what happens to you (like in a diary), but what you think about it. Write down reactions to what you have read or heard on the news or seen in a movie or talked with a friend about. You may want to keep a specific kind of journal—a dream journal, a gardening journal, a travel journal—to record one specific activity you enjoy.

Write thank you notes. Be as specific as you can in describing what the other person has done that you appreciate.

Write an E-mail to someone. Remember your audience when you write.

Write a love letter. Try to find new ways to describe your feelings.

Write what you would like to say to someone you are upset with. (You don't have to show it to anyone.)

Write a letter to a politician or a letter to the editor. Discuss an issue that is important to you.

Write some instructions for a friend. Describe how to do something you do particularly well.

Make a list. Keep track of books you've read or movies you've seen.

Write down some of your childhood memories. Include stories told by other family members.

continued on next page

continued from previous page

Write a letter to someone you have a problem with. Try to resolve the problem.

Write to learn for an exam. Outline your notes.

Write your own questions for an exam.

READING, WRITING, THINKING, AND THIS BOOK

This book is based on the idea that your success in college and in the work you choose to do will partly depend on your ability to continue to improve your reading, writing, and thinking skills. This book also assumes that focusing on reading and writing together to write essays is one of the most efficient ways to use both skills to improve your ability to think. As you work in each chapter, you'll see that we frequently ask you to use reading as a way to improve your writing and to use writing as a way to help your reading. You will not use all the options we offer, but you will find some that will help you to become a better reader and writer. We hope that this process will also help you see your ideas more clearly—and that you will be proud of the essays you will be writing.

Essential Tools for College Writers
Essays, Computers, the Internet, MLA, ESL

Reading, writing, and **critical thinking** will probably continue to be essential skills for you as a worker and as a citizen for the rest of your life. During the time that you're in college, however, you will need to focus on some very specific skills that you'll need to develop in order to succeed in many of your courses. You must learn to write **essays**, a format for writing that underlies many types of writing required in college. In many essays, you will be responding to one or more readings, but sometimes you will write more generally, drawing mainly on your experience of the world. In yet other assignments, you will need to locate information and ideas from other sources, so your essays will include research, and you will need to learn to use the computer efficiently as a writer and researcher. If you're learning English as a new language, you may need also to learn some ways of approaching **academic writing** that may be different from your former practices.

All of these skills will be presented throughout this book at specific points where they are especially appropriate to the reading-writing-thinking process. In this chapter, you will find icons (see the top of page 26, for example) which will highlight certain skills. A list of pages where each skill is discussed is also provided. You can also use the table of contents and the index to help you locate the information that you need.

THE ESSAY: A FORMAT COMBINING READING, WRITING, AND CRITICAL THINKING

Reading, writing, and critical thinking come together in the basic form of academic writing: the essay. Your college essay assignments will require you to demonstrate your understanding of readings and to report what you understand, along with your response to the reading as well as to your instructor's and classmates' perception of the reading. Sometimes your essays will focus on your response to one reading, but in others, you may use a variety of readings to **support** larger ideas. In later courses, your instructors may call these essays by many names—research papers, critical papers, reports, analyses, **critiques**. But no matter what the name, you will still use the basic principles of the essay: relating your reading to your own writing.

Before you go on to learn all the various kinds of **academic** and business **writing** you may encounter in your life, you must first master the format of the essay. All other longer papers are variations on this basic format, which consists of three parts:

- The **introduction** gives your reader an idea of what the essay will be about.
- The **body** is always divided into several parts, and each part supports the main idea in some way, and develops each part completely.
- The **conclusion** returns to the main idea to show the reader how the parts of the body do support that main idea.

Almost any complete piece of writing will have these three parts, whether it's a business proposal, a chemistry lab report, or a psychology research paper. In short essays (like those you'll write for the assignments in this book), each part may be just one paragraph, but in longer papers, a part may be several paragraphs or even pages.

When you write for a specific situation, whether it's a college course or a business transaction, each of these three parts will be subdivided into other parts. Part of learning to write an essay will involve learning how to subdivide your writing. This course is intended to teach you to relate your reading to your writing and thinking, so the required parts will reflect that relationship. Let's now look again at the parts of the essay with the subdivisions added (a complete explanation of how to develop each part is found on the pages in parentheses):

Parts of an Essay Based on Critical Reading

Introduction (pp. 126–141):

- **lead-in** involves reader in topic
- **author and title of reading**
- **main idea of reading** gives idea of what reading is about
- **student writer's thesis** tells your main idea

continued on next page

continued from previous page

Body (pp. 142–152):

■ **several paragraphs** divided according to different reasons why thesis is true, or ways that it is true

■ **each paragraph consists of**

> **topic sentence**—gives main idea of paragraph
>
> **examples and ideas from reading**—makes author's ideas clear
>
> **examples and ideas from student writer**—makes clear student writer's support for main idea of paragraph
>
> **concluding sentence**—reminds reader how support relates to main idea

Conclusion (pp. 153-161):

■ **return to main idea** reminds reader how body paragraphs support thesis

Here is an essay written in response to George Orwell's "A Hanging" (pp. 54–58). The major parts of the essay are labeled on the left side and the parts of each paragraph are labeled on the right. Chapters 8, 9, and 10 (pp. 126–161) will present a complete explanation of how to write all the parts of an essay.

Obeying Orders

INTRODUCTION

1   Most people go through their lives following orders, without questioning whether they should obey so readily. The military is based upon the assumption that all orders will be carried out without question. Laws and regulations work only when we expect people to obey them without question. Safety of children often depends on their following adults' orders and rules without question. Even at work, we have agreed to follow the company's orders just to carry out our jobs. Although people do follow most of the orders given on a daily basis, some situations force a person to question whether or not an order should be followed. *— lead-in* One such situation is depicted in George Orwell's "A Hanging," in which Orwell and fellow *— author, title of reading* British police officers in Burma execute a man. In the essay, Orwell makes an argument against capital punishment. But *— main idea of reading* the essay can also be read to show us why we should not always follow orders. When an order conflicts with our morals or *— THESIS* risks the lives of other people, it should not be carried out.

BODY PARAGRAPHS —

2   Whenever we must decide whether to follow an order, we should first ask ourselves if following the order will risk the safety of others. — topic sentence

Orwell was a police officer and was expected to enforce British law in colonial Burma. In this job, he should have expected to see people die. — examples and ideas from reading

However, faced with an execution Orwell discovers that he believes it is wrong to take another person's life: "Until that moment I had never realized what it means to destroy a healthy, conscious man. When I saw the prisoner step aside to avoid the puddle I saw the mystery, the unspeakable wrongness, of cutting a life short when it is in full tide" (56). By coming face to face with the condemned man, Orwell realizes that killing another human is wrong. Even when we do not know the persons involved, we should not follow orders if there is a possibility that someone may get hurt. I encountered such a situation last week when an angry customer called to complain about her toaster exploding. I reported her story to my supervisor because I thought the Quality Management staff should be made aware of the possible safety problem. My supervisor ordered me to send the customer a new toaster, but not to send a copy of the complaint to Quality Management. He was concerned that it would create needless work and worry since this complaint was the first report of any problems with this model of toaster. Even though I disagreed with my supervisor, I did what he said at the time. However, I feel guilty when I think that a faulty toaster produced by my company may cause families to lose their homes and maybe even their lives. — examples and ideas from student writer

I now have to make a choice—follow my boss' orders or follow my own morals. — concluding sentence

BODY PARAGRAPHS —

3   It seems obvious that one should follow one's own morals if they conflict with an order. However, acting on this belief is difficult. — topic sentence

I may have to risk my job to let Quality Management know about the complaint. The company may even decide not to investigate the safety of the toaster. Then, I may have to choose to inform the public, and such action may prevent me from getting another job. These are the same decisions Orwell faces as a young man. He realizes that capital punishment is wrong, but as an individual member of the police force, he does not try to prevent the execution and does — examples and ideas from student writer

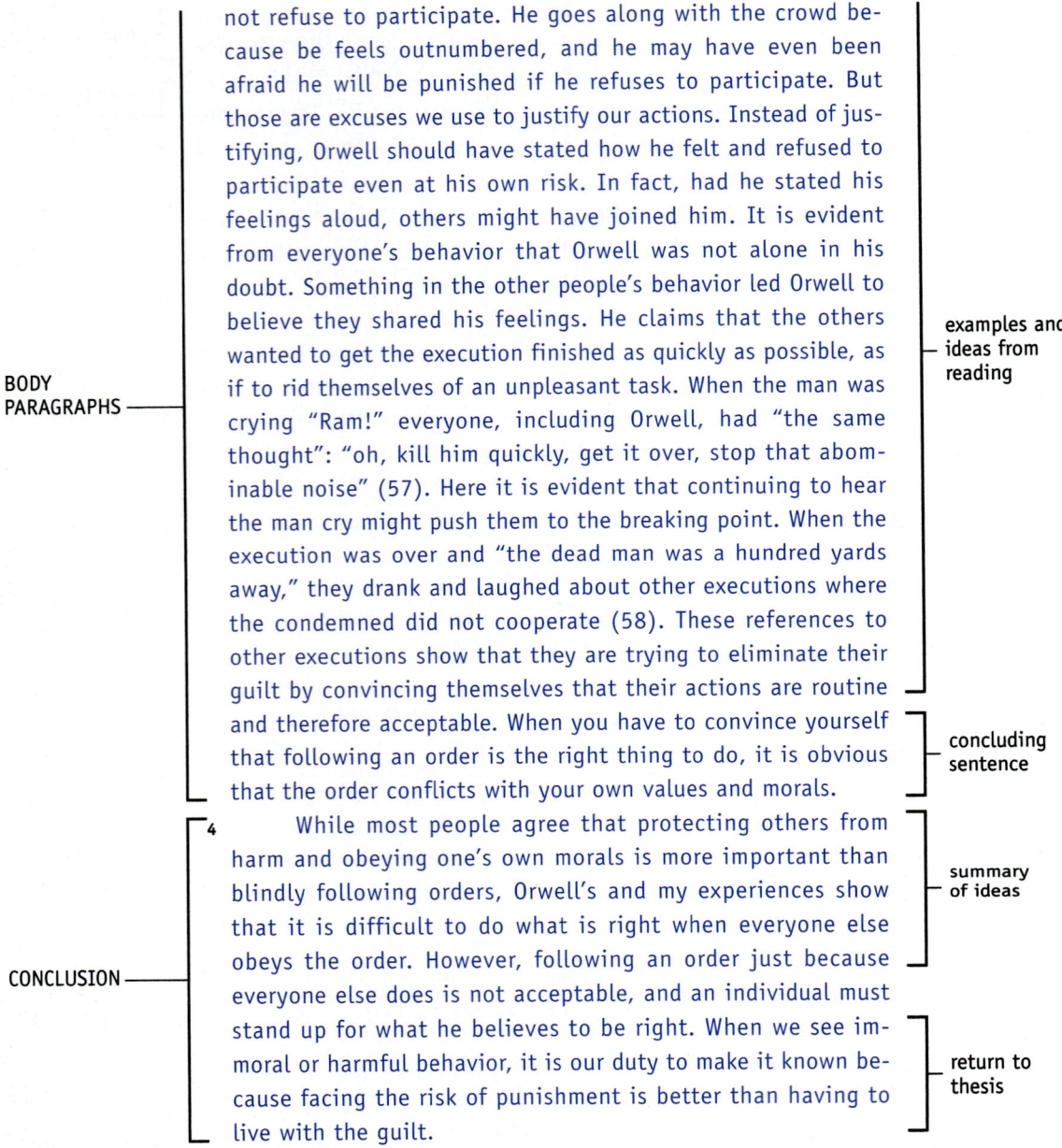

BODY PARAGRAPHS

not refuse to participate. He goes along with the crowd because he feels outnumbered, and he may have even been afraid he will be punished if he refuses to participate. But those are excuses we use to justify our actions. Instead of justifying, Orwell should have stated how he felt and refused to participate even at his own risk. In fact, had he stated his feelings aloud, others might have joined him. It is evident from everyone's behavior that Orwell was not alone in his doubt. Something in the other people's behavior led Orwell to believe they shared his feelings. He claims that the others wanted to get the execution finished as quickly as possible, as if to rid themselves of an unpleasant task. When the man was crying "Ram!" everyone, including Orwell, had "the same thought": "oh, kill him quickly, get it over, stop that abominable noise" (57). Here it is evident that continuing to hear the man cry might push them to the breaking point. When the execution was over and "the dead man was a hundred yards away," they drank and laughed about other executions where the condemned did not cooperate (58). These references to other executions show that they are trying to eliminate their guilt by convincing themselves that their actions are routine and therefore acceptable. When you have to convince yourself that following an order is the right thing to do, it is obvious that the order conflicts with your own values and morals.

examples and ideas from reading

concluding sentence

CONCLUSION

4   While most people agree that protecting others from harm and obeying one's own morals is more important than blindly following orders, Orwell's and my experiences show that it is difficult to do what is right when everyone else obeys the order. However, following an order just because everyone else does is not acceptable, and an individual must stand up for what he believes to be right. When we see immoral or harmful behavior, it is our duty to make it known because facing the risk of punishment is better than having to live with the guilt.

summary of ideas

return to thesis

This example illustrates all the parts of the essay. You can see that the student writer can make many choices about where to put a certain part. For example, in the first body paragraph, the discussion of material from the reading comes first, followed by the student's own example and explanation. These parts are in a different order in the second body paragraph, where the student's own material comes before the ideas from the reading.

As you become more experienced in writing essays, you will learn to write many variations on this basic pattern. For example, you'll learn to decide when you must clearly state your thesis in the introduction and when you can save it for the conclusion, or when you can imply the topic sentence of a paragraph or introduce it in between two examples. Many instructors will want you to be sure that you can write an essay with all these parts clearly stated before you begin to try the variations. Also, you'll find that you may use any number of body paragraphs. The examples we'll show in this book will usually have from two to four body paragraphs, because short essays are easier to control than long ones. In later courses, you'll need to write much longer essays, and you may find that you will need more than one paragraph for the introduction and conclusion.

However, some essential aspects of the essay will be the same, no matter how long the essay is or how many variations you use. Essays always focus on one central point, they always use supporting ideas to develop that point, and they always have some ways of developing those ideas, whether they are examples, quotations, facts, summaries, explanations, or comparisons.

RESEARCH IN ACADEMIC WRITING: USING MLA, AVOIDING PLAGIARISM

Writing in college may mean that you must not only respond to something you read, but also that you must locate additional material at some point in your essay. Instructors in writing and other college courses may assign many different types of research, and may use different names for the kinds of papers they assign. Be sure that you understand what kind of research your instructor wants you to do, and what format you should use. These are the main types of research assignments:

- *Research papers:* Papers based almost totally on outside sources; usually fairly long, but basically organized like an essay
- *Essays with research:* Papers based primarily on student's own ideas, supported by research
- *Summaries and critiques:* Summaries give the main ideas of one or more sources; critiques also give your evaluation of the source
- *Annotated bibliographies:* **Citations** for sources followed by brief summaries or critiques; may stand alone or be part of a paper

Different types of assignments will require you to do research at one or more distinct points in the writing process. For this reason, you will find information on different stages of research at several points in this book. Look for the symbol **RES** in the margin. Here's a brief list of the main sections on research:

> ## For Information on Research
>
> Locating material and using the library: pp. 261–263, 280–285
>
> Evaluating sources: pp. 264–270, 281–282
>
> Taking notes: pp. 254–258, 396–399
>
> Organizing the paper: pp. 90–91, 110–111, 300–302
>
> Writing with sources: pp. 139, 388–392
>
> Documenting sources: pp. 393–403

Avoiding Plagiarism

When you research a topic, or when you write in response to another writer, you will need to be careful to avoid **plagiarism**. Plagiarism means using someone else's ideas, facts, or words as if they were your own. In colleges, universities, and schools in the United States, it is very important to make a clear distinction between your own work and someone else's. If you use ideas, facts, or words from another writer and don't explain clearly who wrote them, your instructor may believe that you are cheating, and may give you a low grade or make you rewrite the paper. In some cases, you could face even greater punishment, such as failing the course or being asked to leave the college.

Some students believe that if they can find papers on the Internet that were written by other students and turn them in as their own, the instructor won't know that the papers are not original. This is a big mistake. Instructors quickly learn your individual writing style and recognize any change; also, a paper someone else wrote for another class will not be likely to fit your assignment. Furthermore, your instructor may ask you to turn in notes and **drafts**, and you will not have those. Realize, too, that instructors also know how to use the Internet and they will probably be able to find any paper that you can find—and often more easily than you did. Of course, the real reason for doing your own work is that you will need to acquire the reading and writing skills taught in the course you are taking in order to succeed in later courses and jobs. You must *practice* those skills to be able to improve your ability.

Other students have no intention of cheating, but they aren't sure how to let the reader know that they are using another writer's work. This book will help you find easy ways to do this; it is called **documentation**. When you use accepted ways of documenting sources, the reader can easily see which ideas, facts, and words are your own and which belong to another writer.

Using MLA Style

To help you learn to document your sources, this book will help you learn how to use **MLA** style. What does this mean? *Style* refers to the format you use to show where you found your material: what information comes first, how it is punctuated, etc. *MLA* is the abbreviation for Modern Language Association, which is the professional organization for scholars who research and write about literature and language. Most English instructors will expect you to learn this style first, so this book will teach you the basics of this style. Once you learn MLA, you will understand how documentation works, and why it is important. If you write a paper for another kind of course, you may be asked to use a very different style. Psychology and other social sciences use **APA** (American Psychological Association) style, and some sciences use **CBE** (Council of Biological Editors). These formats usually include the same information as MLA, but may put it in a different order or use different punctuation. If you do write a paper for another kind of course, be sure to ask the instructor what style you should use. Libraries and writing centers usually have many different books explaining each style in detail, and there are also excellent web sites on each. The advantage of finding the style on a web site is that the information will be more current, since these styles often change as ways of research and writing change. Common use of the Internet and word processing programs has caused great changes in MLA and other styles recently.

Like other aspects of research, documentation will be introduced in this book at the points where you might be likely to use it. Look at the following pages for details of MLA style:

For Details of MLA Style
Parenthetical Documentation: p. 403
Citations: pp. 399–402

THE ESSAY: A FORMAT USING ONLY YOUR OWN THOUGHTS

Not every essay you write will respond to something written by another author. Sometimes you will write an essay relying only on your own thoughts and experiences. The format of the essay and the process of writing it are pretty much the same, whether you respond directly to another writer or develop your ideas entirely on your own. The box below shows a list of the parts of the essay when no outside reading is used.

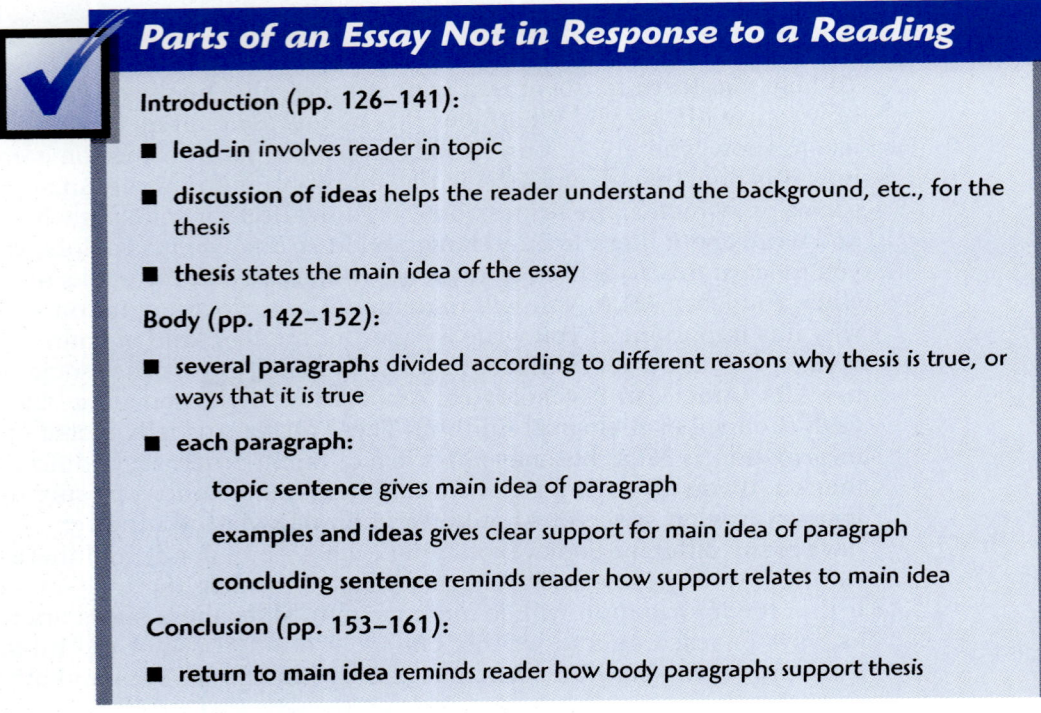

Parts of an Essay Not in Response to a Reading

Introduction (pp. 126–141):

■ **lead-in** involves reader in topic

■ **discussion of ideas** helps the reader understand the background, etc., for the thesis

■ **thesis** states the main idea of the essay

Body (pp. 142–152):

■ **several paragraphs** divided according to different reasons why thesis is true, or ways that it is true

■ **each paragraph:**

   topic sentence gives main idea of paragraph

   examples and ideas gives clear support for main idea of paragraph

   concluding sentence reminds reader how support relates to main idea

Conclusion (pp. 153–161):

■ **return to main idea** reminds reader how body paragraphs support thesis

In the sample essay below, you'll find each of these divisions and subdivisions of the essay labeled. Notice how the entire essay continues to focus on one central idea.

There's No Such Thing as "Just Following Orders"

INTRODUCTION —

1   I have what I call a "button board." It is like a bulletin board, but it only contains buttons. In the middle of my board are my two favorites: "Question Authority" and "No B.S. Please." The two are closely related in my mind. One is an obvious reminder that just because something or someone is an authority, they should not be automatically accepted. The second explains why authorities sometimes cannot be trusted. Sometimes following orders involves just following unreasonable and arbitrary rules. Of course, sometimes, following orders prevents chaos. But I believe that there are certain situations when people should not follow orders. I can imagine at least three situations in which not following orders

— lead-in

discussion of ideas

THESIS

INTRODUCTION

or not obeying an authority is preferable to following orders. The most obvious situation is one in which someone tells you to do something that is clearly against your morals. Another situation is one in which the orders or instructions you are given seem to be harmful to the larger society around us. A different kind of situation is when a person just has to stand up for common sense and reasonable behavior, even if following orders does not do anyone specific harm or damage.

BODY PARAGRAPH

2   We are all familiar with what is referred to as "the Holocaust" in Nazi Germany during World War II. This must be for many people the epitome of what happens when many people follow orders that were immoral, and it was definitely one time when those immoral orders should not have been followed. — topic sentence

Of course, authority there was fragmented. Not every "undesirable" was arrested and sent to concentration camps in one moment—some people just vanished. Although Adolf Hitler was elected as Chancellor of Germany, the population did not have a referendum and vote "yes" or "no" on a proposition like: "arrest, steal from, put into concentration camps, starve, work until exhaustion, physically abuse, and then kill all undesirable people." No, the people just did their little parts in obeying orders, like just identifying suspicious individuals, just driving the transport trains, just guarding the individuals, just collecting property, just making an inventory of individuals, just taking "abandoned" property, etc. The list could be very long, but each little act followed an immoral order, in the long run, although only a few people actually pulled triggers, pushed buttons, or turned knobs that delivered physical pain and death. And of course, everyone could rationalize their little part by saying that this was a wartime situation and different rules applied and that after the war everything would be better and you could afford to have scruples then. — ideas and examples

But even war is no excuse for following immoral orders. — concluding sentence

BODY PARAGRAPH

3   Usually obeying an authority in a situation like the Holocaust also involves fear. The individuals who obey authority are afraid of what might happen to other people they care for like family members. It doesn't take a holocaust to make that fear real. For example, people who work for a business or company that does harm to other individuals or the

public in general might be afraid to disobey because they will lose their jobs and their families will suffer—but they need to learn to look beyond that fear and see the great harm they are causing by following orders that are not always as clearly immoral as the Holocaust. People who have worked for companies that fail to advance people of different races, ethnic backgrounds, or members of one sex may complain about the company's policies, but they do not refuse to work—and they should. The personnel managers continue to hire, fire, and promote those people their bosses tell them to, even if they may disagree about who is really more qualified for a particular position. Similarly, people who work for companies that pollute or wastefully use more resources than they are entitled to may keep their jobs because they fear to lose the money and benefits provided to themselves and their family members. For example, a public facility may refuse to let a non-profit organization reserve its space in advance because it wants to hold it in reserve for potentially paying companies. That is, the administrator is reinterpreting her position as caretaker of public facilities; she wants to generate funds by using those public facilities. In this case, the person making reservations may be told to tell a middle-school enrichment program for at-risk students that the facilities are unavailable because an insurance company has inquired—just inquired—about using the facilities to host a management training seminar. But the facilities were built with public monies allocated for the public use, and were not intended as a money-making resource for the public. Should the reservation assistant follow orders and tell the at-risk program coordinator to call back later? Or should she make a reservation for 50 seventh graders who need positive experiences with public facilities, who need to learn that official programs do not mean detention or summer school? This is definitely a time to disobey orders. The effect of this bad order was not as drastically harmful as the effect of the Holocaust, but ultimately society would have benefited if this bureaucrat had put morals before profit.

4   Some orders may not violate moral principles, but go against common sense. These orders, too, should be disobeyed. Once I had a job searching for information on-line

BODY PARAGRAPH

and in a special library for a project on allocation of public funds according to demographic factors—people's different backgrounds and socioeconomic status. It was just a summer job, but I enjoyed it. I made folders of related information, and I got to decide how to organize the information and what supporting documentation and photocopies to include for support. I compared expenditures per student in Minnesota to expenditures per student in my own state. But there was one drawback. The project administrator kept calling meetings. He would call them whenever he wanted to communicate with us. (Of course, he could have used the Internet for most of them!) He would call them without any notice. He would call them at 9:00 a.m. for 11:00 a.m. There was no crisis. He just called meetings. I wrote a letter asking for at least 24-hours notice for meetings that did not have at least that much notice. I said I could not guarantee that I would attend meetings if I did not have at least that much notice. And I got fired. Is this really an example of not following orders? In a way, no. But, in another way, yes. If something does not make sense, just "because someone says to" is not enough reason to do it. People should not follow orders that are motivatied only by an individual's ego. People should follow orders that are reasonable. If people get into a habit of not questioning orders and people who give orders become complacent about having to justify their orders—even to employees, the world could become a dangerous place.

ideas and examples

concluding sentence

CONCLUSION

5   Should we follow orders? Yes, if they make sense and do no harm, or less harm than not following them. Sometimes, in a moment of crisis, following orders of an authority figure, such as a park ranger or medical professional, is the right thing to do. In such moments, the person giving the orders clearly has the other person's best interests in mind. But in most other situations, it is always a good idea to question authority and to evaluate the reasons underlying any order. Even getting used to "just following orders" without thinking is dangerous in a free society. It is also true that sometimes there may be great pressures on people to try to survive, but surviving at the expense of ethical and moral behavior, maybe even at the expense of other people's chances for advancement, health, or even lives only makes us part of the immoral and unethical

return to main idea

CONCLUSION ———

behavior. Even if we are only a small part of a larger organization, we are still responsible for what we agree to do. If more people would question authority and refuse to mindlessly follow orders, the world would be a better place. Not only would there be less B.S., but there might even be less corruption, discrimination, and other unethical and immoral behavior.

The chapters of this book that explain how to develop an essay will show you steps that respond to readings, but many of the steps are the same when you are not responding to a reading. You'll find this symbol in the margin to help you recognize sections that will be especially useful when writing this kind of essay: **OWN**. Here's a brief list of the pages you'll use if you are *not* writing about a reading:

For Writing an Essay Not in Response to a Reading

Analyzing the assignment: pp. 79–82

Prewriting: pp. 95–103

Organizing: pp. 115–121

Writing the draft: pp. 128–131, 136–138, 146–147, 305–307

Revising: pp. 164–165, 180–181

Editing: pp. 194–211

CYBER COLLEGE: WRITING, READING, THINKING— AND COMPUTERS

Computers provide a way to improve your work efficiently, without recopying your paper between drafts. This is important because when you revise or edit your drafts, you may improve the parts you are working on, but you are very likely to introduce new errors if you are just copying what is correct. (Try it. Copy this entire paragraph in a hurry and see if you are accurate or if you have made some mistakes.) Another reason computers are good writing tools is that you can rearrange either large parts of your writing or individual sentences many times to discover which order is best. There are many other reasons to use a computer when writing. You can probably add to the list below.

■ Word-processed papers can be saved and reprinted.

■ Word-processed papers can become parts of larger projects.

■ Group work is easier if everyone has an electronic version of their contributions and the parts can be merged together to create a larger uniform document.

■ More individual help in revising and editing is available on computers. These computer program aids include **spell checks**, **grammar checks**, style checks, and format checks. Grammar and spelling tutorials are also available as computer software.

■ Keeping an **Editing Log** (see pp. 341–346) is easier using a computer.

■ If you are unable to come to class, you can E-mail your paper to your instructor (and not lose points because the paper is late).

■ An instructor can E-mail comments back to you, even if it is not possible physically to go the instructor's office hours.

■ Employers assume more and more that all employees will have some kinds of word-processing skills.

The Computer Skills You'll Need

Because computers can make your reading, writing, and thinking in college much easier, and can also improve the quality of the work you do, you'll want to be ready to use them as soon as you can. Even if you seem to lose time in mastering computer skills at first, you will eventually save much more time. Here are the essential skills you should try to master as soon as you come to college:

Keyboarding—learning to type by touch.

Word processing—learning a recently published and commonly used program such as Word for Windows or WordPerfect.

Sending E-mail—sending and receiving messages and attachments.

Finding information on the web—using **search engines** and databases.

Downloading files—moving information from the Internet to your own computer.

Chatrooms, Discussion webs, Listservs—using the Internet for conversations, especially about classes.

Evaluating Internet material—learning to distinguish good information from bad.

Some Computer Dos and Don'ts

Although using a computer to write papers has many advantages, there are also some potential problems you should try to avoid. Follow the tips below to use computers more efficiently in your own work.

Saving Your Work

■ **Always save your work on a diskette.** Do not use public hard drives, such as the hard drives on computers in a writing center or a learning center. Lab assistants and tutors periodically clean all documents off the hard drives, so your paper may be deleted as a matter of lab policy.

You may also be unable to get to the computer you saved your document on. If the computers are not networked, you will not be able to retrieve your document unless you work on the same computer.

■ **Make back-up copies of your files.** You may lose a diskette or the diskette may become damaged or corrupted.

■ **Save your revised work with a new name** (using *Save as*). You will need to keep older drafts. If you save a file with the same name, the most recent version will replace the older draft and the older draft will be lost. If you had some good ideas, notes, or prewriting that might be useful in a later revision, you should save the new draft under a different name.

■ **Name your files obvious names.** (Paper1 or Essay3 is easy to remember.)

■ **Label the diskette you are working on** so you do not bring the wrong diskette to class or the computer lab.

■ **Beware of viruses.** Learn how to use virus checkers and do not use pirated software. Be careful when you copy material from the Internet. You may also get viruses from using public labs.

Spell Checkers

Learn to use the spell checker in your word processor program, but check each word that is highlighted/underlined by the spell checker. Why?

■ Most names are not part of the dictionary of spell checkers. Last names like *Bronski* will be underlined, even if they are correct.

■ Spell checkers just check the word against a list. They do not check to see if the word makes sense in that context. For example, *doe snot* may not be underlined, even if you intended to write *does not*.

ESL ■ Spell checkers usually count repeated words as mistakes. However, read the sentence. Sometimes a word needs to be repeated because it serves different functions, as in *That that that I deleted should have been left in.*

■ Because most people are not efficient and accurate keyboarders, they make more spelling mistakes. They may type *van* for *can*, or *nut* for *but*. Read your paper aloud to catch this type of typographical error.

Grammar Checkers

Most grammar checkers are not very accurate. They are no substitute for a good tutor or instructor.

■ While grammar checkers can help you see if a sentence is very long, this does not necessarily mean all long sentences should be changed. Some long sentences are effective. For example, you may need a long, balanced list of equally important points.

■ Grammar checkers may not allow you to have compound words like *student work assistants*. They may also suggest that you add an *-s* to a present tense verb following an irregular plural: *The electronic media support this type of regulation.*

Formatting Your Paper

Learn to use the tool bars to format your paper according to your instructor's specifications.

■ Be sure to leave 1" margins on all sides, insert page numbers (with your name), and double-space the body of the paper. Center headings and include identification information on the first page or the title page (if you have a separate one). Indent using the tab, and only use the **ENTER** (**RETURN**) key if you want to start a new paragraph.

■ Ask your instructor what **format** you should follow for the *Works Cited* or *References* section. Usually you will need to have a **hanging indent**. Only use a hard return (the **ENTER** key) between separate works. Do not line up the indented lines using the **TAB** key.

E-mailing your document

You should become familiar with how your instructor wants you to send electronic versions of your paper. Sending a file as an attachment will save most of the formatting. Also, you can probably cut and paste a file inside of a regular email message, although most of the formatting will be lost.

Tips for Using a Computer Effectively

Always save your document on a diskette.

Keep back-up copies.

Learn to "Save as" with a new name.

Watch out for viruses.

Check the spell checker.

Don't rely on grammar checkers.

Be careful formatting your paper.

Learn to E-mail your work.

ENGLISH AS A SECOND LANGUAGE (ESL) AND THIS BOOK

If you have learned English as a Second Language, you will find that many of the sections of this book will be especially helpful to you. Many of your fellow students who have always spoken English are actually learning a new language in this course, too—they are learning to read and write Academic

English, instead of the more informal English they have always used for speaking and writing. In many parts of the book, you'll find that the information and explanations you need as an ESL student are included as parts of the chapters intended for all students. To find those sections easily, look for the symbol **ESL** in the margin. For easy reference, here are some sections you should find useful.

ESL

> ## Useful Pages for Solving ESL Problems
>
> Reading: pp. 68–69, 73–74, 79–80, 258–261
>
> Analyzing the assignment: pp. 76–80, 274–275
>
> Prewriting: pp. 94–95
>
> Organizing: pp. 114, 297–298
>
> Writing: pp. 133–136, 144, 153–154
>
> Revising: pp. 165–169, 320
>
> Editing: pp. 194–224, 326–346
>
> Handbook: pp. 350–354, 365–371, 403–418

Reading and Vocabulary

Learning new vocabulary is one big task in learning a new language. When you first began to study English, you may have memorized lists of words. You may still want to work on memory, but as much as possible you should now try to learn to understand words from their **context**, which is exactly what native speakers must also do (see p. 68). Be sure that you have two dictionaries: don't rely on just your ESL dictionary; also use a college-level dictionary for native speakers. You may find useful explanations in either dictionary, but be sure to look for the appropriate meaning for the sentence (see p. 69).

Keeping Lists

Keeping a list in a small notebook that you can always keep with you is one additional way to increase your knowledge of English words. You may encounter words in your textbooks for many subjects, in advertisements, in newspapers, and in many other places. Write down the word and your best guess at the meaning; then check the meaning in a dictionary when you have time.

However, words alone may not be enough. You also need to know how words are used. In English and in other languages, certain words are customarily used together. For example, take the word *bill*, meaning *money owed for services or goods*. You might hear American English speakers say *pay the bill* but you would not hear them say *pay for the bill* or *cash the bill* or *spend the bill*, although the dictionary meanings of some of these words may seem to be very close to the meaning of *pay*. These common combinations of words are called **collocations**, and you may want to keep a vocabulary list that includes the phrase where you found the word. You can ask instructors, tutors, and other students for other possible collocations for your words, so leave room in your list to add more possible collocations.

Some combinations of words have meanings that are entirely different from the meaning of the individual words. These are called **idioms**, and you may want to keep a special section of your notebook for idioms. Idioms are more common in spoken language and slang, but you will find idioms even in academic writing, and certain subjects (like computer science) may have their own idioms. For example, when someone says that she *crashed her hard drive*, she means that the main part of her computer doesn't work anymore, but she does not mean that it is physically broken. If your college has a writing center, it may have a dictionary of idioms, but you may still want to keep your own list.

Steps in the Reading and Writing Process

You may find that the many steps outlined in this book are helpful, or you may not understand why you need to do so many different things before, during, and after you read an article or write an essay, especially if you are accustomed to reading difficult material and writing academic essays about it. The explanations in the chapters should help you understand how the steps lead to the kind of reading and writing expected in colleges in the United States. If you try the steps, you may find them helpful, but if you've already developed the skills of reading, writing, and thinking, you may need to spend your time working with vocabulary and editing.

You may find that the kind of reading and writing expected in this course is very similar to the kind you've done in other classes, but you should not be surprised if your instructor asks for something different from what you've done before. Look at the examples in these chapters, especially the explanations with the **ESL** icon, and ask your instructor if you still don't understand what the terms mean. Also check the Glossary (pp. 630–636) and Index (pp. 639–644) to find more explanation.

Look especially at the sections on stating the **thesis** sentence (pp. 128–138). This is a very important element in academic writing in the United States. Sometimes you may feel that the central idea of your essay does not need to be clearly stated, but your instructors will prefer that you do state the main idea clearly. Also, look at sections on support (pp. 143–151), which tell you the kinds of facts, examples, and explanations expected in this kind of writing.

Also, be sure you understand plagiarism (pp. 26–27). In college writing in the United States, as in many other places, instructors feel very strongly that every word or idea that you do not think of yourself must be documented (pp. 393–403). This means that you must always state very explicitly where you found the words or ideas (also called sources). Some instructors may mistakenly believe that you are trying to cheat if you do not document sources.

Group Work

One common activity in different stages of reading and writing is group work. You may be very accustomed to this way of learning, or you may not be. You may feel that only the instructor can help you to improve your writing. However, many instructors want you to learn to understand different points of view about articles that you read, and they may want you to learn to write to many different kinds of audiences, so they will ask you to discuss your reactions to articles written by your fellow students as well as professional writers. They may also ask you to check each other's writing for errors in grammar, spelling, and punctuation, called **editing**. Especially if this kind of classwork is new to you, you should read the sections on **peer editing** (pp. 206–208). You may find that working with other students is very helpful, because often they will see problems in your writing that you may not recognize, and also you may find that looking for other students' problems helps you learn to find your own.

USING THE SKILLS OF COLLEGE READING, WRITING, AND THINKING

In the rest of this book, you will find much more material on writing essays, using sources, using the computer, and using the English language. This book will help you to improve in those areas, and will help you find specific remedies for problems you encounter in your writing assignments. Talk with your instructor, tutors, and fellow students to find the sections that will help you the most. Read the sections carefully, try the exercises, and review when you go on to use the skill in your reading and writing. This book will work if you will work.

3

Five Readings for Analysis

The five essays in this chapter will be used as examples throughout the rest of the book. You may want to read them as you come to them in the following chapters, or you may want to read them early in the course so that you can understand the references as you encounter them.

Measuring Success

by Renee Loth

Renee Loth, writing in the Boston Globe Magazine *in 1997, questions our definitions of success. Is success only financial, or can it mean other things?*

1   Back when I was a callow college student, I devised a neat grid system for what I hoped would be my life's achievements. I could count my life a good one, I thought, if I could attain both success and happiness. So I set about analyzing the component parts of each: Happiness I subdivided into sections labeled health and love; success, I determined, was composed of wealth and fame.

2   Once I actually entered the world of work, however, I learned that success is not so easy to define. For one thing, when I made my simple calculation, I never took into account the joy of creation; the approbation of one's peers; the energy of collaboration; or the sheer satisfaction of a job well done. These are real qualities of success that live outside of wealth or fame.

3   Also, I found that definitions of success are mutable, shifting along with our changing values. If we stick with our chosen fields long enough, we sometimes have an opportunity to meet our heroes, people we thought wildly successful when we were young. A musician friend told me that he spent most of his youth wanting to play like the greats, until he started getting to know some of them. To his surprise, many turned out to be embittered, dulled by drink or boredom, unable to hold together a marriage, or wantonly jealous of others. That's when he realized he wanted to play like himself.

4   Success is defined differently by different people. For some, it is symbolized by the number of buttons on the office phone. For others, it is having

only one button and a secretary to field the calls. Some think the more nights and weekends they spend at the office, the more successful they must be. For others, success is directly proportional to time off.

5   And what about those qualities I did include in my handy grid system? Wealth—beyond what is needed to provide for oneself and one's family, with a little left over for airfare to someplace subtropical in January—turned out to be superfluous. And the little experience I had with fame turned out to be downright scary.

6   Several years ago, I had occasion to appear on a dull but respected national evening television news show. My performance lasted exactly six minutes, and my name flashed only twice. But when I got home from the live broadcast, my answering machine had maxed out on messages. I heard from a woman I had last seen in Brownie Scouts. I heard from former boyfriends, conspiracy theorists, and celebrity agents. I even got an obscene phone call—what kind of pervert watches PBS?—from someone who might have been an old friend pulling my leg. At least, I hope so.

7   For weeks afterward, I received tons of what an optimist might call fan mail. One fellow insisted that if I froze a particular frame of a political campaign ad I had been discussing, I could see the face of Bill Clinton in the American flag. Somebody sent me a chapter of a novel in progress with a main character disturbingly like me. Several people sent me chain letters. I was relieved when the fickle finger of fame moved on to someone else.

8   When I was young and romanticizing about success, I liked a particular Joni Mitchell lyric: "My struggle for higher achievement and my search for love don't seem to cease." Ah, but the trouble with struggling and searching is that it keeps us in a permanent state of wanting—always reaching for more. The drive to succeed keeps us focused on the future, to the detriment of life in the moment. And the moment is all we ever really have.

9   When I look back at my simplistic little value system, I am a bit chagrined at how absolute I thought life was. But I am also happy to report that the achievements that have come my way are the ones that count. After twenty years of supercharged ambition, I have stumbled upon this bit of wisdom. Who needs wealth and fame? Two out of four ain't bad.

My Father's Tribal Rule

by Mark Mathabane

Mark Mathabane grew up in South Africa and experienced the hardships of the years of apartheid. A college scholarship brought him to the United States. This selection is taken from his autobiography, Kaffir Boy, *published in 1986. Mathabane now lives in North Carolina; his latest book is* Miriam's Song: A Memoir.

1 One night our dingy shack, which had been leaning precipitously on the edge of a *donga*,[1] collapsed. Luckily no one was hurt, but we were forced to move to another one, similarly built. This new shack, like the old one, had two rooms and measured something like fifteen by fifteen feet, and overlooked the same unlit, unpaved, potholed street. It had an interior flaked with old whitewash, a leaky roof of rusted zinc propped up by a thin wall of crumbling adobe, two tiny windows made of cardboard and pieces of glass, a creaky, termite-eaten door too low for a person of average height to pass through without bending double, and a floor made of patches of cement and earth. It was similar to the dozen or so shacks strewn irregularly, like lumps on a leper, upon the cracked greenless piece of ground named yard number thirty-five.

2 In this new shack my brother, George, was weaned. It was amusing to witness my mother do it. The first day she began the process she secretly smeared her breasts with red pepper and then invited my brother to suckle. Unsuspecting, George energetically attacked my mother's breast only to let go of it instantly and start hollering because of the hot pepper. This continued throughout the day whenever he wanted to suckle. Finally, after a few days, he began to dread the sight of my mother's breast, and each time she teased him with it he would turn his face. He was now weaned. My father bought a small white chicken, my mother brewed beer, a few relatives were invited, and a small celebration was held to mark George's passage from infancy to childhood. He was almost two years old. He now had to sleep with Florah and me in the kitchen.

3 Soon after George was weaned my father began teaching him, as he had been teaching me, tribal ways of life. My father belonged to a loosely knit group of black families in the neighborhood to whom tribal traditions were a way of life, and who sought to bring up their offspring according to its laws. He believed that feeding us a steady diet of tribal beliefs, values, and rituals was one way of ensuring our normal growth, so that in the event of our returning to the tribal reserve, something he insistently believed would happen soon, we would blend in perfectly. This diet he administered religiously, seemingly bent on moulding George and me in his image. At first I had tried to resist the diet, but my father's severe looks frightened me.

4 A short, gaunt figure, with a smooth, tight, black-as-coal skin, large prominent jaws, thin, uneven lips whose sole function seemed to be the production of sneers, a broad nose with slightly flaring nostrils, small, bloodshot eyes which never cried, small, close-set ears, and a wide, prominent forehead—such were my father's fearsome features.

5 Born and bred in a tribal reserve and nearly twice my mother's age, my father existed under the illusion, formed as much by a strange innate pride as by a blindness to everything but his own will, that someday all white people would disappear from South Africa, and black people would revert to their old ways of living. To prepare for this eventuality, he ruled the house strictly according to tribal law, tolerating no deviance, particularly from his children. At the same time that he was force-feeding us tribalism we were learning other

---

[1]*donga*: ravine

ways of life, modern ways, from mingling with children whose parents had shed their tribal cloth and embraced Western culture.

6   My father's tribal rule had as its fulcrum the constant performing of rituals spanning the range of day-to-day living. There were rituals to protect the house from evildoers, to ward off starvation, to prevent us from becoming sick, to safeguard his job, to keep the police away, to bring us good luck, to make him earn more money and many others which my young mind could not understand. Somehow they did not make sense to me; they simply awed, confused and embarrassed me, and the only reason I participated in them night after night was because my father made certain that I did, by using, among other things, the whip, and the threat of the retributive powers of my ancestral spirits, whose favor the rituals were designed to curry. Along with the rituals, there were also tribal laws governing manners.

7   One day I intentionally broke one of these laws: I talked while eating.

8   "That's never done in my house," my father screamed at me as he rose from the table where he had been sitting alone, presiding over our meal. I was eating *pap 'n vleis*[2] out of the same bowl with George and Florah. We were sitting on the floor, about the brazier, and my mother was in the bedroom doing something.

9   "You don't have two mouths to afford you such luxury!" he fumed, advancing threateningly toward me, a cold sneer on his thin-lipped, cankerous mouth. He seemed ten feet tall.

10   Terrified, I deserted the *pap 'n vleis* and fled to Mother.

11   "Bring him back here, woman!" my father called through the door as he unbuckled his rawhide belt. "He needs to be taught how to eat properly."

12   I began bawling, sensing I was about to be whipped.

13   My mother led me into the kitchen and pleaded for me. "He won't do it again. He's only a child, and you know how forgetful children are." At this point George and Florah stopped eating and watched with petrified eyes. "Don't give me that," snarled my father. "He's old enough to remember how to eat properly." He tore me away from my mother and lashed me. She tried to intervene, but my father shoved her aside and promised her the same. I never finished my meal; sobbing, I slunk off to bed, my limbs afire with pain where the rawhide had raised welts. The next day, as I nursed my wounds, while my father was at work, I told my mother that I hated him and promised her I would kill him when I grew up.

14   "Don't say that!" my mother reprimanded me.

15   "I will," I said stoutly, "if he won't leave me alone."

16   "He's your father, you know."

17   "He's not my father."

18   "Shut that bad mouth of yours!" My mother threatened to smack me.

19   "Why does he beat me, then?" I protested. "Other fathers don't beat their children." My friends always boasted that their fathers never laid a hand on them.

20   "He's trying to discipline you. He wants you to grow up to be like him."

---

[2]*pap 'n vleis*: porridge with meat

21 "What! Me! Never!" I shook with indignation. "I'm never going to be like him! Why should I?"

22 "Well, in the tribes sons grow up to be like their fathers."

23 "But we're not living in the tribes."

24 "But we're still of the tribes."

25 "I'm not," I said. Trying to focus the conversation on rituals, my nemesis, I said, after a thoughtful pause, "Is that why Papa insists that we do rituals?"

26 "Yes."

27 "But other people don't."

28 "Everybody does rituals, Mr. Mathabane," my mother said. "You just don't notice it because they do theirs differently. Even white people do rituals."

29 "Why do people do rituals, Mama?"

30 "People do rituals because they were born in the tribes. And in the tribes rituals are done every day. They are a way of life."

31 "But we don't live in the tribes," I countered. "Papa should stop doing rituals."

32 My mother laughed. "Well, it's not as simple as that. Your father grew up in the tribes, as you know. He didn't come to the city until he was quite old. It's hard to stop doing things when you're old. I, too, do rituals because I was raised in the tribes. Their meaning, child, will become clear as you grow up. Have patience."

33 But I had no patience with rituals, and I continued hating them.

34 Participation in my father's rituals sometimes led to the most appalling scenes, which invariably made me the laughingstock of my friends, who thought that my father, in his ritual garb, was the most hilarious thing they had ever seen since natives in Tarzan movies. Whenever they laughed at me I would feel embarrassed and would cry. I began seeking ways of distancing myself from my father's rituals. I found one: I decided I would no longer, in the presence of my friends, speak Venda, my father's tribal language. I began speaking Zulu, Sotho, and Tsonga, the languages of my friends. It worked. I was no longer an object of mockery. My masquerade continued until my father got wind of it.

35 "My boy," he began. "Who is ruler of this house?"

36 "You are, Papa," I said with a trembling voice.

37 "Whose son are you?"

38 "Yours and Mama's."

39 "Whose?"

40 "Yours."

41 "That's better. Now tell me, which language do I speak?"

42 "Venda."

43 "Which does your mama speak?"

44 "Venda."

45 "Which should you speak?"

46 "Venda."

47 "Then why do I hear you're speaking other tongues; are you a prophet?"

48 Before I could reply he grabbed me and lashed me thoroughly. Afterward he threatened to cut out my tongue if he ever again heard I wasn't speaking

Venda. As further punishment, he increased the number of rituals I had to participate in. I hated him more for it.

Magic and AIDS: Presumed Innocent

by Michael Bronski

Michael Bronski's article, published in Z Magazine *in 1992, examines the media's portrayals of people with AIDS. Bronski currently writes for newspapers and most recently published a book,* The Pleasure Principle.

1   The buzz began sometime that morning. Television newsrooms and sports desks began calling one another, checking out the almost unbelievable rumor that Magic Johnson was giving a press conference later that afternoon in which he was going to announce his retirement from the sports world because he had tested positively for the HIV virus. This was the sort of news story that held up the evening edition, caused radio DJs to scuttle their preordained playlist, and even interrupted the afternoon's installment of *The Guiding Light*. This was NEWS.

2   Sure enough on Thursday, November 7, basketball star Magic Johnson announced that after having tested positively for the HIV virus—or, as the *New York Times* insists, "the AIDS virus"—he would be leaving the Los Angeles Lakers and devoting his life to helping educate Americans, especially teenagers, about AIDS and safe sex.

3   After the initial announcement there was a moment of startled silence—not for the man himself, who was in apparent good health and made his public revelation in straightforward, unapologetic language—but in anticipation of the media response. The announcement of any public figure—not to mention one as famous and beloved as Magic Johnson—being HIV-positive does not, and cannot, happen in a judgment-free vacuum. Was the media going to embrace him as a poor unfortunate, an "innocent victim" who through no fault of his own had fallen prey to a dreadful calamity? Or was he going to be rejected as a diseased "guilty victim" who was being punished for his own evil actions?

4   That moment of silence ended relatively quickly when almost all of the print and electronic media declared Johnson, because of his honesty and courage, the new hero of the AIDS epidemic. But this declaration of support was not without its unspoken unrest. Initially Magic Johnson never stated, or even indicated, how he contracted the HIV virus. In the face of eventual illness and death such concerns might seem minor, or even insignificant, but in the United States both the quantity and quality of sympathy for people with AIDS has always been predicated upon an understanding of how they contracted the virus and their attendant status as "guilty" or "innocent" victims.

5   The breakdown between "guilty" and "innocent" has traditionally been simple: homosexuals (usually portrayed by the media as white) who get AIDS through "perverted" sex, prostitutes who sell their bodies, and people who shoot drugs (almost always portrayed by the media as black) were almost always "guilty"; children who are infected through their mothers, and hemophiliacs, or anyone who received the virus through a blood transfusion, were "innocent."

6   It is not surprising, therefore, that it took Magic Johnson little more than twenty-four hours to announce on the *Arsenio Hall Show* on Friday, November 8, that "he was the furthest thing from a homosexual" and that he got the HIV virus from "messing around with too many women." A statement which placed him in the discernible, if increasingly fragile, realm of the innocent. For after more than a decade of the AIDS pandemic, the once well-entrenched categories of "guilty" and "innocent" are now becoming less rigid. Not that they are disappearing—they are as secure as any number of socially constructed categories which are used to punish, repress, or control certain socially proscribed behaviors—but as the visible profile of the "typical" person with AIDS is changing both the media and popular opinion are having a difficult time accommodating to the fact that the comforting simplicity (and lie) of "guilty" and "innocent" are now untenable categories. No matter that ACT UP has been saying for more than half a decade that "All people with AIDS are innocent," there is still a rush in the press, as well as the public imagination, to distinguish between those people with AIDS who are morally culpable for their illness and those who "truly" deserve sympathy and compassion.

7   The social structures that support this "guilty" and "innocent" dichotomy are so strong that there was probably no way for Magic Johnson—the private man or the public image—to transcend them. And although there has been increasing variance within the categories lately—the publicity generated by the cases of Marc Christian, Dr. Veronica Prego, and Kimberly Bergalis (and now Magic Johnson) has established the parameters of the debate—the basic structure still holds.

8   The association of moral guilt to physical disease is certainly not a new one. When the great plagues ravaged Europe during the Middle Ages they were seen as divine punishment (as well as the onset of the millennium). There were no "innocent victims" because strict Christian theology taught that all humankind, by nature of their incarnate state, was guilty. Later, during more "enlightened" times, other diseases too took on various moral meanings. TB, at least in upper-class Britain, was seen as a sign of sensitivity and artistic temperament. In the United States, however, it has always been viewed as a disease of the undeserving poor, and those who suffered from it were generally seen as being responsible for their illness as well as their state in life. More recently, diseases like cholera, which is airborne and spreads quickly (and across class lines), never became as stigmatizing as TB, probably because it killed so quickly—there was little time for large-scale stigmatization to occur. Typhoid, in the late nineteenth and early twentieth century, on the other hand, was seen as a disease of "dirty" immigrants (morally as well

as physically suspect) who were guilty of spreading it to the "general population." Mary Mallon, dubbed by the popular press as Typhoid Mary, was branded, hounded, and eventually arrested and quarantined—in 1907 and 1915—by New York health officials when she was suspected of "spreading" the disease to her wealthy employers. Later, polio became a nonstigmatizing disease (FDR, after all, suffered from it) and the polio scares of the mid 1950s—possibly because they involved children—never catered to popular prejudices of "guilt" and "innocence."

9   AIDS is probably the only disease to have spawned simultaneous "guilty" and "innocent" associations in the popular imagination. At first—when it was called GRID (Gay-Related Immune Deficiency) only sexually active gay men were being diagnosed, so *everyone* was guilty. The later addition of IV-drug users did not require any changes of popular perception: shooting drugs in the arm was as bad as taking it up the ass. The quick addition (and then removal) of Haitians from official listing of high-risk groups was accompanied with "factual" data of their immoral proclivities: from prostitution with U.S. gay men to massive uncleanliness to exotic and dangerous voodoo rites. When women were first diagnosed, they were generally seen as IV users or prostitutes.

10   It was probably the advent of "AIDS babies" in the early 1980s which first stirred the idea of the truly "innocent victim" in the popular imagination. But when most of these children turned out to live in the inner city, the offspring of drug-using mothers, they lost not only their "innocence" but their media cachet. The search for the perfect "innocent victim" became, in time, a media obsession. White middle-class hemophiliacs were good choices, and for a long time Ryan White was the media choice. And although the press never turned on him, he did not in the end suit their purposes because he refused to fulfill one of the requirements of truly innocent victim status: to highlight and attack the "guilty victims."

11   The cult of the innocent AIDS victim exists to promote the idea that AIDS is, in some profound sense, a moral fault and that the "general population" (as the mainstream press is fond of saying) is safe—not only from disease, but from moral wrongdoing. From a traditional Christian point of view, Ryan White was practicing the noblest form of "Christian charity"—forgiving the sins of others and helping to correct the wrongs of the world. But in our contemporary culture, which promotes a more judgmental, muscular Christianity, moral wrongdoing must be denounced and punished. That is why the moral outrage of Kimberly Bergalis was enormously appealing and persuasive to so many people.

12   Over the past six years it has become more and more apparent that there is no one-size-suits-all perfect-great-white-innocent victim. Life, as it usually does, intruded on the theologizing and moralizing. Accommodations had to be made. The notions of "guilt" and "innocence" were modified, depending on circumstances and considerations; nuances surfaced and the notions of "guilt" and "innocence" became more byzantine.

13   The case of Rock Hudson and Marc Christian proved to be one of the earliest chances for the popular press (as well as the attendant legal battles) to reconstruct and reinforce the idea of the "innocent victim." After Hudson's

death in 1985 his surviving lover Marc Christian brought a lawsuit against the Hudson estate claiming that the movie star had never disclosed his AIDS diagnosis to him and that, even though he was not infected with the virus, this caused incredible emotional stress: $11 million worth, to be exact. The court awarded Christian a $5.5 million settlement two years later, a decision which was quickly appealed but upheld two months ago by a state appeals court.

14   It is impossible to understand the positive publicity that Christian received with his initial lawsuit without first understanding the impact of Hudson's death on popular culture. When the news was first released that Rock Hudson—a living legend, an icon of Hollywood heterosexuality—was dying of AIDS the immediate response was disbelief. Although rumors of Hudson's homosexuality had long flourished both in and outside of the industry, most people believed he was straight. If Rock Hudson could be gay *and* could get AIDS, longstanding ideas of who was and who wasn't at risk from the disease were shattered.

15   Although most people accepted the fact that Hudson contracted the disease through his own conscious homosexual sexual activity—thus making him a "guilty" victim—neither the press nor the public was willing to brand him a complete villain. That is why there was general relief and satisfaction when Marc Christian brought his lawsuit. The fact that he was HIV-negative—no physical harm had actually been done him by Hudson—was the perfect ironic twist of the situation. The social function of Marc Christian's lawsuit was to distinguish a truly *innocent* victim (Christian) from the guilty, but very well liked, victim (Hudson). The fact that Christian was an HIV-negative, open homosexual also addressed the attendant, widespread anxiety generated by the simultaneous understanding of Hudson's health status and his homosexuality.

16   The fact that Christian, four years later, could still be awarded a substantial sum of money for "emotional distress" speaks to the fact that the images of "guilty" and "innocent" AIDS victims are still strongly embedded in our culture. And although these ideas are a baseline for much popular and media thinking, they are not without variants. In 1990 Dr. Veronica Prego, who had been diagnosed with PCP in 1987, brought a $175 million suit against the New York City Health and Hospital Corporation as well as two doctors, claiming that the needle stick by which she had been infected was caused by one doctor's negligence and that her confidentiality had been violated by another physician. What should have been a trial about AIDS and safety in the workplace soon became a four-star television miniseries in which physicians were calling one another "liar" from the witness stand, and Dr. Prego's wardrobe became as important as her testimony.

17   By all accounts Dr. Prego should have been the ideal "innocent victim": a professional woman with no outstanding slurs against her good name. And even though she wasn't, in media terms, "a white middle-class American" (she was born in Argentina), she was clearly much less culpable than your average junkie or queer. But reading through all of the accounts of the trial, it becomes apparent that the popular press was uncomfortable in presenting Prego as a completely "innocent victim." This had less to do with her ethnicity than with her gender, her professional standing, and what was perceived as her greed in

asking for such a large settlement. Almost all the media accounts present Prego as an unfortunate victim of circumstances—"a terrible tragedy, an accident"—but there were always lingering doubts. What if Dr. Prego was lying? What if she did it to herself and was only blaming the other doctor's negligence? The fact that both doctors were women added to the stereotyped image of a cat fight and unstable emotional responses. But beyond that, $175 million seemed like a lot of money to the average New Yorker. In a city in the midst of a financial crisis, where the health care and hospital system is always under great stress, and where the streets are filled with disenfranchised people who need immediate mental and physical care, the medical needs of Dr. Prego may have seemed, if not inconsequential, at least not worth $175 million.

18   The Prego case was eventually settled out of court for an undisclosed sum but the social myths surrounding the case—the necessity to differentiate "guilty" from "innocent"—remained in place. What was important about the Prego case, however, was the cultural ambivalence about the HIV risk that patients presented to their doctors. One of the subtexts in the reporting on the Prego case was the fact that, although it was a shame that she had AIDS, it was, or at least *may have been,* a risk she ran as a health care provider. This was probably the last time this specific problem was aired in public. And, in fact, since then the situation has been placed in quite the opposite context. The "innocent victim" is no longer the doctor who has contracted AIDS from a patient, but rather the "innocent" patient who is at risk from the "guilty" doctor. A situation which the case of Kimberly Bergalis all too aptly illustrated these past weeks and months.

19   Kimberly Bergalis first became a media sensation in late January 1991, when she was publicly identified as one of five HIV-positive clients of a Florida dentist who had recently died of AIDS. Although it is unclear how the transmission occurred—the most recent, and widely accepted, theory is that the virus was passed along through nonsterile surgical equipment rather than from doctor to patient—Bergalis, who was white, twenty-three years old, and middle-class, became the most visible media example of the "innocent victim." The national media played up the Florida story (without naming names) as the first example of AIDS transmitted by a health care worker and lost no time when Bergalis came forward, in light of a $1 million malpractice settlement. Clearly this was the perfect "innocent victim" for whom the media had been waiting.

20   It wasn't just that she was white, middle class, not a prostitute, and moderately photogenic—Ryan White was all of those things as well as being fourteen years old, really cute, and *really* photogenic. What Kimberly Bergalis had, which White was sorely missing, was an acute sense of rage. White was willing to go on TV and say that his job for the rest of his life was to eradicate AIDS prejudice and help inform all U.S. citizens about the risks of AIDS. But he refused to manifest the fear and loathing that AIDS instills in the popular imagination. Not so Bergalis. Upon being awarded the $1 million from her dentist's insurance company, she announced, "It's not going to buy me a cure." She soon, helped immeasurably by a conservative political climate and the ea-

ger and willing media, began a one-woman campaign to mandate HIV testing for all health care providers.

21   Within two weeks, many newspapers began carrying tacitly homophobic stories on how Bergalis further suffered because "people and organizations don't believe me; they want to believe you were using IV drugs; they want to believe you were sleeping around." Bergalis was clearly speaking of AIDS and gay rights groups who were worried that this single Florida incident would be the catalyst for mandatory HIV testing of health care providers. And they were right. By June 1991 Bergalis was calling for federal laws which would mandate such testing. Racked by physical and emotional pain, Bergalis began giving press conferences in which she used her own condition as the main reason to enact mandatory testing laws. "Who do I blame?" she wrote in a letter to the Florida state health investigators, "Do I blame myself? I sure don't. I never used IV drugs, never slept with anyone, never had a blood transfusion. I blame Dr. Acer [her dentist] and every one of you bastards. Anyone who knew Dr. Acer was infected and had full-blown AIDS and stood by not doing a damn thing about it. You are all just as guilty as he was."

22   What is most surprising about Bergalis is not that she does not identify with the "guilty victims" of AIDS; she doesn't even identify with the "innocent victims." The media has consistently played up Bergalis's sense of her own singularity—we never even hear about the other four clients of Dr. Acer who have been diagnosed—until they would have you believe that Bergalis's AIDS diagnosis epitomizes all of the social issues surrounding AIDS social policy. And while any AIDS diagnosis is tragic, none is more or less tragic than others. There are many social policy issues which might be raised by the Bergalis case—the treatment of women and AIDS, the lack of AIDS education in many nonurban locales, the need for safeguards in health care centers—but Bergalis and the media focused solely, despite overwhelming evidence to the contrary from the presidential AIDS commission as well as the AMA, on the need for mandatory testing of health care providers.

23   It is not surprising that the Bergalis case, as well as that of Prego and Christian, would revolve around financial settlements. The idea of a monetary payment, a settlement, for physical or emotional harm, is common in our legal culture. But these cases—and the massive publicity which surrounds them—hint at a broader meaning. By singling out and rewarding these "innocent victims" the popular press is upholding the traditional, false dichotomy between "guilty" and "innocent" victims.

24   Although there was never any indication that monetary settlements would be sought in the Magic Johnson case—there was no one to sue, for any reason—the matter of his beloved public persona and the attendant income from his commercial endorsements made it imperative for Johnson and his public relations people to situate the sports star firmly in the realm of the "innocent." Although he was recently married and his wife is pregnant, the rumors of Johnson's bisexuality (or homosexuality) were so strong that nearly every newspaper report felt obliged to mention them, even as they rushed to discount them. Johnson's possible drug and steroid use—rampant among some

professional circles—also came under scrutiny as a possible cause of his HIV infection. But in the long run, Johnson's story of becoming infected because he "messed around with a lot of women" became not only the accepted version of how he contracted the virus, but also the main tenet in his status as an "innocent victim."

25   In the first flurry of praise for Johnson, almost all of the media noted how he would be the ideal spokesperson for safe sex for younger people, since he is extremely popular among inner-city and African-American teenagers—a population which evidences the highest incidence of new AIDS diagnoses and which (because of government negligence) obtains very little, if any, safe sex and AIDS education. And certainly Johnson—being the only HIV-positive person of color the mainstream press has ever noticed—is in a unique cultural, historical, and political position. But as much as one would like to believe in the positive effect of Johnson's message on people's lives, there is reason to be cautious, if not wary, of his role as a spokesperson for safe sex and those living with the variety of conditions brought on by HIV infection.

26   The rush to confirm Johnson's status as an "innocent victim" by reaffirming his heterosexuality (as opposed to, say, remaining silent on the possible source of infection) forces the topic of heterosexual transmission to the forefront of public discussion. And while the media have focused on this subject before—usually in the context of repressive, antisex sentiments—they have never really taken or presented it seriously or factually. Unfortunately, although hardly surprising, all of the coverage in the Magic Johnson case has focused on female-to-male transmission. Yet, statistically this is the least probable of all transmission scenarios. The probability of male-to-female transmission, for example, is roughly twenty times the probability of female-to-male transmission. The number of heterosexual males with AIDS who have contracted HIV from a female partner is less than 2 percent of the total AIDS population.

27   The constant media attention on Johnson contracting HIV from "messing around with too many women" not only highlights heterosexual transmission but also works to demonize and brand women, especially sexually active women, as deadly disease carriers. This image has always been historically very popular: from Typhoid Mary through the anti-VD poster campaigns of the First and Second World Wars, to the 1950s film images of fallen women who get young men addicted to alcohol and drugs, the deadly, sexual temptress has been a stock figure in contemporary, misogynist morality plays. The innocent AIDS victim as constructed, by the mainstream media is contingent on the oppositional appearance of a "guilty victim." For Marc Christian it was Rock Hudson, for Kimberly Bergalis it was Dr. Acer, for Magic Johnson it is sexually active women.

28   This rush to confirm Magic Johnson's innocence by making his female partners dangerous disease carriers began only days after his original announcement. A November 10 *New York Sunday Times* sports page ran a long piece entitled "Fast Lane Could Be AIDS Lane," which portrayed professional sports groupies as empty-headed sluts hankering for a famous fuck: "In my

day," they quote Walt Frazier, an ex-player and broadcaster for the New York Knicks, "you at least had to go to parties and have a rap to pick up women. Now you see them lining up against the wall after a game. The stars just take their pick and the other guys get the leftovers." So we shouldn't forget who is at risk, Frazier added, "sex is a human need . . . but these guys need to use their heads." In the November 18 *Sports Illustrated* an article entitled "Dangerous Games" quoted numerous professional athletes on how easily available some women make themselves to sports figures. "We come to town, and the women come out in force. They call the hotel, they follow the bus. They hover and wait to get you," claims Kevin Johnson, a guard with the Phoenix Suns. The piece repeats the story, now an urban AIDS legend, of the woman who had over one hundred pairs of autographed pro-basketball sneakers under her bed. A December 4 *Boston Globe* article reported that a Montreal physician has released information that a female patient, who died of AIDS two years ago, told of having sexual relations with fifty National Hockey League players. "If this revelation," claims the doctor, "can save the life of any athlete in the future, my patient's death will have some meaning." As if her death, and life, had no meaning in and of itself.

29   There is, of course, very little discussion about any of these men—including Magic Johnson—infecting their female partners. There is no question that AIDS consciousness in professional sports is on the rise and that women are being blamed for spreading the disease.

30   While Magic Johnson might be doing the right thing in promoting safe sex (and this remains to be seen), the lingering message that his own personal life is communicating to teenagers who have no access to the hard, realistic facts of HIV transmission, is that it is only bad girls—a socially constructed idea if there ever was one—who give you AIDS. If such skewered notions of transmission and responsibility become attached, in any way, to Johnson's safe-sex information, they undermine any good such education will do.

31   The day after the public announcement of his HIV status, Magic Johnson volunteered to be on the presidential AIDS commission and George Bush (after hesitating to sniff the political winds) quickly agreed. It is ironic that Johnson will be taking the place of the recently deceased Belinda Mason. Mason, a young mother who had contracted AIDS through a transfusion and served on the presidential AIDS commission, explicitly called for no mandatory testing, the lifting of all bans of HIV positive immigrants, and consistently refused to make any distinction between "innocent" and "guilty" victims. Although Johnson has yet to make any statements on public policy, his visibility on the commission will put him under a great deal of pressure to conform to the most conservative tenets of the Bush social and public policy agenda. Already there is talk that Johnson is pulling away from his strong safe-sex line and easing into the more right-wing, Republican-authorized, "just say no" mode of AIDS advice. It is impossible to overestimate the pull of politics on the formation of AIDS education and policy. Last September, Kimberly Bergalis testified, on her deathbed, before the House, on a bill which called for mandatory testing of all health care workers. Not surprisingly, Bergalis's trip to Washington was

paid for by the archconservative Representative William Dannemyer. As Tom Stoddard of Lambda Legal Defense wittily noted in the *New York Times,* "Kimberly Bergalis is the Willie Horton of AIDS."

32   The popular media have a clear economic interest in promoting these images of "guilty" and "innocent" victims; they pander to popular prejudice and help sell papers and TV shows. On an even more dangerous level they not only reflect but help shape public policy—the massive attention Bergalis received for her recent press conferences and Senate appearance has set the stage for widespread mandatory testing and helped ease the way for Illinois Governor Jim Thompson to sign a draconian testing measure last September. The ability of the press to influence public policy adds immeasurably to its own sense of self-importance, and illustrates how susceptible it is to partisan politics and power-brokering.

33   But when all is said and done the problem with the press coverage on all of these cases is that it relies on soap-opera scenarios and flash-and-trash sound-bite journalism. After almost a decade, the press still has no idea of how to write about AIDS clearly and honestly. People living with AIDS have to be labeled as either "guilty" or "innocent" victims; the failings of the health care system to deal with the range and variety of HIV infections is seen as idiosyncratic and not part of a larger social problem, and the reporting of personal tragedy is seen as more important than consistent and useful prevention guidelines and information.

34   The publicity surrounding the cases of Marc Christian, Veronica Prego, Kimberly Bergalis, and now Magic Johnson are further indications that society and the media still have a deeply committed investment to making moral judgments about AIDS and to prove, again and again, that the world is divided into good and bad, us and them, even when those categories are not useful, applicable, or right.

Getting Off the Welfare Carousel

by Teresa McCrary

Teresa McCrary as a single parent relied on government subsidies while attending college. This essay was originally published in Newsweek *in 1993.*

1   I am a welfare mom, and I have one thing to say: stop picking on us! There are 5 million families on welfare in the United States, most of them single women with kids. Is this really such a major financial burden? I believe we're targeted because we're an easy mark. Because we have no money, there are no lobbyists working on our behalf either in Washington , D.C., or in local legislatures. I want to tell you who we are and why we stay home with our children.

2   The stereotypical welfare mom has 10 kids, including a pregnant teenage daughter, all taking advantage of the dole. I have never personally known such a woman. Most of the mothers I know are women who forgo the usual round of job searches and day care so they can mind their homes and children in a loving and responsible way. We may not have paying jobs, but any mother, married or single, working or retired, will tell you that motherhood is a career in itself.

3   Yet we are constantly told we should go out and get real jobs. Yes, most of us are unemployed: do we really have a choice? Last time I looked, the unemployment rate was more than 6 percent. If the unemployed can't find work, where are we moms supposed to look? The only jobs open to us are maid work, fast-food service and other low-paying drudgery with no benefits. How are we expected to support our children? Minimum wage will not pay for housing costs, health care, child care, transportation and work clothes that an untrained, uneducated woman needs to support even one child.

4   Many of us take money under the table for odd jobs, and cash from generous friends and relatives to help support our families. We don't report this money to the Aid to Families with Dependent Children, because we can't afford to. Any cash we get, even birthday money from grandparents, is deducted from the already minuscule benefits. We're allowed between $1,000 and $3,000 in assets including savings and property, automobiles and home furnishings. We are told that if we have more than that amount, we should be able to sell some things and live for a year from the proceeds. Can you imagine living on $3,000 a year?

5   As for child support, unless the money sent to the state by the father is greater than AFDC benefits, the family receives only $50 monthly. We are told that the state intends to prosecute "deadbeat dads" for back support. Seldom do news stories mention that, in the case of welfare families, the state keeps collected back support. Although this reduces the tax burden, none of the money goes to the children. Outsiders are led to believe that the children will benefit, and they do not. No wonder some welfare moms—and their children's fathers—believe it's not worth the effort to try to get the dads to pay up. If we could have depended on these men in the first place, we would not be on welfare.

6   So what about family values? Those of us who do not have a man in our lives do the emotional job of both mother and father. My daughter says she should give me a Father's Day card, because I am just as much a father to her as a mother. On top of these two careers, we are told we should work.

7   We could hold down a minimum-wage job, unarguably the hardest work for the least amount of money, if we could find an employer willing to hire us full time (most low-wage jobs are part time). Unable to afford child care, we'd have latch-key children whose only good meal of the day would be school lunch. The whole paycheck would go to housing and job expenses. When we got home exhausted, we'd clean house, help with homework, listen to how the kids' day went—feeling relieved if none of them had been teased for their garage-sale clothes. We'd pray that nobody got sick, because we couldn't afford a day off work or doctor fees (welfare pays very little, but it has the important benefit of health care). We'd worry about getting laid off at any moment—in tough times, minimum wage jobs are the first to go.

8   These fears cause stress that may result in child abuse. Many times we feel, no matter how hard we try, that in some way our children are being neglected if we are holding down a job. So we stay home. We've learned that we can depend only on ourselves. We don't enjoy living at the poverty level, but we can't see a minimum-wage job as the answer.

9   I believe that we single mothers must become self-sufficient through education and training. And that means both money and patience on the taxpayers' part. I, and the other welfare moms I know at school, maintain a 3.0 grade average or better. Are we exceptions to the rule? Maybe not; perhaps people in my circumstances are more motivated to make better lives for themselves. Fighting the low self-esteem brought on by divorce and poverty, we have taken the difficult step, usually without a support system, of going back to school. By carefully scheduling classes and studying late at night, I have been able to care for my kids while learning TV and radio production.

10   College may be out of reach for many. By raising tuition and entrance requirements, most colleges and universities are barring us from their campuses. Even President Clinton's proposed two-year training program may not help much. Vocational or technical schools mean training for low-paying jobs. Still, we'll be told to find work or lose our benefits.

11   If the government keeps decreasing or eliminating the programs we and the children depend upon for survival, here's what will happen: in a few years, instead of 5 million single women and their children on welfare, there will be 5 million single women and their children on the streets. I don't now how many starving millions the United Nations is trying to help in Somalia. But if people keep picking on us, the United Nations will have to help the United States feed *us*.

A Hanging

by George Orwell

George Orwell is the pen name of Eric Arthur Blair, who worked during the early 1930s to enforce the laws of the British Empire in Burma before becoming a writer in England. His novels 1984 *and* Animal Farm *satirize political oppression. This essay was originally published in* Shooting an Elephant and Other Essays *(1946).*

1   It was in Burma, a sodden morning of the rains. A sickly light, like yellow tinfoil, was slanting over the high walls into the jail yard. We were waiting outside the condemned cells, a row of sheds fronted with double bars, like small animal cages. Each cell measured about ten feet by ten and was quite bare within except for a plank bed and a pot of drinking water. In some of them

brown silent men were squatting at the inner bars, with their blankets draped round them. These were the condemned men, due to be hanged within the next week or two.

2   One prisoner had been brought out of his cell. He was a Hindu, a puny wisp of a man, with a shaven head and vague liquid eyes. He had a thick, sprouting moustache, absurdly too big for his body, rather like the moustache of a comic man on the films. Six tall Indian warders were guarding him and getting him ready for the gallows. Two of them stood by with rifles with fixed bayonets, while the others handcuffed him, passed a chain through his handcuffs and fixed it to their belts, and lashed his arms tight to his sides. They crowded very close about him with their hands always on him in a careful, caressing grip, as though all the while feeling him to make sure he was there. It was like men handling a fish which is still alive and may jump back into the water. But he stood quite unresisting, yielding his arms limply to the ropes, as though he hardly noticed what was happening.

3   Eight o'clock struck and a bugle call, desolately thin in the wet air, floated from the distant barracks. The superintendent of the jail, who was standing apart from the rest of us, moodily prodding the gravel with his stick, raised his head at the sound. He was an army doctor, with a grey toothbrush moustache and a gruff voice. "For God's sake hurry up, Francis," he said irritably.

4   "The man ought to have been dead by this time. Aren't you ready yet?"

5   Francis, the head jailer, a fat Dravidian[1] in a white drill suit and gold spectacles, waved his black hand. "Yes sir, yes sir," he bubbled. "All iss satisfactorily prepared. The hangman iss waiting. We shall proceed."

6   "Well, quick march, then. The prisoners can't get their breakfast till this job's over."

7   We set out for the gallows. Two warders marched on either side of the prisoner, with their files at the slope; two others marched close against him, gripping him by arm and shoulder, as though at once pushing and supporting him. The rest of us, magistrates and the like, followed behind. Suddenly, when we had gone ten yards, the procession stopped short without any order or warning.

8   A dreadful thing had happened—a dog, come goodness knows whence, had appeared in the yard. It came bounding among us with a loud volley of barks, and leapt round us wagging its whole body, wild with glee at finding so many human beings together. It was a large woolly dog, half Airedale, half pariah. For a moment it pranced round us and then, before anyone could stop it, it had made a dash for the prisoner, and jumping up tried to lick his face. Everyone stood aghast, too taken aback even to grab at the dog.

9   "Who let that bloody brute in here?" said the superintendent angrily. "Catch it, someone!"

10   A warder, detached from the escort, charged clumsily after the dog, but it danced and gambolled just out of his reach, taking everything as part of the game. A young Eurasian jailer picked up a handful of gravel and tried to stone the dog away, but it dodged the stones and came after us again. Its yaps

---

[1]*Dravidian*: ethnic group from South Asia

echoed from the jail walls. The prisoner, in the grasp of the two warders, looked on incuriously, as though this was another formality of the hanging. It was several minutes before someone managed to catch the dog. Then we put my handkerchief through its collar and moved off once more, with the dog still straining and whimpering.

11   It was about forty yards to the gallows. I watched the bare brown back of the prisoner marching in front of me. He walked clumsily with his bound arms, but quite steadily, with that bobbing gait of the Indian who never straightens his knees. At each step his muscles slid neatly into place, the lock of hair on his scalp danced up and down, his feet printed themselves on the wet gravel. And once, in spite of the men who gripped him by each shoulder, he stepped slightly aside to avoid a puddle on the path.

12   It is curious, but till that moment I had never realised what it means to destroy a healthy, conscious man. When I saw the prisoner step aside to avoid the puddle, I saw the mystery, the unspeakable wrongness, of cutting a life short when it is in full tide. This man was not dying, he was alive just as we were alive. All the organs of his body were working—bowels digesting food, skin renewing itself, nails growing, tissues forming—all toiling away in solemn foolery. His nails would still be growing when he stood on the drop, when he was falling through the air with a tenth of a second to live. His eyes saw the yellow gravel and the grey walls, and his brain still remembered, foresaw, reasoned—reasoned even about puddles. He and we were a party of men walking together, seeing, hearing, feeling, understanding the same world; and in two minutes with a sudden snap, one of us would be gone—one mind less, one world less.

13   The gallows stood in a small yard, separate from the main grounds of the prison, and overgrown with tall prickly weeds. It was a brick erection like three sides of a shed, with planking on top, and above that two beams and a crossbar with the rope dangling. The hangman, a grey-haired convict in the white uniform of the prison was waiting beside his machine. He greeted us with a servile crouch as we entered. At a word from Francis the two warders, gripping the prisoner more closely than ever, half led, half pushed him to the gallows and helped him clumsily up the ladder. Then the hangman climbed up and fixed the rope round the prisoner's neck.

14   We stood waiting, five yards away. The warders had formed in a rough circle round the gallows. And then, when the noose was fixed the prisoner began crying out on his god. It was a high, reiterated cry of "Ram![2] Ram! Ram! Ram!," not urgent and fearful like a prayer or a cry for help, but steady, rhythmical, almost like the tolling of a bell. The dog answered the sound with a whine. The hangman, standing on the gallows, produced a small cotton bag like a flour bag and drew it down over the prisoner's face. But the sound, muffled by the cloth, still persisted, over and over again: "Ram! Ram! Ram! Ram!"

15   The hangman climbed down and stood ready, holding the lever. Minutes seemed to pass. The steady, muffled crying from the prisoner went on and on, "Ram! Ram! Ram!" never faltering for an instant. The superintendent, his

---

[2]*Ram*: name of deity worshipped in South Asia

head on his chest, was slowly poking the ground with his stick; perhaps he was counting the cries, allowing the prisoner a fixed number—fifty, perhaps, or a hundred. Everyone had changed colour. The Indians had gone grey like bad coffee, and one or two of the bayonets were wavering. We looked at the lashed, hooded man on the drop, and listened to his cries—each cry another second of life; the same thought was in all our minds: oh, kill him quickly, get it over, stop that abominable noise!

16   Suddenly the superintendent made up his mind. Throwing up his head he made a swift motion with his stick. "Chalo!" he shouted almost fiercely.

17   There was a clanking noise, and then dead silence. The prisoner had vanished, and the rope was twisting on itself. I let go of the dog, and it galloped immediately to the back of the gallows; but when it got there it stopped short, barked, and then retreated into a corner of the yard, where it stood among the weeds, looking timorously out at us. We went round the gallows to inspect the prisoner's body. He was dangling with his toes pointed straight downwards, very slowly revolving, as dead as a stone.

18   The superintendent reached out with his stick and poked the bare body; it oscillated, slightly. "*He's* all right," said the superintendent. He backed out from under the gallows, and blew out a deep breath. The moody look had gone out of his face quite suddenly. He glanced at his wristwatch. "Eight minutes past eight. Well, that's all for this morning, thank God."

19   The warders unfixed bayonets and marched away. The dog, sobered and conscious of having misbehaved itself, slipped after them. We walked out of the gallows yard, past the condemned cells with their waiting prisoners, into the big central yard of the prison. The convicts, under the command of warders armed with lathis,[3] were already receiving their breakfast. They squatted in long rows, each man holding a tin pannikin, while two warders with buckets marched round ladling out rice; it seemed quite a homely, jolly scene, after the hanging. An enormous relief had come upon us now that the job was done. One felt an impulse to sing, to break into a run, to snigger. All at once everyone began chattering gaily.

20   The Eurasian boy walking beside me nodded towards the way we had come, with a knowing smile: "DO you know, sir, our friend (he meant the dead man), when he heard his appeal had been dismissed, he pissed on the floor of his cell. From fright—Kindly take one of my cigarettes, sir. Do you not admire my new silver case, sir? From the boxwallah,[4] two rupees eight annas. Classy European style."

21   Several people laughed—at what, nobody seemed certain.

22   Francis was walking by the superintendent, talking garrulously: "Well, sir, all hass passed off with the utmost satisfactoriness. It wass all finished—flick! like that. It iss not always so—oah, no! I have known cases where the doctor wass obliged to go beneath the gallows and pull the prisoner's legs to ensure decease. Most disagreeable!"

---

[3]*lathis*: heavy wood and metal sticks
[4]*boxwallah*: peddler

23   "Wriggling about, eh? That's bad," said the superintendent.

24   "Ach, sir, it iss worse when they become refractory! One man, I recall, clung to the bars of hiss cage when we went to take him out. You will scarcely credit, sir, that it took six warders to dislodge him, three pulling at each leg. We reasoned with him. 'My dear fellow,' we said, 'think of all the pain and trouble you are causing to us!' But no, he would not listen! Ach, he wass very troublesome!"

25   I found that I was laughing quite loudly. Everyone was laughing. Even the superintendent grinned in a tolerant way. "You'd better all come out and have a drink," he said quite genially. "I've got a bottle of whisky in the car. We could do with it."

26   We went through the big double gates of the prison, into the road. "Pulling at his legs!" exclaimed a Burmese magistrate suddenly, and burst into a loud chuckling. We all began laughing again. At that moment Francis's anecdote seemed extraordinarily funny. We all had a drink together, native and European alike, quite amicably. The dead man was a hundred yards away.

PART TWO

Using Essential Strategies for Writing Essays

Reading in College
Surveying, Annotating, Reviewing, Modeling

What You Need to Do First

- Prepare to read by thinking about the topic
- Preview what you'll read to get the main idea
- While you read, keep your mind focused by writing and thinking
- Look back over the reading to be sure you understand it
- Use the reading as an example to follow in your own writing

The Reading Process

Prepare to read.

Survey before reading.

Read actively.

Review.

Model what you've read.

When you read an advertisement, you're not supposed to think about it—you're just supposed to let it slide into your mind. But when you read more serious material, you can't just let the words slide in—especially not if you must prepare a written response. If you have acquired the habit of easy reading that just flows through your mind, you'll need to find some ways of stopping and looking carefully at what you're reading and what you think about it. The ideas in this chapter will help you pay attention to different parts of a reading. If reading is usually slow and painful for you, you'll also find the techniques discussed here to be helpful. These techniques will not help you read faster, but they will help you understand what you've read. Reading carefully usually requires five steps.

STEP 1. PREPARE TO READ: OPEN UP THE TOPIC

The process of reading actually begins before you read, when you make your mind ready to receive an author's ideas. You may prepare simply by thinking about ideas or experiences you've had and comparing them with those suggested by the title or introduction to a reading. Sometimes your instructor will ask you to think or write about a topic before assigning a reading. Usually this kind of writing is not intended to be evaluated, so you should write quickly, without worrying about making sense or being correct; this writing is a way of getting your mind "geared up" for the reading. For example, to prepare for reading the essay "Measuring Success" (pp. 39–40) your instructor might ask you to write about the following:

If you had all the money you wanted, what else would you need to be happy?

You might think about this briefly, and then begin writing something like this:

> In a way I think success means money. I always dream about having a lot of money and buying a car, a house, fabulous clothes, going on trips. Not worrying about the bills. I've had to work at so many crummy jobs and I still don't really have what I want. So if I can get a degree and get a job I think I'll feel good. But really when I think about success I guess I know that's just the beginning. Success is when people look up to you and talk about how good you're doing—like in my family they always talk about my cousin who owns her own business. But then sometimes I think she's not really as happy as my sister who's a nurse, because my sister really helps people and also doesn't have to worry about whether she'll do OK next year—she knows she'll always have a job. I guess success would be when you do something you feel really good about. And right now I'm not quite sure what that will be for me. Maybe I'd be a success if I went into computers or quit college and became a musician, or maybe I'd think I was successful if I just had a happy family.

Once you've written something like this, and you've developed some of your own ideas, you don't need to do anything else for now. This writing has served its purpose by getting you ready to read. Be sure to keep this writing, though, because it might be very useful if you have additional writing assignments related to this reading.

What if your instructor doesn't assign a prereading topic? You can create your own. You might want to look at the title and main idea of an essay (see Step 2, below) and ask yourself what experiences you've had that relate to the ideas, or ask yourself what you already know about the topic (or what you guess will be the topic).

EXERCISE 4.1	Prepare to read "My Father's Tribal Rule" by Mark Mathabane (pp. 40–44). Before you read, think about the following **prompt**:

Can you recall any conflicts between parents and children in your family or among your family members?

Now write a page or two about an idea that will make you ready to think about ideas or events in the reading. Don't worry at this point about organization or editing because you're using this writing to help you understand the reading.

STEP 2. SURVEY BEFORE READING: GET THE BIG PICTURE

When you're trying to understand a reading, making a **survey** of the general idea is very helpful. It's like trying to put together a jigsaw puzzle: you know it's much easier to find the places for different pieces when you can see the picture on the box. The same is true in reading. You will have a clearer understanding of specific details, words, sentences, and even paragraphs when you have some general idea about the reading. To see the overall pattern in written material, try some of these hints:

1. *Read any introductory material.* The notes that are sometimes included before a reading are put there to help you understand the material. Read the introductory notes on page 39. What do you learn? Why might this be important? You might make these observations:

   The notes talk about other definitions of success, and they also explain that the author once defined success as financial success, but now has changed her mind. [This gives you an idea of what to expect.] The notes also say she was recently a college student, and that this article was written for the *Boston Globe Magazine* in 1997. [Now you know that it was written for American readers in the recent past. She will probably expect her readers to know and understand the life of a young American in the late 1990s.]

2. *Look at the important parts: title, first and last paragraphs, and subtitles* (if there are any). Read these important parts for a general idea of the topic. Here is one essay with everything but those parts erased.

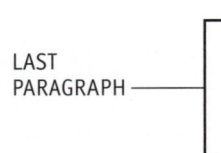

TITLE

FIRST
PARAGRAPH

LAST
PARAGRAPH

Measuring Success

Back when I was a callow college student, I devised a neat grid system for what I hoped would be my life's achievements. I could count my life a good one, I thought, if I could attain both success and happiness. So I set about analyzing the component parts of each: Happiness I subdivided into sections labeled health and love; success, I determined, was composed of wealth and fame.

When I look back at my simplistic little value system, I am a bit chagrined at how absolute I thought life was. But I am also happy to report that the achievements that have come my way are the ones that count. After 20 years of supercharged ambition, I have stumbled upon this bit of wisdom. Who needs wealth and fame? Two out of four ain't bad.

3. *Make some guesses about the main ideas of the reading.* What can you conclude about the reading from the title and first and last paragraphs above? Here are some guesses you might make:

   Title: Suggests that success can be measured.

   First paragraph: Describes the author's original definition of happiness as health and love, and success as fame and money; says that these definitions come from the time when she was in college.

Last paragraph: Says that she has changed her ideas about success. I guess that there's a reason why she changed; maybe something that happened. She says that she doesn't have wealth and fame, but does have "two out of four." Looking back at the introduction, she talks about four things: money, fame, health and love. If she doesn't have money and fame, that leaves two, so I guess that this means she does have health and love. Because she also says "the achievements that have come my way are the ones that count." This means the reading will probably show how "health" and "love" are more valuable than "money" and "fame." As I read, I will look for evidence that "money" and "fame" have become less important.

4. *Ask questions before and during reading.* Questions will help you to keep your mind focused on your reading. Look for the answers to specific questions as you read. The questions you ask before you read might come from the parts you observed in your survey and the guesses you made. You noticed that the author had different ideas when she was a student (mentioned in the first paragraph) from those she has now (mentioned in the last paragraph). This might lead you to some questions about the change:

What caused the change?

What does she mean by *happiness* and *success?*

Is it true that she doesn't have any wealth or fame?

What does she count as health and love?

You should continue to ask questions while you're reading because not all of the ideas will be present in the parts you've surveyed.

5. *Connect your guesses with your experience:* Recall any thinking or writing about your own ideas or experiences you may have done before writing. If you didn't do any writing, you may want to do some after you have made some guesses and asked some questions. You may also want to add to what you have written. If you wrote before reading, you may now want to add a more specific response to the topic as you see it now:

I think there are other things besides money that matter but I don't know how much I'd like life without money. I guess it depends on how much. I sure want to have enough to live on and not worry all the time about bills and getting evicted and things like that.

Once again, keep any writing you do at this point. You may use it later when writing or revising a paper about these readings.

EXERCISE 4.2   Survey "My Father's Tribal Rule" by Mark Mathabane (pp. 40–44). When experienced readers survey a reading, they often do it mentally, but since you may be practicing a new skill, you should write down any responses to the following that you can clearly express:

1. *Read any introductory material:* Look over notes at the beginning or end of the reading. Could it be important to know in what year this was written, or where the author lived?

2. *Look at the important parts.* Check the title, the first and last paragraphs, and subtitles. Does the title hint where the author grew up? Is the last paragraph different from the first paragraph?

3. *Make some guesses about the main ideas of the reading.* Is Mathabane probably writing about his own experience? At what age? What aspects of his life—school, family, work, sports—are involved?

4. *Ask questions before and during the reading.* Try making your guesses into questions. What question could you ask about the title?

5. *Connect your guesses with your experience.* Before writing, you might have thought or written about conflicts you have had with your family. Does the title of the reading suggest that the author might have had a conflict with his father? Was it similar to yours or different?

STEP 3. READ ACTIVELY

Even a reading that seems to make a simple point or tell a clear story may have some complex and interesting ideas. You may miss those ideas if you read too quickly and superficially. To help you look closely for the ideas that are suggested as well as the ones that are openly stated, and to keep your mind focused, you'll need to put your mark on the reading, to read actively. You can do this several ways, as listed in the box below.

How to Read Actively

In your own book or on a photocopy of the reading:

Underline or highlight words, phrases, sentences.

Ask new questions as you go.

Write notes in the margin.

Circle words you don't know.

Because these marks will also be useful to you when you return to the reading while you're writing, you should be sure that you'll still be able to read your signs later on. Don't underline, circle, or highlight everything, because then nothing will stand out. If you don't want to write in the book you're using, you can photocopy the section you're reading. We have included on the opposite page an example of an essay (pp. 39–40) that has been **annotated**.

Measuring Success
Renee Loth

1   Back when I was a callow college student, I devised a neat grid system for what I hoped would be my life's achievements. I could count my life a good one, I thought, if I could attain both success and happiness. So I set about analyzing the component parts of each: Happiness I subdivided into sections labeled health and love; success, I determined, was composed of wealth and fame.

2 out of 4!

2   Once I actually entered the world of work, however, I learned that success is not so easy to define. For one thing, when I made my simple calculation, I never took into account the joy of creation; the approbation of one's peers; the energy of collaboration; or the sheer satisfaction of a job well done. These are real qualities of success that live outside of wealth or fame.

3   Also, I found that definitions of success are mutable, shifting along with our changing values. If we stick with our chosen fields long enough, we sometimes have an opportunity to meet our heroes, people we thought wildly successful when we were young. A musician friend told me that he spent most of his youth wanting to play like the greats, until he started getting to know some of them. To his surprise, many turned out to be embittered, dulled by drink or boredom, unable to hold together a marriage, or wantonly jealous of others. That's when he realized he wanted to play like himself.

caused her to change?

4   Success is defined differently by different people. For some, it is symbolized by the number of buttons on the office phone. For others, it is having only one button and a secretary to field the calls. Some think the more nights and weekends they spend at the office, the more successful they must be. For others, success is directly proportional to time off.

connect to ideas of success? new definition

5   And what about those qualities I did include in my handy grid system? Wealth—beyond what is needed to provide for oneself and one's family, with a little left over for airfare to someplace subtropical in January—turned out to be superfluous. And the little experience I had with fame turned out to be downright scary.

me too

6   Several years ago, I had occasion to appear on a dull but respected national evening television news show. My performance lasted exactly six minutes, and my name flashed only twice. But when I got home from the live broadcast, my answering machine had maxed out on messages.

made her change?

7   I heard from a woman I had last seen in Brownie Scouts. I heard from former boyfriends, conspiracy theorists, and celebrity agents. I even got an obscene phone call—what kind of pervert watches PBS?—from someone who might have been an old friend pulling my leg. At least, I hope so.

not same as love

8   For weeks afterward, I received tons of what an optimist might call fan mail. One fellow insisted that if I froze a particular frame of a political campaign ad I had been discussing, I could see the face of Bill Clinton in the American flag. Somebody sent me a chapter of a novel in progress with a main character disturbingly like me. Several people sent me chain letters.

why? b/c tells why she changed

9   I was relieved when the fickle finger of fame moved on to someone else.

10   When I was young and romanticizing about success, I liked a particular Joni Mitchell lyric: "My struggle for higher achievement and my search for love don't seem to cease." Ah, but the trouble with struggling and searching is that it keeps us in a permanent state of wanting—always reaching for more. The drive to succeed keeps us focused on the future, to the detriment of life in the moment. And the moment is all we ever really have.

can't ever reach success- new definition

11   When I look back at my simplistic little value system, I am a bit chagrined at how absolute I thought life was. But I am also happy to report that the achievements that have come my way are the ones that count. After twenty years of supercharged ambition, I have stumbled upon this bit of wisdom. Who needs wealth and fame? Two out of four ain't bad.

what 2? health + love, not wealth + fame

Below are some approaches for annotating readings. Read these explanations to understand how the annotations work.

1. *Answers and new questions.* Look again at the questions you asked and the guesses you made about "Measuring Success." Since one of your guesses was that something might have made the writer change, underline or put a note beside paragraph 3 describing what she heard from her friend about his disappointment when he met his heroes. Note also her experience with fame that "turned out to be downright scary" in paragraph 5 (with details in paragraphs 6 through 8).

   Look for the answers you can't find. The authors refers to "two out of four" components of success that she does have, but she does not tell us much about those in the body of the essay. You'll thus want to write a question to help you remember that this problem is still not solved.

2. *Surprises.* Look for unexpected ideas. If you didn't guess that the writer would discuss the idea that success can never really be reached, underline that point in paragraph 10, and perhaps write a question beside it.

3. *Connections.* Look for ideas that do—and do not—connect with each other. Some ideas will be clearly connected: in the last paragraph, Loth mentions looking back at her "simplistic little value system" and "two out of four" achievements. These are linked to the definition she gave in paragraph 1. So draw a line or make a note to show the connection. Other times, ideas will not seem to fit with anything else: in paragraph 10, she discusses the idea that we never really achieve satisfaction but are "always reaching for more." Since she has not mentioned this idea anywhere else, you now have a new question: How is this related to her main idea? In paragraph 3 she also brings up a new idea: being yourself rather than imitating other people. You might question why she never discusses this idea again.

4. *Contradictions.* Look for points that seem to contradict other points. Loth says that happiness is love, but then in paragraph 6 she discusses hearing from old boyfriends as a problem that made her realize that fame is not so wonderful. You might ask how these ideas are different.

5. *Repetitions.* Loth repeats certain words over and over: *success or succeed* (title, paragraphs 1, 2, 3, 4, 8,), *define* or *definition* (2, 4), *fame* (1, 2, 5, 9). Think about the effects she achieves by doing this.

6. *Sentences or words that look different on the page.* Paragraph 9 is a single sentence; Loth's other paragraphs all have several sentences. A new question might be why she chooses to write a paragraph with only one sentence.

7. *Solutions to problems.* Sometimes you find the solution to the problems that arise as you read. You asked why paragraph 9 is a single sentence. Looking back, you may realize that she's pointing out one of her changed feelings: her bad experiences with fame made her dislike it, which is the opposite of what she predicted when she was a college student (paragraph 1). Make a note in the margin.

8. *Connections with your own ideas and experience.* In the survey stage, you wrote about money and success (pp. 61–63). You see that Loth's new idea of having enough money rather than extreme wealth—"what is needed to provide for oneself and one's family, with a little left over for airfare to someplace subtropical in January" (paragraph 5)—is very much like yours. Make a note of the similarity.

9. *New words.* Circle words and phrases you don't understand. In Loth's essay these may include *callow, grid, approbation, mutable, embittered, wantonly, superfluous, maxed out on, theorists, fickle, detriment, chagrined.* Think also about familiar words used in a new way—the word *absolute,* for example. Usually you have seen it used with an *-ly* to mean *very,* as in the sentence *That was <u>absolutely</u> fabulous!* If you don't know the word *simplistic,* think about the word *simple,* which you know means *easy, uncomplicated,* or *plain.*

EXERCISE 4.3	Read "My Father's Tribal Rule" (pp. 40–44) actively. Using a copy that you are able to write on, mark the important points in this reading with a highlighter or pen as you read. Don't underline or highlight every sentence because then none will stand out. Also, be sure to write notes about questions, answers, or observations. You may not find all the following categories in any one reading, but many of them will probably be there:

1. *Answers:* Look for answers to the guesses you made and the questions you asked.

2. *Surprises:* Look for anything that seems different from what you expect.

3. *Connections:* Look for ideas that connect with each other and also for those that don't seem related at all.

4. *Contradictions:* Look for points that seem to contradict each other.

5. *Repetitions:* Make a list of or number the important words that are repeated.

6. *Sentences or words that look different on the page:* Note sentences or paragraphs that seem to stand out.

7. *Solutions to new problems:* Make a note in the margin of problems that you find as you read, and note any answers you discover.

8. *Connections with your own ideas and experience:* Look back at ideas you noted before you read. Do you see any connections (even contrasts) with ideas and events you described or explained?

9. *New words:* Circle words and phrases you don't know and familiar words used in a new way.

STEP 4. REVIEW

Review Tools
Check vocabulary
Answer questions
Map the reading
Restate the main idea
Reread

Unless you take the final step of reviewing what you've just read, you may not be aware of any parts you don't understand. Some of the work of active reading can be completed here, and you can use it to help you put all the parts together and make sense of the reading as a whole. So begin by looking back at the guesses you made and the questions you asked before you read, and look also at the words you circled, the points you underlined or highlighted, and the notes you wrote as you read, using five review tools.

Check Vocabulary

When you find words you don't recognize in a reading, you should mark them rather than stopping to look them up or figure them out, because stopping in the middle of reading may confuse you. Look back at the words you circled. You don't have to look up every word in the dictionary, but plan to look up the most unfamiliar words. Make sure you understand all the words you've marked. You have several ways of doing this:

How to Check Vocabulary

Context: Guess the meaning of a word by understanding the rest of the sentence or paragraph.

Notes: Check the definitions at the bottom of the page (footnotes) or the end of the reading (endnotes).

Dictionary: Make sure you know how to use the dictionary. If more than one meaning is given for a word, be sure that you select the one that makes sense in the context of the sentence you are reading.

Sometimes you can use just one of these tools, but often you'll have to use a combination. Let's try using some of them with "Measuring Success" (pp. 39–40).

Context: Some of the words you circle may make sense as you continue to read. In paragraph 3, *mutable* is explained as "shifting along with our changing values." In paragraph 11, Loth refers to her value system as *simplistic* and *little.* You may thus guess that *simplistic* seems related to *simple,* and means *very simple* or *overly simple.*

Notes: Though this essay has no footnotes or endnotes, others do; always check for them.

Dictionary: If you marked *callow* in paragraph 1, you may find that the dictionary offers two meanings for the word: (1) young, inexperienced and (2) unfeathered. Since it makes no sense to speak of a college student as being featherless, you assume that *callow* in this sentence means *inexperienced*. In paragraph 3 if you marked *wantonly*, you won't find it in the dictionary. You will find the word *wanton*, a word that has at least ten meanings, many of them including words you also don't know. The first meaning is the most common: "Done maliciously or unjustifiably." If you don't know those words either, you might want to give up, but you try one more time and find that *maliciously* refers you to *malice*, which finally has a meaning you understand: "a desire to inflict harm on others." You try that in the sentence and it seems to make sense: these successful people may desire to hurt other people that make them jealous. Similar processes help you with the other words you've marked as unknown.

Let's now look at *absolute* in paragraph 9. The first meaning—"complete; perfect"—seems to work, implying that life is not as perfect as Loth thought it was going to be, that her original ideas were too easy.

Answer Your Own Questions

Think back to the questions you had when you first surveyed "Measuring Success," and look back at the questions you asked as you annotated. Try to answer them. Here are some possible answers:

What caused the change? In paragraph 2, she discusses seeing other things she hadn't considered; in paragraphs 3 and 4, she describes her friend's experience with people he thought successful and other definitions of success; finally in paragraphs 5 through 9 she gives details about how unhappy she was when she finally achieved her goal of fame. I'd say that she was changed by her own success and what she saw and heard from other people.

What does she mean by *happiness* and *success*? She gives some examples of success. Her own fame on the evening news, the success of friends. She describes some definitions that she learned later: creativity, approval, working with others, doing something well; enough money to live on. She never really discusses happiness.

Is it true that she doesn't have any wealth or fame? Eventually she does have some fame but she doesn't like it. She isn't poor and she says she realizes that being really rich isn't important but she never says why.

What does she count as health and love? She never says what she thinks about health and love.

Try also to answer any questions that you may have written in the margins as you read.

Why doesn't she say anything about health and love? This is still a problem because she doesn't write about these and also she doesn't really ever tell very much about what wealth is. What she says about fame is mainly that she didn't want it after all. She never did really tell what she means, but she's told a lot about how she changed her mind. The idea of changing her mind must be really important, then.

Why does she say that we are "always wanting more" and why does she bring up the idea that being yourself is more important than being well-known? She also doesn't go into detail about these. Maybe they are more examples of possible things a person could think, and they might even be some things that made her realize that her early ideas were wrong. She brings up a lot of different ideas. Maybe her point is that defining success is very complicated.

What's different about her old boyfriends who call when she's been on TV (an experience she seems to describe as unpleasant) and love, which she still suggests is important? Since she never goes into detail about her idea of love, she must not intend that as the main point she's making, but since she thinks that an old friend may have made an obscene call as a bad joke, she clearly is showing that people who only pay attention when you're famous aren't necessarily kind to you. This must be part of what she learned about the idea of success being more complicated than she thought it was when she was young.

Map the Reading

A **map** is a diagram or drawing that lets you visualize the **organization** of a reading. Different kinds of maps help you see the patterns of different readings: a story might be shown as a line, with different events at points on the line (see pp. 92–100 for more types of maps). A time line might help you see the pattern of a story, but this isn't really a story, so you'll need to think of a different way of showing the organization. Sometimes it's easiest to start with a map that just puts related ideas next to each other, sometimes called a **cluster** map.

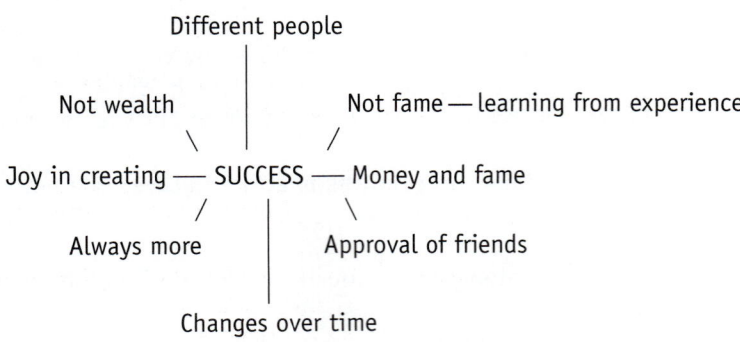

This map doesn't offer much understanding; it seems to be just a jumble of different ideas. Then you think some more and see that the ideas you added at the bottom: "Different people," "always more," and "changes over time" are really different from the ones you listed at the top: "money and fame." You add a second layer of your own ideas to help you see your map:

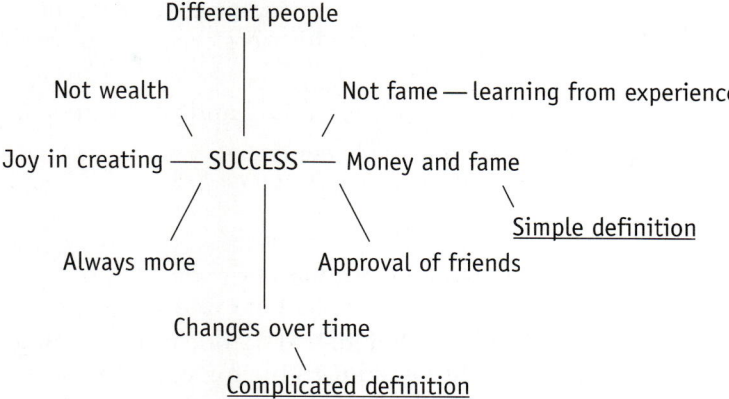

Now you begin to see the main point of the reading: Not just that there are many different definitions of success, but also that Loth's first definitions were really too simple, and her later ideas were more complicated.

Restate the Main Idea In Your Own Words

Restating the main idea of a reading in your own words is a good way to see the point that the author is making. The author's idea becomes a part of your own thinking when you translate it into your own words. If you can't restate the main idea, you may not yet completely understand the reading. If that's the case, go back to Steps 2 and 3, or discuss the reading with your instructor. You might go through the following stages as you develop your statement of the main idea of "Measuring Success."

1. Write the idea in one sentence, answering this question: *What does the author want me to know after reading this?*

   The author wants me to know that success isn't really just wealth and fame, because fame can be a problem.

2. Check this statement of the main idea against the notes and answers you've written. *Is everything in the reading related to this idea?*

   My statement of the idea leaves out the ideas about always wanting more and about different ideas about what success is and about changing our ideas about success over time.

3. If your first attempt doesn't seem to be a statement that really fits the whole reading, look back at the reading and your notes. Try a revised statement that does cover the whole reading: *What does the author want me to know after reading this?*

The author wants me to know that young people often think things like success can be defined very simply as fame and wealth but when they get older they learn that it's more complicated than that.

4. Look again at the reading and your notes. *Is everything in the reading related to this idea?*

This seems to cover it all.

Reread the Material

At this point, it's a good idea to try one more reading of the material. Read this time at a rate that's comfortable for you. If you find new questions or ideas, stop and work with them, but be sure to return after that to one complete, smooth rereading. This will help you see how the details and different parts of the reading all work to support the main idea.

EXERCISE 4.4   Review "My Father's Tribal Rule" (pp. 40–44). Once you've read the material carefully, you are ready to review it. Use the five review tools:

1. *Check vocabulary*: Look back at the unfamiliar words you circled. This reading included some words and phrases from other languages. Did you check footnotes to find the meaning?

2. *Answer your own questions*: Try to answer the questions you had when you first surveyed the reading as well as questions that occurred to you later.

3. *Map the reading*: Try to decide the clearest way to show the different parts of this reading.

4. *Restate the main idea in your own words*: Write the idea in one sentence, answering this question: *What does the author want me to know after reading this?* Check this statement of the main idea against the notes and answers you've made. *Is everything in the reading related to this idea?* If your first attempt doesn't fit the whole reading, look back at the reading and your notes. Try a revised statement that does cover the whole reading: *What does the author want me to know after reading this?* Check again with the reading and your notes. *Is everything in the reading related to this idea?*

5. *Reread the material*: Finish your review by going through the entire reading again at a comfortable pace. You may find that you see some details or events in a different way when you reread. Add any new observations to your annotations.

STEP 5. MODEL THE READING

 If you're sure you understand what you've read and have begun to give some written responses to a reading, you now may want to look at the reading in a different way—and to decide whether you want to use the reading as a **model** for your own writing. A model is an example that you try to imitate in certain ways. Some of the student essays in Chapter 25 can be used as models as can the essays written by professional writers in Chapter 26.

When referring to a model, don't try to imitate everything about it. You should try to write like yourself, not like a copy of another person. Think about the methods you use when learning other skills. If you want to learn to throw a basketball through a hoop, you probably will watch someone else, someone who always makes good shots. You may decide to stand the same way that person stands, or to hold your hands in the same way. The same is true of singing, or driving a car, or even handling a difficult customer at work: You learn how to do things partly by watching or listening to a model. The readings included in this book will thus become your models for how to write; in each one you may find one or two ways of writing that you want to imitate, though you still want to sound like yourself.

Here are some points to consider when you evaluate a model.

How to Evaluate a Reading

Clarity: What is clear in this reading? How does the way it's written help make it clear?

Interest: What is interesting in this reading? How does the writing add to the interest?

Purpose: What is the purpose of this reading? How does it relate to the kind of writing you are trying to do?

Clarity   Look back at the reading and decide which parts gave you the most difficulty. Look at this comment on "Measuring Success":

> I found paragraph 10 hard to follow because I didn't expect it and it didn't seem to fit in with her other ideas, also I don't know who Joni Mitchell is and I don't know why she's talking about "always reaching for more."

If you decide that this paragraph is not a good model, you can look at another one:

> Paragraph 2 tells me she found new kinds of success, and then it goes on to tell what those kinds are. This paragraph is clear because it gives examples and states its idea in simple words.

Interest   Look at the parts you enjoyed reading, the parts you remember the best after you finish. Try to see what made those parts memorable. Paragraphs 6, 7, and 8 may have been particularly interesting:

> In these paragraphs she gives a lot of weird people who tried to get in touch with her when she was on TV, her boyfriends, agents and people who wrote strange books. I also like the way she talks about things like her answering machine had "maxed out." But I think that's slang—can I really write like that? I could try to use more unusual details.

In these paragraphs it is the details and the language that make everything more interesting.

Purpose   When you begin to think about **purpose**, you may notice details about language and use of slang. For example, some writers may use slang because their main purpose is to entertain. Think about Loth's purpose and whether it's like yours:

> She's trying to get us to understand an idea about how we change. I will write about ideas I want people to understand, too, so her writing is like mine in that way. I don't think she's writing for school, though, so she might be different there.

Loth's purpose is clearly not the same as writing for school, which has a special kind of purpose where using slang may not be appropriate. It is also clear that Loth wants to help her reader understand an idea—a goal that is similar to what you want to do. How does she do this? Should you try to imitate her?

> She gives us some ideas of what she's going to explain and then she gives some examples. I could do that.

EXERCISE 4.5	**Evaluate "My Father's Tribal Rule" (pp. 40–44). Decide whether there's anything about the way this essay is written that you'd like to imitate.**

1. *Clarity:* Did any parts give you more difficulty than others? How did the writer help you to understand this different culture? How did he help you with language?

2. *Interest:* What do you remember best from the reading? Why is that so easy to remember? Did the details help you really see the people, places, and events he described?

3. *Purpose:* Was Mathabane explaining an idea or telling a story? How does that affect the way that he writes? How is that similar to your own purpose in writing? How is it different?

Whenever you read an essay thoroughly, you have reached the point of understanding it well enough to move on to write about it.

What You've Done

- ■ *Prepared* to read
- ■ *Surveyed* before reading
- ■ *Read* actively
- ■ *Reviewed* to make sense of what you've read
- ■ *Modeled* what you've read

For More Reading Strategies

- ■ See Chapter 16

The Next Step

- ■ Analyze the assignment (Chapters 5 and 17)

5 Analyzing the Assignment for an Essay
Understanding the Question

What You've Done

- Read and analyzed the assigned reading

What You Need to Do Next

- Analyze the assignment
  Understand the ideas the writing assignment asks you to discuss
  Understand the kind of writing the assignment calls for
  Understand how to use that kind of writing to focus on the ideas

---

What a Prompt Does

Identifies your focus

Identifies expected actions

Links focus and actions

Many terms may be used to refer to writing assignments: question, prompt, assignment, topic. In this book we use the word **prompt**—a statement or a question that directs you to write an essay. We also use the word *assignment*, which refers to all the activities—such as reading, taking notes, discussing ideas, or working in a group—related to addressing the prompt.

Before you begin writing an essay, you must make sure that you understand what you are being asked to do. You can do this by *analyzing the prompt*—taking the prompt apart and carefully looking at its parts. Analyzing the prompt will help you answer the following questions.

WHAT ARE YOU EXPECTED TO FOCUS ON?

To **focus** means to direct your attention to a specific aspect of something. For example, if you are at a football game, you can see many different things on and off the field: the teams, the band, the cheerleaders, your fellow spectators, and the blimp above the field. Since you can't take in everything at the same time, you direct your attention to—you focus on—one thing at a time. If you were given a writing assignment that asked you to comment on fan behavior, you would spend your time focusing on the spectators. When you write, you also select what you want to pay attention to—where your focus will be.

Study the prompt to see how to focus your essay. Because a reading may contain several different ideas or issues, you will want to see if the prompt points you to a particular idea. To find your focus, look for **key focus words**.

How to Identify Key Focus Words

Key focus words point you to the specific ideas or issues you are to write about. They usually fall into three categories:

People: May include the names of individuals (Katherine, Steve), or categories of people (students, parents, employees).

Things: May be specific (my 1997 Nissan Sentra), general (cars), concrete (bicycle), or abstract (transportation).

Ideas: May be abstractions (love, freedom, happiness, justice, pain, prejudice).

ESL

Consider the following prompts:

> *Describe your best friend.*
>
> *Write a letter to the phone company about a mistake that appeared on your bill.*
>
> *Is love at first sight possible?*

The first example is a statement that contains one key focus phrase—*your best friend*. To respond to this statement, you would naturally eliminate the other people in your life who are not your best friend—your overbearing boss, your nosy neighbor, your whiny sister. You know that the reader expects you to limit your comments to (that is, to focus on) your best friend.

The second example contains four key focus words: *letter, phone company, mistake, bill*. To respond to this prompt, you would need to limit your discussion to mistakes in your phone bill (not mistakes in your electric bill or the fact that your phone makes a buzzing noise when you hang up the receiver). While you may want both problems fixed, they are not relevant to your immediate task. Including them may allow your audience to fix one of the minor problems but still not fix your bill.

The third example is a question that names an idea—*love at first sight*. To answer this question, you must first talk about love (what it is and how it is different from friendship, lust, affection, and so on) and you must further talk about whether it can happen when two people meet for the first time.

WHAT ACTIONS ARE YOU EXPECTED TO TAKE?

Once you have found the focus of your essay, you will need to look at action words to determine what you are expected to do with that focus. For example, when you take your car to the shop, you tell the mechanic to focus on the car's problem, such as faulty brakes, and to take action—to diagnose, estimate the cost for, repair, replace, or adjust the brakes.

Just as the mechanic needs to know what action to take to fix your car, you also need to know what action to take by looking at **key action words**.

How to Identify Key Action Words

Key action words can be found in many places:

Direct commands

Indirect or implied commands

Questions

Key action words point you to the specific actions you must do to answer the prompt. Let's look again at the following prompts:

> *Describe your best friend.*
>
> *Write a letter to the phone company about a mistake that appeared on your bill.*
>
> *Is love at first sight possible?*

The first example contains one key action word—*describe*—which is a direct command. To respond to this statement, you would be expected to describe in detail the key focus word—your best friend.

The second example seems to contain a key action word—*write*. However, this word does not specifically direct you to do anything with the focus—a mistake on your phone bill. To respond to this prompt, you would be expected to *identify* and *describe* the mistake and *argue* for a refund.

The third example is a question that contains no direct or implied command. Instead, the prompt asks a question, and you need to find an action that will allow you to answer it. First, you need to determine what the question is asking you to do—in this case, to prove or disprove that love at first sight occurs. To prove or disprove something, you must *argue* a position.

You need to practice identifying key action words in prompts that are given as direct commands, indirect commands, or questions.

If the Prompt Contains Direct Commands

Some instructors use key action words when creating assignments—a process that is like giving a command. The list below contains the general definitions for commonly used key action words. Since some instructors may use these words with slightly different meanings, you may want to ask your instructor what these words mean. As in all writing tasks, it is always a good idea to keep in mind what your audience expects of you.

ESL

Key Action Words That Are Direct Commands

Agree or disagree
To explain why you hold or do not hold an opinion expressed by someone else. During a trial, the prosecution presents a case against the person being tried. Then the jury gives a verdict which shows whether they agree or disagree with the prosecution. When asked, they should be able to explain their position.

Analyze
To examine all aspects of a subject and their relationship to each other. If you are a detective trying to understand what happened at the scene of a crime, you look at the parts of the scene (the bloodstain on the wall, the body on the floor, the knife in the kitchen sink, and the broken window) and make connections between the parts to show how together they present a picture of how the crime was committed.

Argue
To present supporting evidence and reasoning either for or against a view or position. If you are an attorney, you present evidence and reasoning to convince the court of the innocence or guilt of the accused.

Classify
To place various elements of a subject into different categories to reveal their distinctions; for example, criminals can be classified as violent or nonviolent.

Compare
To examine two or more items for their similarities and differences. **Compare** always means both *compare* and *contrast*. For example, if you are an investigator, you might look for similarities and differences between two crime scenes to determine whether the crimes were committed by the same person.

Consider
To include in your thinking process. If you must decide whether to walk home by yourself at night, you might think about (or consider) how late it is, how well-lit the streets are, what kind of neighborhood you will have to walk through, and whether other people will also be walking.

Define
To clarify the elements that make up the subject. If you are asked to define a word, you give its meaning. If you were to prosecute a defendant for first-degree murder, you would need to present and explain the specific points that make an action murder and not something else.

Describe
To give a visual picture or, if the subject is an idea or argument, to reveal the major characteristics. If you have been mugged, you will want to describe your assailant to the police, giving as many visual details as possible (height, weight, skin, hair and eye color, identifying marks, dress, etc.). Sensory details are most important here.

continued on next page

continued from previous page

Determine   To weigh evidence and come to a conclusion or make a final de-cision. If you are asked to determine which of two arguments is the strongest, you will need to decide which is best and why you believe this. If you are serving on a jury, you must decide whether the accused is guilty based on the evidence presented in court.

Discuss   To explore the various aspects of an issue. If you are asked to dis-cuss an author's idea, you must give an in-depth answer rather than a quick summary. Before a jury determines guilt or inno-cence, members discuss the issues by explaining the evidence that has been presented.

Explain   To give more information about an idea or a situation. If your lawyer advises you to plead guilty, you would want him or her to explain why this would be to your advantage and what your pun-ishment might be.

Identify   To point out specific distinguishing characteristics. If you are asked to identify an author's thesis, you must point it out and separate it from other aspects of the text. Think of it as identifying a person in a police line-up. You're pointing him or her out, differentiating between the person you saw and the other people in the line-up.

Trace   To follow the path or progression of an idea. If you are asked to trace the development of an argument or of a process, you must identify a series of steps. Think of reconstructing a crime. You must pinpoint what a suspect did at different points in time, thus trac-ing his or her actions.

If the Prompt Contains Indirect Commands

Sometimes a prompt will ask you to perform an action without using any di-rect action words. In these situations, you must interpret what is being asked for from certain phrases that appear in the prompt. For example, if you take your car to a mechanic and ask her to *look at* the brakes, you will be disap-pointed if all she does is remove the tires and look at the brakes. You expect her to diagnose the problem, recommend a repair, estimate the cost, and per-haps repair or replace the brakes. When you have a writing prompt that con-tains an indirect command, you must also identify more specific actions that will address the prompt.

Let's look at an example of a prompt that does not include any of the di-rect key action words discussed above.

Write a letter to the governor to ask for more funding for schools in your community.

The key action words in this prompt are *write* and *ask*. But you know that simply writing and asking for the money from the governor will not be very effective, so the instructor must be asking you to do more than that. Your job is to select a direct action word that will allow you to complete the assignment. Your instructor has intentionally not given you a direct action so you can choose the action you think will lead to the best essay. There are many actions that you could use—none are right or wrong. You need to pick the best action or combination of actions to fulfill the assignment.

To write to the governor, you could choose any of the following:

- *Analyze* the schools' budget to show why the money is needed.
- *Argue* your position by presenting evidence showing why the money is needed.
- *Compare* the budgets of school districts to show why more money is needed in your community.
- *Define* quality education and show that more money is needed to provide for it.
- *Describe* the conditions of the schools in your community to show where funding is needed.
- *Determine* the impact of lack of money on students.
- *Discuss* why increasing funding to schools is better than supporting other projects.
- *Explain* what will happen if more money is not given to your community.
- *Identify* sources for increasing money for your community.

Often you will need to use more than one key action word to write an effective essay. Be sure to consider combinations of key action words and to look at the prompt to determine if you are required to complete more than one task.

If the Prompt Contains Questions

Questions always provide a focus, just as indirect or implied commands do. Although questions do not contain direct action words, they do imply more specific actions than sentences with indirect or implied commands. Questions do not allow as much leeway but limit the actions you can use to form your answers. Questions usually require a combination of actions. Your task is again to select the best combination that will allow you to write a thoughtful answer.

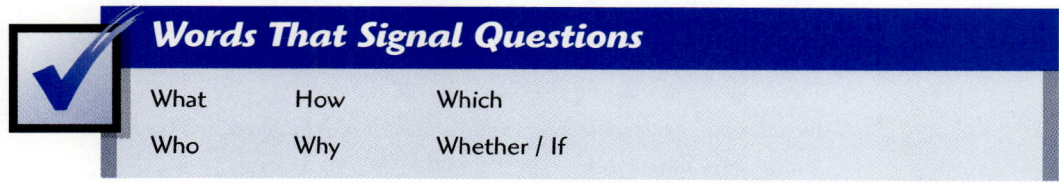

Words That Signal Questions

What	How	Which
Who	Why	Whether / If

Many beginning writers skip the implied actions required to answer questions. For example, when asked "What is the purpose of taxes?" beginning writers tend to argue whether taxes should exist; however, the question implies that taxes do exist and does not ask you to deal with that issue. Instead, the task is to first describe the kinds of taxes (car, sales, property, income) and their purposes. These are the issues your instructor expects you to handle. Once you've done this, you can go beyond the question and argue whether the taxes are fair or whether the revenue is used appropriately, but you cannot substitute these arguments for the implied actions.

Here are example questions and how to answer them:

Who is the best leader?	Define good leadership
	Identify someone who fits this definition
	Describe how this person fits this definition
How can schools be improved?	Identify a problem in schools
	Explain how to solve the problem
Why does racism exist?	Define racism
	Describe it to show it exists
	Determine why it exists
Which candidate should win?	Define the type of person needed for the job
	Identify which person has the qualities needed
	Describe how this person shows these qualities
If we eliminate welfare, what will happen?	Identify the impact of welfare
	Describe what would happen if welfare is stopped
	Compare the results to the present situation

Yes/No Questions   Some prompts involve questions that lead to an answer of **yes** or **no**. All of the questions below can be answered with a yes or a no, or even a **maybe**, but you know that you are expected to write an essay, not a sentence. This kind of prompt asks you to take a position, and, therefore, the key action you are expected to complete is to *argue*. To make your argument convincing, you may also choose other key actions such as *analyze, consider, define, determine,* or *explain*. Consider these questions.

Do you think the welfare system should be eliminated?

Should young adults under 16 be allowed to drive?

Would it be unethical to keep a large sum of money you found on the street?

Is education important?

HOW WILL YOU BRING THE FOCUS AND ACTIONS TOGETHER?

One of the basic requirements of an essay is that you focus clearly on a main idea. Although a prompt may ask you to do several things, you have to find a way to bring the focus and actions together into one essay.

For example, when you are having trouble stopping your car, you may have to take the brakes apart and test each part to find out what you need to do to make everything work properly. Once you have done so, you still have to put the brakes back together before your car will stop safely. In the same way, once you have identified the focus and the actions needed to respond to a prompt, you need to put all your ideas together into one effective essay.

Let's analyze two sample prompts (given below and on page 85). These prompts refer to Mark Mathabane's "My Father's Tribal Rule" (pp. 40–44). In analyzing these prompts, use the questions we discussed:

1. What are you expected to focus on?
2. What actions are you expected to do?
3. How will you bring the focus and actions together?

Sample Prompt 1

Mathabane writes less about his mother than his father or himself. What is her role in the family? Do you think other women play similar roles in their families?

Identifying the Focus

Notice that the first part of the prompt makes a statement about the reading. This statement is an interpretation by your instructor, and gives you an idea of the direction you are expected to take. You should accept this interpretation as valid for the assignment and write your essay based on it. (Chapter 17 will show you how to challenge an interpretation stated in a prompt.) Because this statement contains no direct, indirect, or implied commands and it is not a question, you know that the purpose of this statement is to introduce the assignment, not to give you key action or focus words. To find your action and focus, you must continue reading the prompt.

When you read further, you will see two questions. You should look here for key focus words. They are:

her role   the family   other women   roles   their families

These words focus you on the mother rather than on Mathabane or his father, who are mentioned only in the interpretive statement. You know what part of the reading you are expected to focus on—those parts that deal with Mathabane's mother and her role in the family.

Notice also that the key words require you to consider related material beyond the reading. This means that you will have to add material of your own since Mathabane does not discuss women in other families. These key words limit what you will discuss about these other women. You are expected to discuss only women's activities within the family (not at work, church, school, or in the community, unless these activities are clearly related to the family). You now know the focus of your essay will be Mathabane's mother as well as other women and their roles in their families.

Identifying the Actions

Now that you have the focus, you have to determine what you are being asked to do with that focus. Let's look again at the prompt to determine the actions you are expected to do:

Mathabane writes less about his mother than his father or himself. What is her role in the family? Do you think other women play similar roles in their families?

The first sentence contains no key words or phrases describing actions that involve you. The two questions that follow do. (Remember: questions always require an action on your part.)

The key action words in the first question are *what is*. As described in the example on page 82, *what* indicates that you need to identify the role Mathabane's mother plays and describe what she does to fill that role. Remember that she could play more than one role, and you will want to identify and describe each of them.

The second question in this prompt uses the key action phrases *do you think* and *other women play*. The phrase *do you think* tells you to consider the roles other women play. When you consider these roles, you will identify and describe them just as you did for the roles played by Mathabane's mother.

To summarize, you need to do the following:

- *Identify* and *describe* the role of Mathabane's mother.
- *Identify* and *describe* the role other women play in their families.

Bringing the Focus and the Actions Together

The prompt appears to ask you two different questions, and you have identified two actions that you need to complete. But you are writing one essay, so you must find a way to combine your answers into a single idea. Let's look at the prompt again.

Mathabane writes less about his mother than his father or himself. What is her role in the family? Do you think other women play similar roles in their families?

You have identified all the key focus words (people, things, or ideas) and the key actions (*what is*, or *identify* and *describe*). Many beginning writers stop once they know to identify and describe because they do not notice that the second question requires an additional action. Notice the word *similar* in the prompt. When you are asked whether two things are similar, you are being asked to *compare* (or *contrast*) them. This prompt asks you to compare (or contrast) the roles Mathabane's mother plays and the roles other women play.

You now have three actions to complete:

1. *Identify* and *describe* the role of Mathabane's mother.
2. *Identify* and *describe* the role other women play in their families.
3. *Compare* (or *contrast*) the roles Mathabane's mother plays and the roles other women play.

It is this third action that ties your ideas together to form a complete response to the prompt.

Is All This Really Necessary?   Yes. At first, you will have to consciously and thoroughly analyze the prompt before you begin to write your essay. As you become a more experienced writer, the task of analyzing the prompt will become more automatic, and you will be able to recognize the focus and actions in each prompt quickly and bring them together in your head. Until that time, it is better to address each step individually so that any essay you write will be an effective and complete answer to a prompt. Of course, this process will never become automatic if you don't practice it.

> ### Computer Tip
> Use the word processor to help you analyze a prompt. Type the prompt. Then move the key focus words into one list and the key action words into another. You can also separate the prompt into individual sentences to help you be sure that you are addressing each part of the prompt.

To help you move in this direction, let's practice with another prompt.

Sample Prompt 2

Mathabane has a conflict with his father. Do parents and children always have conflicts? Why or why not? Using Mathabane's essay as well as your own observations and experiences, write an essay in which you answer this question.

Here is a much shorter analysis of what the prompt asks you to do.

Identifying the Focus   This prompt directs your attention to the following:

Mathabane   conflict   his father   parents   children   conflicts

Mathabane's essay   your own observations and experiences

Identifying the Actions   The first part of the prompt is a statement that tells you that Mathabane and his father have conflicts. Your first action is to *identify* these conflicts discussed in the reading and to *describe* them.

The next part of the prompt asks a question. To answer it you first have to determine whether parents and children always have conflicts. There are two answers to this question: *yes* and *no.*

■ If you answer *yes,* you must discuss why this is true using examples from Mathabane's situation and other families you know of. You will need to *identify* and *describe* the conflicts you know about between parents and their children and *compare* these families and Mathabane's.

■ If you answer *no,* you must show that some parents and children do not have conflicts. Since Mathabane's family did have conflicts, you must *describe* examples of parents and children who do not have conflicts and *compare* these families and Mathabane's.

The third part of the prompt asks you *to explain* why conflicts between parents and children do or do not happen. The last part of the prompt instructs you to use Mathabane's essay as well as your own observations and experiences.

Tying the Focus and Actions Together   As you may notice, we have already brought the focus and actions together by recognizing that we have to compare Mathabane's family and other families. As you get more skilled at analyzing prompts, this third step will often require you to just be sure that you have already responded to all parts of the prompt and that you have tied the focus and the actions together.

EXERCISE 5.1   We will be using the following prompt in later chapters to illustrate the entire process of writing an essay in response to a reading. To help you get ready, let's analyze it.

Mathabane says he despises rules and rituals. Is he correct in thinking that rules and rituals have no purpose or value?

1. Identify the focus.
2. Identify the actions.
3. Bring the focus and actions together.

EXERCISE 5.2   Here are additional prompts for analysis:

1. The title of Mathabane's essay is "My Father's Tribal Rule." Is it necessary for a family to be descended from a tribe in order for a parent to exercise "tribal rule"? Why or why not?

2. What does Mathabane's mother mean when she says, "Everybody does rituals, Mr. Mathabane. . . . You just don't notice because they do theirs differently" (paragraph 28)?

3. Mathabane's mother says, "Everybody does rituals, Mr. Mathabane. . . . You just don't notice because they do theirs differently" (paragraph 28). What activities does your family do that could be classified as rituals as Mathabane defines them?

4. Some readers might classify the way Mathabane's father brought up his children as strict. Would he be considered too strict in your community?

5. In "My Father's Tribal Rule" Mathabane says that he hated the rituals that his father made him perform. As an adult, he may have changed his opinion. What makes family relationships change as children get older?

6. Mathabane's family lived in a multi-ethnic neighborhood in a South African township. His friends spoke different languages from the language of his father's tribe. When Mathabane spoke the languages of his friends, his father threatened and punished him. Does a multicultural situation increase the possibility for conflict between parents and children?

7. Mathabane's family lived in a shantytown in a South African township. Does poverty increase the possibility for conflict between parents and children? How? Why?

8. Mathabane says "my father belonged to a loosely knit group of black families in the neighborhood to whom tribal traditions were a way of life" (paragraph 3). He also says that he was "learning other ways of life, modern ways, from mingling with children whose parents had shed their tribal cloth and embraced Western culture" (paragraph 5). Mathabane wishes his father did not insist on a traditional way of life. Would you prefer to follow a more traditional or a more modern way of life?

9. Mathabane's mother says that "It's hard to stop doing things when you're old" (paragraph 32). Do people really get too old to change?

What You've Done

■ Analyzed the prompt by
    Identifying key focus words
    Identifying key action words
    Bringing focus and action together

For More Strategies for Analyzing the Assignment

■ See Chapter 17

The Next Step

■ Understand and practice prewriting (Chapters 6 and 18)

Prewriting
Freewriting, Listing, Mapping, Questioning

What You've Done

■ Analyzed the assignment

What You Need to Do Next

■ Write to explore your ideas about the reading you will be writing about
■ Write to explore your own ideas and experiences related to the topic of the assignment

In Chapter 5, we discussed how to analyze the prompt to focus your writing. After analyzing an assignment and its **prompt** in depth, you probably think that you are now ready to begin the first draft of your essay. However, if you begin writing your essay at this point, you may discover that you don't have as much information as you thought you had or that your essay is not that interesting. To explore all of your options, you need to begin *prewriting*—a process in which you think about the required tasks and record some of your ideas before you begin to write your first draft.

In this chapter, we focus on prewriting based on a reading as well as on your own material. We also show you how to use the writing prompt to focus your reading and generate information.

WHAT IS PREWRITING?

Types of Prewriting
Focused freewriting
Listing
Mapping, clustering
Questioning

Prewriting is private, not public, writing. It is writing that others will not read, writing in which you generate ideas for yourself, not to produce an essay for your readers. There's more to prewriting than just putting words on paper. Reading, talking to other people, and thinking while you do other things are also ways to explore ideas. While you do some of these things, you may jot down some ideas. These notes may be helpful, but there are also more systematic ways to generate ideas that will help you complete the assignment.

To get the most out of your prewriting, you need to follow certain steps:

- Write as much as you can. The more you write, the more choices you have.
- Write down whatever comes to your mind. Don't worry if it seems silly or unrelated.
- Write without worrying about correctness. Do not correct grammar or mechanics. Do not open a dictionary or thesaurus.

This stage of informal prewriting is often called **freewriting**.

How Much Prewriting Is Required?

The amount of prewriting needed depends on a number of factors.

- *Time:* The deadline for the assignment will affect how much prewriting you can do. If you must write a timed, in-class essay or essay exam, you will want to prepare at home, reading and thinking. When you begin your in-class assignment, you will need to limit your prewriting to five to ten minutes. If you are writing an essay out of class and you have two or three days to produce a **draft**, you will want to spend one or two days prewriting. It is better to do one prewriting activity at a time, and then leave the assignment alone for a period of time. Even if you are not actively writing ideas down, your brain continues to work on the tasks subconsciously. When you return to the assignment and attempt another prewriting activity, you should find that you have lots of new ideas or that you have discovered the connections between your ideas.

- *Preference:* Another factor determining how you begin to prewrite is the way you prefer to work. Some writers spend lots of time thinking and jot down a quick list of the ideas they want to include in the draft. Other people think on paper and may produce pages of ideas even though they may use only a few of those ideas in their essay. You will need to find the prewriting activities that help you get your ideas on paper most effectively and efficiently.

- *Assignment:* The nature of the assignment may suggest a particular prewriting activity. For example, if you are writing an essay exam you may want to list the points that must be included to answer the instructor's question. Some assignments may require you to look carefully at the reading. Other assignments may ask you to think about personal experience or do research in the library or on the Internet. The more difficult assignments may take more time and more attempts at prewriting to find the ideas you want to include in your paper.

While all writers have a favorite method of prewriting, they need to understand how to use several prewriting activities. In this chapter, we introduce four methods of prewriting you can use to generate material from a reading and from your own writing; these methods are categorized as focused freewriting, listing, mapping or clustering, and questioning.

PREWRITING ABOUT A READING

RES   Although some college writing assignments will ask you to write only about your own experiences and ideas, other assignments (which we will refer to as prompts), will direct you to respond to ideas in a reading.

When the prompt requires you to respond to a reading, you will probably want to prewrite about the reading before you prewrite to add any of your own material. If you start with your own material, you may generate a lot of information that is not related to the issues in the reading. (See Chapter 5 for more information on analyzing prompts.)

Consider the following prompt related to Mark Mathabane's "My Father's Tribal Rule" (pp. 40–44):

Mathabane says he despises rules and rituals. Is he correct in thinking that rules and rituals have no purpose or value?

Notice that the prompt is specifically concerned about rules and rituals. To prewrite efficiently, you will want to focus your prewriting on those parts of the reading that deal with rules and rituals.

Focused Freewriting

One method of prewriting is to record your first reactions to the general idea about the reading identified in the prompt. The prompt tells you that *Mathabane says he despises rules and rituals.* You might want to write what you think about this idea without looking back at the reading.

Focused freewriting is a prewriting technique that will help you record your first reactions to an idea from a reading. This technique allows you to focus on one idea but gives you the freedom to write anything that comes to your mind while you are thinking about the idea.

You should write in sessions of 15 to 30 minutes. You should try to stay focused on the selected idea. However, if your mind wanders, don't stop writing and don't read what you've already written; just guide your thinking back to the topic.

Let's look at a sample of focused freewriting.

Tribal rule is wrong. Mathabane wants to be like his friends but his father won't let him. He wants him to speak Venda because his tribe speaks Venda. Mathabane want to speak what his friends speak. The father won't let anyone talk at dinner. This is a dumb rule. Why does his father care? Why can't people talk? Does he talk during dinner? Is this rule only for the children? His mother doesn't speak. Can woman speak at the table? Maybe the rules are for the father? He wears the tribal clothing. But Mathabane goes to school and needs to fit in. If his father made him wear the tribal clothing he will be laughed at. The rules and ritual may be ok for old people but not for kids who are our future.

If there are mistakes in freewriting, that is all right, since the object is to write down basic ideas in response to the prompt without worrying about being correct.

While focused freewriting is good for recording your first reactions, you will need to examine the reading carefully to make sure you have identified all the rules and rituals discussed in the reading. One good way to identify the places in the reading is to list them.

Listing

This prewriting method allows you to jot down phrases and important words quickly and works well for identifying places in the reading that relate to your writing prompt. **Listing** works best when you generate more ideas than you may need in your essay. You want to list everything you might use, knowing that you may choose to eliminate ideas later. Extensive listing gives lots of options and allows you to make the best choices for your essay.

In Chapter 5, we asked you to analyze the prompt to identify the key focus words: *rituals*, *rules*, *purpose*, and *value*. To begin dealing with the reading, you first need to identify areas of the reading that relate to these key focus words.

The following paragraphs are related to rituals, rules, purpose, and value:

when George is weaned (paragraph 2)

"George's passage from infancy to childhood" (paragraph 2)

return to old traditions when whites leave (paragraph 5)

Mathabane is more interested in modern ways ("we're not living in the tribes"), but father sticks to tradition (paragraphs 5, 23)

daily rituals for protection, good luck, earning money (paragraph 6)

when Mathabane speaks at the table (paragraph 7)

father says he needs to be "taught how to eat properly" (paragraph 11)

when the father wears tribal clothing (paragraph 34)

when Mathabane speaks languages other than Venda (paragraph 34)

You now have a list of areas of the text that relate to the prompt, but it's not clearly organized into specific topics. You can take this first list and break it into separate lists according to the **key focus words**. Your new list might look like this:

Rituals	Rules	Purpose	Value
George's weaning	Not speaking at table	To be prepared	
		To return to tribes	
Daily rituals	Only speaking Venda	To get protection, good luck, money	Safety, prosperity
Tribal clothing		To move to new stage of life	
		To teach manners	

Notice that there is only one item under the heading *value*. When looking at the reading, there are few direct references to what Mathabane and his family get out of these rituals. You may have to decide what value you think the family gets from these rituals rather than finding it clearly in the reading.

As you do other prewriting methods, you may find the ideas you need to fill in the rest of this list.

You will also need to know how these four topics relate to each other. A good way to see the relationship between the parts of your prompt is to draw yourself a picture or a map that shows the connections.

Mapping and Clustering

Mapping and **clustering** allow you to create a visual picture of your ideas and the relationships among them. This method is good if you have found lots of material and ideas but are not sure how all of them fit together. To create a map, you should start by writing one of the central ideas of the topic in the center of the page and then add ideas that you think are associated with this topic. As you generate ideas, you may want to draw lines and circles to show how these ideas are connected.

Mapping is a way to organize and show the relationships that exist between the items in your lists. Since you already have a list organized by topics, you can start your mapping from your list. According to the prompt, you would expect rules and rituals to each have a purpose and a value. You can begin your mapping by showing the connections between the rules and rituals and purpose and value.

Figure 6.1 shows a map of the relationships you might find between rituals, rules, purposes, and values. Although some parts of the map still aren't connected to anything else, you may find the connections later or you may find out that they aren't really related and can be eliminated.

At this point, you may want to look back at the prompt to see what else it asks you to consider. The prompt states that "Mathabane says he despises rituals." One of the ideas you'll want to explore is why he despises them. Figure 6.2 illustrates how Mathabane's reasons can be added to the map to give you a better picture of his attitudes toward his father's rules and rituals.

In looking at the reasons Mathabane detests rituals that have been identified, notice that there is one ritual—George's weaning—that he doesn't really despise. Since it doesn't relate to the prompt, you probably won't have to talk about it and you can cross it off your map.

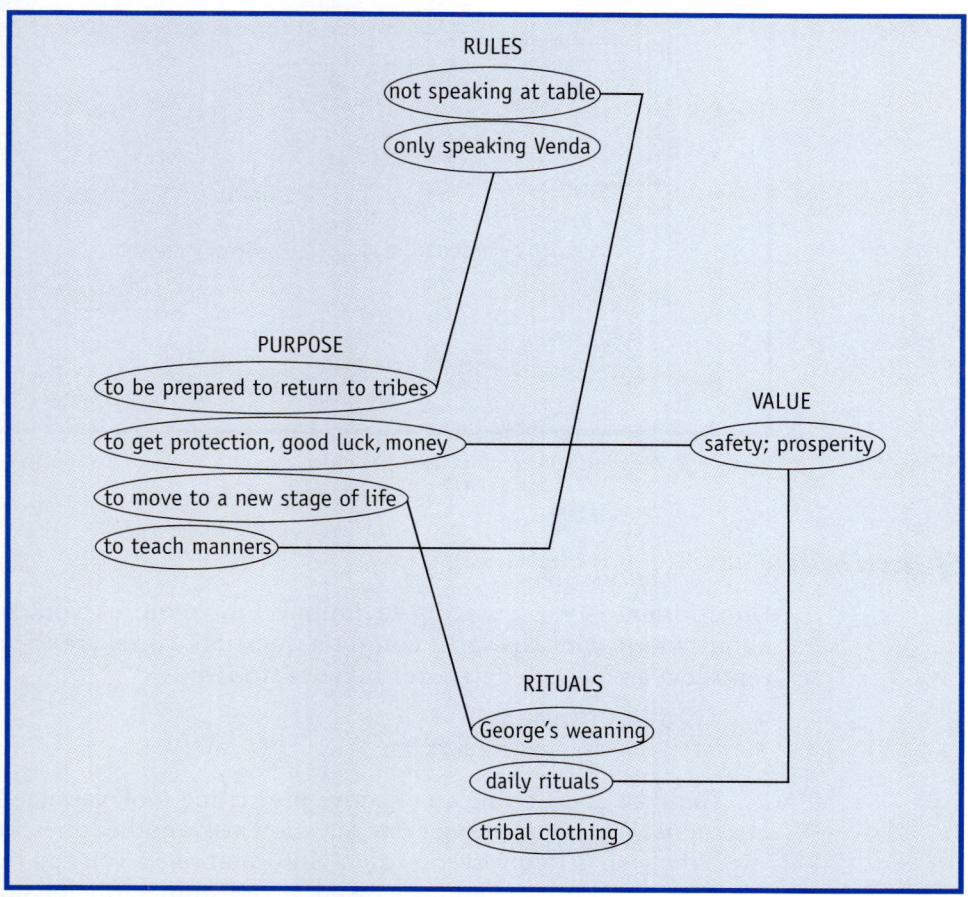

Figure 6.1. Map of Rituals, Rules, Purpose, and Value

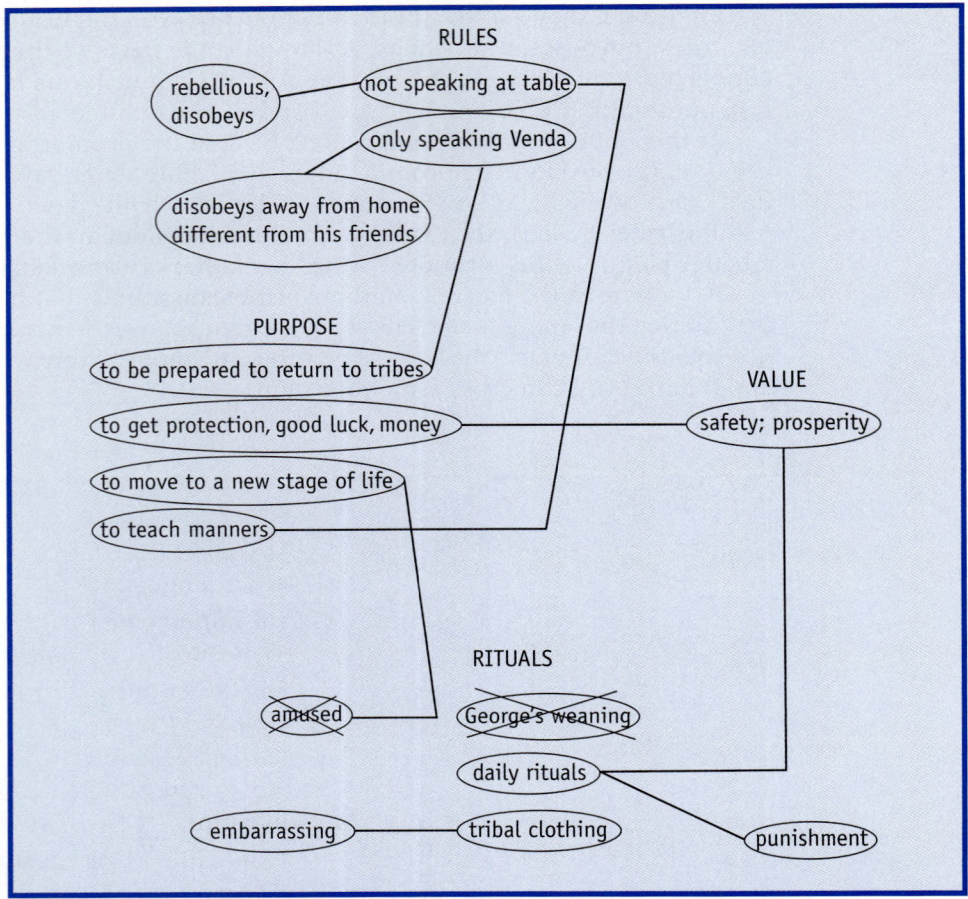

Figure 6.2. Map Including Mathabane's Responses

Questioning

Questioning is a prewriting technique that requires you to ask questions about your topic. The most common question words are the same questions reporters are expected to cover in news stories:

what   who   when   where   why   how

To make questioning an effective prewriting tool, you need to keep asking questions. When you answer one question, ask another question about the answer; the goal is to uncover as much information as you can by asking the difficult and obscure questions as well as the simple, obvious ones. When you continue to ask and answer more specific questions, you get to the core of the issue and reveal the most about the reading.

What rituals does Mathabane and his family participate in?	Weaning George, wearing tribal clothing, daily rituals
What rules does Mathabane have to follow?	Speaking Venda, not speaking at table
Why do they follow these rituals?	Father believes they will return to tribal life, wants them to be ready
Why does Mathabane despise the rules and rituals?	Sometimes used as punishment, his father is unreasonable, he's embarrassed
How does his father punish him?	Beats him, makes him do more rituals
What does Mathabane do?	Sometimes obeys, sometimes disobeys
When does he obey?	Usually when father is there
When does he disobey?	When he's with his friends, and when he's mad at his father
How does he disobey?	He talks at the table, he speaks other languages
Why does he disobey?	He wants to be like his friends, he likes modern ways, he's rebellious
What happens when he disobeys?	His father punishes him, his mother talks to him
What does his mother say?	Father is too old to change, all people do rituals, father wants son to be like him
Why does she say this?	Wants him to understand his father

This is not a complete list of the questions you could ask; it is merely a sample to show how to create and answer questions as a prewriting technique. You need to continue asking questions about the reading and about your answers to those questions until you have identified all aspects of the reading that relate to the prompt and understand how that material will help you respond to the prompt.

After using these four prewriting techniques—focused freewriting, listing, mapping and clustering, questioning—you will have identified which parts of the reading deal with rules and rituals. You will also have discovered what Mathabane's attitude is toward rules and rituals and why he feels that way.

PREWRITING ABOUT YOUR OWN IDEAS AND EXPERIENCES

 The four prewriting techniques we have just discussed can also be used to help you generate your own ideas and identify experiences that you can use to support your **argument**.

When you prewrite about a reading, you have a ready source of examples—the reading itself. Many beginning writers believe that when an assignment requires their own ideas and experiences, they are allowed to discuss only what they have personally done. In fact, these writers often say things like, "I can't write about capital punishment because I've never committed a serious crime." This view of ideas and experiences is much too narrow. While first-hand experience can be very useful, you can also use the experiences of family and friends, what you've heard in the media, or what you've seen happen in the world around you. These experiences—although second-hand—do influence your thoughts and feelings. Even in extreme situations where you've truly had no experience (first-hand or second-hand), you are expected to show your understanding of the issues by creating hypothetical experiences you can use to place yourself in a relevant situation and complete the assignment.

Therefore, when an assignment requires your own ideas and experiences, you need to consider each of these possible areas of experience.

PERSONAL EXPERIENCE:

Have I had any experience with this topic?

EXPERIENCES OF FAMILY MEMBERS OR FRIENDS:

Have I heard of anyone else who has experience with this topic?

CURRENT EVENTS, HISTORICAL EVENTS, OR MEDIA (NEWSPAPERS, MAGAZINES, TELEVISION, MOVIES, RADIO):

Have I seen this topic discussed on TV, in a movie, or in a book?

HYPOTHETICAL SITUATIONS:

Can I make up a scenario in which the topic would be relevant?

To show you how to use these four sources of examples, let us look again at the prompt we are focusing on in this chapter:

Mathabane says he despises rules and rituals. Is he correct in thinking that rules and rituals have no purpose or value?

The second part of the prompt asks if you think (like Mathabane) that rules and rituals have no purpose or value. To complete this part of the prompt, you will have to present your own experiences with rules and rituals so that you can provide clear examples for your reader.

You may have already decided whether or not rules and rituals have purpose and value. If so, you should prewrite to come up with specifics to support your position. If you are undecided, you will probably want to prewrite to find specifics that support both positions, and use this prewriting to help you determine which position you want to take in your essay. You can use prewriting to support your point of view or to find your position on a topic.

Let's examine the four prewriting techniques to show how they can help you produce information and discover your own opinions. Using each of these techniques will help you develop an abundance of material that can be used to strengthen your essay.

Focused Freewriting

A writer did the following focused freewriting on his experiences with the topic of rules and rituals:

In my family, we have a dinnertime ritual. Before dinner, my brothers and my sister and I are supposed to clean the house and get everything ready for dinner. One day I didn't feel like doing it, because I have to do everything. My brothers and my sister hardly do anything. So, I just sat on the couch and watched TV. My father came in and saw me and started to yell at me. He said he worked hard every day to put food on the table and that I was showing disrespect to him, my mother, my brothers and my sister. He sent me to bed without supper.

At first I was really mad. I thought my father was being unfair to me. I'm the oldest, so I wind up doing most of the work. Why should I have to clean the house every day and get the table ready? The more I thought about it, the more I felt bad. He did do a lot for us. Besides providing us with a house and food, he paid for my music lessons, he takes us to the beach in the summer, he drops us off at the movies. He really does do a lot for us and sometimes I think we forget to say thank you. I felt bad for not respecting my father.

This writer has focused on one specific ritual performed in his family. At the end of his entry, he seems to feel regret that he didn't participate in the ritual. His feelings of regret suggest that he does see the value in performing rituals.

He will have to generate other examples to see if he feels the same way about other rules and rituals. If most of his experiences are positive, then he will probably write an essay disagreeing with Mathabane's attitude toward rituals.

Here is another example of focused freewriting:

The instructor in my history class had a ridiculous rule: no gum chewing. One day I forgot that I was chewing gum and went into his class. As he was walking between the rows of desks he saw my jaw moving and then seemed to go nuts. "I warned the class about gum chewing," he shouted at me. "Spit it out and go to the principal's office." This outburst completely disrupted the class and ruined my day. What did I do? I quietly chewed gum with my mouth closed. He couldn't have heard me. I got punished for breaking a stupid rule that authority figures like force on us. These rules make no sense and should be abolished.

This writer has focused on one specific rule. At the end of the paragraph we see this student taking a strong stance against it. If this writer can provide more strong examples showing his disgust with rules and rituals, he will be able to write an essay supporting Mathabane's attitude.

Both of these writers clearly included their attitudes toward rules and rituals as they described their experiences. They now need to come up with additional strong examples to support their positions.

Sometimes you may freewrite about an experience but not clearly understand what it reveals about your opinion. Look back at the prompt and identify the key focus words and **key action words**. Use them to create questions that you can ask about your freewriting. The following questions are based on the prompt for this chapter:

■ Is this focused freewriting about a *rule* or *ritual*?

■ Is there a *purpose* or *value* to this rule or ritual?

■ What is the *purpose* or *value*?

If you ask these questions about all the experiences you write down, you'll be doing a focused freewriting on each of them.

While focused freewriting is good for recording the specifics related to the experience you're discussing, the prompt may require you to come up with several different kinds of experiences. If you are having difficulty remembering other experiences, you will want to try another prewriting technique: listing.

As explained on page 91, listing is a prewriting technique that allows you to jot down words and phrases that come to you as you think about the assignment. The benefits of listing are that you don't have to write in complete sentences or in a logical order. Listing is particularly useful when you have so many ideas that you can't take the time to write in complete sentences without losing some of them.

Listing

The lists below focus on a writer's own experiences related to the two terms *rituals* and *rules:*

Rituals	Rules
Helping with dinner	No TV until homework is done
Clean-up before bedtime	Can't stay out past 10:00
Sunday—church	Chores before play on Saturday
Sunday cookouts	No allowance until chores done

Rituals	**Rules**
Christmas—Thanksgiving	Only one hour TV per night
Birthdays	No phone calls after 8:00
Saturday morning yard work	Can't stay over at friends' houses
Halloween costume party	

This type of list helps you to identify those areas you need to explore in more depth, and it can become the source for more detailed lists. In the list below, this writer has taken one item from the list on rules—only one hour of TV per night—and expanded it, providing more details.

One hour of TV

Each person has their night to choose shows

Parents think one hour of TV is enough

Parents think TV shows "rot your brain"

I miss shows all my friends watch because my brothers choose on those nights

Forced to watch my brothers' stupid action shows

Forced to watch my parents' news shows

Dad can override anybody if there is something he really wants to see—we can't

Mom says it teaches "time management" and "cooperation"

On weekends we vote for shows, but I always lose

This more detailed list begins to reveal attitudes about this rule. Words like *forced*, *stupid*, and *lose* suggest that the rules are unreasonable. This information could be used to support Mathabane's dislike of rules.

Mapping and Clustering

The lists on rituals and rules presented in the previous section give the writer basic ideas or experiences he can examine. However, lists don't necessarily help the writer see how he feels or thinks about the items in the lists. Figure 6.3 on page 100 illustrates how the writer has taken his general list on rules and mapped it.

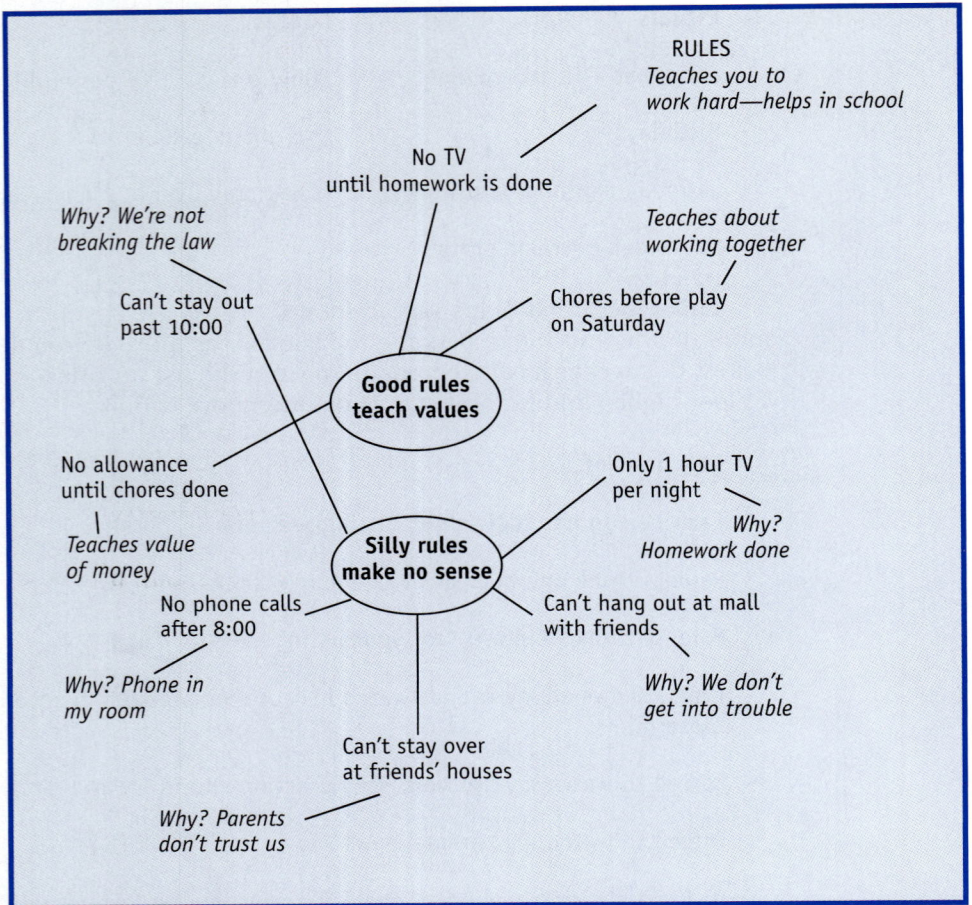

Figure 6.3. Map of Writer's Own Experiences

The diagram identifies which rules are good—and thus have value—and which ones are without value. It identifies the basic reason why each rule is or is not valuable.

Three of the rules have value, but in five of the rules, no value is noted. Since this mapping has identified more rules without value, it could become the basis for an essay agreeing with Mathabane's dislike of rules. Consider the rules with value that are identified. Which are the best examples? Which are most closely related to the prompt and the reading? Examples are provided in the mapping that could be used to agree or disagree with Mathabane's attitude about rules. If this were your mapping, you would now need to decide which position you wish to defend.

Questioning

Questioning is a prewriting technique that requires you to ask questions about your topic. The most common question words are the same questions reporters are expected to cover in news stories: *what? who? when? where? why? how?*

To make questioning an effective prewriting tool, you need to keep asking questions. When you answer one question, ask another question about the answer; the goal is to uncover as much information as you can by asking the difficult and obscure questions as well as the simple, obvious ones. When you continue to ask and answer more specific questions, you get to the core of the issue and reveal the most interesting ideas and information.

The questioning below focuses on a student's prewriting from his own experiences with *rituals*.

What rituals do I do?	Helping with dinner, clean-up before bedtime, church, Sunday get-togethers, Christmas, Thanksgiving, Birthdays, Saturday yard work, Halloween party.
When do we do them?	Some every day. Others on special occasions, holidays.
Why do I do rituals?	Holiday rituals fun—Halloween costumes, Christmas tree decorating. Dinner ritual and clean-up rituals not fun but have to be done.
Who has to do them?	Everybody except Dad.
Why doesn't he do them?	He works all day and gets to relax while we work.
Is that fair?	Not sure. He's at work all day but we're at school working all day.
What happens if we don't do them?	Dad gets angry at us. May punish us.
Why does he get angry?	Feels like we're not helping. Shows disrespect to him and Mom.
How does he punish?	Extra chores, go to room, yells and makes you feel bad.

One question has led to another and the process has helped this writer expand his knowledge of this subject. Notice that there is a question that doesn't contain one of the words *what, who, when, where, why, how*. That's fine. As long as you're asking questions about your subject, you're doing the right thing.

Summary of Prewriting Techniques

Remember that you have many options when prewriting. You can choose the most useful method by thinking about what you need to accomplish in your prewriting:

When you want to	Use
Record your own reactions and explore your ideas	Focused freewriting
Come up with as many ideas as possible	Listing
Explore relationships between ideas	Mapping and clustering
Generate details and pinpoint meaning	Questioning

EXERCISE 6.1   Read the following sample prompt:

Mathabane writes less about his mother than his father or himself. What is the significance of her role in the family? Do you think other women play similar roles in their families?

Prewriting About the Reading

Identify places where Mathabane's mother figures in the reading.

Prewriting About Your Own Experiences

1. Select a prewriting activity to help you add your own examples. Remember to consider the following sources of examples:

   ■ Personal experience

   ■ Experiences of family members or friends

   ■ Current events, historical events, or media (newspapers, magazines, television, movies, radio)

   ■ Hypothetical situations

2. Prewrite about women you know.

3. Choose one of these women and use a prewriting activity to identify the roles she plays or the kinds of things that women are expected to do.

EXERCISE 6.2   Read the following sample prompt:

Mathabane has a conflict with his father. Do parents and children always have conflicts? Why or why not?

Prewriting About the Reading

1. Identify places where Mathabane mentions conflicts in his family.

2. Use a prewriting technique to determine how each of these places in the reading relate to the prompt.

Prewriting About Your Own Experiences

Select a prewriting activity to help you add your own examples to answer the prompt. Remember that the tasks you need to complete to answer the prompt are:

■ Identify and describe the conflicts you know about between parents and children.

■ Identify the similarities between these families and Mathabane's family.

■ Identify parents and children who do not have conflicts.

■ Describe how these families are different from Mathabane's family.

■ Explain why conflicts between parents and children happen (or don't happen).

What You've Done

■ Explored four basic types of prewriting:
  Focused freewriting
  Listing
  Mapping or clustering
  Questioning

■ Applied these methods to
  Writing in response to reading
  Writing from your own experience and ideas

For more Prewriting Strategies

■ See Chapter 18

The Next Step

■ Organize your material (Chapters 7 and 19)

7 Organizing the Material
Planning and Outlining

What You've Done

■ Completed prewriting activities, applying one or more methods to writing either from reading or research, or from your own experience

What You Need to Do Next

■ Be sure you still understand the reading and writing assignment
■ Decide what you can use from the writing you've already done
■ Use that writing to determine the main idea of your own essay

After you have completed **prewriting** activities, it's time to evaluate what you have written and decide what you can use in writing your essay as well as how you can use it.

You probably won't be able to use everything you wrote during prewriting. Don't be surprised or discouraged if you have to cross off some of your ideas because they aren't relevant to the question you are answering. It is much easier to eliminate what you don't need than to make up new ideas or to try to make irrelevant ideas fit into an **essay**. However, do not throw anything away until you have finished **drafting** your paper.

REVIEWING THE PROMPT AND EVALUATING YOUR PREWRITING

Organizing Steps
Review prompt
Review prewriting to:
eliminate
combine
link ideas to details
identify key ideas
Draft a thesis

The first step in organizing your material is to review the **prompt**. Your goal here should be to identify material in the prewriting that you can use in the essay and to eliminate any material not related to the prompt.

Let's look again at the prompt related to Mark Mathabane's "My Father's Tribal Rule" (pp. 40–44).

Mathabane says he despises rules and rituals. Is he correct in thinking that rules and rituals have no purpose or value?

Once again, the **key focus words** are *rules, rituals, purpose,* and *value*.

The second step is to examine the prewriting you have done. When evaluating prewriting, ask three questions:

- What is unrelated to the topic? (Eliminate it.)
- What is repeated? (Choose the best way of saying it or combine statements that repeat the same ideas.)
- What is a main idea and what may be support for that idea? (Match general ideas to related specific details and examples.)

You can start by evaluating either the prewriting on the reading or on your own experiences. There is no right way or order, though many writers start by evaluating the prewriting that contains the most information or that is most familiar.

EVALUATING PREWRITING ABOUT A READING

Let's look at an example of a writer's prewriting:

> Tribal rule is wrong. The father won't let anyone talk at dinner. When Mathabane talks anyway, his father beats him. This is a dumb rule. Mathabane doesn't deserve to be beaten for breaking it. Mathabane also gets punished when he doesn't do the daily rituals. His father must be superstitious. No ritual can possibly bring good luck or keep people from getting sick. It doesn't make sense to waste time doing these things every day like Mathabane's father made him. His father also wears the tribal clothing and Mathabane's friends laugh at his father, calling his clothes Tarzan clothes. Mathabane cries when his friends tease him. He shouldn't have been made to feel bad because of his father's rituals.

Eliminating Unrelated Material or Ideas

RES In many cases, you will easily recognize ideas and examples in your prewriting that are unrelated to your topic, but sometimes you may not be sure. To decide whether material is related to your topic, write one sentence explaining how the idea in your prewriting is related to key focus words. If you cannot explain this relation, your idea may be unrelated and you may choose not to use it. Let's now look at the prewriting from above, one sentence at a time:

Tribal rule is wrong.	The word *rule* is one of the key focus words. The word *wrong* implies a judgment, which also implies *value,* another key focus word. The use of these words makes this sentence related.

The father won't let anyone talk at dinner.	This sentence refers to one of the rules discussed in the reading, so it is clearly related.
When Mathabane talks anyway, his father beats him.	This sentence also refers to one of the rules discussed in the reading, so it is clearly related.
This is a dumb rule.	Like the first sentence of the prewriting, this sentence is clearly related. The word *dumb* implies a purpose or value, both key focus words.
Mathabane doesn't deserve to be beaten for breaking it.	This sentence refers to what happens when Mathabane breaks the rule; it is related.
Mathabane also gets punished when he doesn't do the daily rituals.	This sentence also refers to a set of rituals mentioned in the reading, so it is related.
His father must be superstitious.	No key focus words are used in this sentence. Unless you can write a sentence connecting it to the prompt, it is unrelated.
No ritual can possibly bring good luck or keep people from getting sick.	This sentence includes the key word *ritual*; it is also related.
It doesn't make sense to waste time doing these things every day like Mathabane's father made him.	*These things* refer to rituals, and the words *make sense* and *waste time* relate to the value of the rituals; this sentence is related.
His father also wears the tribal clothing and Mathabane's friends laugh at his father, calling his clothes Tarzan clothes.	Wearing tribal clothing is another ritual.
Mathabane cries when his friends tease him.	This sentence contains no key words and is not clearly related to the prompt.
He shouldn't have been made to feel bad because of his father's rituals.	This sentence also contains the key word *ritual*.

Most of these sentences clearly relate to rules, rituals, purpose, or value. But there are two sentences that may not be related:

Mathabane cries when his friends tease him.

His father must be superstitious.

It is not clear how these ideas relate to the key focus words. Eliminate the ideas if they don't relate. However, before eliminating the sentences, the writer can try to write another sentence or two that shows how the ideas relate to the prompt.

The first sentence refers to Mathabane's reaction when his friends laugh at his father's ritual of wearing tribal clothes. The writer should try to write a sentence that relates Mathabane's reaction to the purpose and value of his father's rules and rituals:

Mathabane is upset because his friends tease him about his father's ritual of wearing tribal clothes. Therefore, this ritual does not have a positive value for him.

The second sentence is an assessment of the father by the writer. Once again, the writer should try to write a sentence that relates this assessment of the father to the purpose or value of his rules and rituals:

I think that the father must be superstitious to think that his rituals will actually bring good luck and protection. Since that is the purpose of his father doing the rituals, I don't think the rituals really have a good purpose.

How to Check for Unrelated Material or Ideas

Find the key focus words from the prompt.

State the relationship between the key focus words and the sentence in the prewriting to determine if the material is unrelated.

Finding Repeated Material

Now that you have determined that all the material is related to the prompt or eliminated what is not related, you need to look for repeated information—that is, where you have said the same thing in two different ways. You want to look for two types of repetition of ideas:

■ Sentences that mean the same thing.

■ Sentences that are close but may contain slightly different or new information.

Sometimes it will be obvious that two sentences are saying the same thing. Other times, you will have to look more carefully at what you have written to discover the repetition because it is easy to confuse repetition with similarity. When you state similar or related ideas, you use many of the same words. Using the same words does not mean that you are repeating yourself. In fact, when you explain ideas fully, you have to repeat key words and phrases so that your reader can understand your ideas and see how they are related. Because you are repeating words, you need to make sure that you are not also repeating ideas.

While there are many ways to check for repetition, one is to group the sentences you have identified as being related to the same focus words and compare them to each other.

- If you are not sure whether two of the writer's ideas are the same, state the difference between the two ideas.
- If you cannot explain the difference between the two ideas, they are probably so close to being the same that you should treat them as one idea.

Let's look at the grouping of the prewriting sentences to see if there are any repeated ideas:

Tribal rule is wrong.

This is a dumb rule.

These sentences both make a judgment about rules and rituals. The first two sentences may seem the same at first glance, but *dumb* and *wrong* mean different things. When people refer to rules as dumb, they generally mean that the rule has no reason or purpose; when people refer to rules as wrong, they usually mean that the rule has a negative effect. These two sentences discuss the same topic, but they give different information about the topic.

The father won't let anyone talk at dinner.

His father also wears the tribal clothing.

These sentences are both related to rules. Each one lists a rule or ritual that Mathabane's father follows.

Mathabane doesn't deserve to be beaten for breaking it.

Mathabane also gets punished when he doesn't do the daily rituals.

These sentences are related because they discuss the consequences of the rules and rituals on Mathabane. The first two sentences state that he is punished when he doesn't follow one of his father's rules and his daily rituals. In addition, the first sentence states the student's opinion about the punishment (Mathabane doesn't deserve it). These two sentences discuss the same topic, but each adds a different piece of information.

Mathabane's friends laugh at his father, calling his clothes Tarzan clothes.

The remaining sentences in this group deal with Mathabane's experience of his father wearing tribal clothes. The first sentence states the consequence: his friends laugh and call his father's clothes Tarzan clothes.

Mathabane cries when his friends tease him.

Mathabane is upset because his friends tease him about his father's ritual of wearing tribal clothes.

The next two sentences describe Mathabane's reaction. The first describes his action (he cries) and the second adds his emotional state (he's upset). These sentences sound very similar, but they do give slightly different information.

He shouldn't have been made to feel bad because of his father's rituals.

The next sentence states the writer's opinion toward the results of the tribal clothing ritual.

Therefore, this ritual does not have a positive value for him.

This last sentence states the writer's conclusion about the value of this ritual.

His father must be superstitious.

I think that the father must be superstitious to think that his rituals will actually bring good luck and protection. Since that is the purpose of his father doing the rituals, I don't think the rituals really have a good purpose.

These three sentences are related since the middle sentence was the one the writer used to show the connection between the other two sentences and the assigned prompt. She can now keep the middle sentence and put the other two aside since the middle sentence incorporates the ideas of both of the other sentences as well as explaining the connection between them and their relationship to the prompt.

No ritual can possibly bring good luck or keep people from getting sick.

It doesn't make sense to waste time doing these things every day like Mathabane's father made him.

This sentence states the writer's opinion of the value of the daily rituals.

How to Check for Repeated Ideas

State the difference between the two ideas.

Matching Main Ideas to Examples and Details

You will now want to match main ideas to examples and specific details. Main ideas are general, and they apply to various people at different times and places. Examples and details (or **supporting** information) apply to specific people at particular times and places. For example, the statement "Dogs make good pets" is a main idea since lots of people throughout the world and throughout history have said this. An example or specific detail focuses on one particular event or instance: "Spot loves to play with the children, and no matter what they do, he never bites them or growls at them."

Let's look again at some prewriting to identify sentences that do not refer to specific people, places, or events, but to general groups.

Tribal rule is wrong.	General idea. It does not identify which tribal rules but makes a statement about all rules of this type.
The father won't let anyone talk at dinner.	Specific.
This is a dumb rule.	Refers to a specific rule but is a general statement about that rule.
Mathabane doesn't deserve to be beaten for breaking it.	Specific.
Mathabane also gets punished when he doesn't do the daily rituals.	Specific.
I think that the father must be superstitious to think that his rituals will actually bring good luck and protection. Since that is the purpose of his father doing the rituals, I don't think the rituals really have a good purpose.	Refers to a specific ritual but makes a general statement about that ritual.
It doesn't make sense to waste time doing these things every day like Mathabane's father made him.	Refers to a specific ritual but makes a general statement about that ritual.

His father also wears the tribal clothing and Mathabane's friends laugh at his father, calling his clothes Tarzan clothes.	Specific.
Mathabane cries when his friends tease him.	Specific.
He shouldn't have been made to feel bad because of his father's rituals.	Refers to a specific ritual but makes a general statement about that ritual.

Determining Which Sentences Are Ideas and Which Are Supporting Examples

Some of these sentences are clearly general or clearly specific. However, some could be both. General ideas are supported by specific examples or by other ideas that further explain them; general ideas also explain the meaning or significance of specific examples. Some sentences serve as support (that is, they support an idea) while also serving as an idea (that is, they explain the significance of an example).

For example, consider the following statements:

It's good to own an animal.

Animals make good companions.

My cat Sherman greets me at the door after a long day and seems happy to see me.

The second sentence "animals make good companions" supports the first sentence "It's good to own an animal." You can test this by asking the following question: Why is it good to own an animal? Because "animals make good companions." But it also serves as a general idea to the third sentence. What are you proving by using the example of "my cat Sherman greets me at the door . . ."? My cat greets me at the door; therefore "animals make good companions." Or you can ask "how do I know that animals make good companions?" You could then answer "because my cat Sherman greets me at the door . . ."

For each sentence in your prewriting, you need to ask two questions:

1. How do I know that this sentence of prewriting is true?
2. What am I proving with this sentence of prewriting?

Any answer to the first question will provide the related supporting example and specifics for this sentence. Any answer to the second question provides the related general idea.

You'll notice that each sentence of the prewriting has corresponding general and specific material. This is because every idea is both general and specific. When you add or include other ideas, you then create a relationship in which one of these sentences is going to be more general or more specific than the other. This relationship creates what instructors sometimes call the "**ladder of abstraction**." It is a ladder because each idea represents a rung on the ladder and you can move up or down the ladder, from general to specific or specific to general, depending on where you start and the direction in which you move.

Now you need to identify the examples and specific details that match each main idea, asking why each idea is true and looking for the answers (examples) in the prewriting. For the main idea "Tribal rule is wrong," let's look at each sentence of the focused **freewriting** that would demonstrate why it is true. The writer needs to write additional information to show the connection between the main idea and the example or specific detail.

The father won't let anyone talk at dinner.	This sentence brings in an example of a rule. The father requires that everyone eat in silence. How does this show that tribal rule is wrong? Perhaps this rule is unfair or doesn't make sense.
This is a dumb rule.	This sentence reveals an attitude about the rule, but doesn't reveal why it is wrong. The writer needs to ask, "Why are dumb rules wrong?" The answer might be: Rules should have a reason or purpose.
Mathabane doesn't deserve to be beaten for breaking it.	The words "doesn't deserve" are a judgment on the part of the writer. The writer needs to state the link between "tribal rule is wrong" and this sentence. Perhaps she would come up with something like: Tribal rule is wrong because it leads to people being treated unfairly.
Mathabane also gets punished when he doesn't do the daily rituals.	This sentence brings in an example of a ritual.
I think that the father must be superstitious to think that his rituals will actually bring good luck and protection. Since that is the purpose of his father doing the rituals, I don't think the rituals really have a good purpose.	This example seems to support the same general idea as the writer stated above: Rituals should have a reason or purpose or they should benefit somebody.

It doesn't make sense to waste time doing these things every day like Mathabane's father made him.

The writer can restate this sentence in more general terms: Rituals ought to make sense and they have no positive value when they don't. Then she can use the daily rituals as examples of rituals that don't make sense.

His father also wears the tribal clothing and Mathabane's friends laugh at his father, calling his clothes Tarzan clothes.

Here is a second example of a ritual—wearing the tribal clothing—as well as an example of the results of the ritual.

Mathabane cries when his friends tease him.

This sentence is a specific example of why rituals have no positive value. It is closely related to the next sentence, which is more general.

He shouldn't have been made to feel bad because of his father's rituals.

Rituals have no positive meaning when they cause embarrassment.

How to Match Ideas and Examples

Label general and specific points.

Match specific ideas and examples to general ideas.

"How do I know this is true?"

"What am I trying to prove with this sentence?"

Write a sentence explaining the connection between ideas and support if the connection isn't clear.

Listing Your Main Ideas

What you have done is to fill in the connections that were in your head but you did not write down. Many inexperienced writers leave out this step and the reasons for their answers remain unclear to their readers. Let's look at a list of just those connections made from the focused freewriting.

They should have a reason or purpose.

It leads to people being treated unfairly.

Rituals should have a reason or purpose or they should benefit somebody.

Rituals ought to make sense and they have no positive value when they don't.

Rituals have no positive meaning when they cause embarrassment

Notice that two of the ideas are very close; you can eliminate one from your list.

Writing a Tentative Thesis

After listing the ideas that respond to a prompt, you will be ready to write a tentative **thesis**, which will state in a sentence or two a clear "answer" to the question asked by the prompt. In this case your list should state your opinion on tribal rule and provide reasons that support that position. Let's look at one writer's tentative thesis and list of main ideas. Note that it is presented in an outline form.

Tribal rule is wrong because:

It leads to people being treated unfairly.

Mathabane gets punished and doesn't deserve it.

Rituals should have a reason or purpose or they should benefit somebody.

The daily rituals won't actually bring good luck and protection, so they don't really have a purpose.

There doesn't seem to be a purpose for not talking at the table.

Rituals ought to make sense and they have no positive value when they don't.

Mathabane has to waste time performing daily rituals.

Rituals have no positive meaning when they cause embarrassment.

Mathabane is embarrassed when his friends laugh at his father's clothes and call them Tarzan clothes.

This writer may have more than can be used in one paper, so she must now decide which ideas would be best to keep. One way to do this is to turn to the prewriting from personal ideas and experience.

EVALUATING PREWRITING ABOUT YOUR OWN REACTIONS AND EXPERIENCE

 Since the prompt asks you to use the reading and your own ideas and experiences, you must also evaluate the prewriting you did about these areas.

Let's review the prompt. You can use the same steps you used when prewriting about the reading:

Mathabane says he despises rules and rituals. Is he correct in thinking that rules and rituals have no purpose or value?

- What is unrelated to the topic? (Eliminate it.)
- What is repeated? (Pick the best way of saying it or combine statements that repeat the same ideas.)
- What is a main idea and what may be support for that idea? (Match general ideas to related specific details and examples.)

Eliminating Unrelated Material or Ideas

Eliminate material that is not related to the prompt. Follow the steps shown in the box.

How to Check for Unrelated Material or Ideas

Find the key focus words from the prompt.

State the relationship between the key focus words and the sentence in the prewriting to determine if the material is unrelated.

Let's look at an example of how one student evaluates the material:

Work Rituals	Work Rules
Draw names to give gifts (Christmas)	can't take more than 5 sick days
Showers for newlyweds and parents	must take lunch hour noon to 1
Mandatory Christmas parties	fill out travel form to leave office on company business
Weekly staff meetings	fill out inventory form to move piece of equipment or furniture
Cakes on birthdays	
Monthly "pep" talks from manager	
July 4th picnic	
Thanksgiving ham or turkey	

The material all seems related to the key focus words (see Chapter 5, Analyzing the Assignment). Because this writer has made a list focused on the key words, she can expect to have little unrelated material. Her results may have been very different had she chosen to freewrite instead.

Finding Repeated Material

As you did with the prewriting about the reading, check for places where you have repeated the same ideas. If you are not sure whether the ideas are the same, use the box below.

How to Check for Repeated Ideas

State the difference between the two ideas.

Since there does not appear to be any repeated material, move to the next step. Again, because this writer has chosen to list material, there is probably not much repetition (just as you would not repeat items on a grocery list). If you did, you would probably just ignore the second time (you wouldn't buy pickles twice if you listed them twice).

Matching Main Ideas to Examples and Details

Finally, as you did with the prewriting about the reading, match ideas with the specific details and examples that support them.

How to Match Ideas and Examples

Label general and specific points.

Match specific ideas and examples to general ideas:

"How do I know this is true?"

"What am I trying to prove with this sentence?"

Write a sentence explaining the connection between ideas and support if the connection isn't clear.

The lists on page 115 give specific examples and details but no ideas. We know this because the writer has listed only rules and rituals that she has experienced; in other words, they apply only to her, not necessarily to everyone. To match ideas to these examples and details, she must do the following:

- ◼ Put the examples and details into categories of rules or rituals to help make sense of them.

- ◼ Write a statement about the purpose or value of each category of rules or rituals.

We can see that the list of rituals refers to several holidays—Christmas, Thanksgiving, birthdays, 4th of July. Inexperienced writers sometimes think because these are separate days that this material is not repeated. They would try to write a paragraph on each of these days and focus their papers on the purpose and value of rituals and rules that apply to holidays. This paper could be written, but it would be a challenging one to write. To write it well, a writer would have to go back to the list and place any material about holidays into categories. The first might be holidays or special days; the second might have to do with specific events at work (showers, parties, staff meetings, pep talks, picnics) and third with specific activities that take place at work. A new list of rituals would look like this:

Special Occasions	Events	Activities
Christmas	Showers	Drawing names
Weddings	Parties	
Births	Picnics	
Birthdays	Staff meetings	
4th of July	Pep talks	
Thanksgiving		

The same process can be followed with the rules list. There may be more than one way to group the parts of this list. One way would be to divide the list into rules that apply to how employees spend time and those that apply to paperwork that must be completed. A grouping might look like this:

Time	Paperwork
Can't take more than 5 sick days	travel forms to leave office on company business
Must take lunch hour from noon to 1	inventory forms to move piece of equipment or furniture

Now the writer can take the category and try to figure out the purpose or value of the entire category, but this can be complicated. Another approach is to choose one rule or ritual from the category and to examine its purpose and value. After the writer has done this, she can check the purpose and value against those for the entire category. Regardless of which option chosen, the writer should come up with very similar ideas.

Let's look at the "paperwork" category. What is the purpose or value of rules governing paperwork that must be completed? The writer might answer that these rules ensure that records are kept accurately. Does this purpose apply to each of these items? Yes. Does the writer have any specific examples? No. While the two items in this list are examples of rules that apply to filling out paperwork, they do not provide specific examples of documenting activities or actions, the purposes of these rules.

You can also start by listing all the purposes or values for one item on the list and applying it to the entire category. This method will lead you to more specific examples of purpose and value. For example, let's take the ritual of drawing names to give gifts at work.

Drawing Names to Give Gifts at Work

$20 limit

everyone gets a gift

all gifts are of similar value

gifts are opened at Christmas party

gives us something to do as a group at the party

we learn names of people we didn't know

I always spend more, I don't want to be thought of as cheap

I never know the person I've drawn

have to guess at a gift

everyone pretends to like the gift

gifts are usually inappropriate or stupid

I gave a basket of meat and wine to a vegetarian who didn't drink

As we did when evaluating pieces of prewriting before, we need to follow the steps of eliminating what isn't related to the prompt, looking for what is repeated, and matching ideas with specific examples and details. Because this list is focused on a single rule, we can assume that everything is related to that rule.

Grouping Related Items

We can start by grouping related items:

$20 limit

gifts are opened at Christmas party

Each of these statements explains how the ritual is done.

everyone gets a gift

all gifts are of similar value

gives us something to do as a group at the party

we learn names of people we didn't know

These statements may indicate the benefits of the ritual or the reasons for following the ritual.

I always spend more, I don't want to be thought of as cheap

I never know the person I've drawn

have to guess at a gift

everyone pretends to like the gift

gifts are usually inappropriate or stupid

I gave a basket of meat and wine to a vegetarian who didn't drink

These statements all concern what can go wrong with the ritual or complaints that the writer has about the ritual.

Do the Groups Complete the Actions Required by the Prompt?

At this point the writer has to take each group of items and determine if these groups allow a response to the actions required by the prompt. After grouping her ideas, she has generated material that clearly provides examples of rituals and rules. But the prompt also asks the writer to determine what each group reveals about purpose or value.

$20 limit	These statements just explain the rules of the ritual—that is, how it is performed. If there is a value here, perhaps it is the following: The ritual does limit how much individuals have to spend on gifts
gifts are opened at Christmas party	
everyone gets a gift	These statements seem to explain a common purpose: The ritual ensures that people are treated equally
all gifts are of similar value	
gives us something to do as a group at the party	These two statements also seem to explain a purpose or value: This ritual serves a social purpose by providing something for people to do together and a way get to know each other
we learn names of people we didn't know	
I always spend more, I don't want to be thought of as cheap	This statement shows how the ritual sometimes doesn't fulfill its purpose: instead of limiting the amount people spend to a reasonable sum, people end up spending more.
I never know the person I've drawn	These statements show that people don't feel good about the gifts they've given or received. Instead of bringing people together, this ritual makes people feel even more uncomfortable because they have to lie about liking the gift and because they know their gifts aren't appropriate.
have to guess at a gift	
everyone pretends to like the gift	
gifts are usually inappropriate or stupid	
I gave a basket of meat and wine to a vegetarian who didn't drink	

Listing Your Main Ideas

Let's now look at a list of the writer's main ideas:

The ritual does limit how much individuals have to spend on gifts.

The ritual ensures that people are treated equally.

This ritual serves a social purpose by providing something for people to do together and a way to get to know each other.

The ritual sometimes doesn't fulfill its purposes—instead of limiting the amount people spend to a reasonable sum, people end up spending more.

Instead of bringing people together, rituals may make people feel even more uncomfortable.

The writer now has a number of lists and should not throw any of them away. She can refer to these specific examples and ideas as she is drafting her essay.

IS ALL THIS REALLY NECESSARY?

Yes. Good writers go through all of these steps. As you gain more experience and skill, you may find that you can do these steps faster, perform multiple steps at a time, or do some of them in your head. Until that time, you should continue to go through these steps on paper.

COMBINING THE PARTS OF YOUR PREWRITING

The prompt we have been working with instructs you to use both the reading and your own ideas and observations. Now that you have generated ideas and examples from each of these sources, you need to combine them so it makes sense to use both in the same paper.

Let's compare this writer's tentative thesis and list of ideas from the reading (first given on page 114) to her list of her own ideas and experiences.

The thesis is:

Tribal rule is wrong.

List from the reading:

It leads to people being treated unfairly.

Mathabane gets punished and doesn't deserve it.

Rituals should have a reason or purpose or they should benefit somebody.

The daily rituals won't actually bring good luck and protection, so they don't really have a purpose.

There doesn't seem to be a purpose for not talking at the table.

Rituals ought to make sense and they have no positive value when they don't.

Mathabane has to waste time performing daily rituals.

Rituals have no positive meaning when they cause embarrassment.

Mathabane is embarrassed when his friends laugh at his father's clothes and call them Tarzan clothes.

List of the writer's own ideas and experiences:

The ritual does limit how much individuals have to spend on gifts.

No more than $20

The ritual ensures that people are treated equally.

Everyone gets a gift of similar value.

This ritual serves a social purpose by providing something for people to do together and a way get to know each other.

We exchange the gifts at the party.

The ritual sometimes doesn't fulfill its purposes.

Instead of limiting the amount people spend to a reasonable sum, people end up spending more.

Instead of bringing people together, rituals may make people feel even more uncomfortable.

Gifts may be inappropriate.

The tentative answer to the prompt is that tribal rule is wrong. The writer now should read each idea and decide if it supports that answer. If any ideas seem to say that tribal rule is right or good, they need to be eliminated. For example, "the ritual does limit how much people spend," "the ritual ensures that people are treated equally," and "this ritual serves a social purpose by providing something for people to do together and a way get to know each other" sound more like reasons why rules might be good than why they might be wrong, so they will not help this writer's essay.

Since the prompt specifies using both the reading and personal experience, the next step is to match the ideas from each source. By omitting the two ideas that contradict the thesis and by combining the two lists, the writer has ended up with the following list:

Tribal rule is wrong because:

It leads to people being treated unfairly.

Mathabane gets punished and doesn't deserve it.

Rituals should have a reason or purpose or they should benefit somebody.

The daily rituals won't actually bring good luck and protection, so they don't really have a purpose.

There doesn't seem to be a purpose for not talking at the table.

Rituals ought to make sense and they have no positive value when they don't.

Mathabane has to waste time performing daily rituals.

Rituals have no positive meaning when they cause embarrassment.

Mathabane is embarrassed when his friends laugh at his father's clothes and call them Tarzan clothes.

The ritual sometimes doesn't fulfill its purposes.

Instead of limiting the amount people spend to a reasonable sum, people end up spending more.

Instead of bringing people together, rituals may make people feel even more uncomfortable.

Gifts may be inappropriate.

This writer has generated a number of ideas and has a lot of material from prewriting. If she were to try to write a paper incorporating all of this material, she would have a very long paper. She should now choose the best ideas, the ones she has the most to say about and the most support for. She should also return to her other prewriting to find additional examples that fit her ideas. She might choose the following four ideas:

1. Tribal rule is wrong because it can lead to people being treated unfairly.

   From the reading: Mathabane gets punishment he doesn't deserve.

   From the writer's experience: My pay is docked when I have to take a sick day to care for my children.

2. Rules should have a reason or purpose or they should benefit somebody.

From the reading:

> The daily rituals won't actually bring good luck and protection, so they don't really have a purpose.

> There doesn't seem to be a purpose for not talking at the table.

From the writer's experience:

> The ritual sometimes doesn't fulfill its purposes—instead of limiting the amount people spend to a reasonable sum, people end up spending more.

> Instead of bringing people together, rituals may make people feel even more uncomfortable. Gifts are sometimes inappropriate.

3. Rituals ought to make sense and they have no positive value when they don't.

From the reading: Mathabane has to waste time performing daily rituals.

4. Rituals have no positive meaning when they cause embarrassment.

From the reading: Mathabane is embarrassed when his friends laugh at his father's clothes and call them Tarzan clothes.

From the writer's experience: I'm embarrassed when I give inappropriate gifts.

These four ideas with examples from the reading and from prewriting form the plan for an essay. The next step is to **draft** your essay.

EXERCISE 7.1   **Use the following steps to organize and evaluate the prewriting you produced in the exercises from Chapter 6 (pp. 102–103).**

1. Check for unrelated material or ideas:

   A. In your prewriting on Mathabane's essay

   B. In your prewriting about your own ideas and experiences

2. Check for repeated material:

   A. In your prewriting on Mathabane's essay

   B. In your prewriting about your own ideas and experiences

3. Match main ideas to examples and details:

   A. In your prewriting on Mathabane's essay

   B. In your prewriting about your own ideas and experiences

4. List your main ideas:

   A. Check to see that each idea in your list responds to the prompt

   B. Check to see if your list provides ideas for all of the actions required to complete the assignment

5. Write a tentative thesis.

What You've Done

■ Reviewed the prompt
■ Evaluated your prewriting
■ Drafted a thesis

For More Organizing Strategies

■ See Chapter 19

The Next Step

■ Draft the introduction (Chapters 8 and 20)

8 Writing Introductions

What You've Done

- Evaluated prewriting from the reading
- Evaluated prewriting on your own ideas and experiences
- Combined material to form a thesis and main ideas

What You Need to Do Next

- Begin your essay with a paragraph that prepares the reader to understand your ideas by:
    Providing an interesting opening
    Letting the reader know that you're responding to a reading
    Making the main idea of your essay clear to the reader

Since most college-level writing responds to the ideas of others, the model essay presented in Chapters 8, 9, and 10 will stress a structure in which the writer is responding to a reading. Additional essay structures are presented in Part Three.

Getting started may be one of the most difficult things to do in writing an essay. At first the assignment might seem to be an overwhelming task. However, if you break the writing process down into steps, as we have shown you in the last few chapters, you will find it easier to decide what you need to do. If you have difficulty starting, don't give up. There are several strategies you can use to get started.

- *Go back to the **prompt** or assignment:* What are you specifically being asked to do? Going back to the prompt may help focus your thinking and get you started writing (see Chapter 5).
- *Go back to the reading:* What topics are being discussed? How do you feel about those topics? Do you agree or disagree with what is said? What related personal experiences have you had? (see Chapter 4).
- *Go back to your **prewriting**:* Prewriting activities help you generate information and give you more material to work with (see Chapter 6).

CREATING DRAFTS

At the end of Chapter 7, the information generated by the writer's prewriting was organized into a basic outline. The plan developed from your prewriting will serve as a framework for your essay. Chapters 8, 9, and 10 will show you how to expand and strengthen the framework you've created.

After examining the prompt, the reading, and your prewriting, you should be ready to begin creating a **draft**—a preliminary version of a final paper. It's important to realize that well-written essays require several drafts and that your first draft will probably be revised many times. You will find that as you write your ideas change, and you will have to reconsider your original ideas. As you discover new ideas, you may also need to return to the reading to find quotes for support. Here are some points to keep in mind when you begin your first drafts.

- For all your early drafts, choose whatever method—pen, pencil, typewriter, word processor—is most comfortable to you. Be sure to leave enough room on your paper to be able to make additions and changes. Leave wide margins, and double-space or even triple-space the lines, if you are writing on lined paper.

- Don't let fine details of **editing** distract you while you create your first drafts. If you stop to look up words in the dictionary as you write, you will lose your train of thought. But do jot down notes about punctuation, grammar, and spelling so that you won't forget to fix them later on.

- Write the paragraphs in early drafts in any order. If you're having trouble with your introduction, you can leave it and work on body paragraphs. Later you can come back to your introduction. See what works best for you.

Completing the exercises in Chapters 8, 9, and 10 will help you create your own essay.

THE INTRODUCTION

An **introduction** is an essential part of an essay. It provides readers with the background information they will need to understand the details presented in the **body** paragraphs. It also determines the scope and thesis of the essay, by defining and limiting what you will discuss.

What the Introduction Does

Provides background information.

Familiarizes your reader with the topic.

Defines and limits your discussion.

Clarifies the thesis or main idea of your essay.

An Introduction Provides
A lead-in
Source of a reading
Overview of a reading
Author's thesis
Your thesis
A plan of development

The following elements usually appear in the introduction to an essay responding to a reading:

■ *A general **lead-in** to the topic:* Lets your readers know the basic topic you will be discussing.

■ *Author and title of the reading:* Describes who the author is and which of that writer's particular works you will discuss.

■ *An **overview** of the reading:* Provides a synopsis of what the reading discusses.

■ *The author's **thesis** or point:* Defines the purpose or main idea of the reading.

■ *Your thesis statement:* Clarifies what you will discuss and defines the main idea or purpose of your essay.

■ *A **plan of development**:* Tells your reader how you will approach your subject and/or what specific issues you will discuss.

Here are some questions to think about when you are writing an introductory paragraph.

Can I start with a thesis statement? It depends on your readers and their familiarity with the subject. If you are discussing an issue everyone is familiar with—for example, capital punishment—you could begin with a thesis statement because your audience will already have an understanding of the topic. However, if you begin with a thesis statement on astrophysics, you will probably confuse your readers.

What goes in an introduction? The content of an opening paragraph is determined by your topic and your reason for discussing that topic. If you are writing about a personal experience—rather than responding to a reading—your introduction would not contain certain elements: an author's name, title of essay, overview of that reading.

Should the information come in a particular order? The information in your introduction does not have to come in the order presented earlier. However, this order is a reliable way to proceed because it will lead your reader into your essay, from the most general to the most specific information. However, there is no rule that says you must follow this approach. (See Chapter 20 for other ways to structure an introduction.)

PROVIDING LEAD-INS

Lead-ins introduce your reader to the general topic you are discussing. If you are responding to a writer who favors gun control, then your lead-in would discuss the topic of gun control, but it would not discuss the writer's specific argument on gun control. Providing a lead-in identifies the issue your essay will explore, and it prepares the reader for the more detailed information that you will present.

A lead-in performs these functions:

- Makes your introduction unique.
- Helps you to avoid making a generic introduction (the type everyone uses).
- Clarifies the topic or issue.
- Helps readers understand the specific information that will follow.

Purpose of a Lead-in

Distinguishes your introduction

Clarifies the topic

Provides background

How do you create a lead-in? You begin by asking what is the first and most basic thing the reader needs to know—the general topic under discussion. Are you discussing the auto industry, extraterrestrial life, education, or politics? If you are discussing an essay or story you have read, what is the general topic: war, love, technology? What issue or theme in the reading are you responding to?

To guide your reader into the specific topic of your essay, provide a lead-in that begins with the general topic under discussion in the reading. Rather than starting with a sentence that identifies author and title—"In Mark Mathabane's 'My Father's Tribal Rule' . . . ,"—focus on the general topic you will discuss. Will you discuss rituals? Will you discuss parent-child conflicts? Will you discuss traditional versus modern ways? ("My Father's Tribal Rule" appears on pages 40–44.)

If you begin your essay with your own discussion of a general topic, your essay will be clearly distinguished from the other essays written in the class, even if everyone is writing in response to Mathabane. Since Mathabane detests rituals, you might begin your lead-in with a discussion of the negative aspects of rituals.

When you're responding to a reading, the lead-in should guide the reader into that reading without discussing the specific ideas that an author is putting forth. A lead-in should not directly discuss what an author says in an essay. It should simply be used to set up the general topic that the author is discussing.

Let's look at some suggestions for creating lead-ins on the topic of capital punishment:

- Present an opinion on the topic that many people would hold.

    Many Americans favor capital punishment because they believe it brings about justice. They see capital punishment as a way to make murderers pay for their crimes. Justice requires punishment.

- Present a view opposite to the one the author holds. (Assume that the author's essay is in favor of capital punishment.)

    There are several reasons why some people believe that capital punishment is wrong. We have laws against killing yet we murder someone who breaks the laws. Only a hypocrite would say don't kill or I'll kill you.

■ Present the same view as the author but provide different ideas. (Assume that the author is in favor of capital punishment because he believes it protects society.)

> Capital punishment is necessary in our society because it serves to deter others from committing the same crime. When a criminal is executed, it sends the message to other criminals that society will not permit their behavior. If criminals know they will be executed for certain crimes, they will be less likely to commit them.

■ Relate a personal experience.

> I never thought much about capital punishment. If someone had asked me if I was for it or against it, I would probably have said I was for it. However, one day when I was listening to the news, I heard that some TV personality wanted to show an execution on TV live. The more I thought about it, the more disgusted I was. It was then that I decided I was against capital punishment.

■ Provide background information.

> Capital punishment is a state sanctioned execution. In other words, it is a killing authorized by a government, either on the state or federal level. In the United States, the death penalty is only used for the most evil crime: first degree murder. Although capital punishment is legal in the United States, not every state in the union carries it out.

Note that these lead-ins discuss the topic of capital punishment, but they do not discuss the author's argument.

To show how lead-ins can help the flow of your introduction, let's look at two examples, one without a lead-in and one with a lead-in.

EXAMPLE WITHOUT A LEAD-IN

> In Mark Mathabane's "My Father's Tribal Rule," he talks about rituals and how he doesn't like them.

Notice that this example leaps right into the author's name and the title of the essay.

EXAMPLE WITH LEAD-IN

> Many people feel that rituals are a thing of the past, practiced only by primitive people. They feel that rituals have little place in a modern society that is driven by technology and science. Rituals, they would say, are just superstitions acted out.

This example discusses the general topic of rituals and the attitude many people have toward them. This prepares the reader for Mathabane's essay and what the reading has to say about rituals.

EXERCISE 8.1 Read the following lead-in to Mark Mathabane's "My Father's Tribal Rule." See if you can determine what subject the writer is intending to focus on.

As children we are always told what to do by our parents and teachers. We may resent what adults force us to do and become rebellious. We may even grow to hate the adults that are always trying to make us do something we do not want to do. Adults tell us that they know what is best for us, but we think we know what is really best. As we grow older, however, we sometimes come to realize that our parents and other adults really were looking out for our best interests.

The following example of a lead-in takes another approach to the reading. What topic in Mathabane's essay does this lead-in focus on?

The role that women play in a family is stereotypically the mother and the housekeeper. However, women may perform several other functions in the family that we often don't think about. Sometimes women are the breadwinners. Sometimes they are teachers who instruct their children on manners and etiquette. Sometimes they are like close friends who listen to your troubles or give you advice. Many mothers are more than just caretakers for their children.

EXERCISE 8.2 Write several lead-ins for introductions on one of the following prompts. Use the suggestions for creating lead-ins discussed earlier in this chapter. Remember not to discuss what the reading says on these topics. Discuss the general topic suggested by the prompt.

Mathabane writes less about his mother than his father or himself. What is the significance of her role in the family? Do you think most women play similar roles in their families?

Mathabane has a conflict with his father. Do parents and children always have conflicts? Why or why not? Using your own ideas and observations, write an essay in which you answer this question.

AUTHOR, TITLE, AND OVERVIEW OF THE READING

After completing your lead-in, you need to:

■ Identify the author and title of the reading you're discussing. These elements do not have to directly follow the lead-in, but they do need to appear early in your introduction.

■ Provide an overview or summary of the piece to provide background and context for your reader. Your reader may have never read the story or essay you are responding to. If you are responding to a story or a narrative, the reader needs to know the general **story line**, setting, and cast of important characters. If you are discussing an essay, your reader needs a brief summary of the writer's ideas.

Let's continue the development of the two lead-ins just discussed by adding the author's name, the title of the reading, and an overview of the reading. If you had never read Mathabane's essay, which introduction would give you a better understanding of the text?

In Mark Mathabane's "My Father's Tribal Rule," he talks about rituals and how he doesn't like them. He talks about his brother, his mother, and his sister. His family had to move to a shack. Mathabane really dislikes his father because his father beats him. The father doesn't beat the other children like he beats his son Mark. Mark Mathabane wants to be like the other boys he plays with. He wants to speak other languages.

Many people feel that rituals are a thing of the past, practiced only by primitive people. They feel that rituals have little place in a modern society that is driven by technology and science. Rituals, they would say, are just superstitions acted out. Mark Mathabane is one of those people who detests rituals. In "My Father's Tribal Rule," he tells us about his experiences growing up in South Africa in a shantytown of rundown huts for people who had been forced off their ancestral, tribal lands. Even though Mathabane and the children in the area were interested in modern ways, Mathabane's father insisted that their family stick to the tribal traditions. If Mathabane failed to follow the tribal rules and rituals, his father would severely punish him. Mathabane eventually came to hate his father for making him follow the tribal rituals.

In the first example, there is no lead-in and very little overview of the text. Someone who had not read Mathabane's essay would not have a clear picture of the particular situation or the setting. The second example gives a good overview of the story that provides more information for the reader (but it doesn't go into specific details—they belong in body paragraphs). Someone who had never read the essay would get a much better understanding of what "My Father's Tribal Rule" is about from the second example.

EXERCISE 8.3   Write overviews for the following two prompts. Provide your reader with a summary of the reading, but focus that summary on the issue raised in the prompt.

Mathabane writes less about his mother than his father or himself. What is the significance of her role in the family? Do you think other women play similar roles in their families?

> *Mathabane has a conflict with his father. Do parents and children always have conflicts? Why or why not? Using your own ideas and observations, write an essay in which you answer this question.*

THE AUTHOR'S THESIS OR MAIN POINT

Purpose of an Author's Thesis
Defines the writer's argument
Clarifies the writer's message

After you have provided an overview, you need to clarify the author's thesis. A thesis statement is the main point of an author's essay. For instance, in an essay presenting several arguments against capital punishment, the author's thesis would be that capital punishment is wrong. To define the author's thesis, ask the following questions:

- What is the point of the reading?
- What is the author arguing?

If you are reading an **argumentative** essay—an essay where the writer is arguing for or against something—the writer will generally have a thesis statement that tells the reader what he or she will argue (for example, money should be spent on drug rehabilitation programs rather than new jails). However, a narrative, like "My Father's Tribal Rule" or a short story like Flannery O'Connor's "Revelation," may not have a thesis statement that defines the writer's point. Instead the writer may use images, situations, or dialogue to get his or her message across.

If you look back at Mathabane's essay (pp. 40–44), you will see that the point of his **narrative** is never clearly stated. Is his point about rules and rituals, his mother, his father, their life in South Africa? What is Mathabane trying to get across to his readers? You need to provide this information for your readers, so they will know what Mathabane's point is. In some essays, the author may make several points, and it is up to the writer to decide which ones to focus the reader on. Looking again at the topics of rules and rituals in Mathabane's article, we can say that each of the following convey the general point of the essay:

To Mathabane, rules and rituals make no sense.

Mathabane hated rules and rituals and felt he should rebel against them.

Because he was forced to follow the rules and rituals, Mathabane came to hate his father.

When it comes to the topic of rules and rituals, all of these statements convey the general point of Mathabane's essay. Notice, however, that certain words in each example suggest a different focus on the essay. The first example focuses on Mathabane's lack of understanding; the second stresses Mathabane's rebellion; the third directs our attention to his relationship with his father.

When providing the author's thesis or point, be sure to carefully word it so that it stresses the idea or topic you will discuss.

Let's attach the author's point to our lead-in and overview. We will use the first example on page 133 but reword it to better flow with the overview.

> Many people feel that rituals are a thing of the past, practiced only by primitive people. They feel that rituals have little place in a modern society that is driven by technology and science. Rituals, they would say, are just superstitions acted out. Mark Mathabane is one of those people who detests rituals. In "My Father's Tribal Rule," he tells us about his experiences growing up in South Africa in a shantytown of rundown huts for people who had been forced off their ancestral, tribal lands. Even though Mathabane and the children in the area were interested in modern ways, Mathabane's father insisted that their family stick to the tribal traditions. Mathabane eventually came to hate his father for making him follow the tribal rituals. *Despite his father's insistence that he follow the rules and practice the rituals, Mathabane thought they made no sense.*

At this point, we have provided a lead-in to introduce the general topic being discussed, the author and the title of the reading, an overview for someone who has never read the essay, and—in the last sentence—the author's thesis, a statement that defines how Mathabane felt about rules and rituals.

EXERCISE 8.4 Look for the general topics in the prompts below and then write a sentence or more that clarifies what you see as the reading's point or thesis. Is there a specific point that Mathabane is trying to make about these issues? If Mathabane isn't trying to make a point about these issues, what point does the reading convey to you?

Mathabane writes less about his mother than his father or himself. What is the significance of her role in the family? Do you think other women play similar roles in their families?

Mathabane has a conflict with his father. Do parents and children always have conflicts? Why or why not?

YOUR THESIS STATEMENT

Purpose of a Thesis

Clarifies the main idea of an essay.

Whereas the author's thesis statement defines the main idea of his or her essay, your thesis statement defines the main idea of your essay. Your thesis statement clarifies where you stand in response to what the author has said.

After you have explained what the reading says, you need to present a thesis statement—a sentence (or more) that tells your reader what you intend to argue or reveal. It defines the main idea of your essay. Will you argue that the author is right or wrong on an issue? Will you reveal that Mathabane's mother serves more roles in the family than just that of mother? Another way to think about a thesis statement is that it is a sentence that tells the reader what you believe and why you believe it. A thesis statement defines the main idea of your paper and thus must be more than an obvious comment about what you're planning to do:

> In this paper, I will discuss Mathabane's essay.

This statement doesn't clarify your reason for writing. It just leaves your reader wondering: Is your purpose to agree with Mathabane's ideas about rituals? Will you examine the relationship between Mathabane's father and mother? You thus need to provide your reader with more than just a general statement. A good thesis clearly defines what you will argue in your essay.

Creating a thesis statement can seem difficult. However, a strong thesis can be created by doing two basic things. If your instructor's assignment is presented as a question, respond to that prompt. Since this assignment is phrased as a question, your answer is your thesis statement. If your instructor has not given you a specific question and expects you to develop your own thesis, then you should use your prewriting to determine your thesis. The following discussions will explain how to use your instructor's assignment or your own prewriting to develop a strong thesis statement.

Using the Prompt to Determine Your Thesis

Keep in mind that an easy way to create a thesis statement is to respond to the **prompt** directly. Another way is to turn the prompt (a question) into a statement. Let's look again at the prompt we have been using:

> *Mathabane says he despises rules and rituals. Is he correct in thinking that rules and rituals have no value?*

If you haven't analyzed this prompt, do so by going back to Chapter 5 where you can review the process of analyzing the assignment. Use the exercises there to determine what this prompt asks you to do.

Let's look at the prompt again and the thesis statement from Chapter 7 to see if it fully responds to the prompt.

Prompt/Question

> *Mathabane says he despises rules and rituals. Is he correct in thinking that rules and rituals have no value?*

Response/Answer

> Tribal rule is wrong.

Does this tentative thesis statement fully respond to the prompt? The prompt asks about rules and rituals in general, not about tribal rules. The thesis statement above mentions rules but not rituals (although it may be possible to write an essay on one or the other). The second part of the prompt asks if you think Mathabane is correct that rules and rituals have no value. This thesis statement doesn't directly respond to the question contained in the prompt. To complete the thesis, some additions need to be made. The question in the prompt requires a yes or no answer. Is Mathabane right or is he wrong? (If you're not sure, then you need to analyze your prewriting to see what your examples suggest. We'll discuss that presently.)

Here is the same thesis statement reworded:

Mathabane is right to think that many rules and rituals serve no purpose.

This thesis statement responds to the question in the prompt (*Is he correct in thinking that rules and rituals have no value?*). This thesis also refers to rules and rituals. (Your prewriting might lead you to focus on one or the other rather than both.) The phrase *serve no purpose* in the thesis lets the reader know what the writer thinks about rules and rituals. Remember, when your instructor gives you a prompt in the form of a question, your *direct response* to that question is your thesis statement.

Using Your Prewriting to Determine Your Thesis

After analyzing a prompt to help you determine your thesis, you should then examine your prewriting. Chapter 6 presented several examples on prewriting. One way to determine what your thesis should be is to reexamine the examples you produced while prewriting about your own experiences. The examples you develop can help you determine what your attitude is about a topic. Let's look again at the prompt that asks if you agree with Mathabane's negative attitude toward rules and rituals. Examine the examples below to see if they suggest whether these experiences confirm or contradict Mathabane's attitude toward rules and rituals.

EXERCISE 8.5   **Examine the following examples to see if they suggest agreement or disagreement with Mathabane's belief that rules and rituals have no purpose or value.**

EXAMPLE 1

In my family, we have a dinnertime ritual. Before dinner, my brothers and my sister and I are supposed to clean the house and get everything ready for dinner. One day I didn't feel like doing it, because I have to do everything. My brothers and my sister hardly do anything. So, I just sat on the couch and watched TV. My father came in and saw me and started to yell at me. He said he worked hard every day to put food on the table and that I was showing disrespect to him, my mother, my brothers and my sister. He sent me to bed without supper. At first I was really mad. I thought my father was being unfair to me. I'm the oldest, so I wind up doing most of the work. Why should I have to clean the house every day and get the table ready? The more I thought about it, the more I felt bad. He did do a lot for us. Besides providing us with a house and food, he paid for my music lessons, he takes us to the beach in the summer, he drops us off at the movies. He really does do a lot for us and sometimes I think we forget to say thank you. I felt bad for not respecting my father.

Does this example suggest rules and rituals do or do not have value?

EXAMPLE 2

Where I work, we are given five sick days a year. After that, your pay is docked for each day you're out. I'm never out sick more than two or three days a year. I don't abuse the policy by taking "mental health" days. However, each of the last two years, I've had my pay docked because I used more than my allotted sick days. I wasn't abusing this rule. I was simply taking care of my child as any mother would. I can't help it if my daughter is too sick to go to school or needs to go to the doctor. Women with children should have additional sick leave for these emergencies. When I have to call in with a sick child, my supervisor always makes me feel like I'm avoiding doing my work, like I'm not a good employee. Five days of sick leave is not enough for a mother, because she has to have sick days for herself and her child. Although I don't intentionally break this rule like Mathabane did, I still pay for breaking it. Some rules are good, but this one needs to be rethought.

Does this example suggest rules and rituals do or do not have value?

EXAMPLE 3

I personally have experienced first hand the negative effects of rituals. There is a ritual we perform every year at work. We select names out of a hat, so we can be someone's Santa for that Christmas. Every year I go through the same thing. I don't know what to buy the person. Although there is a twenty dollar limit on the gift, I always spend more, because I don't want this person I hardly know to think I'm cheap—and I'm sure everyone else is going through the same thing. Then on the last day of work before Christmas, we open our gifts and pretend to be overjoyed at a present we don't even want. Last year was the worst. I bought a basket of cheeses, smoked meats, and wine for a coworker who turned out to be an herb tea sipping vegetarian. It wasn't my fault because I didn't really know him, but I was humiliated when I found out.

Does this example suggest rules and rituals do or do not have value?

EXAMPLE 4

My parents believe in doing little rituals, thinking that they will protect them. Recently my dad was helping set the table. He knocked over the salt shaker. He picked up a pinch of salt to throw it over his shoulder. He always said that throwing salt over your shoulder would ward off bad luck. He happened to throw the salt over his shoulder right as my mother was walking in carrying a bowl of mashed potatoes. She ducked to avoid the salt and dropped the bowl. The bowl broke and threw mashed potatoes all over the floor and the wall. Obviously the salt over the shoulder didn't ward off bad luck.

Does this example suggest rules and rituals do or do not have value?

What attitude was expressed in each example? Do your answers match the ones below?

Example 1 suggests that rituals do have a value: they teach respect.

Example 2 suggests that rules don't have value because mothers deserve extra consideration.

Example 3 suggests that rituals don't have value: they lead to humiliation.

Example 4 suggests that rituals don't have value: they are just superstitions.

Since there are more examples saying that rules and rituals don't have value, it is best to create a thesis statement that supports examples 2, 3, and 4.

Earlier in this chapter, we used the prompt to help determine a thesis. Does the thesis statement below point ahead to the ideas in prewriting examples 2, 3, and 4?

Mathabane is right to think that many rules and rituals serve no purpose.

This thesis statement will work for the three topics we've chosen. However, the specific focus that the writer will take is still unclear. A reader might ask why rules and rituals serve no purpose. A thesis can be focused by adding a plan of development.

EXERCISE 8.6   **Write your own thesis statement in response to one of the two prompts below.**

Mathabane writes less about his mother than his father or himself. What is the significance of her role in the family? Do you think other women play similar roles in their families?

Mathabane has a conflict with his father. Do parents and children always have conflicts? Why or why not? Using your own ideas and observations, write an essay in which you answer this question.

PLAN OF DEVELOPMENT

Having a Plan
Defines what areas of the reading you will discuss
Defines the general points you will bring out

A **plan of development** either tells your reader specifically which parts of the reading you will focus on, or it tells your reader what the focus of your arguments will be. It thus tells your reader what you will and will not be examining. A plan of development is generally one or more sentences following your thesis; however, a plan of development may also be found in the same sentence(s) as your thesis. Your plan of development can be determined by examining your prewriting. What points did your prewriting lead to? Chapters 6 and 7 explain how your prewriting leads to several points, or supporting ideas, used to plan your essay.

Below are two plans of development that have been attached to our thesis statement. Which one points to the reading and which one focuses the reader on the general points the writer will make?

> Mathabane is right to think that rules and rituals serve no purpose. This is especially clear in the scenes where Mathabane speaks at the table, when he decides not to speak Venda, and when his father embarrasses him by wearing tribal clothing.

> Mathabane is right to think that many rules and rituals serve no purpose. Rules are supposed to be applied equally; however, they often unfairly punish certain people. Although some rituals have a value, there are many pointless rituals which people blindly follow. Certain rituals force people to do things they don't want to do and can lead to embarrassing situations.

The first example of a plan of development tells the reader which areas of the reading the writer will discuss: when Mathabane speaks at the table, when he refuses to speak Venda, and when he is embarrassed by his father. The second plan of development lets us know what the writer will argue: rules can be unfair, many rituals are pointless, and rituals create embarrassing situations. Either one of these plans of development will give the reader an idea of what will come in the essay.

EXERCISE 8.7 Write two plans of development for each of the prompts below. Write one plan of development that tells the reader what areas of the reading you will discuss. Write the other to suggest the points you will make in your body paragraphs.

Mathabane writes less about his mother than his father or himself. What is the significance of her role in the family? Do you think other women play similar roles in their families?

Mathabane has a conflict with his father. Do parents and children always have conflicts? Why or why not? Using your own ideas and observations, write an essay in which you answer this question.

PUTTING THE INTRODUCTION TOGETHER

At this point you should be ready to put together the various parts of your introduction. Let's first compare two possible introductory paragraphs:

> In Mark Mathabane's "My Father's Tribal Rule," he talks about rituals and rules. He talks about his brother, his mother, and his sister. His family had to moved to a shack. Mathabane really dislikes his father because his father beats him. The father doesn't beat the other children like he beats his son Mark. Mark Mathabane wants to be like the other boys he plays with. He wants to speak other languages. In this paper I will discuss Mathabane's essay.

This example lacks a lead-in to the general topic under discussion. The overview of the reading is too brief to convey an understanding of the essay as a whole. Someone who has not read "My Father's Tribal Rule" would have little understanding of what the reading is about. This example doesn't clarify what the point of Mathabane's writing is. There is no thesis statement and there is no plan of development. A reader would be confused by this introduction because it lacks essential information that the reader needs to understand what will follow in the rest of the essay. Now compare the example above with the one that follows.

> Many people feel that rituals are a thing of the past, practiced only by primitive people. They feel that rituals have little place in a modern society that is driven by technology and science. Rituals, they would say, are just superstitions acted out. **[lead-in]** Mark Mathabane is one of those people who detests rituals. In "My Father's Tribal Rule," he tells us about **[author and title of reading]** his experiences growing up in South Africa in a shantytown of rundown huts for people who had been forced off their ancestral, tribal lands. Even though Mathabane and the children in the area were interested in modern ways, Mathabane's father insisted that their family stick to the tribal traditions. Mathabane eventually came to hate his father for making him follow the tribal rituals. **[overview of reading]** Despite his father's insistence that he follow the rules and practice the rituals, Mathabane thought they made no sense. **[author's thesis]** Mathabane is right to think that many rules and rituals serve no purpose. **[writer's thesis]** Rules are supposed to be applied equally; however, they often unfairly punish certain people. Although some rituals have value, there are many pointless rituals which people blindly follow. Certain rituals force people to do things they don't want to do and can lead to embarrassing situations **[plan of development]**

In the second example, we are given a lead-in that discusses the general topic of rituals and focuses on the commonly held view. The overview of the reading provides more information for the reader who has never read it. The point of Mathabane's essay—his thesis statement—is provided for the reader. The writer's thesis statement clarifies what the writer believes and responds directly to the prompt. It is followed by a plan of development, which lets the reader know that the writer will discuss such topics as the unfairness of some rules. The writer will also discuss how rituals are sometimes pointless and can lead to embarrassing situations. There is a clear response to the prompt; we know that this writer will agree with Mathabane's attitude about rules and rituals.

Remember that this is only one possible way to construct an introduction. Other assignments may require a different structure. The structure of the introduction on page 140 is designed to move the reader from the most general information to the most specific. (See Chapter 20 for drafting strategies that can be used for other patterns of introduction.)

EXERCISE 8.8   Examine the prompts below and write an introductory paragraph with the six elements we've just discussed. (Go back to Chapter 5 if you need help understanding what the prompt is asking; go back to Chapter 6 if you need to analyze the reading or develop samples of prewriting.) If you have been following the exercises in this chapter, you will have the elements that make up an introduction. Try to put them all together. You'll need to check your wording to make sure the different parts flow together into a whole.

Mathabane writes less about his mother than his father or himself. What is the significance of her role in the family? Do you think other women play similar roles in their families?

Mathabane has a conflict with his father. Do parents and children always have conflicts? Why or why not? Using your own ideas and observations, write an essay in which you answer this question.

What You've Done

- Familiarized your reader with the topic and your focus
- Presented your plan of development

For More Strategies for Introductions

- See Chapter 20
    Introductions Without Readings
    Lead-ins
    Introductions Using Readings

The Next Step

- Write body paragraphs (Chapter 9)

9 Writing Body Paragraphs

What You've Done

■ Created an introduction

What You Need to Do Next

■ Write paragraphs that develop the main idea of the essay:
   Write sentences to state the main idea of each paragraph
   Make the ideas from the reading clear
   Use your own ideas and examples to respond to the reading
   End each paragraph with a point supporting your thesis

In contrast to **introductions**, which supply general information, **body** paragraphs present specific information and details for your reader. The most commonly asked question about body paragraphs is how many are needed. Although some writing textbooks suggest that an essay include at least three body paragraphs, we recommend that the number of body paragraphs be determined by the reading or the material you're discussing. For instance, when we discussed Mathabane's essay "My Father's Tribal Rule" in Chapter 3, we saw that this reading discusses two rules: not speaking at the table and speaking only Venda. We also saw that there were three rituals: weaning George, wearing tribal clothing, and doing daily rituals. If your assignment was to write about the rules in Mathabane's narrative, you would most likely have only two body paragraphs because rules are only discussed in two places in the reading. Similarly, if your assignment was to write about rituals, you would have three body paragraphs, one for each ritual in the reading. If you were asked to write about both the rules and the rituals, you could have five body paragraphs.

Even though there are five areas of the reading that discuss rules and rituals, you need to focus on two questions: Which areas can you respond to with the best examples or strongest arguments? Which areas are directly related to your **thesis** or the **prompt**? For instance, there are three rituals discussed in the reading. If the prompt asks you to discuss Mathabane's dislike of rituals, you could eliminate one of the three. Mathabane says nothing negative about the ritual surrounding George's weaning. You could then focus on the two he does dislike.

Remember: Use the reading, your **prewriting**, and the assignment to help you determine how many body paragraphs you need.

THE COMPONENTS OF BODY PARAGRAPHS

Body Paragraphs

Topic sentence

Transitions

Discussing author's ideas

Your argument

Conclusion

Because many of the assignments you are given in college will require you to respond to the ideas of others, we will focus on a model of a paragraph that creates a balance between the author's ideas and your own. This is only one way to construct body paragraphs. As your assignments change, other structures might be recommended. Although there is more than one way to construct your body paragraphs, they usually contain the general elements that an entire essay does: an introduction (**topic sentence**), a body (discussion of reading and your response), and a conclusion (the point you are trying to make).

Following is an example of a balanced body paragraph structure.

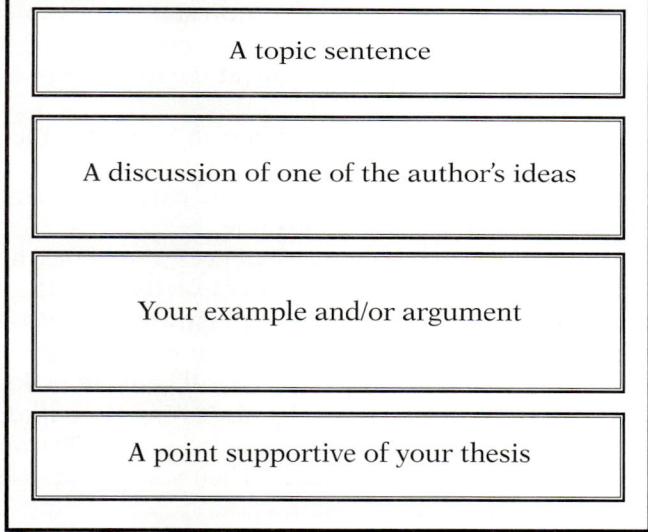

A topic sentence

A discussion of one of the author's ideas

Your example and/or argument

A point supportive of your thesis

This structure creates a balance between the author's ideas and your response to those ideas. The author's ideas are usually presented first, because you are responding to what the author has said. Since many of your assignments will require you to respond to an author's ideas, you must first clarify what those ideas are. Once you have explained the author's position on one issue, you can then directly respond to what he or she has said.

A body paragraph should contain only *one topic*. Any example or discussion of the reading must relate to the topic of your paragraph. This will help you keep a clear focus in each body paragraph, and it will allow you to better select your own examples which best relate to the specific point the author is making. If you have more than one topic in a body paragraph, you may confuse the reader, lose your focus, and never make a clear point.

Throughout the rest of this chapter, we will discuss each element of the body paragraph and provide examples for you to study.

TOPIC SENTENCES

Topic Sentences

Introduce the topic

Provide transitions

A *topic sentence* announces the specific subject that will be discussed in the paragraph. Topic sentences let the reader know what you will discuss, and they also help you to keep a sharp focus on one topic. These sentences:

■ Set up the *topic*—the main idea of the paragraph

■ Act as a *transition*—by linking new information that will come in the new paragraph to information that has been presented in previous paragraphs.

They are important because your reader needs to know what you will discuss. It is important that you present your topic sentence immediately—in your introductory sentence. The topic you set up should be the *only* topic discussed in the paragraph. Look at the following example:

Some rituals are practiced in such a way that they become meaningless.

This introductory sentence to the paragraph sets up the topic of rituals and how they can lose their meaning.

When setting up topic sentences, remember not to start with quotes or examples. Quotes show the reader exactly what the author said, but they do not constitute a topic. Examples illustrate a point the author is trying to make, but they cannot be considered a topic. In other words, a writer may give an example of an incident in a football game to make a point about teamwork. If you begin your paragraph by discussing the author's example, your reader will think the topic of the paragraph is football. Teamwork would be the topic you would set up for your reader. Then you would discuss the author's example to reveal his point about teamwork.

When it's time for you to write your body paragraphs, don't jump right into them. Think about your reader. Provide a topic sentence that clearly reveals whatever single topic you will discuss in your paragraph.

TRANSITIONS

Your first body paragraph doesn't need a transition, because it is not following another body paragraph. However, as you move from one body paragraph to another, it helps if you can link your discussions together for your reader. **Transitions** help the readers to see how the new information is related to the information in the last paragraph they read. To make an opening sentence work as a transition, add a reference to the topic or point of the previous paragraph. If the first body paragraph focuses on meaningless rituals, the following sentence would serve as a transition into the next topic:

Some rituals seem senseless, but some rituals can make us act in ways we don't want to and can lead to embarrassing situations.

This sentence serves as a transition because it points back to a previous discussion about senseless rituals, and it points ahead to the new topic that will be discussed: rituals force us to do things we don't want to do and can be embarrassing.

Topic sentences that serve as transitions do the following:

■ Refer to the topic and/or point of the previous paragraph.

■ Set up the new topic the writer will discuss.

EXERCISE 9.1

Pretend that you are writing an essay in which these are the main ideas presented in your body paragraphs.

Mathabane's relationship with his father

The relationship between Mathabane's father and mother

The relationship between Mathabane and his mother

1. Write topic sentences for each of these ideas.

2. Determine which order these ideas should be presented in an essay. In other words, what order would work for the body paragraphs based on these ideas.

3. Once you have determined the order, add transitional words or phrases to the second and third topic sentences.

Repeat all three steps in the exercise above for these main ideas:

Mathabane's feelings about only speaking Venda

Mathabane's feelings about not speaking at the table

Mathabane's feelings about his father wearing tribal clothing

CLARIFYING THE AUTHOR'S IDEAS

Body Development

Present author's ideas

Provide evidence

Explain ideas

Respond to author's ideas

If you are responding to a reading, your reader needs to know exactly what the author says on a specific point. After you have set up your topic sentence, you need to do the following:

■ Paraphrase or summarize the author's ideas.

■ Quote passages that demonstrate these ideas clearly.

■ Explain the author's idea or point in your own words.

Even if you are going to disagree with the author, you need to present his or her ideas clearly and fairly. In the next example, the introductory sentence we discussed earlier will be followed by an explanation of what is said in the reading:

Rituals can make us act in ways we don't want to and can lead to embarrassing situations. Mathabane tells about his father wearing the traditional tribal clothing while he wanted to wear modern clothing. He says that when his father wore his tribal clothes, the other children would laugh at both of them. Mathabane says he became "the laughingstock of [his] friends." He goes on to say, "Whenever they laughed at me I would feel embarrassed and would cry." I'm sure Mathabane wanted to be proud of his father, but this ritual just embarrassed him and made him cry.

Someone who had never read the essay would understand the situation being described here. This example has given enough detail for readers to have an understanding of how Mathabane feels about this ritual. The last sentence uses the phrase "embarrassed him and made him cry," which echoes the subject set up in the topic sentence: rituals can lead to embarrassing situations.

RESPONDING TO THE AUTHOR

After you have presented the author's position, you need to respond with your own ideas and examples to reveal what you feel about the topic you're discussing. To explain whether or not you agree or disagree with the ideas contained in the reading, you must present arguments and/or examples that provide specific details for your reader. Consider the following example:

We have a lot of rituals around our house. There are rituals from dad's side of the family and some from my mother's side. There's a ritual for every holiday. Sometimes I wish we could just ignore them. I don't see why we need to do the same thing every year in the same way.

This example lacks development and specifics. What are the rituals? Which rituals are from the father's side of the family? Which ones are from the mother's side? Is there any difference between them? Why doesn't the writer want to perform the same rituals every year? There are many things that the reader would be uncertain about. A reader would never remember this example because there is nothing concrete that the reader can hold on to.

Let's look at another sample of prewriting from Chapter 8.

I personally have experienced firsthand the negative effects of rituals. There is a ritual we perform every year at work. We select names out of a hat, so we can be someone's Santa for that Christmas. Every year I go through the same thing. I don't know what to buy the person. Although there is a twenty dollar limit on the gift, I always spend more, because I don't want this person I hardly know to think I'm cheap. I'm sure everyone else goes through the same thing. Then on the last day of work before Christmas, we open our gifts and pretend to be overjoyed at a present we don't even want. Last year was the worst. I bought a basket of cheeses, smoked meats, and wine for a coworker who turned out to be an herb tea sipping vegetarian. It wasn't my fault. I didn't really know him, but I was humiliated when I found out.

This example provides much more detail for the reader. A specific ritual is discussed. There are details given about a specific incident. The way the writer feels about this ritual is spelled out for the reader. This is an example the reader will remember because it has specific details.

You will notice that this example is different from Mathabane's example about his father's tribal clothes, but the situation is very similar. The reader should be able to see the parallel between the two situations: both Mathabane and the writer have to follow a ritual, Mathabane is embarrassed by his ritual, just as this writer is humiliated by the ritual she partakes in.

Your examples don't have to be exactly the same as the author's, but they do need to focus on the same issue. For instance, if you were responding to an article describing how important determination and hard work are in learning to play a musical instrument, you could provide an example discussing how important determination and hard work are in learning math. Math and music are different topics, but the issue of determination and hard work in learning these skills is the same.

CONCLUDING YOUR BODY PARAGRAPH

Examples cannot stand on their own, and they cannot serve as an ending to a body paragraph. An example will illustrate your point, but it isn't your point. Body paragraphs need to end with a statement that sums up your point for the reader.

Let's look at the prompt again and see if the last sentence from the writer's example above is directly responding to the prompt.

Prompt/Question

Mathabane says he despises rules and rituals. Is he correct in thinking that rules and rituals have no value?

Response/Answer

It wasn't my fault. I didn't really know him, but I was humiliated when I found out.

Do these last sentences from the previous example respond to the prompt and support the writer's thesis? The prompt asks if you agree or disagree with Mathabane's attitude toward rules and rituals. You can see that the last sentence in the example doesn't respond to the prompt or support the writer's thesis, which agrees with Mathabane's attitude.

You must explain how your example is related to the issue in the reading. Since the purpose of your paragraph is to support or clarify your thesis, you need to explain to your reader how the example illustrates your point and supports your thesis. Here is the same example of the writer's personal experience with a concluding point:

> I personally have experienced firsthand the negative effects of rituals. There is a ritual we perform every year at work. We select names out of a hat, so we can be someone's Santa for that Christmas. Every year I go through the same thing. I don't know what to buy the person. Although there is a twenty dollar limit on the gift, I always spend more, because I don't want this person I hardly know to think I'm cheap. I'm sure everyone else goes through the same thing. Then on the last day of work before Christmas, we open our gifts and pretend to be overjoyed at a present we don't even want. Last year was the worst. I bought a basket of cheeses, smoked meats, and wine for a coworker who turned out to be an herb tea sipping vegetarian. It wasn't my fault. I didn't really know him, but I was humiliated when I found out. *Mathabane's father's rituals brought shame on him, just as this office ritual humiliated me. Some rituals should be abolished because they embarrass people.*

This conclusion to the paragraph explains the point of the example: *Some rituals should be abolished because they embarrass people*. It is worded to relate the writer's example to Mathabane's experience. Furthermore, it is supportive of the thesis that is set up in the introductory paragraph: *Mathabane is right to think that rules and rituals serve no purpose*. Essentially, it summarizes what has been discussed in the paragraph and is worded to support the writer's thesis.

PUTTING THE BODY PARAGRAPH TOGETHER

Here is the whole paragraph with all the components put together.

> Rituals can make us act in ways we don't want to and   — topic sentence
> can lead to embarrassing situations. Mathabane tells about
> his father wearing the traditional tribal clothing while he
> wanted to wear modern clothing. He says that when his father
> wore his tribal clothes, the other children would laugh at both   — discussion of
> of them. Mathabane says he became "the laughingstock of   the reading
> [his] friends." He goes on to say, "Whenever they laughed at

me I would feel embarrassed and would cry." I'm sure Mathabane wanted to be proud of his father, but this ritual just embarrassed him and made him cry. I personally have experienced firsthand the negative effects of rituals. There is a
ritual we perform every year at work. We select names out of a
hat, so we can be someone's Santa for that Christmas. Every
year I go through the same thing. I don't know what to buy
the person. Although there is a twenty dollar limit on the gift,
I always spend more, because I don't want this person I hardly
know to think I'm cheap. I'm sure everyone else goes through
the same thing. Then on the last day of work before Christmas,
we open our gifts and pretend to be overjoyed at a present we
don't even want. Last year was the worst. I bought a basket of
cheeses, smoked meats, and wine for a coworker who turned
out to be an herb tea sipping vegetarian. It wasn't my fault. I
didn't really know him, but I was humiliated when I found
out. Mathabane's father's rituals brought shame on him, just
as this office ritual humiliated me. Some rituals should be
abolished because they embarrass people.

> discussion of
> the reading
>
> writer's
> example
>
> concluding
> point support-
> ive of the
> writer's thesis

ADDITIONAL BODY PARAGRAPHS

As we discussed at the beginning of this chapter, an essay needs more than
one paragraph to provide support for a thesis. Additional body paragraphs
should examine either new issues (related to the focus of your thesis) or different areas of the reading. The body paragraph we have just looked at discusses the section of the reading where Mathabane is embarrassed by his
father's tribal clothes. Additional body paragraphs should focus on other sections of the reading where rules and rituals are discussed.

EXERCISE 9.2

Examine the body paragraphs that follow. Do they contain the four basic elements
of the model paragraph we have been discussing? Answer the five questions below
for each paragraph.

1. What is the topic sentence?
2. Is there a discussion of one area of the reading? What is it?
3. Does the writer provide a specific example? What is it?
4. Does the paragraph end with a concluding point?
5. Does the concluding point support a thesis? What would the
   thesis be?

EXAMPLE 1

Like Mathabane, I find that some rituals don't make sense. There's one specific ritual that makes little sense to me. The fourth Thursday of November, my husband, my daughter, and I go to my parents' house for Thanksgiving. It is always held at my parents' house, even though they live the farthest out of town. My mother won't let anyone else host the gathering. Each member of the family is assigned a specific dish to bring. We arrive along with cousins, aunts, and uncles, many of whom we have little in common with. Then we all try to be pleasant, make small talk, and smile. Dinner is always a disaster. When the potatoes are done, the turkey isn't. When the turkey is done, the potatoes are dry and cold. The women, of course, do all the work. For the most part, we just get in each other's way as we try to prepare the meal. Even before we sit down to eat, I'm battling a severe case of stress. Thanksgiving is the day when you're supposed to give thanks, but the only thing I'm thankful for is when it's over. When the Pilgrims celebrated the first Thanksgiving, its purpose was clear to them. They had survived in a new and bountiful land. We never share what we are thankful for. Because our family has lost sight of the purpose of this ritual, it makes no sense to celebrate it.

EXAMPLE 2

Mathabane said he had to do daily rituals. Some of the rituals were to "protect the house from evil doers." The family also did rituals to keep them from being sick or hungry. There were other rituals to keep the police away, but I don't know why you would want to do that. The police are there to protect and serve. I would think that you would want a ritual to keep criminals away. They also had rituals to help them get more money. Mathabane says that these rituals "did not make sense." He had to do a lot of rituals, and if he didn't, his father would threaten to beat him. That's not fair and would be considered child abuse.

EXAMPLE 3

Rules can often lead to certain people being treated unfairly. Mathabane's father didn't allow talking at the dinner table. When Mathabane did talk, he was unfairly punished. Where I work, we are given five sick days a year. After that, your pay is docked for each day you're out. I'm never out sick more than two or three days a year. I don't abuse the policy by taking "mental health" days. However, each of the last two years, I've had my pay docked because I used more than my allotted sick days. I wasn't abusing this rule, I was simply taking care of my child as any mother would. I can't help it if my daughter is too sick to go to school or needs to go to the doctor. Women with children should have additional sick leave for these emergencies. When I have to call in with a sick child, my supervisor always makes me feel like I'm avoiding doing my work, like I'm not a good employee. Five days of sick leave is not enough for a mother, because she has to have sick days for herself and her child.

EXAMPLE 4

We have a big ritual on the 4th of July. All the families on our street know each other. Most of the families have children. We put on a block party fireworks show. The object is to put on the best display, or my strategy, which is to save the best for last. Some of the neighbors set out picnic tables and we all contribute some food. Someone always has a barbecue going. These are rituals because we do them the same way every year. It's always the same.

EXAMPLE 5

Another problem with rituals is that they are just based on superstitions. Rituals can't protect you. Although he doesn't explain what he had to do, Mathabane tells us that he had to perform "rituals spanning the range of day-to-day living." He had to do rituals "to prevent us from becoming sick, to safeguard his [father's] job, to keep the police away, to bring [the family] good luck" and more. Mathabane said that these rituals didn't make any sense to him. How can performing rituals bring luck or prevent you from becoming sick? When I was younger, I was like Mathabane's father. I had a ritual for almost everything. I had a ritual for going to sleep: 20 deep breaths and count backward from 100. I had rituals for getting high scores on my tests in school: using a new pen or pencil or repeating the word <u>luck</u> over and over before the test. But as I got older, my views changed and are now like Mathabane's. Luck doesn't have anything to do with knowing the answers on a quiz. I know how well I'll do on a test, because I know how much I've studied. Luck isn't going to make information pop into my head. When I stopped relying on rituals and started to rely on studying, my grades went up. Rituals are just baseless superstitions. Following rituals is senseless and Mathabane is right to think they are useless.

EXERCISE 9.3 | **Group Activity**

Which of the paragraphs in the exercise above lack one or more of the four elements? Working in small groups, see if you can rewrite these paragraphs to better match the structure of the example body paragraph we discussed on page 143.

What You've Done

■ Constructed body paragraphs that include:
   A topic sentence
   A discussion of one of the author's ideas
   Examples and your argument
   A conclusion supporting your thesis

For More Strategies for Body Paragraphs

■ See Chapter 20
   Body Paragraphs
   Narration
   Description
   Process
   Comparison and Contrast
   Classification
   Cause and Effect

The Next Step

■ Write a conclusion (Chapter 10)

10 Writing Conclusions

What You've Done

- Created an introduction
- Created body paragraphs

What You Need to Do Next

- Write a final paragraph to end the essay, to:
  Summarize ideas from the reading
  Review the main points you've made responding to the reading
  Review your own main idea
- Put the entire essay together

Many inexperienced writers are so grateful to reach the point of writing a **conclusion** that they are tempted to put almost anything in the last paragraph. Experienced writers remember that the conclusion gives the reader the last impression of their writing and that it's important to end an essay well—with power, with style, with something substantial still to say. The conclusion can make or break the essay.

THE COMPONENTS OF A CONCLUSION

ESL Although a conclusion can function in several different ways, it generally should recap the major ideas presented in your essay. You should quickly remind the reader of the following:

- The author's **thesis** or point of the reading you're discussing.
- The main points from the reading you're discussing.
- The main points you have made in response to the reading.
- Your thesis (reworded so it isn't a repetition of the thesis in your introduction).

The Conclusion
The author's thesis
Main points of the reading
Your main points
Restated thesis

A good conclusion should wrap up an essay and present one final thought. You can discuss how you feel about the issue described in the reading, you can present a solution to a problem described in the essay, you can make a prediction about what will happen in the future, or you can finish something you started in the **introduction**—answer a question, finish a story (these alternative structures are discussed in Chapter 20). What you don't want to do is merely repeat the thesis in your conclusion and do nothing else.

EXAMPLE 1

I think rituals are bad because of the negative effect they have on the family. Mathabane didn't like to participate in them. He was often punished for not following the rules or rituals that his father followed. My experiences have been very similar.

In this conclusion, the writer has only restated the thesis and provided generalizations. Such a conclusion certainly lets the reader know that the writer is at the end, but it doesn't strongly pull together the writer's main ideas and points, indicating to the reader that the writer has nothing more to say. This conclusion makes little reference to the reading. After reading several pages of an essay, a reader needs a good **summary** that reviews the essay's main ideas.

EXAMPLE 2

Rules can help keep things running smoothly, and rituals can help us preserve traditions, but sometimes they can create problems. The rules and rituals Mathabane had to follow confused and embarrassed him because they were lacking a valid purpose. } Author's thesis and main points

Like Mathabane, I have had to follow senseless rules. I have witnessed people engaging in rituals that are meaningless, and I have been humiliated by participating in rituals. } Writer's main points

My experiences lead me to agree with Mathabane: rules and rituals are often senseless and without purpose or value. } Writer's thesis

This conclusion does more than simply restate the thesis. It also refers to the reading as well as the main points the writer has made. These statements sum up the major ideas presented in the essay.

PUTTING IT ALL TOGETHER

Let's now take a look at a whole essay with all the parts put together. We've selected some of the sample **body** paragraphs we examined earlier in Chapter 9. **Transitions** have been added to help unite the body paragraphs. The second body paragraph in the following essay is based on the model paragraph presented in Chapter 9 (p. 146). Because it appears as the second body paragraph, a transition has been added to relate it to the paragraph it follows.

Many people feel that rituals are a thing of the past, practiced only by primitive people. They feel that rituals have little place in a modern society that is driven by technology and science. Rituals, they would say, are just superstitions acted out. Mark Mathabane is one of those people who detests rituals. In "My Father's Tribal Rule," he tells us about his experiences growing up in South Africa in a shantytown of rundown huts for people who had been forced off their ancestral, tribal lands. Even though Mathabane and the children in the area were interested in modern ways, Mathabane's father insisted that their family stick to the tribal traditions. Mathabane eventually came to hate his father for making him follow the tribal rituals. Despite his father's insistence that he follow the rules and practice the rituals, Mathabane thought they made no sense. Mathabane is right to think that many rules and rituals serve no purpose. Rules are supposed to be applied equally; however, they often unfairly punish certain people. Although some rituals have value, there are many pointless rituals which people blindly follow. Certain rituals force people to do things they don't want to do and can lead to embarrassing situations

— Lead-in

— Author and title of reading

— Overview of reading

— Author's thesis

— Writer's thesis

— Plan of development

Even though many rituals are meaningful, some rituals are practiced in such a way that they become meaningless. Although Mathabane doesn't explain what he had to do, he tells us that he had to perform "rituals spanning the range of day-to-day living." He had to do rituals "to prevent [the family] from becoming sick, to safeguard his [father's] job, to keep the police away, to bring [the family] good luck" and more. Mathabane said that these rituals didn't make any sense to him. How can performing rituals bring luck or prevent you from becoming sick? There's one specific ritual that makes little sense to me. The fourth Thursday of November, my husband, my daughter, and I go to my parents' house for Thanksgiving. It is always held at my parents' house. My mother won't let anyone else host the gathering. We arrive along with cousins, aunts, and uncles, many of whom we have little in common with. Then we all try to be pleasant, make

— Topic sentence

— Discussion of reading

— Writer's example

small talk, and smile. Dinner is always a disaster. When the potatoes are done, the turkey isn't. When the turkey is done, the potatoes are dry and cold. The women, of course, do all the work. For the most part, we just get in each other's way as we try to prepare the meal. Even before we sit down to eat, I'm battling a severe case of stress. Thanksgiving is the day when you're supposed to give thanks, but the only thing I'm thankful for is when it's over. When the Pilgrims celebrated the first Thanksgiving, its purpose was clear to them.

> Writer's example

They had survived in a new and bountiful land. We never share what we are thankful for. Because our family has lost sight of the purpose of this ritual, it is as senseless as the confusing rituals Mathabane had to follow.

> Concluding point supportive of the writer's thesis

Some rituals seem senseless, but some rituals can make us act in ways we don't want to and can lead to embarrassing situations. Mathabane tells about his father wearing the tra-

> Topic sentence with transition

ditional tribal clothing while he wanted to wear modern clothing. He says that when his father wore his traditional tribal clothes, the other children would laugh at both of them. Mathabane says he became "the laughingstock of [his] friends." He goes on to say, "Whenever they laughed at me I would feel embarrassed and would cry." I'm sure Mathabane wanted to be proud of his father, but this ritual just embarrassed him and made him cry. I personally have experienced

> Discussion of the reading

firsthand the negative effects of rituals. There is a ritual we perform every year at work. We select names out of a hat, so we can be someone's Santa for that Christmas. Every year I go through the same thing. I don't know what to buy the person. Although there is a twenty dollar limit on the gift, I always spend more, because I don't want this person I hardly know to think I'm cheap. I'm sure everyone else goes through the same thing. Then on the last day of work before Christmas, we open our gifts and pretend to be overjoyed at a present we don't even want. Last year was the worst. I bought

> Writer's example

a basket of cheeses, smoked meats, and wine for a coworker who turned out to be an herb tea sipping vegetarian. It wasn't my fault. I didn't really know him, but I was humiliated when I found out. Mathabane's father's rituals brought shame on him, just as this office ritual embarrassed me. Some rituals should be abolished because they embarrass people.

> Concluding point supportive of the writer's thesis

Whereas rituals can be embarrassing, rules can often lead to certain people being treated unfairly. Mathabane's father didn't allow talking at the dinner table. Mathabane tells us that "One day I intentionally broke one of these laws; I talked while eating." His father's response was to beat young Mathabane with his belt. Mathabane's father never explains why this rule exists. Like many rules, they exist, but no one questions the fairness of the rule. When Mathabane did, he was unfairly punished. Where I work, we have a rule that causes some people to be unfairly punished. We are given five sick days a year. After that, your pay is docked for each day you're out. I'm never out sick more than two or three days a year. I don't abuse the policy by taking "mental health" days. However, each of the last two years, I've had my pay docked because I used more than my allotted sick days. I wasn't abusing this rule. I was simply taking care of my child as any mother would. I can't help it if my daughter is too sick to go to school or needs to go to the doctor. Women with children should have additional sick leave for these emergencies. When I have to call in with a sick child, my supervisor always makes me feel like I'm avoiding doing my work, like I'm not a good employee. Five days of sick leave is not enough for a mother, because she has to have sick days for herself and her child. Mathabane was unfairly punished for the "crime" he committed, just as I am unfairly punished. Although I don't intentionally break this rule like Mathabane did, I still pay for breaking it. Some rules are good, but some need to be changed or eliminated.

> *Topic sentence with transition*

> *Discussion of the reading*

> *Writer's example*

> *Concluding point supportive of the writer's thesis*

Rules can help keep things running smoothly, and rituals can help us preserve traditions, but sometimes they can create problems. The rules and rituals Mathabane had to follow confused and embarrassed him because they were lacking a valid purpose. Like Mathabane, I have had to follow senseless rules. I have witnessed people engaging in rituals that are meaningless, and I have been humiliated by participating in rituals. My experiences lead me to agree with Mathabane: rules and rituals are often senseless and without purpose or value.

> *Author's thesis and main points*

> *Writer's main points*

> *Writer's thesis*

The essay above contains all the general elements needed for an essay that responds to a reading.

In Exercise 10.1, we look at another essay written on the same **prompt**. This essay, however, takes the opposite approach to the prompt, arguing that Mathabane's attitude toward rituals is wrong and that rules and rituals do have value and purpose. In the next chapter, this essay, a first **draft** with many problems, will be revised.

Parts of an Essay

Does the introduction contain the following?

- ■ A **lead-in**
- ■ An identification of the author and title of the reading
- ■ An **overview** of the reading
- ■ The author's thesis or point
- ■ A **thesis statement** (responding to the prompt)
- ■ A **plan of development**

Do the body paragraphs contain the following?

- ■ A **topic sentence** (with transitions in paragraphs 3 and 4)
- ■ A focus on a specific area of the reading
- ■ An example from the writer's experiences
- ■ A point to conclude the paragraph

Does the conclusion contain the following elements?

- ■ The author's thesis or point of the reading
- ■ The main points from the reading
- ■ The main points you have made in response to the reading
- ■ A restatement of the thesis (reworded so it isn't a repetition of the thesis in the introduction)

EXERCISE 10.1   **Read the following essay to see if it contains the elements discussed in Chapters 8 through 10. What problems do you see? What changes need to be made? Examine this essay and try to identify the problems. Then look at the analysis in the next chapter to see how many of the problems in the essay you identified.**

Rules and rituals are things people do. Everyday we follow some kind of rules. We also participate in rituals, although we might not know it. Mark Mathabane knew he participated in rituals. More than he wanted to. He lived with his family in a poor section of South Africa. His father was from the tribes, but they were now living around people who had accepted modern ways. Ways that Mathabane wanted to follow. His father insisted that the whole family follow tribal rules and rituals, he became angry and violent when Mathabane wouldn't obey the rules or follow the traditions. Mathabane writes about his hatred of rules and rituals in "My Father's Tribal Rule" but I think that rules and rituals do have purpose and value.

Mathabane tells about the rule his father had about not speaking at the table. He tells us that "One day I intentionally broke one of these laws." He spoke during dinner and his father got really mad then he threatened to beat Mathabane. What Mathabane didn't understand was that his father got mad because Mathabane wasn't respecting him. In my family, we have a dinnertime ritual too. Before dinner, my brothers and my sister and I are supposed to clean the house and get everything ready for dinner. One day I didn't feel like doing it, because I have to do everything. My brothers and my sister hardly do anything. So, I just sat on the couch and watched TV. My father came in and saw me and started to yell at me. He said he worked hard every day to put food on the table and that I was showing disrespect to him, my mother, my brothers and my sister. He sent me to bed without supper. At first I was really mad. But the more I thought about it, the more I felt bad for not respecting my father. I learned through this rule to respect my father, Mathabane didn't see the valuable things you can learn from rules.

Following rituals can also help us be more mature. Mathabane showed that he was immature because he disobeyed his father simply for the purpose of rebelling. He had no reason to talk at the table except he wanted to make his father angry and see what he would do. When I was younger, I was suppose to clean my room first thing every Saturday morning. Since I would rather play than clean my room, I would put it off as long as possible. If I had been more mature, I would have realized that cleaning my room was my responsibility and I would have done it without trying to get out of it. Also I should have realized that my jobs before dinner were my jobs, whether my brothers and sister did their jobs or not should not have mattered. Being that I was the oldest, I should have had the maturity to set a good example for them by obeying the rules. Mathabane could have shown his maturity by obeying his father's rules rather than disobeying him just because he didn't like it. Doing rituals, particularly if they aren't ones we enjoy, builds maturity because we will have to do things we don't like our whole lives.

Mathabane tells us about his little brother George. It was time for George to be weaned and so "she smeared her breasts with red pepper and then invited my brother to suckle." Of course, George's mouth must of burned like fire so he stopped nursing. Mathabane thought, "It was amusing to witness my mother do it." He just saw this ritual as being funny. He didn't understand that it had a purpose "to mark George's passage from infancy to childhood." My friend Alan went through a passage similar to George's. Alan's family has alot of money. His parents had bought cars for his older brother and sister when they turned sixteen. They bought Alan one when he turned sixteen, but they told him that driving a car meant that he had to be very responsible. They told him that driving a car meant that he was no longer a kid, he was now a adult. It's strange, but owning that car really did change him. I guess he realized that you can't act irresponsibly when your driving several tons of steel.

Also, the rituals we do everyday can help the whole family. Mathabane had to do "rituals spanning the range of day-to-day living." Everybody does daily rituals. In our house, these daily rituals are divided up. Every evening before bed, for instance, its my job to make sure all the doors are locked and the windows shut and latched. My sister irons my father's shirts so he'll have a fresh one for work. My father gets lunch ready for everybody. My mother supervises and helps who ever needs help. Although Mathabane may be confused by these rituals, I'm not.

In conclusion, Mathabane just doesn't get it. He thinks rules and rituals are just a waste of time. He doesn't see how they can help us learn to respect others and be more courteous to them. I think that Mathabane was too immature to understand that rituals can help us grow up. They can help develop self-responsibility, which is something most people could use more of. Mathabane only thinks about himself and that's why he doesn't want to do the rituals that help the whole family. Basically he wrong. Rules and rituals are something we should follow and practice.

The last three chapters have shown you how to develop an introduction, body paragraphs, and a conclusion, and how to put them all together. For good writers, this isn't the end of the process. Revising what you've done may be as important as developing your first draft. The next few chapters will help you polish your essays through revision and editing. In Chapter 11, we will re-examine the previous essay to determine what needs to be added, deleted, or changed.

What You've Done

- Created a conclusion, to summarize:
    The author's thesis and main points
    Your response and final evaluation
- Put the components of an essay together

For More Strategies for Conclusions

■ See Chapter 20, Conclusions

The Next Step

■ Revise your essay (Chapter 11)

Revising

Improving Ideas, Organization, and Style

> ### What You've Done
>
> ■ Drafted your conclusion and seen how this combines with other components of an essay
>
> ### What You Need to Do Next
>
> ■ Prepare to revise the essay
> ■ Look again at the organization of the essay
> ■ Look again at the explanations and examples in the essay

You have already done more work on this paper than you probably thought possible—and you may be tired of working on it, or you may have run out of time to continue improving it. However, you should not stop here. Just as the difference between a hacker and a good golfer often involves the follow-through on a shot, the difference between a mediocre essay and a good essay is how well the writer follows through in finishing the paper.

To follow through, you need to revise, edit, and proofread. It's important to realize that *each of these is a separate step,* though in each of them you are making changes in your **draft**, and in each of them you may use similar techniques to recognize changes that must be made. Let's look at each step briefly:

1. *Revising:* When you revise your draft, *you are essentially rewriting it.* You will make big changes—you may even decide that you need to change your thesis. You may improve your ideas, organization, or development. You may reconsider the ideas in a reading and how your ideas relate to them. You may also revise at the sentence level, choosing words that are more interesting and creating sentences that express your meaning more clearly.

2. *Editing:* When you edit, *you are making your writing correct* by following the rules of written English. You may edit for clarity, grammar and usage, transitions, punctuation, and spelling.

3. *Formatting and proofreading:* When you proofread, *you are eliminating careless errors.* You are checking to make sure that the words and punctuation on the paper are the ones that you intended to write, not accidents. You may proofread for typographical errors, left out words, inaccurate quotations, incomplete punctuation, and errors created by revising and editing. You also make sure the format of your essay is correct.

All three of these steps may overlap. You may not realize until you begin editing that you have made a mistake interpreting a quotation which leads you to revise a whole paragraph, or you may edit typographical errors as you are revising for the first time. When you proofread for careless errors, you may find that you need to return to some of the steps of editing to make sure you know correct word forms. That's fine. The point is that you must be sure that you *set aside a separate time for each of the three tasks,* because each is essential. This chapter and the next two examine these three steps in detail.

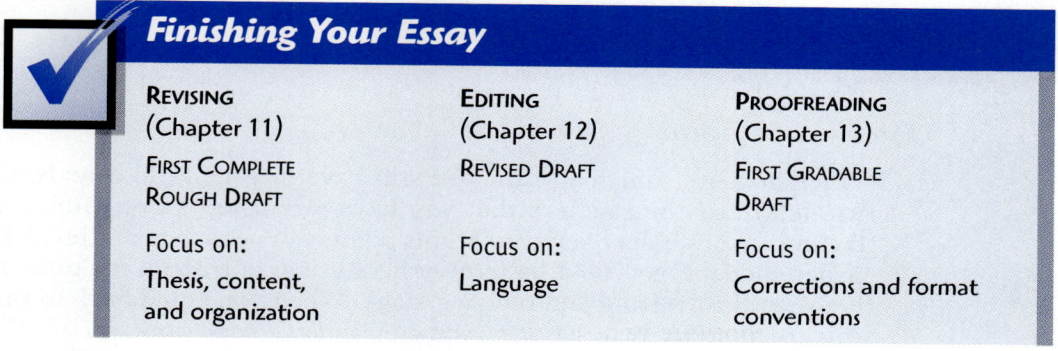

Finishing Your Essay

REVISING (Chapter 11)	**EDITING** (Chapter 12)	**PROOFREADING** (Chapter 13)
FIRST COMPLETE ROUGH DRAFT	REVISED DRAFT	FIRST GRADABLE DRAFT
Focus on: Thesis, content, and organization	Focus on: Language	Focus on: Corrections and format conventions

THE PROCESS OF REVISION

Steps for Revision

Preparing to revise

Checking structure and organization

Checking development

If you think that revision means recopying everything neatly to finish your paper, you are mistaken. Revision is a messy process. You are expected to write on your paper, mark out sections, write in the margins or between lines, draw arrows, or even cut your paper into pieces so that you can move the parts of the essay around physically. If your draft is neat after you have revised, you haven't done it right.

It is easier to revise when you have a systematic way of looking for possible improvements. For example, it might be a waste of time to revise your examples if your **thesis** doesn't answer the **prompt**. You would want to be sure that you were fulfilling the assignment before you try to change anything else.

This chapter presents the three main steps that you should follow during revision. It will help you find an organized way to revise all areas of the essay. You may need to repeat some steps, you may need to rethink your thesis, and you may wind up revising your essay several times. And all of this will only mean that you are doing things right.

Computer Tip

The revision process is easier if you use a word proessing program such as Word or WordPerfect. These programs allow you to move around parts of your essay and try out different alternatives without recopying or retyping. Here is a list of commands that are useful in revising on a word processor:

- *Cut*—allows you to delete (or erase) text you no longer want
- *Copy*—allows you to make a copy of a section of text so that you can move it somewhere else
- *Paste*—allows you to add text you have copied or cut from another location
- *Save as*—allows you to make a new copy of the file with a new name so you can make changes to it while keeping the old copy intact
- *Insert*—allows you to insert complete files with new material into an existing file

STEP 1. PREPARING TO REVISE

Letting the Paper Cool

When you first finish a draft, you still have in your head exactly what you wanted to say and believe that you have exhausted all of your ideas, producing the best paper you can. At this point, you need to take a break from the paper and let it get "cold," a term writers use to talk about the time they take between the drafting and revising stage. When you come back to the paper, you are more likely to see ways you can improve your work.

Too often, beginning writers do not allow themselves enough time to adequately complete this step. The amount of time you allow the paper to cool will vary with the amount of time that you have. Ideally, wait half a day to a day. If you have less time, at least go do something else so you are not consciously thinking about the paper.

Reading the Paper Again

Pretend that you, like your reader, have not read your essay before. Forget what you meant to say, and try to focus on only what you have said. Read the entire draft all the way through, preferably aloud.

When you read, mark anything that doesn't seem to convey what you meant. Don't worry about grammar, **mechanics**, and usage at this point. Avoid wasting energy correcting sentence level problems when you may not even keep the sentence. Don't change anything at this point; just mark the places that you have concerns about so you can come back to them in a later step.

Consulting a Reader

Asking someone else to read the paper is another helpful revision technique:

- If you have problems reading your own words objectively, ask someone else to read the paper to you.
- If you are going to automatically assume that readers will know what you are writing about, ask someone to read your paper and then answer questions about it. This way you can find out what parts of your paper readers might have difficulty understanding.

Here are some things to consider when working with another reader in revising:

- Make sure the reader has time to really consider your paper.
- Tell the reader what your assignment is.
- Tell the reader not to correct grammar or comment on your handwriting or typing skills.
- Make sure the reader knows that he or she is helping you improve the paper, not praising or attacking the paper (or you!).
- Ask the reader to follow the same steps that you follow in revising.
- Ask the reader for specific feedback on what works and what doesn't, as well as for suggestions on how to improve.
- Check out possible solutions with your reader. If your reader says that one of your examples is unclear, try out another example before writing it into your paper.
- Accept your readers' comments as their attempt to be helpful and don't argue with them. You will decide what to change about your paper, so you don't need to defend your work.

Evaluating Your Thesis

ESL **Does Your Thesis Address the Prompt?**   Remember that your thesis is the answer to a prompt and must clearly respond to it. Let's look again at Mark Mathabane's "My Father's Tribal Rule" (pp. 40–44) and the prompt we have been using.

✔ Checking the Prompt

Do the **key focus words** from the prompt appear in the thesis?

Do the actions you are performing in the thesis match the **key action** specified in the prompt?

Mathabane says he despises rules and rituals. Is he correct in thinking that rules and rituals have no purpose or value?

Let's now look at some thesis sentences and analyze how well each of them answers the prompt.

- **Thesis 1: Mathabane talks about rules and rituals. I agree with him.** This thesis does contain the key words "rules" and "rituals," but it does not connect rules and rituals to the remaining key words "purpose" and "value." Saying what a writer "talks about" does not explain the writer's idea. Since the idea is not explained or restated, readers will not understand what the writer is agreeing with when the student writes "I agree with him."

- **Thesis 2: In the essay, Mathabane talks about how he hates the rules and rituals his father made him do. I have to follow stupid rules too.** This thesis also contains the key words "rules" and "rituals" and states Mathabane's attitude toward his father's rules and rituals. This statement almost gets to the key words "purpose" and "value" by mentioning hate, which implies that Mathabane does not see any purpose or value in the rules and rituals he discusses. The second sentence of the thesis does contain the writer's response but it does not fulfill the requirements of the prompt because it does not agree or disagree. It just compares experiences. While the word "stupid" is similar to the word "hate" and implies a judgment of value and purpose, it does not clearly state whether there is purpose and value in the rules and rituals Mathabane and the writer had to follow.

- **Thesis 3: It's wrong for parents to punish their children for not obeying their rules or following their rituals.** This thesis does contain some of the key words but it does not complete the key action given in the prompt—to agree or disagree with Mathabane's attitude toward the purpose and value of rules and rituals. Whether or not parents should punish their children for not obeying rules or following rituals is not the same issue as whether those rules and rituals have purpose and value. The idea of obedience and punishment is not related to the question posed in the prompt.

- **Thesis 4: Mathabane is wrong because rules and rituals do help young people grow up to be good adults.** This thesis does state the direction of the paper—that rules and rituals help young people grow up to be good adults. However, unless the writer has already explained what Mathabane believes about rules and rituals, this sentence alone does not fully reflect Mathabane's idea although it is more specific about the writer's idea.

Let's look at the thesis of the paper drafted in Chapter 10 (pp. 158–160) and check to see that it addresses the prompt:

> Mathabane writes about his hatred of rules and rituals in "My Father's Tribal Rule," but I think that rules and rituals do have purpose and value.

This thesis does contain the key words—"rules," "rituals," "purpose," and "value." It also implies the key action of disagreeing (as shown in the word "but." However, it doesn't clearly state Mathabane's ideas.)

> Mathabane writes that he hates rules and rituals in "My Father's Tribal Rule." Although Mathabane disliked rules and rituals he didn't see that they can be valuable and that they do have a purpose.

Using "that" instead of "about" and adding the phrase "although Mathabane disliked rules and rituals" reveals Mathabane's ideas more clearly. The phrase "he didn't see that" makes it clear that the writer sees purpose and value that Mathabane does not, implying disagreement.

Does Everything in Your Thesis Clearly Relate to the Prompt?   Once you have determined that you have addressed the prompt by using the key focus words and key action words, you will need to be sure that everything in your thesis is related to the prompt. Many times the parts of your thesis will be connected to the prompt, but that connection may not be clear to your reader.

Looking for Connections

1. State the connection between the parts of your paper.
2. Write that connection down.
3. Revise the connection to fit in your paper.

For example, consider the following thesis sentence:

> Mathabane is right to think that rules and rituals are worthless, especially when they have no purpose and they benefit no one. Rules are just something authority figures use to push people around. Furthermore, they can make you feel separated from other people.

The thesis does contain the key words—"rules," "rituals," and "purpose," and refers to "value" by using the word "worthless." It also performs the key action of agreeing (as shown in "Mathabane is right"). The second sentence of the thesis, however, is more about why we have rules than whether they have value.

Using the revising steps regarding connections, shown in the box above, state the relationship between the three ideas in the thesis and the answer that rules and rituals are worthless. The first idea is already connected:

> Rules and rituals are worthless, especially when they have no purpose and they benefit no one.

What is the connection between the answer and the second idea? You may conclude that if rules are just used to push people around, then they don't have a good purpose and so are worthless.

> Rules and rituals are worthless if their only purpose is so authority figures can push other people around.

What is the connection between the answer and the third idea? "Making people feel separated" is not really about a purpose; it's more about having a bad effect.

> Rules and rituals are worthless if they make you feel separated from other people.

Now we can put the parts of the thesis back together again, showing the relationship between the answer and each of the main ideas.

> Rules and rituals are worthless when they have no purpose and benefit no one, if their only purpose is so authority figures can push people around, and if they make you feel separated from other people.

| **EXERCISE 11.1** | **Revise thesis sentences 1–4 on page 166.** |

| **EXERCISE 11.2** | **Use the suggestions for revision to evaluate how well the following thesis sentences match the writing prompts. Revise them if necessary.** |

1. Mathabane writes less about his mother than about his father or himself. What is the significance of her role in the family? Do you think other women play similar roles in their families?

   A. Mathabane's mother plays an important role in his family.

   B. I agree with Mathabane that women play the role of peacemaker in their families.

   C. I think other women play similar roles in their families as Mathabane's mother.

   D. The women I know are caregivers, peacemakers, and housewives, just like Mathabane's mother.

2. Mathabane has a conflict with his father. Do parents and children always have conflicts? Why or why not?

   A. No, they don't have to have conflicts if parents would just consider their children's feelings.

   B. I have conflicts with my parents just like Mathabane.

   C. Yes, because the older generation never understands the younger generation.

   D. Parents and children have to have conflicts in order for the children to grow into independent adults.

3. Mathabane says he despises rules and rituals. Is he correct in thinking that rules and rituals have no purpose or value?

   A. I disagree with Mathabane because rituals do have a purpose even though children are not able to understand.

   B. I agree with Mathabane because I had to make similar choices and I resented them.

   C. Mathabane is correct in saying that rules and rituals have no purpose or value.

   D. Although rituals do have good purposes, parents should allow their children the freedom to choose between the family's rituals and those of their friends.

STEP 2. CHECKING STRUCTURE AND ORGANIZATION

Are All the Parts of the Essay Present?

Label the parts of your paper (**introduction**, **body** paragraphs, and **conclusion**). If you cannot find one of the parts, the chances are that your reader won't either. You will need to write the missing part.

As we discussed in Chapters 8–10, you would expect to have the components shown here in any essay responding to a reading:

Parts of an Essay

Introduction
- A lead-in
- An overview of the reading
- A thesis statement (responding to the prompt)
- A plan of development

Body paragraphs
- A topic sentence (with transitions in paragraphs 3 and 4)
- A focus on a specific area of the reading
- An example from the writer's experiences
- A point to conclude the paragraph

Conclusion
- The author's thesis or point of the reading you're discussing
- The main points from the reading you're discussing
- The main points you have made in response to the reading
- A restatement of the thesis (reworded so it isn't a repetition of the thesis in the introduction)

Using the checklist on page 169, label the parts of the following essay.

Rules and rituals are things people do. Everyday we follow some kind of rules. We also participate in rituals, although we might not know it. Mark Mathabane knew he participated in rituals. More than he wanted to. He lived with his family in a poor section of South Africa. His father was from the tribes, but they were now living around people who had accepted modern ways. Ways that Mathabane wanted to follow. His father insisted that the whole family follow tribal rules and rituals, and he became angry and violent when Mathabane wouldn't obey the rules or follow the traditions. Mathabane writes about his hatred of rules and rituals in "My Father's Tribal Rule" but I think that rules and rituals do have purpose and value.

Mathabane tells about the rule his father had about not speaking at the table. He tells us that "One day I intentionally broke one of these laws." He spoke during dinner and his father got really mad then he threatened to beat Mathabane. What Mathabane didn't understand was that his father got mad because Mathabane wasn't respecting him. In my family, we have a dinnertime ritual too. Before dinner, my brothers and my sister and I are supposed to clean the house and get everything ready for dinner. One day I didn't feel like doing it, because I have to do everything. My brothers and my sister hardly do anything and I didn't think it was fair that they played in the yard with their friends while I was working. So, I just sat on the couch and watched T.V. My father came in and saw me and started to yell at me. He said he worked hard every day to put food on the table and that I was showing disrespect to him, my mother, my brothers and my sister. He sent me to bed without supper. At first I was really mad. But the more I thought about it, the more I felt bad for not respecting my father. I learned through this rule to respect my father, Mathabane didn't see the valuable things you can learn from rules.

Following rituals can also help us be more mature. Mathabane showed that he was immature because he disobeyed his father simply for the purpose of rebelling. He had no reason to talk at the table except he wanted to make his father angry and see what he would do. When I was younger, I was suppose to clean my room first thing every Saturday morning. Since I would rather play than clean my room, I would put it off as long as possible. If I had been more mature, I would have realized that cleaning my room was my responsibility and I would have done it without trying to get out of it. Also I should have realized that my jobs before dinner were my jobs, whether my brothers and sister did their jobs are not should not have mattered. Being that I was the oldest, I should have had the maturity to set a good example for them by obeying the rules. Mathabane could have shown his maturity by obeying his father's rules rather than disobeying him just because he didn't like it. Doing rituals, particularly if they aren't ones we enjoy, builds maturity because we will have to do things we don't like our whole lives.

Mathabane tells us about his little brother George. It was time for George to be weaned and so "she smeared her breasts with red pepper and then invited my brother to suckle." Of course, George's mouth must have burned like fire so he stopped nursing. Mathabane thought, "It was amusing to witness my mother do it." He just saw this ritual as being funny. He didn't understand that it had a purpose "to mark George's passage from infancy to childhood." Some rituals help us to grow up and realize our new responsibilities. My friend Alan went through a passage similar to George's. Alan's family has alot of money. His parents had bought cars for his older brother and sister when they turned sixteen. They bought Alan one when he turned sixteen, but they told him that driving a car meant that he had to be very responsible. They told him that driving a car meant that he was no longer a kid, he was now a adult. It's strange, but owning that car really did change him. I guess he realized that you can't act irresponsibly when your driving several tons of steel.

Also, the rituals we do everyday can help the whole family. Mathabane had to do "rituals spanning the range of day-to-day living." Everybody does daily rituals. In our house, these daily rituals are divided up. Every evening before bed, for instance, its my job to make sure all the doors are locked and the windows shut and latched. My sister irons my father's shirts so he'll have a fresh one for work. My father gets lunch ready for everybody. My mother supervises and helps who ever needs help. Although Mathabane may be confused by these rituals, I'm not.

In conclusion, Mathabane just doesn't get it. He thinks rules and rituals are just a waste of time. He doesn't see how they can help us learn to respect others and be more courteous to them. I think that Mathabane was too immature to understand that rituals can help us grow up. They can help develop self-responsibility, which is something most people could use more of. Basically he wrong. Rules and rituals are something you should follow and practice. If everyone followed the rules and rituals they were taught at home, the world would be a better place.

Does the Main Idea of Each Body Paragraph Correspond to Some Part of the Thesis?

ESL Since the main ideas of each body paragraph are ways of supporting the thesis, the main ideas and the thesis should match. If they don't match, you have two options. You can revise the main idea and paragraph that does not match the thesis, or you can revise the thesis so that it includes the main idea.

However, if you choose this second option, you must be sure that your thesis still answers the prompt.

Let's now look at the revised thesis sentence from the essay drafted in Chapter 10, and reprinted on pages 170–171, along with a list of the main ideas from each of the body paragraphs.

> Mathabane writes about his hatred of rules and rituals in "My Father's Tribal Rule" but I think that rules and rituals do have purpose and value.

■ **Main idea of body paragraph 1:** There is no clear main idea in this paragraph that states a general purpose or value of rules and rituals. The two examples (Mathabane's experience and the writer's experience) are clearly related, but there is not one sentence that clearly ties them together. Using the checklist Looking for Connections on page 167, state the connection between the two examples and write that connection down.

> Rules and rituals help us learn to show respect for others.

While the main idea of a body paragraph does not have to be the first sentence, it is often helpful to have a clear topic sentence to begin the first body paragraph. Inserting this sentence at the beginning of the paragraph helps your reader connect your thesis and your first body paragraph.

■ **Main idea of body paragraph 2:**

> Following rituals can also help us be more mature.

This main idea is the first sentence of the paragraph and is clearly related to the thesis since it states another benefit or value of rituals.

■ **Main idea of body paragraph 3:**

> Some rituals help us to grow up and realize our new responsibilities.

In other body paragraphs, it may be helpful to give some introductory information before the main idea. The first six sentences of this paragraph provide that information, which leads into the seventh sentence. It is this sentence that really states the idea that governs the body paragraph.

■ **Main idea of body paragraph 4:**

> Also, the rituals we do everyday can help the whole family.

This main idea is the first sentence of the paragraph and is clearly related to the thesis since it states another benefit or value of rituals.

EXERCISE 11.4   **Use the suggestions for revision to evaluate how well the following main ideas match the corresponding thesis sentences:**

1. Parents and children have to have conflicts in order for the children to grow into independent adults.

    A. Children have to learn to think for themselves.

    B. It's normal for children to break rules just for fun and to find out what will happen.

    C. Parents are old-fashioned and children want to keep up with the times by listening to the newest music and wearing the coolest clothes.

    D. Parents do know what's best but children still have to rebel.

2. If children honor their parents the way they should, then parents and children won't have conflicts.

    A. Honoring parents means obeying them.

    B. Children should obey their parents until they are at least 18 and out on their own.

    C. Conflicts are okay between parents and children as long as children learn that their parents are always right.

    D. When children have kids of their own, then they'll understand that their parents were right.

3. Like Mathabane's mother, the women I know act as peacemakers, caregivers, and teachers in their families.

    A. Many women act as peacemakers, making sure family members talk to each other instead of sulking.

    B. Most women take care of the children and the men in the family.

    C. Many modern men are also taking care of the children.

    D. Whenever I didn't understand why my parents wouldn't let me do something I wanted to do, my aunt would always explain in a way that I could understand their point.

Are the Paragraphs Arranged in the Best Order?

You will want to give your ideas in an order that your reader will understand and that will have the effect on the reader that you want. Since the purpose, audience, and effect for every writing task is different, no one **organization** will fit every time. You will want to choose the organization that is most appropriate for what you are trying to do in your essay.

The order of the paragraphs should reveal a reason—in other words, the reader can see why the paragraphs are ordered as they are. (Review the types of organization presented on drafting in Chapter 7.)

Often when responding to a reading, inexperienced writers organize their paper by discussing the reading in one section and their own ideas and experiences in another. While this can be an acceptable way to organize an essay, it also tends to be simplistic and should be avoided.

EXERCISE 11.5

Turn back to the essay on pages 170–171, and do the following.

1. Write down the thesis of the paper. Then list the main idea of each paragraph below the thesis.

2. Using the suggestions for organization presented in this chapter, determine the organizational pattern the writer has used for ordering the body paragraphs.

3. Suggest a more effective order for the body paragraphs. Be sure that you can explain why you think your order is more effective.

For more practice, complete steps 2 and 3 with the thesis and main ideas listed below.

■ Thesis

Mathabane is right to think that rules and rituals are worthless. Rules and rituals are worthless when they have no purpose and benefit no one, if their only purpose is so authority figures can push people around, and if they make you feel separated from other people.

■ Main idea of body paragraph 1

Rules and rituals are worthless if they make you feel separated from other people.

■ Main idea of body paragraph 2

Parents should always explain why they want their children to follow their rules when they are different from their friends.

■ Main idea of body paragraph 3

The problem is not that parents insist that the children keep the ritual; it's that parents don't explain to the children what the ritual means and why it is important.

■ Main idea of body paragraph 4

In addition to lessons about respecting others, rituals can teach us about traditions.

STEP 3. CHECKING DEVELOPMENT

Evaluating Your Introduction

How many paragraphs make up your introduction? In short papers, usually one paragraph is enough. Often students will write one paragraph for the **lead-in**, one for the summary of the reading, and one for their thesis. However, if these sections are relatively short, they should be combined into one introductory paragraph.

In Chapter 8, we suggested a five-part introduction when responding to a reading. At this point, you need to check your introduction to see if the essay includes these sections and if what you have written fits together. Beginning writers tend to evaluate the introduction as a whole to see if it all makes sense together. However, good revising requires that you break the introduction into its parts and evaluate each part by itself to ensure that it can stand alone and still make sense to the reader.

Evaluating Your Lead-in   The lead-in should include all material after the title of the essay until the summary of the reading. Now that you have separated it from the rest of the introduction, evaluate your lead-in based on the checklist below.

Checklist for Lead-ins

Does the introduction include a lead-in?

Is the lead-in too long and/or too detailed for the paper?

Is the lead-in too short and/or too sparse for the paper?

Does the lead-in relate to the summary of the reading and the thesis?

Does the lead-in present interesting material that makes the reader want to continue reading?

Let's look at the following lead-in for an essay.

> Rules and rituals are things people do. Everyday we follow some kind of rules. We also participate in rituals, although we might not no it. Mark Mathabane knew he participated in rituals. More than he wanted too.

The lead-in introduces the topic of rules and rituals and but says nothing about purpose and value. In addition, the information provided is not especially helpful—"things people do" does not distinguish rules and rituals from many other things—or interesting.

To revise, you might want to go back to Chapter 8 and review the types of lead-ins you can choose from. Here's an example of a more compelling lead-in:

> As a child, I assumed that every family did things exactly like mine did. It wasn't until I spent a summer vacation with my best friend's family that I realized this wasn't true. The members of his family got up and grabbed a poptart for breakfast whenever they were hungry, while my family always sat down to pancakes or scrambled eggs every morning. In my family, we all had assigned chores, but in his family, his mother took care of the house by herself. That summer I learned that I participated in rules and rituals that other families didn't necessarily follow. Mark Mathabane knew he participated in rituals. More than he wanted too.

This new lead-in provides a story, a technique that often can catch a reader's interest. The story also provides an example of a ritual and of a rule so the writer doesn't have to actually define them. In addition, this lead-in provides a direct connection to the summary of the reading—the idea of realizing that the writer participated in rituals.

| **EXERCISE 11.6** | Using the checklist for lead-ins on page 175, evaluate the effectiveness of the following lead-ins to essays on this topic. |

1. My father had weird rules when I was young.

2. Do you have to follow rules?

3. Rules are good for young people.

4. Webster defines rules as "an authoritative prescribed direction for conduct." Webster defines rituals as "a ceremonial act or series of such acts."

5. Have you ever been to South Africa? Have you ever had to wear tribal clothes?

Evaluating the Summary   Based on the model we've discussed in this book, the **summary** of the reading is the material between the lead-in and the thesis. It includes information about the reading and the author's thesis. Once you have separated your summary of the reading from the rest of the introduction, evaluate it based on the checklist below.

Summary of the Reading

Does the summary adequately introduce the reading and the author of the reading?

Does the summary really address the main point of the reading?

Does the summary provide adequate information for the reader to understand how the summary relates to the lead-in?

Does the summary provide adequate information for the reader to understand how the summary relates to the thesis?

Let's look at the summary from the essay:

> He lived with his family in a poor section of South Africa. His father was from the tribes, but they were now living around people who had accepted modern ways. Ways that Mathabane wanted to follow. His father insisted that the whole family follow tribal rules and rituals, and he became angry and violent when Mathabane wouldn't obey the rules or follow the traditions.

This summary does include the author of the reading but not the title. You may remember that the title is mentioned in the thesis, but it may be more helpful to your reader to move it to where you first mention the author.

> In Mathabane's essay "My Father's Tribal Rule," he says that he lived with his family in a poor section of South Africa.

The rest of the summary does give background information that helps the reader understand the context of the main idea, but it does not clearly state the main idea that relates to the thesis. Remember that the thesis also refers to Mathabane's attitude toward rules and rituals, so you may be able to state the main idea there.

> Mathabane writes about his hatred of rules and rituals in "My Father's Tribal Rule" but I think that rules and rituals do have purpose and value.

This sentence doesn't state Mathabane's attitude toward rules and rituals; it merely mentions his hatred of them. The word "about" forces you to write a topic, not an idea. Try using the word "that" instead. You have already used the title of the reading, so you can leave it out here. In addition, you need to connect Mathabane's hatred of rules and rituals and your view that rules and rituals do have value and purpose.

> Mathabane writes that he hates his father's rules and rituals. Because he disliked rules and rituals, he didn't see that they can be valuable and that they do have a purpose.

Put back together, the new summary might look like this:

> In Mathabane's essay "My Father's Tribal Rule," he says that he lived with his family in a poor section of South Africa. His father was from the tribes, but they were now living around people who had accepted modern ways. Ways that Mathabane wanted to follow. His father insisted that the whole family follow tribal rules and rituals, and he became angry and violent when Mathabane wouldn't obey the rules or follow the traditions. Mathabane writes that he hates his father's rules and rituals. Because he disliked rules and rituals, he didn't see that they can be valuable and that they do have a purpose.

Summary Revision Tip

Use the word "that" before you restate an author's idea rather than the word "about." "That" forces you to state the author's idea, not just the topic of the author's essay.

EXERCISE 11.7 **Using the suggestions for writing summaries, evaluate the effectiveness of the following summaries for essays on this topic.**

Mark Mathabane tells how he grew up in South Africa. His brother was weaned and his father wears tribal clothes. His father beat him for talking at the table. Now Mathabane hates his father and his tribal rules.

In this story Mark Mathabane is embarrassed by his father who wears tribal clothes and follows tribal rules.

Mark Mathabane writes how he hates rules and rituals because his father beat him.

Mark writes about the rules and rituals his father made him follow when he was living in South Africa. He writes about not being able to talk while eating and about how embarrassed he was when his friends teased him about his father's old fashioned clothes.

In this story, Mark Mathabane writes that he disliked following his father's rules and rituals. When his mother weans his brother by smearing hot stuff on her breast, he thinks this is funny. But when his father insists on wearing tribal clothes, he is embarrassed. His father won't let him speak any language other than the one his tribe speaks, so Mathabane gets in trouble when he speaks the languages his friends speak because he doesn't want to be different. Mathabane also speaks at the dinner table even though his father tells him not to. As punishment, Mathabane has to perform even more rituals that are supposed to help keep the family safe and bring them more money, and he ends up hating his father even more.

Evaluating the Thesis and Plan of Development   The last part of your introduction should be your thesis and plan of development. Once you have separated these parts from the rest of the introduction, evaluate them based on the checklist below.

Checking the Thesis and Plan of Development

Does the thesis clearly relate to the lead-in and the summary of the reading?

Does the thesis clearly relate to the plan of development?

Is the plan of development necessary for the paper?

Is the plan of development clearly stated?

Since we have revised the thesis, we need to check again to see that it addresses the prompt.

Mathabane writes that he hates his father's rules and rituals. Because he disliked rules and rituals, he didn't see that they can be valuable and that they do have a purpose.

The thesis contains the key words "rules," "rituals," "valuable," and "purpose," and it implies the key action disagree by the phrase "he didn't see that."

This thesis clearly relates to the summary since the summary and thesis sentence are combined. However, the thesis has no plan of development. Since the thesis does not indicate how the writer will support his idea that rules and rituals do have value and purpose, it would be helpful to have a plan of development.

To write a plan of development, the writer would need to look back at the main ideas of each paragraph and include an indication of these ideas in the thesis or in another sentence immediately following the thesis.

■ Main idea of body paragraph 1

Rules and rituals help us learn to show respect for others.

■ Main idea of body paragraph 2

Following rituals can also help us be more mature.

■ Main idea of body paragraph 3

Some rituals help us to grow up and realize our new responsibilities.

■ Main idea of body paragraph 4

Also, the rituals we do everyday can help the whole family.

These main ideas can be summarized into the following plan of development.

Rules and rituals can teach us many things. They can teach respect, growing up, and helping the whole family.

In summarizing the main ideas, you may notice that the main ideas of paragraphs 2 and 3 are very similar; in fact, we have summarized them into a single idea in our plan of development. We will have to look at these paragraphs when we revise them to be sure that we do indeed have two different ideas and aren't writing two paragraphs on the same idea.

The new introduction would read as follows:

As a child, I assumed that every family did things exactly like mine did. It wasn't until I spent a summer vacation with my best friend's family that I realized this wasn't true. The members of his family got up and grabbed a poptart for breakfast whenever they were hungry, while my family always sat down to pancakes or scrambled eggs every morning. In my family, we all had assigned chores, but in his family, his mother took care of the house by herself. That summer I learned that I participated in rules and rituals that other families didn't necessarily follow. Mark Mathabane knew he participated in rituals. More than he wanted too. In Mathabane's essay "My Father's Tribal Rule," he says that he lived with his family in a poor section of South Africa. His father was from the tribes, but they were now living around people who had accepted modern ways. Ways that Mathabane wanted to follow. His father insisted that the whole family follow tribal rules and rituals, and he became angry and violent when Mathabane wouldn't obey the rules or follow the traditions. Mathabane writes that he hates his father's rules and rituals. Because he disliked rules and rituals, he didn't see that they can be valuable and that they do have a purpose. Rules and rituals can teach us many things. They can teach respect, growing up, and helping the whole family.

Evaluating Your Body Paragraphs

 What Is Development?   **Development** is the pairing of an idea with an illustration or example and with an explanation. This pairing has to be present; it is not enough to give just the idea or just the example. You must provide both the example and the idea you are trying to prove as well as show the connection between them. As you evaluated your prewriting (see Chapter 7), you paired your ideas with examples that supported them, identifying them as general or specific. You also stated how the example supported the idea or what you were trying to prove with the example. It is this explicit connection that many beginning writers omit. When you revise, you should look for places where you need to add these explanations.

Is Each Idea Adequately Supported?   Beginning writers tend to write too little when explaining their ideas. They assume that their readers know more than they do and that the readers can understand the whole idea from being told just a little of it. Experienced writers have a different attitude. They assume that they know more about their ideas and how they connect to the reading that readers do. They are skilled at explaining ideas as fully as possible. These explanations are the supporting information that you promised your readers in the plan of development that you wrote in your introduction.

Let's look at an example that shows the impact of adding adequate development. Suppose you are writing an essay in which you are arguing that some families are abusing the welfare system. You may use a neighbor as an example:

Some families abuse the welfare system. For example, my neighbors Lou and Ellen receive food stamps to help feed their five kids. Ellen is also pregnant with her sixth, so she'll be getting even more of my tax money. Her husband drives a very nice truck, while my husband drives an old truck that his father gave him. It's not fair that they get help and have a better truck than we do.

The writer has a main idea (some families abuse the welfare system) and a specific example but has not connected the example to the main idea. Adding an explanation of how this example shows families abusing the welfare system will provide adequate development. The writer might add the following sentences to her paragraph:

> Families like my neighbors who accept welfare money to pay for essentials such as food and diapers so they can afford big fancy cars are abusing the welfare system. They could be more like my family and drive a less expensive truck so they could buy their own food and clothing without help from the government.

"Adequate" development is defined as development that is explained in enough detail that the reader understands why it is in the paper, how it connects to the main idea, and how it proves or supports that idea. One way to check for the adequacy of your development is to ask yourself if you would accept the development as a convincing and understandable explanation of the main idea.

Development Using the Reading   Beginning writers tend to use ideas and specifics from the reading without showing the connection between the idea from the reading and the ideas in their essay. Revision is the time to add these connections so that readers will know why the material from the reading is being used and how it relates to the writer's ideas. To evaluate your use of the reading, use the checklist below.

Checking the Use of the Reading

Does the material from the reading clearly relate to your idea?

Have you used the reading accurately?

Have you acknowledged the author when using his or her ideas or words?

Have you used the reading appropriately and adequately?

We have spent much time on connecting ideas, so you should be well prepared to attempt the first question. Now we will help you address the other questions in the checklist.

Beginning writers tend to use ideas, examples, and thoughts from the reading but without letting the reader know that these ideas and examples *came* from the reading. Beginning writers also tend to use parts of an essay out of **context**—that is, they select words or details to fit into their essay but misrepresent what the original author intended or change the meaning or purpose of the original author's words. You may be more familiar with how some politicians use the same tactic. They may intentionally take a phrase from an opponent's speech and use it to mean something entirely different from what the opponent originally said.

During revision, you need to find each place in your essay where you have used words, ideas, or examples from the reading. Then use the following steps to help you identify ways to improve your use of the reading:

1. Underline each place in the essay where you have used the reading.
2. Find the specific part of the reading that you have used.
3. Reread the section from the reading and the place in your essay. If your essay does not accurately and fairly reflect that section of the reading, revise that part of your essay.
4. Ask yourself, "What would the author say about how I've used this part of the reading?" If you can imagine the author protesting that you are being unfair, you need to revise.

Remember that you can show that you agree or disagree with an author without misrepresenting that person's words or ideas by writing careful connections between the material from the reading and your own ideas.

For the third question in the reading checklist, you will need to look at two parts of your essay:

■   Look at the parts of your essay you've underlined to indicate that they refer to the reading. Be sure that your readers will be able to tell which part of your essay came from the reading and which part is your own. If the difference is not clear, revise to give credit to the author for his or her words, ideas, or examples.

■   Look at the rest of your essay (that is, the parts of your essay that you haven't underlined). Have any of the author's words or examples slipped into these parts as well? If so, acknowledge that they belong to the author.

Finally, you will want to look at the amount of your essay that you've underlined to judge whether you have used enough development from the reading. You don't want to use so much of the reading that your ideas are getting lost or that the reading takes up more of the essay than your own ideas; on the other hand, you don't want to use so little of the reading that you aren't fulfilling the assignment.

OWN **Development Using Your Own Ideas and Experiences**   In Chapter 7 we looked at establishing the relationship between examples and ideas. At the beginning of this section, we reviewed this crucial part of development. Just as you checked the parts of your essay where you've used the reading to be sure that you have explained how the reading is connected to your ideas, you must use the same process when you are working with examples from your own ideas and experiences.

In addition, you will want to make sure that your examples truly **support** your ideas and don't contradict them. Finally, you will want to be sure that your examples are different from those used in the reading and not just a rewriting of the author's examples. For example, if the author uses his cousin who dropped out of school as an example and you use your aunt who dropped out of school as an example to prove the same point, your readers will think that you are imitating the author, not adding your own example.

Use the checklist below as a reminder of these steps as you evaluate your development using your own ideas and experiences.

Using Your Own Ideas and Experiences

Do your own examples clearly relate to your idea?

Do your own examples truly support your idea?

Are your examples different enough from the author's that it's clear you aren't just repeating the same example?

Revising a Body Paragraph　Let's look at the first body paragraph from the essay on pages 170–171 including the changes made this far in the revision process.

> Rules and rituals help us learn to show respect for others. Mathabane tells about the rule his father had about not speaking at the table. He tells us that "One day I intentionally broke one of these laws." He spoke during dinner and his father got really mad then he threatened to beat Mathabane. What Mathabane didn't understand was that his father got mad because Mathabane wasn't respecting him. In my family, we have a dinnertime ritual too. Before dinner, my brothers and my sister and I are supposed to clean the house and get everything ready for dinner. One day I didn't feel like doing it, because I have to do everything. My brothers and my sister hardly do anything and I didn't think it was fair that they played in the yard with their friends while I was working. So, I just sat on the couch and watched TV. My father came in and saw me and started to yell at me. He said he worked hard every day to put food on the table and that I was showing disrespect to him, my mother, my brothers and my sister. He sent me to bed without supper. At first I was really mad. But the more I thought about it, the more I felt bad for not respecting my father. I learned through this rule to respect my father, Mathabane didnt see the valuable things you can learn from rules.

This paragraph has the needed parts: a main idea, an example and explanation from the reading, an example and explanation from the writer, and a concluding point that ties the two examples back to the main idea.

The example from the reading accurately describes Mathabane's experience and clearly relates it to the main idea of the paragraph. The writer has included enough information from the reading so that readers understand what happened and that Mathabane misunderstood the purpose of the ritual, showing respect for his father.

The example from the writer's own experience also gives enough information—it describes the rule and it shows how the writer learned to show respect for his father. However, it loses its focus and talks about the rule being unfair. The sentence underlined below gets off track.

In my family, we have a dinnertime ritual too. Before dinner, my brothers and my sister and I are supposed to clean the house and get everything ready for dinner. One day I didn't feel like doing it, because I have to do everything. <u>My brothers and my sister hardly do anything and I didn't think it was fair that they played in the yard with their friends while I was working.</u> So, I just sat on the couch and watched TV. My father came in and saw me and started to yell at me. He said he worked hard every day to put food on the table and that I was showing disrespect to him, my mother, my brothers and my sister. He sent me to bed without supper. At first I was really mad. But the more I thought about it, the more I felt bad for not respecting my father.

Because body paragraphs should be clearly focused on the main idea, the sentence underlined could be omitted.

Body Paragraphs 2 and 3   When we looked at the main ideas of these two paragraphs to ensure that they matched the thesis, we noted that they seemed very similar. To revise these paragraphs, we need to look at both of them together and decide if we have two different ideas or if we are writing two different paragraphs about the same idea.

Following rituals can also help us be more mature. Mathabane showed that he was immature because he disobeyed his father simply for the purpose of rebelling. He had no reason to talk at the table except he wanted to make his father angry and see what he would do. When I was younger, I was suppose to clean my room first thing every Saturday morning. Since I would rather play than clean my room, I would put it off as long as possible. If I had been more mature, I would have realized that cleaning my room was my responsibility and I would have done it without trying to get out of it. Also I should have realized that my jobs before dinner were my jobs, whether my brothers and sister did their jobs are not should not have mattered. Being that I was the oldest, I should have had the maturity to set a good example for them by obeying the rules. Mathabane could have shown his maturity by obeying his father's rules rather than disobeying him just because he didn't like it. Doing rituals, particularly if they aren't ones we enjoy, builds maturity because we will have to do things we don't like our whole lives.

Some rituals help us to grow up and realize our new responsibilities. Mathabane tells us about his little brother George. It was time for George to be weaned and so "she smeared her breasts with red pepper and then invited my brother to suckle." Of course, George's mouth must have burned like fire so he stopped nursing. Mathabane thought, "It was amusing to witness my mother do it." He just saw this ritual as being funny. He didn't understand that it had a purpose "to mark George's passage from infancy to childhood." Some rituals help us to grow up and realize our new responsibilities. My friend Alan went through a passage similar to George's. Alan's family has alot of money. His parents had bought cars for his older brother and sister when they turned sixteen. They bought Alan one when he turned sixteen, but they told him that driving a car meant that he had to be very responsible. They told him that driving a car meant that he was no longer a kid he was now a adult. It's strange, but owning that car really did change him. I guess he realized that you can't act irresponsibly when your driving several tons of steel.

Checking for Repeated Ideas

Can you state the difference between the two ideas? If you can, the ideas are different.

Can you switch the examples supporting one idea with the examples supporting the other idea and still have valid support? If you can, your ideas are probably the same.

In the body paragraphs above, let's focus on the difference between the following two ideas:

Following rituals can also help us be more mature.

Some rituals help us to grow up and realize our new responsibilities.

Most people would define "mature" as meaning "growing up" and "becoming more responsible"; thus these two ideas are very similar.

Is it possible to switch the examples in each paragraph? While we couldn't just pick up the support from one paragraph and use it as support for the other with no changes, we could very easily reword the examples to fit the idea in the other paragraph.

All of this shows us that we do not need both paragraphs. We now have two choices:

Combine the paragraphs in some way.

Eliminate one paragraph.

Although either choice may work, we need to make the choice that strengthens this particular paper. We are going to eliminate the second paragraph and keep the third because it allows us to bring in two entirely new but relevant examples instead of reusing the same ones we discussed in the first body paragraph.

Notice that there is some good writing in the discarded paragraph. However, leaving it there would have made the paper less effective because it simply repeats what is better said somewhere else. As painful as this process may be, we often have to throw out perfectly good examples, ideas, or even whole paragraphs for the sake of an entire paper.

Now we need to evaluate how well we have used the reading and our own examples in the third body paragraph.

> Mathabane tells us about his little brother George. It was time for George to be weaned and so "she smeared her breasts with red pepper and then invited my brother to suckle." Of course, George's mouth must have burned like fire so he stopped nursing. Mathabane thought, "It was amusing to witness my mother do it." He just saw this ritual as being funny. He didn't understand that it had a purpose "to mark George's passage from infancy to childhood." Some rituals help us to grow up and realize our new responsibilities.

The reading is used accurately, and the writer has quoted the words taken from Mathabane's essay. But is it clear how George's weaning is related to helping George to "grow up and realize new responsibilities"? Perhaps adding another sentence would help explain what has changed for George:

> Mathabane tells us about his little brother George. It was time for George to be weaned and so "she smeared her breasts with red pepper and then invited my brother to suckle." Of course, George's mouth must have burned like fire so he stopped nursing. Mathabane thought, "It was amusing to witness my mother do it." He just saw this ritual as being funny. He didn't understand that it had a purpose "to mark George's passage from infancy to childhood." <u>George would no longer be nursed like a baby. He would now have to eat and act like a child. Like the ritual to wean George,</u> some rituals help us to grow up and realize our new responsibilities.

The underlined sentences help explain how the weaning ritual fits the category of rituals that "help us to grow up and realize our new responsibilities."

Now let's look at an example from the writer's own experience:

> My friend Alan went through a passage similar to George's. Alan's family has alot of money. His parents had bought cars for his older brother and sister when they turned sixteen. They bought Alan one when he turned sixteen, but they told him that driving a car meant that he had to be very responsible. They told him that driving a car meant that he was no longer a kid he was now a adult. It's strange, but owning that car really did change him. I guess he realized that you can't act irresponsibly when your driving several tons of steel.

This example is clearly connected to the rest of the paragraph by the first sentence. While the story itself is a good example, we have no sense of what changed for Alan, so adding a couple of details to show the difference would help.

> It's strange, but owning that car really did change him. <u>Instead of urging his friends to drive faster, Alan was very careful to drive the speed limit. Instead of blowing his money on the latest CD or a few slices of pizza, Alan saved his money to pay for gas and insurance.</u> I guess he realized that you can't act irresponsibly when your driving several tons of steel.

These underlined sentences, like the ones added to the example of George's weaning, help to show the growth that results from the ritual.

Body Paragraph 4 This paragraph does contain a main idea, an example from the reading, and an example from the writer.

> Also, the rituals we do everyday can help the whole family. Mathabane had to do "rituals spanning the range of day-to-day living." Everybody does daily rituals. In our house, these daily rituals are divided up. Every evening before bed, for instance, it's my job to make sure all the doors are locked and the windows shut and latched. My sister irons my father's shirts so he'll have a fresh one for work. My father gets lunch ready for everybody. My mother supervises and helps who ever needs help. Although Mathabane may be confused by these rituals, I'm not.

However, it does seem to be lacking. The example of the reading is only one sentence; this alone may be a clue that more information about these daily rituals could be added.

The transition between the two examples focuses on the fact that everyone does daily rituals. However, the focus of the paragraph is that daily rituals benefit everyone in the family. This is another area that can be revised.

Finally, the writer's example does list each person's rituals but does not relate each ritual to how it benefits the entire family.

The revised paragraph might look like this:

Also, the rituals we do everyday can help the whole family. Mathabane had to do "rituals spanning the range of day-to-day living." <u>These rituals are intended to bring good luck to the entire family, to protect the household, to keep family members healthy, and to ensure that the father keeps his job. All of these rituals benefit Mathabane, George, their mother, and their father. Each member of my family also does daily rituals that helps the rest of the family out.</u> Every evening before bed, for instance, it's my job to make sure all the doors are locked and the windows shut and latched, <u>my ritual keeps us safe from intruders.</u> My sister irons my father's shirts so he'll have a fresh one for work, <u>which helps him make a good impression on his job</u>. My father gets lunch ready for everybody <u>so we don't go hungry the next day</u>. My mother supervises and helps who ever needs help. <u>Our rituals help us work together to everyone's benefit.</u> Although Mathabane may be confused by these rituals, I'm not.

| EXERCISE 11.8 | **Evaluate the development in each of these paragraphs. The main idea is underlined for you:** |

<u>Another purpose of rituals is to teach family members to work together.</u> For example, Mark says that his father made him and his brother wear the ritual garb of the Venda tribe even though Mark's friends had shed their tribal cloth and embraced Western culture. The reason his father did this was so that the family would fit in with others in their tribe when the whites left South Africa and they revert to their old ways of living. Teaching children to work with other members of the family is good. The family needs to fit in with the rest of the tribe, too. In my family, my brothers and sisters and I had to clean up the house before dinner. As we got older, we got better and faster at having the house straight for my parents before dinner, this made supper time much calmer and meant that we sometimes had free time after dinner.

Within families, parents make their children do things that they think are valuable. Sometimes these things are different from what the children's friends do. <u>Parents should always explain why they want their children to follow their rules when they are different from their friends.</u> Of course, children still won't always agree with their parents reasons, and then their parents should allow them to choose which rituals to obey unless their is a very good reason. Mark's father should have let him wear Western clothes and speak Zulu with his friends instead of insisting that he stick to the tribal way of living. He certainly should not have beaten Mark for disobeying these rules. He also should have explained why he thought Mark should follow these rituals instead of just telling him he had to. My parents never let me go out on Halloween night with my friends.

They never explained why I couldn't go and I thought it was a really stupid rule. All of my friends would come back to school talking about how much fun they had and asking me why I hadn't gone. I would always make up something like I was sick so I wouldn't have to tell them my parents wouldn't let me. If my parents had explained, I might have not have lied.

<u>Most women take care of the children and the men in the family.</u> Although this is changing as more women go back to work, in most families it's the woman who stays home with the children, feeds them, changes diapers, takes care of them when they are sick, makes sure they have clean clothes and cleans the house. Even though my father knew how to do all of these things, he sat and watched television while my mother rushed around taking care of everything after she had worked as a waitress all day. On weekends when they were both off work, the children stayed with my mother. Even if she needed to go shopping and he was staying home, we all piled into the car with her so she could look out for us. Usually when we got back with the groceries, my dad had cut the grass and was asleep on the couch with the television on. When my mother had put up all the groceries, she would cook dinner for my father.

Evaluating Your Conclusion

The conclusion of a paper, like the last song in a concert, is the part of the performance that the audience or reader is most likely to remember. If you want a standing ovation, you need to conclude your paper with skill.

Use the following checklist to help you write a strong conclusion.

Checklist for Conclusions

Does the conclusion wrap up all the ideas in the essay without restating them exactly?

Does the conclusion avoid contradicting your paper or apologizing for your ideas and opinions?

Does the conclusion provide one more thing without bringing in new information or making wild claims?

Here is the conclusion from the essay on pages 170–171.

In conclusion, Mathabane just doesn't get it. He thinks rules and rituals are just a waste of time. He doesn't see how they can help us learn to respect others and be more courteous to them. I think that Mathabane was too immature to understand that rituals can help us grow up. They can help develop self-responsibility, which is something most people could use more of. Basically he wrong. Rules and rituals are something you should follow and practice. If everyone followed the rules and rituals they were taught at home, the world would be a better place.

This conclusion begins with a cliché opener (see Chapter 10 on drafting conclusions). You should not have to tell your readers you are presenting your conclusion.

This conclusion also restates only two of the main ideas—learning respect and growing up. To conclude the entire essay, the conclusion should also refer to the other main ideas.

In addition, it is jarring that the end of the conclusion switches to the second person (you):

Rules and rituals are something you should follow and practice.

This switch sounds strange coming at the end of this paper as well as preachy, since the writer is telling the reader how to behave. Changing "you" to "people" will help.

The end of this conclusion makes a claim:

If everyone followed the rules and rituals they were taught at home, the world would be a better place.

This is a rather large claim that readers may find unbelievable.

The revised version of this conclusion might look like this:

Mathabane just doesn't get it. He thinks rules and rituals are just a waste of time. He doesn't see how they can help us learn to respect others and be more courteous to them. I think that Mathabane was too immature to understand that rituals can help us grow up. They can help develop self-responsibility, which is something most people could use more of. In addition, if Mathabane had been less selfish, he'd know that rituals benefit everyone in the family. Basically he is wrong. Rules and rituals are something people should follow and practice. If everyone followed the rules and rituals they were taught at home, they could learn respect, responsibility, and how to help others.

EXERCISE 11.8 **Evaluate the following conclusions.**

In conclusion, Mathabane is right to think that rules and rituals are worthless. Rules and rituals are worthless when they have no purpose and benefit no one, if their only purpose is so authority figures can push people around, and if they make you feel separated from other people.

Rules and rituals are worthless when they have bad effects on people. Some rules are good because they teach us about tradition.

I agree with Mathabane that rules and rituals are worthless. For example, my high school wouldn't let us wear baseball caps in class. There was no purpose for this rule. Wearing caps didn't hurt anyone. The teachers just wanted to prove to us that they were in charge. Rules that have no purpose, that are used to push people around, and that separate people are worthless.

Mathabane is right that rules and rituals have no purpose or value. All children should refuse to follow their parents stupid rules. Then the world would be a much better place for us all.

The box below lists the steps we have taken to revise this essay.

A Summary of the Steps for Revision

Step 1:   Preparing to Revise
- Let the paper cool
- Read the paper
- Check to see that the thesis matches the prompt

Step 2:   Checking Structure and Organization
- Ensure that all parts of the essay are present
- Ensure that all main ideas relate to the thesis
- Ensure that your paragraphs are in the best order

Step 3:   Checking Development
- Evaluate your introduction
- Ensure that each main idea is adequately supported
- Evaluate your conclusion

THE REVISED ESSAY

The entire revised essay now reads as follows (however, according to the chart on page 163, we still have to edit and proofread this essay before the paper is finished):

As a child, I assumed that every family did things exactly like mine did. It wasn't until I spent a summer vacation with my best friend's family that I realized this wasn't true. The members of his family got up and grabbed a poptart for breakfast whenever they were hungry, while my family always sat down to pancakes or scrambled eggs every morning. In my family, we all had assigned chores, but in his family, his mother took care of the house by herself. That summer I learned that I participated in rules and rituals that other families didn't necessarily follow. Mark Mathabane knew he participated in rituals more than he wanted too. In Mathabane's essay "My Father's Tribal Rule," he says that he lived with his family in a poor section of South Africa. His father was from the tribes, but they were now living around people who had accepted modern ways. Ways that Mathabane wanted to follow. His father insisted that the whole family follow tribal rules and rituals, he became angry and violent when Mathabane wouldn't obey the rules or follow the traditions. Mathabane writes that he hates his father's rules and rituals. Because he disliked rules and rituals, he didn't see that they can be valuable and that they do have a purpose. Rules and rituals can teach us many things. They can teach respect, growing up, and helping the whole family.

Rules and rituals help us learn to show respect for others. Mathabane tells about the rule his father had about not speaking at the table. He tells us that "One day I intentionally broke one of these laws." He spoke during dinner and his father got really mad then he threatened to beat Mathabane. What Mathabane didn't understand was that his father got mad because Mathabane wasn't respecting him. In my family, we have a dinnertime ritual too. Before dinner, my brothers and my sister and I are supposed to clean the house and get everything ready for dinner. One day I didn't feel like doing it, because I have to do everything. So, I just sat on the couch and watched TV. My father came in and saw me and started to yell at me. He said he worked hard every day to put food on the table and that I was showing disrespect to him, my mother, my brothers and my sister. He sent me to bed without supper. At first I was really mad. But the more I thought about it, the more I felt bad for not respecting my father. I learned through this rule to respect my father, Mathabane didn't see the valuable things you can learn from rules.

Mathabane tells us about his little brother George. It was time for George to be weaned and so "she smeared her breasts with red pepper and then invited my brother to suckle." Of course, George's mouth must have burned like fire so he stopped nursing. Mathabane thought, "It was amusing to witness my mother do it." He just saw this ritual as being funny. He didn't understand that it had a purpose "to mark George's passage from infancy to childhood." George would no longer be nursed like a baby. He would now have to eat and act like a child. Like the ritual to wean George, some rituals help us to grow up and realize our new responsibilities. My friend Alan went through a passage similar to George's. Alan's family has alot of money. His parents had bought cars for his older brother and sister when they turned sixteen. They bought Alan one when he turned sixteen, but they told him that driving a car meant that he had to be very responsible. They told him that driving a car meant that he was no longer a kid he was now a adult. It's strange, but owning that car really did change him. Instead of urging his friends to drive faster, Alan was very careful to drive the speed limit. Instead of blowing his money on the latest CD or a few slices of pizza, Alan saved his money to pay for gas and insurance. I guess he realized that you can't act irresponsibly when your driving several tons of steel.

Also, the rituals we do everyday can help the whole family. Mathabane had to do "rituals spanning the range of day-to-day living." These rituals are intended to bring good luck to the entire family, to protect the household, to keep family members healthy, and to ensure that the father keeps his job. All of these rituals benefit Mathabane, George, their mother, and their father. Each member of my family also does daily rituals that helps the rest of the family out. Every evening before bed, for instance, it's my job to make sure all the doors are locked and the windows shut and latched, my ritual keeps us safe from intruders. My sister irons my father's shirts so he'll have a fresh one for work, which helps him make a good impression on his job. My father gets lunch ready for everybody so we don't go hungry the next day. My mother supervises and helps who ever needs help. Our rituals help us work together to everyones benefit. Although Mathabane may be confused by these rituals, I'm not.

Mathabane just doesn't get it. He thinks rules and rituals are just a waste of time. He doesn't see how they can help us learn to respect others and be more courteous to them. I think that Mathabane was too immature to understand that rituals can help us grow up. They can help develop self-responsibility, which is something most people could use more of. In addition, if Mathabane had been less selfish, he'd know that rituals benefit everyone in the family. Basically he wrong. Rules and rituals are something people should follow and practice. If everyone followed the rules and rituals they were taught at home, they could learn respect, responsibility, and how to help others.

What You've Done

- Drafted your complete essay
- Revised it in terms of thesis, organization, and development

For More Revising Strategies

- See Chapter 21

The Next Step

- Editing your essay (Chapters 12 and 22)

12 Editing
Improving Grammar, Usage, and Punctuation

What You've Done
- Drafted and revised your essay

What You Need to Do Next
- Notice any errors of grammar, spelling, usage, or punctuation
- Learn to use tools to correct the errors you've found
- Keep an editing log to avoid future errors

When you've carefully constructed an essay, you've worked hard to create something to be proud of. But if you don't take the final steps of making sure that the details are correct, you may leave your readers with a bad impression of your work. **Editing** is the step that finishes your essay—it's very much like brushing your teeth or washing your car, the final touch that makes everything presentable. In an essay, you want the words, grammar, punctuation, spelling, and appearance to be as neat and clear as possible.

WRITING AND SPEAKING STANDARD ENGLISH

The language you use when you speak and the language you use when you write are very similar but not exactly the same. Sometimes your spoken language is similar to your written language; other times the two are very different from each other.

All of us—from different parts of the country, of different ages and social groups, with different abilities—have special kinds of English that we use with friends and families, a language that makes us feel comfortable and that we can communicate in easily. But sometimes we encounter problems when we try to communicate with groups who might not understand or feel comfortable with our own style of English. So all of us need to be able to use a common or general kind of English when we're communicating with people we don't know well in the academic, professional, and business world.

The accepted practice in these situations is to use **standard written English**. This means that when you write essays for a class, you need to use this general kind of English unless there's a special reason not to. In fact, for most school and business writing, standard written English is best.

Some aspects of language—such as punctuation and spelling—are the same, no matter what kind of English you write. They follow definite rules that most of us have fortunately learned by now. And if we haven't, there are two tools that help us with the rules we don't remember—handbooks (such as Chapter 23 of this book) and dictionaries. These tools will provide crucial help in those cases where standard English is different from spoken English.

Taking Time to Edit

Sometimes using standard English may be difficult. It's hard to think about grammar rules when you're concentrating on understanding a reading and communicating your ideas about it. If you stop in the middle of drafting or revising to look up words in a dictionary or punctuation rules in a handbook, you will probably lose your train of thought. This is why it is best to plan a separate period of time for editing. You will quickly learn how long that time needs to be for your own style of editing and the type of assignment.

Computer Tip

Most people aren't able to pay attention to details on a computer screen. So it's a good idea to print out a draft to use just for editing. Be sure that it's double-spaced. Some people like to use a larger font so they see individual letters more clearly.

There are two important steps in editing: locating errors and correcting errors.

LOCATING ERRORS

Editing Steps

Locating errors

Correcting errors

The first step in editing should be locating the problems you'll need to repair. This is a little trickier than it may seem. Because you're the author of your paper and already familiar with its ideas and organization, *you will tend to see what you meant to write, rather than what you actually wrote. Note:* You may already have used some of these techniques when you were revising (Chapter 11), but this time you are not looking for ways to make your meaning clear. You are looking for ways to make sure you have followed the rules of standard written English. You'll need some tools and tricks to help you see what is actually on the page:

■ *Edit pen:* Always use a pen or pencil that is a bright, strong color to edit your **draft**. An edit pen should get your attention and be easy to read.

Any pen will do, but you may find it helpful to use several colors: make corrections of a certain type in one color, and mark those you need to look up in another color. A pencil or erasable pen is helpful if there's a chance you'll change your mind. Experiment to find what works best for you. Marking words or punctuation and also writing notes in the margin will help you keep track of where you are.

■ *Pointer:* Use something physical like your finger or your edit pen to actually touch each word. This action will help you see what's really there. Using your edit pen will mean that it's handy when you see something you need to mark or correct.

■ *Read backward:* Read the last sentence of your essay. See any problems? If so, correct them. Then read the next-to-last sentence and make any needed corrections. Then move on to the sentence before that, and continue to read backward, correcting errors, until you've completed the essay. This technique works because good readers automatically predict what will appear in a sentence or what should come next. When good readers read forward, moving from one sentence to the next, they often subconsciously fill in blanks or skip over repeated words. Good readers may "read" words, spellings, and punctuation that aren't actually written. Reading backward will help you think about the way you've written each sentence. It will help you see each sentence individually and make mistakes easier to see.

■ *Read aloud:* Reading aloud will help you in two ways. First, because reading aloud slows your processing of each sentence down, it will help you see the actual words on the page. Second, because punctuation signals how parts of sentences relate to each other, reading aloud will help you decide if the pauses and breaks in sentences—the commas and periods—are correct (see fragments pp. 355–358 and run-ons pp. 358–360).

■ *Peer editing:* Another way to locate errors in papers is through **peer editing**, a technique that is explained and illustrated on pages 206–208. Because peer editing involves working with someone else, it is necessary to consider the roles and responsibilities of both the writer and the reader. Instructors also often assign peer editing as a class activity, so it will be necessary to learn how to follow your own instructor's specific directions.

Combining Tools to Locate Your Own Errors

Using several or all of these techniques to locate your own errors will help you focus even more on the language and individual style of your paper instead of on the general ideas.

Look for the most typical types of errors when editing a draft of your paper.

Typical Trouble Spots

Typographical errors and careless mistakes

Misquoting a reading or other source

Omission or repetition of words, especially small words

Spelling mistakes

Errors in punctuation

Errors listed in your editing log

Errors your instructor has marked in previous drafts of papers

Some of these trouble spots were considered in Chapter 11, which discusses revising. Some problems are also discussed more completely in Chapter 13 under proofreading and in Chapter 22 under editing strategies.

EXERCISE 12.1   Look at the **introductory paragraph** from an essay, below. Read it aloud and mark the errors you find with a colorful edit pen. Try reading from the end of the paragraph sentence-by-sentence to find more errors. One error has been underlined. Compare your ability to locate errors with someone else. Divide a piece of paper into two columns labeled "errors" and "corrections." List the errors you find on the left and write the correction for each error on the right. (See the example below the paragraph.) Compare the number and kinds of errors you find with someone else. Compare your suggestions for correcting these errors.

This technique of listing errors with matching corrections is one that is found where **editing logs** are discussed more fully (pp. 341–345). An editing log will make you aware of the particular weaknesses you should look for in your revised drafts. It will also remind you of how to correct these types of errors.

Rules and Rituals (Introduction)

Rules and rituals are <u>thing</u> people do, everyday we follow some kind of rules. We also paticipate in rituals, although we might not no it. Mark Mathaban knew he participated in rituals. More than he wanted too. He lived with his family in a poor section of South Africa. His father was from the tribes, but they were now living around people who excepted modern ways. Ways that Mataban wanted to follow. His father insist that the whole family follow tribal rules and rituals, he became angry and violent when Mathabane wouldnt obey the rules or follow the traditions. Mathabane writes about his hatred of rules and rituals in My fathers tribal rule. Although Mathabane dislike rules and rituals he didn't see that they can be valuable and that they do have a pupose. Rules and rituals can teach us many things. They can teach respect, growing up, and helping the whole family.

SAMPLE EDITING LOG ENTRY:

Errors	Corrections
Rules and rituals are <u>thing</u> people do	Rules and rituals are <u>things</u> people do

EXERCISE 12.2

Use each of the methods below on the first **body paragraph** (paragraph 2) of this essay: (1) using an edit pen, (2) using a pointer, (3) reading backward, and (4) reading aloud.

After you have finished editing the page, think about what you have done.

- ▨ **What types of errors did you find in the sample paragraph?**
- ▨ **How many mistakes did you find?**
- ▨ **Which techniques did you find most helpful? (These are the ones you might find most helpful in locating errors in your own essays.)**
- ▨ **Could you correct some of these errors?**
- ▨ **Compare the edited paragraph to the original paragraph with mistakes. You should be able to see how your corrections help improve the paragraph.**

Rules and Rituals (Body Paragraph 1)

First, rules teach respect. Mathabane tells about the rule his father had about not speaking at the table. He tells us that "One day I intentionally broke one of these laws. He spoke during dinner and his father got really mad, he said, "You don't have two mouths to afford you such a luxury." Then he threatened to beat Mathabane. By Mathabane not respecting him made his father get mad, but Mathabane did'nt understand it. One time my father got at me to. In my family, we have a dinnertime ritual. Before dinner, my brothers and my sister and I are suppose to clean the house and get everything ready for dinner. One day I didn't feel like doing it, because I have to do everything. My brothers and my sister don't do hardly anything. So, I just sat on the couch and watch TV. My father come in and saw me and started to yell at me. He said he worked hard every day to put food on the table and you are showing disrespect to me, your mother, your brothers and your sister. He sent me to bed without supper. At first I was really mad. Being that my father was unfair to me. I'm the oldest, so I wind up doing most of the work. I don't see why should I have to clean the house every day and get the table ready? The more I thought about it, the more I felt bad. He did do a lot for us. Besides providing us with a house and food, he paid for my music lessons, he takes us to the beach in the summer, he drops us off at the movies. He really does do a lot for us and sometimes I think we forget to say thank you. I felt bad for not respecting my father. I learn through this rule to respect my father, Mathabane didnt see the valuable things you can learn from rules.

EXERCISE 12.3   **Use some or all of the following methods to locate errors in an essay you have written. Do this: (1) using an edit pen, (2) using a pointer, (3) reading backward and (4) reading aloud.**

CORRECTING ERRORS

For many people, locating errors is the most difficult part of editing. Most of the errors that you find, you will probably know how to correct. It's important to mark everything in your paper that you recognize as an error and all of the things you suspect may be an error. You can then correct what you have marked in two stages:

1. Correct the errors you know.
2. Find help in correcting the ones you don't know, or the ones you think might be wrong, even though you're not sure.

Correcting Errors You Understand

Make the correction on the draft as soon as you locate it. Don't expect to recognize the error again later and to remember how you planned to correct it if you will be recopying your essay. Write clearly so that you can read what you've written.

> **Computer Tip**
>
> Handwrite the correction on your draft if it is short; if it is complicated, requiring many changes, write a note on the draft to remind yourself. When you return to the computer, mark off each correction as you find it so you won't skip over it.

When you located the errors in the paragraph on page 197 (in Exercise 12.1), you knew how to correct many of these errors.

Errors You Know How to Correct

1. *Rules and rituals are <u>thing</u> people do.* [You know *rules and rituals* are plural, so *things* must be plural, too.]
2. *. . . although we might not <u>no</u> it.* [You know *no* is the opposite of *yes*, but the word makes no sense in this context. What you want is the word that means *be aware of*. You change the spelling of *no* to *know*.]
3. *Ways that <u>Mathaban</u> wanted to follow.* [You check the spelling of the author's name and correct *Mathaban* to *Mathabane*.]

4. *His father <u>insist</u> that the whole family follow tribal rules and rituals.* [You've been writing about this story in the past tense (*wanted, was, were now living*), so you change *insist* to *insisted*.]

5. *Mathabane <u>wouldnt</u> obey the rules.* [You know *wouldnt* is a contraction of *would* + *not* and needs an apostrophe between *n* and *t*. You correct this word to *wouldn't*.]

Finding Help for Errors You Don't Understand

There are several steps you can follow in finding help. The first is deciding what kind of help you need.

Spell Checkers   The **spell checker** is a computer device that checks each word that is typed in your essay against a list in the computer's memory. Spell checkers are helpful, but they don't work alone. The computer can't understand the meaning of words or sentences in a word processing program, so it can't decide which correctly spelled word is correct for your sentence. You must make the decision as to whether to change the word and how to change it, if you do. Sometimes the spell checker will tell you that a word is wrong even when it's right, because not every word can be on the computer's list. The majority of proper names are often left off those lists, and so are specialized words such as technical words from many fields and words from other languages used in English sentences.

Computer Tip

Spell checkers don't know which words are the best corrections for misspelled words. Don't simply accept the first suggestion the spell checker offers. You will have to think about the meaning of each word to see which fits best in your sentence, and you may need to use a dictionary to help you. Turn off the "Autocorrect" feature so that you will be able to make your own decisions about correcting words. Also many proper names will be marked as misspelled even if they aren't.

The list below shows that some errors can be corrected using a spell checker and others cannot. Be careful. You, not the spell checker, must correct your errors.

Correcting Errors Using a Spell Checker

1. Your spell checker highlights *Mathabane*. You don't need to change this word, because it is the correct spelling of the author's name.

2. Your spell checker highlights *paticipated* and suggests *participated*. This seems correct to you, and in fact it is. If you aren't sure that it is correct, look up *participate(d)* in the dictionary.

3. Your spell checker highlights *pupose* and suggests *puppies*. You read the sentence with *pupose* and determine that *puppies* makes no sense

in that sentence. Another choice the spell checker offers is *purpose,* which you recognize as the word you meant to write.

4. Your spell checker doesn't highlight *no* in *we might not no it,* because *no* is a word that would be correct in some sentences. It's not the correct word in this sentence, but the computer doesn't understand the meaning of the sentence.

Grammar Checkers and Style Checkers Grammar checkers and style checkers are often included as part of the software of a word processing program. Again, these mechanical aids simply compare your phrases and sentences against a list in the computer. But the computer does not understand the meaning of the sentence—it just looks for patterns of words on a list. Unfortunately, sentences and phrases are much more complicated than words, so the checker's suggestions are wrong more often than they are right. Most students find them very confusing. It is probably better to learn how to recognize and correct your own errors.

Dictionaries Dictionaries are helpful in giving spellings and definitions. Don't give up immediately if you can't find the words you're looking for, because not all words are spelled the way they sound. Try to think of other letters that might make the same sound (for example, *chaos* is spelled with *ch,* not *k*).

Also, the word you're looking up may have prefixes like *re-* or suffixes (endings added to make a word a different part of speech) like *-ance* or *-ence.* If you have trouble finding the whole word, try to figure out the root and look that up. See the lists on pages 259–260 in Chapter 16 for help in finding roots.

Correcting Errors Using a Dictionary

1. You try to look up the word *participate,* but you have spelled it *paticpate.* You won't find the word listed under *pat-,* but if you continue to look under *pa-,* you eventually find *participate.*

2. You aren't sure you've spelled *disrespect* correctly, but you don't find it under *dis-.* You know that *dis-* is a prefix meaning *not,* so you look for the word *respect.* You find that *disrespect* is the correct spelling of the word.

Use a college dictionary to edit your work. Other dictionaries have far fewer words, and fewer and less complete definitions for the words.

Handbooks Handbooks can be very helpful for punctuation, grammar, and usage questions. In some courses you will need to learn to use a complete handbook for many different questions, but in this course you can use the shorter handbook that begins on page 347. *The key to using a handbook is being able to name the error you are trying to correct.* You may already know the names of some problems, but you may need to learn the names of others.

Common Problems Covered in the Handbook

Period or comma
■ Fragments (Sentence basics, pp. 349–354; Fragments, pp. 355–358)
■ Run-ons (Run-ons and comma splices, pp. 358–362)
■ Other commas (Commas, pp. 383–386)

Other punctuation
■ Question marks (Question marks, p. 386; Question word, p. 357)
■ Quotation marks (Quotation marks, pp. 381–382, 388–393; Documentation, pp. 399–403)
■ Semicolon (p. 359)
■ Titles (pp. 386–388)
■ Capitals (pp. 386–388)

Word endings (pp. 362–372)
■ *–s* on words
    Plural nouns (p. 363)
    Verbs (Recognizing verbs, p. 350; Final *–s* verbs, pp. 365–369; Subject-verb agreement, pp. 372–374)
    Apostrophes (pp. 363–365)
■ *–ed, –ing* on words (Recognizing verbs, p. 350; Past tense verb endings, pp. 369–371)
■ More on verbs (Irregular verbs, pp. 371–372; Helping verbs, pp. 367–368; Modals, pp. 368–369)
■ Verb tense overview (ESL, pp. 409–413)

Using other writers' work (pp. 393–403)
■ Quotation marks and italics (pp. 387, 388–390)
■ Documentation (pp. 396–403)
    Parenthetical citations (p. 403)
    Works cited list (pp. 399–402)
■ Paraphrase (pp. 381–382)

Unclear sentences (p. 377)
■ Prepositional subjects (pp. 377–380); Recognizing prepositional phrases (pp. 353–354); Subject-verb agreement (pp. 372–374); Prepositions (ESL, pp. 404–409)
■ Articles (ESL, pp. 403–404)
■ Indirect questions (pp. 380–381)
■ Smooth quotations (pp. 381–382, 390–393)
■ Verb tenses (ESL, pp. 409–418)

continued on next page

continued from previous page

Parallelism (Clarity, p. 382)

Pronouns

■ Pronoun agreement (pp. 374–375)

■ Pronouns and point of view (pp. 375, 381–382)

Word choice

■ Similar words and spelling (Clarity, pp. 376–377)

Problems You Can Name   Many times you will know the name of the problem you are trying to correct. To find the section of the handbook that describes that problem, you can do either of two things:

■ Look at the list of items which begins on page 202 (also printed on the rear inside cover).

■ Look in the index at the back of the book under the name of the problem.

When you edit, you should check every period and comma. Let's say you are not sure the period is correct in the group of words below:

Mathabane knew he participated in rituals. More than he wanted to.

You know that using a period sometimes creates a **fragment**. You can now look for the section of the handbook that describes fragments to help you decide whether a period should be used. You find that "more than" is a kind of connecting phrase, so "More than he wanted to" will be a fragment if you put a period before it and after it. You correct the fragment by connecting it to the preceding sentence, since it goes with it.

Mathabane knew he participated in rituals more than he wanted to.

Problems You Can't Name   If you don't know the name of a problem, it will be hard to use a handbook. You will need to ask an instructor, tutor, or classmate for help.

They can teach respect, growing up, and helping the whole family.

You know that this last sentence in Body Paragraph 1 sounds a little strange. You ask your instructor about the sentence, and she tells you that the list at the end of the sentence involves a problem in parallel structure. She explains that the grammatical forms of all items in a list should match; that is, they should all be *-ing* words, or *to* words, or parts of sentences that are alike. You have several options:

■ Using simple verbs after *to*:

> They can teach us to have respect, to grow up, and to help the whole family.

■ Using *-ing* words:

> They can teach us about having respect, growing up, and helping the whole family.

■ Using separate sentences:

> They can teach us to have respect, they can aid us in growing up, and they can help the whole family.

You might decide that the last sentence is the closest to expressing the meaning you want because each sentence adds emphasis to the three separate points your paper will make.

Learning by Using the Handbook

When you find the section of the handbook that describes the problem you are trying to correct, or when someone has suggested that you look at a particular section of the handbook, read over the explanations and examples carefully. Then practice correcting the problem by doing the exercises in the handbook. Write down your answers and check them in the back of the book. (Answers for exercises in Chapters 23 and 24 are found on pp. 605–629.) If you have successfully completed the exercise, return to your paper and make the correction. You can then look at the rest of your paper for similar problems.

EXERCISE 12.4 *Use a spell checker, dictionary, and handbook to correct the errors you located in Exercise 12.2.*

EXERCISE 12.5 *Use a spell checker, dictionary, and handbook to correct the errors you located in your own essay.*

Editing Log   To be able to write independently and avoid repeating the same mistakes, you need to learn the names of the problems you commonly have. One good way to do this is with an **editing log**—a written record that is kept in a notebook. Each time your instructor returns a paper or you edit a paper, write down the names of the errors in your log. Also copy the part of the sentence with the error and mark the correction in a different color. This will help you to learn to recognize and name your own particular errors (see pp. 341–345 for more about editing logs.)

Here is an example of an entry in an editing log, complete with the name of the error in the "Errors" column:

Errors	Corrections
Plural ending missing	
Rules and rituals are <u>thing</u> people do,	Rules and rituals are <u>things</u> people do

When you are editing your paper, you should use your log in two ways:

Using the Editing Log

Check for your typical errors.

Enter new errors when you find them.

■ ***Check for your typical errors:*** If you have already begun to keep an editing log, you will have a list of errors that you have made in other papers. Since you know that these are errors you are likely to make, you should set aside a time to check just for these. For example, you may know that you often leave apostrophes off, so you'll know to look closely at all words that end in -*s* or words that show ownership to see if they need apostrophes or not. You may sometimes need to reread that section in the handbook and work on some exercises.

■ ***Enter new errors when you find them:*** Each time you edit you may find many cases of the same error, or you may find new ones. Very often students who have problems with fragments begin to use commas instead of periods, thus creating run-on sentences. So for a while they might add run-ons, as well as fragments, to their editing logs.

EXERCISE 12.6   Look at the following paragraph (an introduction). It is the same paragraph given in Exercise 12.1 but with some of the errors underlined. Below the paragraph are entries in a mock editing log. Try to name the error that has been underlined so it looks more like a real editing log. The first error identification has been done for you. (You may want to find and add more errors from the paragraph. Not all have been underlined; there are more.)

Rules and Rituals (Introduction)

Rules and rituals are <u>thing</u> people do, everyday we follow some kind of rules. We also <u>paticipate</u> in rituals, although we might not <u>no</u> it. Mark <u>Mathaban</u> knew he participated in rituals. <u>More than he wanted too.</u> He lived with his family in a poor section of South Africa. His father was from the tribes, but they were now living around people who excepted modern ways. Ways that <u>Mataban</u> wanted to follow. His father <u>insist</u> that the whole family follow tribal rules and rituals, he became angry and violent when Mathabane <u>wouldnt</u> obey the rules or follow the traditions. Mathabane writes about his hatred of rules and rituals in My fathers tribal rule. Although Mathabane <u>dislike</u> rules and rituals he didn't see that they can be valuable and that they do have a pupose. Rules and rituals can teach us many things. <u>They can teach respect, growing up, and helping the whole family.</u>

Errors	Corrections
Plural ending missing	
Rules and rituals are <u>thing</u> people do,	Rules and rituals are <u>things</u> people do
We also <u>paticipate</u> in rituals,	We also <u>participate</u> in rituals,
we might not <u>no</u> it.	we might not <u>know</u> it.
Mark <u>Mathaban</u>	Mark <u>Mathabane</u>
Mark Mathabane knew he participated in rituals. <u>More than he wanted too.</u>	Mark Mathabane knew he participated in rituals <u>more than he wanted to.</u>
<u>Mataban</u>	<u>Mathabane</u>
His father <u>insist</u>	His father <u>insisted</u>
<u>wouldnt</u>	<u>wouldn't</u>
<u>dislike</u>	<u>disliked</u>
<u>They can teach respect, growing up, and helping the whole family.</u>	<u>They can teach us to have respect, they can aid us in growing up, and they can help the whole family.</u>

EXERCISE 12.7   Make entries in a mock editing log for the errors you located in body paragraph 1 of the student essay in Exercise 12.2.

EXERCISE 12.8   Make real entries in a personal editing log for the errors you found in your own essay.

ESL   **Peer Editing**   Even the best writers will not be able to locate and correct every error in their writing. A new reader will see your essay with different eyes and will find errors that you understand but overlooked as well as others that you didn't understand. For this reason, many instructors will offer time in class for peer editing—an exercise in which peers (people who are equal to each other) look at each other's papers to find errors and make corrections.

Sometimes students feel that other students can't really help them learn to write, or that they have nothing to offer other students. If you have that idea, you should think about a parallel situation: how you learned to use a computer. You may have learned many things about word processing from an instructor, but you probably also learned from other students. Even beginning students can help each other learn about word processing or using the Internet. Many times, students can help each other more easily than an instructor in a formal lesson can. Learning to write is a similar situation. You will be able to read a classmate's paper and recognize some errors, and that same classmate will recognize different errors in your paper. You can become each other's teachers. During this process, everyone—even good students—can learn from helping students with problems. Looking at other people's errors sharpens your own eyes, and explaining problems helps you understand and remember them.

If your instructor doesn't give you time to peer edit, you might want to form a group out of class with other students, because this is one of the best ways to work on your editing. You can also E-mail drafts to other students for peer editing.

Editing Tip

Peer editing is a cooperative exercise that requires you to correct problems in your own paper. It is very different from handing your paper to a friend and asking him or her to make corrections for you. You won't learn from your friend's corrections, and your instructor might think that you are plagiarizing or cheating by turning in someone else's work as your own. If peer editing has not been assigned by your instructor, make sure that she knows that you are working on papers together and approves of your methods.

Here are some pointers for peer editing:

Attitudes

- Give your partner a legible draft for peer editing so that reading each word is not a struggle.
- Accept the idea that the papers you write will be read by another person besides your teacher; be ready to read your paper aloud to another student.
- Don't be hurt by helpful, constructive criticism. Use your partner's suggestions as ways to learn and improve your paper.
- Don't belittle your partner, or laugh at mistakes, or say something is dumb.
- Don't be afraid to offer constructive criticism. You won't be helpful to your partner if you say that a paper is correct when it is full of errors.

Actions

- Exchange papers with a partner, and use a pen or pencil that's a different color from that used in the paper.
- Read the paper aloud to the writer if possible. If not, read it twice. Skim the paper once to see the overall meaning. Then read slowly and carefully.

■ Do not write corrections on your partner's paper. Instead, mark a small X or dot in the margin. Make one mark for each error you think you see in the line.

■ When the paper has been checked, return it to the writer. When you receive your checked paper from your partner, look at each mark in the margin, and try to locate and correct one error for each mark.

■ If you can't find an error your partner marked or don't understand how to correct it, ask your partner to explain.

■ If you are not sure that your partner's idea is correct, look in the handbook or ask a tutor or your instructor to verify the corrections.

EXERCISE 12.9

Pretend that the body paragraph below was written by one of your classmates. Follow the "actions" for peer editing above to help your classmate improve the essay. Use the techniques discussed earlier under "Locating Errors" to find mistakes that you think your classmate should correct. Be prepared to explain everything you have marked.

Rules and Rituals (Body Paragraph 2)

Second, although rules can teach us things, rituals can help you grow. Mathabane tell us about his little brother George. It was time for George to be weaned and so "she smeared her breasts with red pepper and then invited my brother to suckle.. Of course, Georges mouth must of burned like fire soon he stopped nursing. Mathabane thought, it was amusing to witness my mother do it. He just saw this ritual as funny. He didn't understand that it had a purpose it was to mark George's passage from infancy to childhood. My friend Alan went though a passage similar to Georges. Alans family has a lot of money. Since they were rich, he did what ever he wanted cause he could afford too. He was really irresponsible and wasted money on stupid stuff that he would get tired of in two days. When they were sixteen, his parents bought cars for his older brother and sister. They bought Alan one when he turned sixteen, but they told him that driving a car ment that he had to be very responsable. They told him that driving a car meant that he was no longer a kid he was now a adult. It's strange, but owning that car really did change him. I guess he realized that you can't act irresponsably when your driving several tons of steel. This ritual of getting a car was good for Alan. Georges ritual was good for him because it meant he was no longer a baby. Mathabane was just amused by the weaning ritual, not realizing how rituals help you grow and become more mature.

EXERCISE 12.10

Exchange essays with another student and follow the activities suggested above. Keep your partner's feelings in mind.

Responding to Instructor Comments

Understand the comments

Correct the errors

Enter errors in your editing log

Instructor Comments   If your instructor has looked at an earlier draft of a paper, she may have made comments on the editing. These will be useful suggestions for improving your writing. So be sure to think about and act on these comments. Here are some guidelines:

■ ***Understand the comments:*** When your instructor comments on your drafts, she may use symbols or abbreviations. Look through the handbook for some common symbols and abbreviations. If your instructor has her own system, be sure to ask her to explain anything you don't recognize.

■ ***Correct the errors:*** It's extremely important to correct errors as soon as the paper is returned to you. If you don't, you may not have the opportunity to ask the instructor for assistance later, and you may forget to make the corrections, causing problems in subsequent drafts.

■ ***Enter the errors in your editing log:*** Remember that the goal of correcting your editing is not just to make this one paper correct, but to learn to correct your own errors when a teacher is no longer available. Otherwise you may continue to make the same mistakes over and over again. You will need to enter the errors in your editing log (see pp. 341–345) each time you receive a draft from your instructor.

Annotations (teacher's comments)	*An Instructor's Comments on a Paper*	Annotations (teacher's comments)

Student essay

Third, the rituals we do everyday can help the hole family. Mathabane had to do "rituals spanning the range of day-to-day living. He tells us about all the rituals that "Protect the house from evildoers and to safeguard his job." These sound like good things, but "they simply awed, confused, and embarrassed me." However, everybody dose daily ritual. In our house, these are divided up. Every evening before bed, for instance, its my job to make sure all the doors are locked and the windows shut and latch. This protects us from evildoers who might wont to rob us. I couldnt sleep if I thought I left the front door unlocked. My sister irons my father's shirts so he'll have a fresh one for work. If he doesn't look professional, he could be looked down on by his boss. This ritual protect his job. My father get lunch ready for everybody. Thats his ritual and it helps everybody. My mother supervises and help whoever needs help. These aren't hard things to do and everybody benefit. The house is protected, my dads job is protected. Everybody has their lunch ready to go in the morning. Although Mathabane may be confused by these rituals, I'm not.

Left annotations:
- awk pron in quote
- sp. plural missing
- v ending/ run-on (CS)/ apos-poss
- unclear ref of "these": which ones?

Right annotations:
- sp
- close quote
- awk pron in quote, check quote
- what are "these"?
- apos-contract
- v ending
- sp-wrong word/ apos-contract
- v ending x 2
- apos-contract
- v ending
- pron agr

EXERCISE 12.11   **Look at the instructor's comments on the previous page.**

1. Think about the differences between revising (Chapter 11) and editing (this chapter). Which comments refer to editing and which to revising?

2. What does each comment mean?

3. Make a correction for each editing comment.

4. Enter the errors in your mock editing log.

EXERCISE 12.12   **Work with your instructors's comments on one of your own papers.**

1. Think about the differences between revising (Chapter 11) and editing (this chapter). Which comments refer to editing, and which refer to revising?

2. What does each comment mean?

3. Make a correction for each editing comment.

4. Enter the errors in your own editing log.

EXERCISE 12.13   **Using all the methods suggested in this chapter, edit the conclusion shown below. Compare your results with those of your classmates.**

Rules and Rituals (Conclusion)

In conclusion. Mathabane just doesn't get it. He thinks rules and rituals are just a waste of time. He doesn't see how they can help us learn to respect others and be more courtous to them. I think that Mathabane was to immature to understand that rituals can help us grow up. They can help develop self-responsibility and to become more mature, which is something most people could use more of. Mathabane only thinks about himself and thats why he doesn't want to do the rituals that help the whole family. Basically he wrong. Rules and rituals are something you should follow and practice.

Editing turns a revised draft into a paper that is easy for others to read. The language of an edited paper is easy to understand. But editing takes time and is always a two-step process. First you must learn to locate errors in your paper. Then you must take time to correct them.

Errors are easier to locate if you use techniques that help you focus on the form of what you have written, not just the ideas. You should always use an edit pen. Physically pointing to your paper as you read for errors and reading backward can help you focus on form. Peer editing can help you locate things that need to be edited because your peer reads with a fresh eye.

Errors are also easier to locate if you are aware of your weak areas. Keeping an editing log can help you learn not only what types of errors to look for, but also how to correct them. Because most papers are word processed, you should learn how to use a spell checker efficiently. Dictionaries and handbooks can also help you decide the best way to correct errors.

What You've Done

▪ Learned techniques to locate errors in your revised essay
▪ Learned to use tools to correct errors:
   Checkers for spelling
   Dictionaries and handbooks
▪ Learned the usefulness of editing logs and peer editing

For More Editing Strategies

▪ Chapters 22, 23, and 24

The Next Step

▪ Format and proofread your essay (Chapter 13)

13 Finishing the Essay
Formatting and Proofreading

> ### What You've Done
> - Checked and edited the essay
>
> ### What You Need to Do Next
> - Prepare the final copy of the essay in the correct format
> - Check the final copy for careless errors

FORMATTING YOUR ESSAY

Now that you have **edited** your essay, you're ready to put it into the final **format**. You want to use a format that is clear and easy to read, so that your instructor will be able to concentrate on your writing.

Your instructor may require that papers be written on a computer, but some instructors will accept handwritten **drafts** for evaluation. As far as possible, try to follow the same rules for formatting, whether you're writing on a computer or by hand.

Formatting on a Computer

Writing on a computer is covered in Chapter 2 (pp. 32–35).

Computer Tip
Most word-processing programs have preset margins and fonts called the *default settings.* Use them. If you must set them yourself, set them as follows: Use 1-inch margins on top, sides, and bottom. Use a clear, simple font: size 12 Times New Roman is most common. Do not use italics or bold unless you need them for titles or subheads. Use black ink, not colors. Use left justification only; do not use full justification. Left **justification** means that the left margin is a straight line. Full justification means that the right margin is a straight line, too. (In the production of this book, full justification is generally used, although in lists such as this you will see left justification.) Double-space your essay (set line spacing to 2) and write on one side of the paper only.

If you have problems with your printer, bring the diskette to class, along with the last draft you were able to print out.

Handwritten Papers

Handwritten papers are not as easy to read as word-processed papers. But you can make a handwritten paper easier to read if you follow these formatting suggestions. Most instructors will accept printing as well as cursive writing, but check with your instructor to be sure.

- Write in black ink, one side of the paper only.
- Leave 1-inch margins on all sides, including the bottom.
- Double-space. On lined notebook paper, skip lines and write on alternate lines.
- You may use white-out for some errors, but if you make many corrections, begin the page again.

Headings and Page Numbers

Whether you use a computer or write by hand, you should do the following (or follow the equivalent directions from your instructor):

1. Put your name, instructor's name, course and section, and the date in the upper-left corner of page 1.
2. Center the title two spaces below the date or on the first line of lined paper. Do NOT use bold, italics, all capitals, underlining, or quotation marks, but DO capitalize the first letter of all important words.
3. Indent each paragraph, usually one TAB on most computers. If you are writing by hand, indent the beginning of each paragraph the equivalent of five spaces.
4. Put your last name and the page number in the upper-right corner of every page.

Cover Page and Works Cited List

Most instructors do not require a separate cover page for short papers because they waste paper. Also, most instructors let you put a Works Cited list on the last page of your paper, if you have enough space. But some instructors require a separate works cited page, which follows the style guidelines of the Modern Language Association (see pp. 394–403).

- A cover page has the title of your paper (without any special font and without quotation marks), plus all of the information needed to identify you, the course, the instructor, and the specific assignment. This may include the due date of the paper and name of the paper, such as

Paper 3 or Mathabane Response Paper. All of the information on the cover page should be centered. Lower the title of your paper until it is about one-third of the way down the page.

■ Center the heading for a separate Works Cited page at the top of the paper. Follow the documentation format your instructor requires. For more information on how to write a works cited list, see Documentation (pp. 396–403) in Chapter 23, "A Handbook for Writing Correct Sentences."

Here is part of the essay "Rules and Rituals" that has been edited (in Chapter 12, pp. 194–211) and formatted. But the essay has not yet been **proofread,** so there are still errors. The complete, finished essay is at the end of this chapter (pp. 221–223).

Sanchez 1

Maria Sanchez
Dr. Simpson
ENG 100G10
December 12, 2001

Rules and Rituals

Rules and rituals are things people do. Everyday we follow some kind of rules. We also participate in rituals, although we might not know it. Mark Mathabane knew he participated in rituals, more than he wanted too. He lived with his family in a poor section of South Africa. His father was from the tribes, but they were now living around people who excepted modern ways, ways that Mathabane wanted to follow. His father insisted that the whole family follow tribal rules and rituals. He became angry and violent when Mathabane wouldnt obey the rules or follow the traditions. Mathabane writes about his hatred of rules and rituals in My Father's Tribal Rule. Although Mathabane disliked rules and rituals, he didn't see that they can be valuable and that they do have a purpose. Rules and rituals can teach us many things. They can teach respect, growing up, and helping the whole family.

First, rules teach respect. Mathabane tells about the rule his father had about not speaking at the table. He tells us that "One day I intentionally broke one of these laws" (42). He spoke during dinner and his father got really mad, he said, "You don't have two mouths to afford you such a luxury" (42). Then he threatened to cut out Mathabane's tongue. What Mathabane didn't understand was that his father got mad because Mathabane wasn't respecting him. One time my father got at me to. In my family, we have a dinnertime ritual. Before dinner, my brothers and my sister and I are supposed to clean the house and get everything ready for dinner. One day I didn't feel like doing it, because

I have to do everything. My brothers and my sister don't do hardly anything. So, I just sat on the couch and watched T.V. My father come in and saw me and started to yell at me. He said he worked hard every day to put food on the table and that I was showing disrespect to him, my mother, my brothers and my sister. He sent me to bed without supper. At first I was really mad because I thought that my father was unfair to me. I'm the oldest, so I wind up doing most of the work. Why should I have to clean the house every day and get the table ready? The more I thought about it, the more I felt bad. He did do a lot for us. Besides providing us with a house and food, he paid for the movies. He really does do a lot for us and sometimes I think we forget to say thank you. I felt bad for not respecting my father. I learn through this rule to respect my father, Mathabane didn't see the valuable things you can learn from rules.

[the essay continues below]

In conclusion, Mathabane just doesn't get it. He thinks rules and rituals are just a waste of time. He doesn't see how they can help us learn to respect others and be more courtous to them. I think that Mathabane was too immature to understand that rituals can help us grow up. They can help develop self-responsibility and to become more mature. These are two things most people could use more of. Mathabane seems only to thinks about himself and that's why he doesn't want to do the rituals that help the whole family. Basically he wrong. Rules and rituals are something you should follow and practice

[the following starts a new page]

Sanchez 9

Works Cited

Mathabane, Mark. "My Father's Tribal Rule." *The User's Guide to College Writing.* N. Kreml, et al. New York: Addison Wesley Longman, 2001. 40-41.

PROOFREADING YOUR ESSAY

As you look at the edited draft of your paper in its final format, you're probably assuming it's ready to be turned in.

However, if you look closely, you'll see that there are still some other errors to deal with. As the last step, the edited and formatted paper must be proofread. And proofreading must be a separate, careful step, not just a quick glance.

Proofreading as a Reading Process

When you proofread a paper, you are not trying to improve or change what you have written. You are trying to look at the words you have actually written on the page. Is this what you intended to write? When you were drafting, **revising,** and editing, you were paying attention to one problem at a time, and you may have missed some small errors. Also, if you have written your paper by hand or if you have waited to enter it on the word processor as a final step, there's a very good chance that you may have made some errors when you copied it.

Computer Tip

If you write your first draft on a word processor, you'll find it much easier to create a final draft with fewer errors. You won't need to do any recopying, which means you won't make any new errors.

Looking for Typical Trouble Spots in the Final Draft

As you proofread, you may discover that revising and editing has caused your earlier draft to lose some coherence. That is, changes in word choice or carelessly added examples may make your paper jumpy and hard to follow. If you discover that this has happened, you will need to go back to the earlier steps of revising (Chapter 11) or editing (Chapter 12) to make whatever larger changes are necessary. A change in one place in a sentence in your paper may lead to a complication later. If you revise and edit, you will have to proofread the new draft. Don't be afraid to return to an earlier step if you must.

After you have corrected all of your careless mistakes, you need to reread your paper again to be sure what you have written is what you meant to write. Even if you are an excellent speller and know all your punctuation rules, you've probably made some mistakes even on the final draft. You may have relaxed your attention to details like spelling or punctuation, or you may have just become too tired or distracted to notice certain mistakes.

AN OVERVIEW OF PROOFREADING TECHNIQUES

Proofreading, like any step in writing, takes time. Expect that you'll need to read the essay at least two more times—once to be sure that it all fits together and at least once to look for specific errors. In fact, most writers find that they proofread more than twice. To be sure that you do see exactly what you've written, you'll need to use some of the same tools and techniques you used in locating your errors for editing (see pp. 195–196 for more details).

Proofreading for Coherence: Does It All Fit Together?

Read each sentence and paragraph to see if they still say what you want them to. Focus on each sentence or paragraph as a meaningful unit. This is an essential step for locating problems in coherence: missing words, wrong words, sentences copied twice, etc. After you are satisfied that your essay expresses your ideas clearly, you are ready to proofread for specific errors.

Tools and Techniques for Locating Specific Errors

The tools and techniques for proofreading are the same as those for revising and editing (see Chapters 11 and 12). But you are not reading to rephrase or reorganize your ideas. You are checking to make sure that all of the choices you have made in phrasing, sentence structure, and formatting are accurate and that changes made in revising and editing have not caused other mistakes. As explained in Chapter 12 (see pp. 195–196), you need a variety of tools:

- ▪ *Edit pen*
- ▪ *Pointer*
- ▪ *Reading aloud*
- ▪ *Reading backward*
- ▪ *Your editing log:* Your **editing log** will help you proofread because it will remind you about the errors you usually make. Use the list in your log and check through the paper for each of your typical errors. For example, you might want to check each place you know the reading is used separately for accuracy and proper documentation, or you might know that you often confuse *to* and *too*. Remember that checking your editing log for the mistakes you commonly make is one of the most important steps in proofreading.

Combine Proofreading Tools to Locate Your Own Errors

Using several or all of these methods together will help make your proofreading more effective. Remember that proofreading for coherence, specific errors, and your own typical errors is important and none of these steps should be skipped.

When finishing all your final drafts, remember to be patient and to take a few moments to look over everything one more time. Although someone might be able to understand your paper without one more proofreading, your essay will present your ideas more clearly if there are no little mistakes to confuse or distract the reader. As you proofread, remember to check for all potential trouble spots.

Examples of Errors Corrected in Proofreading

Typical Trouble Spots
Coherence
Typos and carelessness
Misquoting of reading or other sources
Small words
Spelling
Punctuation
Spacing between words
Entries in your editing log

When you proofread, you are checking that earlier revisions and editing are accurate and that they have not caused a new problem. Sometimes one correction may introduce a new problem. Also, some types of errors are simply hard to catch, even at the editing stage. Mistakes involving small words, repeated words, word endings, spelling, and punctuation can be hard to notice. The examples below illustrate the types of errors that can still occur in an edited draft.

Overall Coherence   Check once again to make sure that everything fits together smoothly and makes sense. Were any problems introduced in revising and editing?

Computer Tip

Did you move, add, or delete any words or phrases or sentences? Be sure you didn't create any strange problems by leaving out a word or adding an extra one.

Verb Endings   If you change sentence structure or a verb tense, the ending may change and this will affect the spelling of the word. For example, if you combined the two sentences below into one using *besides* or *in addition to* to emphasize the contrast between the ordinary and the extra, *provide* now has the suffix *-ing* and this changes the spelling. This means that adding or deleting endings always requires checking the spelling of a word.

ORIGINAL

He provides us with a house and food.

He pays for my music lessons, he takes us to the beach in the summer, and he drops us off at the movies.

CHANGED IN EDITING

Besides provideing us with a house and food, he pays for my music lessons, he takes us to the beach in the summer, and he drops us off at the movies.

CORRECTED IN PROOFREADING

Besides providing us with a house and food, he pays for my music lessons, he takes us to the beach in the summer, and he drops us off at the movies.

Rephrasing   Rephrasing can also change forms and spellings of words. For example, if you decide to change the phrase *by intention* to the single word *intentionally,* you will need to be sure that you have spelled it correctly. You can't always just add *-ly* as you do in some words—for example, *slow+ly* Look up any of these changes you are unsure of.

ORIGINAL PHRASING

I also broke one of my father's rules by intention.

CHANGED IN EDITING

I also broke one of my father's rules <u>intentionly.</u>

CORRECTED IN PROOFREADING

I also broke one of my father's rules <u>intentionally.</u>

Typographical Errors and Carelessness   Some spelling mistakes are the result of typing errors or carelessness. Letters can be easily switched, left out, or repeated when typing or writing quickly. In the example below, the spell checker will not identify the misspelling *eve*, but it will probably identify the author's name as a misspelling.

Mathabane <u>eve</u> describes his father as ugly.

Since *eve* is a word, the **spell checker** won't underline it. Both the correct *Mathabane* and the incorrect *Mathaban* will be treated as equally incorrect by most spell checkers. It is up to you to check all names for correct spelling.

Misquoting a Reading or Other Sources   If you've quoted from a reading, you must use exactly the words and punctuation that the author used. Double-check the accuracy of your quote by looking back at the reading. Sometimes paraphrasing the author's ideas is better than quoting the original. However, even a paraphrase must accurately represent the content of the original.

The Little Words

Misspelling or Misusing Little Words   Little words can be easily overlooked by spell checkers since the program will not understand which meaning you intend.

Did you mean *of* or *off*?

Do you mean *he* or *she*?

Did you intend to write *doe snot* or *does not?* Your spell checker probably will not recognize the difference.

Leaving Out Little Words   Little words, like *to* and *be,* often do not contribute much to the meaning of a sentence and are often left out in hurried writing. Reading the final draft aloud slowly can catch small words omitted in the editing and proofreading process. For example, what word has been left out of the sentence below?

They can teach respect, growing up, and helping whole family.

Spacing Between Words   Proofread for spacing between words and sentences. Changes in editing a paper may affect spaces between words, sentences, and punctuation. For example, words can run together:

It was time for George tobe weaned.

Unnecessary spaces can appear before commas.

First , rules teach respect.

Parts of sentences can become fused together. In the example below, correcting a fragment by adding it to the previous sentence has resulted in a spacing problem:

His father was from the tribes, but they were now living around people who accepted modern ways, ways that Mathabane wanted to follow.

Spelling, Punctuation, and Accuracy   Here are some points to focus on:

■ *Spelling and capitalization:* Don't forget to check names and titles.
■ *Mistaken identities:* Check words like *except* and *accept,* or *it's* and *its* (more apostrophes to check).
■ *Periods and commas:* Are you sure that each of these is at the proper place?
■ *Question marks:* You may notice these more easily if you read your essay aloud. Does each question end with a question mark?
■ *Accuracy:* Check what you quoted and what you paraphrased or summarized. Are the quotes accurate? Do you use quotation marks only where needed? Do you include quotation marks at the beginning *and* the end of each quote? Check the rest of the punctuation in the quote and the punctuation of any sentence you are combining with the quote.
■ *Format:* Do you have appropriate headings, titles, indentations, and page numbers?

Proofreading: Checking and Rechecking

Revision and editing often create new mistakes.

Read every sentence and paragraph at least one more time.

Read your paper aloud.

Read backward from the end of the paper.

Check the format one more time.

It's not realistic to expect every final draft you turn in to be absolutely perfect, but the more you check, the sharper your eye for details will become. This is the point at which your paper will be ready to turn in. The results of your paper should be evident on every page.

EXERCISE 13.1   **Proofread the final paragraph of the paper.**

> In conclusion, Mathabane just doesn't get it. He thinks rules and rituals are just a waste of time. He doesn't see how they can help us learn to respect others and be more courtous to them. I think that Mathabane was to immature to understand that rituals can help us grow up. They can help develop self-responsibility and to become more mature, which is something most people could use more of. Mathabane only thinks about himself and thats why he doesn't want to do the rituals that help the whole family. Basically he wrong. Rules and rituals are something you should follow and practice

EXERCISE 13.2   **Proofread an essay that you have written.**

THE FINAL PRODUCT

Let's now look at the final version of "Rules and Rituals," a finished essay that has been proofread carefully and is ready to turn in.

Sanchez 1

Maria Sanchez
Dr. Simpson
ENG 100G10
December 12, 2001

Rules and Rituals

Rules and rituals are things people do. Every day we follow some kind of rules. We also participate in rituals, although we might not know it. Mark Mathabane knew he participated in rituals, more than he wanted to. He lived with his family in a poor section of South Africa. His father was from the tribes, but his family was now living around people who accepted modern ways, ways that Mathabane wanted to follow. His father insisted that the whole family follow tribal rules and rituals. He became angry and violent when Mathabane wouldn't obey the rules or follow the traditions. Mathabane writes about his hatred of rules and rituals in "My Father's Tribal Rule." Maybe because Mathabane disliked rules and rituals, he couldn't see that they can be valuable and that they do have a purpose. Rules and rituals can teach us many things. They can teach us to have respect, they can aid us in growing up, and they can help the whole family.

First, rules teach respect. Mathabane tells about the rule his father had about not speaking at the table. He tells us that "one day [he] intentionally broke one of these laws" (42). He spoke during dinner, and his father got really mad and said, "You don't have two mouths to afford you such a luxury" (42). Then he threatened to cut out Mathabane's tongue. What Mathabane didn't understand was that his father got mad because Mathabane wasn't respecting him. One time my father got mad at me, too. In my family, we have a dinnertime ritual. Before dinner, my brothers, my sister, and I are supposed to clean the house and get everything ready for dinner. One day I didn't feel like doing it, because I usually end up doing most of the work. My brothers and my sister don't do hardly anything. This one time I just sat on the couch and watched TV. My father came in and saw me, and then he started to yell at me. He said he worked hard every day to put food on the table and that I was showing disrespect to him, my mother, my brothers, and my sister. He sent me to bed without supper. At first I was really mad because I thought that my father was unfair to me. I'm the oldest, so I wind up doing most of the work. Why should I have to clean the house every day and get the table ready? But the more I thought about it, the worse I felt. My father does a lot for us. Besides providing us with a house and food, he pays for us to go to the movies. He really does do a lot for us and sometimes I think we forget to say "thank you." I felt bad for not respecting my father. I learned through this rule to respect my father. Unlike me, Mathabane didn't see the valuable things you can learn from rules.

Second, while rules can teach us things, rituals can help us grow. Mathabane tells us about his little brother George. It was time for his mother to wean George and so "she smeared her breasts with red pepper and then invited my brother to suckle" (41). Of course, George's mouth must have burned like fire. Soon he stopped nursing. Mathabane thought, "It was amusing to witness my mother do it" (41). He just saw this ritual as funny. He didn't understand that its purpose was "to mark George's passage from infancy to childhood" (41). My friend Alan went through a passage similar to George's. Alan's family has a lot of money. Since they are rich, he used to do whatever he wanted because he could afford to. He was really irresponsible and wasted money on stupid stuff that he would get tired of in two days. When his older brother and sister were sixteen, his parents bought cars for them. They bought Alan one when he turned sixteen, too, but they told him that driving a car meant that he had to be very responsible. They told him that driving a car meant that he was no longer a kid. He was now an adult. It's strange, but owning that car really did change him. I guess he realized that you can't act irresponsibly when you're driving several tons of steel. This ritual of getting a car was good for Alan. George's ritual was good for him because it meant he was no longer a baby. Mathabane was just amused by the weaning ritual, because he did not realize how rituals help you grow and become more mature.

Third, the rituals we do every day can help the whole family. Mathabane had to do "rituals spanning the range of day-to-day living" (42). He tells us about all the rituals that his father made the family do. He mentions rituals to "protect the house from evildoers and to safeguard his job" (42). These sound like good things, but "they simply awed, confused, and embarrassed" Mathabane (42). However, as Mathabane's mother observed, "everybody does rituals" (43). In our house, the daily rituals are divided up. Every evening before bed, for instance, it's my job to make sure all the doors are locked and the windows shut and latched. This protects us from evildoers who might want to rob us. I couldn't sleep if I thought I had left the front door unlocked. My sister irons my father's shirts so he'll have a fresh one for work. If he doesn't look professional, he could be looked down on by his boss. This ritual protects his job. In the morning, my father gets lunch ready for everybody. That's his ritual and it helps everybody. My mother supervises and helps whoever needs help. These aren't hard things to do and everybody benefits. The house and my dad's job are protected. Everybody has their lunch ready to go in the morning. Although Mathabane may be confused by the purpose of rituals in his family, I'm not confused about their purpose in my family.

In conclusion, Mathabane just doesn't get it. He thinks rules and rituals are just a waste of time. He doesn't see how they can help us learn to respect others and be more courteous to them. I think that Mathabane was too immature to understand that rituals can help us grow up. They can help us to learn responsibility and to become more mature. These are two things most people could use more of. Mathabane seems to think only about himself and that's why he doesn't want to do the rituals that help the whole family. Basically he is wrong. Rules and rituals are something you should follow and practice.

[the following starts a new page]

Sanchez 5

Works Cited

Mathabane, Mark. "My Father's Tribal Rule." *The User's Guide to College Writing.* N. Kreml, et al. New York: Addison Wesley Longman, 2001. 41–42.

What You've Done

- ■ Read thoughtfully
- ■ Analyzed the assignment
- ■ Done prewriting and organized your ideas
- ■ Drafted introductory, body, and concluding paragraphs
- ■ Revised
- ■ Formatted and proofread

For More on Formatting and Proofreading

- ■ Chapters 22 and 23
    For more Writing Options, see Part One
    For additional strategies, see Part Four

14 Writing Essay Exams and Timed Writing

As you can see from Part Two of this book, the writing process can be quite long and involved. However, not every writing task will demand this much time, and you will find that different tasks call for different strategies. This chapter will show you how to modify the process to match your own strengths and weaknesses as well as to match your task. It will also provide some specific tips on writing in-class essay exams.

MODIFYING THE PROCESS TO MEET YOUR NEEDS

All parts of the writing process are necessary if you are going to produce good writing. However, some of the tasks will come more naturally and more easily to you than others. You will need to be mindful of the way that you write so that you can recognize the parts of the process that you can do quickly and naturally as well as those that you really must concentrate on.

For example, some writers have a great deal of life experience and can quickly come up with their own ideas and topics. Their **prewriting** tasks are usually fairly quick and easily completed. However, these same writers often have difficulty using material from other sources. They may have to devote more time to studying an author's ideas and prewriting about them.

To be a successful writer, you will need to identify the steps that are difficult for you and to decide how much time you need to spend on these steps to complete them successfully.

MODIFYING THE PROCESS TO MATCH YOUR TASK

Even after you have experimented with the process enough to know which parts come naturally and which parts you have to wrestle with, you will still have to adapt your process for each task. Different tasks place different demands on writers—constraints of time, formality and correctness, subject matter, complexity—any of these may require you to modify the process you are most comfortable with.

For example, many beginning writers are very articulate about topics they feel they have something to say about. These writers do not spend a great deal of time prewriting because ideas and examples come easily to them. But when they come across a topic they know less about or find less appealing, they find it hard to think of anything to say. The temptation is often to say "This topic is boring so I can't write about it." Instructors (or employers) are not likely to let these writers switch their topics simply for this reason. In such cases, writers need to fall back on prewriting techniques or research to help them find a way to make the topic more appealing and to give them more to say. The good news is that writing depends on techniques that can be learned, not just inspiration that either hits you or doesn't. When you are feeling uninspired or lost, the techniques often offer you a way to get restarted.

Often, time constraints will require you to alter your process. If you have 55 minutes to write an in-class essay, you have a limited amount of time to **prewrite**, **organize**, **draft**, **revise**, and **edit**. If you are accustomed to taking a few hours or days to prewrite before you begin to organize and draft, you obviously must try a different strategy. We'll discuss writing in timed situations in greater detail in the section below.

You will also want to modify steps for the unique challenges presented by different assignments. For example, some writers find that organizing their ideas on shorter papers is easily done by writing a list of their ideas in the order they plan to include them. However, for longer papers, these same writers have difficulty seeing how to fit more ideas and examples into their writing. For these tasks, they might write sections of their prewriting on index cards so that they can physically move the pieces around and try out different organizations.

The important thing is to experiment: try new things; try old things in new ways. The more you experiment, the more tools you can develop and the more flexible you can be in approaching each new writing situation.

MODIFYING THE PROCESS FOR ESSAY EXAMS

Writing essay exams is perhaps the most difficult writing task for many students. The idea of writing an essay with limited time and limited sources (such as notes, textbooks, or outlines) leaves students feeling powerless. Yet there are many things that students can do and ways they can alter their writing process that can help them write successful essay exams.

Prewriting for Essay Exams

To prepare to write in a timed situation, you need to complete your prewriting activities in two steps. First, complete the reading and writing activities that will help you study and organize the information you will need for the exam. Second, prewrite briefly during the exam period. You may want to merge the analysis of the **prompt**, prewriting, and planning into one brief session at the beginning of the exam. On the following pages are some tips for completing these activities in a short period of time.

1. Prewriting Before Class

■ Review the materials—textbook chapters, handouts, essays, articles, literary works—that you are required to use for the exam, and complete the activities discussed in Chapters 4 and 16 (the reading chapters in Parts Two and Four). Obviously, if you have not previously read these materials, you will need to allow adequate time for reading and for completing the necessary prewriting and studying activities.

■ Think of possible exam questions and essay topics. You can prewrite using these topics to help you learn the material as well as prepare for the exam. You may want to determine what writing mode could help you answer the questions.

■ Review other essay exams and papers you have completed for this instructor. Not only do you want to determine what kinds of questions the instructor will ask, but also the kinds of weaknesses in writing that your instructor has previously pointed out so that you can work to improve in these areas.

■ If your instructor gives open-book exams or allows you to use notes, be sure to review these materials and to mark them so you can find information quickly. You don't want to spend all of your class time reading this material and looking for details.

■ Bring plenty of paper or pens and correcting liquid or erasers. If your instructor allows you to use a dictionary, the textbook or other readings, or study guides, be sure to bring them to class as well.

2. Prewriting in Class

■ The typical classroom prewriting process will run about 5 to 10 minutes for full-length essays and about 2 to 3 minutes for short-answer questions. Read the assigned topics carefully and be sure you understand exactly what you are asked to do. If you have a choice of topics, choose the topic you plan to answer carefully. Do not try to prewrite for more topics than you intend to answer.

■ Analyze the prompt. Underline the **key focus words** and **key action words**. If key action words are not provided, determine what writing **mode** will help you focus, develop, and organize your essay in a way that addresses the prompt.

■ Create lists to plan your answer. First, list the two or three main ideas that you will need to develop your essay. Then, for each main idea, make a list of one or two examples and details from your own ideas and experiences, the assigned readings, and your notes.

Planning and Organizing Your Essay in Class

After you have made notes on the main ideas and the supporting examples and details, you will be ready to do the following:

1. Write a **thesis**. Be sure that the thesis clearly responds to the topic or exam question. You can do this by using the language found in the prompt.

2. Decide the order of the discussion of the main ideas. Making a good list can lead you to discover the organizational pattern you want to use. Any of the common patterns (see Chapter 15) listed below will work:

   Chronological

   Least important to most important

   Cause and effect

   Problem and solution

   Side by side or point by point for compare/contrast

3. Write **topic sentences** for each main idea. Be sure to connect each main idea in the topic sentence to the thesis and prompt by using the same language.

With all of this information, you will have created a brief outline of your thesis and the points of the body paragraphs.

Drafting the Paper

Since you will have time to write only one draft, skip lines to leave room for revision. Don't write on the back of the paper—especially if you are writing in ink. (The ink may bleed through, making the back side of the page difficult for you to revise and for your instructor to grade.)

Budget your time. If you have 30 minutes, don't spend more than 6 or 7 minutes on each paragraph.

Don't stop to do complicated editing as you go. Underline words you'll need to look up in a dictionary, but wait until after completing the draft to actually look them up. (That's why you're skipping lines.)

Revising, Editing, and Proofreading

Once you have drafted your essay, allow yourself 10 to 15 minutes to revise, edit, and proofread it. It is important at this point to focus on correctness and clarity rather than neatness. Don't spend time recopying your response. Neatness rarely counts, but readability always does. So spend your time making your essay easier to understand and follow. Along with making changes that strengthen your content, you will want to be sure that your reader can tell where you are inserting material and which material you are scratching out. Unless you are given an additional class period to complete a major revision for the exam, you will not have time to do more than this. However, as you edit and proofread your writing, you should check these basic aspects of the essay:

- Are your paragraph breaks logical? You can always change the beginnings and endings of paragraphs by drawing lines and paragraph symbols.
- Do the thesis and main ideas match?
- If you changed your mind about which main ideas to use in developing your paper or if you changed your **plan of development**, check to see if your thesis still fits the body of your paper.
- If you find that one of the paragraphs doesn't fit your thesis or is a repetition of the same ideas, eliminate the paragraph by crossing out the paragraph with an **X** over the deleted material. If you have time at the end of class, you can write another paragraph to insert in the essay to replace the deleted material.

Recopy as little of your essay as possible. If you have made so many changes in one paragraph that it is extremely hard to read, recopy only that paragraph. Write a note in the margin indicating where your reader can find the new paragraph.

During the editing process, you need to work on word choices and correctness.

- Do you need to change some words to clarify your point? Check for potentially confused words that would alter the meaning of your essay. For example, you don't want to confuse the words *affect* and *effect*.
- Do you need to add words or to clarify how your ideas and sentences are related to each other?
- Have you omitted words when writing or changing sentences?
- Check for these major grammar and usage issues (see Chapter 23 for details):

    Sentence boundaries—**fragments** and **run-ons**

    Verbs

    Punctuation

    Spelling

You may like the idea of using liquid paper because your essays will look neater after you have revised, edited, and proofread. However, you will either spend valuable time waiting for the liquid paper to dry or go on to other tasks and take the risk that you won't remember to write in your correction. It may be better to draw a single line through the words you want to change and neatly write in the new words in the blank line above them.

As in all skills, the more you write timed essays, the better you will become at producing them. Until writing in-class essays becomes natural for you, focus on each of the steps discussed in this chapter.

15

Writing Narration, Definition, Persuasion, and Other Modes

Modes of Writing
Narration
Description
Definition
Classification
Comparison and contrast
Illustration
Process
Persuasion and argument
Cause and effect

In many college writing tasks, you will be asked to respond to an assignment with a specific **critical thinking**, **developing**, and **organizing** strategy—what composition instructors often call the **modes** of writing. For example, a history instructor may ask you to compare America's attitudes toward World Wars I and II. A psychology instructor may ask you to define "mental illness." A computer instructor may ask you to explain the process of segmenting a hard drive. An English instructor may ask you to write a character analysis. These tasks may require a couple of paragraphs or a full-length essay. No matter what the requirements are, you can use the same steps for generating and organizing material. The only difference will be the amount of material you need.

In this chapter, we will provide tips for the common modes of writing.

NARRATION

 Narrative writing is used to describe a sequence of events or actions, and it is very similar to fiction writing found in short stories, novels, plays, and movies.

Purpose

When writing a narrative, you need to reveal a **purpose** that allows the reader to determine the meaning of events and why they matter. For example, are you trying to convey conflict or tension and how this was resolved? Are you trying to demonstrate how you or a place has changed—or stayed the same—over time?

Development

Good narrative writing includes many of the same features as **descriptive** writing—a combination of general as well as specific information and the use of concrete nouns with descriptive adjectives and adverbs. Vivid descriptions of the places, people, and events involved in a narrative add life and meaning to all writing.

Many inexperienced writers have problems with details: they either tend to give too many or not enough, and they don't always understand that readers do not need a description of everything that happened or was said. For example, if you were describing a car accident, you would not discuss every detail: the man grabbed the door handle, pulled the handle, pushed the door open, put one leg on the ground, then the second leg, then stood up, then prepared to walk, and he stopped and said, "Are you okay?" Such minute detail would distract and bore a reader. Although you may want to write down everything that happened and was said during the **prewriting** and **planning** steps, you will need to select the relevant details that convey your purpose and meaning.

Organization

When organizing a narrative, you may choose to tell the events in the order or sequence in which they occurred. To do this, you can make a list of events that happened and then rearrange them in the order they happened. To signal the order of events, writers use words like *first, next, then, after that, while, when,* and *before.*

Sometimes it is more effective to rearrange the order of events, especially if you are trying to create suspense. Flashbacks and flashforwards are two techniques for altering the sequence of events. In a flashback, the narrator goes back to a time before the present sequence of events being described; in a flashforward the narrator describes a sequence of events in the future. Both techniques allow a writer to show relationships among events that may be separated by a long period of time or that may be connected in the narrator's mind even though others may not see the connection.

The box below highlights some techniques useful in writing narration.

Tips for the Narrative Mode

Be careful to establish a point of view and to use verb tenses appropriately. Here are some guidelines to help you do this:

Point of view: Point of view is the position from which the narrative is told. One way to understand point of view is to consider who is telling the story (or narrating it). Think about witnesses at a car accident. The driver, the passenger who wakes up as the crash is occurring, and a bystander who observes the accident from outside the car have all witnessed the same event but their accounts of the event would differ greatly because they saw, felt, and were aware of different things. The different ways of telling the story of this wreck represent different points of view.

To establish the point of view in narrative writing, you need to choose a narrator—the person who will tell the events of the story. You can choose a third-person narrator—a person who will be objective and tell the events from an outsider's

continued on next page

> *continued from previous page*
>
> point of view. This person or voice is usually not involved in the events or may not even exist except in the mind of the reader. Another kind of narrator is a first-person narrator—a character who is experiencing the events while describing them. You may realize that there is such a thing as second-person pronouns, but you don't want to attempt a narrative in second person.
>
> **Verb tense:**   Verb tenses show the passage of time and indicate clearly the order of events. For example, "We walked to the store" indicates an event that has already happened. If your next sentence is "we watched the movie," your reader needs to know the order in which these events occurred as well as their relationship.

The time and relationship of the two events mentioned in the box can be conveyed in many ways:

We walked to the store before we watched the movie.

We watched the movie, and then we walked to the store.

We walked to the store to avoid watching the movie.

We walked to the store instead of watching the movie.

We were expected to walk to the store before we watched the movie.

We had to stop the movie so we could walk to the store.

We walked to the video store so we could rent a movie to watch that night.

The list of possibilities is endless, but the point is simple. To demonstrate time and relationship, we had to vary the verb tenses and the way words were used in the sentence. This same level of attention to verbs is required throughout a narrative so that your readers will not get confused about the sequence of events and how they fit together to create meaning.

Examples of Essays Written in the Narrative Mode
Julia Alverez, "Hold the Mayonnaise," p. 471
Malcolm X, "A Prison Education," p. 507
Elizabeth Wong, "The Struggle to Be an All-American Girl," p. 519

DESCRIPTION

 When writing description, you will be asked to put into words how something looks or appears or the way something acts. You will be expected to focus on details, especially those details that reveal the essence of what is being described.

Often you will be asked to describe something that you are very familiar with (your house, a person close to you, your favorite place) or something very new to you (a painting for an art class, a character in a work of literature, a piece of new machinery used in your field of study). For familiar objects, you will need to find a new way to see them. For new objects, you will have to study them closely in order to understand them. In either case, you will be asked to examine an object in depth, to give all relevant details, and to make the subject come alive.

Purpose

When you begin writing a description, you need to consider your purpose for writing and what the reader is going to do with this knowledge. If you are writing an ad to sell your car, your readers will want to know what the car looks like and its condition. They will not be interested in details about personal items in the car or how you feel about it. However, if you are writing an essay on car ownership, you may want to show how cars reflect personality or values, and you may want to include personal information.

There are two types of descriptive writing: technical and evocative. In **technical description**, the writer provides pictorial data in an orderly manner that reveals the purpose, function, or appearance of a subject. This kind of description is most often found in instructional materials, such as user manuals and technical manuals. The order of the details provided should focus on how the object is constructed and how all the parts relate to each other. Since the writer is not trying to convey any emotional connection to the subject, the tone needs to remain objective and the language will need to be precise and technical. For example, to describe the CPU of your computer you would need to mention the visible parts—such as the power button, the reset button, the 3½-inch disk drive, the CD-ROM drive, and the zip drive. You would also need to describe clearly where these parts are in relation to each other—above, below, 3 inches to the left, and so on. Many technical descriptions include a drawing of the subject with the important components labeled.

In **evocative description** the writer emphasizes the emotional aspects of the subject to create a vivid impression. In this type of writing your goal is to reveal the personal aspects of the subject, to move your readers from being detached to being emotionally involved. While you may be tempted to include a painting, drawing, or photograph of the subject being described, this will not make your task any easier.

Let's say you have been asked to describe a favorite place, and you have chosen to write about what your room looks like. In a technical description, you would give all aspects of the subject equal and objective treatment. In an evocative description, you would want to emphasize some aspects of the subject more than others to encourage an emotional response. You would focus more on **connotation** (the emotional aspect) than **denotation** (the objective meaning). For example, instead of using the word "closet" you might use the phrase "overflowing river" to create an image of a closet so crammed full that stuff falls out of it when the door is opened.

Development

When prewriting and planning a descriptive paper, you will need to answer these questions:

- What is the subject?
- What are its dimensions (size and shape)?
- What materials is it made of?
- What is its purpose or use?
- Where is it made or manufactured?
- Where is it most commonly found?
- When does it appear?
- When does one need it?
- Why is it of value?
- Why is it important for the reader to understand it?
- Who needs or uses it?
- Who made it?
- How is it used?
- How does it work?

Organization

When organizing a piece of descriptive writing, it is important to choose a consistent angle or **point of view** that establishes how each new detail is related to the previous ones. One method is to describe every detail from a single reference point or viewpoint. This works best for if you are describing a stationary object or if you want to capture everything that the reader would see from one particular place. For example, you may be describing something you see when you look out your bedroom window: a new car parked in the driveway. Or you may choose to describe everything you see looking out of your window. Once the reader has an angle or point of view, you can then use words and phrases like *to my left* or *in front of the car.*

Another method for organizing descriptions is *spatial,* which means to move around the object or through the place or scene being described. Instead of describing how the car looks in the driveway, you may choose to walk around the car to describe how it looks. Instead of looking out the window to describe your neighborhood, you may choose to walk down the street. If you are moving, your reader will need words such as *down, along,* and *next* to understand the relationship of details.

Tips for the Descriptive Mode

Use both general and specific language. You may be describing a car in general, but you will want to include the specifics that make it a car as opposed to a truck. You also need to be more specific in describing the particular car by discussing its make, model, year, and features that distinguish it from other cars.

Use concrete nouns—nouns that refer to specific places and physical objects—an important part of descriptive writing. These nouns help your readers visualize the place or thing you are describing. For example, *transportation* is an abstract noun that refers to an idea, not to a specific object; *bicycle, subway, train, airplane, car,*

continued on next page

continued from previous page

and *bus* are concrete nouns that name a specific vehicle. In descriptive writing, it's best to use concrete nouns, so your readers will immediately visualize an object similar to the one you are writing about.

Support concrete nouns with carefully chosen adjectives and adverbs that will help readers focus on the qualities of the subject that you want to convey. For example, if you are writing an evocative description of your first car and want readers to understand that you loved this car even though it was old and rundown, you would not describe it as having a *metallic* paint job because metallic might leave the impression of newness. Using the adjective *dull* will better convey the feeling you are trying to get across.

Use sensory words—words related to our senses of sight, touch, taste, smell, and sound—to create a picture for readers. When writing a descriptive paper, you would probably focus first on sight—how the subject looks. However, sight alone may not be enough to capture the essence of a subject. Therefore, you might need to consider other senses when describing a subject. How does an object feel? Is its texture *smooth, rough, cold, spongelike, soft,* etc.? How does an object taste—*bitter, sour, metallic, burning,* etc.? How an object smells is important not only for foods and perfumed objects but also for clothing materials, plants, animals, etc. You may use words such as *soured, flowery, pungent, rank.* How an object sounds is a way to describe musical instruments as well as machinery and living creatures. Think about words such as *clanking, whining, reedy,* etc.

Examples of Essays Written in the Descriptive Mode

Randall Williams, "Daddy Tucked the Blanket," p. 458
Mark Mathabane, "My Father's Tribal Rule," p. 40
George Orwell, "A Hanging," p. 54

DEFINITION

In a **definition** essay, your aim will be to help readers understand the meaning of words or concepts, particularly those that are abstract or complex. Let's say you are writing about welfare. You might begin by defining this term as government assistance to individuals. But then you'll need to explain that there are several kinds of government programs for assisting both individuals and businesses. One person's use of the word *welfare* may be in reference to one particular type of assistance for unwed mothers, while another person may be referring to medical assistance for the elderly, and yet a third person may mean tax breaks given to individuals and businesses.

Purpose

There are three common purposes of definition papers:

- To explain how a word or phrase should be used (*technical definition*)
- To explain the writer's attitude toward a word or phrase (*personal definition*)
- To show how the meaning of a word has changed or is changing (*historical definition*)

Development

In a definition essay, your role will be to provide more than just a repetition of the meaning listed in a dictionary entry. But the dictionary is a good place to start when prewriting for this kind of essay. You will probably have to read through the several definitions given, each providing a slightly different meaning. You will obviously not discuss all of these; more likely you will find one or two words that fit your purpose and can be used as the basis of your essay.

For example, here is what you might find if you look up the word *love:*

Strong affection for another arising out of kinship or personal ties, such as maternal love for a child

Attraction based on sexual desire, or the affection and tenderness felt by lovers

Attraction based on admiration, benevolence, or common interests, such as love for a friend

Warm attachment, enthusiasm, or devotion to something, such as the love of a sport or place

Unselfish loyalty and benevolent concern for the good of another, such as brotherly love

A person's adoration of a god or religious figure

A beloved person

A term of endearment

An amorous episode, such as an affair

A score of zero in tennis

Obviously, when you use the word *love* in a particular situation, you would not expect the reader or listener to think of all these meanings. In fact, to do so would be inappropriate. But your reader or listener may be thinking of a definition of the word that you did not intend. Therefore, it is important when writing or giving a presentation that you establish the meaning of a word for your audience.

You must also consider whether to discuss the *denotations* of a word—the direct, specific meaning—as well as the connotations—the meanings or emotions triggered by the use of the word. For example, the denotations of the word *welfare* are (1) the state of doing well, especially in respect to good fortune, happiness, well-being, or prosperity, and (2) relating to the improvement of disadvantaged social groups. However, each reader of those meanings will also have certain emotional reactions—connotations—to the word *welfare*, depending on their personal experiences and beliefs. A person who has family members receiving welfare benefits may have a different reaction than a person who has never known anyone who received this assistance.

There are several ways to write a definition. During the prewriting stage of your paper, you may want to try all the methods listed below to determine which works best for you or whether you want to include more than one of these methods of development.

You can define a word by using the following methods:

- Provide other words that mean the same thing; these are known as *synonyms*.
- Compare two or more meanings to distinguish among the meanings.
- Explain the function of the word.
- Provide examples to demonstrate how the word is used.
- Explain what the word does not mean.

For technical definitions, you will need to analyze the object by naming it and all of its parts:

- What is the object and its history?
- What is object made of, or what does it look like?
- What does it do?
- How does it work?
- Who uses it?
- How is the object similar to other words like it?
- How is it different than these objects?

Organization

The organization of a definition paper should suit the purpose and the methods of development used. For historical definitions, you would probably begin with the original use of the word and trace the changes in meaning through the present. In some situations, it might be better to start with the present meaning and trace it back in time to its roots. Either method requires that you organize your material in chronological order.

For technical definitions, you may want to organize the paper by focusing first on the object being defined, as a whole—what does it mean in general and what are its *major* features? Then, you would discuss the individual features of the object—the details of how it is made and used.

For personal definitions, you have more flexibility in organizing the paper, but you do need to be careful to remain focused on your readers' needs and expectations. Remember that your readers may not share your personal definition and will respond emotionally to your words.

Let's look again at how we organized the two denotations of the word *welfare*. We began with the least-used denotation, or definition—the state of doing well, especially in respect to good fortune, happiness, well-being, or prosperity. This placement was intentional, and we suspected that very few readers would think of this meaning of the word. We knew that they would have stronger feelings about the second denotation, or definition—relating to the improvement of disadvantaged social groups. Since we expected strong personal reactions to the second, we thought they would not really pay serious attention to the other denotation. We also wanted to remind them of the original meaning of the word *welfare*—how someone is doing—a meaning having a positive connotation. We realized that the negative connotations most often associated with the second definition may have prevented readers from acknowledging this positive connotation of the original definition.

Tip for the Definitive Mode

Focus on *word choice* and *phrasing*. These are particularly important when writing definitions because you are expected to be as precise as possible in relating the meaning of the term you are defining.

Examples of Essays Written in the Definitive Mode

Dorsett Bennett, "I, Too, Am a Good Parent," p. 468
J.J. Thompson, "Plugging the Kegs," p. 486
Nancy Mairs, "On Being a Cripple," p. 558

CLASSIFICATION

In a **classification** essay you will be analyzing a group of things that have similarities and perhaps breaking certain elements into smaller groups. For example, you might classify types of music—classical, pop, big band, jazz, hiphop, rap, R&B, etc.

In another type of classification, you might be separating one object into parts, pieces, sections, or categories for a close examination of the object. For example, an automobile can be analyzed in terms of thousands of parts or it can be more generally categorized into major parts—its engine, drive or transmission, exterior or body, interior.

Purpose

The purpose of classification essays is to analyze similar things and to show the relationships, differences, connections, and associations among them.

Development

Part of the prewriting process for classification is to find or create clear categories. These categories need to meet the following guidelines:

- The categories need to be the *major* categories of the whole or the general classification. For example, if we are discussing a classification system for transportation, we might use the following major categories, each of which has its own subcategories:

  Airplanes

  Trains

  Ships

  Automobiles

  We would not expect to see a category called *ski lift* because it is not a major mode of transportation.

- The level of categories discussed should be *consistent*. We would not expect any of the list below used to classify modes of transportation since they are categories of automobiles, and therefore, subcategories, not major modes of transportation:

  Sports utility vehicles (SUVs)

  Subcompact cars

  Indy cars

- A *component* of the whole should not fit into two categories. If this occurs, it probably means that the two categories are really two subcategories of a larger group and should be combined into the major category. For example, if we had used the category Subcompact Cars in our list of types of transportation, we would be able to fit a Nissan Sentra in two categories—Automobiles and Subcompact Cars.

- The list of categories needs to be *complete*. When we look back at our list of the major modes of transportation, we should have a list that is complete so that we could find a category for any vehicle that transports people or goods.

- The categories should be *significant* and useful to your readers, who should be convinced that you have conducted an in-depth analysis of the topic. For example, a reader would not find the following classification of modes of transportation very useful:

  Air transportation

  Land transportation

  Sea transportation

However, if you did choose to use these categories, you would still need to create subcategories for each group so that the number of vehicles in each category would not be overwhelming to the reader.

Organization

One way to organize a classification paper is to discuss each of the major categories in an order determined by their relationships. For example, if you are tracing the history of the modes of transportation, you would use a chronological order. If you were conducting an analysis of the best mode of transportation, you might organize your information by moving from worst to best records.

Tips for the Classification Mode

Don't oversimplify. Beginning writers tend to create categories that are too broad. A paper classifying movies should do more than provide a discussion of good movies and bad movies.

Don't stereotype. Too often categories of groups of people tend to be stereotypes, lacking any fair and clear distinctions. Let's say you have been asked to create categories of TV shows. If you decide to create categories based on what shows ethnic groups watch, it would be stereotyping to distinguish them by stating that a group watches shows that include only people in that group or that are about a topic associated with that group. For example, you wouldn't categorize TV shows with Jewish actors (such *Seinfeld*) as those watched by Jewish viewers or shows about the mob (*Wiseguy, The Sopranos*) as those watched by people of Italian descent.

Examples of Essays Written in the Classification Mode

Michael Bronski, "Magic and AIDS: Presumed Innocent," p. 44
Linda Robinson, "Hispanics Don't Exist," p. 568
Karen Wright and Sarah Richardson, "Human in the Age of Mechanical Reproduction," p. 596

COMPARISON AND CONTRAST

 Comparison and contrast papers provide an analysis of the similarities and differences among related items. For example, if you were preparing to buy a car, you would compare the different makes and models of cars to decide which one would best suit your needs.

Purpose

The purpose of comparison and contrast papers is to organize information on related items so that readers can make the best decision about them. Comparison papers can be objective or **persuasive**. If the paper is objective, the reader expects a comparison and contrast of the topic without a recommendation, which means the reader expects to make the decision based on the information provided. If the paper is persuasive, the reader expects to be given a recommendation based on the comparison and contrast of the subject. Whether the purpose is objective or persuasive, the reader expects a fair and complete comparison.

Development

In a comparison paper, you provide the criteria for comparison and then apply all of the criteria to each item being discussed. The first step in prewriting to develop your paper is to determine the criteria. For example, when comparing cars, you might select any of these criteria: size, price, reliability, dependability, style, optional features, cost of maintenance and repair, resale value, expected life of the car, performance of the engine, or safety features. Once you have selected the criteria, you then need to prewrite to find the supporting evidence and the criteria for each item. For example, if you chose resale value as a means of comparison and you were comparing six cars, you would need to find the resale value for all six cars.

After you have gathered your information, you will need to analyze it. If you are writing an objective paper, you may choose to simply list the details. But you can also provide some interpretation or scale for your reader. You might rank the items based on the criteria. For example, if you are comparing the resale values of six cars, you might give a rank of from 1 to 6 for the highest to lowest resale value, an analysis that will help readers interpret the information. However, such rankings do not imply a recommendation of which car to buy because there are other criteria to consider.

If you are writing a persuasive comparison paper, you will need to determine the recommendation by weighing all the criteria. Since one product or item is usually best for one criterion and not as good for another, you will need to discuss fully how you determined which item or product to recommend.

Organization

Comparison papers can be organized in two ways: side-by-side and point-by-point.

Side-by-side organization is arranged according to the items being compared. You would first discuss each item individually, and then in a separate section discuss the similarities and differences among the items. For example, if you were comparing three political candidates, you might begin by discussing each one of them individually (in three separate paragraphs). You would then write several more paragraphs in which you compared candidates based on selected criteria. This organizing method works best if you are comparing two or three items; if there are more, the reader is likely to get lost. Beginning writers tend to discuss each of the items well but they are less likely to provide an adequate and fully developed comparison of items. Without this comparison, the paper is a description, not a comparison, and does not fulfill the readers' expectations.

Here is an example of side-by-side organization for an assignment comparing the types of daytime TV shows:

1. Talk shows
2. Soap operas
3. Game shows
4. Comparison of all three based on the selected criteria
5. Contrast of all three based on the selected criteria

Point-by-point organization is arranged according to the criteria selected for comparison. Let's look again at three criteria you might use to compare the three political candidates. If you decide to discuss all three candidates as you discuss each criterion, you will need to choose the order in which to discuss the criteria; usually from least to most important or from most to least important will work. You can probably choose any order for the items being compared under each criterion, but the order of these items should be the same in each paragraph of criteria.

Here is an example of how point-by-point organization might be used in the assignment comparing daytime TV shows:

1. Educational value
   a. Talk shows
   b. Soap operas
   c. Game shows
2. Entertainment value
   a. Talk shows
   b. Soap operas
   c. Game shows
3. Appropriateness for children
   a. Talk shows
   b. Soap operas
   c. Game shows

Tips for the Compare/Contrast Mode

Pay close attention to *transitions* in all comparison and contrast essays. Since you will be discussing at least two items, your reader may get confused if you are not clear about which item you are discussing. For that reason, you must clearly indicate when you switch from one item to the next. Also, you will need to provide transitions to indicate if you are comparing or contrasting since most comparison papers include discussions of both similarities and differences. Transitional words and phrases such as *on the other hand, similarly,* and *in contrast* will help readers follow your ideas.

Another way to help readers understand all the information provided in a comparison essay is to use *graphics* such as charts and graphs. These visual aids both help organize the ideas and provide a quick reference to the information at a later time.

ILLUSTRATION

 Illustration, sometimes called **exemplification,** is a mode that uses examples to **support** an idea. In previous chapters, we have demonstrated how to use examples to support ideas for all assignments. However, in an illustration essay, the examples are much more fully developed and the writer may include several examples. Since the focus of the paper is the illustrations, the writer does not provide much discussion of the relationships between the thesis and the illustrations or examples.

Purpose

Illustration papers provide the audience with extensive examples that are designed to draw a picture of a situation, place, or event in much the same way description papers do. The difference is that illustration papers usually combine the elements of narration (what happened) with description (what something looks like) so that the reader will have a more in-depth example or several different examples; it is this accumulation of examples and illustrations that allows the reader to find the patterns and relationships among the examples, and therefore, understand the author's point.

Development

When prewriting an illustration paper, you will want to create a list of all possible examples and illustrations that will help make your point or prove your thesis. In fact, sometimes this kind of list is used as a list in the essay to demonstrate the amount of evidence. A list works well if your readers are familiar with the topic and will quickly understand how most of the list proves your point. However, if your list includes only what they previously knew, this method of development will not work. You need either to add more items to the list that provide new information or to make an unusual or surprising point by using a list of items.

If a list of the examples will not work for your assignment, you need to choose a number of examples from the list and prewrite to develop fully the ones you plan to include in your paper. You can use the same techniques for developing narration and description to provide the necessary details and specifics needed for extended illustrations.

When choosing which details and specifics to include in the essay, you will want to focus on those that not only establish the story and describe the situation but also show (or imply) the connections between the illustration and your thesis. This is important since in illustration papers the bulk of the focus is on the example itself rather than the writer's explanation of it. We saw earlier that Michael Bronski gives illustrations in his essay "Magic and AIDS: Presumed Innocent" (pp. 44–52) to show how the media depict the lives of people with HIV to determine the "innocence" or "guilt" of a victim. When you read the essay, you will notice that most of the development focuses on what the media said about each of the people he includes, without much of his own interpretation or discussion. The accumulation of examples and illustrations enables the reader to understand Bronski's conclusion.

Another common feature of illustration papers is the use of several extended examples that may at first glance appear to be random choices. Bronski presents several examples showing patterns of the media's depiction of certain people's lives. He chooses celebrities from the entertainment and sports worlds as well as ordinary people who became famous only because they contracted HIV. At first glance, these examples seem as unrelated as the individuals themselves. But as we read Bronski's essay, we begin to see the pattern being established. As Bronski interprets it for us, we are more likely to reach a point of understanding and acceptance.

Organization

To organize an illustration paper effectively, you must find the order of examples that will best build your case or support your thesis. One way to organize the material is to move from shorter to longer examples. Another way is to move from least important to most important and yet another is to move from most familiar to least familiar. As you can see, there are numerous possibilities, depending on your purpose and audience, including those discussed on page 229.

Tips for the Illustrative Mode

Carefully determine the types and number of *examples* you need to include in your essay. If you use too many, you might bore your readers. If the examples are too obvious, your readers may be insulted. For example, if you are writing an essay on welfare and include every example you can think of related to unwed mothers on welfare, you need to make sure that these examples are not repetitions. Each example should add a new idea or a greater level of understanding for the reader. Also, if you can't think of other examples of people receiving welfare benefits, you may be stereotyping and your illustrations will not lead to new information or understanding for the reader.

Review all *transitions*, an important aspect of an illustration paper. Beginning writers tend to use transitions such as *first, second, third,* and so on, while others use *also, and, another example,* and so on. Neither of these patterns for transitions will work well in an illustration paper. Examples should be organized so that their relationships create the necessary transition. For example, two examples may include similar

continued on next page

> *continued from previous page*
>
> language or use a word in two distinct ways; putting these examples close together can help establish the pattern you want your readers to find. If there are no obvious connections between examples, you will need to provide informative transitions that let the reader know that you have changed from one example to another.

Michael Bronski provides such transitions in "Magic and AIDS." For example, he ends his example about Marc Christian with the following statement:

> The images of "guilty" and "innocent" AIDS victims are still strongly embedded in our culture. And although these ideas are a baseline for much popular and media thinking, they are not without variants.

He immediately begins the next example, that of Dr. Veronica Prego. It is clear to readers that he is beginning an example that shows a variation of the ideas illustrated by the example of Marc Christian.

Examples of Essays Written in the Illustrative Mode

Jack G. Shaheen, "The Media's Image of Arabs," p. 503
Renee Loth, "Measuring Success," p. 39
Jon D. Hull, "Slow Descent to Hell," p. 526

PROCESS

Process papers explain how to do something or how something works. Some are instructions that show readers how to perform a process—for example, how to configure the hard drive on a computer. Others are descriptions that help readers understand what is being done, has been done, or will be done. An example of this would be a description of how to reform the welfare system.

Purpose

The purpose of process papers is to provide readers with the sequence of actions involved in a process or procedure. Process descriptions are intended for those who need to understand the process so that they can make a decision; these readers do not need to perform the process, just understand it. Process instructions should be written so that readers can successfully perform the sequence of actions that lead to, or should lead to, a predictable result.

Development

Process papers, whether descriptions or instructions, must be accurate and specific. Imagine that you are trying to explain why you need more staff working in your department. To demonstrate that more help is needed, you would have to provide detailed and specific evidence of what you do, how you do it, and how long it takes. Without adequate details, a supervisor may argue that you don't do enough and that you don't perform your job efficiently.

When you prewrite, you will want to create a list or **flowchart** of steps involved in the process. If you are writing instructions, you need to include each step in detail; in fact, you need enough detail that the reader will be able to complete the process without having to discuss it with anyone else (including you, the writer). If you have ever purchased an item that required assembly, you probably know how poorly some instructions are written. Your goal is to provide enough detail for your reader to be successful on the first attempt at completing the process.

If you are writing a process description, you will need to determine what details and specifics to include in the overview of the process or procedure. You will also need to determine what the reader already knows about the process. For example, your approach for a paper on reforming the welfare system would be very different if your audience were taxpayers rather than politicians.

You also need to consider adding graphics, such as drawings and flowcharts, so that your reader can visualize the process. Flowcharts are useful if the process is one of sequential steps, while charts and drawings are useful when there are steps that occur at the same time or the order of steps is not important.

Organization

To organize a process paper, you must follow the logical order of actions required to perform or understand the process or procedure. In most situations, you will introduce the process by identifying its purpose and major steps. If you are writing instructions, you will need to include a list of equipment and materials in this introduction.

When organizing the body of the paper, you want to group the steps into manageable chunks. For example, if the process requires fifty pieces of equipment that are used to manufacture five large sections of something, you can divide your process description into five sections as well. The order of these five sections would be determined by their relationships. If one part must be completed before moving to the next, you would organize according to that order. If the five sections can be completed in any order and then merged into one unit, then you would have six sections in your paper: one for each of the five parts and a sixth to show how to combine the five parts.

If you are writing instructions, you will want to include a troubleshooting section at the end of the paper. For process descriptions, you will need to conclude the paper by providing readers with information on the next step or what to do with their knowledge of the process.

Tips for the Process Mode

Start your sentences with verbs that direct readers to the *action to be performed.* An instruction that says "First, you should insert the disk in your computer at home" would be better if written as follows: "Insert disk into the 3½-inch disk drive." Your readers should obviously know where their computer is, and they probably know that the disk is to be inserted somewhere in the computer.

Don't assume that your reader knows any of the steps in a process or that a particular step is obvious. Most likely it won't be. For example, purchasers of new computer software will probably know that the disk containing the new program must be inserted into the floppy drive, but they may not know how to create or change the path the computer looks for when the program is installed.

Remember to *list* which actions readers should avoid when you are giving instructions. If you are providing instructions on how to load a computer program onto the hard drive of a computer, you should include a warning that all virus scanning programs must be disabled before installing the new program. It's best to include such warnings early in the instructions, not at the end.

Example of Essay Written in the Process Mode

Stanley Milgram, "The Perils of Obedience," p. 548

PERSUASION AND ARGUMENT

Persuasion papers seek to cause change by convincing the reader to do or to think something. **Argument** papers present reasons and evidence to support a position without intending a change in action. For example, a persuasion paper would include an argument with reasons and evidence, but would also include a call for action by the readers. An argument paper would focus on explaining a position to simply convey information to the reader.

Purpose

The purpose of persuasion papers is to change the way readers think or act; the purpose of argument papers is to inform or educate readers by explaining a position on an issue.

Development

In both persuasion and argument papers, you must include logical reasons for your position and convincing evidence to support it. You will first want to make a list of all the reasons why you hold a certain position and select the ones that are most logical and convincing. You should ask yourself three questions when choosing the reasons to include in your paper:

- How does this reason support my position?
- Why is this reason important?
- Will the reader be convinced by this reason? Why or why not?

While the reasons for your position are important, the bulk of the paper will be the evidence you use to support your position. As you prewrite, you will want to select the most convincing evidence—examples, personal anecdotes, statistics, and testimony. You should also include quotations, **paraphrases**, and **summaries** and be able to document all such evidence thoroughly.

After you have listed your reasons and provided supporting evidence, you need to answer questions that will show the logic of your thinking and anticipate your readers' reactions to your paper:

Are the reasons logical and convincing rather than based solely on personal taste (likes or dislikes) or unimportant criteria (since person X has this position, I have to take the same position)?

Can you provide logical explanations to connect the reasons and evidence?

What are the weaknesses in the reasons and evidence?

What counterarguments will readers think of while reading the paper?

If you are writing a persuasion paper, you will need to include a discussion of what you want readers to think or do—ideally a specific action as well as something that will impact the situation.

Organization

The first section of a persuasion essay should include background information on the issue or an explanation of why the issue is an important one. This is typically followed by a **thesis,** or position, on the issue.

The body of the essay includes the reasons and the supporting evidence. The order of ideas and evidence in a persuasion paper should be logical and convincing, usually arranged with the most important reason placed either first or last. If the most important or convincing reasons take up the most space in your paper, it's best to place them at the beginning or end of your essay. If your paper is long, place the strongest point at the beginning so that your readers will be compelled to read on; if they don't finish reading the paper, at least they have read the most convincing evidence. If your paper is short, you probably want the strongest argument to end the essay since this is the idea that readers will most likely remember about your position.

Tips for the Persuasive Mode

Demonstrate that you *recognize the weaknesses* in your own argument or position. This acknowledgment shows your reader that you have fully considered the argument and have identified the weaknesses but are still convinced that your position is a valid one and worth sharing.

Anticipate and *refute* any counterarguments that readers may think of when considering your position. Including differing viewpoints shows that you understand the counterarguments and can use them to make your case even stronger.

Examples of Essays Written in the Persuasive Mode

Lynda Barry, "The Sanctity of School," p. 516
Don Feder, "Good News and Bad News: The Trouble with Network News," p. 493
Madeline J. Nash, "The Case for Cloning," p. 586

CAUSE AND EFFECT

Purpose

Cause and effect essays provide readers with an analysis of the reasons for and the results of an event and an examination of the relevant causal relationship. Cause and effect assignments might include the following:

> Discuss the causes of the Revolutionary War.
>
> Analyze the effects of the Revolutionary War.
>
> What are the causes and effects of the Revolutionary War?
>
> Do we need welfare programs such as Medicare and food stamps? Why or why not?
>
> What effect does being on welfare have on children?

Whether you do cause and effect in the same essay depends on the wording of the assignment. If both words are not used, then you need to ask your instructor if you can make any changes to the assignment.

Development

You will have to use your critical thinking skills to prewrite a cause and effect paper, where you will be asked to describe and make clear connections between events or situations and their consequences. Specific prewriting steps can help you do the thinking necessary to make these connections:

1. Make a list of possible causes and effects. Be sure to make the distinction between causes and effects.
2. Group or map major and minor causes and effects. Note that this technique is similar to that of classification; you may want to refer to this mode (pp. 239–241) for more ideas on categorizing.

After you have completed the lists of the causes and effects, you need to prewrite to find the connections between the event and each cause and effect listed. If you cannot discuss this connection clearly so that your reader can also understand this connection, you need to reconsider whether it is related, whether it is a cause or an effect, or if further research is needed to find this connection. When you provide the evidence or the logical connections, you have analyzed the causes and effects.

The connection between an event and its causes and effects does not require that you judge or evaluate the situation. For example, the statement "HIV has a negative impact on the gay community" does not provide any discussion of the effects of HIV. An adequately developed essay would include extensive discussion of the causes and effects, but not necessarily your attitude toward them. You need to check with your instructor to determine if it is appropriate to include a discussion of personal attitudes.

Organization

Once you determine the major causes and effects, you then need to decide the order that you will discuss them in your essay. Many writers choose to move from least to most important. If you are required or choose to include a discussion of your attitudes toward the topics identified in your paper, this discussion would probably work best if placed after an analysis of the causes and effects. This placement ensures that your readers will know that you have fully discussed the causes and effects and that you have the necessary background to make sound judgments. This placement also ensures that readers will not confuse the causes and effects with your attitudes.

Tips for the Cause/Effect Mode

Separate causes clearly and consistently from effects. One way to think about this separation is to place your ideas into two lists or categories: *before* and *after*. For example, to find the causes of AIDS and HIV, list things you think are related that happened before society discovered these illnesses. For example, you might list the wider availability of blood transfusions, the sexual revolution, the increase of IV drug use. To find the effects of AIDS and HIV, list things you think are related that happened after their discovery. For example, use of the term "safer sex,"

continued on next page

continued from previous page

universal precautions, availability of condoms, and debates over sex education in public schools. It is obviously not possible to list everything, but you might try to make a list of related concepts and then make your choices based on logic and supporting evidence.

Discuss clearly the *connection* between an event and its causes and effects—a process similar to drawing a road map that enables you to make logical connections between points. For example, suppose that you have a framed picture on the wall and that a train passes by your house every day at 4 P.M. One day as the train is passing, a family member runs into the room, trips, and hits the wall. After you help the family member get up and sit back down, the picture falls to the floor. What would you say caused the picture to fall? Who is responsible—the train, the family member, or you? What is your evidence? If you try to blame either the railroad company or your family member, you need to sound rational and to provide convincing evidence.

Examples of Essays Written in the Cause/Effect Mode

Michael Dorris, "Fetal Alcohol Syndrome: A National Perspective," p. 483
John Leo, "Punished for the Sins of the Children," p. 465
Cindi Ross Scoppe, "Every Chioce Has Its Consequences—Or At Least It Should," p. 535

For more help using any of these modes, see Chapter 9, Writing Body Paragraphs. That chapter provides paragraph-length examples of these modes.

PART FOUR

Using Additional Strategies to Customize the Process

16 Reading Strategies
Maps, Research, and Evaluation

In Chapter 4, we were first introduced to the five steps of the reading process.

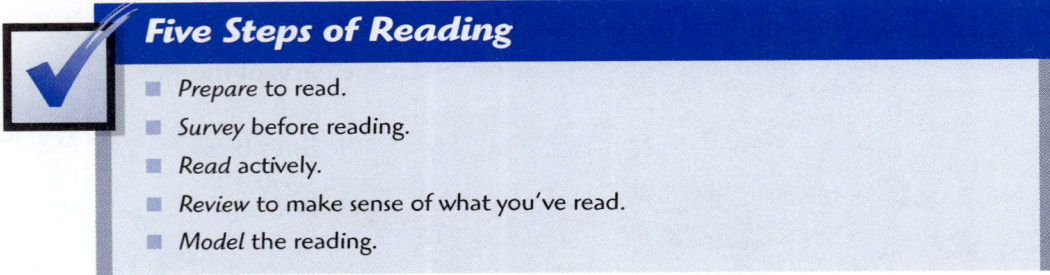

Five Steps of Reading

- *Prepare* to read.
- *Survey* before reading.
- *Read* actively.
- *Review* to make sense of what you've read.
- *Model* the reading.

These five steps are necessary in some form for everything you read. Some readings can be covered very easily, while others may take many repetitions of steps and a good bit of time. But sometimes there are other steps that may be helpful for certain kinds of readings. Try the additional steps described here, but remember to *always* begin reading by following the steps in Chapter 4.

FINDING THE PATTERN

Other Helpful Reading Steps

Find the pattern

Understand words and their parts

Research a topic

Evaluate what you read

Distinguish between speakers

Recognize the author's tone

Recognize your own biases

Readings that are long and complex can be confusing. For this kind of reading, it's important to use strategies to sort out the ideas so that you can see which idea is central and which ideas **support** it. You should still follow the five steps in reading listed in the box above, but you may find that breaking the reading into sections helps you see the big picture. You can use several techniques to do this.

Finding the Pattern by Annotating

You've used **annotating** and note-taking as ways of seeing the meaning of different sections; now try that same technique for seeing the different parts of an essay. Let's look at "Magic and AIDS: Presumed Innocent" by Michael Bronski (pp. 44–52). This is a long essay, so you will need to find the parts to be sure that you are seeing how all the ideas fit together. Look for some of the following clues that a new topic is being discussed. When you find a clue, mark it.

■ *Visual clues:* Subtitles, headings, and spaces between sections.

EXAMPLE: Space between paragraphs 5 and 6.

■ ***Transitional*** *words, phrases, or sentences:* Words such as: *first, second, third; next, also, finally; another kind of; after that; the same kind of*

EXAMPLE: *therefore* in paragraph 6.

■ *Changes of subject:*

EXAMPLES: Paragraphs 1–4 discuss Magic Johnson, but paragraph 5 doesn't focus on him; paragraph 7 brings up other people with AIDS and paragraph 8 is about other diseases.

Each of the points you annotated above is a signal for the beginning of a new part of the essay. Once you've determined some parts of the essay, look at the main idea of each part. Try to be sure you are looking at the idea, not just the topic.

EXAMPLE: We saw that a break in the lines between paragraphs 5 and 6 indicated that the first five paragraphs are one part. This part is about Magic Johnson, but also about how the media portrayed his announcement that he had AIDS.

Now we can look at the rest of the essay and use the clues we found to divide it into at least five parts. We can see the main idea of each. Here are some examples:

■ Part 2, paragraphs 6–9

Clue for breaking into parts: Transitional word *therefore,* change of subject

Main idea: Ideas of "innocent" versus "guilty" victims of AIDS and other diseases

■ Part 3, paragraphs 10–22

Clue for new part: Change of subject

Main idea: Examples of three well-known victims, and analysis of how media presented each as "innocent" or "guilty"

■ Part 4, paragraphs 23–32

Clue for new part: summarizing sentence, change of subject

Main idea: Causes and effects of media's portrayal of "innocent" and "guilty" victims

■ Part 5, paragraphs 33–34

Clue for new part: transitional phrase ("when all is said and done")

Main idea: summary of main idea, conclusion

Using annotation to help you find the pattern is useful if you need to see the way the reading is organized—for example, if you're studying for a test or trying to analyze how a reading is organized. Understanding the pattern of a reading—not just the ideas—is also necessary if you are writing a **critique**, or presenting a formal, balanced **summary**. Seeing the pattern may also help you decide on a point to write about if you are asked to write your own response to an essay.

Finding the Pattern by Mapping

Kinds of Mapping
Time line
Cause and effect
Comparison/Contrast
Outline
Idea Tree

Another strategy to help you see the pattern in a reading is **mapping**—a way of seeing the different parts of an essay in a kind of picture, so that you can see their relationships. Since most readings have more than one kind of pattern, you may need to use different maps for the various sections of the reading:

Time Line Map   A good way to see the different parts of a narrative or a process is to draw a line and show the events or steps in the sequence that they happen. In "My Father's Tribal Rule," we could use this kind of map:

brother weaned—Mark's father tells him rules—Mark disobeys—Mark is punished—his mother tries to help him understand—a final thought or implication: adult Mark looks back with more understanding

Cause and Effect Map   Sometimes a reading becomes clear if you show how causes are related to effects. The fourth part of "Magic and AIDS" has complicated reasoning that may be hard to follow. You might understand this section more easily if you use the cause and effect map below.

Cause	Effect
Because Magic Johnson is famous . . .	. . . papers make money reporting on him
Because media focus on "bad" women as source of AIDS . . .	. . . other, more common causes are ignored
Because Magic got AIDS from women . . .	. . . Magic Johnson's "female partners" were described as "dangerous disease carriers"
Because of myth that "only bad girls . . . give you AIDS" . . .	. . . readers have false idea of AIDS prevention
Because media makes money by appealing to public with false ideas . . .	. . . politicians follow unrealistic ideas about AIDS, which lead to bad laws

Comparison/Contrast Map   A similar kind of map can clarify the similarities and differences between two or more ideas or examples, as in the third part of "Magic and AIDS."

	Kimberly Bergalis	**Ryan White**	**Same or Different?**
How person got AIDS	Medical error	Medical error	SAME
How person feels about others	Blames others	Asks sympathy for all victims	DIFFERENT
How media labels person	Favorable	Less favorable	DIFFERENT

Outline Map   The most common kind of map is the **outline**, which helps us see how smaller points are related to larger ideas. An outline can be very rigid and formal, but if you're making it for yourself—to help you understand and remember what you've read—it can be very rough. Remember though that the point of an outline is to help you see how one big idea is broken down into several smaller ones. There are two kinds of outlines: idea trees and organized outlines.

Idea Tree   The kind of outline that is clearest to see is the **idea tree**—a diagram that shows how outlines break down into each other. To make an idea tree, start with the **thesis**, and then show how the points of the main sections branch out from it and how the details of the section branch out from those. Figure 13.1 illustrates an idea tree for "Magic and Aids."

Notice that the introduction and conclusion are not branches, even though each comprises several paragraphs. Those are not separate ideas, but places where the main idea is stated. Idea trees focus on showing how the body presents support for the thesis (at the top of the tree).

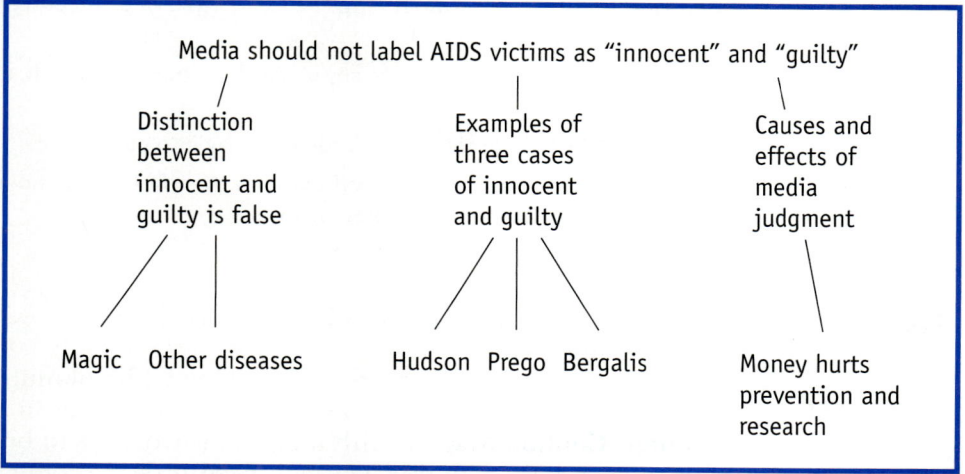

Figure 13.1

Organized Outline   The outline form shows different headings and subheadings. Often we use a different kind of marker (numbers or letters) for each level and indent each sublevel a little more to help us see more clearly:

AIDS victims as "innocent" and "guilty"

   I. False distinction between innocent and guilty

     A. Magic

     B. Other diseases

  II. How three victims have been judged

     A. Hudson

     B. Prego

     C. Bergalis

 III. Causes and effects of media judgment

     A. Financial gain

     B. Hurts real prevention and research

Remember: The purpose of trees or outlines is to help you see how the whole reading fits together.

EXERCISE 16.1	**First use the steps for reading listed on page 254 to read Teresa McCrary's "Getting Off the Welfare Carousel" (pp. 52–54). Then find the pattern in the essay, using these steps:**

    1. Annotate the sections; note any visual clues, transition words, and changes of subject.
    2. Based on your annotations, divide the essay into parts.
    3. Decide which kind of map works best for the whole essay and make it. Compare your map with your classmates' maps.

UNDERSTANDING WORDS AND THEIR PARTS

ESL   In Chapter 4, you learned two ways of working with unfamiliar words: (1) to figure out words from the context and (2) to look up words in a dictionary. Another important way to work with unfamiliar words is to break them down into parts. In order to do this, you will need to learn some typical parts of words.

EXAMPLE: In paragraph 1 of "Magic and AIDS," Bronski says that radio stations changed their *preordained playlist* for the news about Magic Johnson. From the context, you might guess that they did not play the music they had planned to play. But you can also check this by breaking the words into parts. *Playlist* is clear: you know that *play* is a word used to describe putting recorded music on the air, and you know that a list is a series of items. You can see that a *playlist* is probably a series of recorded musical items put on the radio. What about *preordained?* You may not even find that in a dictionary. However, if you break it into parts you will find that it has the prefix (first part) *pre-*, and you know that means *before.* You will find *ordain* in the dictionary, meaning *give orders for.* Now you can see that the list was planned ahead of time.

Parts of Words
Prefix
Root
Suffix

Identifying the parts of words can make it much easier to figure out the meanings, but you must remember to be sure the meaning you guess makes sense in the sentence. Sometimes the same part will have several different spellings, or one spelling will have several possible meanings—just like whole words. You will always need to check your idea of the meaning with the sense of the sentence.

Prefixes

A **prefix** is a part of a word, usually one syllable, that is added to the beginning of the word—usually changing the meaning. In the table below, we list prefixes, their meanings, and examples of words that contain the prefix.

Prefix	Meaning	Examples
a-, an- am-	not	**a**morphous (shapeless) **an**esthetic (no feeling)
a-	to, toward	**a**pply (put to)
bi-	two	**bi**cycle (two wheels)
de-	from	**de**duct (take away from)
circa-, circum-	around	**circum**ference (edge of a circle); **circum**vent (get around)
contra-	against	**contra**dict (speak against)
di-, du-	two	**di**verge (go in two separate directions), **du**et (two singers)
ex-	from or former	**ex**it, **ex**pel, **ex**patriate
in-, im-, il-, ir-	not	**in**sufficient, **im**possible, **il**legal, **ir**responsible
sub-	below	**sub**normal
tele-	far, distance	**tele**vision (seeing from a distance)

Suffixes

A **suffix** is added to the end of a word. Often it shows the part of speech, telling us how to use that form of the word in the sentence. Such suffixes don't really change the meaning. Most kinds of suffixes do change or add to the meaning of a word, and they may also show the word's part of speech.

The table below shows examples of part-of-speech suffixes; some also add to the meaning.

Suffix	Part of Speech	Examples
-ability, -ibility	verb → noun	mov**ability**, deduct**ibility**
-able, -ible	verb → adjective	mov**able**, deduct**ible**
-ate	verb	acceler**ate**
-ence, -ance	verb → noun	excell**ence**, import**ance**
-ent, -ant	verb → adjective	excell**ent**, import**ant**
-ic	noun → adjective	erot**ic** (eros), hero**ic**
-ly	adjective → adverb	quick**ly**
-ness	adjective → noun	lovable**ness**, quiet**ness**
-tion, -ation	verb → noun	examin**ation**

The table below shows examples of suffixes with meanings; some also change the part of speech.

Suffix	Meaning	Examples
-ful	with (noun → adjective)	hope**ful**, care**ful**
-less	without (noun → adjective)	hope**less**, care**less**
-ology	study of	bi**ology**
-ward	in the direction of	after**ward**, south**ward**

Roots

Roots are the central part of a word and contain the basic meaning. Words can also combine two roots for a combined meaning.

Root	Meaning	Examples
bio	life	**bio**logy
-cracy	rule	demo**cracy**
demos	people	**demo**cratic
eros	love	**erot**ic
patrio	homeland	**patrio**t, ex**patria**te
tend	take, carry	ex**tend**

EXERCISE 16.2

Look at the following words from "Magic and AIDS" (the number beside the word is the paragraph where it is found).

unapologetic—3	*negligence*—16
insignificant—4	*ethnicity*—17
variance—7	*inconsequential*—17
nonstigmatizing—8	*immeasurably*—32

1. Find the prefixes, roots, or suffixes of these words. You will need to look up some roots in a dictionary. Form an idea of the meaning of the word. Look at the sentence to check the meaning.

2. Add at least ten items to this list, and then find the meaning or function of the prefixes, suffixes, or roots. *Optional:* Work together in groups to create lists of twenty-five.

3. Find words in "Getting Off the Welfare Carousel"; break them down, guess the meaning, and check it in the sense of the sentence.

RESEARCHING A TOPIC

RES To be able to read well, you must be able to do several things:

- ■ *Respond:* Remember what you already know about the topic.
- ■ *Question:* Realize what you don't know about the topic.
- ■ *Connect:* See relations between your knowledge and the reading, between different parts of the reading, and between your questions and the reading.

Your group work and reading responses help you to remember and make connections with what you already know. **Surveying** and reviewing the text as well as asking questions and trying to answer them have made you aware of some things you don't know about the topic. Some readings don't make sense if there are too many questions and not enough answers. Sometimes in order to read well, you will need to do some research.

Developing Questions for Research

The process of filling in your own knowledge base is as follows:

1. Use your survey/review questions.
2. Look for specific names of people, places, things, events, or ideas.

EXAMPLE: In "Magic and AIDS," Bronski uses many examples to make his point. See if you recognize each of these: *Rock Hudson, Ryan White, Victoria Prego, Kimberly Bergalis, Typhoid Mary, the plague, tuberculosis.* Do you know the difference between *AIDS* and *HIV?* What does each abbreviation stand for? How are the conditions different?

3. Look for other views or more explanation of some of the ideas that are important in the reading.

EXAMPLE: Find information on one of the following topics: *safe sex, transmission of AIDS, media bias.*

4. Find original sources of information. Often writers will base their writing on other readings. Do they report those accurately and completely?

EXAMPLE: "Magic and AIDS" begins with a discussion of the *New York Times* article that appeared when Magic Johnson revealed that he was HIV-positive on November 7, 1991. Find the original article.

Where to Do Your Research

Library   Much of your research can probably be done in the library. Librarians know the quick and easy ways to find many sources. DON'T BE AFRAID TO ASK FOR HELP! Often much more information is available than you might think. Unless you're already familiar with a library system, ask a librarian for assistance in locating any of the following:

books on one topic	books on several topics
magazines	newspapers
microfilm	microfiche
CD-ROM	Infotrac, Searchbank and other indexes
Internet: World Wide Web, Gopher, Telnet, etc.	on-line database services

EXAMPLE: Material on *safe sex* and *transmission of AIDS* can be found in books, which you can locate using the library catalog, and in magazine articles, which you can locate using *Infotrac, Searchbank, Lexis-Nexis,* or another on-line database that contains an index to magazine articles and, in many cases, the entire article. The *New York Times* article dates from 1991, and most libraries will not have an article that old available through a computer. You can find it using the *New York Times* index and the library's microfiche or microfilm.

Research Tip

As you do your research, be sure that you have all the information about the book or other source that you will need for your works cited list. See pages 397–399 for a list of details needed for different kinds of sources. If you have the information, you won't have to go back to the library or have to try to locate a lost Website when you're trying to finish your paper.

Personal Sources   Some of you may want to use your own encyclopedias and computers, a very convenient and often excellent source of information. Be very careful to evaluate your sources when you use the Internet. Remember that there are no controls on who may put a page on the Internet.

> **EXAMPLE:** Most CD-ROM encyclopedias have articles on the major diseases discussed in paragraph 8 of "Magic and AIDS." Those encyclopedias, if published by reputable companies (Encarta, Britannica, etc.), are as reliable as encyclopedias in the library. However, if you look for some of the other examples on the web, you may find some very unreliable sources.

Other Sources   You may also use other sources to do hands-on research: you may want to interview people, clip newspaper articles, visit locations, call agencies, etc. Research doesn't have to take place in a traditional school setting.

> **EXAMPLE:** An interview with someone who volunteers to work with AIDS patients tells us that they do encounter the kinds of prejudices Bronski describes.

Opposing Views   Sometimes it's important to understand the other side of an **argument**. You may find opposing views when you look at Bronski's sources. You may need to search for the other side.

> **EXAMPLE:** Look for articles arguing that medical workers should be tested for HIV.

| EXERCISE 16.3 | **Practice your research skills by doing the following.** |

1. Look for references to unfamiliar topics in "Magic and AIDS," and research them.

2. Look for unfamiliar references in George Orwell's "A Hanging" (pp. 54–58) and research them. Look at the names of people, places, things, and ideas that you don't recognize as well as important topics and unanswered questions you developed for "A Hanging."

3. Do either of the exercises above as a group of four or five students, and share your answers. Then go back to the reading to see how much more you understand now that you share more of the author's knowledge. You might want to make a research plan and divide the research into subtopics or into particular types of reference tools (books, on-line databases, Internet).

4. As a group, survey "Getting Off the Welfare Carousel" (pp. 52–54) by Teresa McCrary. Think of some different views on welfare and research those topics. Each person in the group should share the ideas in the material they located. Then read McCrary's essay and notice where she responds to the opposing arguments. Are those arguments found in your research?

EVALUATING WHAT YOU READ

When you read an assignment from a textbook, you may feel that you don't need to question it, but you should form the habit of evaluating everything you read, whether it's from a textbook, a magazine, or the Internet. Just because something is published does not mean that it is true, especially on the Internet. Here are some questions you should ask about any reading. Even though you will not always be able to answer every question in complete detail, those you can answer will help you be fairly sure of a source's validity; the questions you can't answer mean that you have to keep a question in your mind about that source.

1. **Where did I find this?** Does anyone control in any way what readings are in the location, or can anyone post anything there?

   EXAMPLES:

   "Magic and AIDS" is reprinted in a textbook by a well-known publisher and suggested to you by your instructor. Both of these sources control the material they present to you. This isn't a guarantee of perfect truthfulness in the material, but you do know more about the origins of "Magic and AIDS" than you do about something you receive in the mail from an unknown address. At least you know that this essay was probably not produced by a hate group, or by someone attempting to sell you something.

   If you search for "Magic Johnson" on the Internet, you may well find a page that describes how Magic Johnson made a pornographic movie. Nothing on that page tells you who wrote or published it. Only if you follow links back to the home page will you discover a statement that the whole site is a lie, and that it is intended as satire.

2. **Who originally published this?** Is the publisher at all well-known? What kinds of things does the publisher usually publish?

   EXAMPLE:

   "Magic and AIDS" was originally published in *Z Magazine*. Since this is not a very well-known magazine, you don't know what it usually publishes. You might be able to locate some information about the magazine by searching for it on the Internet or in your library. If you don't find anything about the magazine, then you should be aware that you can't be certain about this essay's validity or lack of bias. You will have to make your judgments in other ways.

3. **When was this written?** Does that matter?

   EXAMPLE:

   "Magic and AIDS" was originally published in 1992, soon after Magic Johnson made the announcement, but long enough that there had been time for the writer to see media coverage of that event. The specific references in the article are a little harder to recognize now. Has the media's attitude toward AIDS changed? This is a question only research could answer.

4. **Who wrote this?** Does this person have enough knowledge to write about this topic? Will this person gain financially or in any other way if readers believe that the writer's view is true?

EXAMPLE:

Michael Bronski is a reporter who writes for different magazines. As a writer, we expect him to know something about the media, but since he's a member of the media, the group he is criticizing, we can say that he is not likely to gain from this article. However, we don't know if he is HIV positive. Would it make a difference if he were?

5. **What are the author's sources of information?** Are those well-known? Biased? Recent?

EXAMPLE:

Bronski is analyzing the media, and he describes some very specific cases of media coverage, as in the *New York Times*, but there are other places where he simply refers to "the media" or "media coverage," and we can't really locate those sources. They seem similar to the ones that he does cite, and those that he mentions are well-known and from the right time period.

6. **Who was the author's target audience** (that is, who did he expect to be the readers)? What did the author expect the audience to know? What did he expect the audience to feel? How are you, the current reader, similar to or different from the target audience?

EXAMPLE:

We can tell that Bronski was writing to people who were familiar with the well-publicized AIDS victims of the 1980s and very early 1990s. Since a good bit of time has passed, you may not be familiar with the people he discusses. He also expected that his audience might have had their feelings toward different AIDS victims shaped by the media, and he wants to change those feelings.

EXERCISE 16.4

Evaluate your sources.

1. Evaluate the publisher(s), author, sources, and target audience of "Getting Off the Welfare Carousel" (pp. 52–54) by Teresa McCrary and "My Father's Tribal Rule" by Mark Mathabane (pp. 40–44). Decide if you can trust the information. You should question the article's bias (does the author want you to see only one side of things?), currency of information (have things changed since

then?), and intended audience (do you have the background you need to understand this?).

2. As a group, evaluate the publisher, author, and sources of "A Hanging" (pp. 54–58). Decide whether you can trust the information. Question the article's bias (does the author want you to see only one side of things?), currency of information (have things changed since then?), and intended audience (do you have the background you need to understand this?). Assign one part of the evaluation to each group member. Then came back together and compile your results. Try to decide on a group opinion about the reading.

3. Try to do additional research on George Orwell and determine whether information about the author's experience and other writings affects your judgment of "A Hanging."

4. Evaluate one of the sources you found while doing a research exercise. Decide whether you can trust the information. You should question the article's bias (does the author want you to see only one side of things?), currency of information (have things changed since then?), and intended audience (do you have the background you need to understand this?).

Whose Ideas?

Often when a reading is long, a reader is tempted to skim and scan to quickly figure out the main idea and identify a few of the supporting details. These techniques may work for some assignments, but they will not work for detailed **academic reading**. One way to check to see if your first reading of an essay is on target is to reread it for specific details, section by section or paragraph by paragraph. Looking for specific types of information in the reading as you reread it is often helpful. Sometimes looking for very specific uses of details can make a pattern in the reading obvious. This will focus your thinking and help prepare you for class discussion. If you have specific ideas or answers to specific questions, you can compare them with those of your classmates.

Identifying the details of a reading will make it easier to see how your own experiences and observations relate to those in the reading. In addition, it will be easier to separate ideas based on fact from those based on popular myths or on stereotypes. You can also keep better track of the source of the ideas in the reading. Obviously, most ideas in a reading will come from the author, but sometimes the author also uses ideas from other individuals or sources. It is important to not only identify these ideas from other sources but also to understand why the author decides to use them, and to recognize the author's opinion of the cited ideas. If you pay close attention to these details as you reread the essay, you will become a more critical reader, better prepared to discuss and write about your response to the reading.

Sometimes a reading, or a part of a reading, will be very much like a conversation that the author is having with other people or sources—the author may report what someone else says in order to agree or disagree with that source. It can be difficult to separate the author's own ideas from ideas of other people or sources, but it is very important to do this; otherwise, you may have an incorrect idea of the author's meaning. Authors signal that they are reporting the ideas of others in several small ways. Be sure not to overlook the use of quotation marks, or brief introductory or explanatory remarks, like *in our contemporary culture, according to the popular view,* or *portrayed by the media as.*

Once again, it is very important to be sure to begin any reading with the steps in Chapter 4, because they will help you have a good idea of what the author means. Some examples follow.

1. What is the title of the reading by Michael Bronski on page 44? Is it clear what it means, or could it mean more than one thing? What do you still need to know in order to clearly explain the significance of the title?

   Who is "Magic"?

   What is "AIDS"?

   "Presumed Innocent": What does the phrase "presumed innocent" remind us of? Why? Who is presuming what?

2. You may have already outlined or mapped the essay into parts. Look over your notes. There is a break after paragraph 5. How does Bronski begin the essay? Is there anything special about paragraphs 1–5? Does the beginning suggest information that will help you answer question 1? Notice the following:

   - ■ The media's response to Magic Johnson's announcement that he has tested positively for the HIV (AIDS) virus
   - ■ The quotation marks around the words "innocent victim" and "guilty victim"

   These suggest that Magic Johnson is being judged by the media. The media classifies people with AIDS as "innocent" or "guilty" victims. Magic has to be categorized with one group or the other.

3. Does Bronski agree with these judgments or not? How do you know? Bronski says that the media's classification "has traditionally been simple."

   He seems to be questioning the validity of this simple breakdown (see paragraph 5).

Work on determining the author's attitude.

1. Review paragraph 12 to identify any unusual words that seem to convey Bronski's attitudes. For example, what do nuances and byzantine suggest in "nuances surfaced and the notions of 'guilt' and 'innocence' became more byzantine" (paragraph 12, last sentence)?

2. Bronski uses quotation marks in different ways in his essay. First, he uses them around special words. He also uses them to quote other individuals or organizations. Look at paragraph 6. What idea is he quoting? Why is Bronski quoting this person (or organization)? Can you tell Bronski's opinion about the ideas in the quote?

Recognizing the Author's Tone

Sometimes authors may say something that is actually the opposite of what they mean; we call this *irony*, or we say that the author is being *ironic*. You have probably noticed that people do this in conversation, but you may have called it *sarcasm* or being *sarcastic* or *facetious*. Sometimes irony is a way of using another's person's ideas. In order to know whether a statement is straightforward or ironic, we need to use all the ways we can to determine what the author's real idea is. We can compare a statement to the rest of the reading, or we can see if the author says anything that seems impossible or greatly exaggerated.

EXAMPLE:

Look at paragraph 5 of "Magic and AIDS." Bronski says: "children who are infected through their mothers, and hemophiliacs or anyone who received the virus through a blood transfusion, were 'innocent.'" Of course, the quotation marks already give us a clue that Bronski is reporting someone else's words, but we can also look at this statement and compare it to what he seems to say in the rest of the essay. That will tell us whether this statement represents his ideas or the opposite. In paragraph 6, Bronski says that it is a "fact that the comforting simplicity (and lie) of 'guilty' and 'innocent' are now untenable categories." This is not a statement that he reports from anyone else. The conclusion, where we might expect to find a clear statement of his thesis, makes a similar point. We can assume that the sentence in paragraph 5 is not Bronski's idea, but an ironic statement of the idea he is arguing against.

Look at the last paragraph of "A Hanging." Compare the behavior of the men described here with Orwell's direct statement of his opinion in paragraph 12. What does that suggest about his attitude toward himself and the other men in the last paragraph? How does the final sentence of paragraph 26 remind us of the final sentence of paragraph 12?

Recognizing Your Own Biases

Sometimes it's hard to read an article because you have very strong feelings and opinions that make it difficult for you to pay attention to what the author is saying. This can be a problem whether you agree or disagree with the author. To become a really good reader, you need to be aware of your own feelings and opinions and try to separate them from the author's. Pay attention to what the reading actually says.

Paying attention to the reading does not mean accepting everything you read without question, but you won't really be able to ask the specific important questions about a reading—or even disagree with the author's support for the thesis of the reading—unless you first read it carefully and see what the author actually says. Then you will be able to ask about an author's assumptions, evidence, attitude, and everything else that's important.

Recognizing your own biases must begin when you first survey a reading. As soon as you see what the topic is, you should take a moment to think about how you feel and what you think. Then remind yourself to listen, no matter how much you disagree.

Of course, sometimes you might make an exception. You will probably not be able to quietly and objectively read anything that is truly offensive, like hate literature. You may not want to waste your time with something from a source that you know is unreliable, like the popular tabloid newspapers in the grocery store checkout line. But when you read something that seems to be from a source that has some credibility, try to set your feelings aside the first time you read it so that you can think, rather than simply reacting emotionally.

EXAMPLE:

When you read paragraph 9 of "Magic and AIDS," you find some "four-letter words." Ordinarily, you may feel that you will not read anything using this kind of language. However, you have recognized that this is a serious article and you have also recognized that Bronski often reports the words and ideas of others, sometimes ironically. You look at this sentence again and note that he is reporting "popular perception." Now you realize that you really need to think about whether Bronski is correct about how people think about victims of AIDS, and you also must consider whether you share this stereotype. You may finally decide that this sentence is correct or incorrect, but you do not let it prevent you from looking seriously at his ideas.

EXERCISE 16.7

Do the following to explore your own biases.

1. Survey "A Hanging." How do you feel about the topic being discussed? Can you put those feelings aside and read the essay to discover Orwell's ideas?

2. Survey "Getting Off the Welfare Carousel." How do you feel about the topic being discussed? Can you put those feelings aside and read the essay to discover McCrary's ideas?

Remember: First follow the general steps in the reading process given in Chapter 4 (see box on p. 60). Whenever you need to evaluate a more difficult reading or you are reading for certain specific purposes, such as writing a critique or getting started on a research project, you may need to repeat steps and add more steps to the reading process. Some steps that may be helpful for certain kinds of readings have been introduced in this chapter in the box on page 254. Ask yourself why you are reading the assignment, and then decide which of these additional steps will help you meet your goals.

17

Strategies for Analyzing the Assignment

Narrowing and Focusing the Topic

In Chapter 5, we discussed how to analyze the **prompt** to determine what you are asked to do in the assignment.

The Prompt Reveals

What you are expected to focus on.

What you are expected to do.

How you will bring the focus and actions together.

This chapter will provide more techniques for analyzing prompts:

- Analyzing more difficult prompts
- Narrowing the prompt
- Refocusing the prompt
- Arguing against the assumption of the prompt

ANALYZING MORE DIFFICULT PROMPTS

Responding to what you've read is a common academic assignment, but it is not the only one you will be required to do. You may also be asked to summarize an author's ideas, analyze how the author uses language or strategies, or evaluate how well the author accomplishes what he or she set out to do. These tasks are known as analysis, rhetorical analysis, and critique.

Analysis

To analyze, you must break a text into its parts and explain how the parts relate to each other to create a whole essay. Consider the following prompt:

How does Orwell use the description of the prisoner to attempt to move his reader to a stance against capital punishment?

This prompt directs you to *identify* a particular part of the text—those parts that describe the prisoner—and to *explain* how they work together to accomplish an effect on the reader.

Rhetorical Analysis

To write a **rhetorical analysis**, you must *identify* and *explain* the strategies or techniques the writer uses to get a point across or to create an effect in the reader. Consider the following prompt:

> *How does McCrary gain sympathy for herself and other women on welfare?*

Critique

To **critique** an essay, you must discuss what the writer is trying to do and how well he or she does it. That is, you must *identify* the writer's strategies, *state* whether they are effective or ineffective, and *explain* why.

This is one of the most difficult assignments for many students, and they often fall back on responding or summarizing, tasks they are more comfortable with. Analyzing critical prompts and sticking to the focus and action are critical in writing successful answers. Consider the following prompt:

> *How successful is McCrary in presenting her argument that women on welfare need government programs to help them provide for their families until they can gain the education to get good jobs?*

To answer this question, you would need to *identify* the strategies that McCrary uses, *describe* each strategy, and *discuss* how effectively she uses each strategy.

Literary Prompts

Literary prompts are a special kind of assignment that requires a response to a reading. They are different for a variety of reasons. First, these prompts ask you to respond to the rhetorical aspects of the reading—how the author presents the ideas and what effect the author expects from the reader. Your role, then, is to serve as an interpreter for your reader who has read the author's work but needs assistance in understanding it. Second, as an interpreter, you are using your own ideas only to explain how you understood the author's ideas. But you are also limited to interpretation. You should be sure that you understand the author's ideas and are not stating what you would have said. You should not give your own opinions or ideas about the subject matter or, unless required by the prompt, evaluate the ideas or the work. Let's take the following prompt:

> *Discuss Orwell's ideas toward capital punishment as revealed in "A Hanging."*

Key focus words:	Orwell's ideas (notice that yours are not included)
	Capital punishment (not other topics he discusses)
Key action words:	Discuss

The **key action word** *discuss,* as you know (see p. 80), gives you a lot of choice as to how to focus what you do in your essay. With a literary prompt, you are not being asked to give Orwell's ideas, but as the prompt says to discuss the ideas as they are *revealed.* The use of the word *revealed* is a hint that Orwell may not state his ideas about capital punishment in an argument. Instead, the prompt suggests that he somehow "reveals" them. Your task then is to explain to your reader how Orwell gets his ideas across without stating them as an argument.

It is important for you to recognize the different types of tasks that may be stated or simply implied by a prompt. The box below matches key action words, types of questions, and types of tasks to help you analyze prompts more fully.

Key Action Words

Key Action Word	Question	Task
Agree/disagree React Discuss Explore	What do you think about what the writer has said or done?	Respond
Summarize Trace Restate Discuss Outline Explore	What does the writer say?	Summarize
Analyze Examine Consider	What does the writer do?	Analyze Discuss Rhetorical or Literary Aspects
Analyze Examine Consider	How does the writer do it?	Discuss Rhetorical or Literary Aspects
Evaluate Critique Assess Consider	How well does the writer do it?	Criticize

Notice that many of the key action words indicate more than one task. You will need to consider the rest of the prompt to determine which task (or how many of them) you are being asked to do.

If your prompt is in the form of a question, you can determine which action to perform by matching the question to the key action word listed on page 273. For example, what would you need to address to be sure you were responding to the following prompt?

> *Trace Bronski's position in his reportage of how the media has covered people with AIDS. How does Bronski let us know his stance on the media's (and the public's) labeling of people with HIV and AIDS as "innocent" and "guilty"?*

Key focus words:	Bronski's position/stance
	Reportage
	Media coverage/labeling
	People with HIV/AIDS
Key action words:	Trace
Key question:	How does

The key action word refers to **summary**. To trace Bronski's position, you would have to *restate* how each news story he mentions shows changes in how people with HIV and AIDS have been labeled. "Trace" implies a process of **development**, so it's not enough just to *list* each entry or *summarize* each point, you must *explain* how Bronski moves from point to point (that is, how he describes the changes that took place from one story to the next).

The key question *how does* refers to analysis. It asks you to *explain* the techniques Bronski uses during his reporting on the news stories to indicate to us what he thinks of the media's labeling of people with AIDS.

To complete these two actions (*trace* and *explain*), you would need to identify the stories that Bronski mentions and explain how the media labels people with HIV/AIDS in each story he presents. You would also need to look at his description of each story (the words he chooses, the tone of his language, the details he has decided to give us) to find words or phrases that indicate what he thinks about the way each story was presented.

What would you need to address to be sure you were responding to the following prompt?

> *Bronski uses the stories of several people with AIDS to illustrate how the media has represented people with AIDS. Analyze his use of each illustration. Has he made his points clearly and fairly? Do his interpretations of these stories and their implications make sense? Are there other interpretations that he neglects to make?*

Key focus words: Stories of several people with AIDS

The media's representation of people with AIDS

His use of each illustration

His points

His interpretations

Implications

Other interpretations

Key action words: Analyze

This is the only specific key action word in the prompt; you could address many topics while performing this task. However, the instructor has given you three questions. You can assume that this additional information is intended to help you focus your answer. If you had no additional questions, you would be asked to shape your own answer. These questions indicate that you should shape your answer to address these issues in your analysis.

Clearly, your audience does not want just a "yes" or "no" answer, so you must decide what type of information you need to provide to give a full in-depth answer.

Has he made his points clearly and fairly?	*Identify* his points. *Define* the standard of clarity and accuracy you plan to use. *Evaluate* his explanation of each point against this standard.
Do his interpretations of these stories and their implications make sense?	*Identify* his interpretation of each story and his explanation of his interpretation. Since there is no standard meaning of "make sense," you will need to *provide your own definition* (ask your instructor how he or she is using this term. Also look over your notes from class discussion to see if this term has been used before). *Evaluate* each interpretation against your definition of "make sense."
Are there other interpretations that he neglects to make?	*Suggest* other explanations that might also explain these stories. You might also offer some explanation about why he ignores or neglects these interpretations. If this question had been worded "What other interpretations does he neglect to make?" the question would then assume that there are other interpretations and you are supposed to find them. In this case, you must answer the question. However, since this question is

worded "Are there," you can skip the question if you have tried to find the other interpretations and haven't been able to identify any. (Does it make sense to you to write a section of your paper on how Bronski has mentioned every possible interpretation?)

NARROWING THE PROMPT

In the previous prompt, you received a great deal of direction from the instructor as to how to frame your answer. Sometimes, however, you may get a prompt that is so broad that you have no clear indication of what you should be discussing. Your first job is to decide what focus you will choose for your paper rather than attempting to give every possible answer. For example:

> *Discuss the impact of AIDS in your community.*

The key focus words are *impact, AIDS,* and *community. Community* can refer to your neighborhood or it can refer to a group of people that you identify with. You may need to let your reader know which definition you are planning to use. Giving this definition is one way to narrow the prompt. *Impact* is also a rather broad term. AIDS may have financial, medical, social, political, religious, or ethical effects on people. You won't be able to discuss every type of effect, so you would need to decide which effects are most important or which ones you have the most to say about.

For example, perhaps you consider your community to be young, single working adults who lose their jobs and their insurance. The impact this community may feel might include financial concerns, access to medical care, or legal protections for people with HIV and AIDS.

Deciding on this focus would mean that you do not have to talk about mothers and children with HIV, gay men, the elderly, or school children. You could also omit discussions of morality, ethics, religion, and social concerns.

REFOCUSING THE PROMPT

Sometimes you may get an assignment that does not address a topic or issue that you can do your best writing about. Other times, you may have an idea that you could write a better paper on, but the prompt doesn't ask you for it. Rather than abandon your idea (and your chance to do your best writing), you need to find a way to refocus the prompt so you can connect your idea to the instructor's assignment. For example:

> *Bronski says that the media focuses on individual tragedy rather than information that would help people protect themselves. Why does the media have this focus?*

It may occur to you that you could write a better paper if you talked about why the media should focus on information and not on why it focuses on entertainment. You can write this paper: you must acknowledge the original prompt to let the instructor know you understand the assignment, but provide a different answer by showing how you will refocus the question. You can do this refocusing either in the introduction or by devoting your first body paragraph to the original question and addressing your own focus in subsequent paragraphs.

Let's look at an example of an introduction in which the writer has decided to refocus the prompt:

> The media is a very useful tool in the daily lives of people. They can find out about the latest medical advances and adjust their lives to help their families stay healthy. I have personally used this tool for years to help me make sure that my family eats right, follows a good exercise program, and takes the right vitamin supplements. When I first starting hearing about HIV and AIDS, I expected the media to help me make my family safe from this disease. But I found little help in the media. Then I read Michael Bronski's essay "Magic and AIDS," in which he explains that the media tend to focus on the tragic lives affected by AIDS and HIV. According to Bronski, this focus reflects our society's attempts to attach morality to a disease. I'm not sure media focus on the lives of individuals coping with this disease. Maybe we are trying to understand how a person contracts the disease so that we can avoid it, or pretend that we won't contract it since we see ourselves differently. While I'm not sure why the media continue to focus on this aspect of AIDS and HIV, I do know that the media should begin to provide more information on how to protect myself and what I can do to help my family protect themselves.

ARGUING AGAINST THE ASSUMPTION OF THE PROMPT

Some prompts ask you to accept an assumption and then to write your essay based on that assumption. If you feel that you can not agree with the assumption, you can answer the prompt by pointing out why you think the assumption is not valid. This strategy allows you some leeway to rewrite the question. Consider the following:

> *Bronski attacks the media's presentation of people with HIV/AIDS. What can the media do to be more fair and accurate?*

This prompt starts with the assumption that Bronski's attack on the media is indeed justified. One way to respond to this prompt is to challenge this assumption by arguing that the media has been fair and that Bronski is wrong.

To successfully argue against the prompt, you have to explicitly tell your readers that this is what you plan to do. You must tell them in your introduction what the author's (or prompt's) assumption is and that you think it is invalid. In the body of your paper, you would need to explain why you think the assumption is invalid and then show how challenging this assumption reinterprets the reading and sets up the thesis which you will prove in your essay.

To argue against the assumption of this prompt, you would have to argue that the media has been fair and accurate in the stories that Bronski presents. Bronski implies that fairness and accuracy would not include personal morality but would include information that would help people prevent infection. You could challenge this assumption by doing the following:

- Arguing that actions do have morality so the media is being fair
- Arguing that these stories do have lessons for prevention as well as giving them a personal touch that attracts the reader

Let's look at an example of an introduction in which the writer challenges the assumption of the prompt and argues against this assumption:

> The media is often criticized for its presentation of people and their lives in this public forum. Princess Diana, OJ Simpson, and every one of the Kennedys have had their personal lives presented in minute detail in newspapers and magazines across the world. Michael Bronski, in his essay "Magic and AIDS: Presumed Innocent," attacks such presentations of people with HIV/AIDS, saying that it is unfair for the media to focus on their personal lives. He claims that the media's judgment of HIV victims as either being "innocent" or "guilty" keeps people from learning how to prevent effectively the transmission of HIV. While I agree with Bronski that the media does need to include more information on effective prevention measures, I do not believe that the media's presentation of HIV victims is unfair. All people's actions, including those infected with HIV, have consequences and therefore are ethical and moral choices. Focusing on a celebrity's personal life and choices helps the audience understand the consequences of risky behavior and may help them make better choices themselves. By presenting this information, the media is being fair and accurate.

This introduction clearly challenges the assumption that the media is unfair, yet addresses the issue of the media's fairness and accuracy. This writer has altered the assignment from "What can the media do to be more fair and accurate?" to "The media is fair and accurate, and I will show this using Bronski's examples."

To complete the essay, the writer would need to use Bronski's stories to show that they can be interpreted as supporting this reinterpretation of this assignment.

EXERCISE 17.1 Analyze the following writing prompts. Try using the techniques in this chapter as they seem helpful.

Teresa McCrary, "Getting Off the Welfare Carousel" (pp. 52–54)

1. How does McCrary use her opposition's arguments to make her own points?

2. Analyze McCrary's use of first, second and third person pronouns—*I, you, they.* What relationship does she set up with people who aren't on welfare? How does she acknowledge their concerns?

3. McCrary asks if she is the exception to the rule of welfare mothers. Is she typical or is she indeed an exception?

4. McCrary represents herself as being like all welfare moms. Does this undercut her argument or make it stronger?

5. McCrary uses few details about herself and talks about welfare moms in general. Is this more effective than writing a personal narrative? Why or why not? What does this allow her to do that she couldn't do in a personal narrative?

6. McCrary assumes all women on welfare are like herself and the women she knows. Does she have just as stereotypical a view as those who think all mothers on welfare have ten children?

7. McCrary identifies two outcomes—keep welfare or have all these women and children on the streets. Evaluate the effectiveness of her conclusion.

8. Summarize the alternatives women on welfare have, according to McCrary. Are there other options she's neglected? Explain.

George Orwell, "A Hanging" (pp. 54–58)

1. How does Orwell use the description of the prisoner to attempt to move his reader to a stance against capital punishment?

2. How does Orwell use the superintendent's feelings about the execution to make a statement about capital punishment?

3. What statement is Orwell making about British colonialism in India?

4. What is the effect of the two threads of Orwell's story—capital punishment and British colonialism? Does he seem more concerned with one than the other? Does one issue detract from the other?

5. The superintendent is a doctor. By carrying out this execution, is he going against his beliefs? How do people reconcile following orders and doing what they believe is right? (You may want to bring in Stanley Milgram's essay "The Perils of Obedience," pp. 548–555, to answer this question.)

Prewriting Strategies
Research

Academic writing is like a conversation among scholars. To join the conversation, you will conduct research to find out what has been said by other scholars.

Think about joining a conversation among your friends. If you give your opinion without listening to others and shaping your words to fit what's already been said, you may appear rude or foolish. You also may merely repeat what someone else has said. To join the conversation, you need to listen and then explain how your opinion fits into what other members of the group have already said.

By using research material in your paper, you are showing that you have something useful to add to the conversation. Even if you don't think you have something to add, you still want to show that you have been listening and that you understand the conversation.

There are two types of research:

- **Primary** (or field) **research**—collecting data and interpreting it
- **Secondary research**—using someone else's report on *his or her* primary research

Throughout your academic career, you will be expected to do both types of research, and occasionally you will have an assignment that requires you to include both kinds in your paper.

In this chapter, we discuss how to use research as a prewriting strategy. We discuss how to conduct secondary research first (since it is the most common in academic settings) and then how to conduct primary research. Finally, we discuss how to select material from your research to use in your writing.

CONDUCTING SECONDARY RESEARCH

Print Sources

Books
Magazines
Newspapers
Scholarly Journals

Secondary research is useful when you want to use information gathered by authorities on a topic. The authorities have conducted primary research and have written books or articles on their findings. Secondary research provides you with some authority without your having to conduct the primary research, and it enables you to find out what other people have already done to investigate the topic.

Types of Sources

There are two types of sources for secondary research—print and electronic. Print sources are those you find on the library shelves: books, magazines, newspapers, journals, encyclopedias, dictionaries. Electronic sources are materials published in cyberspace or for use on a computer: Internet, CD-ROM, Intranet, discussion groups, listservs, or chat rooms.

Evaluating Your Sources

Any time you are using research, you should evaluate the accuracy of your sources. Many print sources have already been evaluated through the publication process. To be printed, the author has had to prove his or her credentials and the validity of his or her ideas. During this process, the staff members of the publishing company and reviewers hired by the company have decided that the material has some worth and that the writer should be paid to publish the material. Articles found in journals have been juried, which means that a board of professionals has agreed that the article is worth publishing.

Some print sources may not be valid for use in academic writing. Some books and magazines are published by the author using what is known as a "vanity press," which allows an author to pay a company to print the materials. You will need to evaluate printed materials to determine if they are reliable and accurate sources.

On the Internet, anyone can publish materials. This means that electronic sources are not consistently reliable. Some electronic sources have printed equivalents, which means that they were juried in the same manner as reliable print sources. Those that do not have printed equivalents may or may not be reliable.

Electronic sources found on Websites that are maintained by universities and colleges, professional groups, publishing companies, and research think tanks have been juried. Sites maintained by individuals are self-published and therefore not juried. Such electronic sources need to be evaluated to determine if they are appropriate for the assignment.

Most instructors want you to avoid using sources that contain only general information (information that can be found in three or more sources). Sources that contain general information include encyclopedias and textbooks. Although these sources are good for giving you background information, college instructors usually do not consider these valid research sources and do not want you to cite them as sources.

The Internet has many sites that are for student use in conjunction with classes. These sites may post papers written by students. Most instructors consider student papers to be invalid sources for research.

Evaluating Websites   You may want to use Websites that have already been evaluated or you may want to evaluate a site yourself. Some Websites offer a service of filtering and evaluating research on the Internet. If you do not feel comfortable evaluating a site yourself, you may want to use one of these screening services, since you know that someone has already checked the sites, at least to some extent, for accuracy and usefulness.

Evaluated Websites	
Argus Clearinghouse	http://www.clearinghouse.net
Best of the Web	http://www.botw.org
Excite	http://www.excite.com (Choose one of the categories such as "education.")
Lycos	http://point.lycos.com (Choose from the Topic Directory.)
Magellan	http://www.mckinley.com (Choose "Green Lite Sites Only.")
Webcrawler	http://www.webcrawler.com (Choose one of the "Channels.")
Yahoo	http://www.yahoo.com (Yahoo does not guarantee the quality of all sites.)

Conducting Searches

Even though you need to be open to what you find during a research project, you have to have a starting point. The first step is to conduct a search for material related to your topic. Obviously you don't have time to wander through the library and look at every book and magazine to find information. Fortunately, others have created devices called **search engines**—research tools that might include a computerized listing of the library's holdings, an index on a CD-ROM, or an Internet browser. Whether you are in the library or on the Internet, you need to understand how to search for the topic and how the search engine provides the information related to your topic.

Identifying Keywords for Searches   The most common way to search for a topic is to provide the search engine with a **keyword**, an identifying word or phrase usually taken from the writing **prompt**. However, you don't want to stop there. An author of an article or book may have used a different term, and you need to search with similar keywords in order to find as much information as you can. For example, if you are searching for information on the death penalty, you would obviously use the words *death penalty* in your search, and then search with other closely related terms such as *execution* and *capital punishment*. If you can't think of related keywords on your own, a good strategy is to look at a few articles or books and make a list of terms that the authors use when discussing the death penalty.

EXERCISE 18.1 **Brainstorm keywords that might help you locate information on the following topics:**

A. AIDS   D. homelessness

B. health insurance   E. abortion

C. domestic violence   F. World Series champions

Narrowing the Subject with Keywords Sometimes keywords provide you with so much information that you can't possibly look at everything, and you will likely miss the best information because you are overwhelmed. A search on *welfare* will provide you with a list of thousands of books and articles published on the topic. Therefore, you will want to narrow your search by combining keywords to make your topic more specific. For example, to search for information on welfare in your home state of California, you would conduct a search combining both keywords *California* and *Welfare*.

Some search engines provide you with a list of categories for broad topics, such as *welfare*. Instead of getting a list of articles on welfare, the computer may give you a list that looks something like this:

Welfare—federal

Welfare—reform

Welfare—state

Welfare—women

You need to select the category you are interested in, and then the computer will provide you a list of articles related to that category and ignore other categories related to welfare.

EXERCISE 18.2 **Brainstorm a list of terms that would help you narrow the focus of the following broad topics:**

A. AIDS   D. homelessness

B. health insurance   E. abortion

C. domestic violence   F. World Series champions

Using the Results of a Search The kind of information provided by search engines varies, so you need to understand what they will and will not do. For example, a search engine may provide you with the following:

■ A list of articles and books

■ A list with short summaries of the article, or annotations

■ A list and the full-text of the article

What you do next will depend on the kind of list provided by the search engine. Here are some suggestions:

If You Get a List of Books and Articles . . .

■ Determine from the title of the article, the author, or the title of the publication if you want to read the article.

■ Determine if you want to find an annotation or summary of the article before you try to find the article.

■ Find the articles and skim them to see if they are relevant to your assignment.

■ Print or photocopy the article, download it to a computer disk, or make notes.

■ Record all the information for documentation of where and how you found the article.

If You Get a List with Annotations . . .

■ Skim the annotation to determine if you want to find the article.

■ Find the articles and skim them to see if they are relevant to your assignment.

■ Photocopy the article or make notes.

■ Record all the information for documentation of where and how you found the article.

If You Get a List with Full-Text Articles . . .

■ Skim the articles to see if they are relevant to your assignment.

■ Print or download the article or make notes.

■ Record all the information for documentation of where and how you found the article.

Computer Tip

Here are some options for reading the information provided by the search engine:

■ Read the material on the screen; this will require lots of time in the library or on the computer and you can't take the information with you unless you make notes, but it is cost effective if you aren't paying for the Internet access or if you pay a flat fee for it.

■ Print the information and take it with you; this saves time but is not cost effective since many libraries charge for excess printing. You will want to be selective about what you print.

■ Download this information; this requires that you provide your own diskette and that you have access to a computer so you can read the information later, but it does save time in the library, it is cost effective, and it allows you to take all the information you want with you.

Making Notes

When you are making notes from research materials, you want to follow these steps:

- Skim the article or book to discover the focus of the article and to determine if you need to do a close reading.
- Look for the author's use of keywords in your topic and for interesting or useful ideas, facts, or quotes.
- When you find something that you might want to use in your own paper, read the section closely to make sense of the author's ideas or data.
- Copy carefully the information, making sure you record it accurately.
- If the material is a direct quote, be sure to use quotation marks or some other notation, so you will remember later that these are the exact words used by the author.
- Be sure to copy the page number, the name of the article and/or book, the author's name, and all publication information related to the idea. This will keep you from having to repeat this step when you get ready to draft your paper and your bibliography or **works cited page**.

Research Tip
As you do your research, be sure that you have all the information about the book or other source that you will need for your works cited list. See page 397 for a list of details needed for different kinds of sources. If you have the information, you won't have to go back to the library to try to locate a lost Website when you're trying to finish your paper.

After you have gathered all notes from the research information, you will want to identify the connections among the ideas as well as identify how they relate to your own ideas and opinions.

CONDUCTING PRIMARY RESEARCH

Advantages to Primary Research

Primary Research

Gathers new information

Evaluates claims

Requires a plan

Primary research is a useful procedure because it provides you with new information and gives you some authority to write about a subject and to find out firsthand what people think or feel about a subject. For example, if you are writing a paper on welfare, you may want to interview someone who is (or was) on welfare. You can also use the Internet to access newsgroups, on-line discussion groups, and listservs related to the subject. These are all electronic means for people who are interested in a topic to exchange ideas and information through the computer.

In addition, primary research may allow you to challenge or verify another writer's claims. For example, some media critics claim that prime-time television is full of sex, violence, and other negative influences that have no positive value for viewers, particularly young ones. To test this hypothesis, you might list the programs shown during prime time, watch some of them, and then use your observations to agree or disagree with the media critics.

Disadvantages to Primary Research

Primary research is very time consuming: you have to design your own research plan, complete the plan yourself, and finally, make sense of the information you've gathered before you report your findings in your paper. Another disadvantage can be the personal aspect of some types of primary research, such as interviews and surveys. While your grandmother may have experienced the Great Depression, others may not consider her an authority on the subject even though she has firsthand knowledge of the event. Therefore, when using primary research, you will need to decide if you need an expert witness. If you are trying to add details and emotions about a topic, you may interview and/or survey anyone—friend, relative, classmate. If you are more interested in interpretations of the event, you will want to rely on expert witnesses, professionals who are qualified to help others understand the topic.

While there are many ways to conduct primary research, we discuss just two types in this chapter:

- ■ Interviews and surveys
- ■ Observations

Interviews and Surveys

In-depth Interviewing   Some of the best resources for information may be people who live in your own community. Before conducting any interview, you should take some time to learn as much about the topic as you can. You do want to convince the person you are interviewing that you are serious as well as prepared. If you do not have a good background understanding of the topic, you will not understand enough of what you have been told to ask follow-up questions or to know if you are getting information that you can use.

You should also be professional when conducting an interview. Any subject who is worth interviewing deserves your professional courtesy. Here are some guidelines for good conduct during an interview:

1. Call for an appointment. Although you need to find a time convenient for both of you, you should expect to have to make the most adjustments to your schedule. Be sure to write down the time and date, as well as the directions to the place where the interview will take place.

2. Do your homework. Complete any background reading you need to do, and prepare a list of questions. (See the section in this chapter called "Designing Opinion Questions.")

3. Gather whatever equipment you need—paper, writing instruments, a tape recorder, and tapes. Be sure to take extras of everything.

4. Be sure to test the recorder before you arrive for the interview.

5. Dress appropriately for the environment in which the interview will be conducted.

6. Arrive early for the appointment.

7. Ask permission to record the interview. If you can record it, you should write down only follow-up questions that you think of, not everything the person says. If you cannot record anything, you will need to write everything that is said; you may read your notes to the person to verify your understanding.

8. Record the full name of the person you are interviewing and the date of the interview. You can add this later to your works cited list.

9. Write a thank-you letter to the person you interviewed.

Surveys

Designing Primary Research Questions   Before you interview or survey others, you want to carefully plan your questions. This type of prewriting allows you to be prepared so you don't forget important questions. More importantly, this **prewriting** activity helps you focus on the material that you have decided is important.

Two kinds of information are gathered during an interview or survey:

- Demographic
- Opinion

Designing Demographic Questions   Demographic information about your subjects is an important but often overlooked aspect of research. For example, you may find that five out of six people support welfare reform. To understand your data, the reader will want to know who these six people are, and you should be prepared to include relevant details about the people you interviewed or surveyed.

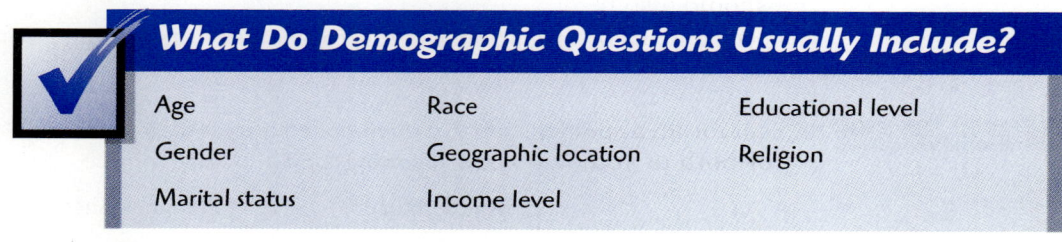

What Do Demographic Questions Usually Include?

Age	Race	Educational level
Gender	Geographic location	Religion
Marital status	Income level	

You will need to add other demographic questions based on the writing prompt or on the group of people you are interviewing or surveying. For example, if you are conducting research on people's perception of those who have HIV disease, you may want to include sexual orientation.

Obviously, demographic questions reveal a great deal about a person's personal life, and many people don't want you to reveal their income level or sexual orientation. For this reason, you need to be clear with the people you survey or interview about how you plan to use the information. If you plan to quote an individual by name, you will need to have permission to use any demographic information. If you plan to report trends, you are then promising to leave out any information that would identify individual participants.

Designing Opinion Questions   Opinion questions get to the heart of primary research. This is the information that, when linked to demographics, can provide insight into the situation. If you are writing a paper on the Great Depression, someone who experienced the event could reveal their opinion about the facts we all know.

When writing opinion questions, you need to consider two types of questions: limited questions and open-ended questions.

Limited questions direct the answer in some way and are useful if you want to gather the same information from all people interviewed or surveyed. Such information usually leads to a yes/no answer or to an answer placed on a scale (strongly agree, agree, neither agree nor disagree, disagree, strongly disagree). Here are some examples of limited questions:

Do you know anyone on welfare?

Have you ever received welfare benefits?

Do you think the mentally or physically disabled should receive financial support from the government?

Open-ended questions allow the person being interviewed or surveyed to provide any kind of response or information she wants. If you want to know the reasons or emotions behind an answer, you will want to include such questions. Examples of open-ended questions are as follows:

What do you think about welfare?

Who do you believe should receive welfare benefits?

How did you feel when you applied for welfare benefits?

To help you write questions, refer to the section on questioning in Chapter 6.

| **EXERCISE 18.3** | Write five limited questions and five open-ended questions that you might ask on a survey or in an interview on the following topics: |

| A. AIDS | C. health insurance | E. homelessness |
| B. abortion | D. domestic violence | F. cloning |

Observations

Observing may include watching a scene or event, but it is not limited to that. You can test a hypothesis by checking out someone's claims.

Designing Observational Research   The key is to identify a question you want to answer or a theory you want to prove or disprove and then design a way of gathering the information that will allow you to find an answer to the question or to prove (or disprove) the theory. Your research design will of course vary based on the information you want to find, the resources you have available to you, and the time you have to complete your project. There are basically two phases of setting up observational research:

1. **Forming a question, answer, or hypothesis**

   Suppose you have read an article in which the author claims that prime-time television is filled with sex and violence and you want to test this claim. You might come up with a question or a statement you want to test:

   Does prime-time television present a lot of sex and violence?

   Prime-time television does (or does not) present a great deal of sex and violence.

2. **Designing research to answer a question or test a hypothesis**

   Once you have pinpointed your question or hypothesis, you must design a plan to find an answer. For the question or hypothesis above, you might decide to do one or more of the following:

   ■ Watch television shows that you feel are representative of those shown on prime time. As you watch, keep track of features you think are presentations of sex and violence. For example, you might count the number of times that characters refer to sex or are shown (or indicated) having sex, and the number of times a character physically attacks or threatens another character.

   ■ Enlist several people to watch shows with you; then interview them about the amount and appropriateness of sex and violence they found in the shows.

Completing the Research

The process of primary research involves three steps:

1. **Conducting the research**

   Be sure to allow yourself enough time to complete your research. If you are conducting interviews or surveys, you are dependent partially on other people's schedules and cooperation, so allow more time than if you are working on your own.

Take notes at the time you are conducting your interviews or observing events. You will find it difficult to remember exactly what you heard and saw if you wait to do so after the fact.

Jot down any ideas or trends you notice while conducting the research. Be sure to keep it separate from the information you are gathering, but you will need to note your ideas and trends for use later.

2. **Compiling the findings**

Once you have completed your surveys, interviews, or observations, you will need to compile your findings. That is, you need to place the answers you received or the insights you gained next to each other to look for patterns. Where are you finding the same type of information? Where are you getting different answers?

If you are doing surveys or interviews in which you have asked limited-answer questions, you would count up the number of persons who gave the same answer to the same question.

3. **Drawing conclusions**

Once you have placed the answers or insights next to each other and looked for patterns, you will need to draw some conclusions: What does the information you gathered mean? How do you make sense of it? What does this information tell you?

If you have conducted interviews or surveys, you might compare the demographic information about your subjects to their answers. Do younger participants tend to answer differently from those who are older? Do female participants tend to answer differently than those who are male? Can you offer an explanation for why one group of participants answers differently than another?

EXERCISE 18.4   As a group, brainstorm ways to investigate the following statements.

1. All rap music contains negative influences, such as profanity, sex, and violence.

2. Children who listen to rap music may repeat the words but they don't understand the meaning of the songs.

3. As Kaminer says, talk shows encourage guests and viewers to consider personal experience (or testimony) but not to think about the larger issues. Guests, studio audiences, and hosts alike concentrate on individuals' personal experience instead of looking objectively at causes, effects, and solutions on a larger scale.

4. *Sports Illustrated* magazine is unfair to female athletes, showing more women in the swimsuit issue than in all other issues during the rest of the year.

5. Parents who want to limit the sex and violence their children are exposed to in music, television, and movies can do so without the help of ratings systems or parental warnings that may entice children.

6. Even though experts says that Americans spend too much time watching TV, in truth most people are doing other things while the TV is on.

7. Adults as well as teenagers are affected by suspenseful and violent movies.

SELECTING MATERIAL TO USE IN YOUR WRITING

Once you have gathered your research material, whether primary or secondary, you must decide how to use the material in your writing. Consider your research prewriting and use the same strategies we discussed in Chapter 7 to evaluate your research as prewriting.

One particularly useful strategy to use with research is to start with the conclusions drawn as you've conducted the research, taken notes, compiled your findings, and evaluated them. These conclusions represent your ideas and could become your **thesis** or **supporting** ideas for your writing. The information that led you to your conclusions then becomes your supporting evidence. Reorganizing your prewriting (by **clustering**, **listing**, charting) into this format may help you see what your ideas and evidence about the topic are.

If you don't have a position on the subject or a clear purpose when you finish your research, use the following questions and activities to help you find your purpose and position for the paper that you will write.

Evaluating Your Research

What did you believe or think about the topic prior to starting the research?

Have you changed your mind about the topic as a result of what you discovered during your research?

Why did you choose the topic?

Why is the topic an important one?

What did you learn during your research that surprised you?

List one to five interesting statistics or facts that you discovered.

List one to five interesting quotes that you discovered.

What did you learn about the topic as result of your research?

What data did you find hard to believe?

What categories or parts of the topic did you find?

What contradictions about the topic did you find?

What errors in fact or perception did you find?

What recurring ideas did you find?

19 Organizing Strategies
Audience Awareness, Ordering Ideas, Rogerian Argument

Once you have analyzed your assignment and completed **prewriting** activities, you are ready to plan what you will actually do in your paper. Sometimes you know what you want to say (your **thesis**) and then need to think about your **audience** and your **purpose**. Other times you may need to consider your audience and purpose to figure out what you want to say.

It's often tempting to start writing now that you have so many ideas. However, your goal should be to write the best paper that you can, not just complete the assignment. One characteristic that distinguishes good writing from mediocre is attention to audience and purpose and how they relate to a thesis.

FORMULATING YOUR THESIS

Organizing Steps
Formulate your thesis
Think about your purpose
Think about your audience
Order ideas
Review the assignment

Usually, by the time you have completed your prewriting, you have identified your thesis (or answer to the writing **prompt**). When you know your thesis, you should write it down as clearly as possible. You then want to decide how you can best support your thesis, given your purpose and your audience as described below. Thinking about your purpose and audience is the next step in planning your paper.

In some situations, you may complete your prewriting and still not have a clear answer or thesis. In this case, you will need to consider your purpose, audience, and grouping of ideas to help you formulate your thesis.

THINKING ABOUT YOUR PURPOSE

One essential part of planning an essay is deciding what you are trying to accomplish. You need to think beyond simply "my instructor assigned it and I want to pass the course." Much of the writing you will do outside of college will not be assigned to you by an instructor. You will have to identify your own purpose for writing to do it effectively. Typically, writers have three purposes:

- *To explain or inform:* Textbooks and encyclopedias are examples of writing that is intended to inform an audience. Writers of these books provide definitions, facts, and statistics.

- *To persuade or convince:* Advertisements are examples of writing that is intended to persuade an audience. Writers of ads try to convince readers to buy a product. They typically provide reasons why the reader would benefit by choosing that particular product.

- *To entertain:* Stories are examples of writing that is intended to entertain an audience. Writers of stories are often trying to cause an emotional response—horror, pity, compassion, fear, enjoyment.

Often you may have to combine purposes to achieve the goal of your paper. For example, advertisers often use entertainment (in the form of a catchy jingle or humor) to capture the audience's attention long enough to persuade them. Other times, advertisers inform the audience about the product as one way of persuading; they talk about the product to show why the reader should buy it. Consider the following prompt on Michael Bronski's "Magic and AIDS":

> According to Bronski, diseases are not a sign of a person's morality. Choose a disease and assess whether or not a judgment can be made about the morality of a person who has this disease.

This question asks you to *choose* and *assess*. The word *assess* asks you to draw a conclusion and convey that conclusion to your audience. In other words it asks you to *persuade*. Before you can persuade your audience of anything about this disease, you will need to ensure that your audience knows what the disease is. So you may need to *inform* your audience by giving a definition or explanation of the disease before you can convince them of your assessment. That suggests that your essay should contain a definition or explanation of the disease followed by your assessment of it. In this case, thinking about your purpose has also helped you think about the order of ideas in your essay. Consider another prompt:

> Discuss the impact of AIDS in your community.

As covered in Chapter 5, *discuss* is a **key action word** that can direct you to other actions as well. When your key words do not give you a clear direction, determine the purpose you want to achieve. Deciding what to include in your answer will depend on what you want to accomplish in your answer:

- If your purpose is to *inform* your reader about the impact of AIDS in your community, select facts and statistics from your prewriting.

- If your purpose is to *persuade* your audience to donate money to local AIDS services organizations, you would have to *teach* your audience what the impact was before you could convince them to give money.

- You might decide to *entertain* your audience as a step in *persuading* them by telling compelling stories of people with AIDS that would get them interested enough to read the facts also and to be moved to act.

EXERCISE 19.1   **What purposes can you identify in the following prompts? How would you go about fulfilling these purposes?**

    A. According to Bronski, diseases are not a sign of a person's morality. Agree or disagree with his opinion.

    B. Why do public figures such as Arthur Ashe feel the need to disclose their own lives to the public and not just to their family, friends, and sexual partners?

    C. What is Bronski's attitude toward the media's representation of people with AIDS? Is his assessment of them fair?

THINKING ABOUT YOUR AUDIENCE

 Another way to help you decide what to include in your paper is to think about your audience. It is tempting to assume that the instructor is the audience. This is not necessarily true; the assignment itself may direct you to another audience or the instructor may specify a different audience (such as your classmates, the governor of your state, or the president of your college).

To address an audience successfully, you need to know who your audience is. For example, if your instructor has assigned an essay in the form of a letter supporting the death penalty, you would want to know whom you are addressing:

■ If you are writing to the readers of the local newspaper, you may need to provide some historical or factual material about the death penalty; if you are writing to lawyers, you might be able to assume they would have this information.

■ If your audience is the members of the local victims' rights group, you would choose a different set of points than if you are addressing a group who wants to abolish the death penalty, since the groups are likely to have different attitudes toward this subject.

In considering your audience, you would need to consider the following:

■ What does your audience already know about the topic?

■ What additional information (or background material) does your audience need to know to understand your ideas?

■ Where might your audience disagree with you?

What Does Your Audience Know?

You need a sense of what your audience knows and what you might need to tell them. This will guide how much detail or what explanations to provide. For example, if you want to discuss the energy crisis in the early 1970s, you would consider the age of your audience as well as their education.

- For audiences born during or before the 1960s, you might assume that they are aware of efforts then to conserve fossil fuels by decreasing speed limits and monitoring thermostats in public buildings, the high price of gas, and the long lines of people waiting to buy gas.
- For audiences born during or after the 1970s, you may need to provide an explanation of what was going on at the time and what the public impact was.

Of course, it's not as simple as age. Perhaps your audience consists of younger people who are interested in ecological and environmental issues; they may already be well-informed on this issue.

Knowing who your audience is and what they are likely to already know can help you decide how much background material you need to supply in your paper.

What Else Does Your Audience Need to Know?

Perhaps your audience remembers the energy crisis and knows that it led to increased gasoline prices and longer waits at gas stations because they experienced it. However, they might not know what impact this crisis had on public policy, on our current attitude toward speed limits and the size of cars, or on the rates of injuries and deaths as a result of car accidents.

If you want to argue that reducing the speed limit increased the fuel efficiency of cars or decreased the number of deaths and injuries as a result of car accidents, you would include any information that supports your claims and not just assume that your audience knows this.

Where Might Your Audience Disagree with You?

To convince an audience, you must deal with their objections to your argument. For example, your audience might say, "Yes, injuries and deaths did decrease as a result of lowering the speed limit, but that's not really necessary anymore because the safety of cars has improved and our road system is much safer. Both the cars and the roads are more capable of handling high speeds than they were in 1974."

To convince your audience that your argument is sound, you would have to acknowledge their disagreement with you and deal with that. Being able to spot how someone else might disagree with you gives you more information on what you need to include as well as where you might need to include it in your paper. The following box lists ways to anticipate your audience's objections to your ideas.

Anticipating Your Audience's Objections

Based on your analysis of the audience, where do your audience's views and values conflict with yours?

What is the weakest part of your argument? Where are you the least sure about yourself?

Look at each of your statements of opinion. Which ones will your audience easily accept? Of the rest, have you provided support so that your audience will accept your opinion?

Write the opposite side of your argument. What would people who disagree with you say? Writing the other side of the argument will help you determine the points you need to convince your audience about.

Let's look at an example from a student paper in response to Bronski's essay:

People with a disease, even a disease like HIV, cannot be thought of as "innocent" or "guilty" regardless of how the disease was contracted. As Bronski points out such labels are "not . . . applicable" (324). Such labels do not apply because people with diseases have not committed an offense which defines what it means to be guilty. For example, people can contract the HIV virus in a variety of ways, most notably through any activity that leads to an exchange of body fluids. Whether that exchange is through sexual activity, sharing a needle or receiving a blood transfusion, the receiver of the HIV virus is not committing an offense. *There is no offense in having sex, regardless of whether the sexual act is heterosexual or homosexual, or whether it is in a committed relationship or in a casual relationship.* The intention of the receiver of the HIV virus was to have sex, not contract a disease. Therefore, if a disease is contracted, the person is not guilty.

If your audience has more traditional ideas and attitudes about sexuality, they may disagree with the italicized sentence. This argument would not be immediately accepted; you would need to prove this statement, and not just assume the audience will agree.

Assessing Your Audience

Environment of the Audience
■ What is his or her physical, social, and economic status?
   (Consider age, environment, health, ethnic ties, class, and income.)

continued on next page

continued from previous page

■ What is his or her educational and cultural experience?

■ What are his or her ethical concerns and hierarchy of values? (Consider home, family, job, success, religion, money, car, social acceptance.)

The Subject Interpreted by the Audience

■ How much does the reader know about the subject?

■ What is the opinion of the reader about the subject?

How strong is that opinion?

How willing is he or she to act on that opinion?

Why does he or she react the way he or she does?

The Relationship of the Audience and the Writer

■ What is the reader's knowledge and attitude toward me?

■ What are our shared experiences, attitudes, values, myths, prejudices? In other words, what kinds of experiences have I had that my readers might have had too?

■ What is my purpose or aim in addressing this audience?

■ Is this an appropriate audience for my subject?

■ What is the role I wish to assign to the audience?

■ What role do I want to assume for the audience?

EXERCISE 19.2 Assume you are writing to the following audiences on the following topics. Analyze the needs of each audience.

A. To sixth graders explaining why the sky is blue.

B. To your supervisor asking for an expensive piece of equipment that will help you do your job more efficiently.

C. To your classmates explaining to them a point you tried to make in a class discussion but don't think you did successfully.

D. To 18-year-olds trying to get them to vote in the next local election.

E. To Teresa McCrary explaining that welfare is not the only option for young untrained single mothers like herself.

F. To an anti-abortion group explaining to them why abortion should remain legal.

ORDERING IDEAS AND INFORMATION

ESL To decide the order of your ideas, you will need to again consider your audience. Think about two helpful questions:

■ What does the reader need to know first to understand your ideas?

■ What order will best convince your reader to accept your ideas?

These questions guide you to think about two issues: What order will make the most sense (be logical and understandable) to your reader? What sequence will be most convincing to your reader?

Common Organizational Patterns

The following are common ways to organize ideas:

Problem/solution: Describe a problem and then explain what your solution is and how your solution would resolve the problem. For example, you might describe the problems of people with AIDS in your community and then recommend a solution that would help.

Overview/parts: Provide an overview of the topic or issue and then explain each of the parts in detail. For example, you might explain that people with AIDS face medical, social, legal, employment, and personal challenges and then discuss each type of challenge in detail.

Definition/analysis or application: Define a term and then apply that term to a situation. For example, to argue whether people with HIV are "guilty," you might define "guilty" and then discuss how this term can be applied to the ways that people contract HIV.

Most readily accepted to least likely to be accepted: Begin with a point that your audience is likely to agree with, and progress to more controversial points. For example, you might argue that adults are responsible for protecting children before you argue that children need to be taught about AIDS in elementary school.

Reasons/conclusion: State your reasons for believing as you do and then give your belief. This strategy is most effective when your belief (or solution) would be rejected by your audience if you stated it at the first. For example, you might have to tell your supervisor why you need a new computer before you ask him or her to approve a purchase order for several thousand dollars. If your supervisor sees convincing reasons before he or she knows what you are asking for, he or she is more likely to agree.

EXERCISE 19.3   For the following thesis sentences, make a list of at least two possible audiences. What method of organization would you suggest for each audience? Why?

    A. All couples should be required to live together for three years before they are married. This would cut down on the number of divorces.

    B. I disagree with Teresa McCrary that welfare is the only option for single mothers who do not have job skills because there are other opportunities for training and job placement.

    C. Bronski has unfairly characterized the media's depiction of persons with AIDS as "guilty" or "not guilty." In using these labels the media is trying to point out that individuals have responsibility for their choices that result in bad consequences.

D. We can help get single mothers off welfare by providing child care and medical insurance.

Rogerian Argument

Psychologist Carl Rogers came up with a way to help people resolve arguments and reach mutual understandings. His technique has been adapted by writers as a **Rogerian argument**.

The organization pattern for a Rogerian argument is based on the theory that an effective way to communicate ideas to an audience is to begin with ideas and values that they accept and believe, and ease them over to a new position or idea one step at a time. Many people write **arguments** as if their audience already agrees with them. Because they make this assumption, they insult people who don't agree with them, mock their beliefs, and do nothing to engage them. There are two problems with this: first, it is a waste of time to write an argumentative essay to an audience who already holds the same views. Second, these essays tend to lack anything that would convince someone who doesn't agree to ever consider the writer's argument, much less change their opinions. Talk shows on television and radio provide many examples of people attacking their opponents without listening to them, trying to understand their point of view, or appealing to them. As a result, we see little resolution of the conflicts presented. Such attacks put the audience on the defensive and they become unwilling to listen. The relationship falls into argument instead of leading to more understanding because the parties have not listened to each other or responded to each other's concerns.

An effective argument must be addressed to those who don't agree or who have not yet made up their minds. Once you've recognized that this is your audience, what you say and how you say it must be altered, and you must organize and develop your essay in a way that shows your audience that you are someone worth taking seriously because you have considered the issue—including their side of it—thoughtfully and politely.

Rogerian argument allows you to get the other person's attention by showing you understand their position. It also requires that you take out insulting or mocking language that might make people defensive. By the conclusion of this type of argument, you've established that you are willing to continue the discussion, to compromise, and to maintain a civil relationship with your audience even though you don't agree with them on this particular issue. Martin Luther King, Jr.'s "Letter from Birmingham Jail" follows the pattern of Rogerian argument, voicing a very strong argument but first addressing the audience's concerns and perceptions, demonstrating that King and his audience have values in common, and using this commonality to show why the audience should change their position to a belief more like King's.

An organization in this pattern would contain the parts shown in the following box.

Rogerian Argument

Introduction: State the subject as a problem rather than as an issue, to interest your audience in reading something they may disagree with.

Fair statement of the audience's position: State the reader's position in a way that seems fair and accurate to the reader.

Statement of contexts in which that position may be valid: Show the reader that you can see that his or her opinion is valid in certain circumstances.

Fair statement of writer's position: State your own position as thoroughly and honestly as you have stated your reader's.

Statement of contexts in which the writer's position is valid: Show how your position is valid in other circumstances or is superior or more effective than the reader's.

Statement of how the audience would benefit by adopting at least some elements of the writer's position: Show how the reader would benefit from changing his or her opinion to be more in line with yours.

EXERCISE 19.4   **Practice argument.**

1. In pairs or in small groups, agree on a controversial topic to discuss. After the first person states his or her opinion, the second person must summarize that opinion to the satisfaction of the first person before stating his or her own. Continue with the discussion, with each speaker summarizing the points or opinions of the previous speaker before stating his or her own.

2. Try this technique as a problem-solving method with someone with whom you are having a disagreement.

Combining Organization Strategies

You may need to use more than one organizational strategy in the same paper. For example, suppose you want to persuade your audience that the key to getting single mothers off welfare is providing child care and medical insurance. You know that your audience accepts the current method of providing welfare benefits for a limit of two years. You could use the Rogerian argument style to organize your paper, stating your audience's opinion first, showing how it works in some ways, and then showing how your alternative solves the problem better. But you might also use the problem/solution organization by describing the problem of single mothers on welfare, describing how your audience's solution does (and does not) solve the problem, and then describing how your solution solves the problem more fully or more beneficially.

Finding an Order

 When all else fails, or when you have massive quantities of material, you may need to physically move your ideas around to find an order. Moving the ideas around can help you see what ideas you have and how they relate to each other.

Ways of Finding an Organization

The following are alternatives for trying your ideas in different orders:

Notecards: Write each of your main ideas on a different 3 x 5 card. Then arrange the cards in different orders to see which one would be most effective.

Cut and paste: Cut apart the ideas and examples in your prewriting that you are planning to use in your paper. Then place the slips of paper into piles according to similar topics. Arrange the piles in an order; then work on ordering the slips within each pile. You will probably have to explain how the pieces of paper within a single pile relate to each other; this explanation will be part of your body paragraphs.

Cut and paste on a computer: Cutting and pasting and the card technique can be very easily accomplished on a computer by using the cut and paste options. By putting each sentence in its own paragraph, you can see each idea individually and move it around easily.

Models of professional writers: Look for interesting and effective organizations as you read essays by professional writers. Try imitating the organization of one of these essays that seems to apply to your topic. (The essay you are using as a model need not be on the same topic as your essay; it does need to show an organization that will work with your topic and purposes.)

EXERCISE 19.5 **Make a photocopy of the paragraphs below and then cut them apart and arrange them into piles to try to find an organization. Remember that the connections between the parts of the prewriting will probably not be here; you haven't discovered them yet. Arranging the parts of your prewriting helps you discover these connections. Remember also that you may not be able to use all of your prewriting in every essay. Try to identify the type of organizations you have found.**

Mathabane's father wore the same clothing that his ancestors wore. Even though they no longer lived in tribal lands. The other children who dressed in modern clothes thought his father "was the most hilarious thing they had ever seen since natives in Tarzan movies."

Mathabane wanted to speak the other languages that his friends did, but his father wanted him to speak Venda. Mathabane spoke these other languages when he was around his friends, but when his father found out, he was very angry.

Mathabane's father had a rule that they couldn't speak at the table. He tells us that "One day I intentionally broke one of these laws." His father got really mad, he said, "You don't have two mouths to afford you such a luxury." Then he threatened to beat Mathabane.

Mathabane had to do "rituals spanning the range of day-to-day living." These rituals were designed to "Protect the house from evildoers" and "to safeguard his job." Mathabane says that these rituals "awed, confused, and embarrassed me."

My friends always made fun of my father playing his bagpipes. They would laugh and pretend they were marching and playing bagpipes. I couldn't understand why my father would embarrass me so much. My mother told me that my father's parents had moved to America before he was born. He had never been to Scotland and this was one way he kept in touch with his roots. She showed me pictures of my great grandparents and other relatives from Scotland. I had never known this about my family's past.

Before dinner, my brothers and my sister and I are supposed to clean the house and get everything ready for dinner. One day I didn't feel like doing it, because I have to do everything. My brothers and my sister hardly do anything. So, I just sat on the couch and watched TV. My father came in and saw me and started to yell at me. He said he worked hard every day to put food on the table and that I was showing disrespect to him, my mother, my brothers and my sister.

My parents always had a rule that my brothers, sister, and I had to wake them up when we came in from a date. It's not that we stayed out that late; another rule was that we had to be home by midnight. My parents would go on to bed but expected us to knock on the door, tell them we were home, and then they would ask how the date went. A lot of times I felt they were treating me like a baby, but sometimes it was nice to talk about my evening.

Everyone in my family has their own assigned ritual. Every night, it's my job to make sure all the doors are locked and the windows shut and latched. My sister irons my father's shirts for the next day. My father gets lunch ready for everybody. My mother supervises and helps whoever needs help.

REVIEWING THE ASSIGNMENT

Now that you have chosen your material and have an idea of how to order it, you need to be sure that your thesis matches the material you have produced. If you have not written a thesis yet, you should now be ready to.

As always, you will need to review the assignment to be sure that you are still addressing it and fulfilling its terms.

Checklist for Reviewing the Assignment

Does your thesis address the prompt you were assigned?

What are your purposes in this essay? Do these purposes allow you to address the prompt?

Does your organization lend itself to addressing this thesis? (Does it allow you to tell your readers what they need to know to understand your point? Does it present your points in an order that readers will accept them? Does it allow you to achieve your purposes?)

Who is your audience? Has your instructor specified an audience or have you had to identify one on your own?

Is everything in your paper related to the prompt? To your purposes?

If research is required, are you incorporating appropriate kinds and amounts?

20 Drafting Strategies
Longer Introductions and Conclusions, Developing Paragraphs Using Modes

There are many ways to organize and develop essays. In Chapters 7, 8, 9, and 10 we saw how to **organize** and **develop** an essay when responding to a reading. In this chapter, we will see how to use additional patterns of organization and development. **Introductions**, **body paragraphs**, and **conclusions** can take many different shapes and contain many different elements.

INTRODUCTIONS WITHOUT READINGS

Chapter 8 points out that when you are writing about a reading, using the structure below is desirable because it moves from the most general information to the most specific. A reader unfamiliar with your topic will thus be led step by step to your **thesis**.

An Introduction to an Essay on a Reading

General lead-in

Author and title of reading

An overview of the reading

The author's thesis or main point

Your thesis statement

A plan of development

However, for some writing purposes, changing, eliminating, or removing some of these elements will strengthen your introduction. If you choose an alternative structure in your introduction, always be sure to consider how the changes will affect the reader's ability to understand. For example, the model introduction above begins with a **lead-in**, which is helpful to readers unfamiliar with your topic, but if you know who your **audience** is and know that they are familiar with your topic, a lead-in can be removed. In another situation, you can eliminate all references to a specific author and reading if you are responding to an issue rather than a reading. Even if you are going to supply quotes from one or more authors to support your **argument**, you need not mention the name(s) of the authors or title(s) of the articles you use. Your introduction would contain the elements shown in the box below.

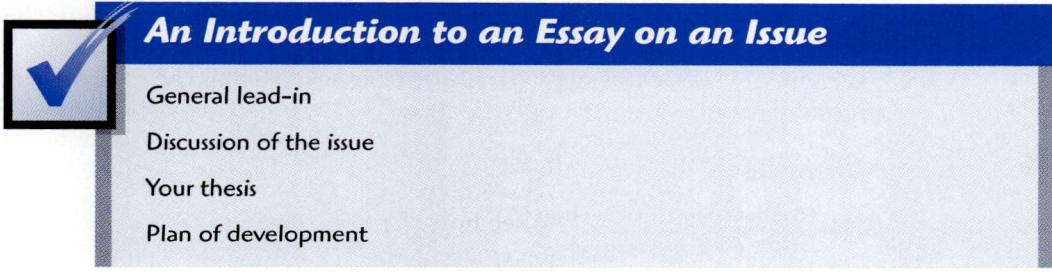

An Introduction to an Essay on an Issue

General lead-in

Discussion of the issue

Your thesis

Plan of development

OWN This structure is reflected in the following example.

> America is considered the land of opportunity, where anyone who is willing to work hard can support his family and himself. As a society, we believe that hard work pays off. We also believe the opposite. If you don't work hard, you deserve what you get—or don't get. Many people look at those on welfare as people who are too lazy to work hard. They believe that welfare recipients are just people who want a free ride. This image is often promoted on television news magazines, which do stories on welfare recipients who abuse the system. We see stories about people illegally trading food stamps or making false claims to bilk the system out of money. We also hear about people who make welfare a life style. Fraud does occur, but the image we have of most welfare recipients is false. Most recipients are people who only use the benefits for a short time between jobs. Other people are unable to work due to disabilities or due to being left a single parent by an uncaring spouse.

This paragraph begins with a lead-in discussing the values Americans hold regarding work. It is followed by a discussion of the issue that the writer is concerned with, the negative image of welfare recipients. The writer's thesis is that our image of welfare recipients is wrong. The writer presents a **plan of development**, noting that he or she will focus on the short time period most people use welfare and on the problems that some people have that won't allow them to work.

Do the elements of the introduction have to come in this order? No, they don't. The previous example uses the general to specific arrangement of information. A writer could choose to skip the lead-in and begin with a discussion of the issue:

- Discussion of issue
- Your thesis
- Plan of development

Since the issue of welfare is one known to most everyone in the United States, a writer could begin with a thesis statement. When a topic is well-known, a writer can start with his or her thesis, using the following organizational pattern:

- Thesis
- Discussion of issue
- Plan of development

Since this structure begins with a thesis, the lead-in is removed. Here is the same paragraph we just examined with this new structure.

> The image that most people have of welfare recipients is false. Many people look at those on welfare as people who are too lazy to work hard. They believe that welfare recipients are just people who want a free ride. This image is often promoted on television news magazines, which do stories on welfare recipients who abuse the system. We see stories about people illegally trading food stamps or making false claims to bilk the system out of money. We also hear about people who make welfare a life style. However, most recipients are people who only use the benefits for a short time between jobs. Other people are unable to work due to disabilities or due to being left a single parent by an uncaring spouse.

Eliminating the lead-in and placing the thesis at the beginning of the introduction required some minor changes in wording, but essentially the paragraph is the same as the previous example. Which one works better? That's a matter of opinion. The first example guides the reader from the general topic of American ideas about the value of hard work to the specific topic of the false image of welfare recipients. The second example begins by seizing the reader's attention with a controversial statement. Both structures will work, but depending on who the writer's audience is, one might work better than the other.

A plan of development is usually placed last in an introductory paragraph, because it tells your reader what specific topics you will address. The issue of capital punishment, for instance, has many subtopics: justice, cruel punishment, protection of society, flaws in the justice system. A plan of development would tell a reader which of those topics you will discuss. However, a plan of development can be incorporated into your discussion of the issue. If your discussion focuses solely on the topic(s) you will examine, a plan of development is not needed at the end of the introduction. Consider the following:

■ Lead-in
■ Discussion of issue with plan of development
■ Your thesis

Use these alternate strategies if you are not responding to one author's ideas, but rather presenting your *own ideas* on an issue. In some essays, you might use quotes from other writers to support your ideas. In that case, you would be examining an issue and not responding to one reading—not to one writer's ideas. Thus, you could create introductions modeled after the examples in this chapter.

Lead-ins

Not only can you change which elements appear in the introduction and change the order the elements come in, you can also *change the nature of the information you present.* For instance, Chapter 8 suggests that a lead-in can do the following:

■ Present what many people would say on a given topic
■ Present a view the same or the opposite of the one you're responding to
■ Discuss a personal experience
■ Provide background information

There are really no limits to what you can use for a lead-in. You might decide to begin your essay by telling a story related to the issue in your essay. Look at the following example to see how a story can bring your reader into the topic you're addressing.

My uncle Robert worked at a tire factory in his small town since he was 16 years old. Two years ago the plant shut down, and my uncle was out on the street with house payments to make and a family to support. He began looking for work but couldn't find any. Eventually, they were forced to sell the house. That was humiliating, but what my uncle said was the worst thing was when he was forced to sign up for welfare benefits. He felt ashamed. He hated being on welfare so much that he began driving to neighboring states looking for work. Five months later, he found a job. My uncle was on welfare, but he was no freeloader. He only took it because he had to feed his family. Although most people on welfare are people like my uncle, too many of us wrongly think that welfare recipients are lazy bums who steal our tax dollars.

This is a long lead-in, but it provides readers with a story they can identify with. The plight of the uncle and his family would touch the reader emotionally. But that is not all it does; it sets the reader up for a discussion of the issue of welfare. Either of the two previous paragraphs we examined could use this lead-in.

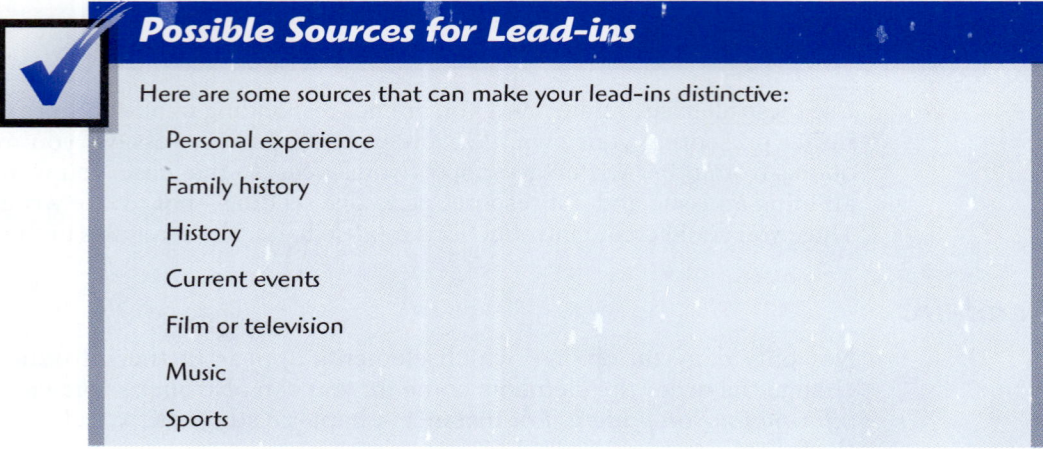

Possible Sources for Lead-ins

Here are some sources that can make your lead-ins distinctive:

Personal experience

Family history

History

Current events

Film or television

Music

Sports

EXERCISE 20.1   Pick *one* of the following issues: crime, space exploration, stereotyping, gun violence, war, adversity, personal courage, overcoming obstacles, relationships, drugs, family conflicts, loyalty. Using sources such as personal experience, family history, history, etc. or other possible sources, write as many lead-ins as you can for *one* issue. For instance one of the topics below is war. What films have you seen about war that you might use as a lead-in? Did the film glorify war or did it stress heroism or war's senselessness? What historical events could you focus on: the D-day invasion, the attack on Pearl Harbor, the dropping of the atomic bomb on Hiroshima, the Gulf War? For each topic, begin by making a list of the examples you might use.

When you choose to start your essay with a lead-in, consider the effect it will have on the audience. Are you trying to provide background information? Are you trying to draw your reader in by personalizing the issue with a personal example or a story? Also consider the appropriateness of your lead-in to the issues you will discuss in your essay. If you provide a story as a lead-in, it should directly relate to the issues you discuss in your essay.

INTRODUCTIONS USING READINGS

When writing about a reading, you can also use structures other than the general-to-specific model described in Chapter 8 and at the beginning of this chapter. However, this structure can be altered. As discussed in this chapter, the elements that make up an introduction can be reorganized or at times eliminated. Examine the following paragraphs and note how their structures are different from the general-to-specific model.

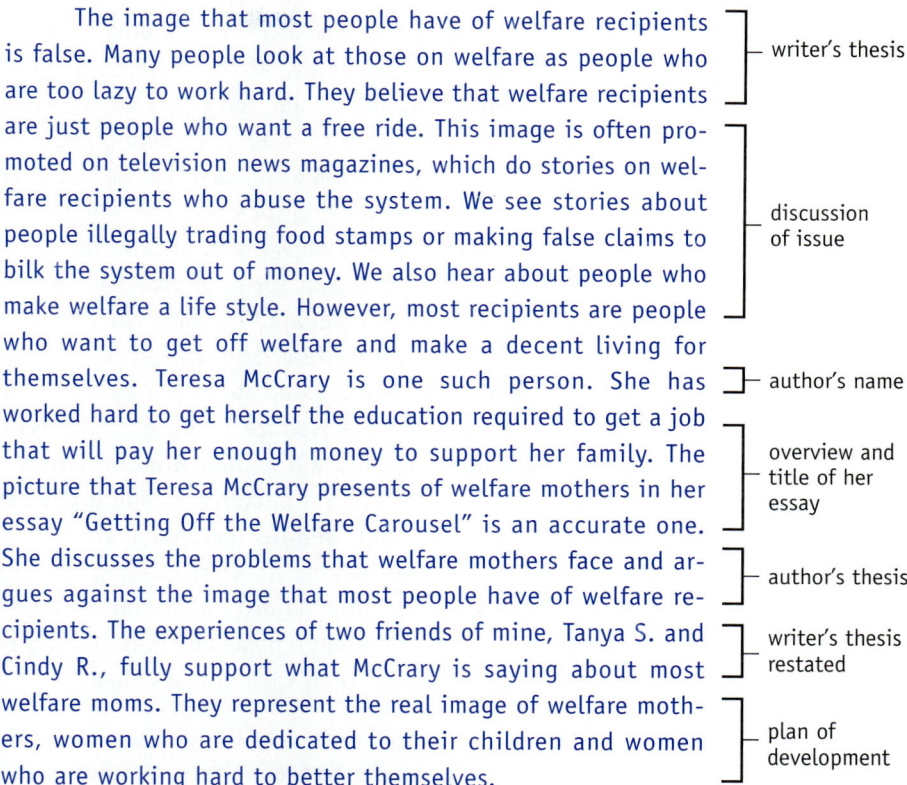

The image that most people have of welfare recipients is false. Many people look at those on welfare as people who are too lazy to work hard. They believe that welfare recipients are just people who want a free ride. — writer's thesis

This image is often promoted on television news magazines, which do stories on welfare recipients who abuse the system. We see stories about people illegally trading food stamps or making false claims to bilk the system out of money. We also hear about people who make welfare a life style. However, most recipients are people who want to get off welfare and make a decent living for themselves. — discussion of issue

Teresa McCrary is one such person. — author's name

She has worked hard to get herself the education required to get a job that will pay her enough money to support her family. The picture that Teresa McCrary presents of welfare mothers in her essay "Getting Off the Welfare Carousel" is an accurate one. — overview and title of her essay

She discusses the problems that welfare mothers face and argues against the image that most people have of welfare recipients. — author's thesis

The experiences of two friends of mine, Tanya S. and Cindy R., fully support what McCrary is saying about most welfare moms. — writer's thesis restated

They represent the real image of welfare mothers, women who are dedicated to their children and women who are working hard to better themselves. — plan of development

In this example, a lead-in has been eliminated and the writer has begun with a thesis statement. The writer has then discussed her concerns about welfare, before discussing McCrary's essay. At the end of the essay this writer has chosen to restate her thesis, in case the reader had forgotten it. The introduction concludes with a plan of development. This structure contains most of the elements of the general-to-specific model, but most of the elements have been rearranged.

The following introductory paragraph begins with a lead-in. Lead-ins can be a very effective way to introduce the topic you are discussing to your reader. Again, you can begin with a story, a narrative about an experience you or someone you know has had. The following example uses the lead-in we discussed earlier in this chapter that sets up the topic by telling a story.

My uncle Robert worked at a tire factory in his small town since he was 16 years old. Two years ago the plant shut down, and my uncle was out on the street with house payments to make and a family to support. He began looking for — lead-in work but couldn't find any. Eventually, they were forced to sell the house. That was humiliating, but what my uncle said was the worst thing was when he was forced to sign up for welfare benefits. He felt ashamed to ask. He only took it because he had to feed his family. Although most people on welfare are people like my uncle, too many of us wrongly think that welfare recipients are lazy bums who steal our tax dollars. He hated being on welfare so much that he began driving to neighboring states looking for work. Five months later, he found a job. My uncle was on welfare, but he was no freeloader. Teresa McCrary is one of those people like my uncle who worked hard to get off welfare. She took the road of education to get herself off welfare. She worked hard to make herself self-sufficient. She tells us about her experiences in her article "Getting Off the Welfare Carousel." She reveals that most welfare recipients are people who are concerned with their family and making a better life. She argues that most people's ideas about welfare recipients are wrong. I fully agree with her. By looking at what McCrary and other writers have to say about the majority of welfare recipients, we can see that they are family/conscious, hardworking people who need more respect than society gives them.

— author's name

— overview of reading

— title of reading

— author's thesis

— writer's thesis

— plan of development

This is the general-to-specific model with a long lead-in. The story of the writer's uncle helps the reader to see welfare recipients as individuals who just need a little help. The story the writer presents also suggests what position he will take on this issue. This lead-in will make the reader more sympathetic to McCrary's concerns.

Keep in mind that the purpose of an introduction is to set up a context for the reader—a framework to help them understand what follows in the essay. In addition, introductions should point ahead to what is to come so the reader won't be baffled by a topic that suddenly appears. The elements of the introduction that we've discussed will help you to provide the information your reader needs. How you present it and in what order you present it, is determined by you and your audience.

BODY PARAGRAPHS

ESL Chapter 9 shows how to put your own ideas into an essay by using personal experiences. When you provide a personal experience, you are using the mode of **narration**. The **modes** are different means to present information to your reader. (See Chapter 15 for more information about the modes.) There are five other modes you might use: **description**, **process**, **comparison/contrast**, **classification**, and **cause and effect**. Providing examples for your reader is just one way to present and support your ideas. The modes can also be used to present your ideas. For instance, if you write in response to a reading that argues that the NASA space program is a waste of taxpayers' money, you might compare and contrast the NASA program with other government-supported programs. Through comparing and contrasting, you might be able to show that less money is spent on NASA than on many other programs or that more benefits are derived from the money spent on NASA than on other programs.

The examples that follow in this chapter are paragraphs written in response to a reading; however, these same approaches can be used in body paragraphs that express your own ideas. If for instance you were writing an essay expressing your own views on capital punishment, you could use narration to tell a story about a man on death row. You might choose to use cause and effect to discuss the effects of capital punishment on families.

The following approaches can be used separately or in combination. In other words, in one body paragraph you might use narration, whereas you might use cause and effect to make a point in another body paragraph.

Narration

Narration is the retelling of an event or experience. In essence, it is relating the story of what occurred. A narration might present the events of a personal experience, like a trouble-filled camping trip or a promising first date. The retelling of historical events is also narration. Previously in this chapter, we presented a lead-in in which the writer discusses his uncle Robert and the story of what happened to him when he was forced to go on welfare. That is one example of narration. Other examples of narration can be found in the examples of body paragraphs in Chapter 9.

Description

Description is a process in which you create a vivid image in the reader's mind, one that will be remembered. The key to description is detail. When describing something for your readers, give them significant details—don't be too vague. Consider the two paragraphs below.

> Although the welfare offices in many cities are dingy, our city's office is designed to make people seeking welfare more comfortable. Our new office is large, airy, and bright. The color scheme is bright and cheery. It's a place where people can feel comfortable.

> One of the difficulties for welfare recipients used to be the welfare office itself. Our local welfare office is designed with people in mind. As soon as you walk in, you can see that they want you to feel comfortable. The

office is painted in blue and pink pastel colors, which are very soothing. The welfare workers aren't hidden behind frosted glass panels; instead, they sit at desks in open areas that give a sense of friendliness. Prints of impressionist paintings by van Gogh and Cezanne brighten the walls. Someone expecting a dingy, green government office will be surprised by the light airy feel of our local office. This may sound luxurious for a welfare office, but it is actually very important. Welfare recipients are looked down on by some people. This creates low self-esteem in recipients. Our new office helps to make recipients feel like they are getting respect. The look of the new office says to the recipient, we want you to feel at ease, comfortable—you are important to us.

The first example isn't very effective, because it lacks detail. It doesn't present the reader with a vivid picture. The second provides a detailed description. Without looking back at the second example, name some of the things attributed to the city's welfare office. The reason you are able to name several things is because you were provided with detailed descriptions. Notice also that the description is used to get the writer's point across about the office's positive effect on clients.

Process

Another way to provide information is through the description of a process. Generally, a writer provides the reader with a description of a process in order to teach or explain. For instance, a writer might describe the process one follows to refinish a piece of furniture or the process one follows to do library research. Essentially, describing a process increases the reader's understanding of each step in the process and how one step leads to the next step. Examine the process revealed in the following paragraph on Teresa McCrary's article "Getting Off the Welfare Carousel."

The welfare system seems to be designed to work against those who receive benefits. McCrary explains to us how the system really works. When a woman with children finds herself divorced, she has to clothe and feed her off spring even though she may have no job skills. Of course her first step is to apply for welfare to protect her children. However, welfare is barely enough to survive on. The woman's next step is to get a job, but because she has no work experience or job skills, "The only jobs open to [her] are maid work, fast-food service and other low-paying drudgery with no benefits," McCrary tells us. This situation leads women on welfare to "take money under the table for odd jobs" so they can make a little more money but not lose their benefits. The system forces women to stay on welfare and take money under the table—for which the government receives no taxes. This system does not benefit the women on it or the government who wants them off it.

This paragraph takes the reader step-by-step through a process. Look back at the paragraph. Write down each step. How does one step lead to another? Also notice that this writer explains the process to the reader in order to make a point about the welfare system.

Comparison and Contrast

You may often get assignments where you are asked to compare two things or contrast two things or compare and contrast two things. When you see the word *compare* in a prompt, it is usually suggesting that you compare or contrast. Likewise, the word *contrast* implies that you compare as well as contrast. When you compare, you are looking for similarities between the things you are examining. When you contrast, you are looking for the differences. Comparing and contrasting are another way to make a point about a topic. In the following paragraph, the writer compares and contrasts her experiences with Teresa McCrary's.

Teresa McCrary tells us about her experiences on welfare and how she used the system to get herself an education. McCrary was a single mother who didn't have any job experience. She says that the only jobs available to her were "maid work, fast-food service and other low-paying" jobs. Rather than take a low-paying job with no benefits, she opted for welfare. McCrary and I are alike in many ways. When I was 27, my husband and I split up. I kept the kids—all four of them. At first my ex-husband sent alimony checks, but one day they stopped. He had left town. I was like McCrary, unmarried, children to support, and no job skills. I thought about welfare, but I didn't want to set a bad example for my children. I got one of those fast-food jobs that McCrary wouldn't take. McCrary is right—it isn't enough money to survive on. I got another job that was part-time. Sometimes I didn't have enough money for rent or food, but my family or friends helped out. It was hard for a long time, but I got promotions and raises. I began taking classes at a community college in accounting and business. A year and a half later, I was offered a job as an assistant manager at a nice restaurant. They let me keep their books. Now I'm the manager. McCrary and I were in the same situation, but our responses were different. McCrary chose to use the welfare system to get by. I chose to work hard and set a good example for my children.

This paragraph points out the similarity (comparison) between the writer's situation and McCrary's. It also reveals the differences (contrast) between their responses to the situation.

Classification

Another way to organize information for your reader is through classification—the process of placing similar items in the same category. For instance, a baseball bat, a football, a tennis racquet, and a golf club are all different items belonging to different sports. However, they could all be classified as sports equipment. Classification helps your reader to see the similarity between the items in a particular category. It may also help your reader to see the similarities or differences between the items in the categories you create. If you were writing about a broad topic like automobiles, you would probably need to classify them, so your reader would better understand your discussion. If your purpose was to decide which car is the best buy, you might create categories such as gas economy, price, cost of maintenance, durability, resale value. With such categories, some cars might appear in more than one list. These classifications, however, will help your reader see each car's particular strengths.

In the following paragraph, the writer has classified three types of people described in McCrary's essay.

> Sometimes what we believe and what is true are two different things. McCrary points out that what most people believe welfare recipients to be like and what they really are like are quite different. McCrary presents us with the image that most people have in their minds when they think of welfare recipients: "The stereotypical welfare mom has 10 kids, including a pregnant teenage daughter, all taking advantage of the dole." So, many people see welfare moms as baby machines who have daughters who are immoral, and all are deviants ripping off the welfare system. In contrast, McCrary describes the welfare mothers she knows. One type she tells us about are the mothers who "mind their homes and children, in a loving responsible way." McCrary is pointing out that many welfare moms' greatest concern is the well-being of their children. These are mothers who believe that their first priority is to provide love and a decent home for their children. She also tells us about another kind of welfare mom, those who are striving to educate themselves so they can improve their lot in life. McCrary tells us that the welfare moms she knows "maintain a 3.0 grade average or better" as they try to get an education which will lead to a high-paying job. The image of the welfare mom with 10 kids is just an illusion we have in our minds. Most welfare moms are working hard to provide a loving environment for their children or working to gain an education which will lead to gainful employment.

In this paragraph, the writer has defined three classes of welfare moms for the reader. Notice, however, that the paragraph is not just a description of different classes. The writer uses these classifications to make a point about the public's misperceptions about welfare moms.

Cause and Effect

A man driving down a steep, winding road on a rainy night loses control and runs off the side of the road and gets stuck in a muddy ditch. What is the effect? What is the cause? What caused the Civil War? What caused World War II? What caused South Africa to abandon its policy of apartheid? You have probably been given many questions asking you to determine cause and effect. Essentially, you are being asked to explain how certain events led to a particular result. The following paragraph shows how causes lead to effects.

One of McCrary's concerns is that children can be negatively affected if mothers choose to work low-paying jobs rather than accept welfare. Our society tells these women to work rather than accept welfare, but most of us don't realize the effect that working a low-wage job has on a family. McCrary describes how a woman working a minimum wage job would be unable to pay for child care. As a result, her children would turn into "latch-key children whose only good meal of the day would be school lunch." When the mother got home from work, she would be tired yet still have all the work a house and children require. McCrary says that a mother working a low-wage job would constantly be worried about being laid off and worrying that she wouldn't be able to pay doctors if she or the children got sick. All these things weigh down on the mother. "These fears cause stress that may result in child abuse," McCrary believes. So, we as a society put pressure on these women to get off welfare and take any low-wage job they can, but McCrary is pointing out what this may lead to—child abuse.

This paragraph describes how the pressures (*cause*) put on women working minimum-wage jobs can cause stress that leads to child abuse (*effect*). The writer has presented this information so that it does more than just describe causes and effects. The paragraph is also condemning society's insistence that these women work any job rather than accept welfare benefits.

Could you also say that this paragraph describes a process? Yes, it does. If you look back a few pages at the section on process, you will see that it not only traces a process but also describes causes and effects. Keep in mind that the modes may be used singly or in combination. A narrative may reveal a process, describe, and show the reader causes and effects. In that case, you would be using three different modes together.

CONCLUSIONS

Conclusions generally serve to sum up the information or argument presented in your essay. However, as we have seen in this chapter, there are alternative approaches that a writer can take. In Chapter 10, the model of a conclusion contained the following elements:

- The author's thesis or point of the reading
- The main points from the reading you're discussing
- The main points you've made in response to the reading
- Your thesis (reworded so it isn't a repetition of the thesis in your introduction)

If you are writing an argumentative essay responding to a reading, these will be the pieces of information you will generally want to present to your reader. However, if you are not, you would want to refer to your main points and restate your thesis. The following examples are all written in response to a reading; however, the strategies suggested would also work for essays that aren't responding to readings.

There are many ways to conclude your essay. For instance, if you are writing on a controversial issue, you might use your conclusion to suggest ways to solve the problems you discussed in your paper. The conclusion that follows discusses solutions to some of the problems McCrary presents in her essay.

> McCrary points out many of the problems that people on welfare encounter. One problem she discusses is that welfare benefits are so low, that welfare mothers can't afford day care for their children. As a result, many mothers are forced to stay at home with their children rather than look for work. Welfare mothers are forced into staying at home because they don't have the money they need for child care. If the government really wants these women off the welfare roles, then the government will have to do more for them. One essential thing the government should do is create day care centers for those on welfare. These centers should be free to those receiving welfare benefits. This would allow a mother to look for work, knowing that her children are being properly fed and cared for. A mother's first priority is her children. If a mother knows that her children are cared for, she can turn to her second priority, finding a job or receiving the training that will lead to a decent job. Without this assistance, it is unlikely that most mothers will ever get off of welfare. This is probably the most important step the government can take to helping welfare moms and, at the same time, reducing welfare roles. Free day care for welfare recipients should be the next addition to the welfare program.

This paragraph focuses on one of the problems that McCrary brings up—welfare mothers are forced to stay at home because they can't afford child care. The writer offers a solution to that problem—free day care for welfare recipients. By providing a solution to the problem raised in the essay, the writer contributes her own original ideas to the issue. Whether or not you are using a reading, offering solutions is often a good way to conclude an essay.

Another strategy is to use your conclusion to make predictions based on the information you have presented in your body paragraphs. See how the following conclusion uses McCrary's article to make some predictions about the future.

> McCrary has revealed several things about the welfare system that need to be changed or our country will continue to suffer the consequences. Since welfare mothers aren't given enough money to pay for day care, they are forced to stay home with their children. Since they must stay home, they can't look for work. Since welfare reform, the amount of time one can stay on welfare is limited. What will happen to these mothers when their time runs out? Five years from now, ten years from now, we will begin to see the results of this policy. Welfare mothers will be expelled from welfare. Where will they go? A likely answer is the streets. Once they are on the streets, who will feed them? These women and their children will probably be fed by relief organizations. And where do these organizations get their money? They get it from the local community. So we will still be paying for these women whether or not they're on welfare. The difference will be that instead of living in the safety of their own homes, they will be living on the streets. If these trends continue, be prepared for the look of your home town to change. You should be prepared to look the other way when you see a tired mother leading her hungry children down an alleyway searching for food.

This conclusion asked the reader to look five to ten years into the future to see what will happen if welfare mothers are not given the support they need. Based on information presented in McCrary's article, it paints a grim picture of the streets of America for the reader to consider. One would not have to be responding to a reading to use this approach.

If you choose the strategy of using a story for your lead-in, you may want to use your conclusion to end the story you've started or refer to it as you make your concluding remarks. At the beginning of this chapter (p. 307) one lead-in told the story of the writer's uncle who was forced out of work and had to rely on welfare. The following conclusion gets back to the story to help the writer make his point.

> Television news shows, even though they purport to be objective, tend to be biased when they do stories on welfare. To boost their ratings, they need a sensational story. They choose to focus on the abuses that take place with welfare. As a result, most people believe that welfare is a lifestyle for people who are conning the system and stealing our tax dollars. However, statistics show that to be untrue. The percentage of people who abuse welfare is very small— smaller than the abuses committed by our elected officials who waste billions

of tax dollars. The great majority of welfare recipients are people like my uncle. He was forced to take welfare and he didn't like it. After he got off welfare, he never got back on it again. He has continued to be a hard working taxpayer like everyone else. He, like most welfare recipients, never returned to the welfare rolls. The next time *60 Minutes* or *20/20* do a story on welfare, they should do a piece on my uncle to fairly portray those who have relied on welfare.

Based on this conclusion, we can see that this writer has written an essay attacking the media's biased presentation of welfare recipients. He has brought the story about his uncle back into his conclusion to underscore his point about the false image the public has of welfare recipients.

A conclusion may serve many purposes. It may sum up what has been said in the essay. It may make a recommendation or predict what will happen in the future. These are just a few of the possibilities. As a writer, you must ask yourself what is best for the type of essay you are writing.

Keep in mind that there are a variety of ways to organize the material in your essays. In addition, the content and structure of your introductions, body paragraphs, and conclusions can be changed to meet the needs of the essays you are writing. For some topics, a lead-in that provides background information may be necessary, especially if your topic is one that few people are familiar with. At other times, a lead-in may be unnecessary. If you are unsure who your readers are, the general-to-specific structure discussed in Chapters 8, 9, and 10 is advantageous. The patterns of organization described in this chapter may be desirable when you know your audience—and thus are aware of their knowledge of the topic—or when you write on a topic that is often in the news or other media.

21 Revision Strategies

To revise effectively, you should have a systematic way to identify the parts of the essay that you can improve. You could just read through your essay and change whatever occurs to you, but you are likely to miss opportunities for improvement. Using a checklist is a good strategy for being sure that you are looking at many ways to improve your essay.

If you are not given a checklist, how can you create the checklist for a course or an assignment? First, read your syllabus and course description to discover the emphasis of a particular course. Then read each assignment carefully to determine what is important about that particular paper. For a **persuasive** essay, clear organization with particular emphasis on **thesis**, **topic sentences**, and summary conclusion may be more important. For a response to a reading, clear attention to the source of ideas and accurate citation of sources and documentation may be more important.

A revision checklist is intended to help you determine if your essay has the content and organization of a good essay and meets the particular assignment.

The simplest revision checklist asks questions like these:

> Does your essay have an introduction, a body, and a conclusion?
>
> Does the introduction have a lead-in and a thesis?
>
> Is the body divided into paragraphs that support the thesis?
>
> Is the conclusion clearly related to the body?

This type of checklist is not very useful, because it is too simple to make most writers analyze their writing in enough detail to improve their rough drafts.

To be useful, a checklist needs to help you evaluate not only the structure but the effectiveness of your essay:

- How well does your paper address the assignment?
- How effectively have you used any reading in the essay?
- Is your organization effective?
- How effectively does the content (main ideas and support) of the essay explain your ideas?

To use the checklist, you need to answer the questions honestly and thoroughly. The purpose of a checklist is not to say you've completed it, but to actually use your answers to improve your paper. The questions will help you identify weaknesses in your paper or essential steps that you have not completed. When you find an omission or a weakness, address it before moving on to the next set of questions.

Beginning writers usually complete the **draft** of a paper by making a clean copy of it, and then they do not complete the necessary revisions because they don't want to mark up the clean and neat draft. However, effective revising requires that you be willing to destroy that clean copy by making marks and notes that help you improve the paper. Throughout this chapter, you will see pencil icons (✎) that signal when you should be writing on your draft.

DOES YOUR ESSAY ADDRESS THE ASSIGNMENT EFFECTIVELY?

ESL   Your first step in revising is being sure that you are addressing the assignment. The following boldfaced questions will help you do so. Remember when you see a pencil icon, you should answer the question or complete the task by writing on your draft.

What is your thesis?

✎ Put an * before and after the sentence(s) which express your thesis. Where is this stated? Is this an appropriate place for your thesis? Why or why not?

Does the thesis provide an appropriate response to the assignment?

Why or why not? Have you used all key focus words from the prompt? If not, should you revise your thesis to include them?

✎ Underline the **key focus words** from the **prompt** in your thesis.

HAVE YOU USED THE READING EFFECTIVELY?

The next step is to be sure that you have used the reading appropriately and effectively.

Have you used the reading accurately? Have you documented your use of it appropriately?

Note that the following checklist is based on a response to a single reading. For some types of papers, such as a research paper or a paper comparing one reading to another, you will need to adapt how you evaluate your use of ideas from someone else. If this paper is a response to an assigned reading, do the following:

✎ Write **RID** (Reading Identification) in the margin where you introduce the reading. Have you included the author's name, the title, and a statement of the main idea?

✎ Write **AUR** (Assigned Use of Reading) in the margin each time you use the reading.

  ✎ Write a question mark (**?**) beside places where it is not clear that you are using the author's material rather than your own.

  ✎ Write an equals sign (**=**) beside ideas from the reading that support your ideas and show that you agree with the author.

  ✎ Write a does not equal sign (**≠**) beside ideas from the reading that you use to show where you disagree with the author.

Turn back to the reading and find material you used in each place where you wrote AUR. Compare these places in the reading to your use of them in the essay to make sure that you:

▪ have accurately reported the author's ideas

▪ have copied quotations correctly

▪ have not used the author's words without enclosing them in quotation marks.

For each ?, review the reading to see if the idea is indeed in the reading. If it is, then revise this section to make it clear where the idea comes from.

Check also to see that all marked uses of the reading are appropriate. As you marked AUR with = and ≠, you may have realized that you used ideas from the reading that are not clearly related to your ideas. You need to omit these uses of the reading, substitute other material from the reading, or provide your own material to show the connection between your ideas and this use of the reading.

Is there an appropriate balance between your ideas and examples and the material from the reading?

If you have more material from the reading than from your own ideas and experiences, then you have probably used the reading too much. Check to see if you have **summarized** large portions of the reading instead of using ideas. Cutting out unnecessary summaries will help you achieve the right balance.

If you've used too much of the reading, this may indicate that you have not spent adequate time developing your own ideas. You need to add more of your own ideas, explanations, and examples.

Before making the changes described above, you may want to also look at the organization of your essay and at the development of your body paragraphs. What you have done here is identified places that may be problems. Evaluating your organization and development may give you more information on how you can improve these sections.

IS YOUR ORGANIZATION EFFECTIVE?

To evaluate your organization, you will need to look at each part of the essay individually as well as how those parts relate to each other.

Introduction

Is the introduction a clearly defined section of your essay?

✎ Draw a line between your introduction and first body paragraph.

✎ Label the parts of your introduction.

Do you need to add or improve any of the following parts of your introduction?

Lead-in: Is the introduction interesting?

Background: Does the introduction have the necessary general background information? Does it introduce relevant ideas from an assigned reading?

Thesis: Is the thesis the main point (or just part) of your whole essay? Your thesis is the key to a good essay. Taking the time now to ensure that your thesis answers the question and clearly states your response is especially important.

Plan of development: Does the introduction suggest how the thesis will be supported?

Body

Is the body divided into parts? Is it more than one paragraph?

✎ *Number the body paragraphs:* Do you have more than one? Do you support your thesis in at least two separate body paragraphs? Does the number of paragraphs seem to match the thesis?

✎ Put an * before and after the sentence which expresses the main idea of each body paragraph (the topic sentence). Ask yourself: Is the point of each body paragraph clear? Is each paragraph clearly on a different point, or do the points overlap too much? Does each paragraph support the thesis? How?

If the main ideas of your body paragraphs do not support your thesis, you have two choices: you can rewrite the thesis to reflect your main ideas (being sure that your thesis still addresses the assignment), or you can change your main idea and body paragraphs to match your thesis. Again, making these changes now will help you be sure that your essay is addressing the assignment and staying on the topic.

Development of Ideas in the Body

✎ Count the number of sentences in each body paragraph; write this number at the end of the paragraph. Although there is no set number of sentences that you must have in a paragraph, counting the number of sentences may help you identify paragraphs that are undeveloped. If you have a paragraph with three or fewer sentences, you want to be sure that your paragraph is that short for a reason that makes your paper better, not just because you couldn't think of anything else to write.

✎ Write **OWN** beside your own ideas, experiences, and observations. For each example you use, ask yourself:

✎ What does each example illustrate?

✎ Is this point related to the main idea of the paragraph? If not, there are options. You might find a different example, one that is related to the main idea of the paragraph, or you might add an explanation to show how the example is related to the main idea.

✎ Is each example given in enough detail so that a reader would understand them? Or does each have *too much* detail, so that your reason for using it gets lost?

✎ Is each explanation detailed enough to be clear to a reader?

✎ Put **DEV** beside each example and explanation that needs more development to be clear. You will need to come back to the sections marked DEV and add more material.

Second Reading Check: Using a Reading for Support

✎ Write **REX** (Reading EXample) beside each idea from the reading used to support the main ideas of your body paragraphs. Is it clear that these ideas are from the reading (and not yours)?

✎ Write **SUM** beside each summary.

✎ Write **PARA** beside each paraphrase.

✎ Write **QUO** beside each quotation.

Do you introduce and explain each paraphrase and quote?

Check each summary, paraphrase, and quotation against the original phrasing in the reading for accuracy.

You have already checked to ensure that you have used the reading in appropriate places and drawn a clear distinction between the ideas and words of the author and those of your own. During this reading check, you are looking at the accuracy of your use of the reading as well as how clearly you explain this use.

Organizing Ideas Within the Body Paragraphs   Now that you have checked your use of the reading, both for location and for accuracy and appropriateness, analyzed your organization, and looked at your development, you are ready to be sure that your thesis, main ideas, and support all fit together.

Beginning writers tend to write paragraphs in the order in which they thought of the ideas. During the revision stage, you need to reconsider how you have organized each paragraph. To do this:

1. Determine how many points you make in the paragraph; you may even want to number each point (1, 2, 3, . . .).

2. Be sure that all sentences related to a point are grouped together. If they are not grouped together, move them or provide adequate transitions so that your reader will know why you are moving back and forth between points.

3. Consider the order these points are presented in. One way to do this is to move each grouping around, read the paragraph with this new order, and then determine which order works best.

4. Once you have chosen the best order for these points, you then need to check transitions between these points to see if they are adequate for this new order.

Conclusion

Is the conclusion a separate part (paragraph) of your essay?

✎ Draw a line between the body of your paper and the conclusion.

Does the conclusion include a summary or a final thought that is related to the whole essay?

✎ Underline the restatement or summary of your thesis. If this restatement is identical to your thesis, reword it.

✎ Put [   ] around the final thought.

Have you contradicted the rest of your paper?

Have you introduced new ideas or examples that would be better used in a body paragraph?

DO YOU NEED RESEARCH TO DEVELOP PARAGRAPHS EFFECTIVELY?

Sometimes you will realize that you need more examples or other information to be able to develop the essay completely, but your personal experience isn't related. If you have time, you may decide to use research to develop your ideas.

Questions for Revising with Research

Introduction

■ Would more background on the topic help the reader understand my thesis?

■ Would more background on the author make the essay more interesting?

Body

■ Where would more examples be helpful?

■ Where would specific facts or figures support my ideas?

Conclusion

■ Would a final example make my conclusion more convincing?

When you find answers to any of the questions listed in the box above, the next step is to locate the material in outside sources. See pages 261–264 and 280–291 for details on how to locate and use material and page 394–403 on how to document sources.

EXERCISE 21.1 Use the checklists in this chapter to revise exercises in Chapter 20.

Use the checklists in this chapter to revise your own essay.

THE NEXT STEP

After you have worked through the revision checklist and have added, changed, moved, or eliminated ideas to improve your essay, you need to be sure that each paragraph and sentence is clear. The next chapter provides a short style checklist to help you check this area of your writing.

22 Editing Strategies:
Editing Checklists and Editing Logs

Tools for the Independent Writer

Style checklist

Grammar and mechanics checklist

Editing logs

One goal in writing is to become independent. Of course, an independent writer develops a **thesis** and plans an essay that **supports** the thesis, but an independent writer also knows how to **revise** and **edit** a paper from the first **draft** to the final draft. Knowing how to use different strategies for revision and editing independently is helpful and often necessary because writers do not always have input from a reader during the different stages of creating a finished paper. Chapter 11 outlined and illustrated the process of revision, and Chapter 12 identified some potentially common errors and different ways to identify and correct these errors. This chapter shows you how to use checklists and an **editing log** to become a more independent writer.

Most instructors expect students to use at least two types of checklists. The first is a *revision checklist*, which was discussed in Chapter 21. This can help you revise your rough drafts for ideas, development, and organization. The second type is an *editing checklist*. There are two basic types of editing checklists to help you improve revised drafts: (1) style checklists and (2) grammar, mechanics, and format checklists. Many instructors expect students to edit for style. You use a style checklist *after* you revise and *before* you edit for grammar and mechanics.

Remember, even though you may be more concerned about content and logical development, all instructors expect your essay to be easy to read and your writing to follow the rules for standard American English. Often an instructor will give a checklist to students for a course or tailored to a particular assignment. But if your instructor does not give you a checklist, you can use the checklists in this chapter. You should pay attention to what the assignment asks you to do. Does the type of assignment require you to check for problems in certain grammar or mechanics? Here are some ways particular assignments might have special problems:

- If you are writing an essay about how personal experience has led to an insight about human nature, you will need to pay special attention to verb tenses.

- If the assignment requires you to respond to a reading, you will need to pay special attention to the mechanics of quoting and using ideas from other writers.

■ If you are writing about cause and effect, you will need to be sure you never confuse the words *effect* and *affect*.

How the essay fulfills the assignment will be evaluated by your instructor.

EDITING FOR STYLE

After you have revised your paper (following directions from your instructor or using the checklist from Chapter 21), you need to be sure that each paragraph and sentence is clear. A short style check can do this.

Sentences that are unclear, confusing, or simply awkward will distract a reader from your ideas. You can find these weak sentences by looking for the parts of sentences that typically cause the problem. Follow the style checklist below to identify the parts of a sentence that are unclear, confusing, or awkward. There is further discussion of each part following the checklist. After you identify each part, you must decide if it is clear or if you can improve the sentence.

If you still have trouble, ask your instructor or lab tutor for help, or go to the relevant section of the Handbook (Chapter 23). You may need to review the meanings of some of the grammar terms or look up correct forms of words. *Note:* You will also find that some of the points in this style checklist are the same or similar to certain points in the grammar and **mechanics** checklist on page 333.

A Simple Style Checklist

Pronouns
■ Is it clear what each pronoun refers to?
■ Does each pronoun agree with what it refers to (its antecedent)?
■ Avoid *it, there, this,* and *that.*
■ Use *you, I,* and *we* only when you mean it.

Verbs
■ Shift tenses only with a reason.
■ Avoid passive: *be + ed* verbs.

Word choice
■ Say what you mean.
■ Vary your word choice: Avoid repetition.

Sentence variety
■ Use a mix of long and short sentences.
■ Avoid very long sentences.
■ Start sentences in a variety of ways.

Pronouns

Clear and correct pronoun use requires you to constantly put yourself in the place of your audience. Check for three types of pronouns separately:

Personal Pronouns That Refer to People   Circle each personal pronoun. (Personal pronouns refer to people. They include words such as *I, we, you, he, she, it,* and *they.* They also include possessive forms such as *her, his, their,* and *our.*)

Is every pronoun clear and unambiguous? To find out, for all pronouns (except *I, we,* and *you*), draw a line to its antecedent (what it refers to). Ask yourself:

- Do the pronoun and its antecedent agree? *Example:* Does *their* (plural) have *each student* (singular) as an antecedent?
- Are the antecedent and pronoun far apart? (They should be close to each other in the same paragraph.)
- Is it clear which antecedent goes with each pronoun? (Is there more than one close antecedent for a pronoun like *her* or *him*? If so, repeat the noun for clarity.)

Remember: If you have trouble finding who or what a pronoun refers to, so will your reader. For additional help, see Handbook (Chapter 23) section 4.2 (p. 374).

Pronouns That Identify Which One   Put every use of *it, this, that,* and *there* in square brackets. Use these words only when they seem to be the only way to express something. Can you rewrite any sentence to eliminate these words? Can you add something after *this* or *that* to make them clear?

EXAMPLE: Bronski addresses <u>this</u> to the general public in America as his audience.
[What is <u>this</u>? What does Bronski address to the general public, the entire essay "Magic and AIDS: Presumed Innocent" or only one part of the essay?]

For additional help, see Handbook section 4.2 (p. 374).

Pronouns That Identify the Reader and the Writer   Put every *you, I,* and *we* in square brackets. Ask yourself: Does *you* really mean all of your readers? If not, rephrase the sentence to eliminate this word. Don't say *if <u>you</u> are a troubled parent, . . .* unless you are sure all of your readers are troubled parents. Say *if <u>someone</u> is a troubled parent,* or *if a <u>parent</u> is <u>troubled</u>.*

Often *I* is unnecessary and just weakens academic writing. Not only will sentences seem wordy, but the main idea will be buried in the middle of a longer sentence. If you really need to use *I* to explain an experience, using *I* is all right, but don't explain the obvious.

EXAMPLE: <u>I personally think that</u> no-fault divorce weakens the institution of marriage because immature partners can marry

without a strong sense of commitment and they can avoid taking responsibility for their selfish actions.
[It is clear to a reader that you are the writer and that you are making a point. Ask yourself: "What is the main point of my sentence—that 'I personally think' something or *what* I am thinking?" If you eliminate *I* (and more), you will have a more forceful and convincing sentence.]

JUST WRITE: No-fault divorce weakens the institution of marriage because immature partners can marry without a strong sense of commitment and they can avoid taking responsibility for their selfish actions.

Verbs

Verb Tenses   Underline each verb. Write SHIFT beside each change in verb tense. Are these shifts necessary and appropriate, or are they lapses to spoken style or a misunderstanding about the time frame of examples?

EXAMPLE: Kimberly Bergalis <u>was</u> a white middle-class female who <u>was</u> 23 years old. She <u>contracted</u> the AIDS virus through her dentist. Bergalis <u>blames</u> the "Florida state health investigators" (Bronski 321).
[Notice that all of the verbs are past tense except the last one. Is it appropriate to use present tense for an action done in the past (by a now dead woman)? No. Change *blames* to *blamed.*]

For additional help, see Handbook sections 3.2 (pp. 365–372) and 8.3 (ESL; pp. 409–413).

Passive Verbs   Underline all forms of the verb *be*—which would include *is, are, was, were, am, been* and *being.*
Do some *be* forms occur with *-ed* verb forms? These are probably passive sentences. Can you rephrase them?

EXAMPLE: AIDS babies <u>are</u> view<u>ed</u> by the media as a whole new "innocent" group of victims.
[This idea can be more directly expressed as *The media <u>view</u> AIDS babies as a whole new "innocent" group of victims.* Note that *media* is a plural word; it means all the types of communication: television, radio, newspaper, magazines, . . .]

Word Choice (Diction)

See Handbook section 5 (pp. 376–377).

Correct Word Choice   Put an X over any word that you are unhappy with— then think about why the word isn't right, why it does not express exactly what you want to say. You'll probably find it most helpful to use a dictionary or a thesaurus to find the word that best suits your ideas.

> **EXAMPLE:** Bronksi uses public figures such as Rock Hudson and Magic Johnson as his examples to have an <u>impounding</u> effect on the public.
> [A quick check in a thesaurus will show that *impounding* means "confining" or "caging." What the writer probably means is simply *great* or *convincing*. The thesaurus gives *important* and *compelling* as synonyms for these words. *Compelling* is probably the best choice because Bronski's paper is persuasive: he wants to *compel* the reader to agree with him.]

Variety and Word Choice   Within each paragraph, put **XX** over every word or word combination that you repeat. Do you use the same word many times? If the repeated word is a key word, repetition is fine. Repeating a key word can hold an essay together and keep it focused on the main point. But if a frequently repeated word is not a key word, use a synonym. Use a thesaurus if you need help.

Look at the example above again:

> Bronksi uses <u>public</u> figures such as Rock Hudson and Magic Johnson as his examples to have a compelling effect on the <u>public</u>.
> [This sentence uses *public* twice. The first use could be replaced by *well-known* and/or the second by *reader* or *audience*.]

Sentence Variety

Sentence Length   Count the number of words in each sentence. Put that number in parentheses at the end of each sentence. If many sentences are about the same length, rewrite some to vary sentence length.

Here are some ways to add variety:

- Combine shorter sentences by using words to show how they are related to each other.
- Break up very long sentences using sentence adverbs to show how the shorter parts are related. Which is better—more long sentences or more short sentences?
- Learn when to use a few short sentences to get across your important ideas directly.

> **EXAMPLE:** Bronski illustrates that the media's role can be more dangerous than merely "pander[ing] to popular prejudice" and selling "news." Popular stereotyping leads to misguided public policy and counterproductive legislation.

[While it would be possible to combine the two sentences above using *because*, using two sentences gives emphasis to the second idea (*misguided public policy*) as well as the first (*what Bronksi shows*).]

■ Avoid a succession of many long sentences. Watch out for sentences that are more than three typed lines. (They make your ideas hard to follow.) Try to break long sentences up or eliminate unnecessary or repeated ideas.

EXAMPLE: In reading the essay "Magic and AIDS: Presumed Innocent" written by Michael Bronski, Bronski attempts to expose the effect that the media has on the general public, when it comes to casting a "guilty" or "innocent" verdict upon people who are infected with the HIV virus, as to the method in which the virus was contracted.

This sentence could be improved in at least three ways:

■ Eliminate some repeated phrases: *written by Bronski* and *Bronski*.
■ Delete unnecessary words: *In reading the essay*.
■ Break up the sentence to focus on the two main ideas: (1) Bronksi's purpose in writing and (2) how the media play a role in judging people.

Here's an edited version:

In "Magic and AIDS: Presumed Innocent," Michael Bronski attempts to expose the effect that the media have on the public's judgment of HIV-infected people as "guilty" or "innocent." Bronksi's essay shows how this verdict depends upon the method in which the virus was contracted.

These two sentences can be further improved by making them more active and eliminating words that do not contribute to the main idea of the sentences:

In "Magic and AIDS: Presumed Innocent," Michael Bronski exposes the effect that the media have on the public's judgment of HIV-infected people as "guilty" or "innocent." Bronski's essay shows how this verdict depends upon how the virus was contracted.

See Sentence Basics, Handbook section 1 (pp. 349–354) and Sentence Boundaries, Handbook section 2 (pp. 354–362) for help in understanding sentence structure. See Handbook section 5 (pp. 376–383) for help in clarity.

Phrasing Circle the first five words of each sentence. Read through the essay, reading only these circled words. If many sentences start with the same pattern, rewrite some to have more variety. For example, in one paragraph about AIDS and the media, a writer has used these first five words to begin sentences:

According to the author, AIDS . . .

According to Bronski, AIDS is . . .

According to the media's portrayal . . .

According to the published story . . .

Some of these can be started in different ways:

Bronski states that AIDS . . .

The media portray AIDS as . . .

The published story implied/claimed/suggested that . . .

Before continuing, review the box on page 327, which summarizes points that can be style problem areas.

EDITING FOR GRAMMAR AND MECHANICS

Each time you read and revise a paper you have written, you will probably catch some grammar and mechanics mistakes. You may also have missed some errors because you were not reading specifically for them or you may have made new errors when you changed one part of a sentence but did not look carefully at the rest of that sentence or the sentences before or after the correction. After you have revised a paper, you must make time to reread it for grammar and mechanics errors. This is a step that cannot be avoided.

What Are Grammar and Mechanics Mistakes?

Typically, grammar and mechanics mistakes are incorrect forms of **standard American English**, misspelled words, confused words, and missing or incorrect punctuation and other **format** conventions.

When you edit for grammar and mechanics, you should ignore the content of your essay. Concentrate just on sentence-level form. Follow the checklist below to edit your paper. (Further discussion of each item follows the checklist.) As you edit your paper, make entries in your editing log to keep track of your progress and to see if you have started to have a different type of grammar or mechanics problem.

Many of the terms in this checklist are discussed and illustrated in the Handbook, Chapter 23. There is an overview of the Handbook on pages 348–349 (as well as on the inside rear cover), and coded tabs will help you

A Grammar and Mechanics Checklist

Sentence boundaries

- Fragments
- Run-ons

Verb endings

- Subject–verb agreement
- Verb tenses: *-d, -ing, -en*

Noun endings

- Apostrophes
- Plurals

Pronouns

- Is it clear what each pronoun refers to?
- Does each pronoun agree with what it refers to?
- Did you get rid of every *it, there, this,* and *that* you could?

Frequently used punctuation

- Commas
- End punctuation
- Capitalization
- Quotation marks

    Use quotation marks (" ") only for exact quotes.

    Provide page numbers of all quotes and paraphrases.

    Verify that all cited names are correct.

Spelling

- Misspelled words
- Homonyms (*there, their,* and *they're*) and confused words (*effect* and *affect*)

Left-out and repeated small words

Final format check

- Identify yourself, course, date, and assignment.
- Use 1" margins.
- Mark the beginning and end of each paragraph clearly.
- Use page numbers.
- List all quoted sources in the works cited list.

locate the specific topic you need. Below we provide cross-references to relevant sections of the Handbook. You can also ask your instructor or a writing center tutor for help. If you have identified some specific problems you need to work on, your instructor or a tutor can help you work with the relevant exercises in Chapter 24.

Sentence Boundaries: Fragments and Run-ons

If you are unsure about some sentences, use the Handbook in Chapter 23 to determine if the group of words is a fragment or a run-on. Try to identify verbs and their subjects.

Hunting for Fragments   Begin reading each "sentence" from the end of the paper backward to the beginning. Put Xs around each sentence you think is a fragment. See Handbook section 2.1 (pp. 355–358).

Remember: All sentences have a tensed verb or a modal: Does each sentence have a tensed verb or a modal?

All verbs have subjects: Does each verb have a subject? A prepositional phrase cannot serve as the subject of a sentence.

> **EXAMPLE:**   <u>In the article by Bronski</u> says that the media influence people's judgment of guilt and innocence.
> [Either *Bronski* says or *the article* says, but *in the article by Bronski* cannot serve as the subject of the sentence.]

Finally, look especially at short sentences and sentences beginning with a subordinator such as *if, because,* or *while.* Look at the last "sentence" in this example. It is a fragment.

> Michael Bronski tells us that the media and society feel that the world is divided between good and bad. The guilty ones are homosexuals, drug users, and prostitutes. <u>While the innocent are children and hemophiliacs.</u>

For further discussion, see Handbook sections 1 and 2 (pp. 349–358).

Hunting for Run-ons   Put Xs around each sentence you think is a run-on.

Look especially at sentences that are very long or have more than one verb. Remember that all sentences either stand alone or are connected to other sentences. Ask yourself the following questions:

- ■ If there is more than one verb in a sentence, are the parts connected correctly?
- ■ Is there a coordinating conjunction such as *and, or,* or *but*? Underline it. Be sure there is a comma before the conjunction.

■ Is one sentence introduced by a subordinating word such as *although, because, that,* or *if* ? If the first sentence starts with a subordinating word, put a comma after that sentence.

■ Are the sentences correctly separated by semicolons?

Look at the run-on in the following example discussing Bronski's use of slang:

> The second is at the end of his essay it can heighten the level of interest to continue reading the essay to get all of the information that is required to correctly interpret Bronski's entire message in the essay, which is how the media can classify an individual an "innocent" victim of the HIV virus or "guilty."

Here is a better and more correct way to phrase this example:

> The second [place Bronski uses slang] is at the end of his essay. This [use of slang] heightens the reader's interest to continue reading to get all of the information required to correctly interpret Bronski's message in the essay, which is how the media can classify an individual as an "innocent" victim of the HIV virus or "guilty."

For further discussion, see Handbook section 2 (pp. 358–362).

Word Endings: Verb Endings

Subject-Verb Agreement   Circle each tensed verb, and draw a line to its subject. Read each pair to see if they agree. *Remember:* Not all plurals end in *-s* (*people, mice, women*). Some foreign-based words may be plural, even though they do not end in *-s* (<u>data</u> are . . . , <u>media</u> are . . .).

> **EXAMPLE:** <u>The press and the public</u> **characterizes** people the AIDS virus as being irresponsible or guiltless.
> [Notice that *the public* is part of a conjoined larger subject: *the press and the public.* This is a plural subject and no *-s* is needed on the verb.]

For further discussion, see Handbook sections 3.2 and 4.1 (pp. 365–369, 372–374).

Verb Tense   Look at the circled verbs. Are any verb endings missing? Read each verb to see if you have left off any endings: *-ed, -en, -ing.*

Check especially every sentence with a form of *be* or *have.* These helping verbs usually require the main verb to have an ending.

> **EXAMPLE:** For instance, homosexuals ,who <u>are</u> usually <u>portray</u> as white, who got the AIDS virus through . . .
> [The verb *portray* needs an *-ed.*]

For further discussion, see Handbook sections 3.2 (pp. 369–372) and 8.3 (pp. 409–413).

Endings on Nouns

Checking Apostrophes   Put an X over each word with an apostrophe. Is the word a contraction, or is it a noun plus possessive *-s*? If the word is not a contraction or a possessive noun, delete the apostrophe.

Finding Missing or Unnecessary Apostrophes   If you often leave off apostrophes, look for *-s* at the ends of words.

- *Apostrophes on verbs:* Unless the verb is in a contraction, it should not have an apostrophe.

  EXAMPLE OF A VERB ENDING IN -S: Bronski claim**s** that the media . . .

  EXAMPLE OF A CONTRACTION: Bronski doe**s**n't consider . . .

- *Apostrophes on nouns:* If the noun is only plural, don't use an apostrophe:

  EXAMPLE OF A POSSESSIVE NOUN: Bronski**'s** point is that . . .

  EXAMPLE OF A PLURAL NOUN: The point**s** that I disagree with are . . .

  A noun can be both plural and possessive:

  EXAMPLE OF A PLURAL + POSSESSIVE: The editor**s'** decisions were . . .

- *Apostrophes and pronouns:* Any pronoun with an apostrophe must be a contraction. Remember that possessive pronouns do not have apostrophes:

  EXAMPLES OF CONTRACTION OF A PRONOUN + AN AUXILIARY VERB:

  He's unable to answer.

  It's not likely.

  EXAMPLES OF CORRECT POSSESSIVE PRONOUNS:

  He lost **his** job. The dog hurt **its** paw.

  EXAMPLE OF A POSSESSIVE PRONOUN WITH AN UNNEEDED APOSTROPHE:

  He's assumption is that there is a moral issue in any kind of sex. [Change *he's* to *his.*]

For further discussion, see Handbook section 3 (pp. 363–365).

Pronoun Forms

Checking Your Pronouns Again   Be sure all your pronouns are correct and who or what they refer to is clear. Underline each pronoun. What does each pronoun refer to? Does it agree with the word or phrase it refers to?

The unclear pronouns are underlined in the following example:

The media tends to label women as bad girls that spread the AIDS virus. **He** gives a quote from Walt Frazier, an ex-ball player and broadcaster for the New York Knicks, "you at least had to go to parties and have a rap to pick up women. Now you see them lining up against the wall after a game." Of course, we hear little discussion about the men— including Magic Johnson—infecting their partners. **It**'s always being told as, "I contracted the virus by messing around with too many women."

This writer is assuming that the reader knows that "he" refers to Michael Bronski, the author of the essay. Do you think this will be obvious? In such cases it's always best to repeat the name whenever you begin a new paragraph.

What about _it_? This is an empty pronoun, without a real antecedent. The writer really means: _Such men always say_,"I contracted the virus by messing around with too many women."

Here's another way to rewrite this: _The story_ is always told as, "I contracted the virus by messing around with too many women." Notice that you sometimes have to rewrite part of a sentence to replace a word.

■ In this example, the pronouns _I, we,_ and _you_ occur within direct quotes, so it is not possible to eliminate them.

For further discussion, see Handbook section 4.2 (pp. 374–375).

Frequently Used Punctuation

For further discussion of punctuation issues, see Handbook section 6 (pp. 383–393).

Commas   Put an X over each comma, and then determine if each one is really needed. Use the Handbook if you need to.
Here's an example of an unnecessary comma:

They are thought of as guilty victims, because of their irresponsible behavior.
[The _because of_ phrase follows the main sentence, so it does not need a comma before it. If the _because of_ phrase occurred before the main sentences, a comma would be needed: _Because of their irresponsible behavior, they are thought of as guilty victims._]

Look at each sentence that does not have a comma. Determine if a comma is needed. Ask yourself the following questions:

■ Is there a phrase (such as _because of public opinion_) or a long word (such as _therefore_) before the subject? Use a comma.

EXAMPLE OF A COMMA USED TO SET OFF AN INTRODUCTORY PHRASE:

Because of public opinion, the media did not appear to want to point out that Magic Johnson and other athletes were also sexually promiscuous.

■ Does a phrase or a long word occur between the subject and the verb? Use a comma.

EXAMPLE OF A PHRASE INTERRUPTING THE CONNECTION BETWEEN THE SUBJECT AND THE VERB:

The media <u>over a period of time</u> has become less rigid at classifying "guilt" or "innocence."
[Put commas around the phrase *over a period of time* because it occurs between the subject and the verb.]

■ Is there a list of more than two items? Use a comma after all of the items except the last one.

EXAMPLE OF LIST NEEDING COMMAS:

Bronski shows how the classification of HIV-infected persons as innocent or guilty is unfair by discussing Kimberly Bergalis, Ryan White, and newborns.

■ Are two complete sentences conjoined? Use a comma.

EXAMPLE OF CONJOINED SENTENCES:

Health educators are aware that the media help shape public opinion about diseases such as HIV, and they should not allow the media to present discriminatory statements regarding AIDS victims.

■ Does a subordinated clause occur before a main clause? Use a comma.

EXAMPLE OF A SUBORDINATE CLAUSE INTRODUCING A SENTENCE:

Because the mothers of AIDS babies usually used illegal drugs, some people found it difficult to classify these sufferers as "innocent."

Punctuation at the Beginning and End of a Sentence   Does each sentence have end punctuation? Look for a period (.), a question mark (?), or an exclamation mark (!).

Determine what's wrong with the end punctuation in the following example from a reading response to "A Hanging":

But I guess they were just following orders: isn't that what we all do.
[The second half of this example is a question, so it should end with a question mark.]

Capital Letters   Does each sentence begin with a capital letter? Are all proper names capitalized correctly?

Here's an example of where capital letters are needed:

AIDS is an acronym and is capitalized.

Quotation Marks   Put an X beside any place you use ideas from someone else. If you are responding to a reading or other source (a speech or interview, for example), you will need to be very careful to show what ideas and words come from someone else.

Exact Quotations.   If you are quoting someone else's exact words, check the following:

■ Did you copy the other person's words exactly?
■ Did you put the quoted words or sentence(s) in quotation marks?
■ Is it clear who is being quoted? Did you spell the name correctly?
■ Did you put the number of the page you are quoting from in parentheses at the end of the sentence?

Paraphrases and Summaries.   If you are not quoting someone else's words exactly, check the following:

■ Did you use quotation marks for a paraphrase or a summary? If you did, remove them.
■ Did you paraphrase or summarize the author's ideas clearly?
■ Did you give the author credit for the ideas?
■ Did you spell the author's name correctly?
■ Ask your instructor: do you need to document the page(s) for summaries and paraphrases? If so, did you put the page(s) in parentheses before the period at the end of the sentence?

For further discussion, see Handbook section 6 (pp. 383–393).

Spelling

Misspelled Words   If you are using a word-processing program with a spell checker, look up every word that is marked as misspelled. But remember:

■ Spell checkers do not include names and many technical or specialized terms.
■ Look up any words you are unsure of.
■ Capitalize proper names such as people, places, or companies.

Homonyms and Other Similar Words   Look up any word that has a similar spelling or pronunciation with another word.

■ Use a dictionary or glossary of usage to check these words.
■ Remember each confused word will distract your reader. And some confused words will actually make your paper wrong.

> **EXAMPLE:** Since Bronski's audience is the general public, what better figures to use to have a powerful <u>affect</u> on the public than Magic Johnson, Ryan White, Dr. Prego, Kimberly Bergalis, and Rock Hudson?
> [Here the writer is commenting on how examples can have a consequence on the reader, so *affect* should be *effect*, as in *cause and effect* or *result*].

For further discussion, see Handbook section 5.1 (pp. 376–377).

Left-out and Repeated Words

For further information, see Chapter 13, Formatting and Proofreading (pages 216–221).

As you write and read focusing on ideas, you may automatically fill in words that have been left out or ignore words that have been repeated if they are function words like *a, the, and,* and *to.* Start at the end of your paper and read each sentence aloud. Speaking will often slow down your reading enough so that you will be able to notice left out or repeated words.

> **EXAMPLE:** We assume Kimberly Bergalis did get the AIDS virus from her dentist, and Typhoid Mary [<u>was</u>] suspected of spreading the typhoid disease to her fellow employees.

> **EXAMPLE:** They are thought <u>of</u> as guilty because of their irresponsible behavior.

Format Check and Proofreading

For further discussion, see Chapter 13, Formatting and Proofreading (pages 212–216).

After you have edited for grammar and mechanics, do a final format check. As you check the format and proofread the final draft, check for the following:

■ Is your name, the date, course title, the instructor's name, and the assignment in the right place?

■ Is the title centered?

■ Is there at least one inch on the top, bottom, and sides?

■ Is each paragraph break clearly marked? If you are indenting paragraphs, is each paragraph indented at least a half inch? If you are using block paragraphing, is there a blank line between each paragraph?

■ Whenever a line is not completely filled, is the next line the beginning of a new paragraph?

■ Is each page numbered (in the right place)?

■ Does your name appear in the upper left or right corner of each page?

■ Have you included a list of works cited or references at the end of your paper? Include only those works you actually use. See Handbook section 7 (pp. 394–403).

EXERCISE 22.1   Use the grammar and mechanics checklist on page 333 to edit the exercises in Chapter 24, pages 419–430.

EXERCISE 22.2   Jigsaw exercise (collaborative): This is a group exercise that asks you to work with Exercises 24.11 and 24.12 (pp. 430–432). Your instructor will assign students to home groups to work on these exercises. Each group will then designate one person to be a specialist in one editing problem (one person will work with fragments, one with verb endings, etc.).

The specialists from each group will meet in new specialist groups. The specialist groups will edit the exercises for the assigned problem (the fragment specialists will correct all fragments, the verb ending specialists will work on verb problems, etc.). The specialists in each group should be sure that they understand why corrections are made and be ready to explain the corrections to other students. The specialists will then return to the home groups and explain the editing work done on their assigned problems (for example in one home group, a fragment specialist would explain the fragments, a verb ending specialist would explain the verb endings, etc.). Thus, each home group will discuss all editing problems.

Note: The home groups can have more than one specialist in each area, if the number of students does not match the nubmer of problems.

EXERCISE 22.3   Use the grammar and mechanics checklist on page 333 to edit one of your own papers for grammar and mechanics. Copy all of the mistakes you found into an editing log (see the following section).

USING AN EDITING LOG

See also Chapter 12 (pages 204–205), where editing logs are introduced.

One of the goals of learning to edit your own work is to be able to write independently. One way to do this is to keep an editing log—a journal or record of problems you have encountered in writing. Keeping such a record is the first step in making an editing log. In order for this record to be helpful, you also need to identify the type of problem with the name used by your instructor or used in the Handbook.

There are many benefits to knowing how to identify the problems you have:

■ You can look up how to correct the problem in the Handbook (see pp. 348–418). You can set aside time to work on the problems you commonly have by doing the suggested activities in the Handbook.

■ You can work with your instructor, classmates, and writing center tutors more effectively if you know what to call specific writing problems.

You will also be more effective in recognizing and acting on their suggestions (see Chapter 11, pp. 206–208, peer review).

■ The editing log provides you with a convenient way of checking your progress in eliminating sentence-level and grammatical problems. That is, when the number of times you enter a particular problem decreases noticeably, you can feel confident that your writing is improving in this area in terms of grammar, editing, and proofreading.

An editing log is often most useful if it is divided into two parts:

■ *Part 1 is the log itself.* Record the name of the mistake you made and how to correct it. Some mistakes can be easily corrected by adding verb endings or punctuation. If you decide to just correct the mistake in the log entry, use a different color pen or circle it, so you can identify it. Include any notes to yourself about checking your corrections with your instructor or in a handbook if you are unsure about them. See the sample entries in the editing log below.

■ *Part 2 is a short summary of the errors you made for a particular assignment.* Make a list of each error type and the number of times you made this error. This summary will help you see if a particular problem is typical of your writing or perhaps just a careless mistake. The summary will help you see if your errors fall into a particular pattern. It can help you identify problems you need to spend more time on or ask for help in learning how to correct.

If your instructor has not assigned a format for an editing log, follow the steps in the box below.

How to Use Editing Logs

Part 1. Creating an Editing Log

1. Make an entry for the paper you are editing—for example, *English 101, Essay 1, 1/21/01: Just Following Orders.*

2. Read your paper carefully, sentence-by-sentence, looking for errors.

3. Copy any sentence with an error: mark the error so you can easily see what part of the sentence is the problem.

4. If others have read your paper and marked a sentence, include any comments they have made beside the error.

5. Identify the error type by name; use the Handbook if necessary.

continued on next page

continued from previous page

6. Using suggestions in the Handbook or your instructor's comments, decide how to correct the error.

7. Write the correction next to the error in your editing log.

Part 2. Making a Summary of Error Types

1. List each error type by name.

2. Count how many times each mistake was made.

3. Identify any problems you should spend extra time working on.

Sample Entries in an Editing Log

The example below illustrates an editing log entry for a daily reading response assignment to George Orwell's essay "A Hanging."

Lena Martin
Reading Response, 1/20/01
George Orwell,"A Hanging"

Errors

Corrections

1. Error/Context: . . . in George Orwell's "A Hanging.

Correction: Close quotation.

Type of error: Closing quotation marks around title

Note: Look up the order of quotation mark and period.

2. Error/Context: After the hanging is over, a Eurasian boy referred to the dead prisoner as . . .

Correction: Change referred to present; maybe change is to was.

Type of error: Tense shift

Note: Ask instructor about which tense would be best to use.

3. Error/Context: Shortly before, the superintendent pokes the dead body and replies . . .

Correction: Change pokes to poked. and replies to replied

Type of error: Wrong tense

Note: This is pretty clearly past, because this is at least before the Eurasian boy talks.

4. Errors/Context: All of paragraph 2:
At the end of the story <u>it</u> <u>seems</u> that
<u>everyone</u> is using humor to release
tension. <u>They</u> *joked* about <u>prisoners</u>
"wriggling about," after they had been
hung (Orwell 57). <u>They</u> also *joked*
about the doctor sometimes having
to "pull the <u>prisoners</u> legs to ensure
decease" (57). The superintendent
offers everyone a drink at eight a.m.
by *replying* that he has "a bottle of
whisky in the car" (58).

Pronoun errors:
Type of error: Use of <u>it</u>
Type of error: Pronouns <u>everyone</u> and
<u>they</u> are unclear. Who is <u>everyone</u> and
who are <u>they</u>?
Correction: *At the end of the essay,*
<u>*all of the prison employees who*</u>
<u>*have participated in the execution*</u> *use
humor to release tension.*

Type of error: Repeated word *joked*

*Correction: rephrase <u>jokes</u> to <u>minimizes
the seriousness</u>*

Type of error: Word choice *by replying,*

*Correction: Develop and rephrase this
sentence as: <u>The superintendent says
that he has</u> "a bottle of whisky in the
car" and offers everyone a drink at
eight o'clock in the morning (58).*

Type of error; tense shift

Correction: [Use present] joked → jokes

Type of error: missing apostrophe
twice?

Correction: [Add apostrophe to plural
noun] prisoners → prisoners'

When to Use Your Editing Log

It is often easiest to learn to use an editing log after you have had help from someone else in recognizing what—or at least where—your errors are on a rough draft. After you have practiced identifying and correcting many of the common problems in your writing, you will be able to use an editing log more independently. You'll also understand when the best time to use your editing log is:

■ Your instructor reads over and comments on a complete rough draft of your paper before you submit it for a final grade. Use your editing log to respond to these comments. Instructors often include the names of an error along with an indication of where the problem is, so identifying the type of error and deciding how to correct it may be easier.

■ You have gotten some feedback from peer review. Remember, many times a fresh reader—even a fellow student—can detect problems more easily than the writer. If your peer editor has marked any particular sentences or phrases as being unclear, awkward, confusing, or wrong, then look at them to see if the problems could be caused by one or more of the common errors you make.

■ As you edit, read your paper twice. One time, look specifically for common errors you noted from your editing log, the second time, look for anything else that seems less than satisfactory: organization, ideas, use of the reading, grammar, mechanics, and format.

Making Your Editing Log Work for You

Using an editing log is most helpful if you are prepared. Being prepared means following steps, setting aside enough time, and using the right resources.

■ Get ready to edit using your log. Unless you have a phenomenal memory, you should read over the lists of errors from your last couple of assignments: What were the most common errors? What are they called? Do you know how to correct them? These are the specific error types you will edit for one time when you are reading your paper.

■ Make a special time to read over your assignment using your editing log. Remember, you have added this extra reading to the overall editing process. Both reading your essay and writing down your errors and their corrections take time.

■ Get help if you have trouble using your editing log. Sometimes looking for your common errors in a draft is very confusing. Get help. Help comes in many forms. Maybe you need to review the error type in the Handbook or with your instructor. You can go to the learning center or writing lab on your campus. You may sometimes need practice in correcting specific problems by working some exercises from the Handbook, too. Use whatever means seem to help you best.

Updating Your Editing Log   Whenever you edit, have peer review, or get comments back from your instructor, enter the errors in your editing log. There are two reasons for this. First, it will help you become more proficient at correcting common errors, since part of each entry for the log includes a correction of the error. Think of this practice as individualized exercises. Second, your writing will change over the course of the term and you will need to learn to correct for any changes in the types of errors you make.

Why Do Error Types Change?   Errors may change because your writing changes. Very often students who have problems with fragments begin to use commas where they had once used periods. This may correct many fragment errors, but it can also create run-on sentences. These run-ons need to be added to the editing log.

In addition, different types of assignments can cause writers to write very differently. A paper that involves responding to a reading may have quotations and summaries that may lead to documentation errors and unneeded tense shifts. A paper that argues for a position may have unclear or inappropriate pronoun use or added-on detail fragments.

Remember: Your goal is to become efficient at finding, identifying, and correcting problems in whatever you write. Keep an editing log and keep it up to date. Become an independent writer.

How to Use an Editing Log

Make a list of your common errors, and read your drafts specifically for these errors.

Review the process of correcting these common errors.

If you are not sure:

■ Use the Handbook.

■ Ask your instructor.

■ Practice with some exercises.

Add new errors when you find them.

EXERCISE 22.4 Make mock entries in an editing log for the errors in Exercises 11 and 12 in Chapter 24, pages 430–432.

EXERCISE 22.5 Make real entries for the errors you find in an essay you have written.

PART FIVE

Working on Sentences

23 A Handbook for Writing Correct Sentences

HOW TO USE THE HANDBOOK

This handbook explains the most common problems you are likely to find when **editing**. If you discover that you make the same errors frequently in your writing, or if a teacher, tutor, or writing partner suggests that you need to review a certain kind of problem, then you should follow the steps listed here.

How to Use this Handbook

1. Read the explanation of the problem in the handbook.
2. Try the exercise.
3. Check the answers on pages 605–629.
4. Ask your instructor for help with any problems you don't understand.
5. Check your writing for the problem and make corrections.

After reading the explanation of each problem area, you should try the corresponding exercise and check the answers in the back of the book. If you didn't miss any, go on to check your paper for the same problem. If you did miss something in the exercise, reread the explanation. If you continue to have difficulty understanding the problem, talk with your teacher or tutor.

Here is an overview of this handbook. Note the eight abbreviations in the parentheses; they are found on tabs in this chapter to help you locate the specific explanation you need at any given time.

Problems Discussed in the Handbook

1. **Sentence basics (BAS)**
   - 1.1 Recognizing verbs (p. 350)
   - 1.2 Recognizing subjects (p. 351)
   - 1.3 More complicated subjects and verbs (p. 351)
   - 1.4 Recognizing prepositional phrases (p. 353)

continued on next page

continued from previous page

1. SENTENCE BASICS

ESL   Before you can understand how to deal with the problems in your writing, you will need to know how the basic building blocks of sentences—verbs, subjects, and prepositional phrases—are used in sentences.

BAS

1.1   RECOGNIZING VERBS

The Building Blocks of a Sentence

Verbs

Subjects

Prepositional phrases

You must first learn to recognize a **verb**—a word that shows action or state of being.

<small>ACTION</small> The firefighter **will extinguish** the fire.

<small>ACTION</small> We **considered** our choices.

<small>STATE OF BEING</small> Sri Lanka **is** the name of the island country just south of India.

If this definition seems confusing, you might find it helpful to use an additional definition: A verb is a word in a sentence that changes when the time of the sentence is changed.

<small>PRESENT</small> The firefighter **will extinguish** the fire tomorrow.

<small>PAST</small> The firefighter **extinguished** the fire yesterday.

<small>PAST</small> We **considered** our choices last week.

<small>PRESENT</small> We **are considering** our choices today.

<small>PRESENT</small> Sri Lanka **is** now the name of the island country just south of India.

<small>PAST</small> Ceylon **was** once the name of the island country just south of India.

As you can see in these examples, sometimes a verb is just one word, and sometimes it is several words, called a **verb phrase**. The word that carries the meaning of the verb is called the **main verb** and the other parts of the verb are known as the **auxiliary** or **helping verbs** or **helpers**.

Auxiliary	**Main**
will	*extinguish*
are	*considering*

BAS EXERCISE 1   Underline each verb twice. Be sure to underline all the parts of the verbs, including main verbs and all auxiliaries (or helping verbs).

The story of the Heike is a very sad story from Japanese history. The emperor (whose family was called the Heike) was fighting his enemies, who chased him until finally he boarded a ship with his family and followers. A nurse carried the baby, the son of the emperor. When the enemies captured the ship, she took the baby emperor to the prow of the ship and jumped into the water where she and the baby drowned, but escaped their enemy in death. All the family and soldiers of the Heike were killed and their bodies were lost at sea. Now the crabs who are caught in that part of the ocean have strange markings on their shells. Local people call them the faces of the Heike.

1.2 RECOGNIZING SUBJECTS

After locating the verb in a sentence, you must now find the **subject**—the word that tells you who or what performed the action of the verb. Just read the sentence again and find the verb:

> The firefighter **will extinguish** the fire.

Now put a mental blank before the verb, and fill it in:

> _____ will extinguish

> **firefighter** will extinguish

Now you know that *firefighter* is the subject.

> We **considered** our choices.

> _____ considered

> **We** considered

This process works the same way with verbs that don't name an action:

> Sri Lanka **is** the name of the island country just south of India.

> _____ is

> **Sri Lanka** is

BAS EXERCISE 2   In the following paragraph, underline the verb in each sentence twice. Underline the subject once.

> A very old story from the Middle East is called *Gilgamesh*. Gilgamesh was the ruler of his country, and he was very strong and handsome. Another man in that country was called Enkidu. Enkidu lived in the forest and had only animals for friends. Gilgamesh sent a woman to Enkidu, and when the animals saw him with another human, they became afraid of him. Enkidu left the forest. He and Gilgamesh fought each other, but finally became good friends. The importance of friendship is a theme of the story.

1.3 MORE COMPLICATED VERBS AND SUBJECTS

Not every sentence you write will be as simple as those above. Here are some hints about how to deal with the more complex sentences you will be writing. If you remember the basic rules, you'll see that problems can be easily avoided.

What Do We Know About Verbs and Subjects?

Verbs are words that must be changed when the time of the sentence changes.

Subjects are words that tell who or what performed the action of the verb.

Now let's look at some ways the words in your sentences may change.

1.3.1 Infinitives

An infinitive (*TO* + *word*) or an -*ing* word with no helper (gerund or participle) cannot be the verb of the sentence. An infinitive (**TO + word**) is a phrase such as:

to sing   to explain   to capture   to inspect

A gerund or participle (**-ing, no helper verb**) is a word ending in -*ing* that does not have auxiliaries or helping verbs such as *is, were, will be, have been:*

peeling the potatoes   taking the test   remembering the past   a flying bird

You might see sentences like these:

I wanted **to paint** the room yellow last week.

Right now, the supervisor calls Gina **to repair** the gears.

Waiting makes me nervous these days.

Speeding down the street last night, the truck passed every car.

What is the verb in each sentence? To determine that, you can always apply the first verb rule: **Verbs are words that change forms when the time of the sentence changes.** If you change the time of each sentence, you can see which words change forms—those are verbs. The words that do not change are not being used as verbs:

I **want** <u>to paint</u> the room yellow this week.

Tomorrow, the supervisor **will call** Gina <u>to repair</u> the gears.

<u>Waiting</u> **made** me nervous when I was younger.

<u>Speeding</u> down the street, the truck **passes** every car right now.

The words shown above in bold are verbs, because they required different forms when the time of the sentence changed. The underlined words may seem like verbs, but they did not change in form when the time of the sentence changed. To save time, you can remember that a word with *to* before it is not the verb in the sentence, and that a word that ends in -*ing* cannot be the verb *unless* it has auxiliaries or helping verbs.

BAS EXERCISE 3 In the paragraph below, underline the verb twice (be sure to include all helping verbs). Draw a circle around the infinitives (*TO* + *words*) and the gerunds or participles (*-ing, no helper verbs*).

From an ancient African county in Mali comes the story of Son–Jara who was born a prince. His mother was one of the king's wives, but another of the king's wives hated her. Being jealous was a common problem among the king's wives in those days. This woman cursed Son–Jara so that he was unable to walk when he was a child. To be a king's mother was his mother's ambition, so she wanted him to be stronger than other men, but instead he was weaker. His mother's hopes for her son seemed impossible, but she went to ask help from a Djinn, a supernatural creature. Following the Djinn's instructions was difficult, but she obeyed. She sent her son on a Haj, which is a pilgrimage to Mecca. Finally the curse was destroyed, and Son–Jara became a great king.

1.3.2 Parts of Verbs

The parts of a verb phrase can be separated and some parts can come before the subject. Don't expect that the auxiliaries or helping verbs will always come right before the verb. Other words can be placed between the helper and the main verb, and some helpers may even come before the subject:

Nathaniel **was** already **going** on to the last part of the test.

After Saturday, Marta **will** not **live** with her sister.

Are we really **expecting** to find a good car here?

Don't you **want** to enroll in the payroll deduction plan?

BAS EXERCISE 4 In the following paragraph, underline the verb in each sentence twice. Underline the subject once.

Do all people have the same idea about how the world was created? People in different parts of the world can sometimes have very different ideas. Many cultures have asked these questions: Where do we come from? How were we made? The question is often answered by a story. The Mayan people of ancient Guatemala long ago told the story of creation, which, according to the stories they told, had been accomplished by a group of gods. These gods were called Bearer, Begetter, Maker, and Modeler (also called Plumed Serpent). They used many grains, fruits, and vegetables to create the first people.

1.4 RECOGNIZING PREPOSITIONAL PHRASES

A **prepositional phrase** is a **noun** (or **pronoun**) and the preposition that connects it to the sentence. It is a part of a sentence but can never be the subject

BND

or the verb. If you're not sure whether or not a word is a preposition, try inserting it in the blank in the following sentence:

The airplane flew _____ the cloud.

Most prepositions will make sense in that blank: *by, beside, under, through, around, with, beneath, after, before. Note:* One very common preposition that does **not** fit in that sentence is the preposition *of.*

Prepositional phrases can occur in many places in a sentence:

Elevated trains and subways both provide transportation **in Chicago.**

Mathematics is an easier subject **for me** than history.

In summer, days are long and nights are short.

In a prepositional phrase, the preposition does not always come right before the noun. Words can be added to describe the noun, and sometimes they can be combined with a gerund or participle (*-ing, no helper verb*) to describe the noun or even to become the noun itself.

Beside the beautiful young princess sat a frog.

We waited **for the slowly passing cars.**

One **of the most wonderful sights on earth** is Mt. Fuji **in Japan.**

BAS EXERCISE 5   In the following paragraph, put parentheses around each prepositional phrase.

Many of the stories we find in one country are also found in the tales from other countries. For example, the story of a great flood that destroys the earth is found in many stories from all over the world. In ancient China, in Babylon, in Israel, in South America, and probably in many other lands as well, we can read or hear of one man who survives the flood with his family and starts the world again. The story of the flood appears in the Bible and in the Koran. One man suggested a theory about these universal stories. In his book *Man and His Symbols,* Carl Jung called these stories *archetypes,* and reminded us that people in all parts of the world tell similar stories, and also dream similar dreams.

2. SENTENCE BOUNDARIES

Do you have problems choosing between commas and periods? Do your papers often have notes about fragments, run-ons, and comma splices? If so, you need to work on understanding **sentence boundaries**—that is, on knowing what makes a complete sentence and how sentences can be combined. *Note:* Using the grammatical descriptions in this section may not be the simplest way to recognize and correct sentence boundary problems; you may want to review the sections of Chapter 22 (pp. 334–335) that suggest ways of editing for complete sentences and try those ideas first. If you still have problems with sentence boundaries, you may find the grammatical descriptions that follow here helpful.

2.1 FRAGMENTS

A **sentence fragment** is a group of words that does not form a sentence. To avoid writing fragments, you will need to recognize sentences.

> ### What Is a Sentence?
>
> A sentence always has a subject and a verb.
>
> A sentence never has a subordinating word, unless the sentence is joined to another sentence.

2.1.1 Check for Subject and Verb

Review the explanations for locating subjects and verbs in Section 1 (pp. 349–354) if you don't remember them clearly:

■ Verbs are words that must be changed when the time of the sentence changes.

■ Subjects are words that tell who or what did the action of the verb.

Any group of words that does not have a subject and a verb is a fragment. Below are examples of fragments caused by the lack of verb and subject.

NO VERB I was really tired. **Studying all day and working all night.**

Studying all day and working all night has no verb. Try changing the time and you will see that no words must be changed.

NO SUBJECT

Studying all day today and **working** all night tonight.

Studying all day yesterday and **working** all night last night.

Note: A verb that ends in *-ing* must have a helping verb. The helper shows the time change.

When we ask "Who?" before the *studying* or *working,* we cannot find the answer in that sentence. We can thus conclude that *Studying all day and working all night* has no subject.

To revise this fragment, add it to the sentence before it.

REVISION I was really tired, studying all day and working all night.

It can also be revised by adding a subject and verb.

REVISION I was really tired. **I was** working all day and studying all night.

BND EXERCISE 1   **Underline each fragment. On a separate sheet of paper, make whatever revisions are needed to create complete sentences. You may either add a fragment to another sentence, or add subjects and verbs to create new sentences.**

A writer of many plays and poems. William Shakespeare is considered to be the greatest writer in the English language. We usually think of Shakespeare as the writer of tragic plays. Plays about murder and unfortunate deaths. However, Shakespeare also wrote plays referred to as the histories and the romances. Also, twelve plays which are called the comedies. His plays were very popular in his own time. Performed at the Old Globe theater. Today, his plays are perhaps most often seen in movie theaters. Some film directors will update the play and set it in modern times. Rewriting the play's original language so it is more accessible for today's audiences. These directors may also film the play outdoors. Instead of indoors on the stage.

2.1.2 Check for Subordinating (Fragment) Words

Words that are used to connect two sentences are sometimes called **subordinating words** or **fragment words**. (You might have also learned to call these subordinating conjunctions and relative pronouns.) Here are some examples of subordinating words:

although	since	when
after	that	who
because	through	which
if	so that	while
before	how	what
as	until	unless

Because subordinating words connect two sentences, **a group of words that has a subject and verb *and also* has a subordinating word is often a fragment.**

Although I had followed the directions. My hair turned a horrible shade of orange.

Although is a fragment word. It shows the relationship between the two groups of words. Revise this fragment by removing the period and adding a comma between the two parts of the new sentence:

REVISION Although I had followed the directions, my hair turned a horrible shade of orange.

Note: When revising, use a comma if the fragment word is at the beginning of the sentence. Do not use a comma if the fragment word is inside the sentence.

My hair turned a horrible shade of orange <u>although</u> I had followed the directions.

BND EXERCISE 2 Underline each fragment. Then on a separate sheet of paper, if needed, revise to create complete sentences. You may add the fragment to another sentence or you may delete the fragment word.

William Shakespeare, who wrote the play *Hamlet.* Was born in England in 1564. The town of his birth was Stratford-on-Avon, and after his death, he was buried there. Little is known about his father, who some biographers say was a merchant. However, Shakespeare's father may also have been a mayor. Although it is not known for certain. It is believed that Shakespeare attended grammar school where he learned to read and write. At the age of eighteen he became a husband. When he married Anne Hathaway. We think of Shakespeare as a playwright, but he was also known for his acting. While most people have heard of *Hamlet* and *Romeo and Juliet.* Many of us don't realize that he wrote more than thirty other plays. In addition, he was an accomplished poet. Who wrote some of the greatest sonnets in the English language. Because he wrote plays that are still popular today and wrote poems that are still models for aspiring poets. He is considered one of the greatest writers who ever lived.

2.1.3 Check for Fragment Words or Question Words

If sentences that begin with *who, which,* or *that* do not ask a question, they are probably fragments.

<u>SENTENCE</u> **Who** was the woman in the red Miata?

<u>FRAGMENT</u> She was the one. **Who** was in the club.

Sentences that begin with expressions like "The one *who* . . ." or "The car *that*" may also be fragments. Check to be sure that the fragment word joins the sentence parts.

<u>FRAGMENT</u> The cat **who wore the hat.** [*The cat* is not a sentence.]

<u>SENTENCE</u> The woman **who called the police** was furious.
[*The woman was furious* is a sentence.]

Delete the fragment word:

<u>REVISION</u> The cat ~~who~~ wore the hat.

Or add the fragment to another sentence as shown on the following page:

He wanted to read about the cat **who wore the hat.**

She was the one **who was in the club.**

BND EXERCISE 3   Underline each fragment. Revise as needed, on a separate sheet of paper, to make complete sentences. You may either delete the fragment word or add the fragment to another sentence.

One of Shakespeare's outstanding works is *Hamlet*. Which is about a young prince trying to avenge his father's death. The play begins with the ghost of Hamlet's father appearing to Horatio and the sentries on duty. They tell Hamlet about their experience. That night, Hamlet also sees the ghost of his father. Who was the former king of Denmark. The experience that young Hamlet has. Deeply disturbs him. Hamlet discovers that his father was murdered by Hamlet's uncle, Claudius. Who is now the King of Denmark and who has married Hamlet's widowed mother. Hamlet is commanded by his father's ghost to kill Claudius. Although Hamlet seems to know that he must take revenge, he delays. Which leads to the deaths of other characters in the play. It can even be argued that Hamlet's inability to carry out the act of revenge leads to the death of Ophelia. Who was Hamlet's true love. That the play ends on a tragic note. Is a vast understatement. In the final scene there are four dead bodies sprawled across the stage.

BND EXERCISE 4   Underline each fragment. Be sure that you have underlined fragments, not questions. Revise as needed, on a separate sheet of paper, to make complete sentences. You may either delete the fragment word or add the fragment to another sentence.

Because this play has so many problems. Readers have always argued about Hamlet's character. They can't decide whether he is a brave and cautious man. Or just can't make up his mind. A really indecisive character! Why should we care about a fictional character? Some readers see themselves reflected in characters like Hamlet. Who may seem to have unusual problems, but is very human all the same.

2.2 RUN-ON SENTENCES, COMMA SPLICES, AND FUSED SENTENCES

2.2.1 Recognizing Run-on Sentences

A **run-on sentence** is just the opposite of a fragment: it is two or more complete sentences joined together without the correct punctuation. You may hear different terms used for this kind of error. If a comma is used instead of a period, some teachers call it a **comma splice**; if no punctuation is found between the two sentences, it may be called a **fused sentence**. Because the grammatical error is so similar in all three cases, many teachers call all three errors run-ons.

To understand run-ons, you must remember:

■ Verbs are words that must be changed when the time of the sentence changes

■ Subjects are words that tell who or what did the action of the verb

One kind of run-on is very easy to understand, because it simply consists of two sentences that are not separated by a period:

RUN-ON Ryan stepped on the accelerator the car sped away.

In the first group of words, *stepped* is the verb and *Ryan* is the subject. In the second part of the sentence, *sped* is the verb and *car* is the subject. These are two separate sentences and cannot be written as one.

A comma is not the correct punctuation between two sentences:

RUN-ON Ryan stepped on the accelerator, the car sped away.

This is still a run-on, because commas are used within sentences, not between them.

BND EXERCISE 5   Locate each run-on. Draw a vertical line between the two sentences.

One of the most interesting characters in the play *Hamlet* is Ophelia, who is Hamlet's love interest. She is often portrayed as a weak-willed person she is dominated by her father Polonius. In the beginning of the play, Ophelia tells her father that Prince Hamlet has been expressing his love to her. Polonius tells her that she should ignore Hamlet's vows of love, Ophelia obeys him she doesn't even protest. Even though she loves Hamlet and wants to see him, she follows her father's orders. Later in the play when Polonius and the king want to spy on Hamlet, she allows herself to be used she talks to Hamlet while Polonius and the king hide behind the curtains and listen. After this scene, Hamlet never sees her alive again, she is later found dead in a stream. It is said that Hamlet couldn't decide what to do Ophelia couldn't stand up for what she wanted.

2.2.2 Revising Run-ons

Period   The simplest way to correct a run-on is to use a period between two sentences:

SENTENCES Ryan stepped on the accelerator. The car sped away.

Joining Word   There is a small group of joining words that can be used between two sentences:

and	so	or	for
but	yet	nor	

Always put a comma *before* these joining words when you use them between sentences:

SENTENCE Ryan stepped on the accelerator, **so** the car sped away.

SENTENCE Ryan stepped on the accelerator, **and** the car sped away.

Subordinating Word Subordinating words or fragment words can be used to make one sentence a part of another. (See the list of fragment words in Section 2.1.2 p. 356.) If the subordinating word is at the beginning of a sentence, use a comma between the two parts of the new sentence. If the subordinating word is in the middle of the sentence, do not use a comma.

> SENTENCE **When** Ryan stepped on the accelerator, the car sped away.

> SENTENCE Ryan stepped on the accelerator **before** the car sped away.

Semicolon A semicolon (;) can be used instead of a period between two sentences:

> SENTENCE Ryan stepped on the accelerator; the car sped away.

Transitional Words with Periods or Semicolons A word that is often found between sentences (but can also be found within sentences) is called a transitional word.

however	thus	for example
then	therefore	moreover
next		

These words do *not* join sentences; they simply give us some information. When transitional words come between sentences, a semicolon or a period must also be used before the transitional word and a comma must follow the transitional word.

> SENTENCE Ryan stepped on the accelerator; **therefore,** the car sped away.

> SENTENCE Ryan stepped on the accelerator; **then,** the car sped away.

BND EXERCISE 6 **Locate the run-on sentences. Use one of the five types of revision above to make them complete sentences.**

An often overlooked character in the play *Hamlet* is Fortinbras, however, he is very important. Hamlet and Fortinbras are in the same situation, they have both lost their fathers. At the beginning of the play, we learn that Fortinbras has raised an army and is demanding that Denmark return the lands his father lost. This is Fortinbras' way of avenging his father's death Fortinbras is a man of action. Hamlet, like Fortinbras, formulates plans to take revenge for his father's murder he delays he doesn't act. In the middle of the play, Fortinbras' army is allowed to cross Denmark on its way to do battle with the Poles. Again we see that Fortinbras craves action Hamlet, at this point in the play, is being shipped off to England he still hasn't taken action against Claudius, his father's murderer. Fortinbras only appears in the play once. In the very last scene, Fortinbras arrives at the castle he finds Hamlet dead. The man of action has survived, the man of thought has perished.

2.3 DISTINGUISHING FRAGMENTS AND RUN-ONS

As you learn to correct fragments, you may find that at first you create run-ons. And as you learn to correct run-ons, the opposite may happen—you find more fragments in your writing. Don't be discouraged by this. It's normal, because you're trying to establish a clear model of a sentence in your mind. You'll also find that the sentences you write yourself are sometimes more complicated than the examples in books and exercises, and that the errors are more difficult to find in your own writing. For more practice, work on the exercises in this section, which contain both run-ons and fragments.

The Difference Between a Fragment and a Run-on

A fragment

1. Lacks a subject and/or verb

OR

2. Has a subordinating word **that does not join** it to another sentence

A run-on is two or more complete sentences

1. Joined only by a comma

OR

2. Without any punctuation

BND EXERCISE 7   In the paragraphs below, locate all fragments and run-ons. Revise so that all sentences are complete.

> Hamlet believes that his mother, Gertrude, has betrayed his father's memory. After the death of King Hamlet, Gertrude marries Claudius. Who is King Hamlet's brother this infuriates Hamlet. Hamlet sees his father as a god, he sees Claudius as a satyr, a creature half goat. Hamlet cannot understand how his mother could so quickly forget his godlike father, therefore he concludes that women are faithless. In addition to feeling betrayed by his mother, Hamlet also feels that Ophelia has betrayed him. At her father's command, Ophelia rejects Hamlet and she returns the letters and gifts he has given her. This sends Hamlet into a rage, it confirms his belief that women are weak and unfaithful.

BND EXERCISE 8   In the following paragraph, locate all fragments and run-ons. Revise so that all sentences are complete.

> Although *Hamlet* is one of Shakespeare's tragedies, it has moments of humor. One of the most humorous scenes takes place in a graveyard, Hamlet has a dialogue with a gravedigger who won't give Hamlet a straight answer. When Hamlet and his friend Horatio enter, they find the gravedigger in the act of digging a grave. Hamlet

asks to whom the grave belongs, the gravedigger responds that it is his own grave. Hamlet wants to know who will be buried in the grave, however, the gravedigger's logic is that the one who makes the grave owns the grave. This gravedigger is fond of wordplay he is also fond of riddles. Prior to the arrival of Hamlet and Horatio, the gravedigger has asked his fellow worker who builds stronger than a mason, a shipwright, or a carpenter. His co-worker's answer is good he says a gallows–maker. After all, the man who makes the gallows lives longer than those who find them–selves on the gallows. The gravedigger, however, has a better answer. Which he gives to his co-worker. The gravedigger says that a grave maker builds stronger than a ma–son, a shipwright, or a carpenter, his logic is twisted but sound. The grave you are buried in lasts longer than the house a mason might build, therefore, the grave maker builds the strongest.

BND EXERCISE 9   In the paragraph below, locate all fragments and run-ons. Revise so that all sen-tences are complete.

Hamlet's negative view of life is in part the result of the betrayals he has experi-enced. Which leave him with few people to trust. His mother betrayed both King Hamlet and Hamlet by quickly marrying Claudius Ophelia betrayed Hamlet by re-jecting his affections. In addition to these betrayals, Hamlet is also betrayed by Rosencrantz and Guildenstern. Who are friends of Hamlet's. Although Hamlet doesn't know it, his two friends are really spying on him for Claudius. Hamlet finds out they are spying on him, therefore, he decides to toy with them. He asks Guildenstern to play a recorder. Which is a wooden flute. Guildenstern says that he doesn't know how to play the instrument, then Hamlet tells his two friends what he thinks of them. Hamlet says that they think they can play him more easily than one can play a flute. This is not however the end of their betrayal. The King has Hamlet sent to England so he can have Hamlet executed. Rosencrantz and Guildenstern accompany Hamlet they are carrying a letter which requests that Hamlet be killed immediately upon his arrival in England. Hamlet changes the letter now it says that Rosencrantz and Guildenstern should be killed immediately. Rosencrantz and Guildenstern pay dearly for the betrayal of their friend.

3. WORD ENDINGS

Many English words change their meanings slightly when the endings of the words are changed. You know that a person is referring to more than one bird if an *s* is added to make the word *bird* into the word *birds*. You know that the action happened in the past if the verb ends in *-ed*. When you are writing, you may concentrate on the ideas you are expressing and forget to add these im-portant endings or you may accidentally use the wrong one. If this is a prob-lem in your writing, you must learn to form the habit of checking carefully for all word endings as a part of your editing. If you find that you don't under-stand which endings you need to use, study some of the explanations in this section.

3.1 NOUN ENDINGS: PLURALS AND APOSTROPHES

You must often make decisions about the letter *s* at the end of a noun. There are two key rules that tell you how to use the letter *s*:

> ### *Choosing Noun Endings*
>
> ■ To show that a noun is plural, add the letter s.
>
> ■ To show that a word is possessive, add an apostrophe and the letter s (usually).

3.1.1 Forming Plurals

If you want to show that you are talking about more than one of a thing, you usually add an *s* to the word:

three boy**s**	some automobile**s**
those idea**s**	many national**s**

The plurals of some words are formed differently. Here are two ways words might become plural:

■ Form the plural of words that end in *y* or *s* or *sh* or *ch* by changing the spelling:

　　abili**ties**　　los**ses**　　ra**shes**　　chur**ches**

■ Form the plural of some words by changing the spelling **inside** the word, not at the end:

　　wom**e**n　　m**i**ce　　g**e**e**s**e

END EXERCISE 1 Underline each noun that should be plural. Add an *s* to each of those words or change the spelling if necessary.

Many single mother who work have too many responsibility—they can't find enough hour in one day to do all the job that must be done. Their children need lunch for school, the dish need washing, the car needs gas—all at the same time. No magic will give those mother the five extra minute in each hour, but some trick will help them. Mother with too many chore can try this: set a timer for fifteen minute after each meal, and each member of the family must spend those minute putting away object that are out of place. Keep a table or a shelf by the door, and put on it all the book, coat, lunch, key, and other thing that need to be taken when the family leaves.

3.1.2 Forming Possessives

When Should –'s Be Used?　Generally, use an apostrophe (') and an *s* with a noun or a proper name (even if it ends in -*s*) to show possession (ownership):

END

That is Charlie**'s** house.

The dog**'s** bowl is empty.

END

END EXERCISE 2   Circle each word that shows possession. Draw an arrow to the word it possesses. Add an apostrophe (') or 's to the possessive words.

Another problem for single mothers families is keeping the children rooms neat. When a childs toys are scattered everywhere, children fight about them more often. Is the truck in the living room Renita or Roberts truck? Is that Lara paintbrush or her brothers? If the children know each toy place, they will be more likely to put their toys away.

Where Should the Apostrophe Be Placed?   With plurals, the final letter is the key. *Note:* A plural noun ending in *-s* requires only an apostrophe.

the shoes that belong to the boy**s** = the boy**s'** shoes

the choice made by the ladie**s** = the ladie**s'** choice

If a word does not end in *-s*, add an apostrophe and an *-s*. It does not matter whether the word is singular or plural.

the pen that belongs to a studen**t** = the studen**t's** pen

the skates of the childre**n** = the childre**n's** skates

END EXERCISE 3   Underline the possessive words. If the possessive word already has an *-s*, add an apostrophe after the *-s*. If the possessive word does not already have an *-s*, add an apostrophe and then an *-s*.

Keeping children clothes clean is yet another problem for single mother families. If the laundry is just the mother job, then she will be washing her family clothes all day. Each child must learn to be responsible for clothes. If Tara shirt is dirty, or if her brothers sheets need washing, the children themselves must be sure to put them in the hamper. Each child room should have a hamper, and it should also be the children job to put towels in the bathroom hamper.

There are certain times when an apostrophe should **not** be used:

▪ **Do not** use an apostrophe with a plural noun that is *not* possessive.

PLURAL The **roses** are beautiful.

PLURAL The **shirts** were at the laundry.

▪ **Do not** use an apostrophe with a *pronoun* to show possession.

The book lost **its** cover.

That house is **theirs.**

Here are some pronouns that end in -*s* and show possession; you should not use an apostrophe with them:

> yours   ours   hers   his   theirs   its

END EXERCISE 4   Underline all the words that show possession, and draw a circle around the pronouns. Cross out any unneeded apostrophes. Add apostrophes where needed.

What are the most important foods to eat? Whether it's dieters waistline's or athletes muscles, many people are trying to change their bodies', but they need to know their bodies needs. Everybody should eat some foods with protein, some with carbohydrate's, some with fats. Your muscles strength comes from protein—it's found in meats, soybeans, and dairy products. Carbohydrate's give us quick energy for the days work. Carbohydrates are found in bread, candy, alcohol, potatoes, rice, and cereal. Fats store energy to meet your bodys needs at any time. Be sure to give your body enough to meet it's needs. Without any fats, we'd be like bunnies' without batteries, but we only need a few batteries at a time.

END EXERCISE 5   Add apostrophes where needed and cross out any that are not needed.

A students future may not totally depend on her grade's, but grades will help when she looks for job's, so a course in study skills might make a difference in a student's life. Student's sometimes don't want to take these course's, because the credits aren't required for degree's, but they don't realize that what's most important is having a good GPA. When credit's are analyzed at graduation time, a course's grade might be just as important as its credit's.

3.2   VERB ENDINGS

ESL   *3.2.1 Final -s verb endings*

Before you read this section, think about two questions:

- Can you always pick out the complete verb in a sentence? If not, see Section 1.1 (p. 350) before you continue here.
- Can you always recognize the subject of a verb? If not, see Section 1.2 (p. 351) before you continue here.

The verbs in a sentence provide all kinds of information, as do the endings on every verb. Besides telling us the meaning of the word itself, the ending tells us when the sentence takes place and it may indicate whether the subject is singular or plural. Because many people do not pronounce these verb endings when they speak, they also forget to add the endings when they write. When you write, be sure that all verbs have the necessary endings.

Note: Adding an ending may change the spelling of the word. For example, *carry* becomes *carries*.

END

Simple (One-Word) Verbs   A **simple (one-word) verb** in a sentence that describes the present *may* end in *-s*. To determine whether a simple verb should have an *-s*, we must find the subject. If the subject is *I, you, we,* or *they,* a present-tense verb does not need an *-s*. Also, if the subject is a word that could be replaced by *they,* the verb does not need an *-s*.

I walk	you cook	they sing
we settle	dogs bark	airplanes fly

A simple verb needs an *-s* only if it happens in the present and the subject is singular.

Now he *plays* guard.

Today the house *looks* clean.

Every day she *waits* for the bus.

END EXERCISE 6   Underline the verbs in the following sentences. Write P above the ones that happen in the present and add an *–s* to those verbs.

When Lisa plant a garden, she always use lots of fertilizer, just as her mother did when she was a little girl. Her mother told her how to plant, and now Lisa follow that advice. Lisa sometimes buy fertilizer at a discount store but she also get compost from the city. Last fall the city took all the leaves people had raked, and ground them up. Now the compost is ready to use. Each weekend, Lisa spread the compost on her garden and dig it in. Then she rake it smooth.

A simple verb needs an *-s* if the subject is third person *singular*. The third person singular subjects are *he, she,* or *it* **or** a word that can be replaced by one of these words.

(HE)	(SHE)	(IT)
he *walks*	She *cooks*	it *flies*
Alvin *seeks*	Suzette *laughs*	the computer *works*

Do not add an *-s* if the subject is *they* or a word that could be replaced by *they*.

(THEY)	(THEY)
They *walk*	We *cook*
Raymond and John *seek*	Those women *laugh*

END EXERCISE 7   Underline the verbs in the following sentences. Draw an arrow to the subject. Then add an *–s* to the verb if the subject is *he, she, it,* or a word that could be replaced by one of those words.

Sean always take care of his car. He clean it every weekend, he change the oil every three thousand miles, and he take it for a tune-up every thirty thousand miles. The tires take some of his attention, too, because they need to be rotated often so that they wear evenly. Sean's brother Charles take care of the tires for him, but he charge Sean a small amount. Rotating the tires take time and tools, Charles say. Time and tools cost him money, so he want Sean to pay.

Verbs Ending in –s

Remember: Add –s to a verb only if the tense is present and the subject is third person singular.

Check:

1. When is the verb happening?
   - ■ now (use –s)
   - ■ in the past (no –s)
2. What word would replace the subject?
   - ■ he, she, it (use –s)
   - ■ they, you, we (no –s)

END EXERCISE 8 Underline each verb in the following sentences. Add an –s if the verb is in the present tense and the subject is singular.

Computers do exactly what we tell them to do. If we tell a computer to type a letter, the computer type a letter. If we tell a computer to sing a song, it will sing a song. Sometimes when I write, I look back and see that what I have written look really strange. It look strange because I told the computer to write in capital letters or italics. Of course the computer did exactly what I told it to do. Sometimes my hands write words that my brain know, and other times my hands seem to write on their own. It take time to go back and correct these mistakes, but it save more time since I just type the corrections, not the whole paper.

Helping Verbs   Often a verb is actually several words—the main verb and its helpers. **Helping verbs** (also called **auxiliary verbs**) are short, common verbs that give more information about the main verb but do not change its meaning. Here are some examples of helping verbs:

are	can	is
might	does	should
must	have	will

In *most* cases, use the rules above to decide if a verb needs an -s. Then find the *first* helping verb and use the -s form (most helping verbs have many forms).

she *was* skipping   we *were* finished

Marcia and Tom *are* driving   the cat *is* mewing

END

END EXERCISE 9   Underline each verb phrase once, and then underline twice any helping verbs that are part of the verb phrase. Draw a line to the subject. Use the checklist from page 367 to decide if the helping verb should be put in the present tense.

> Trying to lose weight have been really confusing. (It also take a lot of will power, of course.) Some experts were saying that bread make you fat and others have said that butter and cheese make you fat. My friend were reading a book that say exercise work best. My friends Marla and Rene were trying to run a mile every day, and Mike went with them. Mike have been losing weight by not eating any dessert, because he had heard that sugar make you fat.

Modal Verbs   A **modal verb** is a special kind of helping verb that *slightly* changes the meaning of the main verb. Modal verbs tell more than just the time when a verb happens. They suggest ideas like possibility and necessity. Future verbs, especially, use modals:

may	might	can	will
would	could	could	should
must	ought (to)		

Even when these verbs seem to have a present meaning and a third person singular subject, they do not end in -*s*.

> he **can** stay   Lorraine **must** sell

END EXERCISE 10   Correct the use of –*s* in the following paragraph. Use the checks in the box on Verbs Ending in –*s* (p. 367) as well as the information in this section on helping verbs, p. 367. Add –*s* when it is needed and cross it out when it is not.

> We sometimes wonder what would have happened if things in history had been different. For example, things might have been safer for everyone if the nuclear bomb had never been invented. Maybe scientists should think more carefully about what will happen to their inventions. An inventor who make a new way to run cars may think she will help the world but she may really finds that the new invention can kill many people.

Infinitives (*to* + *verbs*)   Most of the verbs we encounter are real verbs, which means that they show time. The **infinitive** is a special kind of verb that does not show time. (You might find the word *infinitive* hard to remember. If so, call it a **To + verb**.) It is written with a *to* before the verb and never has an -*s* added to it.

> I want *to eat* now   they have *to leave* now

END EXERCISE 11   Correct the use of –*s* in the following sentences.

> We'd like to think that the invention of medicine was one way to improves the world. It is certainly better that no child has to catch polio and that no one even

has to get a smallpox vaccination anymore. But now that fewer people die from infectious diseases, there is not enough room for all of us to lives well. We are going to become even more crowded every year. So even the miraculous inventions of a vaccine to cure a terrible disease can turn out to be a problem no one knows how to solves.

Sometimes the *to* in an infinitive is understood (like the subject *you* in a command), but the rules are still the same:

I heard you **sing.**   She lets the dog **eat.**

The infinitive can never be the only verb in a sentence.

END EXERCISE 12   Underline the verbs twice and the subjects once. Circle the infinitives. Add *–s* where needed and correct the helping verbs as necessary.

Sometimes a person want to go on a trip but don't know how to get to her destination. Now there is a site on the Internet that tell you how to get from one place to another. The traveler have to type in the city she is leaving from and the place where she want to go. Then the computer tell her what route to take and also warn her to avoid any delays.

3.2.2 Past Tense Verbs

Regular Verbs   The following discussion covers simple verbs and verbs without helpers. (Can you always recognize the complete verb phrase? If not, review Section 1.1, Recognizing Verbs, before working on this section.)

When a sentence describes the past, the verb should reflect that time. Most simple verbs show past time by ending in *-ed* although the ending may change the spelling.

The men gossip**ed**   Maynard exercis**ed**   she suggest**ed**

A train pass**ed**   the babies cri**ed**   MacIntosh produc**ed**

END EXERCISE 13   Underline the verbs that happen in the past. Add *-ed* to those verbs:

Yesterday Alicia want some ice cream, so she borrow her sister's car. Then she remember that she also need some money, so she ask her sister for money. Her sister laugh. She want some ice cream, too, so she call to Alicia: "When you get to the store, please buy two cones! I want chocolate!" Alicia use the money for the cones of ice cream. She and her sister lick the cones while they watch TV yesterday evening.

In some past tense forms, both the helping verb and the main verb will change. The helping verb usually changes form (see pp. 371–372), but a regular main verb may need an *-ed* ending. Here's a checklist to help you determine when to use *-ed.*

When to Use -ed on a Past Tense Verb

1. The tense is past (which means that the verb happened in the past).
2. The helper is *is, are, was, were, has,* or *had* **and** the verb is past tense.

    macaroni **was** serv**ed**   a form **had been** fil**ed**

    they **were** tir**ed**   those horses **have** jump**ed**

3. The verb is passive, even if it is present tense.

Note: Even present tense verbs with the helpers *is* or *are* need *-ed* endings if the verb is passive (if the action happens *to* the subject):

the toast is burned   the houses are painted

the tires are mended   the hose is filled

END EXERCISE 14 Underline helping verbs once and main verbs twice. Add an *-ed* if needed (use the checklist above), and remember that *to* + verbs don't show change in time.

> If you have ever use a car with a manual shift, you must have notice the clutch. In most cars, clutches are locate on the floor to the left of the brake pedal. When the clutch is push in, the driver is able to change gears with the right hand, using a gearshift on the floor. Drivers who are use to this arrangement are sometimes confuse when they change to an automatic transmission. In these cars, there is no clutch, and the gears are changed by a gear shift that is locate on the steering column.

Do not use *-ed* with the helping verbs *do, does, did, don't, doesn't, didn't.*

I do believe

the car didn't stall

END EXERCISE 15 Underline the helping verbs once and the main verbs twice. Circle the helping verbs *do, does, did, don't, doesn't, didn't.* Add *-ed* to main verbs that have helping verbs that are not circled. Change the spelling of main verbs if necessary. *Note:* Remember that helping verbs are often found in questions or in contractions. Look carefully at the entire verb.

> Did the weather seem warmer this year? Has it rain as much as it usually does? If you aren't worry about the icebergs melting, maybe you don't worry about the ocean rising near the beach, either. When the temperature of the water has been raise only a few degrees, the level of the water will have been raise by a few feet. That's not much, but it doesn't take much to make a difference if you live in Miami or Charleston or Boston.

Do not use *-ed* with modal helpers such as *can, could, may, must, should, would, will, might.* Modal helpers change the meaning of the verb slightly, not the time.

END

END EXERCISE 16 Underline the main verbs twice. Underline the *-ed* helpers once and draw a circle around the modals. Add an *-ed* where needed. *Note:* Remember that one helping verb might fit with two main verbs joined by *and* or *or*.

Have you ever been charge a lot for medicine? People who would pay $50 to see a basketball game will not pay $50 for medicine, will they? Most people say they would think about whether they could find cheaper medicine, and then they might try to wait a few days. If they had learn about another medicine that they could buy, they would buy it. If they hadn't ask their doctor for cheaper medicine, they might call the office and ask the nurse.

Irregular Verbs   Some verbs show past time by changes in the spelling of the entire word:

the quartet **sang**   the boat **sank**

he was **caught**   it has been **said**

Here is a list of some common irregular verbs and the changes in their endings.

Present	Past	Past Participle
beat	beat	beaten
break	broke	broken
bring	brought	brought
buy	bought	bought
catch	caught	caught
come	came	come
drink	drank	drunk
fight	fought	fought
find	found	found
eat	ate	eaten
find	found	found
get	got	gotten
go	went	gone
hold	held	held
know	knew	known
lose	lost	lost
make	made	made
put	put	put
say	said	said
see	saw	seen

END

seek	sought	sought
send	sent	sent
sing	sang	sung
sink	sank	sunk
spend	spent	spent
teach	taught	taught
wind	wound	wound

In the list starting on page 371, three different forms are given for each irregular verb. Here are the ways that each form is used:

Editing Tip

Be sure to proofread all verb endings carefully.

1. *Present form:* Use for present tense, or use with *do, does, did,* etc., and with modals (*can, may,* etc.).
2. *Past form:* Use for simple past tense.
3. *Past participle:* Use with *-ed* helping verbs (*had, has, have, is, are, was, were*).

AGR

END EXERCISE 17   Underline the verb phrase once and the irregular verbs twice. If the irregular verb is not in the correct form, cross it out and write in the correct form.

Why do athletes receive so much money? When a major league pitcher has brung in as much money as Greg Maddux, the fans have gave him their respect. But other athletes haven't came as far as he has, and they don't deserve the salary he makes.

4. AGREEMENT

In order to make writing clear, certain words must "agree" with certain other words. Specifically, pronouns and verbs must match the nouns they're related to in certain ways.

4.1   SUBJECT-VERB AGREEMENT

To Solve Problems in Subject-Verb Agreement

Be sure you understand the material in:

Recognizing subjects and verbs (pp. 350–353)

Recognizing prepositional phrases (pp. 353–354)

Verb endings: present tense (-s) (pp. 365–367)

Subject-verb agreement means that a verb must match its subject in several ways, the most important being number (whether a word is singular or plural). As we saw in Section 3.2.1, present-tense verbs with singular subjects must end in *-s*, so you must be able to recognize the correct subject for the verb. There are many rules for special situations, but those presented in the sections that follow are the ones that most writers use. You can find additional rules in complete handbooks.

To be sure that verbs agree with their subjects, keep the following points in mind.

Checking for Singular or Plural Subjects

Subjects are never in prepositional phrases.

Two singular subjects joined by **and** form a plural subject.

Usually there is an *-s* on **either** the subject **or** the verb, not both.

AGR

4.1.1 Subjects and Prepositional Phrases

There are two ways to be sure that you have located the correct subject of a verb, which can never be in a prepositional phrase:

■ Locate the verb, then ask *Who?* or *What?* before the verb:

The man in the jacket with the red initials has turned the corner.

If you locate the verb, *has turned,* and asked **Who** or **What** *has turned,* you will see that the subject must be *man.* Therefore you will use the verb *has.*

■ Cross out any prepositional phrases (either on the paper or in your mind). The subject will then become clear:

The painters in the truck with the loud radio have turned the corner.

If you cross out the prepositional phrases *in the truck* and *with the loud radio,* you will find that the subject must be *painter.* Therefore you will use the verb *have.*

AGR EXERCISE 1 Draw a line through all prepositional phrases. Underline the verb twice and the subject once. Correct any problems in subject-verb agreement.

One of the biggest problems for students are finding time to keep in shape. In the morning, a student could get up early to run if it is the time of year when mornings are lighted, but in the winter the light of the sun don't appear until almost seven. A woman by herself in the darkness have to be a little more careful than usual. After school, a student could go to the gym, but a student with expenses must work. At night, a student with a family make dinner for them, and a student without a family try to have a little time to be with her friends. Nevertheless, most of the students I know have found some time to get the exercise they needs.

4.1.2 Subjects Joined by And

Remember that one way to recognize a plural subject is to think of the pronoun you would use instead of the nouns. If you choose *they,* the subject will be plural.

Tamara and Ben have bought a new car.

When you find the verb *have bought* and ask *Who?* or *What?* before it, you will find that two people *have bought* the car: *Tamara and Ben.* The pronoun *they* would be used for these two people, so the subject is plural. Therefore you would use *have bought* as the verb.

AGR EXERCISE 2   Underline the verb twice and the complete subject once. Correct any errors in subject-verb agreement.

> If you want to be healthy, eating and exercising is very important subjects to under-stand. Being a healthy vegetarian requires a little knowledge about the foods your body and your health needs. Protein and iron is nutrients you must be sure to have. A milk product and a bean dish usually provides enough protein, but iron is more difficult. A vegetarian often must take an iron supplement.

4.1.3 Only One -s

Language is not always logical. When you think of verbs matching subjects, you may begin to think that a subject that ends in -s should go with a verb that ends in -s, but the opposite is true. You might want to think that you have only one -s to use, and that you can't use it on both the subject and the verb—only one -s to a pair. Review pages 365–367, which discuss the simple present.

AGR EXERCISE 3   Underline the verb twice and the complete subject once. Correct any errors in subject-verb agreement.

> My friends thinks that getting in shape mean getting smaller, period. They don't realize that muscles is healthy and also attractive, even on a woman. Diets and pills is a bad way to lose weight, but eating well and exercising are good ways. Even weightlifting can be healthy for a woman. If she don't want big muscles, small weights helps you to be strong. Muscles and bones benefits from weightlifting, be-cause the pressure of the weights makes bones tougher.

4.2 PRONOUN AGREEMENT

A pronoun is a word that stands for a noun (remember that *-ing* words and *to* + words can be nouns). This means that the pronoun should match the noun it stands for. Usually this means that you must use a plural pronoun to stand for a plural noun:

The crops were withering in the heat. **They** would soon be dead.

The corn was withering in the heat. **It** would soon be dead.

Watering the crops will be expensive. **It** can cost many dollars a day.

The noun that the pronoun stands for should be clear. Avoid using pronouns that could possibly refer to more than one noun in a sentence:

UNCLEAR **Tomas** drove **Luke** to **his** house.

CLEAR **Luke** went home in **Tomas's** car.

Avoiding using *you* to mean *people in general.* You may use *you* to speak directly to the reader.

INCORRECT When **you** get drunk, **you** do not use good judgment.

CORRECT When **people** get drunk, **they** do not use good judgment.

You should also be careful to stay with the same person, especially when you are using pronouns to stand for your reader or for people in general:

INCORRECT **You** must follow these directions whenever **you** attempt to start this machine. Otherwise, **operators** might damage the machine or hurt **themselves.**

CORRECT **Operators** must follow these directions whenever **they** attempt to start this machine. Otherwise, **they** might damage the machine or hurt **themselves.**

CORRECT **You** must follow these directions whenever **you** attempt to start this machine. Otherwise, **you** might damage the machine or hurt **yourself.**

Always try to use the most accurate pronoun for a noun. Avoid using *he* to stand for a noun like *student* that could refer to either a male or female student. One simple way to achieve this is by using plural nouns and pronouns.

INCORRECT **A student** must be careful to put **his** name on all **his** books.

CORRECT **Students** must be careful to put **their** names on all **their** books.

AGR EXERCISE 4 Underline the pronouns in the paragraph below. Draw an arrow to the noun each pronoun stands for. If the pronoun does not agree with the noun, change the pronoun, using a separate sheet of paper if necessary.

Traveling in the summer can be very unpleasant. It can make you want to stay at home forever. Travelers sometimes forget their manners. You have to expect the worst from an airline trip. They can sometimes take twice as long as scheduled. When the traveler comes home, he calls the airline to complain, but they don't offer him a refund.

AGR

5. CLARITY

5.1 CHOOSING THE RIGHT WORD

Because many words look or sound very much alike, you must be extremely careful to choose the one you really want. Here are some commonly confused words that you'll probably be seeing often. There are many others to watch for in grammar reference books and dictionaries.

Word	Meaning
already	earlier, before
all ready	completely ready
course	subject of study, path
coarse	rough, not fine
cloths	more than one cloth
clothes	attire: shirts, pants, shoes, etc.
hear	perceive with ears, listen to
here	in this place, not there
hole	empty space
whole	complete, all
know	be aware of, understand
no	opposite of yes, negative
knew	past tense of *know*, understood
new	not old
lose	misplace
loose	not tight
lost	(verb) past tense of *lose*, misplaced
loss	(noun) something that is gone
passed	past tense of *pass*, went by or succeeded in a course
past	time before now
peace	quiet, harmony, no conflict
piece	section, segment, part
sense	feeling or understanding
since	after
their	belongs to them
there	not here
they're	they are
to	into, in the direction of, toward (used with verb in infinitive)

too	also, very
two	one plus one
want	desire
won't	will not
would of	(no meaning; not standard English)
would have	wanted to
where	in what place
were	past tense of *are*
your	belonging to you
you're	you are

CLR EXERCISE 1   Cross out any incorrectly used words and substitute appropriate ones.

Mathabane was embarrassed because his father insisted on wearing tribal cloths and his friends referred to him as Tarzan. He wanted to live a modern life like his friends did instead of the traditional weigh of life his father wonted him too. My parents always wonted me to dress like nice young man but the cloths that were in style when I was a teenager were those jeans with wholes in the knees. Even though I new that my parents thought that I looked like a hood in those pants, I would change into my favorite jeans the minute I left the house so I would be dressed the way my friends where when I got to school.

CLR EXERCISE 2   Cross out any incorrectly used words and substitute appropriate ones.

When my brother and I would play basketball, I would always loose because I was shorter then him and he used to block every shot I tried to make. In fact, he would tease me sense he could just stand their and still reach higher than me even when I jumped as high as I could. But now that I'm taller then he is, I'm the one whose winning every game. Its nice to get him back for all those games I loss.

5.2   WRITING CLEAR SENTENCES

Some sentences may sound correct when you are speaking but are confusing when written down. In this section we'll show you several kinds of sentences that have this problem. First, we'll explain why these sentences don't work. If you find the grammar in that part confusing, you can skip to the next part: how to repair these sentences.

5.2.1 Prepositional Phrases as Subjects

Note: Before you begin this section, you may want to review Section 1, Sentence Basics (pp. 350–354).

CLR

Here are some examples of sentences that have prepositional phrases as subjects:

INCORRECT **A.** In the article by Samuel Watson says that computers are essential in business.

INCORRECT **B.** By her taking so long to get dressed made us both late to school.

Following are some rules that will help you to understand the errors in these sentences.

A Word Can Do Only One Job in a Sentence   Words can do many different jobs in sentences. They can be verbs, subjects, objects of prepositions, etc. Words can do different jobs in different sentences, but in any one sentence, a word CANNOT do two jobs. If a word is a subject, it cannot also be a verb or an object of a preposition.

The problem in sentence A above is that the word *article* is being forced to do two jobs, which it can't do. Here are the two ways *article* is used in sentence A:

■ *In the article:* Here *article* is the object of the preposition *In.*
■ *The article . . . says:* here *article* is the subject of the verb *says.*

To repair this kind of error, you must choose which job you want the word to do, and then either add or drop a word to take care of the other job. If you choose to make *article* the subject of the verb *says,* you can choose to drop the preposition *In:*

CORRECT   The article by Samuel Watson says that computers are essential in business.

Another way to correct the sentence is by making another word act as the subject of the verb *says:*

CORRECT   In the article by Samuel Watson, **he** says that computers are essential in business.

This sentence is grammatically correct, but wordy and possibly confusing. You could also drop a different preposition to make a slightly different correction that's not so wordy. *Samuel Watson* is the object of the preposition *by.* You can drop this preposition and make *Samuel Watson* the subject:

CORRECT   In the article, Samuel Watson says that computers are essential in business.

A Prepositional Phrase Can't Do the Job of a Subject of a Sentence   In sentence B above, the prepositional phase is used as the subject:

INCORRECT By her taking so long to get dressed made us both late to school.

The verb in this sentence is *made.* If we try to find the subject asking <u>who</u> or <u>what</u> *made us late to school,* the answer we will get is the prepositional phrase *by her taking so long to get dressed.* This phrase can't also be a subject.

To repair a sentence with this problem, you'll often need two steps:

1. Make the prepositional phrase into a *because* clause.
2. Add a word that can be the subject of the sentence.

CORRECT Because she took so long to get dressed, we were both late to school.

Sometimes you'll see sentences that have only done the second part of the repair, adding only a new subject. This makes a sentence that's incorrect because it breaks another rule:

INCORRECT By her taking so long to get dressed, it made us both late to school.

A Pronoun Cannot Stand for a Prepositional Phrase   In the sample sentence above, the pronoun *it* stands for the prepositional phrase *By her taking so long to get dressed.* A pronoun cannot stand for a prepositional phrase, so this sentence is still incorrect.

Revisions   If you see sentences that start with prepositional phrases in your writing, check to make sure that you are not using the phrase or part of the phrase as the subject of the verb. To repair these sentences, you may do the following:

■ Drop words:

INCORRECT In the article by Samuel Watson says that computers are essential in business.

CORRECT The article by Samuel Watson says that computers are essential in business.

CORRECT In the article, Samuel Watson says that computers are essential in business.

■ Add words:

CORRECT In the article by Samuel Watson, he says that computers are essential in business.

■ Change words:

CORRECT Samuel Watson's article says that computers are essential in business.

■ Drop, add, and change words:

INCORRECT By her taking so long to get dressed made us both late to school.

CORRECT Because she took so long to get dressed, we were both late to school.

CLR EXERCISE 3

Mark the verb with a **V** and the subject with an **S** in the five sentences below. Put prepositional phrases in parentheses. If the subject is a prepositional phrase, rewrite the sentence so that the subject is not a prepositional phrase. You may use any method to rewrite: drop, add, and/or change words.

EXAMPLE:

$$\overset{S}{\text{(With me being an only child)}} \overset{V}{\text{meant}} \text{ that I was sometimes lonely.}$$

Because I was an only child, I was sometimes lonely.

OR

As an only child, I was sometimes lonely.

1. By me working very hard was able to pull up my grade in math.
2. With them taking care of my children helped me to have time to study.
3. In the textbook for my math class says that calculators are sometimes necessary.
4. With two children at home, I can't always have time for myself.
5. By knowing about my problems helped my teacher understand how to help me.

5.3 **INDIRECT QUESTIONS**

5.3.1 Sentences and Questions

Word Order In English, we don't use the same words in the same order to ask a question and to make a statement. One difference between questions and statements is the order of the subject and the verb:

STATEMENT You can leave.

QUESTION When can you leave?

In the statement, the subject *you* comes **before** the verb *can*. In the question, the subject *you* comes **after** the verb *can*.

Question Words Another difference between statements and questions is the use of the word *when*. This word can be used as a **question word** in a question or as a **connecting word** in a statement:

<u>QUESTION</u> **When** did you leave? [*When* is a **question word** here]

<u>STATEMENT</u> I told you **when** I left. [*When* is a **connecting word** here]

You can make a statement about asking a question. The sentence below does not ask what you are going to do, but states what I did—I asked you a question.

<u>STATEMENT</u> I asked you **when** you left. [*When* is a connecting word here]

In this statement, the word *when* is used as a **connecting word**, not a question word. Also, the subject *you* comes before the verb *left*. Because it's a statement, not a question, it follows the rule for a statement.

5.4 DIRECT AND INDIRECT QUOTES AND PARAPHRASING

RES

Students often have problems fitting the material from a reading into their own sentences. The first step in learning to do this is to recognize the difference between a direct quote, an indirect quote, and a paraphrase. Let's start with an example of a conversation between Gus and his friend Lara.

<u>ORIGINAL</u> <u>MATERIAL</u>

Gus says:	*I've been working too hard. I need to get away.*
Lara says:	*I have some free time this weekend. Maybe we could go somewhere together.*
Gus says:	*Sounds great. Let's go to the mountains.*
Lara says:	*When can you leave?*

<u>QUOTE</u> Gus's friend Lara said, "I have some free time this weekend. Maybe we could go somewhere together."

The words inside the quotation marks, *"I have some free time this weekend. Maybe we could go somewhere together,"* are a **direct quote**—the exact words spoken by Lara. Whatever appears inside the quotation marks is like a photocopy of her words—which have not been changed in any way.

<u>PARAPHRASE</u> Gus told Lara that he had to have a change of scenery because he was tired.

A **paraphrase** expresses an idea from the original in different words. Gus said: *"I've been working too hard. I need to get away."* If you repeat those words, you are quoting, but if you change the words but keep the same idea, you are paraphrasing. Notice how the ideas stay the same although the words change:

<u>ORIGINAL</u> I've been working too hard.

<u>PARAPHRASE</u> He was tired.

<u>ORIGINAL</u> I need to get away.

<u>PARAPHRASE</u> He had to have a change of scenery.

CLR

CLR EXERCISE 4	Paraphrase Gus's answer to Lara.

Sometimes you can make your writing clearer and easier to follow by combining quotes and paraphrases. This is sometimes called an **indirect quote** because it uses some original words and some that are changed:

INDIRECT QUOTE Gus said that he wanted "to get away."

The words in quotation marks, *"to get away,"* are like a photocopy of the actual words that Gus used. The words not in quotation marks—*that he wanted*—are not his exact words but express his ideas in the writer's words. The rest of Gus's words (*"I want"*) are not quoted but paraphrased as *he wanted.* This allows the quote to fit smoothly into a paragraph:

Gus was talking to Lara yesterday and said that he wanted "to get away." She suggested that they could go somewhere that weekend.

Notice that the pronoun *I* is changed to *he* in the paraphrase, and the verb tense is changed to past to fit with the rest of the paragraph.

CLR EXERCISE 5	Restate the rest of the conversation, using indirect quotes.

CLR

5.5   PARALLELISM

When words in a sentence express similar ideas, they should be stated in a similar form. That means that items in a list or joined by the conjunctions *and, but, not, for, or* should all be words, or phrases, or even complete sentences.

INCORRECT For breakfast, we ate **fish, tomatoes,** and **were toasting some good bread.**

CORRECT For breakfast, we ate **fish, tomatoes,** and **bread.**

CORRECT For breakfast, we **were broiling fish, slicing tomatoes,** and **toasting some good bread.**

INCORRECT I wanted to learn **to make** multimedia presentations and **using** a spreadsheet.

CORRECT I wanted to learn **to make** multimedia presentations and **to use** a spreadsheet.

CLR EXERCISE 6	Underline the items that are in lists or joined by conjunctions such as *and*. If the items are not in similar form, rewrite them, using a separate sheet of paper if necessary.

Pollution is everywhere: out in the country, in the city, and also found in our homes. Pollution is caused by manufacturing processes and we drive cars, as well as to waste many products. For example, when consumers buy broccoli at the store, the vegetable has a wire around it and in a plastic bag, then puts it in a bigger bag with other vegetables. This makes three different wrappings for the broccoli, when one would be enough.

6. FREQUENTLY USED PUNCTUATION AND STYLING MARKS

Frequently Used Punctuation
Commas
Question marks
Titles
Capitals
Quotation marks

This section focuses on some basic rules of punctuation that may seem very small but are in fact an important part of good writing. Again, you will need to consult a complete handbook for many details in unusual sentences. Here we give you the simplest rules for the most common problems.

6.1 COMMAS

Commas are not decorations that you can just sprinkle randomly through your sentences. Every comma added to a sentence has a clear job that is determined by the rules of punctuation. Think about the two general concepts below, and the rules that go with them.

Using Commas

Comma Guide 1: Use a comma only within a sentence or between the parts of one sentence. A comma can do many things in a sentence:

■ Separate introductory material before the subject.

■ Set off words or phrases that could be removed or moved to other places in the sentence.

■ Separate items in a series.

■ Separate two complete sentences if they are joined by conjunctions (and, but, or, nor, for). See Section 2.2.

Comma Guide 2: Use a comma only when you have a reason. If in doubt, leave it out.

6.1.1. Using a Comma to Separate Introductory Material Before the Subject

When you have any introductory words at the beginning of a sentence, the sentence may be hard to follow. Use a comma right *before* the subject to make the main part of the sentence clear.

PUNC

CONFUSING When students are painting their hands may feel cramped.

CLEAR When students are painting, their hands may feel cramped.

PUNC EXERCISE 1 Correct the comma usage in the passage below.

> On my way home I passed a group of older women. Since I could see that they were walking slowly I felt that I should ask if they needed any assistance. One of them thanked me and said she was able to walk but just not very quickly. Although I worried about them I felt that I needed to get to my destination. When I came back, I saw the same ladies. They had walked just one more block while I had walked five.

6.1.2 Using a Comma to Set Off Words or Phrases that Could Be Removed or Moved to Other Places in the Sentence

Commas can be used almost like parentheses to show words and groups of words that are not needed to make a complete sentence. Use commas around material that can be omitted from the sentence:

COMPLETE SENTENCE My sister, the woman in the green boots, has enrolled in computer classes this fall.

Use commas before and after the phrase *the woman in the green boots*. It could be removed from the sentence without creating a fragment:

COMPLETE SENTENCE My sister has enrolled in computer classes this fall.

Use commas around material that can be moved to another place in the sentence without changing the meaning:

SENTENCE I told him, however, that we would also require a written request.

SENTENCE WITH UNCHANGED MEANING I told him that we would also require a written request, however.

SENTENCE WITH UNCHANGED MEANING However, I told him that we would also require a written request.

Note: Be sure to use commas both *before* and *after* this kind of material, unless it comes at the beginning or end of a sentence; see rules for using commas on page 383.

PUNC EXERCISE 2 Correct the use of commas in the following sentences.

> When a single parent is a man he may have more problems however than a woman. My brother the parent of a three-year-old has to work and arrange for child care. With these problems he's just a like a single mother. In the evening though it's hard

for him to find another single father to share child care or to trade babysitting jobs. Surprisingly he doesn't know any other single fathers. He knows single women who have children but they live far away from him.

6.1.3 Using Commas to Separate Items in a Series

When you have a list of words, phrases, or clauses, you should put a comma after each item except the very last one:

LIST OF WORDS Jogging, rowing, and skating are all good aerobic exercise.

LIST OF PHRASES We put notices on the bulletin boards, on the windows, and on the doors to advertise the sale.

LIST OF SENTENCES JOINED WITH CONJUNCTIONS. In this computer lab students are typing papers, lab assistants are sending E-mail, and people are learning to use software.

PUNC EXERCISE 3 Correct the use of commas in the following sentences.

The best rituals in my family were those around holidays birthdays and vacations. Those were the times when we cooked special food visited family, and went on trips. We might visit our cousins they might visit us or we might all go to the beach together. When we went to the beach with my older cousin her favorite rituals were singing silly songs in the car telling ghost stories and playing card games in the middle of the night.

6.1.4 Using a Comma to Separate Two Complete Sentences Joined by Conjunctions

Review the rules on fragments (pp. 355–358) and run-on sentences (pp. 358–361), and make sure you know that you may join two complete sentences with a conjunction (*and, but, or, nor, for, so*). When you do this, you should use a comma *before* the conjunction, not after:

CORRECT Alicia wanted to improve her children's musical ability, so she enrolled them in guitar lessons.

CORRECT The transmission of the car was working well, but the fuel pump needed to be replaced.

Note: Do *not* use a comma before conjunctions that join only two words or two phrases. Be sure the conjunction joins two *complete* sentences:

CORRECT I wanted to visit Africa, so I signed up for the tour.

INCORRECT I wanted to visit Africa, and Korea.

INCORRECT I wanted to visit Africa, and stop in Europe on the way.

PUNC

PUNC EXERCISE 4 Correct the use of commas in the following sentences.

We all react differently to feelings of guilt. Orwell and the prison officials may have felt guilty about hanging the man but they denied their feelings and hid from them by drinking and joking. Other people may use these same ways to hide from guilt or they may get angry at the person they have hurt. Admitting that you feel guilty is a difficult thing to do and many people never can take that step. Thinking about your feelings and your reactions is difficult but necessary.

6.2   QUESTION MARKS

Questions can be direct or indirect (see Section 5.3). **Always use a question mark at the end of a direct question.**

What would be the point of writing all the papers and taking all the exams if you withdrew from the course at the very end?

Why did you come?

Never use a question mark after an indirect question.

She asked me why I came.

PUNC EXERCISE 5 Correct the use of question marks in the following sentences.

The interview with the new governor was really boring, wasn't it. First a reporter asked him if he planned any changes in the next year? He said that he would wait and see what happened. Then another reporter asked, "Will you approve a bill to raise taxes?" The governor replied, "Didn't I just answer that." Would you listen to an interview as boring as that. Why do the sponsors want to pay for boring news. I just don't get it?

6.3   TITLES

6.3.1 Capitals in Titles

There are two basic rules that tell you which words to capitalize in a title:

■ Capitalize the first word and the last word in a title.

In his essay "A Hanging," George Orwell describes his own experience.

To Have and Have Not is the movie assigned for this discussion.

"On His Blindness" is the poem Milton wrote.

■ Capitalize all other words *except* articles, conjunctions, and prepositions.

The Old Man and the Sea is my favorite book.

In "Getting Off the Welfare Carousel," McCrary says that welfare recipients are stereotyped.

Note: Do *not* copy the capitalization as you find it on the title page or in a library or electronic listing. Many times you will see that book covers and title pages do not follow the rules of capitalization. The title may appear in all capital letters or with no capitals at all. When you find a reference to a book in a database or on the Internet, only the first word may be capitalized.

6.3.2 Underlining, Italics, and Quotation Marks

When you want to indicate that a group of words is a title, you must follow certain rules:

- Underline (or italicize) long, complete works such as books, plays, and movies.

  Gone with the Wind is my favorite movie.

  <u>In Our Time</u> is the book assigned for this discussion.

- Use quotation marks for short works or parts of longer works.

  In "Getting Off the Welfare Carousel," McCrary says that welfare recipients are stereotyped.

  "On His Blindness" is the poem Milton wrote.

- Choose the correct format and use only that; do *not* use both underlining and quotation marks for the same title.

  INCORRECT In his essay <u>"A Hanging,"</u> George Orwell describes his own experience.

  CORRECT In his essay "A Hanging," George Orwell describes his own experience.

- Be consistent throughout your essay in the use of either italics or underlining for titles of long and complete works. Do *not* use both.

  INCONSISTENT *Gone with the Wind* is my favorite movie now, not <u>The Wizard of Oz.</u>

  CONSISTENT *Gone with the Wind* is my favorite movie now, not *The Wizard of Oz.*

  CONSISTENT <u>Gone with the Wind</u> is my favorite movie now, not <u>The Wizard of Oz.</u>

PUNC EXERCISE 6 Correct the punctuation of titles in the following sentences.

I found a number of good sources for my paper. I'm going to use a novel called The scarlet Letter, a story entitled <u>"Where I'm calling from,"</u> and a poem called MY PAPA'S WALTZ. The best book I read was **the Firm,** but I don't think I'll use that. I might also discuss the movie <u>How Green Was My Valley</u>, or another movie,

American Beauty. My little sister used the movie "Beauty And The Beast" for her project.

6.4 CAPITALIZATION

Using a capital letter for the first letter of a word has a specific meaning for most readers. Capitalization can be confusing unless it is done correctly, so use capital letters only when you know why you are doing so. Here are some simple rules for capitalization:

- Capitalize proper names of people (including titles and honorifics), ethnic groups, places, countries and states, holidays, institutions, and religions.

the Armenian people	Sri Lanka	Juneteenth
Easter	South Dakota	Ms. Chung
Victory Savings Bank	Buddhism	the Pope
the Inuit	Nelson Mandela	Prime Minister Thatcher

- Capitalize the first word in a sentence or a quoted word, phrase, or sentence of dialogue. But do not capitalize the first word of an indirect quote in paraphrase (see p. 382).

  The most important thing is her answer. If she says, "The men weren't here," then we will know that they were not the criminals.

- Do *not* capitalize words to emphasize them in academic writing.

  INCORRECT That was MY First Real Job.

  CORRECT That was my first real job.

PUNC EXERCISE 7 Correct the capitalization in the following sentences.

Marla went to visit her Aunt in Buffalo, New york. Aunt Mary told her, "don't expect it to be as warm here as it is in California," but marla thought it would be warm anywhere by easter. She took her Tee shirts and plenty of Levis. Her Cousins laughed at her idea of warm clothes, and told her, "you need to go to the Mall to get some REALLY Warm Clothes."

6.5 QUOTATION MARKS

6.5.1 When to Use Quotation Marks

RES Use quotation marks whenever you use the *exact words* of a speaker or a book, even if it is only a few words or something that someone *might* have said.

The essay describes "the poets in the kitchen."

Formal writers should avoid slang, meaning terms like "cool" and "laid back."

Note: If a speaker's or writer's words are introduced by words like "said" or "replied," use a comma to set off the quotation. Don't use a comma after "that."

Robert said, "I'll do that!"

Jefferson says that "life, liberty, and the pursuit of happiness" are every human being's "inalienable rights."

Do not use quotation marks for paraphrases or summaries. Also, single, *very common* words that might be found often in many works do not require quotation marks.

PARAPHRASE Robert thinks he can take care of the problem.

SUMMARY Jefferson described universal entitlements.

COMMON WORD Jefferson lists our **rights.**

Note: Don't mix the speaker's (or writer's) words with yours. Anything in quotation marks should be exactly what was said by someone else; anything *not* in quotation marks should be entirely your own words.

INCORRECT Jefferson described universal entitlements, such as life, liberty, and the pursuit of happiness.

CORRECT Jefferson described universal entitlements, such as "life, liberty, and the pursuit of happiness."

PUNC EXERCISE 8 Assume that the following passage was found on page 156 of the book *Guide to China* by J. L. Sims. Use this paragraph for the exercises that follow.

The city of Beijing is the capital of China and is located in the northeast section of the country. Although Beijing was not the first capital of this ancient country, it has held that position since the fourteenth century. When China's rulers were emperors, they lived in the center of Beijing in a great palace called the Forbidden City. This palace is now a cultural and art museum, open to all of China's people. Also in Beijing are many temples and other museums, but Beijing is not a city of the past. Most visitors delight in the many restaurants serving different kinds of food from every part of China and the world. On one street the restaurants have blazing fires and whole sheep hanging outside; on another street are elegant Sichuanese restaurants where twenty course meals are served on rare porcelain dishes, and on yet another street Pizza Hut competes with McDonald's.

Correct the use of quotation marks in the following student paragraph. Be sure to check with the original above to see where the student is quoting and where she is paraphrasing.

> The capital of the United States is Washington, D.C., and the capital of China is Beijing (Sims 156). Beijing is like Washington is in some ways and different in others. Beijing once had emperors who lived in the center of Beijing in a great palace called the Forbidden City. Washington has the White House and our president lives there now, but the leader of China does not live in the Forbidden City "which is now open to all of the people of China" (Sims 156). Washington and Beijing both have many museums and restaurants, and in both you might find exotic ethnic foods, elegant cuisine, and streets where Pizza Hut competes with McDonald's (Sims 157).

Note: When using **parenthetical citations**, the parentheses come after any quotation marks, but before the period. (See pp. 394–403 on documentation for more information on citing sources.) Here's an example:

> In *An Anthropologist on Mars*, Robert Kellogg says that we are all "wishing for the past" (185).

6.5.2 Quoting Too Much

Is it possible to quote too much? In most cases, you should try to avoid quoting so much material that your own ideas are overshadowed. Quoting too much can confuse your reader because the quotations may not fit together well with each other or with your ideas. Quote only as much as you need to give evidence for your opinions, and quote only the phrases or sentences that are directly related to what you are saying.

> GOOD George Orwell knows that the people of Burma do not like the Europeans. The young priests "stand on street corners and jeer" (175).

> (TOO MUCH QUOTATION) AVOID

> At that college, you may take courses to improve your basic skills. "Business Math I stresses the basic operations of addition, subtraction, multiplication, and division as applied to whole numbers, decimals, fractions, and percentages. Speed and accuracy are emphasized along with some application to consumer and business problems. The course is not open to students who have completed BUS 109 or its equivalency" (Catalogue 143). You may also take courses to improve reading speed and comprehension, spelling, and study skills that will prepare you for many career majors.

6.5.3 Fitting Quotations Smoothly into a Paragraph

Quotations as long as a complete sentence or more need an introduction and explanation to fit them smoothly into the paragraph. Here are some techniques for doing this:

PUNC

■ Introduce a quotation with a sentence or phrase:

Ellis explains what khakis mean to Americans. She says, "the pants have become a tradition" (31).

According to Leibowitz, "Irina was already a legend" (87).

■ After giving a quotation, explain what it means or why it is important:

Ellis explains what khakis mean to Americans. She says, "the pants have become a tradition" (31). **We like them because of their history as well as their usefulness.**

According to Leibowitz, "Irina was already a legend" (87). **They thought she was beautiful partly because of her reputation for courage.**

PUNC EXERCISE 9 Write a paragraph comparing your city to Beijing, using quotations from the selection on page 389. Be sure to introduce and explain your quotes.

6.5.4 Fitting Quotations Smoothly into a Sentence

Shorter quotations—words, phrases, parts of sentences—can fit into sentences without a separate introduction and explanation, but they must fit in smoothly with the grammar of your sentence, and they must make sense. You can do this in several ways.

■ Begin and end quotations at points that fit well with your sentence.

INCORRECT Beber says that being a law school feminist is hard because of "a lawyer means identifying with the people you are trying to defeat" (207).

CORRECT Beber says that it was difficult to be a complete feminist in law school because wanting to be "a lawyer means identifying with the people you are trying to defeat" (207).

■ Reword your sentence to help it fit with the quotation.

INCORRECT Xanadu is a house that "Hearst appeared to have furnished Xanadu largely from estate sales" (112).

CORRECT A visitor might think that "Hearst appeared to have furnished Xanadu largely from estate sales" (112).

PUNC EXERCISE 10 Here is a paragraph from a book. It will be the original text to use in the exercise that follows.

Volcano eruptions are not as common as earthquakes, hurricanes, and tornadoes. Volcanoes look very much like big mountains—they sit there quietly, wearing their

PUNC

snow and glaciers like kindly white-haired grandparents. This is deceptive. Under the cold ice lies a raging furnace that may spew tons of suffocating ashes, torrents of hot mud, or fiery rivers of lava. Any of these eruptions will destroy all life in the path of the outpouring. Mt. St. Helens erupted with ashes and caused destruction in the United States; Mt. Pinatubo in the Philippines and Mt. Fako in Cameroon have also erupted in the last ten years.

Improve the sentences in the student paragraph below by selecting better material from the original above or by rewording the sentence.

Among the natural disasters in the U.S. recently was "Mt. St. Helens erupted with ashes." We don't expect volcanoes. The source says "like kindly white-haired grandparents." We should be afraid of volcanoes "spew tons of suffocating ashes."

6.5.5 Changing Quotations

If necessary, you can make *very small* changes that do not affect the meaning of the original sentence. You may add, delete, or change words. For example, you may need to change the person or number of pronouns or verbs, or substitute a noun for a pronoun.

Leaving Out Words   If you want to leave out some words within quoted material, you must indicate that you have done this with ellipses—three spaced dots that take the place of the words you have left out. Be sure that the meaning is not changed.

SAME MEANING Xanadu is a house that "Hearst appeared to have furnished . . . largely from estate sales" (112).

MEANING CHANGED (AVOID) Not many people know that "Hearst . . . furnished Xanadu largely from estate sales" (112).

PUNC EXERCISE 11   **Improve the use of quotation by using ellipses in the following sentences (the original text is on pp. 391–392).**

1. Some results of volcano eruptions include: "Under the cold ice lies a raging furnace that may spew tons of suffocating ashes, torrents of hot mud, or fiery rivers of lava."

2. Three volcanoes that have erupted recently are "Mt. St. Helens erupted with ashes and caused destruction in the United States; Mt. Pinatubo in the Philippines and Mt. Fako in Cameroon have also erupted in the last ten years."

Adding Words   If you want to add your own explanatory words or comments to a direct quote, place them in square brackets, *not* parentheses. Be sure that the meaning is not changed.

SAME MEANING Beber says that it was difficult to be a complete feminist in law school because "wanting to be a lawyer means identifying with the people [men] you are trying to defeat" (207).

MEANING CHANGED (AVOID)   Beber says that it was difficult to be a complete feminist in law school because "wanting to be a lawyer means [not] identifying with the people you are trying to defeat" (207).

Changing Words   If you want to substitute a word or phrase for something in a direct quote use square brackets. (Do not use ellipses.) Be sure that the meaning is not changed.

SAME MEANING   When they met Irina, the reporters knew that she "[had become] a legend" (87).

MEANING CHANGED (AVOID)   When they met, the reporters knew that "Irina [was going to be] a legend" (87).

PUNC EXERCISE 12   Use brackets to add or change the wording to make the sentences fit smoothly. Be careful not to distort the meaning.

1. People who live near a volcano should be concerned about the eruptions because "These eruptions will destroy all life in the path of the outpouring."

2. Anyone who was climbing a volcano and thought that it was peaceful should have realized that "This is deceptive."

7. MLA STYLE DOCUMENTATION

Identifying the words or ideas of other writers or speakers is known as **documentation**. **Sources** are the places where you found your information: other writers, speakers, library books, computer materials, etc. A **citation** is the specific piece of information about that source.

Documentation involves different details for each possible type of material and fields of study. You will probably need to use a complete handbook when you write complicated research papers. Here we show you how to use the three simplest types of sources: (1) books and selections from anthologies; (2) articles in magazines or newspapers; and (3) Internet sites. The rules we show here are the ones used by most English teachers and are called MLA style, but if you write a paper for a psychology or biology class, you may follow a different documentation style. For those too you will need a complete handbook related to a particular field of study to be able to write research papers. In this book, we will give you only an introduction to documentation to help you understand the basic parts of the process. Once you understand how documentation works, it's not very difficult to adapt to special situations.

DOC

7.1 PURPOSE

When you write in college, you'll need to be sure that you let your readers know clearly when you use another writer's or speaker's ideas, information, or words.

What Must Be Documented

Identify (document) anything from another writer or speaker:

- Exact words of another person (direct quote)
- Ideas of another person (paraphrase or summary)
- Facts from any source (paraphrase, summary, or direct quote)

There are many reasons why you will be expected to document your sources:

1. To let your readers know where your information and ideas come from, so they can judge whether the source is reliable.
2. To let your readers know where to find more information on the topic.
3. To give credit to the writer or researcher who originally found the facts or wrote the words.

Imagine that your readers will be using your citations like maps, taking them to the library or bookstore or computer and finding the same material you found. They should be able to locate every source that you used, not just direct quotations. If you paraphrase someone's ideas or facts, you must document that in the same way that you do a quote.

7.2 PROCESS: PARENTHETICAL DOCUMENTATION AND WORKS CITED

Basically, there are two parts to any citation: (1) a parenthetical citation in the body of an essay that tells your reader exactly which words or ideas are yours and which are someone else's, and (2) a works cited or reference list that gives all the information about the sources used in the essay.

The Two Parts of Documentation

- **Parenthetical citation:** Brief notes in the body of your essay identifying any material that comes from another source.
- **Works cited or references:** Lists at the end of the essay giving detailed information about where each source was found.

The two parts of a citation work together. You must first make the end list, which we call the **works cited** list. The first word or words in each entry in the list will be used as a shorthand in your paper each time you use material from that source. Here's an example of two paragraphs and part of the works cited list from a paper using outside sources. This example follows MLA style (except for the right **justification** used in this book). Notice that every quotation or paraphrase is clearly linked to the first words of one of the entries in the list that follows:

The image that most people have of welfare recipients is false. Many people look at those on welfare as people who are too lazy to work hard. They believe that welfare recipients are just people who want a free ride. According to Chou, "Newt Gingrich [said that they] posed a threat to American civilization" (Chou B15). This image is often promoted on television news magazines which do stories on welfare recipients who abuse the system. We see stories about people illegally trading food stamps or making false claims to bilk the system out of money. We also hear about people who make welfare a lifestyle. However, most recipients are people who want to get off welfare and make a decent living for themselves (McLeod and Donalds 12-27). Teresa McCrary is one such person. She has worked hard to obtain the education required to get a job that will pay her enough money to support her family. The picture that Teresa McCrary presents of welfare mothers in her essay "Getting Off the Welfare Carousel" is an accurate one. The fact is that life is very difficult for women like her, who usually have poorer working conditions than other people (Clemons). She discusses the problems that welfare mothers face and argues against the image that most people have of welfare recipients. The experiences of two friends of mine show this daily, as they struggle to take care of children by volunteering at the elementary school and going to school themselves at night. They represent the real image of welfare mothers, women who are dedicated to their children and women who are working hard to better themselves, yet I've heard neighbors call them "bums," just because they get a few dollars to help feed their children.

The welfare system seems to be designed to work against those who receive benefits. McCrary explains to us how the system really works. When a woman with children finds herself divorced, she has to clothe and feed her offspring even though she may have no job skills (Myron 107). Of course, her first step is to apply for welfare to protect her children. However, welfare is barely enough to survive on. The woman's next step is to get a job, but because she has no work experience or job skills, "The only jobs open to [her] are maid work, fast-food service and other low-paying drudgery with no benefits," McCrary (12) tells us. According to the Clearinghouse for Welfare Information, women are "steer[ed] . . . into working for minimum wage rather than training for better jobs." This situation leads women on welfare to "take money under the table for odd jobs" (McCrary 12) so they can make a little more money but

DOC

not lose their benefits. The system forces women to stay on welfare and take money under the table—for which the government receives no taxes. This system does not benefit the women on it or the government who wants them off it.

Works Cited

Chou, Linda. "Off the Welfare Rolls, On the Payrolls." *New York Times* 2 July 2000: B15.

Clearinghouse for Welfare Information. "You Never Get Free: Transition from Welfare to Work." *Social Work Site.* 15 January 1998. Online. http://www.clearinghouse.org/socialworksite/welfare/transition.htm (18 March 2000).

Clemons, Laurie G. "Welfare Reform and Working Women." *Review of Welfare* May 1999: 79-109. Online. LEXIS-NEXIS Academic Universe. Mountain Public Library, Stanton, MT. 7 April 1998. (http://web.lexis-nexis.com/cis). 21 May 2000.

McCrary, Teresa. "Getting Off the Welfare Carousel." *Newsweek* 6 December 1993: 11.

McLeod, Peggy, and Samuel Donalds. *The Stories of Women at Work and on Welfare.* New York: Ramparts, 1998.

Myron, Wessinger. "Making It Alone: The Single Parent." *Welfare Reform.* Ed. Sandra Mayson. New York: Clarks, 1999. 98-119.

7.3   FORMAT: MLA STYLE

Steps in Documentation

Locate and record all the necessary information

Format that information according to certain rules, no mater how it was formatted in the original source

Documentation is much easier if you understand the process from the beginning of your research. If you know what you are doing and why, you will be able to work efficiently and quickly, and you'll be able to spend your energy on being sure that your ideas are clear.

7.3.1 Locating and Recording Information

Your research activities will become very frustrating if you must return to a source a second time to find a missing piece of information for documentation. To avoid making last-minute trips to the library and midnight searches on the Internet, be sure to *record all necessary documentation information when you find a source.* You may want to record each source on a separate note card, so that you can sort them easily when you start to format your paper. If you are only using a few sources, you may find it easier to use printouts from online sources and photocopies from books and magazines, and write the necessary information on the printout or photocopy. You may prefer to keep a notebook with all your sources listed in one section.

DOC

However you record the information, be sure that you do locate and record every detail. For every source used, you will need to locate and record information in several categories.

Information Needed for Works Cited or References

Author—the name(s) of the writer(s) or speaker(s) of the specific source you are using

Title—the title of the specific source you are using

Page—the exact page where the information or quotation was found

Publication information—information about the book, magazine, or Website where the information was found, including date and place

Author   Be sure that you accurately identify the author of the specific source you are using. For example, if you want to cite "A Hanging" in this book, the reference entry would begin with George Orwell, not the authors of the entire book.

Title   Record the exact title of the specific source you are using. For example, if you are citing Michael Bronksi's essay about AIDS in this book, you would record the title "Magic and AIDS: Presumed Innocent," as well as the title of the entire book.

Page Numbers   Be very careful to record all relevant page numbers for any material taken from an article or book. Websites usually do not have page numbers.

Publication Information   This part of the citation will be different for each type of source. You may need to refer to a complete handbook for additional details.

- **Book:** The following information can be found on the title page or copyright of the book:

    Place of publication: The city, or if it is not a well-known city, the city and the state. If several are given, use the first.

    Publisher: The name of the company that published the book. You do not need to include words such as *Publishers, Company, Press, Inc.,* etc.

    Year: The most recent year that a book was published. Be sure you find the year that comes after the copyright symbol, which appears on the copyright page. Use the most recent if more than one is listed.

If the book is an anthology—a collection of essays, stories, poems, plays, etc.—you will need some additional information:

DOC

Title of entire book: This is the title that appears on the title page. The title of the specific essay cited will be found in the table of contents and on the first page of the essay. Be sure to record both.

Editors of entire book: The names of the editors are listed on the title page. There may be other names listed on the back of the title (copyright) page, but you do not record these.

Page numbers: Write down the first and last page of the essay you are citing.

- **Periodical (magazine or newspaper):** You can find the following information on the front page or cover of most periodicals or in the table of contents:

    Title of periodical: Record the complete title.

    Date: Record the date of publication.

    Page numbers: List the first and last pages of the article. If the article is continued later in the periodical, list the first page and a plus sign (16+). If you are citing a newspaper, be sure to record the section number as well as the page number, since the numbers start over at the beginning of each section. Most newspapers assign a letter to each section followed by a page number—for example, C1 for the first page in section C.

    Volume and issue: For journals, write down volume and issue number, found in Table of Contents.

- **Website:** Websites are much less standardized than books and magazines. Because they may be changed and updated, the site you are citing may not be available later on. In addition, documentation rules for Websites are still being developed, so you may find in a few years that you need to change the way you cite them. For most Web sources, you should first try to find the author of the page you are using. If that is not available, you may have to list an organization as the author. Sometimes you will need to be a detective to find what you need to know about a Web source—following links back to home pages, decoding the URL, looking at the end as well as the beginning of the page. Basically, you must distinguish three types of sites:

    Online versions of print magazines and newspapers.

    Databases and indexes (usually available only through libraries.) The articles found in these sources often exist on paper as well as online.

    Websites that are open to everyone and exist only on the Web.

The first two sites have **print equivalents**, which means that the same article exists printed on paper. You must first give the information that you would give if you had found the source in print. For the third type, you will need to cite only the author of the specific material you are using (if the author is given) and the title of the page you are using.

In general, you will also need the following information for all online sources:

Online date: This is the date that the material was put on the Web; usually it is available on the homepage (the main or central page of the organization maintaining the site). Dates may sometimes be found at the ends of pages, as well.

Site title: This may be difficult or impossible to find, but if you can locate it, it will help your reader greatly to understand what the source is. You may be able to find it by following links to *home.*

Uniform Resource Locator (URL): These are the letters, numbers, and symbols that locate a particular Web page. Often you will find a URL at the bottom or top of the page if you print out a Web page; you can also look at the top of the screen while you have the page online. Usually the URL will be listed as "address" or "go to." It will always begin *http://.* . . . Be sure to copy it exactly.

Your date: This is the day that you actually locate the page. It may also appear at the top or bottom of the page in a printout. If not, you must be sure to record it.

If you cannot find some of this information, it will be even more important that whatever you do have is absolutely accurate.

7.3.2 Works Cited List

In the works cited list, you must be careful to set up the citations exactly as the rules tell you. The rules are guides to a kind of shorthand or code. If you don't follow them exactly, you will confuse your reader. Also, once you learn to follow the rules, you'll be able to understand other people's citations and use them to find sources if you need to. Remember that the rules will be different in different fields of study.

Note: Often you will see the information in a very different format on the book or magazine itself, or in a library or index. You must translate the information so that it is in the format that the rules below describe.

Let's look first at some principles that apply to all citations in English classes. These are called **MLA** style.

■ You must remember the general rules for punctuating titles (see Section 6.3).

■ You must always set up the works cited entry using **hanging indentation**, a type of text formatting in which the first line starts at the left margin and continues all the way to the right margin, and the next line

DOC

is indented five spaces. In the example below, notice that the author's name is easy to see, since there are no words directly underneath it.

Clemons, Laurie G. "Welfare Reform and Working Women." <u>Review of Welfare</u> May 1999: 79-109. Online. LEXIS-NEXIS Academic Universe. Mountain Public Library, Stanton, MT. 7 April 1998. (http://web.lexis-nexis. com/cis). 21 May 2000.

Computer Tip

Don't use the TAB key to indent the entry. Most word-processing programs have a very simple way of creating hanging indents:

1. Place the cursor where you want the entry to begin.
2. Click the FORMAT command on the top of the screen.
3. From the pull-down menu, select PARAGRAPH.
4. (Only in some programs) A dialogue box may appear; if so, click SPECIAL.
5. Select HANGING INDENT
6. Do *not* hit the ENTER key until you reach the end of that entry.
7. Repeat for each entry.

■ Punctuation of titles and use of hanging indentation are the same for all entries. Also, in each entry you must put the information in a certain order, and you must separate the information with the appropriate punctuation. Punctuation must be exactly correct. Look carefully at each mark.

Using the exact punctuation is important, because each comma, period, and colon has a meaning. If you do not use the correct punctuation, your reader will not understand the information about the source. Notice, for example, that a comma comes after the author's last name, but a period comes after the entire name; notice that a colon follows the name of the city.

Book   Give the author, title, place, publisher, and date.

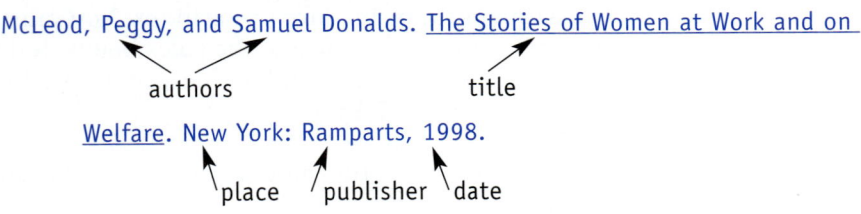

OR

McLeod, Peggy, and Samuel Donalds. *The Stories of Women at Work and on Welfare.* New York: Ramparts, 1998.

In the examples shown here, titles will be underlined, but italic print is always an acceptable alternative if you are using a computer.

Essay in a Book (Anthology)   Give the author, the title of the individual selection, the title of the book, the editor, the city, the publisher, the date, and the pages.

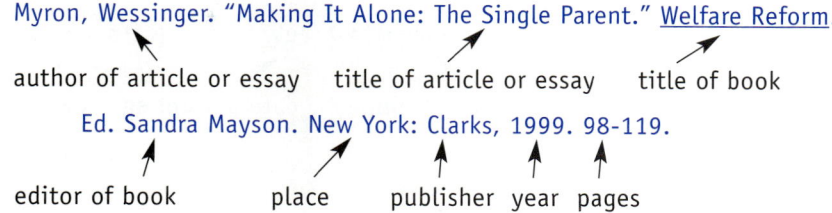

Myron, Wessinger. "Making It Alone: The Single Parent." <u>Welfare Reform</u>.

author of article or essay   title of article or essay   title of book

Ed. Sandra Mayson. New York: Clarks, 1999. 98-119.

editor of book   place   publisher year pages

Article in a Newspaper or Magazine   Give author, title of article, title of magazine, date, and page.

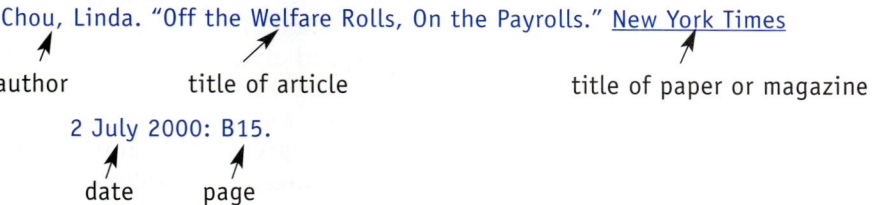

Chou, Linda. "Off the Welfare Rolls, On the Payrolls." <u>New York Times</u>

author   title of article   title of paper or magazine

2 July 2000: B15.

date   page

Online Database   You will often find articles from newspapers, magazines, or journals in *online* or *electronic databases*, such as Lexis-Nexis or Infotrac, which are special sites on the Internet that have many complete articles available to download for reading or printing. You will be able to use most databases if you go through a library, so you want to give your reader two kinds of information about your site.

- *Print-equivalent information:* The version of an article as it was published on paper—in an actual magazine or newspaper—is called the print equivalent. When citing this type of source, you can always start by following the format for periodicals given above.

- *Online source:* Immediately after you have recorded the complete periodical information, you should note whatever information you can find about the online database. Your reference must contain the word *online* to indicate that this is an electronic source. Then give the name of the database, the name of the library where you used it, and the date it was put online (if available) followed by the URL of the database (not the complete URL for the article). Finally, give the date you found the source.

DOC

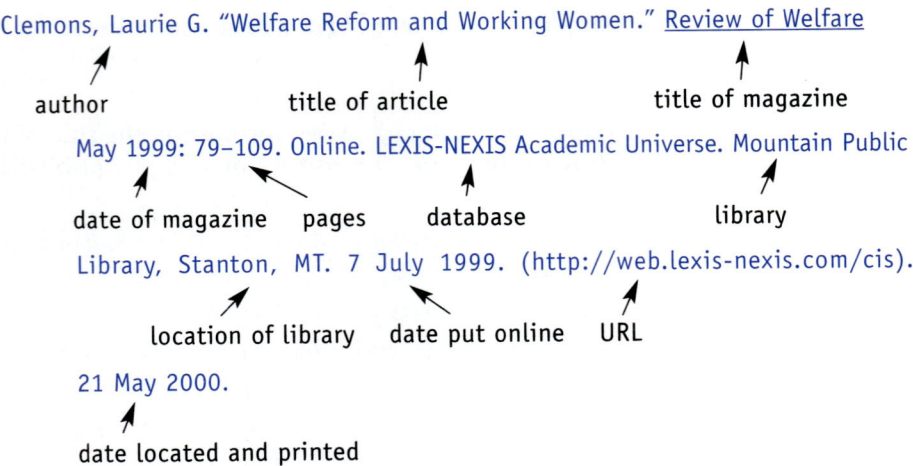

Clemons, Laurie G. "Welfare Reform and Working Women." <u>Review of Welfare</u>

↗ author   ↑ title of article   ↑ title of magazine

May 1999: 79–109. Online. LEXIS-NEXIS Academic Universe. Mountain Public

↗ date of magazine   pages   database   library

Library, Stanton, MT. 7 July 1999. (http://web.lexis-nexis.com/cis).

↗ location of library   ↖ date put online   ↗ URL

21 May 2000.

↗ date located and printed

Web Page or Site   "Web page" or "site" refers to anything you may find on the Internet. Some Websites are official publications of organizations, but others may be the work of one individual. The information that is given for sites varies, so you will not always find all the information listed here. If you cannot find some of the information, you must omit it, but make a note of this somewhere for your own information.

To format the entry, start by giving the name of the organization that sponsors the page or the author's last name followed by first name, followed by a period; the title of the page in quotation marks and followed by a period; the name of the site, underlined and followed by a period; the online date followed by a period, then the URL, and the date you found the site enclosed in parentheses. If the Web page is also available in print, give the information for the print version first, using the guide for magazine or newspaper above. Then give the publication information for a web page.

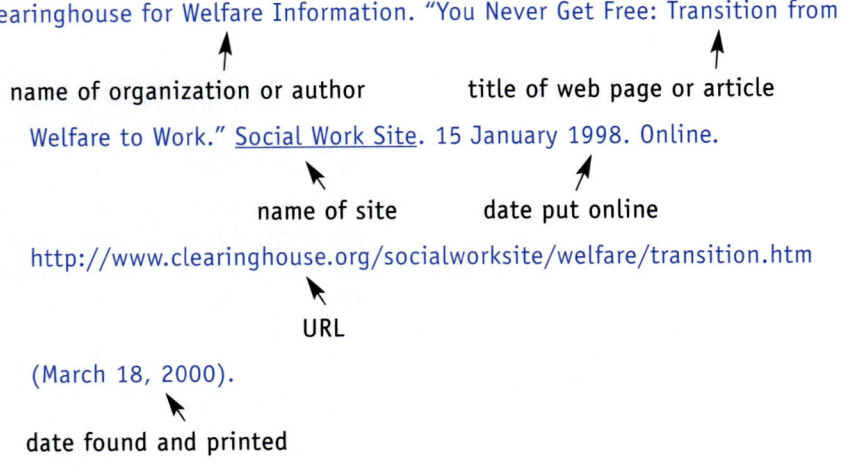

Clearinghouse for Welfare Information. "You Never Get Free: Transition from

↑ name of organization or author   ↑ title of web page or article

Welfare to Work." <u>Social Work Site</u>. 15 January 1998. Online.

↖ name of site   ↗ date put online

http://www.clearinghouse.org/socialworksite/welfare/transition.htm

↖ URL

(March 18, 2000).

↖ date found and printed

DOC

7.3.3 Parenthetical Citations

A key component of documentation is the parenthetical citation—a quick way to show your reader where to find a source in the works cited list. If you learned to use footnotes or end notes or to refer to the items in the works cited list by number, please **forget** that system. The MLA style rules you must follow in college English courses are simpler than that, designed to be easy and clear for reader and writer. Here are a few steps to follow:

1. Select the information that must be cited. If you have used someone else's words, you must put them in quotation marks. If you have incorporated someone else's ideas or information in your own words, you must still include a clear citation.

2. Look at the works cited entry for that source. Usually it will begin with the author's last name, but it may begin with a title. In either case, you will use the first word or two as a code to guide the reader back to that entry. If you must use part of the title, punctuate it as you did the title.

3. Decide how to cite the source in your writing. You may refer to the author or title in the sentence, or you may enclose the entire citation in parentheses. In either case, you must give the page number in parentheses if it is available.

Summary of Documentation

1. Locate and record the information about the source when you find it.
2. Make the works cited entry according to the rules.
3. Use author or title along with the page number in the sentence or in parentheses.
4. Provide a citation when you use an author's ideas or information in your own writing, and also when you quote an author's exact words.

8. ENGLISH AS A SECOND LANGUAGE (ESL)

8.1 ARTICLES

Articles, also called *determiners,* are words that precede many nouns (and any adjectives that go with the nouns). The greatest problems in using determiners arise when you must choose whether to use *a/an* or *the.* Some general rules will guide you correctly for many sentences, but there are many exceptions to these rules. As you read and hear American English, you will gradually develop an intuition for using articles and determiners. Your instructors, tutors, and fellow students who are native speakers will be able to tell you which determiner "sounds right," so use peer editing and teacher comments

ESL

as much as possible. This is a special use of **collocation**, so you might want to add sentences that are new examples of article use to your vocabulary/collocation log. Nevertheless, the rules below will give you some basic guidance. There are two important things to know about a noun when you choose an article or determiner:

1. **Is the noun definite or indefinite?**
   The article *a/an* is **indefinite**: it is used to refer to an item that is not specific, but can be any one of a group. The article *the* is **definite**: it is used for specific or unique items.

   An airplane flew overhead. It was not **the** plane I was meeting.

   A manager gave me **the** application for **the** job.

   The teachers met to grade **the** papers.

   Exception: Many proper names take no article.

   The programmer worked for **Microsoft.**

   Sevena worked for **the software company.**

2. **Can the noun be counted?**
   Use articles to refer to items that can be counted. If the item cannot be counted, use no article.

   Education is important for a student.

   One of **the** ways to lose **weigh**t is to exercise.

   To cook **rice,** use water and salt; make sure a lid is on the pot.

   Exception: If a number or quantity comes before a count noun, no article is needed.

   Three children sat waiting in **the chairs.**

   The children sat waiting in **three chairs.**

ESL EXERCISE 1   In the following paragraph, add the correct article. If no article is needed, do not add anything.

Even though United States is one country with official language which is called English, many people speak dialect which means that they use language differently from people in other parts of country. Person who lives in North Carolina mountains might not understand person who lives in northern city like New York. Sometimes misunderstanding is funny, but sometimes big problem can result.

8.2   PREPOSITIONS

ESL   Prepositions are very common in English, but there are few rules to tell which preposition is best for a particular sentence. Choosing the right preposition for a particular phrase can be very difficult. To become more fluent in choosing and using prepositions, make a special place in your log of English phrases, idioms, and collocations. Sometimes a preposition adds real meaning to a sentence, and then the choice of preposition is not difficult. For example, *before* allows us to relate ideas about time and space:

> Leslie left **before** lunch.

> Alex stood in line **before** Sam.

Note on dialect variation: The use of prepositions can vary from dialect to dialect. For example, in many parts of the United States, people stand *in line*, but in parts of the Northeast (New York or New Jersey, for example), people stand *on line*. But they are doing the same thing; they are waiting for their turn to do something (maybe to see a bank cashier).

8.2.1 Prepositions with Verbs (Phrasal or Prep + Verbs)

Many times the choice of a preposition depends on the other words around it. This means that the preposition is in an **idiom** or a more general collocation—that is, words that are often used in combination with each other. For example, *run into* can mean meet by chance as well as physically run into. The two sentences below mean very different things:

> Alex **ran into** Leslie at the store. (met by chance)

> The truck **ran into** Mary's car at the corner of Main Street and Rosewood Avenue. (had a wreck)

As you add prepositions to your vocabulary log, notice the differences in meaning in different phrases. *Run into* is an example of a verb + preposition combination called **"phrasal verbs"** or **"prep + verbs."** These types of verbs should be learned as a unit, not as separate words. For example, there are different types of phrasal verbs. Some are called *separable,* which means that the preposition can come after the noun it goes with, too. For example, you can say both *throw away* the garbage and *throw the garbage away*. A list of common phrasal verbs in English is found on pages 406–408. The list shows which prepositions can be separated from their verbs and which cannot.

Verb-Preposition-Verb   When a phrasal verb is followed by another verb, the second verb is usually a gerund or *-ing* verb. It's different when a verb is followed by another verb; in that case, usually the second verb is an infinitive or *to* + verb.

> PHRASAL VERB FOLLOWED BY *-ING* VERB: We **planned on going** to the store.

> PHRASAL VERB FOLLOWED BY *-ING* VERB: We **thought about going** to the store.

> VERB FOLLOWED BY *TO* + VERB: We **planned to go** to the store.

> VERB FOLLOWED BY *TO* + VERB: We **wanted to go** to the store.

> INCORRECT: We planned on to go to the store.

ESL

Prepositions with Verbs: Phrasal or Prep + Verbs

In the list below, verbs are listed with the prepositions that often follow them to make up Prep + Verbs. The verbs are in alphabetical order, and the prepositions are in bold. Words in parentheses are optional (they can be left off without changing the meaning of the verb). Separable prep + verbs are marked with an asterisk (*). The meanings of phrases that might not be clear if you have only a dictionary definition are given in italics.

account **for** one's actions, an idea, or a situation
*add something **to** something else
agree **on** something
agree **with** someone
apologize (**to** someone) (**for** something)
apply (**to** a place) **for** something
*apply oneself **to** something
approve **of** something or someone
argue **with** someone **about** something
arrive **at** a specific place (*airport, stadium, building, room, meeting*)
arrive **in** a larger open place (*a city, country*)
*ask (someone) (**about** something or someone)
ask (someone) (**for** something)
*ask someone **out** (**on** a date or **to** an event)

believe **in** something or someone
belong **to** someone or something
*blame someone **for** something
*blame something **on** someone
*borrow something (**from** someone or a source)

*call someone **back**
*call something **off**
call **on/upon** someone (to do something)
*call someone **up** (*on the telephone*)
care **for** someone or something

*compare something or someone **with/to** someone or something
complain **to** someone **about** something
*compliment someone **on** something
come **from** somewhere (**to** another place)
concentrate **on** something (or someone)
consent **to** something or a verb
consist **of** something
*convince someone **of** something (or **to** verb)
*cross something **out**

decide **on/upon** something
depend **on/upon** someone or something (**for** something or **to** verb)
disagree **with** someone (**over** or **about** something)
*discuss something **with** someone
*divide something **up** (or **into** parts)
* divide something **by** something
*do something **over** (*redo*)
dream **about** something or someone or verb + ing
drop **in** (**on** someone) (*visit informally*)
drop **out** (**of** something) (*quit school*)

escape (**from** something)
*excuse someone (**from** a duty)
*excuse someone (**for** a mistake)

*figure something **out**
*fill something **in**
*fill something **out**
*fill something **up**
*find something **out**
fool **around** (**with** something/ someone, *sometimes with a sexual meaning*)
*forgive someone (**for** something)

get **along** (**with** someone)
get **back** (**from** a place)
get **in/into** (a car)
get **off** (*a means of transportation*)
get **on** (*a means of transportation*)
get **out of** (*a means of transportation or avoiding something*)
get **over** something (*such as an illness or problem*)
get rid **of**
get **through** (*with a task*)
*give something **back** (**to** someone)
give **up** (verb + ing/a goal or project)
graduate (**from** an educational institution)
grow **up**

*hand something **in** (**to** someone)
*hand something **out** (**to** someone)
*hang something **up** (**on** a hanger or hook)
*hang the phone **up**
happen **to** someone (involve someone)
*have respect **for** someone or something
hear **about/of** someone or something
hear **from** someone or something
*help someone (**with** something)
*hide something (**from** someone)
hope **for** something (to happen)
*hunt something/someone **down** (*find*)

insist **on/upon**
*introduce someone **to** someone else or something new
*invite someone **to** (an event/a place /verb)

keep **on** (verb + ing) (*continue*)
know **about** something or someone

laugh **at** something/someone
*leave something **out**
listen **for** (*something/someone*)
listen **to** (*something/someone*)
look **after** someone (*watch, care for*)
look **at** (*something/someone*)
look **down on** someone (*disregard*)
look **for** (*something/someone*)
look **forward to** (something/an event/verb + ing)
*look something/someone **over** (*inspect*)
*look some information **up**

*make something **up** (*invent, create*)
make **up** (with someone) (*settle disagreements or differences*)
make **up** one's face (*use cosmetics*)
matter **to** someone
(what is the) matter **with** someone or something (*what is the problem*)

object **to** something/an idea/verb + ing

*pay money **back** (**to** someone) (**for** something)
pay **for** something
*pick something **up** (**from** a place or **for** someone)
plan **on** something/an event
point **at/to** something or someone
protect something or someone (**from** something or someone)
provide **for** something/someone

*provide someone **with** something
*put something **away**
*put something **back** (*in the original place*)
*put something **down** (in a place)
*put someone or an idea **down** (*criticize*)
*put something **off** (*postpone*)
*put someone **off** (*avoid giving a direct answer to someone or discourage someone*)

recover **from** (*an illness/an error*)
rely **on/upon** someone or something (*for something*)
remind someone **of/about** something
result **from** something
run **into** something or someone (*meet by chance*)
run **into** something or someone (*crash or wreck*)
*run someone **off** (*make someone leave*)
run **out** (**of** something)
run **over** something or someone
run **over** (**to** a place) (*visit*)

search **for** something/someone
see **about** something/someone
*separate something or someone **from** someone or something else
*shut something **off**
speak **to** someone (**about** something)
stare **at** something or someone
*start (something) **over**
substitute (something) **for** something/someone
*subtract something **from** (something else)

take care **of** something
*take something **off** (of something)
talk (**to/with** someone) (**about** something/someone/verb + ing)

talk **of/about** something or someone or verb + ing
*tear something **down** (*destroy*)
*tear something **off** (*of something else, like a credit card receipt*)
*tear something **out** (*of something, like paper out of a notebook*)
*tear something **up** (*into pieces*)
*tell (someone) (**about** something)
*thank someone (**for** something)
think **about/of** something/someone/an idea
*throw something **away** or **out**
*tie something/someone **up**
travel **to** a place
*try something **on** (*clothing*)
*try something **out** (*an idea*)
*turn something **down** (*decrease volume or speed*)
*turn someone or something **down** (*refuse*)
*turn something **off** (*a machine, light, noise*)
*turn someone **off** (*offend or repel someone*)
*turn something **on** (*a machine, light, noise*)
*turn someone **on** (*arouse, usually with a sexual meaning*)
*turn someone **on to** something (*make aware of*)
*turn something **up** (*increase volume or speed*)

wait **for** something/someone
wait **on** someone (serve; same as *wait for* in some dialects)
*wake (someone) **up**
watch **out** (*be careful*)
watch **out** (**for** something or someone)
worry **about** someone or something
write (**to** someone) (**about** something)
*write something **down**

Differences Across Languages   One way languages differ that does not seem to follow a pattern is the use of prepositions to add another element to a sentence. For example, English allows some verbs like *tell* or *give* to have two objects without requiring a preposition for the second object: *Tony told Alex a story.* However, not all verbs that express similar ideas have similar patterns. For example you can *explain the answer to him*; you cannot *explain him the answer.* Verbs which can have two objects without the use of a preposition are called *double object verbs.* But even these double object verbs occur with prepositions (usually *to* or *for*): *Tony told a story to Alex.* There are only a few double object verbs in English and most verbs with two objects will need a preposition to express the second object, but verbs like *tell* and *give* are very common.

8.2.2 Prepositions with Other Kinds of Words

Adjectives   Many adjectives occur with prepositions when the situation that the adjective is describing is being explained in more detail. For example, sentences like *Marie is angry* give less information than sentences like *Marie is angry **at Tony*** or *Marie is angry **about the meeting.*** It is best to learn the whole adjective + preposition phrase as a unit. You can enter common uses of adjectives + preposition phrases in your English log to help you remember these phrases.

Nouns (Possessive *of*)   English has two ways to express possession and other related meanings: the apostrophe + *s* (*Tony's friend*) and the preposition *of* (*a friend of Tony*). Possessive *'s* is discussed on pages 363–365.

ESL EXERCISE 2   **In the following paragraph, correct the use of prepositions and prep + verbs.**

When Adam first arrived to this college, he insisted to buy new books. He worried for having the books because he hoped on a good grade in his classes. When he went at the bookstore, he looked to many books. He didn't want to leave out any of his courses. He listened at the salesman explain around new books and used books, and finally Adam decided for the ones he needed to buy. While he stood in line, he met a friend who introduced him with another student who wanted to sell his used books.

ESL EXERCISE 3   **In the following paragraph, correct the use of prepositions.**

Many people have difficulty by living in a climate that is different from their home. They may complain for the cold or the heat. If they become ill, they blame on their illnesses to the climate. They fool over the thermostat in their homes. After living in a new climate for several years, they may get used of the new climate, and may no longer ask of changes in the office's temperature.

8.3   VERB TENSE

Verbs in English can be simple (or one word), but they can also be longer (combining helping verbs and verb endings). Sections 1.1, 1.3, 3.1, and 4.1 give some basic information about verbs, but additionally you will need to understand some other qualities of English verbs:

- **tense** (the time when a verb happens)
- **aspect** (how the verb happens)
- **modals** (the possibility of something happening)
- **voice** (whether the subject does the action or received the action of the verb)

First, be sure that you understand each of these qualities separately and then see how they are combined.

8.3.1 Tense

Tense in English identifies when an event happens or describes a state. It can be in the **past**, the **present**, or **future**. One form of the future is a modal: *will*. There is another way to express future that is very common in American English: *be going to* + verb. The form of *be* agrees with the subject. In the last example below, *are* agrees with students.

PRESENT The students **write** in their journals twice a week.

PAST The students **wrote** in their journals twice a week.

FUTURE (MODAL) The students **will write** in their journals twice a week.

FUTURE (*BE GOING TO*) The students **are going to write** in their journals twice a week.

If a verb is present tense, and the subject is, or can be replaced by, *he, she,* or *it,* the verb must agree with the subject and have an *-s* ending (see Section 4.1). In the example below, *the student* can be replaced by *she.* This form of the verb is called third person singular (present tense).

THIRD PERSON SINGULAR PRESENT The student **writes** in her journal every evening.

Writers use past tense to describe and narrate an event or situation that occurred in the past and is over. Notice how the specific age of *twelve* sets the scene for this narrative.

When I **was** twelve, I **broke** my leg. I **slipped** on the playground on a cold winter morning and **fell.** The bone near my ankle **snapped** with a loud "pop!" Even my friends **heard** it. The teachers **called** my parents, who **came** quickly . . .

Writers use present tense to describe an event or situation that is typical and that can be predicted to occur in the same way again. Notice the phrase *every spring* in the first sentence:

The alligators **come** back to the nesting grounds **every spring.** The grass **grows** thick again and the egrets **build** nests in the trees over the water.

ESL

If a chick **falls** out of the nest, an alligator **is** there. When the chicks **are** mature and **fly** well, the alligators **move** back to the black water swamp.

8.3.2 Aspect

Aspect locates an event in relation to another time, often the present. *Progressive* or *continuous* aspects show that events or states are happening at a particular time. *Perfect* aspect shows that events are completed by a certain time. Progressive and perfect are illustrated below, along with combinations of tense and aspect.

Progressive   **Progressive** verbs contain a form of *be* and add *-ing* to the main verb.

Li **is** work**ing.**

Gloria **was** listen**ing** to the radio.

Thomas **will be** earn**ing** more next year.

I **am** try**ing** to help.

Progressive aspect focuses on the action of an event. *Note:* When people write quickly, they sometimes leave out the *be* verb. Be careful in your writing to include both parts of the progressive. Remember that aspect is an additional quality of verbs, so they may also have tense and modals.

In the example below, the action of writing is occurring now (today or this semester):

PRESENT PROGRESSIVE **Today** some of the students **are writing** in their journals and others **are starting** to prewrite the next essay.

This semester we **are studying** *Don Quixote.*

In the example below, the action of writing was an activity in the past (the class period, the course, or the semester).

PAST PROGRESSIVE The teacher **was conferencing** with some students while other students **were revising** their rough drafts.

In the example below, future progressive represents a prediction or guess.

FUTURE PROGRESSIVE Lena **will be sleeping** if you arrive after ten o'clock.

What is the difference between progressive and habitual? Progressive aspect is most commonly used for events in the present—events that are going on as we speak, but may end at some definite time. On the other hand, the simple present tense (one word) often suggests that an event happens regularly, or that it is habitual. In the following pair, the first sentence suggests that this is a goal of the course, not a specific activity:

ESL

The students **learn** about documenting quotes (every semester when this course is taught).

The students **are learning** about documenting quotes (during this class period).

Simple present is most commonly used for verbs that describe a state, not an activity—verbs such as *is, are, seem, taste, feel,* and others. Using present progressive for this kind of verb suggests that something is not typical about the situation.

Miles **lives** in Charleston.

Miles **is living** in Charleston. [but he hasn't always]

Sally **is** a cooperative child.

Sally **is being** a cooperative child. [but she isn't usually or might not be expected to be cooperative in all situations]

Perfect   **Perfect aspect** has two parts: *have* and a past participle ending of the verb (an *-en* or an *-ed* ending or an irregular form such as *bought* (see Section 3.2.2 for more about past participles of irregular verbs). Perfect means that an activity or situation has been completed by a certain time or began to happen at a certain time. Many verbs must be stated in the present perfect because we often discuss one event as happening before some other event.

PRESENT PERFECT Maureen **has lived** in Charleston since last summer.
                 present perfect   *began in past*
                 [The situation was true in the past (last summer) and is also still true now.]

If the past event was an activity (rather than a state), the verb may also be progressive. In this example, notice that college graduation is a one-time event, but working is an activity that can start in the past and be continuing in the present.

PRESENT PREFECT PROGRESSIVE Maureen **has been working** with that
                             present perfect

company since she **graduated** from college.
            simple past

Past perfect is often used to relate two events in the past, especially if one is a specific event and the other is ongoing. In this example, an ongoing past activity (*had been working*) is related to an activity that happened at one specific time in the past (*decided*).

PAST PERFECT Maureen **had been working** in Washington, but she
              past perfect progressive

decided it was too expensive.
simple past

The future tense can also occur with the perfect aspect. Future perfect makes a prediction that an action will be completed by a certain time in the future. Future perfect can also be progressive.

FUTURE PERFECT Caroline **will have finished** her driver's education class
future perfect

by December.
definite time in the future

She **will have been practicing** for four months by December.
future perfect progressive

ESL EXERCISE 4 | **In the following paragraph, correct the use of verb tense and aspect.**

Tomorrow we will going to our new apartment. We are owning too much furniture, so we will hiring a van to help us move. We will had worked all day packing things when the van arrives. Last time we were moving, we had tried to do all the work ourselves. We are having better judgment this time, even though it will be costing us more money. However, we will saved money if the dishes are not breaked and the chairs is not lose.

8.3.3 Modals

Modals express possibility, obligation, or inferences about what the speaker believes to be true.

The Use of Modals

Modals are often used in polite forms (instead of simple commands).

Modals can mean different things in different sentences. The context makes clear which meaning is intended.

When modals are combined with other verb forms, the meaning usually changes.

Modals do not combine with tense, although some modals (such as *could* or *would*) look as if they could be a past tense form. Also, using modals with the perfect aspect can express a past meaning (for more on Modals, see page 368). One modal, *can,* does not occur with perfect aspect. The following list (continued on p. 414) gives the meanings of modals with other aspects:

| **Modal** | *They **could go**.* | (ability, possibility, permission; a polite form) |
| **Modal + progressive** | *They **could be going**.* | (a prediction or guess) |

ESL

| **Modal + perfect** | *They **could have gone.*** | (a guess or a past possibility or a missed possibility) |
| **Modal + perfect + progressive** | *They **could have been going.*** | (a missed or past possibility or a guess) |

There are two types of modals: true modals that are simple (one word + verb) and phrasal modals (several words + verb or infinitive).

SIMPLE **might** read

PHRASAL **might be able** to read

Only one modal can be used with each verb, but a simple modal can occur with a phrasal modal:

Lena **might be able** to read that story by tomorrow.

Note: Using two modals, such as *might could,* is a regional spoken dialect, and not written, unless you are quoting someone who speaks this local variety of English.
The following modals occur with bare verb forms (bare verbs do not have tense; they are usually the same as the simple present):

can

could

had better

may

might

must

shall

should

will (future)

would

The following phrasal verbs are like modals, but they occur with an infinitive (*to* + verb). (The forms preceded by an asterisk can be stated in different tenses.) They usually have the same meaning as a simple modal:

*be able to (can)

*be going to (will)

*be supposed to (should)

*have to (must)

*have got to (must)

ESL

ought to (should)

supposed to (should)

used to (would)

In speaking, modals are often used to express polite requests for oneself:

May I go? **Could** I go? **Can** I go?

I **would** like some coffee.

Some modals are used to ask someone to do something:

Could you do this? [the speaker is not sure you can]

Would you do this? [the speaker assumes you can]

Can you do this? [a little more informal than **could**]

Some modals express obligation, advice, or necessity:

All students **should** keep their journals up to date. [advice, an obligation]

All students **must** take the placement exam. [a necessity]

All students **have to** take the final exam. [a necessity]

All students **had to** take the final exam. [a past necessity]

All students **have got to** turn in their final essays on Monday. [a necessity]

Some modals express degrees of certainty:

■ With verbs that show a state rather than an activity, *must, may, might,* and *could* represent a belief or a guess.

Maureen **must be** tired; she usually goes to bed later. [sure]

Maureen **could be** sick. [less sure]

■ With actions, the perfect is used to express certainty or guesses.

Maureen **must have done** her assignment. [sure]

Maureen **could have done** well on the test. [less sure]

Maureen **might not have gone** to the library. [less sure]

Some modals show predictions can be made about the future:

Maureen **will do well** on the test. [sure future]

Maureen **should do well** on the test. [sure future]

ESL

Obligation plus perfect implies expectations may not be met:

> Maureen **should have done well** on the test, but maybe she didn't. [unsure future]

Some modals change their meaning when they are negative, and others do not:

> NEED We **have to tell** the rest of the class about the project before the end of the semester.

> NO NEED We **do not (don't) have to tell** the rest of the class about the project before the end of the semester.

> NEED We **must tell** the rest of the class about the project before the end of the semester.

> PROHIBITED We **must not (mustn't) tell** the rest of the class about the project before the end of the semester.

Some other modals with special meanings are often used:

- *Used to* expresses a typical past state or activity that is no longer true.

  > They **used to** live in Illinois.

  > Before Jim got ill, he and Marie **used to** travel more.

- *Supposed to* expresses an obligation, like *should,* but also suggests that the obligation may not be met.

  > They were **supposed to** arrive at noon, but they didn't.

- *Had better* is usually stronger than other modals of obligation or advice.

  > Students **had better** get their papers in on time, or their grades will be lowered.

ESL EXERCISE 5 | In the following paragraph, correct the use of modals.

> Lee must hopes to make a high salary, because he will majoring in computer science. He thinks he ought start at a salary as high as many people make with several years' experience because he goes to study many new aspects of computers. He can be very unhappy if he received a lower salary. He can would make more than his friends who study art, but they might enjoys their work, even if their salaries may be low.

8.3.4 Voice

Verbs in English also have the quality of "voice," which tells whether the subject does the action of the verb (**active voice**) or receives the action of the verb (**passive voice**).

> ACTIVE The <u>dinosaur</u> ate the tree.
>   [*dinosaur*, the subject, performs the action]

ESL

PASSIVE The <u>tree</u> was eaten by the dinosaur. (*tree*, the subject, receives the action)

Passive sentences use the helping verb *be* and the past participle form of the verb occurs (usually the *-ed* or *-en* form, or an irregular form like *bought* from *buy*—see Section 3.2.2 for more on verb parts and endings). The agent (the doer of the action) occurs at the end of the sentence after the preposition *by*, but it can be left out. Many times people use passive voice because only the thing affected by the verb is important and they want to leave out the agent or they don't know the agent.

> The accident occurred around midnight. The windshield of the mini-van **was broken** and the fender of the hatch back **was smashed.** A guardrail **was bent** and **may have to be replaced.** Fortunately, the teenaged drivers of the two cars **were not** seriously **injured,** although they **were taken** to the hospital for observation. The parents of the drivers **have been notified.**

The form of *be* depends on the modal, tense, and aspect of the verb in the active form.

TENSE, ASPECT (MODAL)	ACTIVE	PASSIVE
Past, simple	The lawyer **wrote** the letter.	The letter **was written** [by the lawyer].
Past, simple	Someone **knocked** over my bicycle.	My bicycle **was knocked** over [by someone].
Past, perfect	The company **has bought** the building.	The building **has been bought** [by the company].
Past, progressive	Someone **was telling** the rumors at work.	Rumors **were being told** at work [by someone].
Past, simple, possibility	The class **might finish** the project soon.	The project **might be finished** [by the class] soon.

If a verb has more than one object, only the first object can become the passive subject.

ACTIVE	PASSIVE
The family sent a **nice birthday present** to Caroline.	**A nice birthday present** was sent to Caroline [by the family].
The family gave **Caroline** a nice birthday present.	**Caroline** was given a nice birthday present [by the family].

ESL

Sometimes *get* occurs with past participles with a passive-like meaning:

The couple **got married** last week [by someone].

The children **are getting excited** about the state fair [by someone/something].

The squirrel almost **got run over** in the street [by a car].

8.3.5 Verb Form Combinations

Helping verbs are often combined, as some examples have shown. The different forms must be placed in a certain order: tense or modal, perfect, progressive. Passive can follow either tense or a modal. The endings that express the concepts of tense, perfect, progressive, and passive are added to the verb after the helper or modal.

Past	+	**Progressive**	+	**Passive**	+	**Verb**
Past form		*be* + *ing*		*be* + *-en/-ed*		eat
was		*being*				eat*en*

The corn **was being eaten** by wild animals all summer so none is left now.

For more details about verb endings, see these sections of the handbook: Past forms (pp. 369–371), irregular verbs (pp. 371–372), present third person singular *-s* (Section 3.2.1). Also, you should check every sentence with a helping verb for endings on the verb, since any verb using the helpers *be* or *have* also needs an ending (see pp. 365–369). Look as well at subject-verb agreement (pp. 372–374). You should keep a record of mistakes you make using verb forms in your editing log to help you discover any pattern of error in verb forms.

ESL EXERCISE 6   **In the following paragraph, correct the verb usage.**

I am owning a car now, and it can being a big responsibility. I must to worry about gasoline, repairs, and insurance. Because my car is paint white, it is getting dirty very easily. My brother teaches me how to take care of the car. He is driving to work every day, and he must parks in a garage, which is also costing him more money. One day I was driving my car and I can hear a terrible sound. I was very worried, but then I saw that the door was open and the seat belt dragged on the road.

24 Applying the Tools
Additional Exercises

The exercises in this chapter are based on essays and paragraphs that are examples of both good and bad writing. Most focus on specific types of problems related to revision as well as editing and proofreading.

These exercises were designed to be used with the checklists in Chapters 21 and 22. Your instructor may ask you to work independently with the exercises. If so, you may want to use these along with the editing log (pp. 341–346) and the Handbook (Chapter 23). Once you have determined the kinds of problems you need to practice solving, find the exercise that focuses on that type of problem. Complete one paragraph of an exercise, and then check the answers (starting on p. 605). Then try the next paragraph. If you need to practice proofreading rather than focus on specific problems, the last two essays contain a mixture of problems.

REVISING FOR THESIS SUPPORT AND EDITING FOR SENTENCE BOUNDARIES

Reading: "Magic and AIDS: Presumed Innocent" by Michael Bronski

Prompt

In this essay, Bronski suggests that the media often distort the truth. Do you agree or disagree with this view? Use your own ideas and observations as well as Bronski's to support your view.

EXERCISE 24.1 In the following essay, read carefully to recognize the problems listed below, as well as any others you may notice. When you have determined the revision and editing needed, make the necessary improvements. You will need to rewrite the essay (or the parts you change) on a separate sheet of paper.

Revision Problem: Relating support paragraphs to thesis

Editing Problem: Sentence boundaries—fragments

Be Fair to Teens

"Teenagers set off bomb!" "Fifteen-year-old held in shooting!" Headlines such as these appear every day. Suggesting that teenagers are violent, angry people. Newspapers make similar judgments about AIDS victims, according to Michael Bronksi. In his essay "Magic and AIDS: Presumed Innocent." Bronski shows how the media increase prejudice by portraying some people with AIDS as innocent. Others as guilty. He says that the media's unfair judgment creates problems for everyone, and I agree. I believe that the media are not accurate in many cases.

Sometimes the media make innocent people appear guilty. By presenting stereotypes of groups. Bronski shows how the media make it seem that some people deserve AIDS: "Sympathy for people with AIDS has *always* been predicated upon an understanding of how they contracted the virus." TV news also stereotypes teenagers as violent. People who are always involved in crimes. If it's a young person who commits a crime. That person's age is part of the headline. Whether it's a bomb threat or a drive-by shooting. We never see headlines saying "middle-aged man holds up bank," or "40-year-old woman held in husband's murder." Why is age always mentioned when teenagers are the suspects? To stereotype teens as the media often do. This is a way of distorting the truth.

But sometimes the media are accurate and fair. For example, natural disasters. When a hurricane or flood comes, we need the media to tell us about the problem. If we know that a hurricane will come to our city, we can prepare. Storing water, buying batteries, and putting up shutters. Even in the case of diseases, Bronski shows how media could help prevent the spread of AIDS. Describing real safety precautions like abstinence, use of condoms, and regular testing. Which is one way that media can be helpful and accurate.

With fair reporting, media can be an asset to the community. Media should focus on being helpful to readers and viewers. By giving us real information that we can use to live safer lives.

| EXERCISE 24.2 | In the following essay, read carefully to recognize the problems listed below, as well as any others you may notice. When you have determined the revision and editing needed, make the necessary improvements. You will need to rewrite the essay (or the parts you change) on a separate sheet of paper. |

Revision Problem: Relating support paragraphs to thesis

Editing Problem: Sentence boundaries—run-ons

Sports and the Media

Once there was a time when children looked at Michael Jordan as a real hero, every kid wanted to "be like Mike!" Athletes like Michael Jordan and Magic Johnson get special treatment from the media, suggests Michael Bronski in "Magic and AIDS: Presumed Innocent." Bronski focuses on athletes like Magic Johnson he misses the media's unfavorable pictures of other athletes like Mike

Tyson and Charles Barkley, who are shown to be as violent as anyone. I don't think the media always distort when they describes athletes, they actually show us many views of athletes, both good and bad.

The media may sometimes give extra credit to a well-known athlete as they did when Michael Jordan left baseball and returned to basketball, fans and media alike were so happy for his return that there was no criticism they only praised him. Also, Bronski shows how media immediately began to portray Magic as an innocent victim of bad women with AIDS, they didn't focus on Magic's own irresponsible actions of having unsafe, promiscuous sex. However, other athletes are shown as bad by the media. Mike Tyson and Pete Rose both committed crimes. Few papers sympathized with Tyson against the charge of rape many sportscasters criticized Rose for gambling.

But why should we expect sports heroes to be wonderful people? Michael Jordan was hired because he was a good basketball player, not because he was a good person. Many people live moral, honest lives, for example, my father always worked hard and defended his country in the Vietnam War. But my father isn't famous because he can't help a team win the NBA championship. Charles Barkley was another famous basketball player he was often criticized for rough playing. He asked why we expect basketball players to be good role models just because they are good at sports. Bronski says that "media declared Johnson . . . the new hero of the AIDS epidemic," does it make sense to call him a hero and a role model just because he's a good ball player?

So the media isn't really unfair to athletes, we see descriptions of both good and bad people as athletes, not just a distorted picture of one kind of person. The media does not stereotype athletes.

EXERCISE 24.3

In the following essay, read carefully to recognize the problems listed below, as well as any others you may notice. When you have determined the revision and editing needed, make the necessary improvements. You will need to rewrite the essay (or the parts you change) on a separate sheet of paper.

<u>Revision Problem:</u> Relating support paragraphs to thesis

<u>Editing Problem:</u> Sentence boundaries—fragments and run-ons

Be Fair

Do the media distort the truth? Bronski, in "Magic and AIDS: Presumed Innocent," says that the media are unfair to people with AIDS. By classifying them as "innocent" and "guilty." He shows how some famous people were considered "innocent" while others were "guilty," I agree that the media often make unfair judgments.

The media do judge AIDS patients unfairly. Bronski describes how gays and drug users are blamed for contracting AIDS, other people with the disease, like Kimberly Bergalis, are seen as being innocent victims. Bronski says that media "distinguish between those people with AIDS who are morally culpable for their illness and those who 'truly' deserve sympathy and compassion." This is an accurate statement, I've seen this happen in my own family. When my cousin contracted AIDS. Because he might have gotten the disease from drug use, some people in my family thought he was a bad person, they never visited him or helped him in any way. But we didn't really know how he got AIDS, so they weren't being fair. To treat him as a guilty person.

If we don't know about a person's life, we shouldn't judge them for being sick. There are many ways to get AIDS. Including blood transfusions and other things. Maybe my cousin had not gotten AIDS from drug use. We should not have blamed him when he need our help, instead we should have brought him food, medicine, and moral support. As some members of the family tried to do. As Bronski says, we shouldn't put AIDS victims into categories. Especially if we don't know how they got the disease.

So I do agree that the media is unfair. In the way that it stereotypes and categorizes AIDS victims. I hope everyone will realize that AIDS victims need all the sympathy and support we can give them. Without worrying about how they got the disease. "All people with AIDS Are Innocent" is a good slogan from ACT UP, according to Bronski, we should all accept it.

REVISING FOR FOCUS IN EACH SUPPORTING PARAGRAPH AND EDITING FOR WORD ENDINGS

Reading: "*Getting Off the Welfare Carousel*" *by Teresa McCrary*

Prompt

McCrary explains many reasons why welfare is necessary for single mothers. Decide whether you believe that a single parent can support a child without government assistance, and write an essay defending your idea. Use your own ideas and observations as well as McCrary's to support your view.

EXERCISE 24.4

In the following essay, read carefully to recognize the problems listed below, as well as any others you may notice. When you have determined the revision and editing needed, make the necessary improvements. You will need to rewrite the essay (or the parts you change) on a separate sheet of paper.

Revision Problem: Paragraph unity and difference

Editing Problem: Verb endings (–s)

All Alone?

You're nineteen, you've just graduated from high school, and you're not married. Now you discovers that you're pregnant. Will you be able to raise your child on your own? "No," says Teresa McCrary, author of "Getting Off the Welfare Carousel." She believe that an uneducated parent must have government assistance. I agree that welfare is necessary for single parents who is young and alone.

First of all, a young, single parent who is uneducated will need to continue their education to be able to get a good job in the future. This mean attending college, and while the parent is in class, who will cares for the child? The parent also have to do homework, because college is much more difficult than high school. You really needs to be dedicated and give your whole attention to college, because instructors expects you to do work for every class. You may have to read several chapters of economics, work ten hard math problems, and write an English paper in one evening.

Also, a single parent have many expenses, and often can't afford to do everything without some assistance from welfare. But welfare have too many rules and really try to hold people back. Welfare expects the parent to report any gifts or family assistance, including money from the child's father, according to McCrary. Welfare need to be more realistic, because children needs both parents to grow up happy and healthy. A mother has to be both mother and father, and that's difficult. She have to do a lot of school work and still have time to play with the children and help them with their homework. That is not easy.

Last of all, minimum wage jobs don't pay enough to live. As McCrary say, when people makes minimum wage, "the whole paycheck would go to housing and job expenses," and it is very hard not to be able to buy your baby all the things she need and also not to buy the things you need for yourself. My advice is to wait until you are married or has a well-paying job before you have children. You should not get involved with boys if you are not ready to be a parent. It is hard for a young woman because there is a lot of peer pressure to be popular, but she have to be strong and respect herself. She can't lets her boyfriend talk her into having sex if she don't feel ready.

In conclusion, single mothers can't raise children without welfare. It's too hard to work, go to school, and be a parent, so some government assistance is necessary.

EXERCISE 24.5 **In the following essay, read carefully to recognize the problems listed on page 424, as well as any others you may notice. When you have determined the revision and editing needed, make the necessary improvements. You will need to rewrite the essay (or the parts you change) on a separate sheet of paper.**

<u>Revision Problem:</u> Paragraph unity and difference

<u>Editing Problem:</u> Verb endings (*-ed*)

You Can Do It!

Raising a child is very difficult for any parent, but especially for one who must worked or attend school. It's even more difficult for parents who are unmarry. Teresa McCrary, in " Getting Off the Welfare Carousel," says that government assistance is require for young single mothers to be good parents. Perhaps this is true, but I believe that it is possible to be a good single parent without relying on welfare.

The first requirement for survival as a single parent is a stable income. McCrary says that single parents "could hold down a minimum wage job, unarguably the hardest work for the least amount of money," with no medical benefits, but not all jobs have these problems. When I graduate from high school, I already had work for the same company for a year in retail sales, and I was promote to supervisor, which gaved me higher pay, regular working hours, and medical benefits. When I realize that I was pregnant, I was afraid I would losed my job, but I only miss six weeks at work. Fortunately my aunt and my grandmother help me financially, so I was able to survived without welfare until I returned to work. With a good job and family support, I did not needed government assistance.

A single parent does need assistance, but it can come from family instead of the government. McCrary points out that "those of us who do not have a man in our lives do the emotional job of both mother and father." The government cannot give emotional assistance but your family can. When I was feeling lonely and sad because I want to go out and buy nice clothes, my aunt help by giving me some money to buy a new coat. I was really worry about being able to meet all my expenses, but my grandmother also helped. She cover the rent after the baby was born. My family was always ready to helped me when I needed them. I will never forget how they all assist me, and it seem much better to me because it didn't come from the government.

So McCrary was wrong when she claim that single parents must relied on government assistance. If a parent has good family support, they will not required welfare to be able to supported the child and raise it well.

EXERCISE 24.6   In the following essay, read carefully to recognize the problems listed on page 425, as well as any others you may notice. When you have determined the revision and editing needed, make the necessary improvements. You will need to rewrite the essay (or the parts you change) on a separate sheet of paper.

<u>Revision Problem:</u> Paragraph unity

<u>Editing Problem:</u> Word endings (*–'s* and *–s*)

Welfare and Single Parents

Can single parent's raise a child well without the governments assistance? In my experience, thats a very hard thing to do. In Teresa McCrary essay, "Getting Off the Welfare Carousel," she explain's why single parents may need welfare to be good parent's. This is true. Single parent's must have some assistance to be able to raise a child well, and many time its the government that must provide assistance.

A single parent who is young and alone will have a very hard time. There are so many problem's to face. McCrary says that a minimum wage job "will not pay for housing costs, health care, child care, transportation, and work clothes that an untrained, uneducated woman need's to support even one child." My friends situation was similar to McCrarys. Anna was a young single mother and at first she didn't want to tell her parents that she was pregnant. Annas parent's had always expected her to be a good student. She was in the church choir and she knew that her parent's would be disappointed with her. When she heard about Anna pregnancy, her mother cried, but then her mother and father told her that she could bring the baby to live at the parents' house. She had a very hard time with the baby birth and almost died, but the doctor's did a C-section. When we found out that she'd be all right, we were so happy. We loved the baby when we saw it's face. Its times like this that let you know who your friends are. But then the next problem was that the baby father wouldn't give her any money, because he wasnt sure that it was his baby. So then my friend had to apply for welfare, but then her baby's father changed his mind.

Also single parents have many lonely feeling's. My friend was used to going out with her friends every weekend. Of course she should have been more careful and used birth control, so she wouldn't have gotten pregnant. However, some teenagers' use birth control and get pregnant anyway. Thats why some people think teenagers should not have sex, and I agree. You can't tell when you might become pregnant. McCrary say's that a single parent has to be both mother and father and I agree that government assistance is necessary.

So there are very many problem's for young single parents, including money and emotions. For these reasons, the government assistance is necessary, especially for young mothers who can't raise a child alone. The childs welfare is the most important thing.

EXERCISE 24.7   **In the following essay, read carefully to recognize the problems listed below, as well as any others you may notice. When you have determined the revision and editing needed, make the necessary improvements. You will need to rewrite the essay (or the parts you change) on a separate sheet of paper.**

Revision Problem: Paragraph unity and difference

Editing Problem: Word endings

The Successful Single Parent

Diaper's, babysitter's, doctor's, clothes—there are so many expense for a parent. If the parents is young and single, they may not believed that they can manage these expense's all alone. Teresa McCrary, in "Getting Off the Welfare Carousel," says "any mother, married or single, will tell you that motherhood is a career in itself." I agree that raising a child alone is difficult, but its not necessary for every single parent to has government assistance. If the parent use all the resources available to them, then they won't need to depends on welfare.

Many necessity of life are expensive, but if a parent try, she can often choose a cheaper alternative. For example, baby formula is a very costly way to feeds a baby, but breastfeeding is free, and its better for the baby health. For older childrens dinner's, a dinner at McDonalds cost $5.00 per child, and a frozen dinner cost $3.00, but vegetable soup can be prepare at home for about $1.00 per child, especially if big pots is cook and frozen for later use. Clothes can be bought on sale, pass down from friend's, or bought at second-hand store—sometimes these are just as good as new one's. The librarys books is free, and the child will remember an hour spent with the parent reading *The Cat in the Hat* long after he forget the latest Pokemon or computer game. McCrary say that a single parent can't meet all the expenses', but a parent whos careful can takes care of a child on very little money.

Its also difficult to manage the responsibility of raising a child if a parents alone. As McCrary say, sick children is a real problem for a working parents, because most day care's and schools dont wants sick children. All parents can planned ahead for their children normal childhood disease's and use family, friends, church and community as back-up child care. Parent's can get to know other single parents who's working hours are different so that they can trade babysitting for emergencies. The parent will know that the child have receive good care and met many different kind's of people. The parents also feels less lonely and isolate.

The worst problems for single parents is facing the future. A young parent can become discourage if they work at a low-paying job and comes home to face a parent responsibilities alone. Life seem to be a trap, or a cycle without an end. Its true that with the government assistance, a parent can go to college full time to prepare for a new career and improves her children future. McCrary essay describe's how she use her time to be a good parent; she go to college to be educate so she eventually won't need to be on welfare. But many parent also takes one or two courses at a time, when the children is in school. Many college's now offers courses on the internet or on videotape, so parents actually takes the whole course at home. Babysitting can be easier to arrange if a parent takes a class that meet only once a week, and some colleges offer cheap daycare for students children.

Not every single parent are ready for working hard and making sacrifice's. Just being a responsible parent is a big enough challenge for some young parents. However, for those who really want independence, its possible to be a good parent without government assistance. Parent's who aren't assist by the government has to plan carefully, but they can succeed.

REVISING FOR PARAGRAPH DEVELOPMENT AND EDITING FOR AGREEMENT, WORD CHOICE, AND PUNCTUATION OF TITLES AND QUOTATIONS

Reading: "Measuring Success" by Renee Loth

Prompt

What is success? Explain how you would define success. Use your own ideas and observations as well as Loth's to support your view.

EXERCISE 24.8

In the following essay, read carefully to recognize the problems listed below, as well as any others you may notice. When you have determined the revision and editing needed, make the necessary improvements. You will need to rewrite the essay (or the parts you change) on a separate sheet of paper.

Revision Problem: Paragraph development

Editing Problem: Pronoun and verb agreement

My Successful Career

Success—what do it mean? In "Measuring Success," Renee Loth says that "fame and money" is what success mean to her, but I think it's having a good career.

First a good career is one that's meaningful, not just a job. It is just a way to make money but a career really means something to you.

Second a good career is secure. You know you can feel sure about it. Loth says you change and things change. I don't want a bad change to happen, like losing my career. One of the things I want to accomplish are having security.

Third, a good career is suited to me. I want a job that's right for me, and I'm willing to wait and look for them. I don't want to settle for a job that's not the best one for my abilities.

So success to me means all of this. Having a career that's meaningful, secure, and suited to me are my ideas of success.

EXERCISE 24.9 **In the following essay, read carefully to recognize the problems listed below, as well as any others you may notice. When you have determined the revision and editing needed, make the necessary improvements. You will need to rewrite the essay (or the parts you change) on a separate sheet of paper.**

<u>Revision Problem:</u> Paragraph development

<u>Editing Problem:</u> Confused words

Success Is a Family

According to Loth, "success . . . means different things to different people." I have a clear idea of success. To me, success would be having a loving family.

Whatever job I may have, even if I'm a star basketball player like Michael Jordan or a rich computer genius like Bill Gates, I want feel successful if I'm lonely. I'd need my wife too share my success if I make money or become well-known. If I'm poor and unknown, a loving wife would change failure to success. My wife can laugh at my jokes, eat the hole diner that I cook, and somehow no when I'm tired or sick. I don't know what I would of done without her, but life would be to hard. There are times also when she shares her own success with me, so when she gets a raise or gets promoted, I feel good, too. She and I do things together, like collecting food for a church project or going to the mountains for a walk. We where meant too be together. My wife is the first peace of my success.

Along with my wife, I have a vision of another part of success, which is raising a family. We have all ready one son and plan to have another child soon. If my children grow up healthy and happy, I'll have another big part of my success. If your like me, you'll know that children can make you a knew person. I've really changed myself since my son was born so that I'll be ready to help him as he grows up. Whenever I feel like being lazy at work or going to a party instead of studying for an exam at school, I think about the things I want to do for my son and I'm ready to work hard. Thanks to him, I past all my coarses this semester. I want to be able to send my children to college and I want to here them say they admire me. If I can do these things for them, I'll be a real success.

So money, fame, and other things may make some people feel successful, but for me, success is my family. Everything I do is for them. There my hole life.

EXERCISE 24.10

In the following essay, read carefully to recognize the problems listed below, as well as any others you may notice. When you have determined the revision and editing needed, make the necessary improvements. You will need to rewrite the essay (or the parts you change) on a separate sheet of paper.

<u>Revision Problem:</u> Paragraph development

<u>Editing Problem:</u> Punctuating titles and quotations

<u>"Make mine money"</u>

Some people may think of success as being "famous" for their accomplishments, and others may think that it's being an important executive or politician. Renee Loth in Measuring success says that her own ideas of success have changed. As I grow older, my ideas may also change, but right now I know what success means to me. It's money. I'll feel successful when I'm really rich.

Loth says that "success is defined differently by different people." She also says that wealth is superfluous if it goes beyond being able to take care of your family and have something left over for airfare to someplace sub-tropical in January. She obviously has a different idea about being wealthy. She doesn't really feel the need to be rich.

The trouble with struggling and searching is that it keeps us in a permanent state of wanting—always reaching for more. I don't see what's wrong with wanting more. As Loth says, "The drive to succeed keeps us focused on the future. Wanting to have more in the future is important, and my desire to be wealthy causes me to put forth effort in the present.

Loth tells "how she disliked fame when she finally achieved it." It was downright scary. She doesn't tell how the money she earned affected her, but I don't think I'll be disappointed. I believe I'd know how to use my money if I ever became rich.

I realize that I may change in many ways as I grow older, but I don't expect to lose sight of my most important goal. I hope I'll be healthy and happy, but I won't really feel that I'm a success until I'm "really" wealthy. For me, there are no real qualities of success that live outside of wealth.

EDITING FOR ALL PROBLEMS

Reading: "A Hanging" by George Orwell

Prompt

Orwell describes an execution he witnessed in another country. Do you agree or disagree with his reaction to the execution?

The essays in this section respond to the prompt above. They do not have major revision problems, but they may have many different types of editing problems: fragments, run-ons, incorrect verb and noun endings, agreement problems, confused words, and incorrect punctuation of titles and quotations. Correct all errors.

EXERCISE 24.11

Killing is wrong

I have never saw a person die, I hope I never will. But when I read George Orwell description of an execution in "A Hanging. I realized that I also never won't to be responsible for another persons death. Even if that person have commit a terrible crime. Though Orwell never state's his position on the death penalty, his story leaves little doubt that he would oppose it, I to believe that we have know right to take a life, "for any reason."

Many people argue for the death penalty on the ground's that it will prevent murders of other people. Yet is there any logical reason to think that this would be true. If the death penalty really deterred criminals. They're should be no murders in states with the death penalty. Like "South carolina "and Texas. Yet hardly a week go by without a murder being report in the newspaper. Just this morning while I drove to school. I heard of a womans body being found in an abandon trailer in South Carolina, and a gunman shooting several people at an office in Texas, clearly these murderer's did not cared about the death penalty.

However, Orwell do not discuss execution as a possible deterrent too crime. He is more concern with the effect that the execution have on the executioner's. He tell how he went to drink and laugh with the guards after the execution. Even though he had earlier realized the mystery, the unspeakable wrongness, of cutting a life short when it is in full tide. Reading this passage made me think that I too am often doing the same thing. Enjoying myself at the same time that a person is being execute hear in my state, I care nothing for the person life. As a citizen of the state, I two am really a peace of the execution. So I am like Orwell I am blinding myself to the realities' of what I am doing. Like Orwell, I do'nt have the power to stop the execution, but now I think that I should have been more aware of whats happening and what the government do in my name. Now I think I should paid attention when my government class discuss' constitutional right's. Try to listen when the news report on trials, so that Im not just acting like the guards at the end of Orwell's essay.

We could find many argument in favor of it, but one of the strongest argument's against it seem to be the one that Orwell makes. He show us that execution may not stop a crime, it is a crime.

EXERCISE 24.12

THE RIGHT THING TO DO

When we read an essay like "A Hanging" by George Orwell, our first reaction is sympathy with the prisoner we sees' many reasons to care for him, because Orwell show him as powerless and pathetic. By showing only the appealing side of the prisoner makes the reader believe that killing him is wrong. But perhaps if we new the whole story. Wed know that the execution was the right punishment for this criminal. I understands Orwell reaction to the execution, but I ca'nt agree with him. I believe that some crime's should be punish "by death."

Orwell make the prisoner appealing by showing that he prays when he know's that death is near "when the noose was fixed, the prisoner began crying out to his god." His belief cause him to call for help, but my belief say that crimes should be punish. "An eye for an eye," says the Bible, a criminal should be willing to suffer in the same way that he makes other people suffer. We don't know what crime the prisoner in Orwell's essay commit, but in this country, it would of been murder. He have taken a life, he should pay by giving his life.

We has too think about the victim. Orwell make us think about the prisoner, he tells detail's such as the fact that his cell is "like a small animal cage, and that he has "a shaven head and vague liquid eyes." He seem very real Orwell's horror at the man death is easy to see. "He and we were a party of men walking together, seeing hearing, feeling, understandin the same world; and in two minutes, with a sudden snap, one of us would be gone—one mind less, one world less." But Orwell do not give us any information about the victim of the crime. If this man is a murderer. His victim also use to be a live person with a mind and feelings, like him—did he stopped too think about the victim feelings when he committed the murder? Maybe his victim was a child, who had big brown eyes. Who liked to play with his kitten. Maybe his victim parents where poor and lonely. Id like to ask if we might of react differently if we knew about the victim as well as the prisoner?

Finally, we has too think about the purpose of execution, its intended to prevent crime. Orwell have not told us much about the time or place, so we can't know what crimes were common than. But if we look at our present time, with "schoolyard shooting's" and airplane bombings. We know that many of them does'nt care what happens to them. That's why we has to make it impossible for them ever to commit another crime. If we just puts them in jail. They could eventually be free to continue their crimes. Just last week I read of a man who return home to kill his wife only a month after being release from prison for beating her execution is the only certain way to make sure these criminals never kills again.

Orwell is a good writer, but his one-sided description of this event could maked a person agree that execution is wrong. Ive thought about the things Orwell have told us and the things he haven't told us and I've decide that I do not share his reaction, I believe that execution is sometimes necessary and right.

PART SIX

Essays and Readings

25 Essays by Student Writers

Rituals . . . for the Love of a Parent

by Keenan Johnson

In this essay, Keenan Johnson uses vivid details to demonstrate that the apparently unreasonable rules and rituals of a parent may in fact have a serious purpose in the future lives of the children, which the children do not understand. He first gives the example of a friend whose father hoped to instill a respect for culture in children by punishment, and then goes on to show how he himself has adopted his own rituals of luck as a result of his family's practices. Most complete of all is his explanation for the rational basis of the prohibition against talking while eating.

1   In the essay, "My Father's Tribal Rule," Mark Mathabane portrays his hatred toward his father's tribal rituals. All through the story Mathabane tells of his father making him practice tribal rituals and his rebellion toward these rituals. Although his father is doing all of this for his own reasons, he is also doing it for love. Mathabane has a hatred for all the rituals that his father forces him to participate in, as do most children who are unwillingly forced to do certain rituals, although all parents who make their children perform such rituals have some purpose for doing this.

2   One purpose for forcing rituals upon young children is the parent's desire for the preservation of culture. In Mathabane's essay, Mathabane is forced to speak his father's native language of Venda. When he is caught speaking another language, his father gets angry and punishes him by lashing him and making him participate in more daily rituals. Mathabane's father just wants his son to grow up knowing the culture and language that the father grew up with. I agree that Mathabane's father went about making his son learn about his culture the wrong way, but he is raising his children the way he was raised.

3   Many people today have the same type of problem Mathabane faced as a child. My best friend's father is from a small island named Guam. The island is a very different place than the States. My friend's father was raised in a harsh way. When he disobeyed his father he was hit, not just spanked with a belt, but hit with a fist. When my friend was growing up, his father tried to force the native language on him. He refused to learn the language, saying, "We aren't on the islands and I probably will never go there." My friend's father was furious at this and hit him, just like the father had been hit when he was a child. Now that my friend is older, he understands that his father was just trying to keep the island culture alive through him.

4   Some of the rituals described were supposed to bring good luck, money, and safety. Mathabane as a child hated doing these rituals because in his youth he did not understand the necessity of them. As a young kid I did not understand some of the rituals my parents made me do. Some include eating collard greens on New Year's Day. This was said to bring money. Also, I didn't understand why my grandfather kept a horseshoe hung over the barn door. This was to ensure luck. Now that I am older, I have some rituals that I participate in that I believe help me. Before every football game I wore the same shirt and boots. Now every time I need luck I wear them. Also, when I need luck I carry around a green Monopoly hotel. I think it is lucky because all hotels in that game are red, and I got a green one the only time I have ever won that game. Every culture and every person has different ways of trying to make luck and has different superstitions about things. Just as my parents did for me, Mathabane's father was just passing down the ways to get these things.

5   In one part of the essay, Mathabane is punished for talking at the dinner table. His father gets very angry about this and tells him, "You don't have two mouths to afford such luxury!" (42). I believe that Mathabane's father is just looking out for the well-being of his children. By that I mean if a family is poor and doesn't have much to eat, they need to spend all their meal time eating and not talking. One of my good friends just moved to Greenville, South Carolina, where she teaches the second grade. During lunch time she has to punish her children when they talk, so that they will get finished eating in time to get back to work. I think it is necessary to keep the talking down during a meal because it is a time of nourishment and not a social time.

6   Although as a child I hated the rituals my parents forced upon me as much as Mathabane hated the rituals forced upon him, they all had a purpose. In every instance Mathabane was forced to do rituals, his father had a clear purpose for enforcing them. Mathabane's father might have had a harsh way in teaching the rituals to his children, but he did it for the love he had for his children. He loved his children enough to take the time to teach his kids these rituals and punish them for not doing them. When a parent punishes children for not doing something, it is done in love. All these rituals did have a pupose in one way or another to his father and his father just wanted Mathabane to learn them as the father did.

Rituals: A Way of Life

by J. P. Myers

The following essay by Mr. Myers argues that children resent being forced to follow rules and customs that they do not understand. He uses a brief description of his bitterness toward his father after being forced to do his sister's chores, and follows with a concrete and memorable description of the clothes he was required to

*wear, showing how similar his problems were to those experienced by Mathabane.
An obvious conclusion would be the restatement of the thesis that parents cannot
accomplish their goals by intimidation, since that only creates more resistance.*

1   Growing up through life, my father had rules and values to which I never
grew accustomed. Their purpose was to mold me into the best person my father could imagine. In the essay "My Father's Tribal Rule," Mark Mathabane
reflects on his life growing up with his father's tribal rules and rituals. He discusses the differences between the way everyone else around him lives, and
the strict rules and rituals his father instills in the household. Mathabane despises his father's rules so much that he develops animosity toward his father
and the beliefs. I agree with Mathabane on his belief that rules and rituals
have no purpose or value because my father's rules and rituals served only to
intimidate, embarrass, and develop resentfulness in me because he felt I
should be like him.

2   My father, whom I feared, stood six feet tall and weighed three hundred
pounds and intimidated me something fierce. Although rebellious against certain rules, I had no alternative but to follow them or get switched. Mathabane
says, "Somehow they did not make sense to me; they simply awed, confused,
and embarrassed me, and the only reason I participated in them night after
night was because my father made certain that I did by using, among other
things, the whip, and the threat of the retributive powers of my ancestral
sprits, whose favor the rituals were designed to curry" (42). For example, one
afternoon I was asked by my father to do one of my sister's chores. Although I
disagreed, my father stood up with the belt and that intimidation alone frightened me into doing his wishes. I will never forget the control my father had
over me when it came to obedience.

3   As a child and a teenager, my father set strict rules pertaining to the type
of clothes I was allowed to wear. His philosophy was that I should wear plaid
shirts with pockets and a collar, corduroy pants, and loafers. He felt that this
type of attire would help me to look presentable and gain respect from others,
at least in his eyes. Mathabane says "Participation in my father's rituals sometimes led to the most appalling scenes, which invariably made me the laughingstock of my friends, who thought that my father, in his ritual garb, was the
most hilarious thing they had ever seen since natives in Tarzan movies" (43).
For example, one day I had to wear brown corduroy pants, a plaid shirt, and
cowboy boots to school. At this time kids normally wore blue jeans, cool
T-shirts, and Nikes. Every kid in class made fun of me all the time because I
looked ridiculous, like a geek. However, for this embarrassment my father
never seemed to care and never respected my wishes to wear what I felt was
normal clothes.

4   When it came time for dinner, my father's rules seemed to aggravate me
most. He believed you should eat poultry, beef, and lots of green vegetables.
Every meal my mother cooked consisted of these items. Mathabane says,
"This diet he administered religiously, seemingly bent on moulding George
and me in his image. At first I had tried to resist the diet, but my father's se-

vere looks frightened me" (41). For example, my mother always seemed to prepare liver and broccoli a numerous amount of times in my life. This particular meal was my father's favorite. I remember having to eat this horrid meal, and having really no chance to be excused from the table. All I ever wanted was a peanut butter sandwich or even a cheeseburger and french fries every now and again.

5   In conclusion, my father's rules and values were supposed to serve a purpose. In fact the only purposes they served were intimidation, fear, embarrassing clothes, and resentfulness for eating horrible foods. Consequently, it was my belief and aggravation that my father imagined me as if he was growing up himself all over again. I can't say that I hated him for his values, but I believe it would have been very close. Mathabane says, "As further punishment, he increased the number of rituals I had to participate in. I hated him more for it" (44). I believe my father enjoyed having control and developing rules and values that he knew must be obeyed growing up. My hatred is not so much at him but for his lack of understanding that times do and always will change.

WORKS CITED

Mathabane, Mark. "My Father's Tribal Rule." *The User's Guide to College Writing: Reading, Analyzing, and Writing.* Nancy Kreml et al. New York: Addison-Wesley-Longman, 2001. 40-44.

The Woman Chain: A Reflection of Women's Roles

by Meg Christmas

In this essay, the strong introduction and conclusion help focus on the thesis that the roles of women are roles of strength rather than weakness. In the body paragraphs, the deft paraphrases and quotes chosen by Meg Christmas show the details of the roles of women in Mathabane's writing, and parallel examples from her own experience show how much information can be inferred from small details, such as the fact that the mother was busy while the rest of the family ate. Ms. Christmas also explains how the role of peacemaker played by Mathabane's mother does not really undercut her support of her husband, showing how the mother cooperates with the father in maintaining a united front. The wealth of detail and thoroughness of examples make the argument convincing.

1   We come from our mothers. They have been with us over the course of our entire lives. Whether we were brought up by our natural mothers, grandmothers, adopted mothers, aunts, or a father that played the role of an absent mother, these people were the ones that cared for us when we were ill. They

fought with us when we were at battle, and provided for us a sense of love and belonging that only a mother can provide for her child. Women have played an integral part in most people's lives, whether directly or indirectly, throughout history. In Mathabane's essay, "My Father's Tribal Rule," he shows us how his mother and his experiences with her parallel other experiences we might have had in our own families. Mothers and women throughout time have proclaimed love and family above all else, not only in our era, but in any time, any place, and in any country in the world. A mother's love shines as the brightest beacon in the night, provides a safe harbor in any storm, and comforts in any tragedy.

2   Mathabane first introduces us to his mother in a positive light. He says, "It was amusing to witness my mother do it [wean George]." This shows us that he likes her, which reflects that she is, in turn, a good mother. It shows us her human side, not just a mother-like characteristic; it makes her a person. It brings us to a place in our hearts that is instinctively sensitive and warm when we think about our mothers. He shows her as a friend, someone he can take delight in and feel comfortable around. Women throughout time have played a similar role in the family, whether it be Elizabethan-Age to Turn-of-the-Century mothers or mothers of the 1960s or mothers of the 1990s. I believe we all strive to maintain good rapport with our children. Providing love and affection, helping our children grow up healthy and happy in their lives, is the role of most mothers.

3   Mathabane also shows his mother as a nurturer. The woman is usually in charge of preparing meals, feeding children, washing clothes and washing dishes. He illustrates this point when he was talking about mealtime. He says, "We were sitting on the floor, about the brazier, and my mother was in the bedroom doing something" (42). This might have been part of a tribal rule, one that states that women must wait to eat after everyone else has had their fill. I know that to be true because in my family, the men and children are always seated at the table and served before the women even think about sitting down themselves. If in a large family group and eating, the women are busy serving and making sure everything has been taken care of. One might be tending to children and the other in the kitchen washing dishes. But when it is just my mother and no other woman around, she still waits for every one to get a plate and then eats afterwards. Some might call it being polite, but I think it's much deeper than that. She is putting the family before herself. And I see that as what Mathabane is saying about his mother when she is found in the other room while all the others are eating. Women sacrifice. I also see Mathabane placing his mother in the role of protector. He says in his essay, "My mother led me into the kitchen and pleaded for me" (42). He also states, "She tried to intervene" (42). This evokes scenes of mother bears and their cubs, the natural feeling a female gets in protection of her offspring. No mother wishes harm to befall her child. In my experiences, I have seen mothers fight tooth and nail for the well-being of their children from bodily harm and from emotional distress. Women are inbred with this natural protection device, some say to ensure the progression of the species, and I am sure that

it is so in some cases. But to protect what is hers, what a mother or woman loves, especially a child, is a far greater inbred desire than any survival of the species theory I have ever heard.

4   Women are also disciplinarians. Mathabane uses his mother as an example of this when he begins to tell her he hates his father. Her reaction is one of a loyal wife. She begins by saying, "Don't say that!" followed by Mathabane's interpretation "My mother reprimanded me . . .'He's your father, you know . . . Shut that bad mouth of yours!' " and he says she threatened to smack him (42). In saying these things to her son, she is ingraining the values and rituals her husband has taught in the home. This enlightens us in that we see her as a loyal wife and a believer in the customs that her husband dictates. In a wife-husband relationship, it is customary that the wife is submissive to the husband. What the husband enforces, the wife follows and teaches to her children. I say this because it is usually the mother that can better relate to her children than the father, simply because she is usually the one to take more time with them. This enables her to communicate better than the father. In threatening to hit her son, she is also being a loyal wife by using the same method of hand-to-rod discipline that the father doles out. This leaves no room for the children to be confused by a different method of treatment. Instead of her just talking to the children and offering some lesser punishment such as not being able to have dinner, she is right on the heels of her husband in promising the same punishment for her children as the father would give if he were there himself. This shows unity in the couple—a trait that all women hope to find in a good marriage.

5   Mathabane also shows us a softer side of his mother. After disciplining her son, she begins to teach him by example why things are the way they are. She defends her husband and says, "He's trying to discipline you. He wants you to grow up to be like him" (42). She then goes on to explain calmly and rationally the reasons why. "Well, in the tribes sons grow up to be like their fathers" (43), and goes further by saying, "But we're still of the tribes" (43) at Mathabane's "indignation." She includes not only her husband and her son when she says "we" but also herself, now showing a family unity, not just a wife-husband unity. She then is seen in the role of philosopher. "Everybody does rituals, Mr. Mathabane" (43). She elaborates so that the child can understand her. She is not forceful in tone or in body, but simply states to him the reasoning behind her statement. Women generally take up a steady vigil of maintaining peace in their homes. They play the part of peacemaker and justifier, teacher and judge of what is said and how it means to be interpreted. In this case, the son is having problems with what his father is enforcing, and the mother has stepped in to aid in the communication process. Just as in any modern day home, the woman plays the same role. We might call it refereeing in this day, but the task remains the same: keeping peace in the home and explaining why certain rules are in place.

6   "My mother laughed" (43). Mathabane brings us to his mother again in a personal way. At the end of his essay, he brings us to her as a solitary person, not in conjunction with his father, showing us that he still likes her, that his

mother is a person of positive reflection and that she can laugh in the midst of things when they seem heavy. But at the very closing of Mathabane's essay, he last mentions his mother with his father. His father asks, "Whose son are you? . . . Yours and Mama's . . . Whose? . . . Yours" (43). I hear Mathabane saying that no matter what he might think of his mother, once the father steps in she is no longer an issue in what he deems as right and necessary. Again I see this submissive female role in society even today in a world where we all try to see everyone as a person, not as male or female. It wasn't until recently that women were actually credited with equal stature as men as far as their capability is concerned. Women were thought to be inferior to men and not deemed worthy of equal work for equal pay.

7   Women have always been in the forefront of their family's lives. They have played the same roles, taught the same lessons, and eaten of the same philosophies that their societies have given them. In valuing family above all, women have nurtured the well-being of their loved ones in a way that only a woman can. Throughout history, women have been the backbone of their families. They administer the same strength and knowledge that was taught to them by their mothers. Women are ensuring the role of the woman by handing down the teachings of our mothers to our children, and by our children to our children's children, generation after generation, until the end of time.

Family Roles in South Africa

by Jaime Cox

Jaime Cox explores the role of Mark Mathabane's mother in "My Father's Tribal Rule." Her paper illustrates how a person who seems to play a minor role in a Venda household in apartheid South Africa is central to the family structure. The strength of Ms. Cox's essay lies in paying attention to details in Mathabane's essay as she discusses the risks Mathabane's mother takes in trying to mediate the conflict between Mark Mathabane and his father. In a very difficult situation, Mathabane's mother still expects her son to recognize the source of his father's actions. The first and second body paragraphs work well together to present a unified picture of the mother's role as mediator. In completing her evaluation of the role of Mathabane's mother, Ms. Cox also points out how some of the mother's odd means of child rearing can be viewed as selfless and ultimately nurturing.

1   In many cultures, men seem to play a dominant role within the family construct. Many men assume roles in which they feel they are the source of the family's values and they feel the need at all costs to instill their beliefs within

each family member so that in their patriarchal mind-set the family will function. In Mark Mathabane's essay "My Father's Tribal Rule," he displays the character roles in a South African family. The essay focuses on Mathabane's issues with his father. Mathabane illustrates how his striving to accept non-traditional values conflicts with his father's desire to remain strictly within the confines of the old Venda tradition. Mathabane's mother is portrayed as playing a submissive role to her husband, who takes on the responsibility of teaching his children his values. Mathabane also exposes the extent of physical abuse and strict control his father displays toward any violation of his rules. As shown in the essay, Mathabane's mother seemingly plays a very small part within the family. However, in actuality, Mathabane's mother is the strongest figure due to her centrality within the family.

2   In Mathabane's essay, he portrays the overbearing control his father casts over the family; however, the mother actually has the greatest amount of influence over each family member. For instance, Mathabane's father's lack of complete control motivates him to enforce his rules by physical abuse. His methods of coercion only tempt Mathabane to resist his domination. On the other hand, Mathabane's mother has an open line of communication with her son to try to make him understand what her husband is trying to accomplish. Even with this open communication with his mother, Mathabane fails to realize that she has more of an influence over the way he perceives his parents' tribal ways. For instance, when Mathabane asks his mother, "Why do people do rituals?" (43) he is allowing himself more acceptance of her explanation than the acceptance he allows his father. Traditionally, in Venda culture, women are not allowed to question the behavior or child rearing techniques men display. However, Mathabane's mother contradicts her traditional role and "tr[ies] to intervene" (42) in order to prevent her son from being lashed. Her attempt to stop her husband from lashing her son did not work; nevertheless, her action of opposition shed light on his lack of control of not only his son, but his wife as well. In contradiction to the impression Mathabane gives that his father has complete control over the family, his mother has much more authority than she is given credit for.

3   Unlike the first impression received from the text, Mark Mathabane's mother has a very large role within the family. She is a mediator between her husband and her children. By her efforts to try to bring Mathabane and his father closer to an understanding, she ultimately holds the family together. When Mathabane tells his mother how he feels about his father by saying that he "hate[d] him and promised her that [he] would kill him when [he] grew up" (42), she quickly discourages him from feeling this way toward his father. She further explains to Mathabane that his father means well and only wants him to grow up to be an efficient Venda tribesman. She also tells Mathabane that his father "grew up in the tribes" (43) and moved to the city when he was older and was already set in his ways. The mother's mediation between Mathabane and his father soothes the intensity of angry emotions and motivates him to understand the father's point of view. Her efforts to make her husband

and son more acceptable in each other's eyes seem to reach Mathabane more than her husband, which will have a lasting effect on generations to come. Mathabane's mother's role as a peacekeeper is not referred to directly in the essay; nevertheless, her efforts to keep peace benefit the entire family immensely.

4   Mathabane's mother also plays a large role in rearing the children because they turn to her for understanding and explanations of her husband's demands. Mathabane's mother humbly weans the children to become independent of her instead of refusing them. For example, when Mathabane's younger brother, George, is weaned from suckling, she does not reject him in her efforts to do so. She uses hot pepper on her breast so that George withdraws from suckling on his own accord instead of her physically pushing him away. Although Mathabane's father is portrayed as the figure who teaches and disciplines the children, the mother also teaches the children by a more nurturing method and explains their disciplinary actions in a way they can understand why they have been punished.

5   In cultures such as those in South Africa, men seem to draw more attention to their authority by their dominating nature. Conversely, as we have seen in Mark Mathabane's essay, the mother figure also plays an essential part in the family. Her method of weaning her children promotes a sense of independence because they are motivated to withdraw themselves from suckling. Mathabane's mother's veiled manner in which she has the tendency to try to implement authority in tense situations allows the reader some insight as to the nature of her true personality. Because Mathabane's mother attempts to be the line of communication between her husband and her son, her contribution as a mediator between the two keeps the family together. Contrary to the impression received from the text, her role as a wife and mother is a far-reaching influential component, which determines the outcome of the family as whole.

WORKS CITED

Mathabane, Mark. "My Father's Tribal Rule." *The User's Guide to College Writing: Reading, Analyzing, and Writing.* Nancy Kreml et al. New York: Addison-Wesley-Longman, 2001. pp. 40-44.

Single Parents' Adversities

by Larry Evans

In a brief response to Teresa McCrary's "Getting Off the Welfare Carousel," Larry Evans asks if welfare assistance is warranted for single parents experi-

encing financial difficulties and concludes that some assistance is better than the alternative. His reflections focus on two benefits of welfare assistance— health care and housing. His observations regarding the complex issue of health care are more complete, although the reader is left to make the connection between his points and the argument he cites from McCrary. Regarding housing, Mr. Evans suggests that poverty creates living arrangements that are especially stressful for the children involved. Finally, in a very brief conclusion, Mr. Evans hints that political energy would be better spent on trying to find solutions to poverty rather than trying to avoid a situation because we do not feel responsible for it.

1   Single parents with children experience hardship in raising their children. It is almost impossible for single parents to raise children without an adequate job or any type of assistance. In a recent article, Teresa McCrary, a single parent on welfare, wrote that "single mothers were told to get off of welfare and get a job." I agree that single parents can not raise their children without any type of assistance from welfare or another government source.

2   Health care is probably the most important concern for single parents because parents want to know that their children have secure health coverage. Welfare provides health care for parents and their children. If single parents with children did not have any type of health coverage, they would be putting their children in a state of health poverty. Health care for one child alone can cost thousands of dollars a year. A recent article in *USA Today* tells how some health providers have organized a low income plan for single parents with children to provide adequate health coverage for them. McCrary said, "When the only jobs open to us are maid work, fast-food service and other low-paying drudgery with no benefits, how are we expected to support our children? Minimum wage will not pay for housing cost, health care, transportation and work clothes that an untrained, uneducated woman needs to support even one child. Although welfare pays very little, it provides adequate health coverage for single parents with children."

3   Single parents without any assistance can not afford adequate housing for their children. A house on the market today is very expensive for a person who has a secure job and can afford it. An apartment can cost hundreds of dollars a month. Many single parents and their children stay with other family members or friends because they can not afford adequate housing of their own. This may create a situation where too many are in the home and cause hardship on the children. The Department of Housing and Urban League has a program set up for families. Without this type of government assistance, many single parents could not afford housing for their children.

        Parents and their children are in such a position that no matter what they do, the solution is that they will suffer. No, we did not put them in the position they are in, but we can help them find a solution to their problem, by voicing our opinion to Congress or our state Representative.

Give the Needy a Break

by Rodell S. Johnson

Rodell S. Johnson's discussion of issues raised in Teresa McCrary's essay "Getting Off the Welfare Carousel" suggests that the failures of the welfare system are a consequence of the system itself. His topic sentences in paragraphs 2 and 3 clearly present his two main ideas: Minimum wage is not enough to support a family and the system penalizes those who try to get ahead. Building on Mc-Crary's comments, Mr. Johnson shows some of the absurd and unreasonable consequences of a system that seems designed to punish the poor. Overall, Mr. Johnson's paper reflects an appreciation of McCrary's position and argues that we should "Give the Needy a Break."

1   We Americans dramatize ourselves as being a kind, friendly, and caring nation which reaches out to help other countries in their time of need. Yet, why does the United States of America, a country that represents a great pillar for humanity, find it so difficult to lend a giving hand to single parents with children? In the article "Getting Off the Welfare Carousel," by Teresa McCrary, she describes how single mothers who are supported by the welfare system find it difficult to raise their families because of the inadequate support in today's society. I agree with the author that single parents find it difficult to raise their families because of inadequate support.

2   It is very difficult for a single woman with kids to support her family financially while earning minimum wages. McCrary cites how single parents who undertake the impossible task of managing, with minimum wage support, a family with one child. McCrary explains in paragraph 3 how single mothers take money from other sources, such as "odd jobs, and cash from generous friends, and relatives" to make ends meet without reporting it to the Aid To Families With Dependent Children. They are allowed to have up to three thousand dollars in total assets, and possessing anything more would reduce their benefits. I understand that the government wants to prevent people from taking unfair advantage of the system. For example, a welfare recipient could be receiving aid while owning an expensive automobile valued at thirty-five thousand dollars. I am sure if such recipients can afford to own an expensive vehicle and make the monthly payments, they should not be supported by financial aid at the taxpayers' expense. However, it doesn't take a degree in accounting to figure out a recipient's problem. Earning the minimum wage of five dollars and seventy-five cents an hour and at forty hours a week, totaling fifty-two weeks a year, minus twenty-five percent in taxes, she will earn an average salary of eight thousand and nine hundred dollars a year to support her family. Out of her net income she must make allowances for rent, daycare, clothes, insurance, utilities, school supplies, and a used car that isn't valued over her allowed assets. As a result of her net worth totaling three thousand dollars, she cannot afford a good car or the repairs. A single parent must balance her lim-

ited income and overcome the financial strains that choke her family out of their independence and deprive her children of social normalcy.

3   Welfare recipients shouldn't be penalized for people wanting to help them. The author goes on to explain that unless child support from fathers is paid to the state and is greater than AFDC benefits, the mother is given only fifty dollars more, while at the same time reducing her allowances in food stamps. She also mentions that the state keeps collected back child support that is paid by fathers and none of the money is given back to the children. I ask you, is this concept conducive to improving their economics? Instead, our government has developed a system to keep families who are dependent on welfare wondering about their next meal. They live from paycheck to paycheck, because they have no contingency plan to obtain financial freedom from poverty. The system amputates any means of families having a better life. Let's consider that the deadbeat dad finally comes out of his comatose state of mind, and he decides to do the morally right thing. That is, he starts being responsible and supports his children in the principal state of fatherhood. Maybe their dad is earning minimum wages too, and he can only afford to give a small amount of what he earns. Should we deduct the amount from the family's total assets worth three thousand dollars? In addition, a neighbor who is a good samaritan has purchased a new living room set, and he wants to donate to the welfare recipient his used set that's valued at fifteen hundred dollars. Now the AFDC penalizes her, and literally reduces her support, because her total net worth is more that three thousand. It is appalling to think how the United States has supported other countries with billions of dollars, such as Bosnia, to improve their economic situation, which I have seen with my own eyes, while at the same time, the government puts a choke chain on welfare recipients and deprives their families of the right to a better life.

4   Our government should not penalize the needy for their economic situation and social status. Just because they are poor, society should not have a prejudiced heart. I have seen pets receive better treatment. For example, a pet obeys a command, or does a trick; we reward them with a bone. A welfare recipient does more to improve on their economics and what is expected of them, and the government penalizes them by cutting back on their benefits, as if they were being punished by taking their bone back, and treating them like pets.

The Single Female Families
by Benjamin W. Munden, Sr.

Benjamin W. Munden, Sr., explores his own response to times when his wife was essentially a single parent while he was posted overseas with the military. The strengths of this essay lie in Munden's ability to connect the details of his own family's limited single-parent experience with the larger picture of hardships

Teresa McCrary discusses in "Getting Off the Welfare Carousel." Mr. Munden points out there was an emotional toll to his long military-related absences, even though his family was not poor. In addition to the emotional toll the "second shift at home" took on his wife, Mr. Munden also offers his children's reactions to their mother's stress, and he also recognizes that in some single-parent situations, physical hardship and stress may lead to abuse. In his conclusion, Mr. Munden returns to McCrary's position that public assistance should provide opportunities for education and training, including life skills that encourage single parents to learn to better balance education and child care.

1   A single-parent family is likely to be headed by a woman. Most women who live in a single-parent family do not choose to do so. The single mother has the enormous responsibility of taking care of a child's emotional and physical well-being. The biggest problem of being a single mother is financial. I agree with Teresa McCrary's idea that it is almost impossible for a single parent to rear children with no assistance.

2   As Teresa McCrary says, "We may not have paying jobs, but any mother, married or single, working or retired, will tell you that motherhood is a career in itself" (53). I empathize with any mother who works and has the responsibility of caring for her children. For example, during my military career, my wife and children remained in the States several times when the military transferred me to a foreign country. We thought at the time that it would enable the children to remain in the same school system. As we discussed it, I thought that remaining in the States was more beneficial for the children's education. My wife and I felt that it would also be wise for economical reasons. Meanwhile, my wife was employed full time on a job and pulled second shift at home with housework, children, and checking homework. I felt guilty about the situation for leaving her behind with the children and I couldn't help her as I wanted. In fact, I felt I was not doing my part as a spouse. Nevertheless, my guilty feeling was replaced by the justification that I was supporting my family. At times, I wondered whether it would be more beneficial if she did not work. Her salary was spent on babysitters and transportation. Adding more to the downside, she didn't spend enough quality time with the children.

3   My wife stated that the children asked her not to check their homework, because she used their papers as pillows when she fell asleep from fatigue. Her make-up was a telltale sign on their papers. She said, "The only consolation I had was the knowledge that you'd come eventually, to help with the children." She stated, "During those times, I often thought about the single mothers' plight with no help in sight." I questioned myself about the pressure and stress that single mothers undergo when the threat of utilities being disconnected presents itself. It's difficult enough caring for children alone. Add the fear of no shelter, food, or clothing, and get total disaster. Many times abuse comes into play. Teresa McCrary says, "These fears cause stress that may result in child abuse" (53). When some single mothers worry about how they are going to help their children without assistance from welfare, family, or friends, they

hurt the children. They seem to use this as an outlet. Most often, help from family, friends, or welfare assistance can alleviate this. However, single mothers should not turn welfare assistance into careers. They should use these measures as a measure to get off that role into a more independent role of self-sustaining.

4   Teresa McCrary says, "I believe that we single mothers must become self-sufficient through education and training" (53). Education and training are vital elements in moving to the right direction. Through self-motivation a single mother can devise a plan or schedule to accommodate time for studying and caring for her children.

Capital Punishment

by Lois Johnson

Lois Johnson has clearly presented her analysis of Orwell's essay. She uses detailed evidence to demonstrate how Orwell "manipulates" rather than makes an argument. She presents this analysis by writing a clear thesis that indicates the areas she will discuss, providing transitions between body paragraphs, and including specific details and quotes from Orwell. The strength of her essay lies mainly in her explanations of the details and quotes she uses as support for each of her main ideas and in her concluding sentences that remind readers how her examples are related to her main ideas.

1   What does one have to do to be put on death row? Is capital punishment right or wrong? In George Orwell's narration of "A Hanging," he tells us of a prisoner being put to death in the early 1900s, in Burma. Orwell manipulates the reader against capital punishment by not telling the reader what the prisoner did to be put to death. Although Orwell doesn't present an argument, he uses the prisoner's religion, size, personality and physiological description to persuade us that capital punishment is wrong.

2   One of the things Orwell wants us to see is that the prisoner is a religious man. Orwell tells us he is "a Hindu," (55) who worships all life. The prisoner is described as having "a shaved head" with "a lock of hair" (55). He was demonstrating his religion. Even when the prisoner was about to be hanged, he cried "RAM! RAM! RAM!" (56) All he was thinking about was his god and he was calling out to him. When we think of a religious man, we have the impression that he is a good, nice man and one who tries not to do anything wrong. This is what Orwell wants us to see, that the prisoner is a religious man who is nice and friendly.

3   Another thing Orwell wants us to see about the prisoner is his personality. Orwell tells us that, when the warders were taking the prisoner to the gallows,

he "stood quite unresisting, yielding his arms limply to the ropes" (55). Even though they had his arms bound to his sides, he was calm. This tells us that the prisoner is not violent, that he is peaceful and calm. When the dog came out of nowhere and was excited to see many people, he picked the prisoner out of every person there to jump on him and lick his face. That tells us the prisoner is a friendly man, because dogs are known to have a sixth sense. When we think of someone who is peaceful and calm, we think of them as nice and easygoing, even when mad. The calmness suggests that he's an OK guy. Orwell wants us to see that the prisoner was calm even when he knew he was going to die. Orwell wants us to see that the prisoner is a calm, easygoing and friendly man.

4   Orwell also wants us to take into consideration the prisoner's size. Orwell tells us that the prisoner was a "puny wisp of a man" with a "thick, sprouting mustache, absurdly too big for his body" (55). We picture somebody who's small and skinny. Orwell tells us there were "six tall Indian warders" (55) guarding the prisoner. Orwell describes the warders as being tall standing beside the prisoner, so the prisoner must also be short. Orwell wants us to see that the prisoner is short and skinny, which means that he is a small man.

5   The last thing Orwell wants us to see about the prisoner is that he is a living human being just like everybody else. Orwell says that "all the organs of his body were working—bowels digesting food, skin renewing itself, nails growing, tissues forming—all toiling away in solemn foolery" (56). Orwell is trying to tell us that the prisoner is alive, that all his body parts are working, even though he is being put to death. When we think of someone whose organs are working in his body and their tissues forming, we picture someone who is alive just as we are. That is what Orwell wants us to see about the prisoner: he is alive and breathing, just like all us other humans.

6   Orwell manipulates the reader into thinking that capital punishment is wrong by using the description of the prisoner. He tells us that the prisoner is a religious man, he has a good personality, and he is short and skinny and that he is just like all other human beings. From the descriptions, we picture this man as nice and friendly. If the prisoner is all these nice things, then what could he have possibly done to be put to death? Orwell wants us to see that the prisoner was just like us and since he's just like us he shouldn't be put to death. Therefore, capital punishment is wrong.

Exposure of Public Executions

by Jane Smith

This essay discusses whether or not executions should be televised—a topic that has been debated in recent years. In her introduction, Jane Smith uses quotes from George Orwell's "A Hanging" to show the reader where she stands on this issue.

She returns to Orwell in her last body paragraph, quoting a passage that condemns the death penalty. In the rest of her essay, Ms. Smith presents her own ideas as to why executions shouldn't be televised and strengthens them with passages from Orwell's description of an execution.

1   If public executions were televised or made admissable to the public by any means, I believe society would become so accustomed to the exposure of people murdered legally as an everyday occurrence that executions may become common enough not to affect the general public in a conscious fashion. In George Orwell's essay "A Hanging," he says, "but till that moment I had never realized what it means to destroy a healthy, conscious man" (56). Life is very precious to me, no matter what form it may be in, and to purposely take a life has to be wrong, unless in self-defense. Publicizing executions is wrong. It could give people that are watching them the idea that somehow killing someone is O.K. as long as you have a good reason. In Orwell's essay he says, "an enormous relief had come upon us now that the job was done. One felt an impulse to sing, to break into a run, to snigger. All at once everyone began chattering gayly" (57). Viewing an execution could become such a common occurrence that we might just find it easier not to feel anything as long as it doesn't take longer than our lunch hour.

2   A lot of people in the past have murdered in cold blood and felt no remorse. Soldiers have to be trained to kill the enemy soldiers. With every body count, killing becomes maybe not easier, but perhaps automatic. Television sometimes puts crazy ideas into people. There is enough violence on television today even though most of it may be fiction. We don't need to give people in our society, especially those people that are already unstable, any reasons to think that killing is fine as long as you have a good reason. Look what Hitler did to the Jews. Who knows where he got his ideas for his executions of Jews? There are just too many unstable people in the world today. There seem to be no good reasons why we should add more exposure to killing than society is already exposed to by television, or in our homes, or streets.

3   What effect would it have on young minds to see someone being killed? Children are so vulnerable at young ages. What they see and hear sometimes may have everlasting effects on children. This public display of executions would be wrong because the very young mind might not be able to grasp the legal ethics of killing someone, whatever the reason. There are enough statistics involving children, children that are committing crimes and crimes that are committed on them, without exposing our young ones to this kind of killing, even though it is supposed to be legal.

4   The public should also take into consideration, especially if people have never witnessed someone dying, that it's not a pretty sight to see. Taking someone's life away may affect the human side of people more than we would expect. I don't believe God created people so that they could kill one another for any reason other than self-defense. There is a lot of humanity left in our society, even though people might have to remind themselves of this at times.

For some people it just comes naturally to let the "human" side of them show. Orwell says, "When I saw the prisoner step aside to avoid the puddle I saw the mystery, the unspeakable wrongness, of cutting a life short when it is in full tide" (56).

5   It is not in our human nature to take a life for any other reason than survival unless there is an unbalanced side to us. Having to carry out the task of escorting someone to their death could not be a very pleasant job. Public executions should not be completely open to the public, unless you have a good reason to witness such displays.

AIDS and the Media: A True Assessment

by Brian Murray

Brian Murray argues against Bronski's essay, addressing three of Bronski's points directly, one in each of his body paragraphs. One of the strengths of Mr. Murray's essay is his reporting of Bronski's idea before he presents his own objection and examples. He uses research on actual reporting of AIDS-related stories to demonstrate that Bronski's thesis is not accurate. After describing at least one of Bronski's examples, he also provides a thorough description of his own example, showing how other reporters have presented a less judgmental picture of people with AIDS.

1   The mass media—radio, television, newspapers, and magazines—are, for most people, the primary source of daily news. Often the news we receive reflects the dominant culture and society's tastes. What we read or listen to dramatically affects the way we shape our lives and beliefs. Therefore, it is not surprising that every so often an issue will arise that gives people an offensive view of the media. In "Magic and AIDS: Presumed Innocent," Michael Bronski discusses just how biased the media can be towards HIV victims, depending on their social class and the way that they were infected with the deadly virus. Bronski's concern is how the media portrays certain groups within the AIDS community as either guilty or innocent. Homosexuals and drug addicts are seen by the media as guilty because they have "perverted sex" and "shoot drugs" (45). Children who have been born with AIDS or have been infected through blood transfusions are seen as innocent by the media. When Magic Johnson announced on November 7, 1991, that he had tested positive for HIV, the media "placed him in the discernible, if increasingly fragile, realm of the innocent" (45). Bronski's attitude towards the media is one of disgust, and he believes the media "relies on soap-opera scenarios and flash-and-trash sound bite journalism," (52) because "the press still has no idea how to write about AIDS" (52). In addition, Bronski adds that the media reports only on "per-

sonal tragedy and not useful preventive guidelines and information," (52) and believes the media divides the world into "good and bad . . . them and us," (52) when it comes to moral judgment. Unfortunately, Bronski fails to notice numerous articles published throughout the United States and abroad that refute his assessment of the media. Upon researching , I found five major newspaper articles that educate or show hope and determination for AIDS victims, as well as views that AIDS is not contracted only through "perverted sex" and "drug use" (45). Although understandable, Bronski's assessment of the media is narrow-minded and unfair.

2   One of Bronski's leading arguments against the media is that "the press still has no idea how to write about AIDS" (52). An example of this happened when the actor Rock Hudson died of AIDS in 1985. After his death, the media began running articles of his homosexuality, naming his lover and telling how there had been rumors of his gay lifestyle before his death. In addition, when the singer Freddie Mercury died, the media once again began to use the opportunity to drag his name and memory through the dirt, by exposing details of his past relationships. It is exactly this type of reporting that brings Bronski to his argument of how the media writes about AIDS. However, *The Wilmington News* article, "AIDS Drugs and Prevention," is a 3-page article on how certain drugs have "almost cleared the AIDS virus from the bloodstream" (Simons 1), yet the virus still continues to infect new cells. In another article in *The Chicago Leader,* headlines read "Topical Cream Shields against AIDS" (Marvell G11). The article outlines a vaginal cream that will protect women from AIDS and other sexually transmitted diseases. This new and still unapproved cream has "reportedly been found to prevent the transmission of the virus" (Marvell G11). Upon reading these and other articles, Bronski would have seen just how educational and informative the media can be. How many lives will be spared because of articles like these? Many women and AIDS victims will be aware of such products available in the prevention and care of AIDS. Unfortunately, since trash articles do sell newspapers and air time, the public and Bronski must be aware of just how educational and informative the media can be.

3   Bronski's second argument is that the media only reports "personal tragedy," and not "useful prevention guidelines and information" (52). Unfortunately, it is true that in every newspaper throughout the United States there are stories of death and sorrow. Often families lose loved ones to car accidents, cancer, murder, and AIDS. All of these stories are tragic, but none more so than the story of Aaron Washington. *Sports* published the story of the life and death of this remarkable man (Hewlett-Lopez). Washington was a nurse, a veteran, an AIDS victim, and a father. Washington accomplished many wonderful things in his life; he worked in local hospitals and treated patients who had tropical diseases, was a marathon runner, and worked with the Gay Olympic Games. In addition, he raised and was extremely proud of his son Tom. In the last few weeks of life, Washington suffered from Kaposi's syndrome and terrible pain. Aaron Washington died in his home from AIDS (Hewlet-Lopez 27). It is a sad, regrettable fact of life that AIDS brings death

and therefore tragedy will follow, but for Bronski to report that the media is more interested in "personal tragedy" than passing on information is false. A good example of reporting that is educational through tragedy was published in *Good Homes*. Cindy and Richard Travis had made their decision to have a child, but unfortunately, the decision came with much risk. Richard was diagnosed with the AIDS virus and unprotected sex could be deadly for Cindy. After six months of doctors' visits and bad news, the couple discovered a technique that could possibly allow them to conceive a child. Sperm washing had been a technique not used in the United States, but after researching the facts through an Italian doctor, they were able to locate a physician in the United States willing to perform the controversial procedure (Ramos 40-42). This is an extremely informative article that, although showing personal tragedy and heartache, also shows hope and determination. If Bronski were more open-minded, he would see that there are many articles published that do show educational information.

4   When Magic Johnson announced he was HIV positive, some media sources reported his action was heroic, while some judged him as either immoral or irresponsible. Depending which newspaper you read or television station you watched would affect how Johnson was portrayed. In Bronski's last argument he states that the media makes "moral judgment[s]" (52) about AIDS victims by placing them in categories of either "good or bad . . . them and us" (52), for contracting AIDS. For Bronski to say that the media in general is to blame for such labeling is outrageous. No one can argue that certain articles do indeed judge and blame AIDS victims, but these articles reflect the reporters' opinion and views, not the media as a whole. There are reporters who do not make moral judgments on their subjects. Marian Moeller, a reporter for *The San Francisco Times*, writes about a woman she compares to herself. Tracy Thomas and Moeller are both in their 40's, grew up in small towns, and went to small colleges. Even as professional women their lives were very similar; they both worked long hours and juggled family and friends. However, as parallel as their lives were, in 1984 Thomas' life changed forever. Like Moeller, Thomas was married, but in 1984 she became infected with the AIDS virus from her husband. In Moeller's piece, she never passes judgment on Thomas. She points out how easily people's lives change and how infection with AIDS does not come just from "perverted sex" (45), or drug use. Moeller states how there are thousands of young women living exactly as Thomas lived and how easily they could be a victim of AIDS. Bronski is correct that moral judgment is passed on AIDS victims, but it is not by the media as a whole, but from the reporters' attitude and beliefs.

5   In order to get a complete and true assessment of how the media portrays AIDS, we must look beyond the trash articles. Bronski firmly believes that the media has "no idea how to write about AIDS" (52), and therefore, relies on stories of personal tragedy to hold the reader's attention. Bronski also states that the media makes "moral judgements" (52) against AIDS victims by placing them into categories. In national and international newspapers and magazines, articles are found that argue against Bronski's assessment. The article from *The*

Chicago Leader suggests that a cream may have the potential to save millions of women's lives. The story of the Travis family's personal tragedy of AIDS shows that through hope and determination their decision to conceive a child was fulfilled. Articles such as these do indeed educate and provide information on new methods of the prevention and cure of AIDS. Marian Moeller's article is an extremely good example of unbiased and nonjudgmental reporting. At no time does Moeller place Thomas into a category. Moeller writes a piece that not only educates, but compares an AIDS victim's life to her own, thus stating how easily anyone can become infected. Bronski would be well advised to read Moeller's article and realize that it is not the entire media who place moral judgment on AIDS victims, but only certain narrow-minded reporters. Bronski's assessment of the media is not only shallow, but also irresponsible.

WORKS CITED

Bronski, Michael. "Magic and AIDS: Presumed Innocent." *The User's Guide to College Writing: Reading, Analyzing, and Writing.* Nancy Kreml et al. New York: Addison-Wesley-Longman, 2000. 44-52.

Hewlett-Lopez, Tamina. "Real Heroes." *Sports* 17 April 1997: 25-29.

Marvell, Linda. "Topical Cream Shields against AIDS." *The Chicago Leader* 25 September 1999: G11.

Moeller, Marion. "Staying Alive." *The San Francisco Times* 27 July 1999: B39+.

Ramos, Cara. "Living On." *Good Homes* 14 January 2000: 39-45.

Simons, Cary. "AIDS Drugs and Prevention." *The Wilmington News* 10 March 1998: C1-3.

Diseases and Morality

by Stacey Hawkins

Stacey Hawkins argues against Bronski's essay. The long lead-in provides an analogy between irresponsible behaviors in sports and irresponsible behavior pertaining to health. In the first body paragraph, Mr. Hawkins acknowledges areas in which he agrees with Bronski, while in the other two body paragraphs, he shows areas in which he disagrees with Bronski.

1   Injuries are a big part of any sport. Football is probably the sport with the most injuries. Blame is usually addressed after injuries occur. A dirty player who uses cheap tactics and bends the rules is ostracized. A player who is the victim of a dirty play gains much sympathy. The NFL (National Football League) a few years back had a problem with cheap tactics. Players were being hurt by others' negligence. The most rampant cheap tactic in the NFL was using the

crown of your helmet as a battering ram to deliver the biggest hit on an opposing player. This would cause concussions and even career-threatening injuries.
This was before a backlash to the incidents happened. The NFL decided to fine
the player guilty of giving out the hit. Chuck Cecil, a strong safety, was the
posterboy for these dangerous hits. Whenever the opportunity presented itself,
he would use the crown of his helmet. Cecil became one of the first recipients
of the fines to curb this dangerous play. Later, Cecil received a serious concus-
sion as a result of one of his hits. No one felt bad because it was his own actions that led to the injury. The next year Cecil, a solid player, couldn't find
work; he had been blackballed because of his dirty play. His negligence led to
an injury and then his exit from the league. This is similar to a disease caused
by negligence or lack of morals. In the article "Magic and AIDS: Presumed Innocent," Michael Bronski says that diseases are not caused by someone's moral
ideals. He gives examples of diseases throughout history that had nothing to
do with morality. He says the idea of innocent and guilty victims isn't plausible
or relevant to the problem of the disease. The evidence shows a link between
morality and catching a disease today. Bronski gives some examples, but fails
to mention many diseases prevalent today. Alcoholism and compulsive gambling are diseases with links to morals of people who acquire the disease.

2   Bronski says there is no connection between morals and disease. He
shows how media and others brand a disease unfairly with immoral behavior.
This is basically a stamp given to those people that shows a consequence to
not having morals. This is regardless of whether there is a direct connection
or not. He says, "When the great plagues ravaged Europe during the Middle
Ages, they were seen as divine punishment" (45). The plagues had no connection with morals, but were given a connection. TB is another disease that
Bronski says has nothing to do with morals. In Britain, TB "was seen as a sign
of sensitivity and artistic temperament"; however, in the United States it has
always been viewed "as a disease of the undeserving poor," showing a distinction for the same disease (45). The two opposite viewpoints show no connection with morals. Typhoid is another disease stamped with moral deficencies.
Bronski says it "was seen as a disease of 'dirty' immigrants who were guilty of
spreading it" (45–46). This is saying typhoid was labeled as a disease spread
by people different from us who infected us with it. These are all examples of
diseases that have no connection to the morals of the people who contract
them. The victims were unfairly stamped with a moral judgment.

3   Alcoholism is a disease rampant in America today. Almost anyone can tell
you what an AA meeting is. Alcoholism is a disease that comes as a consequence of the person's actions. A person has to have a conscience when it
comes to alcohol. Drinkers have to limit how much and how often they drink.
Alcoholics aren't able to do this because they allowed their bodies to become
dependent on alcohol. Alcoholics drink too much, too often, until their self
control is pretty much gone. Their morals did not tell them that immersing
your existence in alcohol is wrong. Liver cancer is another disease acquired
from overuse of alcohol. A person's morality directly coincides with their use
of alcohol until they finally become an alcoholic.

4   Morality also comes into play when a person becomes a compulsive gambler. No one can debate whether this is true or not. People become compulsive gamblers as a result of their own actions. This is a disease that takes away people's willpower. They must keep gambling no matter how much money they've lost. They falsely think they're lucky. The only way to look at gambling is that it's wrong. There are many signs a gambler chooses to ignore. Gambling is illegal in many states. Our laws are in many instances based on morals. The moral standard in the United States, the Bible, also condemns it. When two of our main bases condemn something morally, and people do it, their morals should be questioned.

5   Michael Bronski makes good points that typhoid and TB aren't traced to morality, but diseases out there are. Alcoholism comes from the user's inability to show restraint. The same thing can be said about a compulsive gambler. A gambler ignores the signs that this is not right. Alcoholism and gambling diseases do not grip people immediately, so they can see their problem coming. It is by people's own fault they have these diseases and that in itself shows their lack of morals.

Moral Judgments

by Ave Givens

Ms. Givens's essay takes an approach to organization different from some of the other student essays in this section. Her introduction follows the general-to-specific model in Chapter 8; however, she has chosen a pattern of organization for her body paragraphs that is different from the one described in Chapter 9. She uses used her first two body paragraphs to discuss the ideas of author Michael Bronski. She uses the third and fourth body paragraphs to present her own arguments. For this organization to be successful, writers must word their own discussions so they clearly refer back to the ideas of the author. Givens's research on the symptoms of typhoid and syphilis add to the credibility of her argument that some diseases may legitimately be linked with the victim's morality.

1   Picture yourself on your way home, driving down the street. You see three police cars outside of a neighbor's house. As you drive by, you see the police drag a middle-aged black man to the police car. In your mind, you are thinking that he has just been arrested for an illegal drug charge. Whether your thinking is right or wrong, it is a prejudgment. Everyone has prejudgments about many things. Most of our judgments deal with a particular person's morality. Michael Bronski, an activist as well as a reporter on gay issues, has written many articles discussing prejudgments and morality. In a specific article, "Magic and AIDS: Presumed Innocent," he tells how the media has two different classes

when it comes to a person's morality. The two classes are innocent and guilty. Bronski goes on to discuss specific diseases that people have personal judgments about, therefore judging the human being as well. He strongly believes that diseases are not a sign of a person's morality. He uses examples such as AIDs and typhoid. On the other hand, there are many diseases where it may be appropiate for judgments to be made about the person's morality. This point will be proven by discussing two specific diseases, alcoholism and syphilis.

2   In Bronski's article he discusses Magic Johnson's announcement that he was HIV positive. The media, however, gave him an innocent title. At this time they did not know the reason he contracted this disease but felt he should be labeled innocent because he came straight out with the truth. Bronski brought out how the people who had AIDs were viewed before this event. At first all AIDs victims were guilty. The thinking was that a victim had to be a homosexual, prostitute, or IV-user. The only cases that were considered innocent were those of children who contracted the disease from their mothers. The very next day after the announcement, on the *Arsenio Hall Show,* Magic Johnson told that he contracted HIV from "messing around with too many women" (45). Johnson was still considered innocent and the blame was placed on women. This falls out of the simple guilty or innocent description. Now we have reason to believe that not everyone who contracts the HIV virus except for children is guilty. The media brings out that medical care workers may contract HIV from an accident at work, and blood transfusions, and even doctors can infect their patients if not careful at work. Here Bronski shows that the simple guilty or innocent judgment is very questionable and unfair in many cases.

3   Bronski then goes on to show how the media seemed to be looking for the "perfect . . . victim" (47). There was a case concerning a woman named Dr. Prego who worked at a hospital and was stuck by a needle and contracted HIV. She blamed the doctor for leaving the infected needle out. She was thought of as the perfect victim at first, but because of her large settlement in court she become questionable. There was another "perfect" victim named Ryan White. He was a young boy who had a bad transfusion. The media, however, did not like him because he didn't blame anyone. Bronski brings out, by using these examples, that there is not a perfect innocent or guilty victim. The other disease about which inappropriate moral judgments were made is typhoid. Typhoid fever is "a communicable disease marked by fever, diarrhea, prostration, headache, and intestinal inflammation" (Epidemiology). This was thought to be a disease of dirty immigrants who would be "guilty of spreading the disease to the 'general population'" (46). An Irish woman named Mary Mallon was arrested and quarantined for spreading this disease to others. This is another example of how Bronski expresses his strong dislike for the stigmatization occurring with diseases.

4   On the other hand, consider the disease of alcoholism. Alcoholism is defined as a continued excessive or compulsive use of alcoholic drinks. When we think of an alcoholic, we have the judgment of a person who constantly drinks and puts everything else such as family and occupation aside. This, however,

is a moral judgment about a disease that is true. Alcoholics make drinking an everyday and all day activity. They begin to stop communication with others. They may not go to work and may forget about all of their responsibilities. This disease may be brought to an end if the person decides to. There are many centers where alcoholics can check in to get rid of this illness. People have to want to be helped in order to receive help. That is a decision they must make for themselves. Because people can choose to be cured, alcoholism is a disease that gives a sure sign of individuals' morality.

5   Another disease that is correctly linked to morality is syphilis. Syphilis is a sexually transmitted disease defined as "a chronic contagious usually venereal and often congenital disease caused by a bacteria spirochete and if left untreated characterized by a clinical course in three stages may continue over many years" (Doctor's Line). Someone who has this disease is known to have had sexual intercourse with numerous partners. Syphilis is another prime example of moral judgments being rightly placed on diseases. This disease can be treated. The person then has a chance to change their sexual course of actions. This disease could have been prevented by protected sex and sex with one partner who would be your long-term mate. This disease is also an example of true moral judgments.

6   It is often sad for persons to be told they have a disease, whether it is curable or not. However, things could have been different in some cases if precautions had been taken. With the examples of alcoholism and syphilis, we see how Bronski is wrong in his view that moral judgments cannot be placed on diseases. In many cases, the actual morality of a person becomes the cause of the disease. Many people could have had a better outcome if they had made a better choice or decision in life.

WORKS CITED

Bronski, Michael. "Magic and AIDS: Presumed Innocent." *The User's Guide to College Writing: Reading, Analyzing, Writing.* Nancy Kreml et al. New York: Addison-Wesley-Longman, 2000. 44-52.

Doctor's Line. "Syphilis." *Sexually Transmitted Diseases.* 8 December 1998. Online. http://www.std.com/std/sym/syphilis.html (16 March 2000).

Epidemiology Association of California. "Typhoid." *Diseases and Symptoms* 12 January 2000. Online. http://www.publichealth.org/edpical/dis/typhoid.html (18 March 2000).

Readings by Professional Writers

Family

Exploring the Theme

- What helps a family stay united? Do difficult times bring family members together, or tear them apart?
- How should parents shape and guide their children's behavior? What works best to help children grow into responsible adults—punishment or reward?
- How do our cultural, ethnic, or religious backgrounds support our families?
- How do institutions and bureaucracies help families? How do they cause harm to families?
- What should our society do to protect families? Should there be limits on government interference with family problems?
- What is a good parent? Who should decide?

PREREADING SUGGESTIONS

1. Can you recall a house or an apartment that you lived in when you were a child? Write a brief passage describing that place and your feelings about it.
2. What to you would be the most damaging part of being poor?

Daddy Tucked the Blanket

by Randall Williams

Randall Williams describes his own experiences in this essay. He later went to college on a scholarship and became a writer, but vividly recalls the problems of his earlier life. This article was first published in 1975 in the New York Times.

1   About the time I turned 16, my folks began to wonder why I didn't stay home any more. I always had an excuse for them, but what I didn't say was that I had found my freedom and I was getting out.

2 I went through four years of high school in semirural Alabama and became active in clubs and sports; I made a lot of friends and became a regular guy, if you know what I mean. But one thing was irregular about me: I managed those four years without ever having a friend visit at my house.

I was ashamed of where I lived. I had been ashamed for as long as I had been conscious of class.

3 We had a big family. There were several of us sleeping in one room, but that's not so bad if you get along, and we always did. As you get older, though, it gets worse.

4 Being poor is a humiliating experience for a young person trying hard to be accepted. Even now—several years removed—it is hard to talk about. And I resent the weakness of these words to make you feel what it was really like.

5 We lived in a lot of old houses. We moved a lot because we were always looking for something just a little bit better than what we had. You have to understand that my folks worked harder than most people. My mother was always at home, but for her that was a full-time job—and no fun, either. But my father worked his head off from the time I can remember in construction and shops. It was hard, physical work.

6 I tell you this to show that we weren't shiftless. No matter how much money Daddy made, we never made much progress up the social ladder. I got out thanks to a college scholarship and because I was a little more articulate than the average.

7 I have seen my Daddy wrap copper wire through the soles of his boots to keep them together in the wintertime. He couldn't buy new boots because he had used the money for food and shoes for us. We lived like hell, but we went to school well-clothed and with a full stomach.

8 It really is hell to live in a house that was in bad shape 10 years before you moved in. And a big family puts a lot of wear and tear on a new house, too, so you can imagine how one goes downhill if it is teetering when you move in. But we lived in houses that were sweltering in summer and freezing in winter. I woke up every morning for a year and a half with plaster on my face where it had fallen out of the ceiling during the night.

9 This wasn't during the Depression; this was the late 60's and early 70's.

10 When we boys got old enough to learn trades in school, we would try to fix up the old houses we lived in. But have you ever tried to paint a wall that crumbled when the roller went across it? And bright paint emphasized the holes in the wall. You end up more frustrated than when you began, especially when you know that at best you might come up with only enough money to improve one of the six rooms in the house. And we might move out soon after, anyway.

11 The same goes for keeping a house like that clean. If you have a house full of kids and the house is deteriorating, you'll never keep it clean. Daddy used to yell at Mama about that, but she couldn't do anything. I think Daddy knew it inside, but he had to have an outlet for his rage somewhere, and at least yelling isn't as bad as hitting, which they never did to each other.

12 But you have a kitchen which has no counter space and no hot water, and you will have dirty dishes stacked up. That sounds like an excuse, but try it.

You'll go mad from the sheer sense of futility. It's the same thing in a house with no closets. You can't keep clothes clean and rooms in order if they have to be stacked up with things.

13   Living in a bad house is generally worse on girls. For one thing, they traditionally help their mother with the housework. We boys could get outside and work in the field or cut wood or even play ball and forget about living conditions. The sky was still pretty.

14   But the girls got the pressure, and as they got older it became worse. Would they accept dates knowing they had to "receive" the young man in a dirty hallway with broken windows, peeling wallpaper and a cracked ceiling? You have to live it to understand it, but it creates a shame which drives the soul of a young person inward.

15   I'm thankful none of us ever blamed our parents for this, because it would have crippled our relationships. As it worked out, only the relationship between our parents was damaged. And I think the harshness which they expressed to each other was just an outlet to get rid of their anger at the trap their lives were in. It ruined their marriage because they had no one to yell at but each other. I knew other families where the kids got the abuse, but we were too much loved for that.

16   Once I was about 16 and Mama and Daddy had had a particularly violent argument about the washing machine, which had broken down. Daddy was on the back porch—that's where the only water faucet was—trying to fix it and Mama had a washtub out there washing school clothes for the next day and they were screaming at each other.

17   Later that night everyone was in bed and I heard Daddy get up from the couch where he was reading. I looked out from my bed across the hall into their room. He was standing right over Mama and she was already asleep. He pulled the blanket up and tucked it around her shoulders and just stood there and tears were dropping off his cheeks and I thought I could faintly hear them splashing against the linoleum rug.

18   Now they're divorced.

19   I had courses in college where housing was discussed, but the sociologists never put enough emphasis on the impact living in substandard housing has on a person's psyche. Especially children's.

20   Small children have a hard time understanding poverty. They want the same things children from more affluent families have. They want the same things they see advertised on television, and they don't understand why they can't have them.

21   Other children can be incredibly cruel. I was in elementary school in Georgia—and this is interesting because it is the only thing I remember about that particular school—when I was about eight or nine.

22   After Christmas vacation had ended, my teacher made each student describe all his or her Christmas presents. I became more and more uncomfortable as the privilege passed around the room toward me. Other children were reciting the names of the dolls they had been given, the kinds of bicycles and the grandeur of their games and toys. Some had lists which seemed to go on and on for hours.

23   It took me only a few seconds to tell the class that I had gotten for Christmas a belt and a pair of gloves. And then I was laughed at—because I cried—by a roomful of children and a teacher. I never forgave them, and that night I made my mother cry when I told her about it.

24   In retrospect, I am grateful for that moment, but I remember wanting to die at the time.

READING QUESTIONS

1. Why was the author ashamed of his home? What were some of the physical problems in the house he lived in? Why does the author think that the house was a bigger problem for the girls in the family than for the boys?

2. Why did his parents argue about the washing machine? When the author's father watches the mother sleeping, why does he cry? Why do you think they divorced?

3. How do the children expect other people to react to their poverty? Do other people react as the children expect them to? Why does the author say he's "grateful" for the laughter of the children in his class?

4. What is the effect of poverty on children, according to this writer? How does he suggest poverty affects family relationships?

5. Poverty can affect many parts of life: medical care, education, food, clothing, etc. What aspect of poverty does this essay emphasize? Why is that aspect so important?

WRITING TOPICS

1. Williams suggests that the house we live in can affect our lives in many ways. Write an essay showing how a house can cause problems or benefits for the people who live in it.

2. Williams shows how children and adolescents often judge other people by their money and possessions. Is this still true in our society? Write an essay explaining your views.

3. Williams's parents divorced, and he suggests that the problems of their housing could have been one of the causes. Can money problems cause disruption in a family? Write an essay arguing your point.

GROUP ACTIVITIES

1. This essay shows how lack of money affects people psychologically and socially. List and discuss other ways that poverty can affect people.

2. Find specific details describing the problems of the house that the Williams family lived in. Why are the details important?

RESEARCH TOPICS

1. Find information to support or refute Williams's ideas. Do poor families have more divorces?

2. Find information on problems of poverty in another part of the world. How do those problems compare with those Williams describes?

PREREADING SUGGESTIONS

1. Were you required to do chores as a child? Write about one that you remember.
2. What work do you enjoy as an adult?

The Case Against Chores

by Jane Smiley

Jane Smiley is the author of several novels, including A Thousand Acres *(1992),* Moo *(1996), and* The All-True Travels and Adventures of Lidie Newton *(1998), which take a realistic and sometimes humorous look at the lives of her heroines. This article was first published in 1995 in* Harper's Magazine.

1   I've lived in the upper Midwest for twenty-one years now, and I'm here to tell you that the pressure to put your children to work is unrelenting. So far I've squirmed out from under it, and my daughters have led a life of almost tropical idleness, much to their benefit. My son, however, may not be so lucky. His father was himself raised in Iowa and put to work at an early age, and you never know when, in spite of all my husband's best intentions, that early training might kick in.

2   Although "chores" are so sacred in my neck of the woods that almost no one ever discusses their purpose, I have over the years gleaned some of the reasons parents give for assigning them. I'm not impressed. Mostly the reasons have to do with developing good work habits or, in the absence of good work habits, at least the habits of working. No such thing as a free lunch, any job worth doing is worth doing right, work before play, all of that. According to this reasoning, the world is full of jobs that no one wants to do. If we divide them up and get them over with, then we can go on to pastimes we like. If we do them "right," then we won't have to do them again. Lots of times, though, in a family, that *we* doesn't operate. The operative word is *you*. The practical result of almost every child-labor scheme that I've witnessed is the child doing the dirty work and the parent getting the fun: Mom cooks and Sis does the dishes; the parents plan and plant the garden, the kids weed it. To me, what this teaches the child is the lesson of alienated labor: not to love the work but to get it over with; not to feel pride in one's contribution but to feel resentment at the waste of one's time.

3   Another goal of chores: the child contributes to the work of maintaining the family. According to this rationale, the child comes to understand what it takes to have a family, and to feel that he or she is an important, even indispensable

member of it. But come on. Would you really want to feel loved primarily because you're the one who gets all the floors mopped? Wouldn't you rather feel that your family's love simply exists all around you, no matter what your contribution? And don't the parents love their children anyway, whether the children vacuum or not? Why lie about it just to get the housework done? Let's be frank about the other half of the equation too. In this day and age, it doesn't take much work at all to manage a household, at least in the middle class—maybe four hours a week to clean the house and another four to throw the laundry into the washing machine, move it to the dryer, and fold it. Is it really a good idea to set the sort of example my former neighbors used to set, of mopping the floor every two days, cleaning the toilets every week, vacuuming every day, dusting, dusting, dusting? Didn't they have anything better to do than serve their house?

4   Let me confess that I wasn't expected to lift a finger when I was growing up. Even when my mother had a full-time job, she cleaned up after me, as did my grandmother. Later there was a housekeeper. I would leave my room in a mess when I headed off for school and find it miraculously neat when I returned. Once in a while I vacuumed just because I liked the pattern the Hoover made on the carpet. I did learn how to run water in my cereal bowl before setting it in the sink.

5   Where I discovered work was at the stable, and, in fact, there is no housework like horse-work. You've got to clean the horses' stalls, feed them, groom them, tack them up, wrap their legs, exercise them, turn them out, and catch them. You've got to clip them and shave them. You have to sweep the aisle, clean your tack and your boots, carry bales of hay and buckets of water. Minimal horsekeeping, rising just to the level of humaneness, requires many more hours than making a few beds, and horsework turned out to be a good preparation for the real work of adulthood, which is rearing children. It was a good preparation not only because it was similar in many ways but also because my desire to do it, and to do a good job of it, grew out of my love and interest in my horse. I can't say that cleaning out her bucket when she manured in it was an actual joy, but I knew she wasn't going to do it herself. I saw the purpose of my labor, and I wasn't alienated from it.

6   Probably to the surprise of some of those who knew me as a child, I have turned out to be gainfully employed. I remember when I was in seventh grade, one of my teachers said to me, strongly disapproving, "The trouble with you is you only do what you want to do!" That continues to be the trouble with me, except that over the years I have wanted to do more and more.

7   My husband worked hard as a child, out-Iowa-ing the Iowans, if such a thing is possible. His dad had him mixing cement with a stick when he was five, pushing wheelbarrows not long after. It's a long sad tale on the order of two miles to school and both ways uphill. The result is, he's a great worker, much better than I am, but all the while he's doing it he wishes he weren't. He thinks of it as work; he's torn between doing a good job and longing not to be doing it at all. Later, when he's out on the golf course, where he really wants to be, he feels a little guilty, knowing there's work that should have been done before he gave in and took advantage of the beautiful day.

8   Good work is not the work we assign children but the work they want to do, whether it's reading in bed (where would I be today if my parents had rousted me out and put me to scrubbing floors?) or cleaning their rooms or practicing the flute or making roasted potatoes with rosemary and Parmesan for the family dinner. It's good for a teenager to suddenly decide that the bathtub is so disgusting she'd better clean it herself. I admit that for the parent, this can involve years of waiting. But if she doesn't want to wait, she can always spend her time dusting.

READING QUESTIONS

1. In this essay, the author sometimes gives her own ideas, but often also reports the ideas of other people. Underline three places where she reports the ideas of other people.

2. What are chores? What do parents in her community expect children to learn from chores? Does Smiley agree that children do learn these things?

3. What is another benefit of chores, according to the parents who assign them? How does Smiley argue against them?

4. What work did Smiley do as a child, and why? In what ways was this work good preparation for her future life? Why were her feelings about the work important?

5. What work did her husband do as a child, and why? How does he feel about work now?

WRITING TOPICS

1. Smiley says: "Good work is not the work we assign children but the work they want to do." Explain what this statement means, and write an essay that agrees or disagrees with it.

2. Smiley suggests that modern households require so little real work that the children's contributions are not really necessary. Write an essay agreeing or disagreeing with this idea.

3. Smiley says that chores teach children the wrong lessons, that they learn to hate work rather than to enjoy it. In your experience, is this true? Did your childhood experiences with work cause you to resent or enjoy the work you do as an adult?

GROUP ACTIVITIES

1. Work as a group to make a chart comparing Smiley and her husband. What work did each do as a child? Why? How does each one feel about work now? How do you know?

2. Does it matter whether we enjoy our work or not? Make a list of the work each person in the group enjoys and another list of the work each dislikes. What seems to motivate each group member?

RESEARCH TOPICS

1. Research to find information on motivation and work performance. Is it true that people are better workers if they feel that they have some choice in what they do?

2. Research the work done by children in some other part of the world. How are those children's lives different from the lives described by Smiley?

PREREADING SUGGESTIONS

1. Recall a time when your parents or guardians tried to control your behavior. What was the result?

2. Briefly describe a recent crime committed by teenagers or children.

Punished for the Sins of the Children

by John Leo

John Leo has written for well-known magazines and newspapers for many years, including the New York Times *and* Time. *He was also a commissioner for the New York Environmental Protection Agency. This article was first published in 1995 in* U.S. News and World Report.

1   In a burst of mostly patronizing publicity from the national media, the small town of Silverton, Oregon, and the Oregon state legislature have moved to hold parents responsible for offenses committed by their children.

2   "Both stigmatize parents with their assumption that a child's misbehavior results from a failure of parental supervision," clucked a Page 1 *New York Times* report. And the reporter for public TV's "MacNeil/Lehrer Newshour" explained that Silverton's belief that parents are responsible for children up to age 18 is "a homespun philosophy from a homespun town." (Translation: We are dealing here with a town full of rubes.)

3   What the reporter seemed to think was some sort of rural aberration is actually part of a fast-growing national trend. Hundreds of exasperated communities, large and small, are holding parents responsible for curfew violations, graffiti damage and crimes by their children. Often they impose fines or community service and sometimes require attendance at basic classes on how to parent.

4   Many changes in welfare plans also make parents responsible for their children's attendance at school, and in some public housing, a parent can be evicted if a child is found to be dealing drugs out of the family apartment.

5   In some cases, these laws are popping up in basically stable, but apprehensive, communities. By big-city standards, the level of vandalism and youth

crime in Silverton seems quite low. And in the dozens of Chicago-area communities that now have parental responsibility laws, the targets seem to be illegal teen drinking parties and drunken driving. In these cases, the tactic is chiefly to embarrass well-off parents into taking charge.

6   In devastated urban areas, however, the practical and ethical problems are very different. It can look as though poor mothers are being punished for the sins of children they can't control. Patricia Holdaway, the first parent charged under the curfew law of Roanoke, Virginia, said: "I went through so much with these kids. I'm just ready to just call it quits." Her 16-year-old son, arrested at 5 a.m. for his fifth curfew violation and for driving without a license, said, "I just left. It's not her fault. She shouldn't be held responsible. I know right from wrong."

7   Roanoke's policy is a reasonable one—it wants to work with at-risk youngsters and keep things out of court, if possible. It wants to establish the principle that parents should supervise a youngster in trouble. But in this case, the policy led to a $100 fine and a 10-day jail sentence for a woman who already agreed with the principle of parental responsibility but couldn't enforce it. She is appealing the conviction.

8   Very few parental responsibility laws allow jail terms. But given the stresses on the poor, many of them single mothers, even mandatory community service or $100 fines can be very punitive. That's why parental responsibility laws catch so many of us leaning both ways, pro and con. Are these laws attempts to reassert reasonable civic expectations about parenting, or are they desperate attempts to use the coercive force of the state to solve a cultural problem?

9   "When a culture is in free fall, as ours is, and our nonlegal institutions are falling apart, there's a temptation to move in with laws and government," said David Blankenhorn, president of the Institute for American Values. And the laws work best with parents who are already in control and merely need a wake-up call; they work poorly, or not at all, when the no-parenting ethic is ingrained or passed on from one generation to the next.

10   Still many communities are so besieged that something must be tried. It's hard to keep kids off the streets during early morning hours when gangs are roaming if parents don't cooperate. And the detachment of many parents from the fate of their young is a crucial problem—many don't even bother to go down to a police station to collect an arrested son or daughter.

11   "These laws are signs that the antibodies are starting to kick in," said Roger Conner, head of the American Alliance for Rights and Responsibilities. "But they have to be regarded as experiments. We have to find out what works, what encourages responsibility without resorting to draconian penalties." Conner thinks the Silverton ordinance is too strong—it allows a fine for a first offense, requires parental responsibility to age 18, and has been applied to cover teens caught smoking.

12   The statewide Oregon measure, which has passed the legislature and has to be signed into law by the governor, is more carefully constructed. The law

covers responsibility for children up to age 15—a way of recognizing that older teens are much harder to deal with and sometimes beyond parental control. The first offense draws only a warning. The second time a parent faces mandatory attendance at a parenting class. Only after a third offense is a fine likely, and even then not if a parent can show reasonable efforts to control the child. The offense is civil, not criminal, and parents cannot be jailed.

13   With feedback from the community, these laws can be adjusted depending on results and a changing social consensus. Let the experiments continue.

READING QUESTIONS

1. What new laws does this article describe in the first paragraphs? What does the *New York Times* reporter say about those laws? Paraphrase his statement.
2. Does Leo agree with the reporters? How can you tell?
3. What similar laws does he describe next? How do these laws affect poor parents more than wealthy ones?
4. Why are such laws needed, according to Leo?
5. What are some more reasonable penalties in other communities? Why are these penalties better?
6. What is Leo's position? Does he favor or oppose laws that hold parents responsible for their children's behavior?

WRITING TOPICS

1. Is it necessary to have laws that make parents responsible for their children's behavior? Why or why not?
2. Do you believe that it is possible for a single mother to control the behavior of an older teenager? Write an essay explaining why it would or would not be possible.
3. Do you agree or disagree that some punishments are less fair to poor parents than to rich ones? Write an essay supporting your views.

GROUP ACTIVITIES

1. Leo suggests that laws are used because cultural controls, like families, neighborhoods, or communities no longer work. Is there any other way, besides laws, to help families and neighborhoods restore control over children? Brainstorm ideas.
2. Leo uses a very difficult vocabulary. Pick three difficult sentences and paraphrase them in language a young teenager could understand. Then compare your paraphrases. Which is closest to the original in meaning?

RESEARCH TOPICS

1. Conduct your own research to find ways that children and teenagers were controlled in the past.
   a. Interview members of your family or community.
   b. Look for material in the library and on the Internet comparing parental control over teenagers in the past and in the present.
2. What are the laws in your state concerning parents' responsibility for teenagers' actions?

PREREADING SUGGESTIONS

1. Do you know families in which the father is the parent who contributes most to the children's care? Write a brief description of their abilities.
2. Why is it sometimes difficult for a father to be a good parent?

I, Too, Am a Good Parent

by Dorsett Bennett

This essay was originally published in the "My Turn" column in Newsweek *magazine. Dorsett Bennett lives in Roswell, New Mexico, where he is an attorney. This article was first published in 1994.*

1   Divorce is a fact of modern life. A great number of people simply decide that they do not wish to stay married to their spouse. A divorce is not a tremendously difficult situation unless there are minor children born to a couple. If there are no minor children you simply divided the assets and debts. But you cannot divide a child. The child needs to be placed with the appropriate parent.

2   In my own case, my former wife chose not to remain married to me. That is her right and I do not fault her decision. My problem is that I do not believe it is her right to deny me the privilege of raising our children. Some fathers want to go to the parent/teacher conferences, school plays, carnivals, and to help their kids with homework. I have always looked forward to participating on a daily basis in my children's lives. I can no longer enjoy that privilege—the children live with their mother, who has moved to a northern Midwest state.

3   I tried so hard to gain custody of my children. I believe the evidence is uncontradicted as to what an excellent father (and more important, parent) I am. My ex-wife is a fairly good mother, but unbiased opinions unanimously agreed I was the better parent. Testimonials were videotaped from witnesses who could not attend the out-of-state custody hearing. I choose to be a father.

When I was three years old, my own father left my family. While I've loved my father for many years, I did and still do reject his parental pattern.

4 A couple of centuries ago, a father and mother might have shared equally in the care and raising of children above the age of infancy. But with the coming of the Industrial Revolution the father went to work during the day, leaving the full-time care of the young to the mother, who stayed at home. It was easier to decide who should get child custody under those circumstances. That would be true today even if the mother were put into the position of working outside the home after the divorce.

5 Now, a majority of married mothers are in the workplace—often because the family needs the second income to survive. With the advent of the working mother, we have also seen a change in child care. Not only have we seen an increase in third-party caregivers, there is a decided difference in how fathers interact with their children. Fathers are even starting to help raise their children. I admit that in a great many families there is an uneven distribution of child-care responsibilities. But there are fathers who do as much to raise the children as the mother, and there are many examples where men are full-time parents.

6 But, because we have this past history of the mother being the principal child caregiver, the mother has almost always been favored in any contested child-custody case. The law of every state is replete with decisions showing that the mother is the favored custodial parent. The changes in our lifestyles are now being reflected in our laws. In most, if not all, states, the legislature has recognized the change in child-care responsibilities and enacted legislation that is gender blind. The statutes that deal with child custody now say that the children should be placed with the parent whose care and control of the child will be in the child's best interest.

7 This legislation is enlightened and correct. Society has changed. We no longer bring up our children as we did years ago. But it is still necessary to have someone make the choice in the child's best interest if the parents are divorcing and cannot agree on who takes care of the kids. So we have judges to make that enormous decision.

8 The state legislature can pass laws that say neither parent is favored because of their gender. But it is judges who make the ultimate choice. And those judges are usually *older males* who practiced law during the time when mothers were the favored guardians under the law. These same judges mostly come from a background where mothers stayed home and were the primary caregivers. By training and by personal experience they have a strong natural bias in favor of the mother in a child-custody case. That belief is regressive and fails to acknowledge the changed realities of our present way of life. Someone must be appointed to render a decision when parents cannot agree. I would ask that those judges who make these critical decisions reexamine their attitudes and prejudices against placing children with fathers.

9 After the videotaped testimony was completed, one of my lawyers said he had "never seen a father put together a better custody case." "But," he asked me, "can you prove that she is unfit?" A father should not be placed in the position of having to prove the mother is unfit in order to gain custody. He

should not have to prove that she has two heads, participates in child sacrifice or eats live snakes. The father should only have to prove that he is the
more suitable parent.

10   Fathers should not be discriminated against as I was. It took me three
years to get a trial on the merits in the Minnesota court. And Minnesota has a
law directing its courts to give a high priority to child-custody cases. What
was even worse was that the judge seemed to ignore the overwhelming weight
of the evidence and granted custody to my ex-wife. At the trial, her argument
was, "I am their mother." Other than that statement she hardly put on a case.
Being the mother of the children was apparently deemed enough to outweigh
evidence that all the witnesses who knew us both felt I was the better parent;
that those witnesses who knew only me said what an excellent parent I was;
that our children's behavior always improved dramatically after spending
time with me; that my daughter wished to live with me, and that I had a better child-custody evaluation than my wife.

11   So I say to the trial judges who decide these cases: "Become part of the solution to this dilemma of child custody. Don't remain part of the problem." It is
too late for me. If this backward way of thinking is changed, then perhaps it
won't be too late for other fathers who should have custody of their children.

READING QUESTIONS

1. Why does Bennett want custody of his children?

2. Trace the changes in the history of parenting, according to Bennett.
   How does he think changes in women's work patterns have affected
   childcare? How does this new legislation in many states reflect these
   changes?

3. If the new laws are fair to fathers, why are mothers often given custody? Who decides how the laws are applied? Do the people who make
   the decisions have backgrounds that would cause them to be biased?
   How?

4. What proof did Bennett feel he needed to produce? What evidence did
   his wife need to give? Why does he feel that the courts were unfair?

WRITING TOPICS

1. Can fathers ever be better parents than mothers? Write an essay illustrating your answer.

2. What are some standards for being a good parent that courts should
   use for determining child custody? Write an essay explaining why
   these are important characteristics of a parent.

3. Bennett says that "the child needs to be placed with the appropriate
   parent" (paragraph 1). In your opinion, what is more important: the
   parent's behavior in the marriage or the parent's ability to care for the
   child? Write an essay arguing your point of view.

4. This essay focuses on a parent's ability to care for children. Why is this
   so important in the case of divorce? Write an essay explaining some of

the ways that divorce can affect children. *Optional:* Do research to learn about some of these effects.

5. Is it possible for divorced parents to share the custody of the children? Write an essay examining the dangers as well as the benefits of sharing custody.

GROUP ACTIVITIES

1. Act as judges in the case of Bennett versus his wife. Find the evidence supporting each one's case for custody of the children.

2. List the qualities of an ideal parent. Give an example of each.

RESEARCH TOPICS

1. Find the laws governing child custody in your state.

2. Find statistics on the percentages of single fathers in your state or in the country.

PREREADING SUGGESTIONS

1. When you were a child, was there a food you really hated? Why?

2. What would be some of the problems of being a stepparent?

Hold the Mayonnaise

by Julia Alvarez

Julia Alvarez left the Dominican Republic when she was ten years old because of her father's political activities. Her experiences as a political refugee are described in her book Time of the Butterflies *(1994). She has also written* How the Garcia Girls Lost Their Accents *(1991) and a sequel,* Yo! *This article was first published in 1992 in the* New York Times Magazine.

1   "If I die first and Papi ever gets remarried," Mami used to tease when we were kids, "don't you accept a new woman in my house. Make her life impossible, you hear?" My sisters and I nodded obediently and a filial shudder would go through us. We were Catholics, so of course, the only kind of remarriage we could imagine had to involve our mother's death.

2   We were also Dominicans, recently arrived in Jamaica, Queens, in the early 60's, before waves of other Latin Americans began arriving. So, when we imagined who exactly my father might possibly ever think of remarrying, only American women came to mind. It would be bad enough having a *madrastra,* but a "stepmother." . . .

3   All I could think of was that she would make me eat mayonnaise, a food I identified with the United States and which I detested. Mami understood, of course, that I wasn't used to that kind of food. Even a madrastra, accustomed

to our rice and beans and tostones and pollo frito, would understand. But an American stepmother would think it was normal to put mayonnaise on food, and if she were at all strict and a little mean, which all stepmothers, of course, were, she would make me eat potato salad and such. I had plenty of my own reasons to make a potential stepmother's life impossible. When I nodded obediently with my sisters, I was imagining not just something foreign in our house, but in our refrigerator.

4   So it's strange now, almost 35 years later, to find myself a Latina stepmother of my husband's two tall, strapping, blond, mayonnaise-eating daughters. To be honest, neither of them is a real aficionado of the condiment, but it's a fair thing to add to a bowl of tuna fish or diced potatoes. Their American food, I think of it, and when they head to their mother's or off to school, I push the jar back in the refrigerator behind their chocolate pudding and several open cans of Diet Coke.

5   What I can't push as successfully out of sight are my own immigrant childhood fears of having a *gringa* stepmother with foreign tastes in our house. Except now, I am the foreign stepmother in a gringa household. I've wondered what my husband's two daughters think of this stranger in their family. It must be doubly strange for them that I am from another culture.

6   Of course, there are mitigating circumstances—my husband's two daughters were teenagers when we married, older, more mature, able to understand differences. They had also traveled when they were children with their father, an eye doctor, who worked on short-term international projects with various eye foundations. But still, it's one thing to visit a foreign country, another altogether to find it brought home—a real bear plopped down in a Goldilocks house.

7   Sometimes, a whole extended family of bears. My warm, loud Latino family came up for the wedding: my *tía* from Santo Domingo; three dramatic, enthusiastic sisters and their families; my papi, with a thick accent I could tell the girls found it hard to understand; and my mami, who had her eye trained on my soon-to-be stepdaughters for any sign that they were about to make my life impossible. "How are they behaving themselves?" she asked me, as if they were 7 and 3, not 19 and 16. "They're wonderful girls," I replied, already feeling protective of them.

8   I looked around for the girls in the meadow in front of the house we were building, where we were holding the outdoor wedding ceremony and party. The older hung out with a group of her own friends. The younger one whizzed in briefly for the ceremony, then left again before the congratulations started up. There was not much mixing with me and mine. What was there for them to celebrate on a day so full of confusion and effort?

9   On my side, being the newcomer in someone else's territory is a role I'm used to. I can tap into that struggling English speaker, that skinny, dark-haired, olive-skinned girl in a sixth grade of mostly blond and blue-eyed giants. Those tall, freckled boys would push me around in the playground. "Go back to where you came from!" *"No comprendo!"* I'd reply, though of course there was no misunderstanding the fierce looks on their faces.

10   Even now, my first response to a scowl is that old pulling away. (My husband calls it "checking out.") I remember times early on in the marriage when the girls would be with us, and I'd get out of school and drive around doing errands,

killing time, until my husband, their father, would be leaving work. I am not proud of my fears, but I understand—as the lingo goes—where they come from.

11   And I understand, more than I'd like to sometimes, my stepdaughters' pain. But with me, they need never fear that I'll usurp a mother's place. No one has ever come up and held their faces and then addressed me, "They look just like you." If anything, strangers to the remarriage are probably playing Mr. Potato Head in their minds, trying to figure out how my foreign features and my husband's fair Nebraskan features got put together in these two tall, blond girls. "My husband's daughters," I kept introducing them.

12   Once, when one of them visited my class and I introduced her as such, two students asked me why. "I'd be so hurt if my stepmom introduced me that way," the young man said. That night I told my stepdaughter what my students had said. She scowled at me and agreed. "It's so weird how you call me Papa's daughter. Like you don't want to be related to me or something."

13   "I didn't want to presume," I explained. "So it's O.K. if I call you my stepdaughter?"

14   "That's what I am," she said. Relieved, I took it for a teensy inch of acceptance. The takings are small in this stepworld, I've discovered. Sort of like being a minority. It feels as if all the goodies have gone somewhere else.

15   Day to day, I guess I follow my papi's advice. When we first came, he would talk to his children about how to make it in our new country. "Just do your work and put in your heart, and they will accept you!" In this age of remaining true to your roots, of keeping your Spanish, of fighting from inside your culture, that assimilationist approach is highly suspect. My Latino students—who don't want to be called Hispanics anymore—would ditch me as faculty adviser if I came up with that play-nice message.

16   But in a stepfamily where everyone is starting a new life together, it isn't bad advice. Like a potluck supper, an American concept my *mami* never took to. ("Why invite people to your house and then ask them to bring the food?") You put what you've got together with what everyone else brought and see what comes out of the pot. The luck part is if everyone brings something you like. No potato salad, no deviled eggs, no little party sandwiches with you know what in them.

READING QUESTIONS

1. Why did the author and her sisters think about having a stepmother? What was so terrible about mayonnaise to them?

2. What does the author mean when she describes herself as "a real bear plopped down in a Goldilocks house" (paragraph 6)?

3. How did her stepchildren interact with her own family on the day of the wedding? How does she think the children must have felt? What childhood memories still affect the author as an adult?

4. How do she and her daughters resolve the problem of introductions? What does this show about their developing relationship?

5. Why does she compare a stepfamily to a potluck dinner?

WRITING TOPICS

1. Do you think it is possible for marriages between people from different cultures to be successful? Write an essay giving evidence for your belief.

2. Alvarez says she is "relieved . . . for a teensy inch of acceptance" (paragraph 14). Do you think her cautious approach to her stepdaughters is appropriate? Write an essay explaining how a stepparent can win the stepchildren's approval and acceptance.

3. Alvarez says that assimilation is necessary in a family, but may not be accepted in a community. What does *assimilation* mean? Write an essay comparing assimilation in families and communities.

4. Write an essay narrating your own encounter with a different culture.

GROUP ACTIVITIES

1. Outline the essay. What is the main idea of each section? What is the main idea of the essay?

2. What foods are important to members of the group? List the foods you hated and the foods you loved as a child. What is a new food each has learned to like as an adult? Are any of these foods related to your family's customs?

RESEARCH TOPICS

1. Research the origins of mayonnaise. Was it originally an American food? What are some foods eaten in Puerto Rico that are now available in other parts of the United States?

2. How successful are second marriages? Find statistics comparing the success of second marriages to the success of first marriages.

Drugs

Exploring the Theme

■ Califano argues against the legalization of drugs whereas the editorial "Legalize It" argues in favor of legalization. Use library sources to examine other writers' ideas on this controversial topic. Which side presents the strongest argument?

■ The editorial "Legalize It" discusses the public's fear of crime and the public's perception that drugs are directly related to crime. What percentage of crimes have studies directly linked to drug use? Is the association the public makes between drugs and crime valid? Is this an irrational fear created by the rhetoric associated with the war on drugs? Use library research to validate or invalidate this perception by the public.

■ We have a "war on drugs," but we don't have a "war on alcohol." Which is the most dangerous and which costs our society more in terms of money, life, and ruined lives? Support your argument with research.

PREREADING SUGGESTIONS

1. Find definitions for *cirrhosis, psychosis, revisionist, civil liberties.*
2. What was Prohibition and when did it take place?

Legalization of Narcotics: Myths and Reality
by Joseph A. Califano

Many have argued that the "war on drugs" is a failure. After decades of fighting drug pushers, growers, and manufacturers, drugs still flow in large quantities into the United States. In response, critics of our drug policies have called for legalization, arguing that it is the only means we have to control the drug problem. In the following article, Joseph A. Califano examines the claims of those who favor the legalization of drugs. Mr. Califano, president of The National Center on Addiction and Substance Abuse at Columbia University, New York, was Secretary of Health, Education, and Welfare during the Carter Administration and served as President Lyndon Johnson's top aide for domestic affairs from 1965 to 1969. This article was first published in 1997 in USA Today.

1 When the high priests of America's political right and left as articulate as the *National Review*'s William F. Buckley and the *New York Times*' Anthony Lewis peddle the same drug legalization line, it is time to shout caveat emptor—buyer beware. The boomlet to legalize drugs like heroin, cocaine, and marijuana that they, and magazines like *New York*, are trying to propagate is founded in myths, not realities, and it is the nation's children who could suffer long-lasting, permanent damage.

2   *Myth:* There has been no progress in the war on drugs.

3   *Reality:* The U.S. Department of Health and Human Services' National Household Drug Survey, the nation's most extensive assessment of drug usage, reports that, from 1979 to 1994, marijuana users dropped from 23,000,000 to 10,000,000, while cocaine users fell from 4,400,000 to 1,400,000. The drug-using segment of the population also is aging. In 1979, 10 percent were over age 34; today, almost 30 percent are. The number of hardcore addicts has held steady at around 6,000,000, a situation most experts attribute to the unavailability of treatment and the large number of addicts in the pipeline.

4   *Myth:* Whether to use drugs and become hooked is an adult decision.

5   *Reality:* It is children who choose. Hardly anyone in America begins drug use after age twenty-one. Based on everything known, an individual who does not smoke, use drugs, or abuse alcohol by twenty-one is virtually certain never to do so. The nicotine pushers understand this, which is why they fight so strenuously to kill efforts to keep their stuff away from kids.

6   *Myth:* Legalized drugs would be only for adults and not available to children.

7   *Reality:* Nothing in the American experience gives any credence to the ability to keep legal drugs out of the hands of children. It is illegal for them to purchase cigarettes, beer, and liquor. Nevertheless, 3,000,000 adolescents smoke, an average of half a pack a day, constituting a $1,000,000,000-a-year market; and 12,000,000 underage Americans drink, a $10,000,000,000-a-year market.

8   *Myth:* Legalization would reduce crime and social problems.

9   *Reality:* Any short-term reduction in arrests from repealing drug laws would evaporate quickly as use increased and the criminal conduct—assault, murder, rape, child molestation, vandalism, and other violence—that drugs like cocaine and methamphetamines spawn exploded. The U.S. Department of Justice reports that criminals commit six times as many homicides, four times as many assaults, and almost one and a half times as many robberies under the influence of drugs as they do in order to get money to buy drugs.

10   *Myth:* The American experience with prohibition of alcohol supports drug legalization.

11   *Reality:* This ignores two important distinctions: Possession of alcohol for personal consumption was not illegal, and alcohol, unlike illegal drugs such as heroin and cocaine, has a long history of broad social acceptance dating back to the Old Testament and ancient Greece. Largely because of this, the public and political consensus favoring Prohibition was short-lived. By the early 1930s, most Americans no longer supported it. Today, though, the public overwhelmingly favors keeping illegal drugs illegal.

12   Despite these differences, which made Prohibition more difficult to enforce than the current drug laws, alcohol consumption dropped from 1.96 gallons per person in 1919 to .97 gallons per person in 1934, the first full year after Prohibition ended. Death rates from cirrhosis among men came down from 29.5 per 100,000 in 1911 to 10.7 per 100,000 in 1929. During Prohibition, admission to mental health institutions for alcohol psychosis dropped 60 percent; arrests for drunk and disorderly conduct went down 50 percent; welfare agencies reported significant declines in cases due to alcohol-related family problems; and the death rate from impure alcohol did not rise.

13   Neither did Prohibition generate a crime wave. Homicide increased at a higher rate between 1900 and 1910 than during Prohibition, and organized crime was well-established in the cities before 1920.

14   I put these facts on the record not to support a return to Prohibition, something I strongly oppose, but to set the historical record straight and temper the revisionist view of legalizers who take their history from celluloid images of 1930s gangster movies.

15   *Myth:* Greater availability and legal acceptability of drugs would not increase use.

16   *Reality:* This defies not only experience, but human nature. In the 1970s, the United States de facto decriminalized marijuana. The Shafer Commission appointed by President Richard Nixon recommended decriminalization, as did President Jimmy Carter. The result was a soaring increase in marijuana use, particularly among youngsters. Today, just 11 percent of Americans report seeing drugs available in the area where they live; after legalization, there could be a place to purchase drugs in every neighborhood.

17   Today, the United States has 50,000,000 nicotine addicts, 18,000,000 alcoholics and alcohol abusers, and 6,000,000 illegal drug addicts. It is logical to conclude that, if drugs are easier to obtain, less expensive, and socially acceptable, more individuals will use them. Experts such as Columbia University's Herbert Kleber believe that, with legalization, the number of cocaine addicts alone would jump beyond the number of alcoholics.

18   *Myth:* Legalization will save money by allowing the government to spend less on law enforcement and permit taxation of drug sales.

19   *Reality:* While legalization temporarily might take some of the burden off the criminal justice system, such a policy would impose heavy additional costs on the health care and social service systems, schools, and the workplace. Like advocates of legalization today, opponents of alcohol prohibition claimed that taxes on the legal sale of alcohol would increase revenues dramatically and help erase the deficit. The real-world result has been quite different.

20   *Myth:* Drug use is an issue of civil liberties.

21   *Reality:* This is a convenient misreading of John Stuart Mill's *On Liberty*. Legalizers cite Mill to argue that the state has no right to interfere in the private life of a citizen who uses drugs; only when an action harms someone else may the state take steps to prevent it. They ignore the fact that Mill's conception of freedom does not extend to the right of individuals to enslave themselves or to decide that they will give up their liberty. Mill wrote with blunt clarity: "The principle of freedom cannot require that he should be free not to be free. It is not freedom to be allowed to alienate his freedom."

22   Drug addiction is a form of enslavement. It "alters pathologically the nature and character of abusers," says Phoenix House president Mitchell Rosenthal. Even Mill at his most expansive would admit that the state can take action not just to free addicts from chains of chemical dependency that take away the freedom to be all that God meant them to be, but to prevent those bonds from shackling them. A nation devoted to individual freedom has an obligation to nourish a society and legal structure that protect people from the slavery of drug addiction.

23   Even Mill's most libertarian contention—that the state can regulate only those actions which directly affect others—does not support individual drug abuse and addiction. Such conduct does affect others directly, from the abused spouse and baby involuntarily addicted through the mother's umbilical cord to innocent bystanders injured or killed by adolescents high on crack

cocaine. The drug abuser's conduct has a direct and substantial impact on every taxpayer who foots the bill for the criminal and health cost consequences of such actions.

24   Certainly a society that recognizes the state's compelling interest in banning (and stopping individuals from using) lead paint, asbestos insulation, unsafe toys, and flammable fabrics hardly can ignore its interest in banning cocaine, heroin, marijuana, methamphetamines, and hallucinogens. Indeed, refusing to include drug use in the right of privacy, the Supreme Court has approved state laws that prohibit even the sacramental use of peyote. With the exception of Alaska, state courts have held that possession of marijuana in the home is not protected by the right of privacy.

25   *Myth:* Legalization works well in European countries.

26   *Reality:* The ventures of Switzerland, England, the Netherlands, and Italy into drug legalization have had disastrous consequences. Switzerland's "Needle Park," touted as a way to restrict a few hundred heroin addicts to a small area, turned into a grotesque tourist attraction of 20,000 heroin addicts and junkies that had to be closed down before it infected the city of Zurich. England's foray into allowing any doctor to prescribe heroin quickly was curbed as heroin use increased.

27   In the Netherlands, anyone over age 17 can drop into a marijuana "coffee shop" and pick types of marijuana like one might choose flavors of ice cream. Adolescent pot use there jumped nearly 200 percent while it was dropping by 66 percent in the United States. As crime and availability of drugs rose and complaints from city residents about the decline in their quality of life multiplied, the Dutch parliament moved to trim back the number of marijuana distribution shops in Amsterdam. Dutch persistence in selling pot has angered European neighbors because its wide-open attitude toward marijuana is believed to be spreading pot and other drugs beyond the Netherlands' borders.

28   Italy infrequently is mentioned by advocates of legalization, despite its lenient drug laws. Personal possession of small amounts of drugs has not been a crime in Italy since 1975, other than a brief period of recriminalization between 1990 and 1993. (Even then, Italy permitted an individual to possess one dose of a drug.) Under decriminalization, possession of two to three doses of drugs such as heroin generally was exempt from criminal sanction. Today, Italy has 300,000 addicts, the highest rate of heroin addiction in Europe. Seventy percent of all AIDS cases in Italy are attributable to drug use.

29   In contrast, Sweden offers an example of a successful restrictive drug policy. After a brief period of permitting doctors to give drugs to addicts, Sweden adopted the American policy of seeking a drug-free society in 1980. By 1988, Sweden had seen drug use among young Army conscripts drop 75 percent and use by nine-graders fall 66 percent.

30   What is most disturbing about the arguments for legalization is that they glide over the impact such a policy would have on American children. The United States assuredly is not the Garden of Eden of the Old Testament. Dealing with evil, including drugs, is part of the human experience. Nevertheless, there is a special obligation to protect youngsters from evil, and drugs are first

and foremost an issue about children. It is adolescent experimentation that leads to abuse and addiction.

31   Today, most kids don't use illicit drugs, but all of them, particularly the poorest, are vulnerable to abuse and addiction. Russian roulette is not a game anyone should play. Legalizing drugs not only is playing Russian roulette with children, it is slipping a couple of extra bullets into the chamber.

READING QUESTIONS

1. In the first sentence, Califano refers to the "political right and left." Who are we generally referring to when using those terms? What ideas or policies are generally attributed to the political right? What ideas or policies are generally associated with the political left?

2. In paragraph 5, Califano mentions the "nicotine pushers." Who is he referring to? How does what he says about nicotine relate to drug use?

WRITING TOPICS

1. Califano believes that legalization of drugs would cause more problems than it would solve. Is Califano right? Would legalization lead to greater problems or would legalization solve many of the problems we now have?

2. Califano dismisses the civil liberties argument which states that we as citizens have the right to do whatever we want as long as we don't harm other people. Do you agree with Califano or the civil libertarians on this issue?

GROUP ACTIVITIES

1. Califano presents his reader the arguments for legalization in one sentence and then provides us with a paragraph arguing against that position. As readers, we are never given a full explanation of the arguments for legalization. Have each member of the group take one or more arguments for legalization. Write a paragraph that more fully explains the argument for legalization.

2. Form small groups and assign an argument for legalization to each member. Research that topic in the library. After seeing the full arguments for legalization, do you find Califano's arguments as strong? Share the information you gather with the rest of your group.

RESEARCH TOPIC

Califano believes that experiments with drug legalization in Europe have failed. Research this topic to see what opinions others have on this subject. Who presents the strongest argument concerning the failure or success of European drug laws?

PREREADING SUGGESTIONS

1. Make a list of the things you associate with illegal drug use.
2. Explain what you think the connection is between drug use and crime.
3. Describe what you think the typical drug user is like.

Legalize It

As the following article points out, most citizens are concerned with crime and drugs. When we think about the drug problem, we often think of the sleazy, playground pusher trying to get kids hooked on drugs. We think of machine-gun-toting drug dealers, willing to kill to see that their drugs hit the streets. We think of the poor victims of drug use, hooked on the drug, unable to stop until an overdose kills them. The writer of this editorial suggests that our notions about drug problems may be all wrong. This selection was first published in 1993 as an editorial in the New Statesman & Society.

1   Tony Blair is partly right. Responding, at the weekend, to the latest announcements in Home Secretary Michael Howard's 27-step plan to combat crime, he said that proposed new laws to deal with hunt saboteurs and new age travelers were side-issues compared with what most people were really concerned about—violent crime, muggings, burglaries . . . and drugs.

2   The shadow home secretary is partly right because virtually everything Howard has announced since the Tories went big on retribution and small on thinking at their Blackpool conference has been either irrelevant, wrong-headed or downright counter-productive. More people in prison, more austere prison regimes, less sympathy for the criminal, more for the victim—it sounds good from the platform (or it did to the audience at Blackpool, at any rate), but it will do about as much good in reducing crime as will cutting off people's benefits in reducing unemployment.

3   The concentration on minor "problems," moreover, and the minorities associated with them, reflects the void at the heart of government policy-making. The fact is that, beyond a vague rhetoric around the belief that tougher punishments will reverse rising crime, the Tories are at a loss about what to do. Like the public at large, they are confused and distressed about a society that, in terms of the extent and—sometimes—the nature of criminal behavior, seems to be coming apart at the seams. But, deprived of an adequate explanation, still less a strategy, to deal with the country's criminal ills, increasingly they lash out indiscriminately, seeking not so much solutions as scapegoats: single mothers, squatters, new age travelers, hunt saboteurs.

4   Far from bringing down the crime figures, the outcome of such scapegoating, ironically, will be to create completely new classes of criminals. It is a sign of a government that has wholly lost its way in criminal policy that it is now countenancing laws whose principal effect will be to make potential criminals

out of 50,000 squatters, 10,000 or so travelers and many thousands more anti-hunt campaigners who will have done nothing worse than to partake in peaceful protests. These groups have nothing to do with rising crime (or where they do, existing laws are adequate to deal with them). Their criminalization is both irrelevant to the real problem and an indication of a nasty, narrow (and often wholly disingenuous) suburban moralism now being elevated to the pretense of a political philosophy by John Major and his ministers.

5   In this small-minded universe, drugs are the demon king. They go to the heart of every fear of petty prejudice, blinding the judgment of those who would blame them for all social ills as surely as they blind the judgment of those for whom they become a destructive addiction. And it is here that Tony Blair is wrong. Drugs may be central to public concern about crime, although the evidence is patchy. But such concern is in large part to do with the exaggerated association by politicians and the media of drug-taking with criminal behavior.

6   Of course, the production and supply of illicit drugs is, by definition, part of a criminal subculture. Of course, the very illegality of drugs brings users into contact with that subculture and turns them into potential offenders. Of course, the combination of addiction, high prices, and limited availability means some users turn to crime to finance their habits.

7   The normal reality of drug supply and use, however, is a long way from the media stereotype of gun-toting Yardie dealers preying on needle-scarred, AIDS-carrying junkies, who prostitute their bodies and steal from their neighbors in a cycle of personal and social decline. The more typical picture is one of recreational drug use, as represented by the recent survey showing that up to half of young people take illegal drugs regularly. (This was roundly dismissed, incidentally, by one government minister on *Question Time,* who said that the people running the survey obviously didn't talk to the same young people as he did. This represents another trait in government policy-making: if you don't like the figures, deny their veracity—and hence disregard the problem.)

8   Such drug use is, broadly speaking, harmless—or at any rate no more harmful than the kind of alcohol and nicotine consumption that passes as usual social behavior. Certainly, it should not be subject to criminal sanctions.

9   The fact is that the criminal law works no better in combating illicit drug consumption today than when it was employed against alcohol during Prohibition. As Alexander Cockburn writes, in the United States, 54 federal agencies, with a budget of $13 billion, have achieved nothing in their "war on drugs" other than the criminalization of large sections of the population. As the numbers in U.S. prisons doubled during the 1980s, to almost one million today, it was crimes of simple drug possession that put many of the new prisoners behind bars. And the switch to crack-cocaine, the scourge of black inner cities, was itself brought about because the war on drugs made it so much more difficult to distribute the more bulky (and less profitable, weight-for-weight) marijuana.

10   The British police have so far taken a more sensible approach. More than half of those arrested for possession of cannabis now receive cautions, compared with 2 percent ten years ago. Even so, people are still being sent to jail

for simple possession, and of 72,000 seizures in 1992, 57,700 involved cannabis. Only 880 involved crack, 2,400 MDMA (Ecstasy) and 3,000 heroin. The "war on drugs" remains primarily a war on one soft drug, cannabis. If it "succeeds," its principal effect, as in the United States, is likely to be to push suppliers into dealing in other, hard drugs.

11   Biting the bullet of decriminalization (with the war on addiction being fought through education and treatment) may be more than any politician is prepared to take on yet. But until they do, Tony Blair—or whoever—will never be more than partly right.

READING QUESTIONS

1. What does the editorial suggest is the image most people have of drug users?

2. When it comes to crime, what does the article say most citizens are concerned with?

3. What are new age travelers? (Look at how the term is used in the essay.)

4. What are hunt saboteurs? (Look at how the term is used in the essay.)

5. Who does the editorial say is being blamed for the rise in crime? Why?

6. The article says that "drugs may be central to public concern about crime" (paragraph 5). Why is it believed that drugs are related to crime?

7. According to the article, the general perception we have about drug users is wrong. What does the article suggest is a truer image of drug users?

8. What, according to the editorial, has been the effect of drug laws and the "war on drugs"?

9. In 1992, we are told, 57,000 seizures of marijuana were made and 3,000 seizures of heroin. What point is the author making?

10. What does the article seem to suggest should be done about the drug "problem"?

WRITING TOPICS

1. Several sections of this article suggest that there really isn't a drug problem or that it isn't as bad as we perceive it to be. Do you find this assertion valid?

2. The editorial states that "drug use is, broadly speaking, harmless—or at any rate no more harmful than the kind of alcohol and nicotine consumption that passes as usual social behavior" (paragraph 8). What is the rationale behind this statement? Do you agree?

3. We are told that in Great Britain, "a more sensible approach" (paragraph 10) is being taken toward the possession of marijuana—violators are issued a caution rather than being arrested. Is it sensible to decriminalize marijuana? Use the reading and your own ideas.

GROUP ACTIVITIES

1. The editorial argues that the drug problem isn't really the problem we think it is. If the article is right, then our society is taking time and money away from more serious problems. As a group, discuss other problems our nation faces that may be even more harmful to our society than drugs.

2. Although the article downplays the harmful effects of drugs on our society as a whole, politicians and citizens have been so concerned that for decades we have waged a "war on drugs." List and discuss the arguments on each side. As a group, try to come to a decision as to who is right.

RESEARCH TOPIC

The article argues that the "war on drugs" has been a failure. Use library research to defend or attack this statement. Look for information supportive of the "war on drugs" effort. Which is the stronger argument?

PREREADING SUGGESTION

What is fetal alcohol syndrome (FAS)? What causes it? When was it first identified?

Fetal Alcohol Syndrome: A National Perspective

by Michael Dorris

Alcohol abuse is a destructive force we usually associate with auto fatalities and abuse within the family. Michael Dorris focuses on another problem related to alcohol abuse, fetal alcohol syndrome (FAS). Dorris had first-hand experience with the effects of FAS: his adopted son was a victim of FAS. This selection is from Paper Trail *(1994) by Michael Dorris.*

1 At the time I adopted my oldest son, Abel, in 1971, I knew that his birth mother had been a heavy drinker, but even the medical textbooks in those days stated that exposure to alcohol could not damage a developing fetus. I knew that Abel had been born small and premature, had "failed to thrive," and was an initially slow learner, but for ten years as a single parent I convinced myself that nurture, a stimulating environment, and love could open up life to my little boy.

2 It wasn't true. At the University of Washington and elsewhere, biochemists and psychologists now confirm that for some women even moderate doses of prenatal exposure to alcohol can permanently stunt a human being's potential. According to the U.S. surgeon general, *no* level of ethanol is guaranteed to be "safe."

3   My grown son has a full range of physical disorders: seizures; curvature of the spine; poor coordination, sight, and hearing. But his most disabling legacy has to do with his impaired ability to reason. Fetal alcohol syndrome (FAS) victims are known for their poor judgment, their impulsiveness, their persistent confusions over handling money, telling time, and in distinguishing right from wrong.

4   Since the publication of *The Broken Cord* last August, I have received an outpouring of wrenching letters from literally hundreds of readers—rural and urban, religious and agnostic, of all ethnic and economic backgrounds—who share experiences of heartache, grief, and frustration uncannily identical to my wife's and mine. Their sons, daughters, or grandchildren have been repeatedly misdiagnosed with the same amorphous labels: retarded, sociopathic, attention-deficit, unteachable troublemakers.

5   A majority of full-blown FAS victims are adopted or in state care, but many children who are less drastically impaired (i.e., with fetal alcohol effect [FAE]) remain with their natural parents. Depending on the term of pregnancy in which the harmful drinking occurred, these individuals may look perfectly healthy and test in the normal range for intelligence, yet by early adolescence they show unmistakable signs of comprehension problems or uncontrollable rage. It is currently estimated that in the United States some eight thousand babies are born annually with full FAS and another sixty-five thousand with a degree of FAE. Nothing will ever restore them to the people they might otherwise have been.

6   And it seems that's far less than the half of it. An additional three hundred thousand babies prenatally bombarded with illegal drugs will be born in this country in 1990. Recent studies indicate that crack cocaine, if smoked during pregnancy, causes learning deficits in offspring similar to those caused by alcohol. The "first generation" of children from the 1980s' crack epidemic is about to enter public school, and these children are consistently described as "remorseless," "without a conscience," and passive, apparently lacking that essential empathy, that motivation toward cooperation, upon which a peaceful and harmonious classroom—and society—so depends.

7   No curriculum or training program has so far proven to be completely effective for people with this totally preventable affliction, and a Los Angeles pilot education project costs taxpayers $15,000 a year per pupil. However, the price of doing nothing, of ignoring the issue, is beyond measure.

8   Nothing like crack—a baby shower gift of choice in certain populations because it is reputed to speed and ease labor—has occurred before. According to one survey, upwards of 11 percent of all U.S. infants in 1988 tested positive for cocaine or alcohol the first time their blood was drawn. A New York City Health Department official estimated that births to drug-abusing mothers had increased there by about 3,000 percent in the past ten years.

9   Why? Some explanations have to do with a paucity of available services and support. Too many fathers regard their baby's health as solely their partner's concern. Only one residential treatment program specifically for chemi-

cally dependent pregnant women exists in New York City, where the State Assembly Committee on Alcoholism and Drug Abuse estimates that "twelve thousand babies will be born addicted . . . in 1989, and the number of children in foster care has doubled in two years from twenty-seven thousand in 1987 to more than fifty thousand today, mainly because of prenatal drug abuse." The system has broken down. Sixteen percent of all American mothers have had insufficient prenatal medical attention—increasing to 33 percent for unmarried or teenage mothers, 30 percent for Hispanic women, and 27 percent for black women.

10   At last, thanks to a 1989 act of Congress, liquor bottle labels must include a warning, and signs posted in many bars proclaim the hazards of alcohol to unborn children. But what happens when public education doesn't work as a deterrent, when a pregnant woman herself is a victim of FAS or prenatal crack and therefore cannot understand the long-term disastrous consequences for the life of another resulting from what she drinks or inhales? It isn't that these women don't love the *idea* of their babies. They just can't foresee the cruel realities.

11   The conflict of competing rights—of protecting immediate civil liberty versus avoiding future civil strife—is incredibly complex, with no unambiguously right or easy answers, but as a nation it's unconscionable to delay the debate. If we close our eyes, we condemn children not yet even conceived to existences of sorrow and deprivation governed by prison, victimization, and premature death.

12   My wife and I think of these tragedies as we wait for our son to have brain surgery that may reduce the intensity of his seizures, though not eliminate them. At twenty-two, despite all of our efforts and his best intentions, he remains forever unable to live independently, to manage a paycheck, or to follow the plot of a TV sitcom, and we worry about the very fabric of society when hundreds of thousands of others with problems similar to his or worse become teenagers, become adults, beyond the year 2000.

READING QUESTIONS

1. What are some of the effects that FAS has on children?
2. What difficulties do children face who have FAS?
3. What difficulties do parents face who have a child with FAS?
4. Based on what Dorris presents, what are the differences between the symptoms of FAS and the symptoms of children whose mothers smoked crack during pregnancy?

WRITING TOPICS

1. Although it is now well-known that using alcohol during pregnancy can harm a fetus, some women continue to drink and use drugs while pregnant. Dorris states, "the price of doing nothing, of ignoring the issue, is beyond measure" (paragraph 7). What things have been done

that Dorris mentions? What further steps can be taken to reduce the number of women who abuse drugs and alcohol during pregnancy?

2. Women who abuse alcohol and drugs during pregnancy show a lack of responsibility for their actions and show a lack of concern for the impact their actions will have on the fetus. Referring to the reading and your own ideas, discuss other ways people act irresponsibly and disregard the safety of others.

GROUP ACTIVITY

Alcohol isn't illegal. There are no laws that say women can't drink during pregnancy. Should there be laws against drinking while pregnant? Could they be enforced? If a child is born with alcohol in its system, should the mother be prosecuted by the law for child abuse? As a group, discuss these issues. What conclusions can you draw? Is there a solution to this problem?

RESEARCH TOPICS

1. How much alcohol must a women drink to cause FAS in her child? Is it only at certain times during the pregnancy that drinking can lead to FAS? Will beer or wine cause any harm or is it only hard liquor that leads to FAS? Research FAS to see what is currently known about this disorder.

2. Dorris informs his readers that babies are also being born with cocaine in their systems. What effects do drugs like cocaine have on a developing fetus? Are they the same as the effects of alcohol? Use library sources to investigate the effects of drugs other than alcohol on a fetus.

PREREADING SUGGESTION

What has been your experience with alcohol in college? What kinds of stories have you heard about students drinking once they go off to college? Write down as many specific instances as you can.

Plugging the Kegs

by J. J. Thompson

Toga! Toga! That was the chant of the characters in the film Animal House *before their fraternity launched a party fueled by gallons and gallons of alcohol. The film's comic look into college fraternity life avoided the serious ramifications of college drinking. Thompson gives his readers a more sober look at the true cost of alcohol abuse in our colleges. This article was first published in 1998 in* U.S. News and World Report.

1 Jason McCray remembers drinking shots at JB's in Tallahassee, Florida, but after that the details of his twenty-first birthday fade. The college senior knows from photos his buddies took that, several pubs later, he forced down double shots of whiskey and later vomited under the bar. (They got photos of that, too.) "They had to carry me out," he says.

2 Thus ended McCray's Tennessee Waltz, a coming-of-legal-age ritual in which Florida State University students celebrate turning twenty-one with a free drink, in addition to those bought by friends, at each of the half-dozen or so bars along Tennessee Street.

3 McCray denies that his birthday binge is the way he typically drinks. But it does represent the manner of drinking that too many expect and experience at college. Surveys show that up to 85 percent of all college students imbibe and that nearly half drink heavily. In 1949, when the first thorough study of college drinking was made, undergraduates drank no more than others their age, and college life did not encourage excessive tippling. The same can't be said today. College students drink more because college officials are less strict and many young people drink in high school or before. The result is that students now enter college cultures in which drinking is not only common but is done mainly to get drunk.

4 Schools tend to respond with hand-wringing, saying there is little they can do. Recent research, including a study by *U.S. News,* indicates that's not so. *U.S. News* got responses from 69 percent of the 1,320 presidents of four-year colleges and universities it surveyed to learn what makes a difference. The survey found that while college presidents try to highlight the evils of student alcohol abuse, many don't see how common binge drinking really is. Only 3 percent of the presidents responding to the questionnaire estimated a rate as high as that found by a Harvard University study and, remarkably, 21 percent couldn't say how common it was on their campuses. Some researchers argue that it is a good idea to teach students when to say when; others say it may be even better for schools to prohibit them from drinking. The *U.S. News* survey and follow-up reporting suggest that schools that allow drinking on campus are up to three times more likely to experience high numbers of binge drinkers.

5 College students don't just down more alcohol, experts say; many often swill stronger forms, such as "PGA" (pure grain alcohol) and potent concoctions of several alcoholic beverages—sometimes through funnels or directly from the keg taps, while hanging upside down. "When I was in school, if you got drunk once a week, you were thought to be somebody no one wanted to hang out with, never mind [getting drunk] three or four times a week," says Fran Cohen, 52, director of the Office of Student Life at the University of Rhode Island. Now she deals with students who don't seem to mind the drunken behavior, wooziness, vomiting, and passing out that accompany too much alcohol.

6 A late-fall fraternity bash at DePauw University in Greencastle, Indiana, proves her point. Guests—many of whom had already achieved a buzz at smaller parties and at the football game against rival Wabash College—tossed empty beer bottles from the balcony of the Delta Tau Delta house,

watching them smash in the courtyard. Their target was the fraternity crest, and guests knew to walk far clear of the area when a big bash was going on. Inside, several hundred people, many of them riding on another's shoulders, screamed over the stereo's throbbing bass. Men and women waited their turns to lie on their backs and have beer or schnapps poured out of a bell, the trophy of that day's football victory, into their mouths. After each student gulped—be it one or twelve—he or she rose to the cheers of the crowd and the clanking of the bell. Meanwhile, a nauseated woman leaned over a plastic trash can for several minutes, a man holding her so she wouldn't topple in headfirst.

7   Social scientists call this "binge drinking," defined as five or more drinks for a man at any one time within a two-week period, four or more drinks for a woman. This definition doesn't mean getting falling-down drunk, says Dr. Henry Wechsler, principal investigator in the Harvard study of college drinking. Instead, having five drinks in a row indicates problems associated with drinking. What's more, he found that few students who consume five fail to drink six or more. "It's right there, it's free, it's in front of you, and the next thing you know you've had twelve drinks in an hour and you can't move," one college senior explains.

8   The Harvard study showed that 44 percent of all undergraduates in the United States binge drink—a rate that has been fairly constant for almost 20 years. It also found that 23 percent of the men and 17 percent of the women were frequent binge drinkers—downing a bunch of drinks three or more times in two weeks.

9   This much drinking takes its toll. Tim Anderl, an Ohio University senior, says that typically, "By the end of the fall, you're broke and your grades are in the gutter." Indeed, many students spend more money in a semester on alcohol—over $300—than they do on books. There's also a correlation between drinking and grades. One study found that A students have, on average, three drinks a week, while those making D's and F's average 11 drinks a week.

10   *Sex and Violence*   Problems with grades aren't the only ones plaguing binge drinkers. They are two to five times as likely as other drinkers to engage in unplanned or unprotected sex, get injured, damage property, argue, fight, or face trouble with the police.

11   And some die. Scott Krueger, eighteen, a high-achieving freshman at Massachusetts Institute of Technology, overdosed on alcohol at a fraternity party in September, slipped into a coma, and died three days later. Leslie Anne Baltz was a twenty-one-year-old honor student at the University of Virginia until November, when she drank too much at a pregame party, was left alone by friends to sleep it off, somehow tumbled down a flight of stairs, hit her head, and died. Alcohol poisoning or alcohol-related accidents killed at least five other undergraduates nationwide during the 1997 fall term. While no one counts the number of college students who die from alcohol use, Dr. David Anderson of George Mason University in Fairfax, Va., estimates that at least fifty die each year.

12   Binge drinkers also make life difficult for students who don't drink so heavily. At schools where more than 50 percent of the students binge drink, Wechsler found that a majority of the nonbingeing students complain of the secondhand effects of binge drinking, ranging "from assault to sexual assault to vandalism to just being a pain all the way around."

13   College administrators often identify student alcohol abuse as one of the biggest challenges they face. Yet, funding for prevention programs, on the increase until 1994, has never averaged more than a few dollars per student, not counting staff salaries. Experts complain that many alcohol education programs seldom involve more than a few posters, some brochures, and an Alcohol Awareness Week, all of which students say are largely ignored.

14   Bill DeJong, director of the Higher Education Center for Alcohol and Other Drug Prevention in Boston, thinks colleges have to change the way they recruit students. "If their view books show scenes of small groups socializing rather than football games, tailgate parties, and so on, they will attract a different kind of student," he argues. The *U.S. News* survey of college presidents suggests that when schools included their alcohol policies and the associated penalties in recruiting materials, they were about half as likely to have high numbers of binge drinkers.

15   That's the strategy being adopted by the University of Rhode Island, once rated a top party school. On a sunny fall afternoon, URI junior Denis Guay guides a tour of the campus for prospective students and their parents to a freshman dormitory room. After pointing out the route to the bathrooms, he states the school's alcohol policy: no drinking anywhere on campus by anyone under 21 and only one six-pack at a time per legal-age student in the dorm rooms. The first offense earns a fine of $50; the second, $100; the third, suspension.

16   Lee and Judi Kroll, on the tour with their son Jon, were glad to hear of the low-tolerance alcohol policy. Jon doubted the measures were actually enforced. While a number of URI students said it was possible to discreetly drink on campus, more agreed with sophomore Kira Edler, who said, "If you get caught, there are prices to pay." As a result, URI is less of a party school. Since 1990, kegs have been banned from campus, alcohol prohibited from social events, and fines instituted and raised. While the number of violations for possessing alcohol is up, other violations involving alcohol, such as violence or vandalism, have fallen sharply.

17   The argument against such policies has always been that it pushes drinking underground. Harvard's Wechsler argues that administrators who say that are shunning responsibility. "If you let them drink on campus, it doesn't mean they'll only drink on campus," he says. He maintains that there is less binge drinking on campuses where students are encouraged to focus on other activities. One reason could be that schools with such tough antidrinking policies attract fewer students who want to party.

18   A number of students at Earlham College in Richmond, Indiana, said that the school's dry policy influenced their decision to attend the liberal arts college. "One thing I like about it is that if you don't want to see drinking, you can avoid it," says student Roscoe Klausing.

19   Writing more-restrictive policies—which 30 percent of the campuses reporting to the *U.S. News* did within the past two years—is no panacea. Consistent enforcement is key, as is filling students' days and nights with meaningful activities. Friday classes are a joke on too many campuses, and grade inflation has allowed students to spend even less time on coursework. "There's nothing else to do but drink" is a common lament among college students.

20   *Keep Them Busy*   In general, presidents of colleges in urban areas, where there are more recreational and cultural events to lure students, report lower binge drinking rates on campus than those running schools in less urban settings. In addition, schools with lots of older or part-time students report low binge-drinking rates, probably because those students have families, jobs, or responsibilities that keep them away from the party circuit.

21   Many experts agree that alcohol abuse is perhaps most rampant and causes the most trouble in places where colleges have little or no authority, such as the fraternity system. Studies show that residents of fraternity and sorority row are up to four times as likely to be binge drinkers as other students, and their leaders are the most likely of all.

22   But an organization doesn't have to be Greek to encourage drinking. At St. John's University, an all-male Catholic college in central Minnesota, the school's unofficial rugby club initiated its new members one cold Saturday night at an off-campus party house known by the locals as the Far Side. The behavior is as bizarre as a Gary Larson cartoon. A chant of "Drink, [expletive]! Drink, [expletive]! Drink, [expletive]! Drink!" rings out. Two kegs of beer chill outside while inside a fifth of Jack Daniels waits on a table for the team's rookies—boys clad only in bras and panties. St. John's officials insist that the incident is not typical there, and they have met with the rugby team to plan alternatives for initiating new members.

23   Often, though, such behavior at most colleges has received little more than a "boys will be boys" response until student injuries or deaths, as well as lawsuits and rising insurance premiums, prompt some action. Nationally, two fraternities have committed to having dry houses by 2000. In December, all 66 member fraternities of the National Interfraternity Conference passed a resolution recommending alcohol-free chapter houses. URI's Carothers has moved all but two fraternities onto campus, where they must comply with school rules. The University of Iowa's interfraternity council has mandated that official Greek parties be alcohol free starting next fall.

24   *Cheap Beer*   While some colleges and Greek organizations are making headway, the pubs and liquor stores near colleges tend to be much less cooperative. One Cornell University senior says, "I was seventeen when I got to school and I could get a drink anywhere," including several bars and convenience stores near campus, where students often present false proof of age. Ads in college newspapers tempt students with "Nickel Beer," "Beat the Clock," and "Penny 'til you Pee" nights, where drinks are discounted or served free with a small cover charge. In the crowded parking lot outside Caesar's, an oceanside bar running a busy "Slug Fest" special about five miles from URI, senior

25 Anthony Antorino was insisting that students there know their drinking limits when he had to interrupt himself. "Oh my God!" he exclaimed. "Well, there's an exception." He pointed to a young woman who had just squatted by the front wheel of a car to relieve herself.

26 Some college administrators have joined community leaders on "town and gown" councils to tackle this and other problems. Experts say that schools can wield their economic clout to compel local governments and alcohol control boards to action. The Presidents Leadership Group of the Higher Education Center for Alcohol and Other Drug Prevention goes a step further, urging their colleagues to work at the state level for more stringent laws. A peeved Bill Sheen knows such efforts work. After the Tallahassee police started their weekend "Party Patrol," the sophomore business major was fined $195 for holding a cup of Coke and Jim Beam whiskey outside a rowdy apartment gathering. "It sucks. We can't have a party," he says.

27 Colleges and universities will never rid themselves of alcohol abuse completely, Wechsler says; instead, the goal is to change the norm. Look at what happened with smoking. "No Smoking" signs are obeyed with few complaints. The designated driver, an idea unheard of fifteen years ago, is now a common practice, even for partying college kids. Alcohol education did reach some of the more moderate drinkers, experts say. Now it's time to target heavy drinkers.

READING QUESTIONS

1. What is binge drinking?

2. How does binge drinking differ from other types of drinking?

3. Thompson relies heavily on studies and reports from sources like *U.S. News and World Report*. Which type of sources best support his concern for binge drinking: studies and reports or comments from students and educators? Why?

4. Thompson never provides his reader with a thesis; he just presents the results of surveys and the comments of students and others. Even though he doesn't present a thesis, is Thompson presenting an argument?

5. Since we are never presented a direct thesis, what do you think Thompson's thesis is?

WRITING TOPICS

1. Thompson relays some of the strict policies some schools use to combat binge drinking, but he notes, "The argument against such policies has always been that it pushes drinking underground" (paragraph 17). Using the reading as well as your own ideas, explain what you believe is the best way to combat binge drinking.

2. The funding of prevention programs "has never averaged more than a few dollars per student" (paragraph 13), Thompson tells us. According to Thompson, what is being done now? If more money was available, what could special programs do to reduce binge drinking?

3. Thompson reports that college students drink more than others their ages. Why do you believe this is true? Be sure to use Thompson's ideas as well as your own.

GROUP ACTIVITIES

1. As a group, list as many reasons as you can to explain why students binge drink. Can the reasons be organized into categories?

2. Thompson tells us that some people fear that strict rules against drinking will drive drinking underground where it will be out of sight and out of the control of the college. What guidelines should a college use? As a group, write what you believe would be the best guidelines for a college to adopt when it comes to drinking.

RESEARCH TOPIC

Thompson's article appeared in January 1998. Use library research to determine what changes have occurred since the article was published. Have colleges become more restrictive about drinking? Are there more educational programs on campuses now? Has the number of students involved in binge drinking gone up, down, or stayed the same? Have the number of deaths related to binge drinking changed? What is being done now that was not being done when Thompson wrote the article?

Media

Exploring the Theme

■ All the essays in this section criticize television for one reason or another. In what ways are these criticisms unfair? What is good about television that is too often overlooked?

■ Most of the articles presented here attack the way television is today. Barbara Raab suggests that, at least in terms of the news media, things have improved. In what other ways has television improved over the years?

PREREADING SUGGESTIONS

1. Do you know what the ideals and political views of liberalism are? Do you know what the ideals and political views of conservatism are? Use the dictionary to look up these words. Also discuss these terms with parents or people you know who are knowledgeable about politics.

2. Look up the definition of Gresham's law.

3. What does the term *Sino-Soviet* refer to?

4. What does the word *poignancy* mean?

Good News and Bad News: The Trouble with Network News

by Don Feder

Don Feder is a columnist whose writings often support the ideas of political conservatives. Feder is also an attorney whose legal knowledge led him to work for the Second Amendment Foundation, which strives to increase the public's knowledge about the second amendment, which guarantees citizens the right to keep and bear arms. In "Good News and Bad News," Feder focuses his sights on another topic: network news. This article was first published in 1997 in The American Enterprise.

1 Conservatives complain incessantly about liberal bias in television news, but while well-founded, this criticism misses a larger point: Network news today is frivolous, fluffy, sensational, tabloid, dumbed-down, and just plain stupid. If *People* merged with the *National Enquirer,* the result would be network news. The medium had a built-in bias against objectivity, calm reflection, and historical consciousness, and in favor of sloppy sentimentality, victimology, and convenient blame location—that is to say, in favor of liberalism and against conservatism.

2 The increasing lack of substance in nightly newscasts, their growing predilection for razzmatazz over reality, has drawn the notice of the medium's venerable elders. Walter Cronkite charges: "The networks now do news as entertainment," while Robert MacNeil (formerly a chatting cranium at PBS) complains, "All the trends in television journalism are towards the sensational, the hype, the hyperactive."

3 Marvin Kalb, formerly of CBS and now at Harvard, explains that although the evening news once told viewers what they should know to stay informed on world events, "now they're telling you what they think you want to know about." What they think you want to know about—what will pull you in to boost their ratings—is celebrity gossip, scandal, disasters and threats, conspiracies and the paranormal, and health and lifestyle features (billed as "news you can use").

4 There is a fascination, verging on obsession, with anything health-related: Alzheimer's, antihistamines, arthritis, brain injuries, clot busters, diabetes, estrogen, fibroids (uterine tumors), grapes (to reduce the risks of cancer), memory loss, osteoporosis and the like. And this in the first quarter of 1997 alone.

5 Network news is lousy with features on the meaning of dreams and daydreams, how to find quality day care, rescue services for pets, exposés of

Internet sex, the fantasies of UFO cultists, fear of flying, and how telephone psychics rip you off. The tide of fluff and helpful stuff (which qualifies as news only in the remotest sense of the term) is still advancing. In a media variation on Gresham's Law, flab drives out hard news. According to the watchdog *Tyndall Report*, in the past decade, real news coverage declined by at least 7 to 8 percent. But the trend is long term. In the mid-1960's, network news shows regularly had 20 real news items. Today, half a dozen is closer to the norm.

6   Take the top evening news stories of 1996. ABC devoted almost as much time to the TWA Flight 800 crash as to the Dole campaign. CBS was more interested in the O.J. Simpson civil trial than the Whitewater investigations. NBC rated the Atlanta Olympics above the Middle East peace process, the war in the Balkans, and the GOP's San Diego convention (in fact, Olympic coverage almost beat out the other three combined). In short, these days it's "The CBS Evening Entertainment and News Snippets with Dan Rather."

7   In his book *The Inarticulate Society*, Tom Shachtman examined the declining quality of oral communication. In one chapter, Shachtman recounted the contribution of television news to this deterioration. He looked at the quality of language on "The CBS Evening News" from 1963 to 1993. The first broadcast he examined was on August 29, 1963, the maiden voyage of CBS's half-hour format. There were few visuals. Cronkite read the news from a script, and journalists filed their reports. The vocabulary appealed to the reasonably educated. Shachtman: "The sentences have dependent clauses and often run to 18–25 words. Each sentence contains such conceptual and abstract words as 'unanimous,' 'reduction,' 'underdeveloped,' and 'colonial,' and such phrases as 'using the Sino-Soviet ideological dispute as a cover.' Absolutely no pictures accompany these reports." In addition, "the television reporters' sentences are full, sometimes near to bursting from the effort of condensing information. Their sentences are also complete, have dependent clauses, and are highly grammatical; they are often longer than can be uttered with a single breath."

8   Thirty years later, Shachtman found that correspondents and those interviewed (especially politicians and government officials) are driven to produce quotable sound bites, having learned that this is often the only way to get attention. This, as much as anything, has reduced campaigns to slogans and public-policy debates to dueling clichés. Vocabulary is now at a seventh-grade level. Sentences are 12 to 15 words. (Shachtman comments that correspondents will soon be "talking in headlines.") "The language of the broadcast is tending toward complete union with the few thousand words that we utter in our everyday conversation . . . . Whereas the first Cronkite news of 1963 was clearly based on full literacy, this 1993 broadcast exists in theoretical limbo, between the written language and the spoken language." This vocabulary signals the surrender of seriousness. News of politics, government, the economy, and foreign affairs requires language an articulate adult would use. But when journalism becomes tabloidism, a seventh-grade vocabulary will suffice.

9   That the networks are retreating from hard news is probably for the best, given the institutional biases against objectivity, sound analysis, historical

consciousness, and in-depth reporting. Network news is great at dramatizing the plight of victims (welfare mothers, illegal immigrants, the homeless), but seemingly incapable of showing the other side—the impact on our culture of illegality, irresponsibility, and fragmentation.

10   Emotions are what TV news does best—the tenant who tearfully doubts he'll be able to afford an apartment once rent control ends; the assembly-line worker who doesn't know what he'll do if Washington allows the merger to go through and he's laid off; the woman on welfare who wonders how she'll be able to afford day care and medical insurance on a $7-an-hour job once her benefits end; the agonized civil-rights leader who assures an interviewer that if affirmative action is abolished, inner-city youth will lose their opportunity for higher education and a ticket out of the ghetto; the widow of a crime victim who's just sure that if it weren't for "the ready availability of handguns," her husband would still be alive.

11   Broadcast news thrives on poignancy: the angry charge, the tearful confession, the admission of despair. All can be conveyed in a matter of seconds, with facial expressions (the picture worth a 1,000 words), and crisp but evocative commentary supplementing the sound bites. Where network news fails is at conveying any sense of how a situation developed. Why is there a shortage of affordable housing? How does a 27-year old end up alone with a junior-high education and five kids? How have government policies and judicial decisions conspired to create a burgeoning predator population?

12   One side of these stories transfers easily to film; the other does not. For people who believe that national problems need to be solved through reason rather than emotion, that presents a big problem.

READING QUESTIONS

1. What is victimology? Can you define it from its use in the essay?
2. In paragraph 3, Feder quotes Marvin Kalb, who believes that television news tells "you what they think you want to know about" rather than what you really want to know. What is the difference?
3. What is Feder's thesis?
4. What point is Feder trying to make about the differences between the lengths of sentences in broadcasts in the 1960s and today?
5. What are the different complaints Feder has about television news? Identify each one.

WRITING TOPICS

1. Feder says that network news is fluff, filled with reports about UFO cultists and Internet sex. Is network news more fluff than objective reporting of real news?
2. Watch your local news and the national news. Keep a record of each story they discuss. Does what you see on the news confirm Feder's assertions?

3. Feder believes that news broadcasts focus on the emotions associated with a story, rather than the situation that led up to the story. Does what you see on news programs support what Feder says?

GROUP ACTIVITY

Assign each member of your group to watch the local and national news on different channels. Compare the results. Did each station cover the same stories? Of the stories presented, which ones just presented the facts in an objective manner? Which stories focused on emotional elements? What kind of balance is there between objective reporting and reporting that focuses on the emotional aspect of the story? Is there a difference between the local and national news? Is there a difference between the way each station presents the news?

RESEARCH TOPIC

Feder and others complain about the content and presentation on network news broadcasts. What do the defenders of today's news programs have to say? Use library research to see how television journalists have defended themselves against the attacks of critics like Feder.

PREREADING SUGGESTION

How many gay or lesbian newscasters do you see on television? Do you see gays and lesbians in other areas of television? Identify what type(s) of programs.

Gays, Lesbians, and the Media: The Slow Road to Acceptance

by Barbara Raab

Barbara Raab is a NBC producer who is concerned with gay and lesbian issues. She is particularly concerned with the way the media handles issues like AIDS and gay and lesbian life. In the following article, she examines how these issues were handled in the past. She also reveals the changes that have occurred in the way these issues are now reported. This article was first published in 1996 in USA Today.

1   In 1990, ABC lost half its advertisers and $1,000,000 for an episode of "thirtysomething" showing two men in bed. Just a few years ago, "Roseanne" was slammed for an on-screen lesbian kiss with Mariel Hemingway, and the Fox network got cold feet and cut a gay kiss from its ultra-hip "Melrose Place."

2   That was then. This is now: "Friends" celebrated a lesbian wedding in which Speaker of the House Newt Gingrich's real-life lesbian half-sister Candace officiated as a minister. Transvestite RuPaul made a guest appearance as a flight attendant on "The Crew," a Fox comedy. On "Mad About You," the male lead's sister announced she is a lesbian. A gay precinct receptionist is a regular character on "NYPD Blue" and there was an openly gay secretary on "High Society." The list goes on and on. According to *US* magazine, during the 1994–95 television season alone, there were more than 15 lesbian and gay recurring characters on regular prime-time shows. In 1996, the gay and lesbian presence in prime-time television is unprecedented.

3   On cable, the Comedy Central network has presented several successful editions of a program called "Out There," a showcase for gay comedians. MTV carried the story of the late Pedro Zamora, a young gay Cuban man with AIDS, on "The Real World." It also has announced that lesbians and gays will be included in at least one episode of the network's dating game show, "Singled Out." (Imagine the old "Dating Game" letting bachelorettes question bachelorettes.)

4   On public television, there's a long-running gay and lesbian program called "In the Life." Television talk shows, though often crass and tacky, constantly are giving gays and lesbians a forum for shattering the silence about their lives. "Oprah," for example, did a show on gay marriage.

5   Over on the news side of television, where I work, though stories about and images of gays and lesbians have been slower in coming and less integrated into overall coverage, there have been big changes in a relatively short time. Take, for instance, the way NBC News has covered one specific event that has taken place three times: the gay rights marches on Washington, first in 1979, then in 1987, and most recently in the spring of 1993.

6   In the 1979 broadcast, anchorwoman Jessica Savitch told the story of the march in approximately 25 seconds, in "voice-over" format, in which viewers see videotape of the event, but do not hear from any participants. At one point, Savitch clearly was perplexed by the word "homophobia" in the script she was reading; she said the word as though she never had heard of it before. Today, of course, "homophobia" is used widely.

7   Coverage of the 1987 march lasted approximately 35 seconds, again in voice-over format, although anchorman Garrick Utley put the march in better perspective. He reported that the demonstrators came to Washington to demand more protection from discrimination, as well as more money for AIDS research. The report used the term "AIDS victim," which people with AIDS always have found offensive, and ended by noting that "police reported no arrests and no incidents," a rather odd thing to say given that the videotape showed a very peaceful and compliant crowd.

8   By 1993, the news media had a much better sense of what the gay rights march was all about and had elevated its importance in its coverage. On NBC, Utley was broadcasting live from Moscow on the night of the march. Normally, when an anchorman is on location, he's there for a journalistic reason that almost always is the lead story. On this night, though, the top story was that hundreds of thousands of "men and women gathered in the nation's capital, raising

their voices and demanding change." Rather than a short voice-over read by the anchorman, it was reported by a correspondent live on the scene, with a taped report in which many participants were interviewed. The reporter took notice of the fact that organizers disputed the Park Police's crowd estimates and explained that the event was meant to be "more than just a gay rights march. It was an attempt to demonstrate gay political power." In 1993, print coverage was far more extensive as well, both leading up to and after the march. Almost every daily newspaper in the United States featured a photograph of the march on its front page the following morning.

9   Coverage of the three marches is typical of the expansion and improvement of television news coverage of the "big ticket" stories involving gay issues. Topics such as homosexuals in the military, AIDS, and gay-bashing are too big for the news media to ignore.

10   There also has been some integration of lesbian and gay lives into over-all television news reporting. On Father's Day, 1995, for example, the "CBS Evening News" did a story about two men raising their two sons together. A broadcast of CNN's "Inside Business" series focused on marketing to the gay and lesbian consumer. On ABC, when Barbara Walters did a long profile of Hollywood billionaire David Geffen, they matter of factly discussed his homosexuality. The same thing occurred when Jane Pauley profiled breast cancer surgeon Susan Love on "Dateline NBC," as the doctor's lesbian partner was included in the story. In 1995, my show, "NBC Nightly News," won an award from the Gay and Lesbian Alliance Against Defamation media watchdog group for a three-part series called "Gay in America."

11   The print news media greatly have increased their reporting on gays and lesbians, and some newspapers, including the *New York Times,* have an official gay beat. Deb Price is a nationally syndicated lesbian columnist for the Gannett chain, and other newspapers around the country have openly gay columnists as well.

12   Magazines, too, are paying attention. A July, 1995, cover story in *Newsweek* was about bisexuals. In the August issue of *New Woman,* the mother of a gay son who just had come out of the closet asked the magazine's columnist whether she should send him to a psychiatrist. Dr. Harriet Lerner's advice was absolutely not; homosexuality, she said, is as normal as heterosexuality, and "the right to be who we are, is the most precious right we have." The executive editor of *Essence,* Linda Villarosa, is an African-American lesbian who came out of the closet in the pages of her own magazine and since has written another article on what it's like to live openly as a black Christian lesbian. *Advertising Age* assigns a reporter to the gay beat; *Entertainment Weekly* devoted an entire issue to "The Gay 90s"; and *People's* coverage of rock star Melissa Ethridge's birthday celebration noted that "the party's crowning moment came when her live-in lover took off her blouse and danced topless."

13   On the silver screen, there has been an explosion of movies with gay themes and characters: "Philadelphia," "To Wong Foo, Thanks for Everything! Julie Newmar," "Four Weddings and a Funeral," and even "The Brady Bunch," to name just a few. More than a dozen gay and lesbian films debuted in 1996 at the prestigious Sundance Film Festival.

14   Let's not forget about the music industry, where k.d. lang, Boy George, Janis Ian, and other openly homosexual musicians are writing songs and making videos about same-sex love that are selling like hotcakes.

Gays and lesbians are moving from the media margins to the media mainstream at a fast and furious pace. That indeed is encouraging to those of us who believe that, no matter who you are, what you see and hear in our powerful popular culture should be a true, fair, and accurate picture of our world. It's not the entire story, though.

15   Despite all the mainstream media attention, gays and lesbians continue to struggle with the same basic issues we always have struggled with: coming out, overcoming shame and self-hatred, how to convey the reality of our lives, how to live free from violence, and how to live and raise families as openly gay people. Mainstream media visibility has not taken the sting out of the facts of gay life.

Double Standards

16   In many ways, the mainstream media continues to keep lesbian and gay people on the margins. There are the double standards; visible affection between gay people, for instance, remains taboo. A kiss is much more than a kiss when a gay or lesbian character is the kisser. The simplest same-sex kiss somehow is more controversial than the steamiest heterosexual one or a typical love scene in a typical daytime soap opera. The "Friends" wedding did not include a kiss. ABC rescheduled the "December Bride" episode of "Roseanne" about the wedding of two gay male characters so that it would be seen later in the evening than usual.

17   Advertisers sometimes exert a lot of pressure on the networks when they include gay and lesbian characters or story lines, and that may be one reason why gays and lesbians get portrayed in the most bland ways. Our individuality and our differences are minimized and erased so that we are acceptable to the mainstream.

18   The news media marginalizes gay men and lesbians by ghettoizing us and seldom integrating us into ordinary everyday news and feature coverage. When was the last time you saw a gay or lesbian couple in a news story about home-buying, tax-planning, or workplace issues? Gays and lesbians usually are covered in stories about being gay, and not about being homebuyers, taxpayers, or workers. Gay people thus are marginalized in supposedly fact-based coverage even though we are the readers' and viewers' family, friends, neighbors, and co-workers.

19   Here's a glaring example: in 1993, the Fourth International Gay Games competition in New York City drew more participants than the Olympics. Nevertheless, there was not one word about the Gay Games in *Sports Illustrated*. Despite the fact that some of the athletes set world records, the editors viewed the event as a gay story, not as a sports one. That is marginalizing.

20   Lesbians tend to be particularly marginalized in television news coverage, along with women in general. Most gay people who appear on news programs are white men, even though they represent only a portion of gay Americans. One of the interesting angles on the Million Man March, for example, was the

dilemma facing gay black men who supported the goals of the march, but were offended deeply by what they saw as Nation of Islam leader Louis Far-rakhan's blatant homophobia. With the exception of an article in the *New York Times,* however, that part of an otherwise extensively covered story remained invisible, on the margins.

21   Another double standard that seems to be disappearing is the mandate that reporters "balance" their coverage of gay rights with opposing views. You don't see the mainstream media seeking out an opinion from white suprema-cists each time it presents a story about the NAACP, so why must there be an "anti-gay" spokesperson in all stories about gay rights?

22   There is the issue of invisibility in high-profile news media positions. How many openly gay newscasters can you name? Chances are, the answer is none.

23   Why, when there are gay characters in movies, sitcoms, talk shows, and soap operas, are there not openly gay and lesbian TV anchorpeople and news reporters? There *are* a few openly gay men on the air at various local news sta-tions around the country—Los Angeles, San Francisco, Miami—but not in New York. Moreover, there are no openly gay men or women on any of the na-tional newscasts.

24   It's not that there aren't any gay people working in these places—trust me, there are—but many of them earn a lot of money and are afraid that coming out could be a career killer. There is some evidence to support their fears. A few years ago, I coordinated a survey of news directors in local stations around the country for the National Lesbian and Gay Journalists Association (NLGJA). One of the questions was: "Would you be willing to put an openly gay reporter or anchor on the air, or to keep that person on the air if he or she came out?" The majority of the news directors in the survey said they weren't sure. No wonder nobody wants to take a chance.

Workplace Dilemmas

25   Gay and lesbian employees remain on the margins of their workplaces in some other very profound ways that are not visible to the viewer or the reader. Coming out and being out at work remains a complicated and stressful propo-sition for many lesbians and gay men who work in the media. NBC knew I was gay when I was hired, and I never have regretted the decision to be "out" from the start. Yet, it can be frightening to come out at work, so many gay people stay closeted, and that can feel very marginalizing because it means those employees hesitate to suggest stories about gay issues, never bring a same-sex partner to company functions, and never join gay and lesbian em-ployee groups where they can get support and encouragement.

26   When gay employees in the newsroom do come out, they often face a new dilemma: the danger of being perceived as having "an agenda." We know that many of our co-workers suspect us of being gay activists just by virtue of be-ing honest about who we are, so, to counter that, we may hesitate to bring up interesting and important news stories that we know about. We silence our-selves and bend over backwards to prove that we are generalists, rather than

"special interest" journalists. That is marginalizing, and it diminishes the editorial product.

27   Then there's the flip side. When we do work on stories involving gay issues, we worry about the response we may get from our gay friends. Will they think it's good enough? Will they be angry that there are some characters in the story who don't support their views? It's a constant mind game: worrying, on the one hand, that our mainstream media companies will marginalize us for being biased; worrying, on the other hand, that gay people will view us as "too mainstream."

28   Gay employees also can be marginalized when homophobia in the workplace is accepted passively, or when heterosexual employees are permitted time off to care for an ailing spouse, but bereavement leave for a partner's death from AIDS is denied. Gay employees feel marginalized when it feels too awkward to bring a same-sex partner to office parties. We are marginalized when our health and other company benefits are not extended to our same-sex partners. We are marginalized when the newspapers we work for refuse to print same-sex wedding announcements or mention same-sex partners in obituaries. We are marginalized when there are no standards set for acceptable language in stores about homosexuality; thus, Reuters' use of the term "normal heterosexual sex" in a story about HIV transmission. (The error, once called to Reuters' attention, promptly was corrected.) We are marginalized when reporters are not expected to cultivate contacts in the local gay and lesbian community, the way they do in other communities. We are marginalized when workplace diversity seminars do not address sexual orientation. We are marginalized when editors practice a double-standard about revealing the sexual identities of public and political leaders.

29   The mainstream media can help bring gay and lesbian employees off the margins by making it clear that it is safe to come out; by explicitly including sexual orientation in company-wide non-discrimination policies and diversity training seminars; and by making it clear that "fag jokes" and other homophobic behavior are not acceptable, just as racist and sexist remarks and behavior are unacceptable. An increasing number of mainstream media companies are recognizing the relationships of their gay employees by extending so-called domestic partner benefits to their same-sex partners; it's a benefit that is both economic and psychological. When the mainstream media is willing to recognize same-sex relationships in obituaries and social announcements and to tell the truth about the relevant personal lives of public and political figures, gay people inside and outside the newsroom will be far less marginalized.

30   Finally, gays and lesbians in the media are facing a backlash by radical right-wing forces determined to stop the momentum from margin to mainstream. Pat Robertson's "700 Club," for instance, ran a report on the NLGJA. The report, and an accompanying "fact sheet" available at no cost through an 800 number, asserted that today's mainstream media "overwhelmingly support the homosexual agenda"; that gay people are rising to newsroom management positions and are infecting news coverage with "pro-homosexual perspectives"; and that, according to Robertson, "the truth is that the so-called

mainstream media are becoming more and more marginalized because they are so far outside the mainstream of America."

31   These kinds of allegations have a marginalizing effect. I have heard some openly gay journalists say their news outlets are pulling way back on gay coverage or are subjecting certain stories to a higher standard before they can get in the paper or on the air.

32   There are several organizations working hard to assure gays and lesbians are not marginalized in the media or in their workplaces. One is the National Lesbian and Gay Journalists Association, which has nearly 1,200 members in eighteen chapters. The organization's mission is to promote, from within the news industry, fair portrayal of gay and lesbian people, equal treatment of gay and lesbian journalists, and the elimination of gay bias in newsrooms. NLGJA has helped to move gay journalists and journalism on gay subjects toward the mainstream, in large part by giving many gay and lesbian journalists the courage to come out in their workplaces and take an active role in contributing to coverage.

33   The Gay and Lesbian Alliance Against Defamation's West Coast headquarters monitors the entertainment industry, while its East Coast office pays close attention to the news media. Hollywood Supports is a Los Angeles-based organization founded by leading figures in the entertainment industry to counter workplace fears and discrimination based on sexual orientation and HIV status. It successfully has lobbied for adoption of domestic partnership benefits at over 40 entertainment companies, including all but one of the major studios.

34   In the end, new technologies may marginalize the mainstream media itself. The Internet, for example, is allowing every single one of us to communicate with the entire world on whatever subject we want. Until that happens, the fact remains that being visible in the mainstream media is to achieve a certain measure of cultural legitimacy. That is why gays and lesbians want their stories, in their voices, told and why gay people who work in the media want to have the same freedom as their straight co-workers to be who they really are.

READING QUESTIONS

1. In the first four paragraphs, Raab mentions several shows that focus on gay and lesbian issues. What is she trying to point out to the reader?

2. What is Raab's complaint about the coverage of the Gay Rights March in 1987?

3. Why does Raab consider the news coverage of the 1993 march better?

4. Although gays and lesbians aren't shunned by the media like they used to be, Raab notes that there are still taboos. What are they?

5. How are gays and lesbians ghettoized and marginalized?

6. What problems do gays and lesbians face in the workplace?

7. What does Raab say the mainstream media can do to help gay and lesbian employees?

8. At the end of her article, Raab tells us about gay and lesbian organizations. What goals are these organizations working toward?

WRITING TOPICS

1. Raab relates that "gays and lesbians want their stories, in their voices, told" (paragraph 35). Can a media that is largely made up of straight, heterosexual males fairly present the stories of gays and lesbians? Can our current journalists fairly present discussions of gay and lesbian issues? Use the essay as well as your own reasoning and observations.

2. Raab quotes Pat Robertson who charges that the mainstream media "overwhelmingly support the homosexual agenda" and that the mainstream media, with their "pro-homosexual perspectives" has gotten "far outside the mainstream of America." Has the media's focus on gay and lesbian issues led it to become disassociated with American values, or has the media just come to better represent the values of modern America?

GROUP ACTIVITY

According to Raab, the media's bias toward gays and lesbians is in part due to the lack of gays and lesbians in positions of power and influence in the media. Since most prominent television broadcasters are middle-aged, white, heterosexual males, can they fairly and accurately present the issues associated with woman, the elderly, teenagers, or minority ethnic groups? Form small discussion groups and list reasons why the typical television broadcaster might have difficulty giving an accurate portrayal of these or other groups.

RESEARCH TOPIC

Many critics charge that the media's failure to realize that the AIDS epidemic concerned everyone and not just gay men led the media to disregard the seriousness of the topic. As a result, AIDS spread at a faster rate than it would have if the public had been made aware. Using sources in the library, trace the media's involvement in the AIDS crisis. How much blame should be placed on the media?

PREREADING SUGGESTION

Make a list of Arabs you have seen in the media (on the news, in movies, on television.) How would you characterize each?

The Media's Image of Arabs

by Jack G. Shaheen

Arabs make up more than 100 million of the world's population. Most live in Saudi Arabia, Jordan, Qatar, Kuwait, Oman, the United Arab Emirates, Bahrain, Yemen, Iraq, Egypt, Syria, Israel, Lebanon, Libya, Algeria, Morocco, the Sudan,

Tunisia, and Turkey, although Arabs also live in the Americas. Shaheen, a first-generation Lebanese-American, has written The TV Arab *and* The Hollywood Arab. *The essay that appears here was first published in* Newsweek *in 1988.*

1   America's bogeyman is the Arab. Until the nightly news brought us TV pictures of Palestinian boys being punched and beaten, almost all portraits of Arabs seen in America were dangerously threatening. Arabs were either billionaires or bombers—rarely victims. They were hardly ever seen as ordinary people practicing law, driving taxis, singing lullabies or healing the sick. Though TV news may portray them more sympathetically now, the absence of positive media images nurtures suspicion and stereotype. As an Arab-American, I have found that ugly caricatures have had an enduring impact on my family.

2   I was sheltered from prejudicial portraits at first. My parents came from Lebanon in the 1920s; they met and married in America. Our home in the steel city of Clairton, Pa., was a center for ethnic sharing—black, white, Jew and gentile. There was only one major source of media images then, at the State movie theater where I was lucky enough to get a part-time job as an usher. But in the late 1940s, Westerns and war movies were popular, not Middle Eastern dramas. Memories of World War II were fresh, and the screen heavies were the Japanese and the Germans. True to the cliché of the times, the only good Indian was a dead Indian. But when I mimicked or mocked the bad guys, my mother cautioned me. She explained that stereotypes blur our vision and corrupt the imagination. "Have compassion for all people, Jackie," she said. "This way, you'll learn to experience the joy of accepting people as they are, and not as they appear in films. Stereotypes hurt."

3   Mother was right. I can remember the Saturday afternoon when my son, Michael, who was seven, and my daughter, Michele, six, suddenly called out: "Daddy, Daddy, they've got some bad Arabs on TV!" They were watching that great American morality play, TV wrestling. Akbar the Great, who liked to hear the cracking of bones, and Abdullah the Butcher, a dirty fighter who liked to inflict pain, were pinning their foes with "camel locks." From that day on, I knew I had to try to neutralize the media caricatures.

4   It hasn't been easy. With my children, I have watched animated heroes Heckle and Jeckle pull the rug from under "Ali Boo-Boo, the Desert Rat," and Laverne and Shirley stop "Sheik Ha-Mean-le" from conquering "the U.S. and the world." I have read comic books like the "Fantastic Four" and "G.I. Combat" whose characters have sketched Arabs as "lowlifes" and "human hyenas." Negative stereotypes were everywhere. A dictionary informed my youngsters that an Arab is a "vagabond, drifter, hobo and vagrant." Whatever happened, my wife wondered, to Aladdin's good genie?

5   To a child, the world is simple: good versus evil. But my children and others with Arab roots grew up without ever having seen a humane Arab on the silver screen, someone to pattern their lives after. Is it easier for a camel to go through the eye of a needle than for a screen Arab to appear as a genuine human being?

6   Hollywood producers must have an instant Ali Baba kit that contains scimitars, veils, sunglasses and such Arab clothing as *chadors* and *kafiyahs*. In the mythical "Ay-rabland," oil wells, tents, mosques, goats and shepherds prevail. Between the sand dunes, the camera focuses on a mock-up of a palace from "Arabian Nights"—or a military air base. Recent movies suggest that Americans are at war with Arabs, forgetting the fact that out of 21 Arab nations, America is friendly with 19 of them. And in "Wanted Dead or Alive," a movie that starred Gene Simmons, the leader of the rock group Kiss, the war comes home when an Arab terrorist comes to the United States dressed as a rabbi and, among other things, conspires with Arab-Americans to poison the people of Los Angeles. The movie was released last year.

7   **Racial slurs:** The Arab remains American culture's favorite whipping boy. In his memoirs, Terrel Bell, Ronald Reagan's first secretary of education, writes about an "apparent bias among mid-level, right-wing staffers at the White House" who dismissed Arabs as "sand niggers." Sadly, the racial slurs continue. At a recent teacher's conference, I met a woman from Sioux Falls, S.D., who told me about the persistence of discrimination. She was in the process of adopting a baby when an agency staffer warned her that the infant had a problem. When she asked whether the child was mentally ill, or physically handicapped, there was silence. Finally, the worker said: "The baby is Jordanian."

8   To me, the Arab demon of today is much like the Jewish demon of yesterday. We deplore the false portrait of Jews as a swarthy menace. Yet a similar portrait has been accepted and transferred to another group of Semites—the Arabs. Print and broadcast journalists have started to challenge this stereotype. They are not revealing more humane images of Palestinian Arabs, a people who traditionally suffered from the myth that Palestinian equals terrorist. Others could follow that lead and retire the stereotypical Arab to a media Valhalla.

9   It would be a step in the right direction if movie and TV producers developed characters modeled after real-life Arab-Americans. We could then see a White House correspondent like Helen Thomas, whose father came from Lebanon, in "The Golden Girls," a heart surgeon patterned after Dr. Michael DeBakey on "St. Elsewhere," or a Syrian-American playing tournament chess like Yasser Seirawan, the Seattle grandmaster.

10   Politicians, too, should speak out against the cardboard caricatures. They should refer to Arabs as friends, not just as moderates. And religious leaders could state that Islam like Christianity and Judaism maintains that all mankind is one family in the care of God. When all imagemakers rightfully begin to treat Arabs and all other minorities with respect and dignity, we may begin to unlearn our prejudices.

READING QUESTION

According to Shaheen, how are Arabs depicted in the media? What is objectionable to him about these depictions? What effects does he attribute to these depictions?

WRITING TOPICS

1. Shaheen writes that Arabs are portrayed negatively in the media. Write an essay in which you describe another group of people who are depicted stereotypically in the media.

2. Shaheen writes that people's attitudes toward Arabs are affected by the stereotypes they see in media. Do you think that people's behavior is affected by what they see or hear in the media?

GROUP ACTIVITY

Have each member of the group make a list of news events that focused on Arabs. Explain whether your impression was positive or negative. What in the media's portrayal led you to your positive or negative perception? How many positive portrayals were recorded in your group? How many negative?

RESEARCH TOPICS

1. Research one or all of the events and people mentioned in this article. Share your findings with your class in discussion or a brief written summary.

2. Search for recent articles and cartoons on topics related to Arabic countries, such as oil, Middle East peace agreements, etc. Do these recent articles reflect the biases that Shaheen discusses?

3. Search for more information about contributions of Americans of Arabic descent, either in the nation or in your own locality. Report on those findings to your class.

Education

Exploring the Theme

■ Why is education so important? Has the need for education changed in the last fifty years? In what ways?

■ What motivates people to learn?

■ Why are some students better than others? How are some teachers and schools better than others?

■ Does our family or cultural background influence our education? Should it? Does education affect the way we relate to our friends and family?

■ Who should make decisions about what is taught in our schools? Is going to school the only way to become educated?

PREREADING SUGGESTIONS

1. Do you remember when you first learned to read? Write a brief description of how this happened.
2. What are your reasons for needing an education?

A Prison Education

by Malcolm X

Malcolm X was a famous and controversial African-American leader. After his release from prison in 1949, he went on to become a great writer, speaker, and leader, first in the Nation of Islam, then in his own organization. He was assassinated in 1965. This selection is from The Autobiography of Malcolm X *(1965).*

1   It was because of my letters that I happened to stumble upon starting to acquire some kind of a homemade education.

2   I became increasingly frustrated at not being able to express what I wanted to convey in letters that I wrote, especially those to Mr. Elijah Muhammad. In the street, I had been the most articulate hustler out there—I had commanded attention when I said something. But now, trying to write simple English, I not only wasn't articulate, I wasn't even functional. How would I sound writing in slang, the way I would *say* it, something such as, "Look, daddy, let me pull your coat about a cat, Elijah Muhammad—"

3   Many who today hear me somewhere in person, or on television, or those who read something I've said, will think I went to school far beyond the eighth grade. This impression is due entirely to my prison studies.

4   It had really begun back in the Charlestown Prison, when Bimbi first made me feel envy of his stock of knowledge. Bimbi had always taken charge of any conversation he was in, and I had tried to emulate him. But every book I picked up had few sentences which didn't contain anywhere from one to nearly all of the words that might as well have been in Chinese. When I just skipped those words, of course, I really ended up with little idea of what the book said. So I had come to the Norfolk Prison Colony still going through only book-reading motions. Pretty soon, I would have quit even these motions, unless I had received the motivation that I did.

5   I saw that the best thing I could do was get hold of a dictionary—to study, to learn some words. I was lucky enough to reason also that I should try to improve my penmanship. It was sad. I couldn't even write in a straight line. It was both ideas together that moved me to request a dictionary along with some tablets and pencils from the Norfolk Prison Colony school.

6   I spent two days just riffling uncertainly through the dictionary's pages. I'd never realized so many words existed! I didn't know *which* words I needed to learn. Finally, just to start some kind of action, I began copying.

7   In my slow, painstaking, ragged handwriting, I copied into my tablet everything printed on that first page, down to the punctuation marks.

8   I believe it took me a day. Then, aloud, I read back, to myself, everything I'd written on the tablet. Over and over, aloud, to myself, I read my own hand-writing.

9   I woke up the next morning, thinking about these words—immensely proud to realize that not only had I written so much at one time, but I'd writ-ten words that I never knew were in the world. Moreover, with a little effort, I also could remember what many of these words meant. I reviewed the words whose meanings I didn't remember. Funny thing, from the dictionary first page right now, that "aardvark" springs to my mind. The dictionary had a pic-ture of it, a long-tailed, long-eared, burrowing African mammal, which lives off termites caught by sticking out its tongue as an anteater does for ants.

10   I was so fascinated that I went on—I copied the dictionary's next page. And the same experience came when I studied that. With every succeeding page, I also learned of people and places and events from history. Actually the dictionary is like a miniature encyclopedia. Finally the dictionary's A section had filled a whole tablet—and I went on into the B's. That was the way I started copying what eventually became the entire dictionary. It went a lot faster after so much practice helped me to pick up handwriting speed. Be-tween what I wrote in my tablet, and writing letters, during the rest of my time in prison I would guess I wrote a million words.

11   I suppose it was inevitable that as my word-base broadened, I could for the first time pick up a book and read and now begin to understand what the book was saying. Anyone who has read a great deal can imagine the new world that opened. Let me tell you something: from then until I left that prison, in every free moment I had, if I was not reading in the library, I was reading on my bunk. You couldn't have gotten me out of books with a wedge. Between Mr. Muham-mad's teachings, my correspondence, my visitors—usually Ella and Reginald—and my reading of books, months passed without my even thinking about being imprisoned. In fact, up to then, I never had been so truly free in my life.

12   The Norfolk Prison Colony's library was in the school building. A variety of classes was taught there by instructors who came from such places as Har-vard and Boston universities. The weekly debates between inmate teams were also held in the school building. You would be astonished to know how worked up convict debaters and audiences would get over subjects like "Should Babies Be Fed Milk?"

13   Available on the prison library's shelves were books on just about every general subject. Much of the big private collection that Parkhurst had willed to the prison was still in crates and boxes in the back of the library—thou-sands of old books. Some of them looked ancient: covers faded, old-time parchment-looking binding. Parkhurst, I've mentioned, seemed to have been principally interested in history and religion. He had the money and the spe-cial interest to have a lot of books that you wouldn't have in general circula-tion. Any college library would have been lucky to get that collection.

14   As you can imagine, especially in a prison where there was heavy empha-sis on rehabilitation, an inmate was smiled upon if he demonstrated an unusually intense interest in books. There was a sizable number of well-read inmates, especially the popular debaters. Some were said by many to be prac-

tically walking encyclopedias. They were almost celebrities. No university would ask any student to devour literature as I did when this new world opened up to me, of being able to read and *understand*.

15   I read more in my room than in the library itself. An inmate who was known to read a lot could check out more than the permitted maximum number of books. I preferred reading in the total isolation of my own room.

16   When I had progressed to really serious reading, every night at about ten P.M. I would be outraged with the "lights out." It always seemed to catch me right in the middle of something engrossing.

17   Fortunately, right outside my door was a corridor light that cast a glow into my room. The glow was enough to read by, once my eyes adjusted to it. So when "lights out" came, I would sit on the floor where I could continue reading in that glow.

18   At one-hour intervals the night guards paced past every room. Each time I heard the approaching footsteps, I jumped into bed and feigned sleep. And as soon as the guard passed, I got back out of bed onto the floor area of that light-glow, where I would read for another fifty-eight minutes—until the guard approached again. That went on until three or four every morning. Three or four hours of sleep a night was enough for me. Often in the years in the streets I had slept less than that.

19   Every time I catch a plane, I have with me a book that I want to read—and that's a lot of books these days. If I weren't out here every day battling the white man, I could spend the rest of my life reading, just satisfying my curiosity—because you can hardly mention anything I'm not curious about. I don't think anybody ever got more out of going to prison than I did. In fact, prison enabled me to study far more intensively than I would have if my life had gone differently and I had attended some college. I imagine that one of the biggest troubles with colleges is there are too many distractions, too much panty-raiding, fraternities, and boola-boola and all of that. Where else but in a prison could I have attacked my ignorance by being able to study intensely sometimes as much as fifteen hours a day?

READING QUESTIONS

1. How well could Malcolm X read and write when he went to prison? What motivated him to learn to read well?

2. What was the process he used to begin learning to read?

3. What was the next stage in his education? What problems did he have in continuing to educate himself in prison?

4. What does he say about prison as a place to become educated, compared to college?

5. How did his ability to read change his life?

WRITING TOPICS

1. Write an essay comparing Malcolm X's educational experience to your own.

2. Malcolm X was inspired to become educated by two people. What motivates you to become educated? Write a paper explaining your reasons for needing an education.

3. Malcolm X says that prison was probably a better place to become educated than a college. Do you agree or disagree? Write a paper supporting your argument.

4. Prison was a terrible place, but Malcolm X turned that disaster into an opportunity. Write a paper narrating a time when you turned a bad experience into a good one.

GROUP ACTIVITIES

1. In paragraphs 1–5, Malcolm X narrates some events that led to his beginning to educate himself. He tells those events out of order. As a group, make a list of the events in those paragraphs, and rearrange them in chronological order. Why did he write them out of order?

2. Have all group members discuss what motivates them to become educated. Has their motivation changed as they have gotten older?

RESEARCH TOPICS

1. Research more about the life of Malcolm X. In what ways was he a person of great moral courage?

2. Malcolm X became a Muslim. What are some beliefs of Islam?
   a. What are the Five Pillars of Islam?
   b. What was Malcolm X's Muslim name? What does "El Hajj" mean?
   c. What is the Nation of Islam? How many Americans are members of that group?

PREREADING SUGGESTIONS

1. What characteristics of your own cultural, ethnic, or national background make you proud?

2. What are some of the choices that are available to you only if you are educated?

A Letter to a Child Like Me

by Jose Torres

Jose Torres is a former professional boxer (light heavyweight champion, 1965). He now writes about sports, including In This Corner, Fire and Fear: The Inside Story of Mike Tyson *(1989). This essay was first published in 1991 in* Parade *magazine.*

1 DEAR PEDRITO:

2   You're 13 now, and you must certainly be aware that there are some people in this country who refer to you as "Hispanic." That is, you're a member of a minority group. You read newspapers and magazines, you watch television, so you know that the world is moving into the 21st century faced with big problems, enormous possibilities, huge mysteries. I worry that you might not be fully prepared for the journey.

3   The statistics are scary. They show us Hispanics facing a sea of trouble. The United States has 250 million people, a little more than 20 million of whom are of Hispanic descent. That's only 8 percent of this nation's total population. We're also the youngest ethnic group in the nation. We earn the lowest salaries, and, in cities where we have a large concentration of Hispanics, we have the highest school dropout rate. In New York City, for example, we compromise 25.7 percent of the high school dropouts, 42.7 percent of pregnant teenagers and 8.9 percent of the unemployed.

4   It should not be too hard for you to understand, my friend, that these statistics hurt us a lot. That means that many of our young people end up badly, as both victims and perpetrators. Some blame us for these conditions, despite our minuscule stock in this country and the fact the overwhelming majority of us are hardworking, decent, law-abiding citizens.

5   Still, you should realize that the world is not made up of statistics but of individuals. By the year 2030, you'll be my age, and what you do now is going to determine what you'll be doing then.

6   I've had my defeats; I've made my share of mistakes. But I've also learned something along the way. Let me tell you about a few of them. You didn't ask for this advice, but I'm going to give it to you anyway.

7   Let's start with a fundamental human problem, and I don't mean race or religion or origin. I mean fear. Fright, my young friend, may be the first serious enemy you have to face in our society. It's the most destructive emotional bogeyman there is. Cold feet, panic, depression, and violence are all symptoms of fear—when it's out of control. But this feeling, ironically, can also trigger courage, alertness, objectivity. You must learn not to try to rid yourself of this basic human emotion but to manipulate it for your own advantage. You cannot surrender to fear, but you *can* use it as a kind of fuel. Once you learn to control fear—to make it work for you—it will become one of your best friends.

8   I learned this the hard way. I was a boxer. I became world champion, but on my way up the ladder I found Frankie Kid Anslem, a tough young Philadelphian made of steel. The match proceeded, to my increasing dismay, with me hitting and Anslem smiling. At one point, I remember I let go a particularly strong left hook–right cross combination. The punches landed flush on his jaw, but he simply riposted with a smile—and some hard leather of his own.

9   Suddenly, I found myself struggling for my life. I was afraid. For two rounds—the eighth and ninth—Anslem and I seemed contestants in an evil struggle. My punches seemed to give him energy and pleasure! Unexpectedly, my chest began to burn, my legs weakened, my lungs gasped for air. I felt

exhausted. I was dying! Thoughts of defeat and humiliation assailed me. I was grappling with these facts when I saw Anslem's jaw exposed and, reaching from somewhere beyond my terror, I threw a straight right with all my might. And Anslem lost his smile and dropped like an old shoe.

10   My fatigue disappeared. I felt good, happy, invigorated. Fear had overtaken me, been recognized, then resolved and manipulated for a positive result.

11   I was obliged to learn about handling fear through the brutal trade of boxing. I didn't have the option now open to you, my young friend. I was one of seven poor kids who lived under many layers of an underdeveloped subculture. I chose a tough profession because two black boxers—a heavyweight champion named Joe Louis, and a middleweight marvel called Sugar Ray Robinson—showed me the way. They lived far away from my hometown in Puerto Rico. But I knew them. I wanted to be like them.

12   Looking back, I wonder what my choice would have been if real alternatives had been available when I was your age. Don't get me wrong. I'm very proud of my first profession. To be recognized as the best in the world at what you do, even if only for a moment, is a wonderful experience. Still, I was very much aware that boxing was a temporary activity intended only for the young. And so I had a pretty good idea of what your choice should not be if you're given a chance to become an artist, a corporate executive, a doctor, a lawyer, an engineer, a writer, or a prizefighter—though it should be *my* choice.

13   Whatever your ambition, you must educate yourself. School is a great gift our society offers you. It provides the key for your future. You must accept this gift, not disdain it. School is where you'll learn about your country and your world and your life in both. You also discover the conflicts and contradictions of history. You'll unlock the treasure chest of the world's literature and begin to sense the beauty of music and art. You'll acquire the tools of abstract thinking, of science and mathematics—and the computer, perhaps the primary instrument of the world you'll inherit.

14   At home, you should learn about compassion and dignity and care. You should realize that the workings of an individual's heart and soul can be as important as the histories of the great battles, military generals, dictators and kings. Most of all, you should learn that it's *you* who are responsible for your future.

15   There is a basic principle you should never forget: Don't be ruled by other people's low expectation of you! It almost happened to me. I grew up in Playa de Ponce, a small *barrio* in the southern part of Puerto Rico, an island 100 miles long and 35 miles wide, with a dense population today more than 3.3 million—1,000 human beings per square mile. I was only five when I first noticed the American military men—many of them tall, blond, and blue-eyed—wearing a variety of uniforms, roaming the streets of my neighborhood and picking up the prettiest girls. They seemed to own Playa de Ponce. Their attitude in the streets and their country's constant military victories, which we witnessed at the movie houses, became symbols of these young men's "obvious superiority." By comparison, we Puerto Ricans felt limited, inadequate.

16   To catch up, I volunteered to serve in the U.S. Army as soon as I became of age. And, for some mysterious reason, I joined its boxing team. My first four opponents were two compatriots and two black men from the Virgin Islands, all of whom I had no trouble disposing of. But just before my fifth fight— against one of those tall, blond, blue-eyed "superior" American soldiers, doubt started to creep into my mind. Yet, despite my worries, after three rounds of tough boxing, I overcame. I won! I had discovered the equality of the human race.

17   Your best defense against the ignorance of bigots and haters is pride in your own heritage. That's why you must learn your own history. Do it now. Don't wait until you are in college. You don't need teachers. Go to the library. Ask your parents and relatives and friends.

18   Be proud of your ethnicity and language. Don't be afraid to use it. Don't give up to the stupidity of those know-nothings who insist one language is better than two or three. You should know, and be proud, that in the Western Hemisphere more people speak Spanish than English; that Español was the language of the Hemisphere's first university—the Santo Tomás de Aquino University in the Dominican Republic, founded in 1538—and of the books in its first library. When you discover the long and honorable tradition to which you belong, your pride will soar.

19   So do not lose the language of your parents, which is also yours. Instead, refine your skill in it. If you're having trouble with grammar or writing, take courses in Spanish. Go to the library and read Cervantes's *Don Quixote,* the first full-fledged novel, or the works of the hundreds of great modern Hispanic authors, such as Gabriel García Marquez, Lola Rodriguez de Tió, Carlos Fuentes, Mario Vargas Llosa, Octavio Paz, Jorge Luis Borges, and Oscar Hijuelos, the 1990 Pulitzer Prize winner in fiction (who writes in English). Read them in both languages; know the strength of both. This is the treasure that no one can ever beat.

20   Puerto Rico is a nearly imperceptible dot on the map, my friend. Still, this small island recently had five boxing champions at the same time. And consider this: baseball star Reggie Jackson; the great entertainer Sammy Davis, Jr.; Dr. Joaquín Balaguer, poet, writer and six-time president of the Dominican Republic; the renowned cellist Paolo Casals all had one thing in common—one of their parents was Puerto Rican. The film and stage star Rita Moreno, a Puerto Rican, is one of the few performers ever to win an Oscar, a Tony, a Grammy, and an Emmy award. José Ferrer, a proud Puerto Rican, was once selected as the American citizen with the finest English diction in the United States. Ferrer also won an Oscar for his brilliant performance in the classic film *Cyrano de Bergerac.* Dr. Raul García Rinaidi, a physician of world prominence and a native Puerto Rican, helped invent six instruments now used in cardiovascular surgery. Arturo Alfonso Schomburg, a native Puerto Rican, made an extensive investigation into Black history. In his honor, the New York Public Library system erected the Schomburg Center for Research in Black Culture.

21   The contribution of Hispanics to the development of the United States of America has been vast and unquestionable. But much more remains to be

done, my friend. Every member of society must work together in order to survive together.

22   We live in a country where more than 27 million people can't read or write well enough to take a driving test, and many can't recognize "danger," or "poison." Every eight seconds of the school day a student drops out; every sixty seconds a teenager has a baby; every six minutes a child is arrested for drugs; every year, the schools graduate 700,000 who cannot read their diplomas.

23   Most of them are *not* Hispanics. Yet many of these victims are the same people who, day after day, throw themselves in front of a TV set and become passive, docile ghosts, allowing their lives to be easily controlled by others. Television, with its emphasis on package images and quick bites, discourages thought and imagination. Studies indicate that chronic televiewers develop problems with their thinking processes and articulation. Excessive viewing dulls the most indispensable muscle—the brain.

24   Instead of watching TV, read and write. Words are the symbols of reality, and a well-read person, skilled at decoding those symbols, is better able to comprehend and think about the real world.

25   Many years ago, the great Japanese artist, Katsushika Hokusai lay on his deathbed at age 89. Experts say no one could paint better than Hokusai during his prime, and many are convinced that his work is as good as—or better than—today's top artists. But Hokusai was never satisfied with his triumphs and success. "If I could live one more year," he said, "I could learn how to draw."

26   You, my young friend, would do well to become like Hokusai—a person who can lead a humble but useful and productive life, free of harm and, most important, free of the influences that generate hate, murder, suicide, and death. If you choose to spend your time not reading, thinking, and creating, but watching TV and learning how to deceive, cheat, and lie, then you become another person out there perpetuating the cycle of ignorance that leads to poverty, suffering, and despair. But if you commit yourself to a lifetime of honest work—if you assure yourself that a day in which you are unable to produce anything positive is a tragically misspent day—then, my friend, the 21st century is yours.

27   Go and get it!

READING QUESTIONS

1. Why did Torres become a boxer? Why does he say that his first lesson was learning how to benefit from fear?

2. Why does Torres say that "other people's low expectation of you" (paragraph 14) can harm you? Why is this a particular problem for Hispanic people?

3. Why is it important not to "lose the language of your parents" (paragraph 18)?

4. What are some accomplishments of Puerto Rican people?

5. Torres tells the story of the death of a Japanese artist. What lesson does he hope a Hispanic child will learn from this story?

6. Torres says that his reader is a young Hispanic person. Could readers of other ethnic backgrounds and ages also learn something from his advice?

WRITING TOPICS

1. Torres writes that education gives us more choices as to what we might become in the future. Write an essay comparing some choices you will be able to make with an education.

2. Torres explains why it is important for Puerto Ricans to be proud of their ethnic heritage. Write a paper illustrating how a person could be proud of his or her ethnic, national, or family background.

3. Fear became a positive force for Torres as a young boxer. Have you ever overcome or benefited from fear? Write an essay arguing that fear can be positive.

4. Hokusai was a Japanese painter whom Torres describes as still wanting to learn more when he died at 89. If time and money were no problem, what would you like to learn about now? Write an essay explaining what you'd like to learn and why.

5. Torres tells his reader that the "best defense against the ignorance of bigots and haters is pride in your own heritage" (paragraph 16). How could schools be changed to help students learn to be proud of their own heritage? Write an essay describing the changes you'd like to see.

GROUP ACTIVITIES

1. As a group, list the different "rules" that Torres suggests a child like him should follow. What examples does he give to support each rule?

2. Torres tells his reader some benefits of an education. As a group, list those benefits and add at least three more items to the list. Give an example of each one that you add.

RESEARCH TOPICS

1. Research the accomplishments of a person from your ethnic or national background.

2. Learn more about one of the famous Hispanics named by Torres.

PREREADING SUGGESTIONS

1. What does sanctuary mean?

2. When you were seven, where did you feel safest? Why?

3. What is the purpose of school?

4. What role should school play in the life of a child?

The Sanctuary of School

by Lynda Barry

Lynda Barry is a cartoonist and writer. In "The Sanctuary of School," she reflects on her own experience in grade school in Seattle, Washington. This article was first published in the "Educational Life" section of the New York Times *in 1992.*

1   I was 7 years old the first time I snuck out of the house in the dark. It was winter and my parents had been fighting all night. They were short on money and long on relatives who kept "temporarily" moving into our house because they had nowhere else to go.

2   My brother and I were used to giving up our bedroom. We slept on the couch, something we actually liked because it put us that much closer to the light of our lives, our television.

3   At night when everyone was asleep, we lay on our pillows watching it with the sound off. We watched Steve Allen's mouth moving. We watched Johnny Carson's mouth moving. We watched movies filled with gangsters shooting machine guns into packed rooms, dying soldiers hurling a last grenade and beautiful women crying at windows. Then the sign-off finally came and we tried to sleep.

4   The morning I snuck out, I woke up filled with a panic about needing to get to school. The sun wasn't quite up yet but my anxiety was so fierce that I just got dressed, walked quietly across the kitchen and let myself out the back door.

5   It was quiet outside. Stars were still out. Nothing moved and no one was in the street. It was as if someone had turned the sound off on the world.

6   I walked the alley, breaking thin ice over the puddles with my shoes. I didn't know why I was walking to school in the dark. I didn't think about it. All I knew was a feeling of panic, like the panic that strikes kids when they realize they are lost.

7   That feeling eased the moment I turned the corner and saw the dark outline of my school at the top of the hill. My school was made up of about 15 nondescript portable classrooms set down on a fenced concrete lot in a rundown Seattle neighborhood, but it had the most beautiful view of the Cascade Mountains. You could see them from anywhere on the playfield and you could see them from the windows of my classroom—Room 2.

8   I walked over to the monkey bars and hooked my arms around the cold metal. I stood for a long time just looking across Rainier Valley. The sky was beginning to whiten and I could hear a few birds.

9   In a perfect world my absence at home would not have gone unnoticed. I would have had two parents in a panic to locate me, instead of two parents in a panic to locate an answer to the hard question of survival during a deep financial and emotional crisis.

10   But in an overcrowded and unhappy home, it's incredibly easy for any child to slip away. The high levels of frustration, depression and anger in my house made my brother and me invisible. We were children with the sound turned off.

And for us, as for the steadily increasing number of neglected children in this country, the only place where we could count on being noticed was at school.

11 "Hey there, young lady. Did you forget to go home last night?" It was Mr. Gunderson, our janitor, whom we all loved. He was nice and he was funny and he was old with white hair, thick glasses and an unbelievable number of keys. I could hear them jingling as he walked across the playfield. I felt incredibly happy to see him.

12 He let me push his wheeled garbage can between the different portables as he unlocked each room. He let me turn on the lights and raise the window shades and I saw my school slowly come to life. I saw Mrs. Holman, our school secretary, walk into the office without her orange lipstick on yet. She waved.

13 I saw the fifth-grade teacher Mr. Cunningham, walking under the breeze-way eating a hard roll. He waved.

14 And I saw my teacher, Mrs. Claire LeSane, walking toward us in a red coat and calling my name in a very happy and surprised way, and suddenly my throat got tight and my eyes stung and I ran toward her crying. It was something that surprised us both.

15 It's only thinking about it now, 28 years later, that I realize I was crying from relief. I was with my teacher, and in a while I was going to sit at my desk, with my crayons and pencils and books and classmates all around me, and for the next six hours I was going to enjoy a thoroughly secure, warm and stable world. It was a world I absolutely relied on. Without it, I don't know where I would have gone that morning.

16 Mrs. LeSane asked me what was wrong and when I said "Nothing," she seemingly left it at that. But she asked me if I would carry her purse for her, an honor above all honors, and she asked if I wanted to come into Room 2 early and paint.

17 She believed in the natural healing power of painting and drawing for troubled children. In the back of her room there was always a drawing table and an easel with plenty of supplies, and sometimes during the day she would come up to you for what seemed like no good reason and quietly ask if you wanted to go to the back table and "make some pictures for Mrs. LeSane." We all had a chance at it—to sit apart from the class for a while to paint, draw and silently work out impossible problems on 11×17 sheets of newsprint.

18 Drawing came to mean everything to me. At the back table in Room 2, I learned to build myself a life preserver that I could carry into my home.

19 We all know that a good education system saves lives, but the people of this country are still told that cutting the budget for public schools is neces-sary, that poor salaries for teachers are all we can manage and that art, music and all creative activities must be the first to go when times are lean.

20 Before- and after-school programs are cut and we are told that public schools are not made for baby-sitting children. If parents are neglectful tem-porarily or permanently, for whatever reason, it's certainly sad, but their un-lucky children must fend for themselves. Or slip through the cracks. Or wan-der in a dark night alone.

21 We are told in a thousand ways that not only are public schools not impor-tant, but that the children who attend them, the children who need them most,

are not important either. We leave them to learn from the blind eye of a television, or to the mercy of "a thousand points of light"* that can be as far away as stars.

22   I was lucky. I had Mrs. LeSane. I had Mr. Gunderson. I had an abundance of art supplies. And I had a particular brand of neglect in my home that allowed me to slip away and get to them. But what about the rest of the kids who weren't as lucky? What happened to them?

23   By the time the bell rang that morning I had finished my drawing and Mrs. LeSane pinned it up on the special bulletin board she reserved for drawings from the back table. It was the same picture I always drew—a sun in the corner of a blue sky over a nice house with flowers all around it.

24   Mrs. LeSane asked us to please stand, face the flag, place our right hands over our hearts and say the Pledge of Allegiance. Children across the country do it faithfully. I wonder now when the country will face its children and say a pledge right back.

READING QUESTIONS

1. Why did Barry sneak out of the house?
2. Why does Barry discuss her and her brother's watching television? What is the relationship between her feelings about television and school?
3. Paraphrase paragraphs 9 and 10.
4. Why does Barry describe all those who spoke to her? What effect does this have on a reader?
5. What discovery does Barry make while writing about the morning at school?
6. What role did art play for Barry when she was a child? What role does art play in her adult life?
7. What does Barry mean when she says "I learned to build myself a life preserver that I could carry into my home" (paragraph 18)?
8. Why is Barry telling the story of her experience at school? What does she want the reader to do or to think after reading her story of her grade school?
9. Why does Barry refer to the Pledge of Allegiance in her concluding paragraph?

WRITING TOPICS

1. Describe a place that you thought of as a sanctuary when you were a child.
2. Barry points out that school is often a substitute home for some and that society should recognize and financially support this role. Do you agree? Why or why not?
3. Do you think art, band, and other creative activities should be part of the school curriculum and supported by public funds? Why or why not?

---

*"A thousand points of light" is a phrase from President Bush's State of the Union Address.

GROUP ACTIVITIES

1. Identify the places where Barry is narrating the story of her morning at school when she was seven and the places where she is commenting on those events as an adult.
2. Work as a group to conduct research on the school schedule and budget in Research Topic 1.
3. Working as a group, make a list of all the purposes—official and unofficial—of school.

RESEARCH TOPICS

1. Conduct research to determine if the local school provides time and supplies for creative activities, such as music, art, and band. What percent of the time and budget goes to the personnel and supplies for these activities? What academic subjects are taught? How much time is given to each? What other kinds of activities such as PE, sports, clubs, etc., does the school support financially and by allotting students the time to participate? Using your findings, write a letter to the school board asking for more money and support for a particular activity you think is important but not adequately supported. (Or you can write asking for a decrease in funding and support for an activity you think is less important.)
2. Conduct research to determine if public funding for schools has changed in the last 5 years. How much of this money reaches the classroom? What is the dollar amount spent per student in the state or in the school district? How does this compare to other states or school districts? Write a report in which you provide the results of your research.

PREREADING SUGGESTIONS

1. Have you ever been embarrassed by feeling different from other people?
2. Think of someone you've learned to appreciate better as you grew more mature.

The Struggle to Be an All-American Girl

by Elizabeth Wong

Elizabeth Wong grew up in the United States, but her family came here from China. She describes problems caused by her two cultures in this essay. This article was first published in 1980 in the Los Angeles Times.

1   It's still there, the Chinese school on Yale Street where my brother and I used to go. Despite the new coat of paint and the high wire fence, the school I knew ten years ago remains remarkably, stoically the same.

2   Every day at 5 P.M., instead of playing with our fourth- and fifth-grade friends or sneaking out to the empty lot to hunt ghosts and animal bones, my brother and I had to go to Chinese school. No amount of kicking, screaming, or pleading could dissuade my mother, who was solidly determined to have us learn the language of our heritage.

3   Forcibly, she walked us the seven long, hilly blocks from our home to school, depositing our defiant tearful faces before the stern principal. My only memory of him is that he swayed on his heels like a palm tree, and he always clasped his impatient twitching hands behind his back. I recognized him as a repressed maniacal child killer, and knew that if we ever saw his hands we'd be in big trouble.

4   We all sat in little chairs in an empty auditorium. The room smelled like Chinese medicine, an imported faraway mustiness. Like ancient mothballs or dirty closets. I hated that smell. I favored crisp new scents. Like the soft French perfume that my American teacher wore in public school.

5   There was a stage far to the right, flanked by an American flag and the flag of the Nationalist Republic of China, which was also red, white and blue but not as pretty.

6   Although the emphasis at the school was mainly language—speaking, reading, writing—the lessons always began with an exercise in politeness. With the entrance of the teacher, the best student would tap a bell and everyone would get up, kowtow, and chant, "Sing san ho," the phonetic for "How are you, teacher?"

7   Being ten years old, I had better things to learn than ideographs copied painstakingly in lines that ran right to left from the tip of a *moc but*, a real ink pen that had to be held in an awkward way if blotches were to be avoided. After all, I could do the multiplication tables, name the satellites of Mars, and write reports on *Little Women* and *Black Beauty*. Nancy Drew, my favorite book heroine, never spoke Chinese.

8   The language was a source of embarrassment. More times than not, I had tried to disassociate myself from the nagging loud voice that followed me wherever I wandered in the nearby American supermarket outside Chinatown. The voice belonged to my grandmother, a fragile women in her seventies who could outshout the best of the street vendors. Her humor was raunchy, her Chinese rhythmless, patternless. It was quick, it was loud, it was unbeautiful. It was not like the quiet, lilting romance of French or the gentle refinement of the American South. Chinese sounded pedestrian in public.

9   In Chinatown, the comings and goings of hundreds of Chinese on their daily tasks sounded chaotic and frenzied. I did not want to be thought of as mad, as talking gibberish. When I spoke English, people nodded at me, smiled sweetly, said encouraging words. Even the people in my culture would cluck and say that I'd do well in life. "My, doesn't she move her lips fast," they would say, meaning that I'd be able to keep up with the world outside Chinatown.

10   My brother was even more fanatical than I about speaking English. He was especially hard on my mother, criticizing her, often cruelly, for her pidgin speech—smatterings of Chinese scattered like chop suey in her conversation.

"It's not 'What it is,' Mom," he'd say in exasperation. " It's 'What *is* it, what *is* it, what *is* it'!" Sometimes Mom might leave out an occasional "the" or "a," or perhaps a verb of being. He would stop her in midsentence: "Say it again, Mom. Say it right." When he tripped over his own tongue, he'd blame it on her: "See, Mom, it's all your fault. You set a bad example."

11   What infuriated my mother most was when my brother cornered her on her consonants, especially "r." My father had played a cruel joke on Mom by assigning her an American name that her tongue wouldn't allow her to say. No matter how hard she tried, "Ruth" always ended up "Luth" or "Roof."

12   After two years of writing with a *moc but* and reciting words with multiples of meanings, I finally was granted a cultural divorce. I was permitted to stop Chinese school.

13   I thought of myself as multicultural. I preferred tacos to egg rolls; I enjoyed Cinco de Mayo more than Chinese New Year.

14   At last, I was one of you; I wasn't one of them.

15   Sadly, I still am.

READING QUESTIONS

1. What was "Chinese school"? How did Wong feel about going there?
2. Was the principal really a child killer? Why does she say that she recognized him as one?
3. What was Wong proud of knowing?
4. How did she feel about the Chinese language? How did she and her brother react to their mother's way of speaking?
5. Why does she say she was "granted a cultural divorce" (paragraph 12)? How does she feel about that now?

WRITING TOPICS

1. Has there ever been a time when you wanted to be very different from the rest of your family? Write an essay comparing your experience to Elizabeth Wong's.
2. Should parents force their children to follow the ways of a culture that is different from the ones their friends follow? Write an essay supporting your opinion.
3. Wong did not want to learn about her family's culture when she was young, but now she feels sad that she is not more like her family. How can adults learn more about the cultures of their families? Write an essay explaining how a person could learn about your family's background.

GROUP ACTIVITIES

1. Elizabeth Wong is an adult writing about her feelings and behavior as a child. Find three places where she hints that as a child she misunderstood something.

2. What are the best ways for parents to help children appreciate their own culture when it is different from that of their friends?

RESEARCH TOPICS

1. Research some information on the background of your family and write an essay explaining what is most important to you.
2. Are there any cultural schools in your community? Locate one resource that would help a person learn more about one culture in your area.

Haves and Have-Nots

Exploring the Theme

■ What is your community doing to address the needs of poor people? What should it be doing?

■ Homelessness and poverty are usually depicted as having a negative impact on people. Can these situations have a positive impact as well? Why or why not?

■ This unit describes how little many people live with. What would you need for you (and your family) to survive? What would you be willing to do to get these needs met?

PREREADING SUGGESTION

What kind of exposure did you have to computers in school? What did you learn to do? How did you learn to do it?

The Haves and the Have-Nots

by LynNell Hancock

Computers have become an increasingly well-established part of the workplace. Since even fast food restaurants and gas stations are run by computers, the ability to use computers is crucial to being able to get a job. In this essay Hancock describes the great discrepancy in schoolchildren's access to computers and analyzes the effects. This article was first published in 1995 in Newsweek.

1   Aaron Smith is a teenager on the techno track. In America's breathless race to achieve information nirvana, the senior from Issaqua, a middle-class district east of Seattle, has the hardware and hookups to run the route. Aaron and 600

of his fellow students at Liberty High School have their own electronic-mail address. They can log on to the Internet every day, joining only about 15 percent of America's schoolchildren who can now forage on their own for documents in European libraries or chat with experts around the world. At home, the 18-year-old e-mails his teachers, when he is not prowling the World Wide Web to track down snowboarding conditions on his favorite Cascade mountain passes. "We have the newest, greatest thing," Aaron says.

2   On the opposite coast, in Boston's South End, Marilee Colon scoots a mouse along a grimy Apple pad, playing a Kid Pix game on an old black-and-white terminal. It's Wednesday at a neighborhood center, Marilee's only chance to poke around on a computer. Her mom, a secretary at the center, can't afford one in their home. Marilee's public-school classroom doesn't have any either. The 10-year-old from Roxbury depends on the United South End Settlement Center and its less than state-of-the-art Macs and IBMs perched on mismatched desks. Marilee has never heard of the Internet. She is thrilled to double-click on the stick of dynamite and watch her teddy-bear creation fly off the screen. "It's fun blowing it up," says the delicate fifth grader, twisting a brown ponytail around her finger.

3   Certainly Aaron was born with a stack of statistical advantages over Marilee. He is white and middle class and lives with two working parents who both have higher degrees. Economists say the swift pace of high-tech advances will only drive a further wedge between these youngsters. To have an edge in America's job search, it used to be enough to be well educated. Now, say the experts, it's critical to be digital. Employees who are adept at technology "earn roughly 10 to 15 percent higher pay," according to Alan Krueger, chief economist for the U.S. Labor Department. Some argue that this pay gap has less to do with technology than with industries' efforts to streamline their work forces during the recession. . . . Still, nearly every American business from Wall Street to McDonald's requires some computer knowledge. Taco Bell is modeling its cash registers after Nintendo controls, according to Rosabeth Moss Kanter. The "haves," says the Harvard Business School professor, will be able to communicate around the globe. The "have-nots" will be consigned to the "rural backwater of the information society."

4   Like it or not, America is a land of inequities. And technology, despite its potential to level the social landscape, is not yet blind to race, wealth and age. The richer the family, the more likely it is to own and use a computer, according to 1993 census data. White families are three times as likely as blacks or Hispanics to have computers at home. Seventy-four percent of Americans making more than $75,000 own at least one terminal, but not even one third of all Americans own computers. A small fraction—only about 7 percent—of students' families subscribe to online services that transform the plastic terminal into a telecommunications port.

5   At least in public schools, the computer gap is closing. More than half the students have some kind of computer, even if it's obsolete. But schools with the biggest concentration of poor children have the least equipment, according to Jeanne Hayes of Quality Education Data. Ten years ago schools had one computer for every 125 children, according to Hayes. Today that figure is one for 12.

6   Though the gap is slowly closing, technology is advancing so fast, and at such huge costs, that it's nearly impossible for cash-strapped municipalities to catch up. Seattle is taking bids for one company to wire each ZIP code with fiber optics, so everyone—rich or poor—can hook up to video, audio and other multimedia services. Estimated cost: $500 million. Prosperous Montgomery County, Md., has an $81 million plan to put every classroom online. Next door, the District of Columbia public schools have the same ambitious plan but less than $1 million in the budget to accomplish it.

7   New ideas—and demands—for the schools are announced every week. The '90s populist slogan is no longer "A chicken in every pot" but "A computer on every desk." Vice President Al Gore has appealed to the telecommunications industry to cut costs and wire all schools, a task Education Secretary Richard Riley estimates will cost $10 billion. House Speaker Newt Gingrich stumbled into the discussion with a suggestion that every poor family get a laptop from Uncle Sam. Rep. Ed Markey wants a computer sitting on every school desk within 10 years. "The opportunities are enormous," Markey says.

8   Enormous, yes, but who is going to pay for them? Some successful school projects have relied heavily on the kindness of strangers. In Union City, N.J., school officials renovated the guts of a 100-year-old building five years ago, overhauling the curriculum and wiring every classroom in Christopher Columbus Middle School for high tech. Bell Atlantic provided wiring free and agreed to give each student in last year's seventh-grade class a computer to take home. Even parents, most of whom are South American immigrants, can use their children's computers to e-mail the principal in Spanish. He uses translation software and answers them electronically. The results have shown up in test scores. In a school where 80 percent of the children are poor, reading, math, attendance and writing scores are now the best in the district. "We believe that technology will improve our everyday life," says principal Bob Fazio. "And that other schools will piggyback and learn from us."

9   Still, for every Christopher Columbus, there are far more schools like Jordan High School in South-Central Los Angeles. Only 30 computers in the school's lab, most of them 12 to 15 years old, are available for Jordan's 2,000 students, many of whom live in the nearby Jordan Downs housing project. "I am teaching these kids on a system that will do them no good in the real world when they get out there," says Robert Doornbos, Jordan's computer-science instructor. "The school system has not made these kids' getting on the Information Highway a priority."

10   *Donkey Kong*   Having enough terminals to go around is one problem. But another important question is what the equipment is used for. Not much beyond rote drills and word processing, according to Linda Roberts, a technology consultant for the U.S. Department of Education. A 1992 National Assessment of Educational Progress survey found that most fourth-grade math students were using computers to play games "like Donkey Kong." By the eighth grade, most math students weren't using them at all.

11   Many school officials think that access to the Internet could become the most effective equalizer in the educational lives of students. With a modem attached, even the most ancient terminals can connect children in rural Mississippi to universities in Asia. A Department of Education report last week found that 35 percent of schools have at least one computer with a modem. But only half the schools let students use it. Apparently administrators and teachers are hogging the Info Highway for themselves.

12   There is another gap to be considered. Not just between rich and poor, but between the young and the used-to-be-young. Of the 100 million Americans who use computers at home, school or work, nearly 60 percent are 17 younger, according to the census. Children, for the most part, rule cyberspace, leaving the over-40 set to browse through the almanac.

13   The gap between the generations may be the most important, says MIT guru Nicholas Negroponte, author of the new book "Being Digital." Adults are the true "digitally homeless, the needy," he says. In other words, adults like Debbie Needleman, 43, an office manager at Wallpaper Warehouse in Natick, Mass., are wary of the digital age. "I really don't mind that the rest of the world passes me by as long as I can still earn a living," she says.

14   These aging choose-nots become a more serious issue when they are teachers in schools. Even if schools manage to acquire state-of-the-art equipment, there is no guarantee that trained adults will be available to understand them. This is something that tries Aaron Smith's patience. "A lot of my teachers are quite illiterate," says Aaron, the fully equipped Issaqua teenager. "You have to explain it to them real slow to make sure they understand everything." Fast or slow, Marilee Colon, Roxbury's fifth-grade computer lover, would like her chance to understand everything too.

READING QUESTIONS

1. What does Hancock mean by her terms "haves" and "have-nots"?
2. Compare the access the "haves" have to computers with that of the "have-nots." Include a comparison of what each group tends to use their access for.
3. How have public schools tried to keep up with the changes in computer technology? How successful have they been?
4. Who are the "choose-nots"? What impact does Hancock think they will have on children's ability to learn computer technology?

WRITING TOPICS

1. Hancock argues that access to and knowledge of computers has divided children into two groups—the haves and the have-nots. Write an essay in which you agree or disagree.
2. Assuming that Hancock is right, what should be done to ensure that all children have access to computer technology?
3. Hancock quotes Nicholas Negroponte as saying that "the gap" between the children who have learned the new technology and the adults who

have not "may be the most important" (paragraph 13). Write an essay in which you illustrate to what extent such a gap exists.

GROUP ACTIVITY

Compare your answers to the Prereading Suggestion on page 522. Taking into account the size and economics of each high school represented by your group as well as the age of your group members, what generalities can you draw? Do your findings support Hancock's claims? If not, can you make some guesses as to why not?

RESEARCH TOPICS

1. In many communities, schools, businesses, and individuals have tried to address the inequities Hancock writes about. Find out what is being done in your community to provide more access to computers for schoolchildren. (Consider gifts to schools from corporations, computers set up in community centers for use after school, etc.)

2. Hancock writes that "many school officials think that access to the Internet could become the most effective equalizer in the educational lives of students" (paragraph 11). Log on to the Internet to find out what students can find access to. How could such access make up for a lack of other resources?

PREREADING SUGGESTION

1. Do you know anyone who has been homeless? If so, what was their experience like? If not, what do you imagine homelessness to be like?

2. Why do you think some people are homeless?

3. What do you think homeless people are like?

4. How would your life change if you became homeless?

Slow Descent into Hell

by Jon D. Hull

As a correspondent for Time *magazine, Jon D. Hull decided to live on the streets with the homeless to find out for himself what the homeless experience. This article was first published in 1987 in* Time.

1   A smooth bar of soap, wrapped neatly in a white handkerchief and tucked safely in the breast pocket of a faded leather jacket, is all that keeps George from losing himself to the streets. When he wakes each morning from his makeshift bed of newspapers in the subway tunnels of Philadelphia, he heads

for the rest room of a nearby bus station or McDonald's and begins an elaborate ritual of washing off the dirt and smells of homelessness: first the hands and forearms, then the face and neck and finally the fingernails and teeth. Twice a week he takes off his worn Converse high tops and socks and washes his feet in the sink, ignoring the cold stares of well-dressed commuters.

2   George, 28, is a stocky, round-faced former high school basketball star who once made a living as a construction worker. But after he lost his job just over a year ago, his wife kicked him out of the house. For a few weeks he lived on the couches of friends, but the friendships soon wore thin. Since then he has been on the street, starting from scratch and looking for a job. "I got to get my life back," George says after rinsing his face for the fourth time. He begins brushing his teeth with his forefinger. "If I don't stay clean," he mutters, "the world ain't even going to look me in the face. I just couldn't take that."

3   George lives in a world where time is meaningless and it's possible to go months without being touched by anyone but a thug. Lack of sleep, food or conversation breeds confusion and depression. He feels himself slipping but struggles to remember what he once had and to figure out how to get it back. He rarely drinks alcohol and keeps his light brown corduroy pants and red-checked shirt meticulously clean. Underneath, he wears two other shirts to fight off the cold, and he sleeps with his large hands buried deep within his coat pockets amid old sandwiches and doughnuts from the soup kitchens and garbage cans.

4   Last fall he held a job for six weeks at a pizza joint, making $3.65 an hour kneading dough and clearing tables. Before work, he would take off two of his three shirts and hide them in an alley. It pleases him that no one knew he was homeless. Says George: "Sure I could have spent that money on some good drink or food, but you gotta suffer to save. You gotta have money to get out of here and I gotta get out of here." Some days he was scolded for eating too much of the food. He often worked without sleep, and with no alarm clock to wake him from the subways or abandoned tenements, he missed several days and was finally fired. He observes, "Can't get no job without a home, and you can't get a home without a job. They take one and you lose both."

5   George had $64 tucked in his pocket on the evening he was beaten senseless in an alley near the Continental Trailways station. "Those damn chumps," he says, gritting his teeth, "took every goddam penny. I'm gonna kill 'em." Violence is a constant threat to the homeless. It's only a matter of time before newcomers are beaten, robbed or raped. The young prey on the old, the big on the small, and groups attack lonely individuals in the back alleys and subway tunnels. After it's over, there is no one to tell about the pain, nothing to do but walk away.

6   Behind a Dumpster sits a man who calls himself Red enjoying the last drops of a bottle of wine called Wild Irish Rose. It's 1 a.m., and the thermometer hovers around 20 degrees, with a biting wind. His nickname comes from a golden retriever his family once had back in Memphis, and a sparkle comes to his eyes as he recalls examples of the dog's loyalty. One day he plans to get another dog, and says, "I'm getting to the point where I can't talk to people. They're always telling me to do something or get out of their way. But a dog is different."

7   At 35, he looks 50, and his gaunt face carries discolored scars from the falls and fights of three years on the streets. An upper incisor is missing, and his lower teeth jut outward against his lower lip, giving the impression that he can't close his mouth. His baggy pants are about five inches too long and when he walks, their frayed ends drag on the ground. "You know something?" he asks, holding up the bottle. "I wasn't stuck to this stuff until the cold got to me. Now I'll freeze without it. I could go to Florida or someplace, but I know this town and I know who the creeps are. Besides, it's not too bad in the summer."

8   Finishing the bottle, and not yet drunk enough to sleep out in the cold, he gathers his blanket around his neck and heads for the subways beneath city hall, where hundreds of the homeless seek warmth. Once inside, the game of cat-and-mouse begins with the police, who patrol the maze of tunnels and stairways and insist that everybody remain off the floor and keep moving. Sitting can be an invitation to trouble, and the choice between sleep and warmth becomes agonizing as the night wears on.

9   For the first hour, Red shuffles through the tunnels, stopping occasionally to urinate against the graffiti-covered walls. Then he picks a spot and stands for half an hour, peering out from the large hood of his coat. In the distance, the barking of German shepherds echoes through the tunnels as a canine unit patrols the darker recesses of the underground. Nearby, a young man in a ragged trench coat stands against the wall, slapping his palms against his sides and muttering, "I've got to get some paperwork done. I've just got to get some paperwork done!" Red shakes his head. "Home sweet home," he says. Finally exhausted, he curls up on the littered floor, lying on his side with his hands in his pockets and his hood pulled all the way over his face to keep the rats away. He is asleep instantly.

10   Whack! A police baton slaps his legs and a voice booms, "Get the hell up, you're outta here. Right now!" Another police officer whacks his nightstick against a metal grating as the twelve men sprawled along the tunnel crawl to their feet. Red pulls himself up and walks slowly up the stairs to the street, never looking back.

11   Pausing at every pay phone to check the coin-return slots, he makes his way to a long steam grate whose warm hiss bears the acrid smell of a dry cleaner's shop. He searches for newspaper and cardboard to block the moisture but retain the heat. With his makeshift bed made, he curls up again, but the rest is short-lived. "This s.o.b. use to give off more heat," he says, staring with disgust at the grates. He gathers the newspapers and moves down the block, all the while muttering about the differences among grates. "Some are good, some are bad. I remember I was getting a beautiful sleep on this one baby and then all this honking starts. I was laying right in a damn driveway and nearly got run over by a garbage truck."

12   Stopping at a small circular vent shooting jets of steam, Red shakes his head and curses: "This one is too wet, and it'll go off sometimes, leaving you to freeze." Shaking now with the cold, he walks four more blocks and finds another grate, where he curls up and fishes a half-spent cigarette from his pocket. The grate is warm, but soon the moisture from the steam has soaked

his newspapers and begins to gather on his clothes. Too tired to find another grate, he sets down more newspapers, throws his blanket over his head and sprawls across the grate. By morning he is soaked.

13   At the St. John's Hospice for Men, close to the red neon marquees of the porno shops near city hall, a crowd begins to gather at 4 p.m. Men and women dressed in ill-fitting clothes stamp their feet to ward off the cold and keep their arms pressed against their sides. Some are drunk; others simply talk aloud to nobody in words that none can understand. Most are loners who stand in silence with the sullen expression of the tired and hungry.

14   A hospice worker lets in a stream of women and old men. The young men must wait until 5 p.m., and the crowd of more than 200 are asked to form four rows behind a yellow line and watch their language. It seems an impossible task. A trembling man who goes by the name Carper cries, "What goddam row am I in!" as he pulls his red wool hat down until it covers his eyebrows. Carper has spent five to six years on the streets, and thinks he may be 33. The smell of putrid wine and decaying teeth poisons his breath; the fluid running from his swollen eyes streaks his dirty cheeks before disappearing into his beard. "Am I in a goddam row? Who the hell's running the rows?" he swears. An older man with a thick gray beard informs Carper he is in Row 3 and assures him it is the best of them all. Carper's face softens into a smile; he stuffs his hands under his armpits and begins rocking his shoulders with delight.

15   Beds at the shelters are scarce, and fill up first with the old, the very young, and women. Young men have little hope of getting a bed, and some have even come to scorn the shelters. Says Michael Brown, 24: "It stinks to high heaven in those places. They're just packed with people and when the lights go out, it's everybody for themselves." Michael, a short, self-described con man, has been living on the streets three years, ever since holding up a convenience store in Little Rock. He fled, fearing capture, but now misses the two young children he left behind. He says he is tired of the streets and plans to turn himself in to serve his time.

16   Michael refuses to eat at the soup kitchens, preferring to panhandle for a meal: "I don't like to be around those people. It makes you feel like some sort of crazy. Before you know it, you're one of them." He keeps a tear in the left seam of his pants, just below the pocket; when he panhandles among commuters, he tells them that his subway fare fell out of his pants. When that fails, he wanders past fast-food outlets, waiting for a large group eating near the door to get up and leave. Then he snatches the remaining food off the table and heads down the street, smiling all the more if the food is still warm. At night he sleeps in the subway stations, catnapping between police rounds amid the thunder of the trains. "Some of these guys sleep right on the damn floor," he says. "Not me. I always use two newspapers and lay them out neatly. Then I pray the rats don't get me."

17   It was the last swig of the bottle, and the cheap red wine contained flotsam from the mouths of three men gathered in a vacant lot in northeast Philadelphia. Moments before, a homeless and dying man named Gary had vomited. The stench and nausea were dulled only by exhaustion and the cold.

Gary, wheezing noisily, his lips dripping with puke, was the last to drink from the half-gallon jug of Thunderbird before passing it on, but no one seemed to care. There was no way to avoid the honor of downing the last few drops. It was an offer to share extended by those with nothing, and there was no time to think about the sores on the lips of the previous drinkers or the strange things floating in the bottle or the fact that it was daybreak and time for breakfast. It was better to drink and stay warm and forget about everything.

18   Though he is now dying on the streets, Gary used to be a respectable citizen. His full name is Gary Shaw, 48, and he is a lifelong resident of Philadelphia and a father of three. He once worked as a precision machinist, making metal dies for casting tools. "I could work with my eyes closed," he says. "I was the best there was." But he lost his job and wife to alcohol. Now his home is an old red couch with the springs exposed in a garbage-strewn clearing amid abandoned tenements. Nearby, wood pulled from buildings burns in a 55-gallon metal drum while the Thunderbird is passed around. When evening falls, Gary has trouble standing, and he believes his liver and kidneys are on the verge of failing. His thighs carry deep burn marks from sleeping on grates, and a severe beating the previous night has left bruises on his lower back and a long scab across his nose. The pain is apparent in his eyes, still brilliant blue, and the handsome features of his face are hidden beneath a layer of grime.

19   By 3 a.m., Gary's back pains are unbearable, and he begins rocking back and fourth wile others try to keep him warm. "Ah, please God help me. I'm f — — — ing dying, man. I'm dying." Two friends try to wave down a patrol car. After 45 minutes, a suspicious cop rolls up to the curb and listens impatiently to their plea: "It's not drugs, man, I promise. The guy was beat up bad and he's dying. Come on, man, you've got to take us to the hospital." The cop nods and points his thumb toward the car. As Gary screams, his two friends carefully lift him into the back seat for the ride to St. Mary Hospital.

20   In the emergency room, half an hour passes before a nurse appears with a clipboard. Address: unknown. No insurance. After an X–ray, Gary is told that a bone in his back may be chipped. He is advised to go home, put some ice on it and get some rest. "I don't have a goddam home!" he cries, his face twisted in pain. "Don't you know what I am? I'm a goddam bum, that's what, and I'm dying!" After an awkward moment, he is told to come back tomorrow and see the radiologist. The hospital pays his cab fare back to the couch.

21   Gary returns in time to share another bottle of Thunderbird, and the warm rush brings his spirits up. "What the hell are we doing in the city?" asks Ray Kelly, 37, who was once a merchant seaman. "I know a place in Vermont where the fishing's great and you can build a whole damn house in the woods. There's nobody to bother you and plenty of food." Gary interrupts to recall fishing as a boy, and the memories prior to his six years on the street come back with crystal clarity. "You got it, man, we're all getting out of here tomorrow," he says with a grin. In the spirit of celebration, King, a 34-year-old from Puerto Rico, removes a tube of glue from his pocket with the care of a sommelier, sniffs it and passes it around.

22   When the sun rises, Ray and King are fast asleep under a blanket on the couch. Gary is sitting at the other end, staring straight ahead and breathing heavily in the cold air. Curling his numb and swollen fingers around the arm of the couch, he tries to pull himself up but it fails. When another try fails, he sits motionless and closes his eyes. Then the pain hits his back again and he starts to cry. He won't be getting out of here today, and probably not tomorrow either.

23   Meanwhile, somewhere across town in the washroom of a McDonald's, George braces for another day of job hunting, washing the streets from his face so that nobody knows where he lives.

READING QUESTIONS

1. What problems do the homeless people in Hull's article face? How do they try to resolve these problems? What obstacles do they face? What options do they have?

2. Hull gives examples of several people who are homeless. What point is he trying to make? How do you know? What kinds of details does he choose to include? What tone does he use? How do his details and tone contribute to his point?

3. Hull's examples are all men. What portion of the homeless population has he omitted? Why? What is the effect of leaving out these people?

4. Hull uses only stories of homeless men, but no facts or statistics. What does he gain by this strategy? What facts would you like to know?

WRITING TOPICS

1. What can be done to cope with homeless populations? If you can answer the research question on page 532, you may want to suggest how your own community can better respond to people who are homeless.

2. Many people respond to those who are homeless by saying that they deserve what they get because they have brought it on themselves. Using Hull's essay and your own ideas and observations, write an essay in which you agree or disagree with this idea.

GROUP ACTIVITIES

1. Statistics also say that most people are only a few paychecks away from homelessness. Using current prices for your community, calculate how much money it would take to get a job, eat, and move into an apartment (and have utilities) if you were starting from scratch. Consider needs such as child care, work clothes, transportation.

2. Financial advisors say that households should spend 25 to 33 percent of their income on housing. People who live in poverty usually spend 50 percent of their income on housing. Using the calculations you used above, what effect would this have on their ability to obtain other necessities?

RESEARCH TOPICS

1. Hull wrote his article in 1987. Find more recent figures about the number of homeless people.

2. What resources does your community have for people who are homeless? Who do these resources serve? How are they funded? What type of help do they provide?

PREREADING SUGGESTION

Our culture tends to think of poor people in two opposite ways: either as dirty and criminal or as honest and goodhearted. What examples in the media or popular culture can you think of that support each view?

Experiencing Poverty Might Do Us All Good

by Ernest L. Wiggins

Ernest Wiggins is a journalism professor at the University of South Carolina. He has written editorials for The State *newspaper, often focusing on minority issues. This article was first published in 1998 in* The State *newspaper.*

1 A student came to me, concerned that the use of the phrase "poor people" in an exercise was inappropriate. I said I didn't understand her concern. She said she'd been taught the expression is rude.

2 This struck me as odd, odder yet when other students voiced the same opinion. Why would "poor people" be considered rude by some folks? In its context in the exercise it was accurate and meaningful. But then I thought about it.

3 Perhaps it is considered damning by some. There is, after all, the Protestant ethic of hard work and thrift in which poverty is tantamount to godlessness, prosperity to righteousness.

4 Or, perhaps, it is thought ill-mannered to point out the deficiencies in others of God's children. Maybe they believe it is like referring to another's disability.

5 Whatever the reason, I was, and am, intrigued.

6 Millions of us in this country know or have known need. We are the most acquisitive society in the world, and yet 16 percent of us live *below* the poverty level. For those of us who are black and brown, the figure is 30 percent, though the rate is decreasing for blacks.

7 And yet, I fear, not nearly enough of us have known need.

8 I believe that need—be it hunger or chill—can enliven as well as destroy. Need inspires in many of us the resolve to overcome obstacles and venture forward. In this way we survive.

9 And yet, if the obstacles are tremendous and we are without the resources—spiritual or material—to scale them, we will, most assuredly, perish. In these instances, we need the help of others to pull ourselves up and

over. It is because too many of us have not known need that so many others are despairing of life. It is in this way that our lack of need can actually be destructive.

10   For the lack of need skews our values.

11   I was stunned by reports of McDonald's customers throwing away scores of Happy Meals after pulling the prized Beanie Babies out of them. Unless I'm mistaken, much of the public outrage has been over the measures some folks have used to acquire these plush toys. Little was said about the waste of food. Would one who had known hunger be so cavalier?

12   Likewise, the lack of need numbs us to people's suffering. We spend hundreds of dollars for purebred canines to do "potty" at the curb and avert our eyes from the poor living on the streets.

13   How many of us have even faced uncertainty day after day as we tried to ensure the survival of our children, wondering if the day would ever come when we would accept that our children will never thrive as others do? Would we maintain a vise grip on the hope that more and better is in store for our offspring if we press on?

14   And yet we daily hear men and women—associates and leaders—who cannot understand how hope might be crushed under the unyielding pressures of modern living. I'm not talking about the urbane pressure of choosing between investments or refinancing schemes, but the maddening pressure of choosing between keeping a fatiguing, low-paying job and gambling on a "retraining" opportunity that might pay off, and then might not.

15   If more of us had known need, plans to scuttle public assistance would not have overlooked such disheartening dilemmas.

16   Those of us who have not known need cannot fabricate an experience so that we might, if we desired, know better how to assist the poor. But we can listen, without bias and with compassion, maybe even trust, when the poor talk to us.

17   Our public leaders and the media rarely do listen. That lends credence to my belief that the most destructive consequence of our lack of need is our blindness to the poverty of humanity within us.

READING QUESTIONS

1. Who can benefit from experiencing poverty? How can they benefit?
2. What is the Protestant work ethic? How does it affect people's attitude towards poverty?
3. What solutions does Wiggins offer to getting out of poverty?
4. What does Wiggins mean by "the lack of need skews our values" (paragraph 10)?
5. What would happen if more people had experienced need?
6. What alternative does Wiggins offer to direct experience of need?

WRITING TOPICS

1. Wiggins says that poverty "can enliven as well as destroy" (paragraph 8). Using Wiggins' essay and your own ideas and experiences, write an

essay in which you discuss whether poverty is more likely to enliven or to destroy.

2. Wiggins says "that our lack of need can actually be destructive" (paragraph 9). Write an essay in which you discuss how lacking bad experiences may be detrimental.

GROUP ACTIVITIES

1. Wiggins says that his student expressed concern over his use of the term "poor people" because she thought it was rude. Make a list of terms your group has heard used to refer to poor people. Are some of these undesirable terms? Why or why not?

2. Pick another group of people (the disabled, mentally ill, etc.) and make a list of terms used to refer to this group. Are some of these undesirable terms? Why or why not?

RESEARCH TOPICS

1. Wiggins says in 1998 that 16 percent of Americans lived below the poverty line. Conduct research to find out the dollar amount of the poverty line and how many Americans live below this line today. Has this number increased or decreased? If there is a difference, what do you think has caused this change?

2. Using the current government definition of the poverty level you researched in question 1 above, make a budget, using typical prices for your community. What can you afford? What can you not afford? What choices will you have to make to ensure your survival? How would you make those choices?

Making Choices

Exploring the Theme

■ What does it mean to be responsible?

■ What do you think the average adult ought to be responsible for?

■ What should be the role of society in regulating the individual's actions? What should the individual do if society requires him/her to act against his/her conscience?

PREREADING SUGGESTIONS

1. Have there been any laws regulating public behavior that you or others you know have not wanted to accept? What are they? Why have you or others rejected these laws?

2. Do you think health insurance rates or car insurance rates are equitable? Or do you think your rates are unfairly high because of the risky behavior of other people?

Every Choice Has Its Consequences— Or at Least It Should

by Cindi Ross Scoppe

Cindi Ross Scoppe is an editorial writer for The State *newspaper in Columbia, South Carolina. This article was first published in 1999 in* The State *newspaper.*

1   Once again, it seems, highway safety will be done in by the cholesterol police. When his colleagues tried recently to make the state's safety belt law enforceable, Senator Glenn McConnell decried the idea of "government getting involved in micromanaging people's lives." Since fried foods lead to poor health and higher insurance rates, he warned, the state will soon try to ban them.

2   Yes, dictating diets sounds outrageous. And in a world in which we were all responsible for our actions, it would be. But we're not living in that world. Not anymore.

3   Once upon a time, we understood that with rights come responsibilities. When my rights come into conflict with the rights of others, a balance must be struck. Striking that balance is what society—and our mechanism for maintaining society, government—is all about. Before we exercise our rights, our covenant with society requires us to consider the impact our actions will have on others.

4   But little by little, we have put the rights of some individuals above the legitimate interests of society, which just happens to be made up of individuals. We have constructed our laws so that individuals don't have to suffer the consequences of their actions. Society as a whole (in other words, all the other individuals in the community) pays for their irresponsibility, usually through higher insurance rates or taxes or higher prices on goods and services.

5   These protections become so normal that people tend to forget about them. So when society as a whole tries to impose reasonable restrictions on individuals' activities in order to reduce the burden the rest of us must bear, a few people scream bloody murder.

6   So we back down, and we are left with an inherently unfair situation— most of us must subsidize the irresponsibility of a few.

7   Of course, there is an alternative. Instead of imposing reasonable restrictions on your activities, we could tear down those artificial protections that society offers you from yourself. And the rest of us could take back *our* rights.

8   Go ahead, exercise your right to drive without a seat belt. Then when you slam head-on into another car and your body goes flying through the windshield, the insurance company can refuse to pay your hospital bills. After all, the rest of the people who have the same insurance company have the right to refuse payment for higher premiums to cover your irresponsibility.

9   Don't want Image Data to have your picture in its database? Fine. Let's give your bank the right to make you cover the checks that thief wrote on your account—as well as all the five-figure credit card bills he ran up.

10   Smoke all you want. It's your right. But shouldn't it be the right of businesses to refuse to hire you, since your employment will make the company's insurance rates skyrocket? Or maybe we should just let insurance companies exercise the right to refuse to cover you and other people who make unhealthy lifestyle choices—even through group insurance coverage. And as a society, shouldn't we have the right to refuse to subsidize unhealthy behavior through Medicare and Medicaid? (Economists estimate that within the next decade, a full 17 percent of the nation's gross domestic product will be devoted to treating preventable diseases.)

11   Need to cut a few corners on safety measures in order for your company to save money? OK. Do it. But then when your product inevitably injures your customers, they have the right to sue for damages. (Yes, that right already exists. But the same legislators who want to protect your right to drive without a seat belt also want to take the right to sue away from your customers.)

12   You want your own children so much that you're willing to use fertility treatments that exponentially increase the chance of expensive and dangerous multiple births? Go ahead. But certainly you'll understand when the rest of us exercise our right to refuse to have our insurance rates go up to pay for the treatment.

13   If we carry the idea of removing artificial protections to its logical conclusion, we would also exercise our right to refuse to pay for the extra expense of all those extra births. (Of course, even the most radical libertarians understand that we don't condemn children for the choices of their parents.)

14   My colleague Claudia Brinson tells me that a similar approach is fashionable in parenting. It's called "logical consequences." You teach your children about the consequences of their actions by allowing those consequences to play out naturally. When your child leaves his keys at home for the 10th time, you let him sit on the stoop for an hour before you come to his rescue.

15   I imagine that could be pretty effective. But I would guess that most parents would rather come up with a combination of reasonable limits and protections that would prevent them from having to subject their children to the consequences of bad behavior. Do we, as a society, really want anything different for ourselves?

READING QUESTIONS

1. What does Senator Glenn McConnell's criticism of the "'government getting involved in micromanaging people's lives'" (paragraph 2) mean? Give some examples of this type of legislation.

2. What fault does Scoppe find with putting "the rights of some individuals above the legitimate interests of society" (paragraph 5)?

3. What alternative to subsidizing the irresponsible behavior of theirs does Scoppe give? What is problematic about this solution?

4. What are some examples that Scoppe gives of irresponsible behavior?

5. Scoppe points out that an approach to parenting "called 'logical conse- quences'" is popular (Brinson, quoted in paragraph 15). Does she sug- gest that we follow this approach in dealing with the irresponsible be- havior in society? Why or why not?

WRITING TOPICS

1. Scoppe says "we are left with an inherently unfair situation—most of us must subsidize the irresponsibility of a few" (paragraph 7). Do you agree that this is unfair? Why or why not?

2. Scoppe provides several examples of behavior that can be classified as irresponsible. There are, of course, other types of risky behavior. Pre- sent an analysis of another type of behavior that is in some ways so- cially irresponsible. How should society respond to individuals who practice this type of behavior? Is there a simple solution to the prob- lems associated with this type of behavior?

3. Is it overly simplistic to suggest that individuals who practice irrespon- sible or risky behavior must accept all of the consequences of their ac- tions? Why or why not?

4. Do you agree with the title of Scoppe's essay? Why or why not?

GROUP ACTIVITIES

1. Think about your lifestyle. Do you have any habits or activities that someone could label "bad"? What is bad about these habits? Whom do they negatively impact? Compare the results of your self-assessment with the self-assessment of others in your group.

2. List other habits or activities that society pays for. As a group, discuss which ones should be solely the responsibility of the individual and which should be subsidized by others. Then state guidelines that would help another group come up with the same decisions your group made.

RESEARCH TOPICS

1. Explore car/driver insurance rates. What factors affect the cost of in- surance? What is your opinion of these relative costs?

2. Explore health insurance rates. What factors affect the cost of health insurance? Can individuals be considered responsible for these fac- tors? Explain.

PREREADING SUGGESTIONS

1. How did your parents reward you when you did what you were sup- posed to do as a child? If you are a parent, how do you reward your children?

2. What is the point in doing what is right? What do you expect to get out of doing the right thing?

Money for Morality

by Mary Arguelles

Mary Arguelles is a freelance writer whose articles are often published in magazines for parents. This essay first appeared in Newsweek's *"My Turn" column in October 1991.*

1   I recently read a newspaper article about an 8-year-old boy who found an envelope containing more than $600 and returned it to the bank whose name appeared on the envelope. The bank traced the money to its rightful owner and returned it to him. God's in his heaven and all's right with the world. Right? Wrong.

2   As a reward, the man who lost the money gave the boy $3. Not a lot, but a token of his appreciation nonetheless and not mandatory. After all, returning the money should not be considered extraordinary. A simple "thank you" is adequate. But some of the teachers at the boy's school felt a reward was not only appropriate, but required. Outraged at the apparent stinginess of the person who lost the cash, these teachers took up a collection for the boy. About a week or so later, they presented the good Samaritan with a $150 savings bond, explaining they felt his honesty should be recognized. Evidently the virtues of honesty and kindness have become commodities that, like everything else, have succumbed to inflation. I can't help but wonder what dollar amount these teachers would have deemed a sufficient reward. Certainly they didn't expect the individual who lost the money to give the child $150. Would $25 have been respectable? How about $10? Suppose that lost money had to cover mortgage, utilities and food for the week. In light of that, perhaps $3 was generous. A reward is a gift; any gift should at least be met with the presumption of genuine gratitude on the part of the giver.

3   What does this episode say about our society? It seems the role models our children look up to these days—in this case, teachers—are more confused and misguided about values than their young charges. A young boy, obviously well guided by his parents, finds money that does not belong to him and he returns it. He did the right thing. Yet doing the right thing seems to be insufficient motivation for action in our materialistic world. The legacy of the '80s has left us with the ubiquitous question: what's in it for me? The promise of the golden rule—that someone might do a good turn for you—has become worthless collateral for the social interactions of the mercenary and fast-paced '90s. It is in fact this fast pace that is, in part, a source of the problem. Modern communication has catapulted us into an instant world. Television makes history of events before any of us had a chance to absorb them in the first place. An ad for major-league baseball entices viewers with the reassurance that "the memories are waiting"; an event that has yet to occur has already been packaged as the past. With the world racing by us, we have no patience for a rain check on good deeds.

4 Misplaced virtues are running rampant through our culture. I don't know how many times my 13-year-old son has told me about classmates who received $10 for each A they receive on their report cards—hinting that I should do the same for him should he ever receive an A (or maybe he was working on $5 for a B). Whenever he approaches me on this subject, I give him the same reply: "Doing well is its own reward. The A just confirms that." In other words, forget it! This is not to say that I would never praise my son for doing well in school. But my praise is not meant to reward or elicit future achievements, but rather to express my genuine delight in the satisfaction he feels at having done his best. Throwing $10 at that sends out the message that the feeling alone isn't good enough.

5 *Kowtowing to ice cream* As a society, we seem to be losing a grip on our internal control—the ethical thermostat that guides our actions and feelings toward ourselves, others, and the world around us. Instead, we rely on external "stuff" as a measure of our worth. We pass this message to our children. We offer them money for honesty and good grades. Pizza is given as a reward for reading. In fact, in one national reading program, a pizza party awaits the entire class if each child reads a certain amount of books within a four-month period. We call these things incentives, telling ourselves that if we can just reel them in and get them hooked, then the built-in rewards will follow. I recently saw a television program where unmarried, teenaged mothers were featured as the participants in a parenting program that offers $10 a week "incentive" if these young women don't get pregnant again. Isn't the daily struggle of being a single, teenaged mother enough of a deterrent? No, it isn't, because we as a society won't allow it to be. Nothing is permitted to succeed or fail on its own merits anymore.

6 I remember when I was pregnant with my son I read countless child-care books that offered the same advice: don't bribe your child with ice cream to get him to eat spinach; it makes the spinach look bad. While some may say spinach doesn't need any help looking bad, I submit it's from years of kowtowing to ice cream. Similarly, our moral taste buds have been dulled by an endless onslaught of artificial sweeteners. A steady diet of candy bars and banana splits makes an ordinary apple or orange seem sour. So too does an endless parade of incentives make us incapable of feeling a genuine sense of inner peace (or inner turmoil).

7 The simple virtues of honesty, kindness and integrity suffer from an image problem and are in desperate need of a makeover. One way to do this is by example. If my son sees me feeling happy after I've helped out a friend, then he may do likewise. If my daughter sees me spending a rainy afternoon curled up with a book instead of spending money at the mall, she may get the message that there are some simple pleasures that don't require a purchase. I fear that in our so-called upwardly mobile world we are on a downward spiral toward moral bankruptcy. Like pre–World War II Germany, where the basket holding the money was more valuable than the money itself, we too may render ourselves internally worthless while desperately clinging to a shell of appearances.

READING QUESTIONS

1. Why were the teachers "outraged" that the boy who returned the $600 received only $3 as a reward? Why does Arguelles think that these teachers are "confused and misguided about values" (paragraph 3)?

2. How does Arguelles feel about paying children for making good grades? Why? What is the connection between this example and her opening example?

3. What other payments to children does Arguelles object to?

4. What point is Arguelles illustrating with the example of ice cream and spinach (paragraph 6)? How does this example relate to the point she has made so far in the essay?

5. According to Arguelles, how can we give "the simple virtues of honesty, kindness, and integrity" a "makeover" (paragraph 7)?

6. What other values does Arguelles praise in this essay?

WRITING TOPICS

1. Arguelles implies that virtue is its own reward and that rewarding children for doing the right thing teaches them to value the reward rather than the behavior itself. Should people be rewarded for doing what is right?

2. Arguelles writes that "as a society, we seem to be losing a grip on our internal control" and that "instead we rely on external 'stuff' as measure of our worth." Do you agree with Arguelles that we seem to find our self-worth outside ourselves instead of within?

3. According to Arguelles, the golden rule no longer motivates us because our fast-paced lives have caused us to expect an immediate payoff for our deeds. Do you agree that we are impatient when it comes to seeing results of our actions? Why or why not?

GROUP ACTIVITIES

1. Plan a debate in which you address the major issue brought up in Arguelles' first examples: should children be financially rewarded for honesty or hard work? Assign one half of your group to each side of the issue and have each half explain as clearly as possible the arguments that support that side.

2. Arguelles says that "the role models our children look up to these days—in this case, teachers—are more confused and misguided about values than their young charges" (paragraph 3). List specific role models your group is familiar with that children look up to. In each case, what values does the role model present to children? Are these values positive or negative examples for children?

RESEARCH TOPICS

1. Survey parents of school-age children, asking them whether they reward their children for good grades. Also ask how well the children do in school. Can you draw any conclusions from the presence or absence of a reward and the child's school success?

2. Arguelles lists a variety of programs that offer children incentives to behave in certain ways to participate in certain activities. Find other programs that offer such incentives and look for evidence of their effectiveness. Write a report in which you present your findings. Do they support Arguelles' argument or provide evidence against it?

PREREADING SUGGESTIONS

1. Would you tell a friend that the person they are dating has a drinking problem? Would you tell your mother not to use her employer's photocopier to reproduce the annual family newsletter?

2. Do you often act on impulse or do you sometimes defer your actions until you have had time to think about the consequences? Describe one time when you acted on impulse and another time when you waited to act. How were the situations similar or different?

On Restoring the Moral Voice: Virtue and Community Pressure

by Amatai Etzioni

Amatai Etzioni, a sociologist, calls himself a communitarian, a person who believes in a balance between individual rights and group responsibilities. This article was first published in 1994 in Current.

1 Audiences that are quite enthusiastic about the communitarian message, which I carry these days to all who will listen, cringe when I turn to discuss the moral voice. One of my best friends took me aside and gently advised me to speak of "concern" rather than morality, warning that otherwise I would "sound like the Moral Majority." During most call-in radio shows in which I participate, sooner or later some caller exclaims that "nobody should tell us what to do." *Time* magazine, in an otherwise highly favorable cover story on communitarian thinking, warned against busybodies "humorlessly imposing on others arbitrary (meaning their own) standards of behavior, health and thought." Studies of an American suburb by sociologist M. P. Baumgartner found a disturbing unwillingness of people to make moral claims on one

another. Most people did not feel it was their place to express their convictions when someone did something that was wrong.

2   At the same time, the overwhelming majority of Americans, public opinion polls show, recognize that our moral fabric has worn rather thin. A typical finding is that while school teachers in the forties listed as their top problems talking out of turn, making noise, cutting line, and littering, they now list drug abuse, alcohol abuse, pregnancy, and suicide. Wanton taking of life, often for a few bucks to buy a vial of crack or to gain a pair of sneakers, is much more common than it is in other civilized societies or than it used to be in America. Countless teenagers bring infants into the world to satisfy their ego needs, with little attention to the long term consequences for the children, themselves, or society.

How We Lost Our Moral Voice

3   How can people recognize the enormous moral deficit we face and at the same time be so reluctant to lay moral claims on one another? One reason is that they see immorality not in their friends and neighborhoods but practically everyplace else. (In the same vein, they find members of Congress in general to be corrupt but often re-elect "their" representative because he or she is "O.K.," just as they complain frequently about physicians but find their doctors above reproach.) This phenomenon may be referred to as moral myopia; a phenomenon for which there seems to be no ready cure.

4   In addition, many Americans seem to have internalized the writings of Dale Carnegie on how to win friends and influence people: you are supposed to work hard at flattering the other person and never chastise anyone. Otherwise, generations of Americans have been told by their parents, you may lose a "friend" and set back your "networking." A study found that when college coeds were asked whether or not they would tell their best friend if, in their eyes, the person the friend had chosen to wed was utterly unsuitable, most said they would refrain. They would rather she go ahead and hurt herself rather than endanger the friendship. Also, Daniel Patrick Moynihan has argued convincingly in his recent article in the *American Scholar*, "Defining Deviancy Down," that people have been so bombarded with evidence of social ills that they have developed moral calluses, which make them relatively inured to immorality.

5   When Americans do contemplate moral reform, many are rather asociological: they believe that our problem is primarily one of individual conscience. If youngsters could be taught again to tell right from wrong by their families and schools, if churches could reach them again, our moral and social order would be on the mend. They focus on what is only one, albeit important, component of the moral equation: the inner voice.

6   In the process many Americans disregard the crucial role of the community in reinforcing the individual's moral commitments. To document the importance of the community, I must turn to the question: what constitutes a moral person?

7   I build here on the writings of Harry Frankfurt, Albert Hirschman, and others who have argued that humans differ from animals in that, while both species experience impulses, humans have the capacity to pass judgments on their impulses. I choose my words carefully: It is not suggested that humans can "control" their impulses, but that they can defer responding to them long enough to evaluate the behavior toward which they feel inclined. Once this evaluation takes place, sometimes the judgments win, sometimes the impulses. If the judgments always took precedence, we would be saintly; if the impulses always won, we would be psychopaths or animals. The human fate is a constant struggle between the noble and the debased parts of human nature. While I reach this conclusion from social science findings and observations, I am often challenged by those who exclaim "Why, this is what religion taught us!" or as one heckler cried out "What about the rest of the catechism?" As I see it, while some may find it surprising that religions contain social truths, I see no reason to doubt that the distillation of centuries of human experience by those entrusted historically with moral education, has resulted in some empirically solid, sociologically valid observations.

8   It is to the struggle between judgments and impulses that the moral voice of the community speaks. The never-ending struggle within the human soul over which course to follow is not limited to intra-individual dialogues between impulses that tempt us to disregard our marital vows, to be deceitful, or to be selfish, and the values we previously internalized, which warn us against yielding to these temptations. In making our moral choices (to be precise, our choices between moral and immoral conduct rather than among moral claims), we are influenced by the approbation and censure of others, especially of those with whom we have close relations—family members, friends, neighbors; in short, our communities. It may not flatter our view of ourselves, but human nature is such that if these community voices speak in unison and with clarity (without being shrill), we are much more likely to follow our inner judgments than if these voices are silent, conflicted, or speak too softly. Hence, the pivotal importance of community voices in raising the moral level of their members.

The Critics

9 I need to respond to various challenges to this line of argumentation, beyond the general unarticulated uneasiness it seems to evoke in a generation that has largely lost its moral voice. Some argue that the reliance on community points to conformism, to "other-directed" individuals who merely seek to satisfy whatever pleases their community. This is not the vision evoked here. The community voice as depicted here is not the only voice that lays claims on individuals as to the course they ought to follow, but rather is a voice that speaks in addition to the inner one. When the community's voice and the inner voice are in harmony, this is not a case of conformism, of one "party" yielding to the other, but one of two tributaries flowing into the same channel (e.g., if I firmly believe that it is wrong to leave my children unattended

and so do my neighbors, and I stay home, this is hardly an instance of conformism). If these two voices conflict, I must pass judgment not only vis-a-vis my impulses (should I yield or follow the dictates of my conscience?) but also pass judgment on whether or not I shall heed my fellow community members, or follow my own lead. In short, the very existence of a community moral voice does not necessarily spell conformism. Conformism occurs only if and when one automatically or routinely sets aside personal judgements to grant supremacy to the community. That happens when personal voices are weak—far from a necessary condition for the existence of a community voice. To put it differently, while conformism is a danger so is the absence of the reinforcing effects of the communal voice. The antidote to conformism is not to undermine the community's voice but to seek to ensure that the personal one is also firmly instilled.

Pluralism

10   Above all, it must be noted that while the moral voice urges and counsels us, it is unable to force us. Whatever friends, neighbors, ministers, or community leaders say, the ultimate judgment call is up to the individual. (True, in some limited situations, as when a community ostracizes or hounds someone, the pressure can be quite intense, but this rarely happens to modern-day communities because individuals are able to move to other communities when they are unduly pressured, and because they often are members of two or more communities—say of residence and of work—and hence are able to psychologically to draw on one community to ward off excessive pressure from the other.)

11   Others argue that the community voice is largely lost because of American pluralism. Individuals are subject to the voices of numerous communities, each pulling in a different direction and thus neutralizing the others. Or the cacophony is so high that no clear voice can be heard. The notion that no community is right and all claims have equal standing, championed by multiculturalists, further diminishes the claim of the moral voice. The fact is that there is no way to return to the days of simple, homogeneous communities. In any case, these communities were often rather oppressive. The contemporary solution, if not salvation, lies in seeking and developing an evolving framework of shared values—one which all subcultures will be expected to endorse and support without losing their distinct identities. Thus, Muslim-Americans can be free to follow the dictates of their religion, cherish their music and cuisine, and be proud of select parts of their history (no group should be encouraged to embrace all of its history). But at the same time they (and all other communities that make up the American society) need to accept the dignity of the individual, the basic value of liberty, the democratic form of government, and other such core values. On these matters we should expect and encourage all communities to speak in one voice.

12   Other critics argue that the essence of individual freedom is every person following his own course and social institutions leaving us alone. (More techni-

cally, economists write about the primacy of our preferences and scoff at intellectuals and ideologues who want to impose their "tastes" on others.) In honoring this pivotal value of free society one must be careful not to confuse allusions to freedom from the state's coercion and controls with freedom from the moral urgings of our fellow community members. One can be as opposed to state intervention and regulation as a diehard libertarian and still see a great deal of merit in people encouraging one another to do what is right. (Technically speaking, the reference here is not to frustrating people and preventing them from acting on their preferences, which is what the coercive state does, but rather appealing to their better selves to change or reorder their preferences.)

13   Indeed, a strong case can be made that it is precisely the bonding together of community members that enables us to remain independent of the state. The anchoring of individuals in viable families, webs of friendships, communities of faith, and neighborhoods—in short, in communities—best sustains their ability to resist the pressures of the state. The absence of these social foundations opens isolated individuals to totalitarian pressures. (This, of course, is a point Tocqueville makes in *Democracy in America*.)

Getting Our Voice Back

14   In my discussions with students and others about the moral voice, I have borrowed a leaf from Joel Feinberg's seminal work *Offense to Others*. In this book, Feinberg provides a list of activities others may engage in that he believes we will find offensive. He asks us to imagine we are riding on a full bus, which we cannot readily leave. He then presents a series of hypothetical scenes which would cause offense, such as playing loud music, scratching a metallic surface, handling what looks like a real grenade, engaging in sexual behavior, and so on.

15   I am interested not so much in the question of what members of the community find tolerable versus unbearable, but what will make them speak up. Hence I asked students and colleagues "imagine you are in a supermarket and a mother beats the daylights out of a three year old child—would you speak up?" (I say "mother" because I learned that if I just say "someone" most of my respondents state that they would not react because they would fear that the other person might clobber them.) Practically everyone I asked responded that they would not speak up. They would at most try to "distract" the mother, "find out what the child really did," and so on. However, when I asked "imagine you are resting on the shore of a pristine lake; a picnicking family, about to depart, leaves behind a trail of trash—would you suggest they clean up after themselves?" Here again, many demurred but a fair number were willing to consider saying something.

Environment

16   Possibly, my informal sample is skewed. However, it seems to me something else is at work: we had a consensus-building grand dialogue about the environment. While there are still sharp disagreements about numerous details

(for instance, about the relative standing of spotted owls vs. loggers), there is a basic consensus that we must be mindful of the environment and cannot trash it. However, we have had neither a grand dialogue nor a new consensus about the way to treat children. This would suggest one more reason our moral voice is so feeble and reluctant: too many of us, too often, are no longer sure what to state.

17   A return to a firm moral voice thus will require a major town hall meeting of sorts, the kind we have when Americans spend billions of hours in bowling alleys, next to water coolers, and on call-in shows, to form a new consensus, the kind we had about the environment, civil rights, and excessive general regulation, and are now beginning to have about gay rights. This time we need to agree with one another that the common good requires that we speak up and enunciate the values for which we speak. To reiterate, heeding such consensus should never be automatic; we need to examine the values the community urges upon us to determine whether or not they square with our conscience and the basic values we sense no person or community has a right to violate. However, here the focus is on the other side of the coin; it is not enough individually to be able to tell right from wrong, as crucial as that is. We must also be willing to encourage others to attend to values we as a community share.

READING QUESTIONS

1. What is "moral myopia"? Do you agree that individuals fail to notice the moral shortcomings of those who are closest to them? Why or why not?

2. What "constant struggle" does Etzioni identify? Do you agree that humans are in a state of inner conflict?

3. Etzioni identifies a second opposition, one between the inner voice and community voices. How is this opposition sometimes in conflict and sometimes in harmony?

4. Etzioni discusses a connection between pluralism and the community moral voice. According to Etzioni, what should this connection be? What other possible connections does he reject? Why?

5. Etzioni writes that "a strong case can be made that it is precisely the bonding together of community members that enables us to remain independent of the state" (paragraph 13). What point is he trying to make? How well is this idea developed? Is he convincing?

WRITING TOPICS

1. Etzioni identifies a conflict between acting on impulse and acting on judgment. He suggests that it is always more appropriate to act on judgment. Do you agree? Why or why not?

2. What connection does Etzioni note between social science observations and religion? Do you find this connection surprising? Why or why not?

3. Etzioni contrasts the role of "the inner voice" with "community voices" (paragraphs 5, 8). Do you agree with his claim that "the never-ending struggle within the human soul . . . is not limited to intra-individual dialogues between impulses to tempt us . . . and the values we previously internalized" (paragraph 8)? Why or why not?

4. Etzioni writes that "while the moral voice [of the community] urges and counsels us, it is unable to force us" (paragraph 10). Do you agree that individuals have that much choice in making decisions? That is, can they follow their inner voice instead of conforming to pressure from the "moral voice" of the community?

GROUP ACTIVITIES

1. In paragraph 5, Etzioni identifies a shortcoming in addressing the problems resulting from poor moral decisions by youth. In a small group, make a list of specific, concrete programs that he is criticizing. Do you think these programs make a difference? Why or why not?

2. Do the activities described in paragraphs 14 and 15 (the bus and the child in the supermarket). Compare your responses with those of others in your group. Write some of your own "moral voice" activities. What issues are being explored by each activity?

3. Etzioni suggests that America has already formed a new consensus on "the environment, civil rights, and excessive general regulation," and that one of gay rights is beginning. What are areas of disagreement in America? In your state or local community? Why did you list these areas? What are the differing positions on these issues? Do you think it is possible to begin to have a dialogue that will lead to a new consensus? Why or why not?

RESEARCH TOPICS

1. What is the Moral Majority? Who are its leaders? What are its goals? Who are libertarians? What are their goals?

2. Etzioni says "Wanton taking of life . . . is much more common than it is in other civilized societies or than it used to be in America. Countless teenagers bring infants into the world to satisfy their ego needs, . . ." (paragraph 2). Are there statistics to back up his claims? Are violent crime and teenage pregnancy really increasing?

3. Who is Dale Carnegie? What is he famous—and rich—for?

4. Who is Daniel Patrick Moynihan? Etzioni cites him as an authority on moral judgment. Is he an appropriate authority figure? Why or why not?

5. What is multiculturalism? What is pluralism? How are they the same? How are they different?

6. Etzioni refers to the work of other writers. These include Harry Frank-fort, Albert Hirschman, Tocqueville, Joel Feinberg. Find out more about these people. What do you think about their ideas?

PREREADING SUGGESTIONS

1. Have you ever done anything you did not think you should do because you were expected to do so by someone else?
2. What kinds of professions have a very tight chain of command? Why is this chain of command so rigid?

The Perils of Obedience

by Stanley Milgram

Stanley Milgram, a social psychologist at Yale University, studied the conflict between obedience to authority and personal conscience as a means of understanding the genocide of World War II. This selection is from Obedience to Authority *(1974) by Stanley Milgram.*

1   Obedience is as basic an element in the structure of social life as one can point to. Some system of authority is a requirement of all communal living, and it is only the person dwelling in isolation who is not forced to respond, with defiance or submission, to the commands of others. For many people, obedience is a deeply ingrained behavior tendency, indeed a potent impulse overriding training in ethics, sympathy, and moral conduct.

2   The dilemma inherent in submission to authority is ancient, as old as the story of Abraham, and the question of whether one should obey when commands conflict with conscience has been argued by Plato, dramatized in *Antigone,* and treated to philosophic analysis in almost every historical epoch. Conservative philosophers argue that the very fabric of society is threatened by disobedience, while humanists stress the primacy of the individual conscience.

3   The legal and philosophic aspects of obedience are of enormous import, but they say very little about how most people behave in concrete situations. I set up a simple experiment at Yale University to test how much pain an ordinary citizen would inflict on another person simply because he was ordered to by an experimental scientist. Stark authority was pitted against the subjects' strongest moral imperatives against hurting others, and, with the subjects' ears ringing with the screams of the victims, authority won more often than not. The extreme willingness of adults to go to almost any lengths on the command of an authority constitutes the chief finding of the study and the fact most urgently demanding explanation.

4   In the basic experimental design, two people come to a psychology laboratory to take part in a study of memory and learning. One of them is desig-

nated as a "teacher" and the other a "learner." The experimenter explains that the study is concerned with the effects of punishment on learning. The learner is conducted into a room, seated in a kind of miniature electric chair; his arms are strapped to prevent excessive movement, and an electrode is attached to his wrist. He is told that he will be read lists of simple word pairs, and that he will then be tested on his ability to remember the second word of a pair when he hears the first one again. Whenever he makes an error, he will receive electric shocks of increasing intensity.

5   The real focus of the experiment is the teacher. After watching the learner being strapped into place, he is seated before an impressive shock generator. The instrument panel consists of thirty lever switches set in a horizontal line. Each switch is clearly labeled with a voltage designation ranging from 15 to 450 volts. The following designations are clearly indicated for groups of four switches, going from left to right: Slight Shock, Moderate Shock, Strong Shock, Very Strong Shock, Intense Shock, Extreme Intensity Shock, Danger: Severe Shock. (Two switches after this last designation are simply marked XXX.)

6   When a switch is depressed, a pilot light corresponding to each switch is illuminated in bright red; an electric buzzing is heard; a blue light, labeled "voltage energizer," flashes; the dial on the voltage meter swings to the right; various relay clicks sound off.

7   The upper left-hand corner of the generator is labeled SHOCK GENERATOR, TYPE ZLB, DYSON INSTRUMENT COMPANY, WALTHAM, MASS. OUTPUT 15 VOLTS–450 VOLTS.

8   Each subject is given a sample 45-volt shock from the generator before his run as teacher, and the jolt strengthens his belief in the authenticity of the machine.

9   The teacher is a genuinely naïve subject who has come to the laboratory for the experiment. The learner, or victim, is actually an actor who receives no shock at all. The point of the experiment is to see how far a person will proceed in a concrete and measurable situation in which he is ordered to inflict increasing pain on a protesting victim.

10   Conflict arises when the man receiving the shock begins to show that he is experiencing discomfort. At 75 volts, he grunts; at 120 volts, he complains loudly; at 150, he demands to be released from the experiment. As the voltage increases, his protests become more vehement and emotional. At 285 volts, his response can be described only as an agonized scream. Soon thereafter, he makes no sound at all.

11   For the teacher, the situation quickly becomes one of gripping tension. It is not a game for him; conflict is intense and obvious. The manifest suffering of the learner presses him to quit; but each time he hesitates to administer a shock, the experimenter orders him to continue. To extricate himself from this plight, the subject must make a clear break with authority.

12   The subject, Gretchen Brandt,* is an attractive thirty-one-year-old medical technician who works at the Yale Medical School. She had emigrated from Germany five years before.

---

*Names of subjects described in this piece have been changed.

13   On several occasions when the learner complains, she turns to the experimenter coolly and inquires, "Shall I continue?" She promptly returns to her task when the experimenter asks her to do so. At the administration of 210 volts, she turns to the experimenter, remarking firmly, "Well, I'm sorry, I don't think we should continue."

14   EXPERIMENTER: The experiment requires that you go on until he has learned all the word pairs correctly.

15   BRANDT: He has a heart condition, I'm sorry. He told you that before.

16   EXPERIMENTER: The shocks may be painful but they are not dangerous.

17   BRANDT: Well, I'm sorry, I think when shocks continue like this, they are dangerous. You ask him if he wants to get out. It's his free will.

18   EXPERIMENTER: It is absolutely essential that we continue . . .

19   BRANDT: I'd like you to ask him. We came here of our free will. If he wants to continue I'll go ahead. He told you he had a heart condition. I'm sorry. I don't want to be responsible for anything happening to him. I wouldn't like it for me either.

20   EXPERIMENTER: You have no other choice.

21   BRANDT: I think we are here on our own free will. I don't want to be responsible if anything happens to him. Please understand that.

22   She refuses to go further and the experiment is terminated.

23   The woman is firm and resolute throughout. She indicates in the interview that she was in no way tense or nervous, and this corresponds to her controlled appearance during the experiment. She fells that the last shock she administered to the learner was extremely painful and reiterates that she "did not want to be responsible for any harm to him."

24   The woman's straightforward, courteous behavior in the experiment, lack of tension, and total control of her own action seem to make disobedience a simple and rational deed. Her behavior is the very embodiment of what I envisioned would be true for almost all subjects.

25   Before the experiments, I sought predictions about the outcome from various kinds of people—psychiatrists, college sophomores, middle-class adults, graduate students and faculty in the behavioral sciences. With remarkable similarity, they predicted that virtually all subjects would refuse to obey the experimenter. The psychiatrists specifically predicted that most subjects would not go beyond 150 volts, when the victim makes his first explicit demand to be freed. They expected that only 4 percent would reach 300 volts, and that only a pathological fringe of about one in a thousand would administer the highest shock on the board.

26   These predictions were unequivocally wrong. Of the forty subjects in the first experiment, twenty-five obeyed the orders of the experimenter to the end, punishing the victim until they reached the most potent shock available on

the generator. After 450 volts were administered three times, the experimenter called a halt to the sessions. Many obedient subjects then heaved sighs of relief, mopped their brows, rubbed their fingers over their eyes, or nervously fumbled cigarettes. Others displayed only minimal signs of tension from beginning to end.

27   When the very first experiments were carried out, Yale undergraduates were used as subjects, and about 60 percent of them were fully obedient. A colleague of mine immediately dismissed these findings as having no relevance to "ordinary" people, asserting that Yale undergraduates are a highly aggressive, competitive bunch who step on each other's necks on the slightest provocation. He assured me that when "ordinary" people were tested, the results would be quite different. As we moved from the pilot studies to the regular experimental series, people drawn from every stratum of New Haven life came to be employed in the experiment: professionals, white-collar workers, unemployed persons, and industrial workers. *The experimental outcome was the same as we had observed among the students.*

28   Moreover, when the experiments were repeated in Princeton, Munich, Rome, South Africa, and Australia, the level of obedience was invariably somewhat *higher* than found in the investigation reported in this article. Thus one scientist in Munich found 85 percent of his subjects obedient. . . .

29   One theoretical interpretation of this behavior holds that all people harbor deeply aggressive instincts continually pressing for expression, and that the experiment provides institutional justification for the release of these impulses. According to this view, if a person is placed in a situation in which he has complete power over another individual, whom he may punish as much as he likes, all that is sadistic and bestial in man comes to the fore. The impulse to shock the victim is seen to flow from the potent aggressive tendencies, which are part of the motivational life of the individual, and the experiment, because it provides social legitimacy, simply opens the door to their expression.

30   It becomes vital, therefore, to compare the subject's performance when he is under orders and when he is allowed to choose the shock level.

31   The procedure was identical to our standard experiment, except that the teacher was told that he was free to select any shock level on any of the trials. (The experimenter took pains to point out that the teacher could use the highest levels on the generator, the lowest, any in between, or any combination of levels.) Each subject proceeded for thirty critical trials. The learner's protests were coordinated to standard shock levels, his first grunt coming at 75 volts, his first vehement protest at 150 volts.

32   The average shock used during the thirty critical trials was less than 60 volts—lower than the point at which the victim showed the first signs of discomfort. Three of the forty subjects did not go beyond the very lowest level on the board, twenty-eight went no higher than 75 volts, and thirty-eight did not go beyond the first loud protest at 150 volts. Two subjects provided the exception, administering up to 325 and 450 volts, but the overall result was that the great majority of people delivered very low, usually painless, shocks when the choice was explicitly up to them.

33   This condition of the experiment undermines another commonly offered explanation of the subjects' behavior—that those who shocked the victim at the most severe levels came only from the sadistic fringe of society. If one considers that almost two-thirds of the participants fall into the category of "obedient" subjects, and that they represented ordinary people drawn from working, managerial, and professional classes, the argument becomes very shaky. Indeed, it is highly reminiscent of the issue that arose in connection with Hannah Arendt's 1963 book, *Eichmann in Jerusalem.* Arendt contended that the prosecution's effort to depict Eichmann as a sadistic monster was fundamentally wrong, that he came closer to being an uninspired bureaucrat who simply sat at his desk and did his job. For asserting her views, Arendt became the object of considerable scorn, even calumny. Somehow, it was felt that the monstrous deeds carried out by Eichmann required a brutal, twisted personality, evil incarnate. After witnessing hundreds of ordinary persons submit to the authority in our own experiments, I must conclude that Arendt's conception of the banality of evil comes closer to the truth than one might dare imagine. The ordinary person who shocked the victim did so out of a sense of obligation—an impression of his duties as a subject—and not from any peculiarly aggressive tendencies.

34   This is, perhaps, the most fundamental lesson of our study: ordinary people, simply doing their jobs, and without any particular hostility on their part, can become agents in a terrible destructive process. Moreover, even when the destructive effects of their work become patently clear, and they are asked to carry out actions incompatible with fundamental standards of morality, relatively few people have the resources needed to resist authority.

35   Many of the people were in some sense against what they did to the learner, and many protested even while they obeyed. Some were totally convinced of the wrongness of their actions but could not bring themselves to make an open break with authority. They often derived satisfaction from their thoughts and felt that—within themselves, at least—they had been on the side of the angels. They tried to reduce strain by obeying the experimenter but "only slightly," encouraging the learner, touching the generator switches gingerly. When interviewed, such a subject would stress that he had "asserted my humanity" by administering the briefest shock possible. Handling the conflict in this manner was easier than defiance.

36   The situation is constructed so that there is no way the subject can stop shocking the learner without violating the experimenter's definitions of his own competence. The subject fears that he will appear arrogant, untoward, and rude if he breaks off. Although these inhibiting emotions appear small in scope alongside the violence being done to the learner, they suffuse the mind and feelings of the subject, who is miserable at the prospect of having to repudiate the authority to his face. (When the experiment was altered so that the experimenter gave his instructions by telephone instead of in person, only a third as many people were fully obedient through 450 volts.) It is a curious thing that a measure of compassion on the part of the subject—an unwilling-

ness to "hurt" the experimenter's feelings—is part of those binding forces inhibiting his disobedience. The withdrawal of such deference may be as painful to the subject as to the authority he defies.

The subjects do not derive satisfaction from inflicting pain, but they often like the feeling they get from pleasing the experimenter. They are proud of doing a good job, obeying the experimenter under difficult circumstances. While the subjects administered only mild shocks on their own initiative, one experimental variation showed that, under orders, 30 percent of them were willing to deliver 450 volts even when they had to forcibly push the learner's hand down on the electrode.

37   Bruno Batta is a thirty-seven-year-old welder who took part in the variation requiring the use of force. He was born in New Haven, his parents in Italy. He has a rough-hewn face that conveys a conspicuous lack of alertness. He has some difficulty in mastering the experimental procedure and needs to be corrected by the experimenter several times. He shows appreciation for the help and willingness to do what is required. After the 150-volt level, Batta has to force the learner's hand down on the shock plate, since the learner himself refuses to touch it.

38   When the learner first complains, Mr. Batta pays no attention to him. His face remains impassive, as if to dissociate himself from the learner's disruptive behavior. When the experimenter instructs him to force the learner's hand down, he adopts a rigid, mechanical procedure. He tests the generator switch. When it fails to function, he immediately forces the learner's hand onto the shock plate. All the while he maintains the same rigid mask. The learner, seated alongside him, begs him to stop, but with robotic impassivity he continues the procedure.

39   What is extraordinary is his apparent total indifference to the learner; he hardly takes cognizance of him as a human being. Meanwhile, he relates to the experimenter in a submissive and courteous fashion.

40   At the 330-volt level, the learner refuses not only to touch the shock plate but also to provide any answers. Annoyed, Batta turns to him, and chastises him: "You better answer and get it over with. We can't stay here all night." These are the only words he directs to the learner in the course of an hour. Never again does he speak to him. The scene is brutal and depressing, his hard, impassive face showing total indifference as he subdues the screaming learner and gives him shocks. He seems to derive no pleasure from the act itself, only quiet satisfaction at doing his job properly.

41   When he administers 450 volts, he turns to the experimenter and asks, "Where do we go from here, Professor?" His tone is deferential and expresses his willingness to be a cooperative subject, in contrast to the learner's obstinacy.

42   At the end of the session he tells the experimenter how honored he has been to help him, and in a moment of contrition, remarks, "Sir, sorry it couldn't have been a full experiment."

43   He has done his honest best. It is only the deficient behavior of the learner that has denied the experimenter full satisfaction.

44   The essence of obedience is that a person comes to view himself as the instrument for carrying out another person's wishes, and he therefore no longer regards himself as responsible for his actions. Once this critical shift of viewpoint has occurred, all of the essential features of obedience follow. The most far-reaching consequence is that the person feels responsible to the authority directing him but feels no responsibility *for* the content of the actions that the authority prescribes. Morality does not disappear—it acquires a radically different focus: the subordinate person feels shame or pride depending on how adequately he has performed the actions called for by authority.

45   Language provides numerous terms to pinpoint this type of morality: *loyalty, duty, discipline* all are terms heavily saturated with moral meaning and refer to the degree to which a person fulfills his obligations to authority. They refer not to the "goodness" of the person per se but to the adequacy with which a subordinate fulfills his socially defined role. The most frequent defense of the individual who has performed a heinous act under command of authority is that he has simply done his duty. In asserting this defense, the individual is not introducing an alibi concocted for the moment but is reporting honestly on the psychological attitude induced by submission to authority.

46   For a person to feel responsible for his actions, he must sense that the behavior has flowed from "the self." In the situation we have studied, subjects have precisely the opposite view of their actions—namely, they see them as originating in the motives of some other person. Subjects in the experiment frequently said, "If it were up to me, I would not have administered shocks to the learner."

47   Once authority has been isolated as the cause of the subject's behavior, it is legitimate to inquire into the necessary elements of authority and how it must be perceived in order to gain his compliance. We conducted some investigations into the kinds of changes that would cause the experimenter to lose his power and to be disobeyed by the subject. Some of the variations revealed that:

48   *The experimenter's physical presence has a marked impact on his authority.* As cited earlier, obedience dropped off sharply when orders were given by telephone. The experimenter could often induce a disobedient subject to go on by returning to the laboratory.

49   *Conflicting authority severely paralyses action.* When two experimenters of equal status, both seated at the command desk, gave incompatible orders, no shocks were delivered past the point of their disagreement.

50   *The rebellious action of others severely undermines authority.* In one variation, three teachers (two actors and a real subject) administered a test and shocks. When the two actors disobeyed the experimenter and refused to go beyond a certain shock level, thirty-six of forty subjects joined their disobedient peers and refused as well.

51   Although the experimenter's authority was fragile in some respects, it is also true that he had almost none of the tools used in ordinary command structures. For example, the experimenter did not threaten the subjects with punishment—such as loss of income, community ostracism, or jail—for failure to obey. Neither could he offer incentives. Indeed, we should expect the experimenter's authority to be much less than that of someone like a general, since the experimenter has no power to enforce his imperatives, and since participation in a psychological experiment scarcely evokes the sense of urgency and dedication found in warfare. Despite these limitations, he still managed to command a dismaying degree of obedience.

52   I will cite one final variation of the experiment that depicts a dilemma that is more common in everyday life. The subject was not ordered to pull the lever that shocked the victim, but merely perform a subsidiary test (administering the word-pair test) while another person administered the shock. In this situation, thirty-seven of the forty adults continued to the highest level of the shock generator. Predictably, they excused their behavior by saying that the responsibility belonged to the man who actually pulled the switch. This may illustrate a dangerously typical arrangement in a complex society: it is easy to ignore responsibility when one is only an intermediate link in a chain of action.

53   The problem of obedience is not wholly psychological. The form and shape of society and the way it is developing have much to do with it. There was a time, perhaps, when people were able to give a fully human response to any situation because they were fully absorbed in it as human beings. But as soon as there was a division of labor, things changed. Beyond a certain point, the breaking up of society into people carrying out narrow and very special jobs takes away from the human quality of work and life. A person does not get to see the whole situation but only a small part of it, and is thus unable to act without some kind of overall direction. He yields to authority but in doing so is alienated from his own actions.

54   Even Eichmann was sickened when he toured the concentration camps, but he had only to sit at a desk and shuffle papers. At the same time the man in the camp who actually dropped Cyclon-b into the gas chambers was able to justify *his* behavior on the ground that he was only following orders from above. Thus there is a fragmentation of the total human act; no one is confronted with the consequences of his decision to carry out the evil act. The person who assumes responsibility has evaporated. Perhaps this is the most common characteristic of socially organized evil in modern society.

READING QUESTIONS

1. In paragraphs 1–3, Milgram contrasts the more abstract legal and philosophic aspects of obedience with what he is most interested in: "how most people behave in concrete situations." (a) Explain what he means by the more abstract aspects of obedience. (b) What might be examples of more concrete situations?

2. Describe the basic experimental situation. Why is the real focus of the experiment the "teacher"? What does Milgram want to find out?

3. The first "teacher" subject is Gretchen Brandt. How does she behave?

4. How well did the predictions regarding the outcome of the experiment match the actual results in Yale, in New Haven, in other places in the world?

5. Identify the other "teachers" that Milgram describes. How do they behave? What point does Milgram make with Batta?

6. Why does Milgram modify the experiment so "that the teacher was free to select any shock level on any of the trials"? (paragraph 23). What theory is he testing?

7. What does Milgram identify as the most fundamental lesson of the study?

8. Characterize the behavior of the teacher toward the experimenter. What does Milgram learn from this behavior?

9. Milgram writes that when the teacher "no longer regards himself as responsible for his actions," "[m]orality does not disappear—it acquires a radically different focus" (paragraph 37). What does he mean? What are some examples in real life that illustrate this?

10. Paragraphs 41–43 describe several ways Milgram changed the experiment. What effect does he notice with each variation?

11. What is the final variation of the experiment (paragraph 45)? What conclusion does Milgram draw from the results of this variation?

WRITING TOPICS

1. What institutions attempt to serve the interests of the community by preserving social order? Write an essay in which you identify these institutions and describe their methods of operating.

2. Milgram relates his experiments to the killing of Jews and other undesirables in Nazi Germany. What connection do you see? At what point is it necessary for individuals to disobey orders in order to act morally?

3. One implication of Milgram's statement that "Morality does not disappear—it acquires a radically different focus" (paragraph 37) is that different individuals can be in conflict about what is most moral in a given situation. Identify specific situations in which this conflict can affect people's lives. Does this type of conflict arise only during war, or is it a more common situation than that?

4. Milgram claims that "For a person to feel responsible for his actions, he must sense that the behavior has flowed from 'the self'" (paragraph 46). Do you agree with this statement? Why or why not?

GROUP ACTIVITIES

1. Make a large list of professions. Each person in the group should rank the professions on a continuum from the ones demanding the most

obedience to authority to the ones demanding the least obedience to authority. Compare your results.

2. Milgram says that language allows us to make and justify moral and ethical decisions. In other words, how we label a decision can make it sound right or wrong. For example, Milgram points out that people justified shocking the learners by calling their actions obedience rather than harm. Go through the reading and find as many instances of this labeling as you can. Then describe situations or organizations that explain their actions by using words that sound positive but which may mask negative effects on others.

RESEARCH TOPICS

1. Milgram mentions the following names: Antigone, Abraham (from the Old Testament), Eichmann, Hannah Arendt. Who are they? What are they known for? Alone or in a group, look up more information about them.

2. Who were the other undesirables in Nazi Germany?

3. Alone or in a group, select one of the following topics. Research the topic and present a brief background of the situation to your classmates. Explain how some of Milgram's findings relate to the specific situation you researched.

> Civil Rights Movement/life of Martin Luther King, Jr.
> Boston Tea Party or other event of the Revolutionary War
> Underground Railroad or other abolitionist movement
> Nelson Mandela and South African apartheid
> Mahatma Gandhi and the Indian independence movement

Beyond Stereotypes

Exploring the Theme

■ Choose one of the following groups: men, women, African-Americans, Arabs, gays, people with mental illness, Northerners, or any other group of your choice. List as many stereotypes about this group as you can. Identify a possible basis for each stereotype.

■ What can individuals do to fight stereotypes?

PREREADING SUGGESTIONS

1. Imagine that you are unable to walk. What would your life be like? What would you be able/unable to do? What would be important for you to keep doing? What would you have to give up? What would be hardest for you? What would be easiest for you?

2. What words are commonly used to describe people with physical or mental disabilities? What is the effect of using these words to label people?

On Being a Cripple

by Nancy Mairs

The political correctness (PC) movement has focused a new awareness on the language used to describe other people—for example, Native American instead of Indian or African-American instead of black. Nancy Mairs considers the effects of labels on people with disabilities in assigning herself the label "cripple." This selection is from Plaintext *(1986) by Nancy Mairs.*

> To escape is nothing. Not to escape is nothing.
> —Louise Bogan

1   The other day I was thinking of writing an essay on being a cripple. I was thinking hard in one of the stalls of the women's room in my office building, as I was shoving my shirt into my jeans and tugging up my zipper. Preoccupied, I flushed, picked up my bookbag, took my cane down from the hook, and unlatched the door. So many movements unbalanced me, and as I pulled the door open I fell over backward, landing fully clothed on the toilet seat with my legs splayed in front of me; the old beetle-on-its-back routine. Saturday afternoon, the building deserted, I was free to laugh aloud as I wriggled back to my feet, my voice bounding off the yellowish tiles from all directions. Had anyone been there with me, I'd have been still and faint and hot with chagrin. I decided that it was high time to write the essay.

2   First, the matter of semantics. I am a cripple. I choose this word to name me. I choose from among several possibilities, the most common of which are "handicapped" and "disabled." I made the choice a number of years ago, without thinking, unaware of my motives for doing so. Even now, I'm not sure what those motives are, but I recognize that they are complex and not entirely flattering. People—crippled or not—wince at the word "cripple," as they do not at "handicapped" or "disabled." Perhaps I want them to wince. I want them to see me as a tough customer, one to whom the fates/gods/viruses have not been kind, but who can face the brutal truth of her existence squarely. As a cripple, I swagger.

3   But, to be fair to myself, a certain amount of honesty underlies my choice. "Cripple" seems to me a clean word, straightforward and precise. It has an honorable history, having made its first appearance in the Lindisfarne Gospel in the tenth century. As a lover of words, I like the accuracy with which it describes my condition: I have lost the full use of my limbs. "Disabled," by contrast, suggests any incapacity, physical or mental. And I certainly don't like "handicapped," which implies that I have deliberately been put at a disadvantage, by whom I can't imagine (my God is not a Handicapper General), in or-

der to equalize chances in the great race of life. These words seem to me to be moving away from my condition, to be widening the gap between word and reality. Most remote is the recently coined euphemism "differently abled," which partakes of the same semantic hopefulness that transformed countries from "undeveloped" to "underdeveloped," then to "less developed," and finally to "developing" nations. People have continued to starve in those countries during the shift. Some realities do not obey the dictates of language.

4   Mine is one of them. Whatever you call me, I remain crippled. But I don't care what you call me, so long as it isn't "differently abled," which strikes me as pure verbal garbage designed, by its ability to describe anyone, to describe no one. I subscribe to George Orwell's thesis that "the slovenliness of our language makes it easier for us to have foolish thoughts." And I refuse to participate in the degeneration of the language to the extent that I deny that I have lost anything in the course of this calamitous disease; I refuse to pretend that the only differences between you and me are the various ordinary ones that distinguish any one person from another. But call me "disabled" or "handicapped" if you like. I have long since grown accustomed to them; and if they are vague, at least they hint at the truth. Moreover, I use them myself. Society is no readier to accept crippledness than to accept death, war, sex, sweat, or wrinkles. I would never refer to another person as a cripple. It is the word I use to name only myself.

5   I haven't always been crippled, a fact for which I am soundly grateful. To be whole of limb is, I know from experience, infinitely more pleasant and useful than to be crippled; and if that knowledge leaves me open to bitterness at my loss, the physical soundness I once enjoyed (though I did not enjoy it half enough) is well worth the occasional stab of regret. Though never any good at sports, I was a normally active child and young adult. I climbed trees, played hopscotch, jumped rope, skated, swam, rode my bicycle, sailed. I despised team sports, spending some of the wretchedest afternoons of my life, sweaty and humiliated, behind a field-hockey stick and under a basketball hoop. I tramped alone for miles along the bridle paths that webbed the woods behind the house I grew up in. I swayed through countless dim hours in the arms of one man or another under the scattered shot of light from mirrored balls, and gyrated through countless more as Tab Hunter and Johnny Mathis gave way to the Rolling Stones, Creedence Clearwater Revival, Cream. I walked down the aisle. I pushed baby carriages, changed tires in the rain, marched for peace.

6   When I was twenty-eight I started to trip and drop things. What at first seemed my natural clumsiness soon became too pronounced to shrug off. I consulted a neurologist, who told me that I had a brain tumor. A battery of tests, increasingly disagreeable, revealed no tumor. About a year and a half later I developed a blurred spot in one eye. I had, at last, the episodes "disseminated in space and time" requisite for a diagnosis: multiple sclerosis. I have never been sorry for the doctor's initial misdiagnosis, however. For almost a week, until the negative results of the tests were in, I thought that I was going to die right away. Every day for the past nearly ten years, then, has been a kind of gift. I accept all gifts.

7   Multiple sclerosis is a chronic degenerative disease of the central nervous system, in which the myelin that sheathes the nerves is somehow eaten away and scar tissue forms in its place, interrupting the nerves' signals. During its course, which is unpredictable and uncontrollable, one may lose vision, hearing, speech, the ability to walk, control of bladder and/or bowels, strength in any or all extremities, sensitivity to touch, vibration, and/or pain, potency, coordination of movements—the list of possibilities is lengthy and, yes, horrifying. One may also lose one's sense of humor. That's the easiest to lose and the hardest to survive without.

8   In the past ten years, I have sustained some of these losses. Characteristic of MS are sudden attacks, called exacerbations, followed by remissions, and these I have not had. Instead, my disease has been slowly progressive. My left leg is now so weak that I walk with the aid of a brace and a cane; and for distances I use an Amigo, a variation on the electric wheelchair that looks rather like an electrified kiddie car. I no longer have much use of my left hand. Now my right side is weakening as well. I still have the blurred spot in my right eye. Overall, though, I've been lucky so far. My world has, of necessity, been circumscribed by my losses, but the terrain left me has been ample enough for me to continue many of the activities that absorb me: writing, teaching, raising children and cats and plants and snakes, reading, speaking publicly about MS and depression, even playing bridge with people patient and honorable enough to let me scatter cards every which way without sneaking a peek.

9   Lest I begin to sound like Pollyanna, however, let me say that I don't like having MS. I hate it. My life holds realities—harsh ones, some of them—that no right-minded human being ought to accept without grumbling. One of them is fatigue. I know of no one with MS who does not complain of bone-weariness; in a disease that presents an astonishing variety of symptoms, fatigue seems to be a common factor. I wake up in the morning feeling the way most people do at the end of a bad day, and I take it from there. As a result, I spend a lot of time *in extremis* and, impatient with limitation, I tend to ignore my fatigue until my body breaks down in some way and forces rest. Then I miss picnics, dinner parties, poetry readings, the brief visits of old friends from out of town. The offspring of a puritanical tradition of exceptional venerability, I cannot view these lapses without shame. My life often seems a series of small failures to do as I ought.

10   I lead, on the whole, an ordinary life, probably rather like the one I would have led had I not had MS. I am lucky that my predilections were already solitary, sedentary, and bookish—unlike the world-famous French cellist I have read about, or the young woman I talked with one long afternoon who wanted only to be a jockey. I had just begun graduate school when I found out something was wrong with me, and I have remained, interminably, a graduate student. Perhaps I would not have if I'd thought I had the stamina to return to a full-time job as a technical editor; but I've enjoyed my studies.

11   In addition to studying, I teach writing courses. I also teach medical students how to give neurological examinations. I pick up freelance editing jobs here and there. I have raised a foster son and sent him into the world, where

he has made me two grandbabies, and I am still escorting my daughter and son through adolescence. I go to Mass every Saturday. I am a superb, if messy, cook. I am also an enthusiastic laundress, capable of sorting a hamper full of clothes into five subtly differentiated piles, but a terrible housekeeper. I can do italic writing and, in an emergency, bathe an oil-soaked cat. I play a fiendish game of Scrabble. When I have the time and the money, I like to sit on my front steps with my husband, drinking Amaretto and smoking a cigar, as we imagine our counterparts in Leningrad and make sure that the sun gets down once more behind the sharp childish scrawl of the Tucson Mountains.

12   This lively plenty has its bleak complement, of course, in all the things I can no longer do. I will never run again, except in dreams, and one day I may have to write that I will never walk again. I like to go camping, but I can't follow George and the children along the trails that wander out of a campsite through the desert or into the mountains. In fact, even on the level I've learned never to check the weather or try to hold a coherent conversation: I need all my attention for my wayward fee. Of late, I have begun to catch myself wondering how people can propel themselves without canes. With only one usable hand, I have to select my clothing with care not so much for style as for ease of ingress and egress, and even so, dressing can be laborious. I can no longer do fine stitchery, pick up babies, play the piano, braid my hair. I am immobilized by acute attacks of depression, which may or may not be physiologically related to MS but are certainly its logical concomitant.

13   These two elements, the plenty and the privation, are never pure, nor are the delight and wretchedness that accompany them. Almost every pickle that I get into as a result of my weakness and clumsiness—and I get into plenty— is funny as well as maddening and sometimes painful. I recall one May afternoon when a friend and I were going out for a drink after finishing up at school. As we were climbing into opposite sides of my car, chatting, I tripped and fell, flat and hard, onto the asphalt parking lot, my abrupt departure interrupting him in mid-sentence. "Where'd you go?" he called as he came around the back of the car to find me hauling myself up by the door frame. "Are you all right?" Yes, I told him, I was fine, just a bit rattly, and we drove off to find a shady patio and some beer. When I got home an hour or so later, my daughter greeted me with "What have you done to yourself?" I looked down. One elbow of my white turtleneck with the green froggies, one knee of my white trousers, one white kneesock were blood-soaked. We peeled off the clothes and inspected the damage, which was nasty enough but not alarming. That part wasn't funny: The abrasions took a long time to heal, and one got a little infected. Even so, when I think of my friend talking earnestly, suddenly, to the hot thin air while I dropped from his view as though through a trap door, I find the image as silly as something from a Marx Brothers movie.

14   I may find it easier than other cripples to amuse myself because I live propped by the acceptance and the assistance and, sometimes, the amusement of those around me. Grocery clerks tear my checks out of my checkbook for me, and sales clerks find chairs to put into dressing rooms when I want to

try on clothes. The people I work with make sure I teach at times when I am least likely to be fatigued, in places I can get to, with the materials I need. My students, with one anonymous exception (in an end-of-the-semester evaluation), have been unperturbed by my disability. Some even like it. One was immensely cheered by the information that I paint my own fingernails; she decided, she told me, that if I could go to such trouble over fine details, she could keep on writing essays. I suppose I became some sort of bright-fingered muse. She wrote good essays, too.

15   The most important struts in the framework of my existence, of course, are my husband and children. Dismayingly few marriages survive the MS test, and why should they? Most twenty-two- and nineteen-year-olds, like George and me, can vow in clear conscience, after a childhood of chickenpox and summer colds, to keep one another in sickness and in health so long as they both shall live. Not many are equipped for catastrophe: the dismay, the depression, the extra work, the boredom that a degenerative disease can insinuate into a relationship. And our society, with its emphasis on fun and its association of fun with physical performance, offers little encouragement for a whole spouse to stay with a crippled partner. Children experience similar stresses when faced with a crippled parent, and they are more helpless, since parents and children can't usually get divorced. They hate, of course, to be different from their peers, and the child whose mother is tacking down the aisle of a school auditorium packed with proud parents like a Cape Cod dinghy in a stiff breeze jolly well stands out in a crowd. Deprived of legal divorce, the child can at least deny the mother's disability, even her existence, forgetting to tell her about recitals and PTA meetings, refusing to accompany her to stores or church or the movies, never inviting friends to the house. Many do.

16   But I've been limping along for ten years now, and so far George and the children are still at my left elbow, holding tight. Anne and Matthew vacuum floors and dust furniture and haul trash and rake up dog droppings and button my cuffs and bake lasagna and Toll House cookies with just enough grumbling so I know that they don't have brain fever. And far from hiding me, they're forever dragging me by racks of fancy clothes or through teeming school corridors, or welcoming gaggles of friends while I'm wandering through the house in Anne's filmy pink babydoll pajamas. George generally calls before he brings someone home, but he does just as many dumb thankless chores as the children. And they all yell at me, laugh at some of my jokes, write me funny letters when we're apart—in short, treat me as an ordinary human being for whom they have some use. I think they like me. Unless they're faking. . . .

17   Faking. There's the rub. Tugging at the fringes of my consciousness always is the terror that people are kind to me only because I'm a cripple. My mother almost shattered me once, with that instinct mothers have—blind, I think, in this case, but unerring nonetheless—for striking blows along the fault-lines of their children's hearts, by telling me, in an attack on my selfishness, "We all have to make allowances for you, of course, because of the way you are." From the distance of a couple of years, I have to admit that I haven't any idea

just what she meant, and I'm not sure that she knew either. She was awfully angry. But at the time, as the words thudded home, I felt my worst fear, suddenly realized. I could bear being called selfish: I am. But I couldn't bear the corroboration that those around me were doing in fact what I'd always suspected them of doing, professing fondness while silently putting up with me because of the way I am. A cripple. I've been a little cracked ever since.

18   Along with this fear that people are secretly accepting shoddy goods comes a relentless pressure to please—to prove myself worth the burdens I impose, I guess, or to build a substantial account of goodwill against which I may write drafts in times of need. Part of the pressure arises from social expectations. In our society, anyone who deviates from the norm had better find some way to compensate. Like fat people, who are expected to be jolly, cripples must bear their lot meekly and cheerfully. A grumpy cripple isn't playing by the rules. And much of the pressure is self-generated. Early on I vowed that, if I had to have MS, by God I was going to do it well. This is a class act, ladies and gentlemen. No tears, no recriminations, no faint-heartedness.

19   One way and another, then, I wind up feeling like Tiny Tim, peering over the edge of the table at the Christmas goose, waving my crutch, piping down God's blessing on us all. Only sometimes I don't want to play Tiny Tim. I'd rather be Caliban, a most scurvy monster. Fortunately, at home no one much cares whether I'm a good cripple or a bad cripple as long as I make vichyssoise with fair regularity. One evening several years ago, Anne was reading at the dining-room table while I cooked dinner. As I opened a can of tomatoes, the can slipped in my left hand and juice splattered me and the counter with bloody spots. Fatigued and infuriated, I bellowed, "I'm so sick of being crippled!" Anne glanced at me over the top of her book. "There now," she said, "do you feel better?" "Yes," I said, "yes, I do." She went back to her reading. I felt better. That's about all the attention my scurviness ever gets.

20   Because I hate being crippled, I sometimes hate myself for being a cripple. Over the years I have come to expect—even accept—attacks of violent self-loathing. Luckily, in general our society no longer connects deformity and disease directly with evil (though a charismatic once told me that I have MS because a devil is in me) and so I'm allowed to move largely at will, even among small children. But I'm not sure that this revision of attitude has been particularly helpful. Physical imperfection, even freed of moral disapprobation, still defies and violates the ideal, especially for women, whose confinement in their bodies as objects of desire is far from over. Each age, of course, has its ideal, and I doubt that ours is any better or worse than any other. Today's ideal woman, who lives on the glossy pages of dozens of magazines, seems to be between the ages of eighteen and twenty-five; her hair has body, her teeth flash white, her breath smells minty, her underarms are dry; she has a career but is still a fabulous cook, especially of meals that take less than twenty minutes to prepare; she does not ordinarily appear to have a husband or children; she is trim and deeply tanned; she jogs, swims, plays tennis, rides a bicycle, sails; but does not bowl; she travels widely, even to out-of-the-way places like Finland and Samoa, always in the company of the ideal man, who possesses a nearly

identical set of characteristics. There are a few exceptions. Though usually white and often blonde, she may be black, Hispanic, Asian, or Native American, so long as she is usually sleek. She may be old, provided she is selling a laxative or is Lauren Bacall. If she is selling a detergent, she may be married and have a flock of strikingly messy children. But she is never a cripple.

21   Like many women I know, I have always had an uneasy relationship with my body. I was not a popular child, largely, I think now, because I was peculiar: intelligent, intense, moody, shy, given to unexpected actions and inexplicable notions and emotions. But as I entered adolescence, I believed myself unpopular because I was homely: my breasts too flat, my mouth too wide, my hips too narrow, my clothing never quite right in fit or style. I was not, in fact, particularly ugly, old photographs inform me, though I was well off the ideal; but I carried this sense of self-alienation with me into adulthood, where I regenerated in response to the depredations of MS. Even with my brace I walk with a limp so pronounced that, seeing myself on the videotape of a television program on the disabled, I couldn't believe that anything but an inchworm could make progress humping along like that. My shoulders droop and my pelvis thrusts forward as I try to balance myself upright, throwing my frame into a bony S. As a result of contractures, one shoulder is higher than the other and I carry one arm bent in front of me, the fingers curled into a claw. My left arm and leg have wasted into pipe-stems, and I try always to keep them covered. When I think about how my body must look to others, especially to men, to whom I have been trained to display myself, I feel ludicrous, even loathsome.

22   At my age, however, I don't spend much time thinking about my appearance. The burning egocentricity of adolescence, which assures one that all the world is looking all the time, has passed, thank God, and I'm generally too caught up in what I'm doing to step back, as I used to, and watch myself as though upon a stage. I'm also too old to believe in the accuracy of self-image. I know that I'm not a hideous crone, that in fact, when I'm rested, well dressed, and well made up, I look fine. The self-loathing I feel is neither physically nor intellectually substantial. What I hate is not me but a disease.

23   I am not a disease.

24   And a disease is not—at least no singlehandedly—going to determine who I am, though at first it seemed to be going to. Adjusting to a chronic incurable illness, I have moved through a process similar to that outlined by Elizabeth Kübler-Ross in *On Death and Dying*. The major difference—and it is far more significant than most people recognize—is that I can't be sure of the outcome, as the terminally ill cancer patient can. Research studies indicate that, with proper medical care, I may achieve a "normal" life span. And in our society, with its vision of death as the ultimate evil, worse even than decrepitude, the response to such news is, "Oh well, at least you're not going to *die*." Are there worse things than dying? I think that there may be.

25   I think of two women I know, both with MS, both enough older than I to have served me as models. One took to her bed several years ago and has been there ever since. Although she can sit in a high-backed wheelchair, because she is incontinent she refuses to go out at all, even though incontinence pants,

which are readily available at any pharmacy, could protect her from embarrassment. Instead, she stays at home and insists that her husband, a small quiet man, a retired civil servant, stay there with her except for a quick weekly foray to the supermarket. The other woman, whose illness was diagnosed when she was eighteen, a nursing student engaged to a young doctor, finished her training, married her doctor, accompanied him to Germany when he was in the service, bore three sons and a daughter, now grown and gone. When she can, she travels with her husband; she plays bridge, embroiders, swims regularly; she works, like me, as a symptomatic-patient instructor of medical students in neurology. Guess which woman I hope to be.

26   At the beginning, I thought about having MS almost incessantly. And because of the unpredictable course of the disease, my thoughts were always terrified. Each night I'd get into bed wondering whether I'd get out again the next morning, whether I'd be able to see, to speak, to hold a pen between my fingers. Knowing that the day might come when I'd be physically incapable of killing myself, I thought perhaps I ought to do so right away, while I still had the strength. Gradually I came to understand that the Nancy who might one day lie inert under a bedsheet, arms and legs paralyzed, unable to feed or bathe herself, unable to reach out for a gun, a bottle of pills, was not the Nancy I was at present, and that I could not presume to make decisions for that future Nancy, who might well not want in the least to die. Now the only provision I've made for the future Nancy is that when the time comes—and it is likely to come in the form of pneumonia, friend to the weak and the old—I am not to be treated with machines and medications. If she is unable to communicate by then, I hope she will be satisfied with these terms.

27   Thinking all the time about having MS grew tiresome and intrusive, especially in the large and tragic mode in which I was accustomed to considering my plight. Months and even years went by without catastrophe (at least without one related to MS), and really I was awfully busy, what with George and children and snakes and students and poems, and I hadn't the time, let alone the inclination, to devote myself to being a disease. Too, the richer my life became, the funnier it seemed, as though there were some connection between largesse and laughter, and so my tragic stance began to waver until, even with the aid of a brace and a cane, I couldn't hold it for very long at a time.

28   After several years I was satisfied with my adjustment. I had suffered my grief and fury and terror, I thought, but now I was at ease with my lot. Then one summer day I set out with George and the children across the desert for a vacation in California. Part way to Yuma I became aware that my right leg felt funny. "I think I've had an exacerbation," I told George. "What shall we do?" he asked. "I think we'd better get the hell to California," I said, "because I don't know whether I'll ever make it again." So we went on to San Diego and then to Orange, up the Pacific Coast Highway to Santa Cruz, across to Yosemite, down to Sequoia and Joshua Tree, and so back over the desert to home. It was a fine two-week trip, filled with friends and fair weather, and I wouldn't have missed it for the world, though I did in fact make it back to

California two years later. Nor would there have been any point in missing it, since in MS, once the symptoms have appeared, the neurological damage has been done, and there's no way to predict or prevent that damage.

29   The incident spoiled my self-satisfaction, however. It renewed my grief and fury and terror, and I learned that one never finishes adjusting to MS. I don't know now why I thought one would. One does not, after all, finish adjusting to life, and MS is simply a fact of my life—not my favorite fact, of course—but as ordinary as my nose and my tropical fish and my yellow Mazda station wagon. It may at any time get worse, but no amount of worry or anticipation can prepare me for a new loss. My life is a lesson in losses. I learn one at a time.

30   And I had best be patient in the learning, since I'll have to do it like it or not. As any rock fan knows, you can't always get what you want. Particularly when you have MS. You can't, for example, get cured. In recent years researchers and the organizations that fund research have started to pay MS some attention even though it isn't fatal; perhaps they have begun to see that life is something other than a quantitative phenomenon, that one may be very much alive for a very long time in a life that isn't worth living. The researchers have made some progress toward understanding the mechanism of the disease: It may well be an autoimmune reaction triggered by a slow-acting virus. But they are nowhere near its prevention, control, or cure. And most of us want to be cured. Some, unable to accept incurability, grasp at one treatment after another, no matter how bizarre: megavitamin therapy, gluten-free diet, injections of cobra venom, hypothermal suits, lymphocytopharesis, hyperbaric chambers. Many treatments are probably harmless enough, but none are curative.

31   The absence of a cure often makes MS patients bitter toward their doctors. Doctors are, after all, the priests of modern society, the new shamans, whose business is to heal, and many an MS patient roves from one to another, searching for the "good" doctor who will make him well. Doctors too think of themselves as healers, and for this reason many have trouble dealing with MS patients, whose disease in its intransigence defeats their aims and mocks their skills. Too few doctors, it is true, treat their patients as whole human beings, but the reverse is also true. I have always tried to be gentle with my doctors, who often have more at stake in terms of ego than I do. I may be frustrated, maddened, depressed by the incurability of my disease, but I am not diminished by it, and they are. When I push myself up from my seat in the waiting room and stumble toward them, I incarnate the limitation of their powers. The least I can do is refuse to press on their tenderest spots.

32   This gentleness is part of the reason that I'm not sorry to be a cripple. I didn't have it before. Perhaps I'd have developed it anyway—how could I know such a thing?—and I wish I had more of it, but I'm glad of what I have. It has opened and enriched my life enormously, this sense that my frailty and need must be mirrored in others, that in searching for and shaping a stable core in a life wrenched by change and loss, change and loss, I must recognize the same process, under individual conditions, in the lives around me. I do not deprecate such knowledge, however I've come by it.

33   All the same, if a cure were found, would I take it? In a minute. I may be a cripple, but I'm only occasionally a loony and never a saint. Anyway, in my brand of theology God doesn't give bonus points for a limp. I'd take a cure; I just don't need one. A friend who also has MS startled me once by asking, "Do you ever say to yourself, 'Why me, Lord?'" "No, Michael, I don't," I told him, "because whenever I try, the only response I can think of is 'Why not?'" If I could make a cosmic deal, who would I put in my place? What in my life would I give up in exchange for sound limbs and a thrilling rush of energy? No one. Nothing. I might as well do the job myself. Now that I'm getting the hang of it.

READING QUESTIONS

1. Why does Mairs refer to herself as a "cripple" rather than using a term that might be considered nicer?
2. How would you characterize Mairs's life? What is she able to do? What is she no longer able to do?
3. How do her friends, family, and coworkers respond to her illness?
4. What does Mairs fear? How does she deal with these fears?
5. What does Mairs say she has gained, perhaps because of her MS?

WRITING TOPICS

1. Mairs writes that "one's sense of humor [is] . . . the easiest to lose and the hardest to survive without" (paragraph 7). What resources do you think are essential in surviving a traumatic accident or illness?
2. What are your greatest fears about your own body?

GROUP ACTIVITIES

1. Discuss people you know (or know about) who have physical disabilities. What can they do and not do? How have they responded or compensated? How have your views of physical disabilities been affected by your observation of these people?
2. List labels used to refer to people with physical or mental disabilities. Which labels are positive? Which are negative? How do you know?

RESEARCH TOPICS

1. Read Kurt Vonnegut's "Harrison Bergeron" to find out what Mairs is referring to when she says that "my God is not a Handicapper General" (paragraph 3). Why is this short story an appropriate reference for Mairs to use?
2. What is MS? Who does it affect?
3. Identify and research a famous person who has a disability. Compare his/her attitude towards disability with that of Mairs.
4. Find out what accommodations your college makes for persons with disabilities.

PREREADING SUGGESTION

Pick five groups that you belong to (for example, Catholics, college students, young adults, parents, volleyball team). Are all members of this group alike? Are there subgroups within the group? What advantage is gained by considering all members of the group alike? What are the disadvantages of not recognizing the differences among members of the group?

Hispanics Don't Exist

by Linda Robinson

The term Hispanic is not an ethnic description. It refers to native language and to cultural background and contains people of diverse ethnic origins. This article was first published in 1998 in U.S. News and World Report.

1   The growing proportion of Hispanics in the U.S. population constitutes one of the most dramatic demographic shifts in American history. The number of Hispanics is increasing almost four times as fast as the rest of the population, and they are expected to surpass African-Americans as the largest minority group by 2005. It's projected that nearly 1 of every 4 Americans will be Hispanic by the year 2050, up from 1 in 9 today. Yet other Americans often have no clear idea of just who these 29 million people are.

2   One reason is that the label *Hispanic* obscures the enormous diversity among people who come (or whose forbears came) from two dozen countries and whose ancestry ranges from pure Spanish to mixtures of Spanish blood with Native American, African, German, and Italian, to name a few hybrids. While most are bound by a common language, Spanish, many Hispanic-Americans speak only English. This diversity helps explain why Hispanics' political clout remains disproportionately slight. Hispanics even disagree on what they want to be called; most identify themselves by original nationality, while others prefer the term *Latino*.

3   A common Latino subculture doesn't really exist in the United States. True, there are some pockets of pan-Hispanic melding in major cities, and occasional alliances are struck on specific issues; with time, the differences may merge into a shared Latino identity. But for the present, it makes more sense to speak of Hispanics not as one ethnic group but as many. Mexicans are the largest, at 63 percent of the total Hispanic population, yet even they vary by region and experience.

4   How many Hispanic subcultures exist in the United States today? Ethnologists are bound to differ on this question, but *U.S. News* puts the number at 17. We have taken into account the largest communities as well as the smaller (yet, in our unscientific judgment, most culturally distinct) ones. What follows is an overview and taxonomy of the 17 major Latino subcultures in the United States, listed by geographic region.

Californians

5 Hispanics represent 30 percent of the population in California today and by 2020 are projected to outnumber non-Hispanic whites there. Many Latinos, of course, migrated to California back when it was still a part of Mexico. But more than 80 percent of Southern California's Hispanics came after 1970. In 1996, newly naturalized Latinos voted at higher rates than the general population. The galvanizing event was 1994's passage of Proposition 187, which sought to end school and health services for illegal immigrants. (A federal judge has blocked implementation of Prop. 187; the matter is expected to be appealed up to the Supreme Court.)

6 *1. Immigrant Mexicans.* Newcomers to Los Angeles traditionally settle in enclaves like East L.A., but in the past decade they've also poured into low-income black areas like South Central and Compton as well as Huntington Park, a formerly Anglo neighborhood that had become a ghost town. *"Ahora es México,"* says a man standing with his son at the corner of Florence and Pacific while his wife buys tamales and chicken in *mole* from a huge takeout store. "None of this was here when I came 15 years ago," he says, nodding at the Spanish-named car dealerships, shoe stores, bridal shops, and supermarkets stretching for blocks.

7 *2. Middle-class Mexicans.* Many Mexican-Americans in California have moved up the socioeconomic ladder, sometimes in a single generation. Overall, two thirds of Latinos in the United States live above the poverty line; half of Southern California's native Latino families, and one third of those from abroad, are middle class. New arrivals often hold two jobs, leveraging themselves or their children into such middle-income occupations as police officer, manager, and executive secretary. They have migrated from traditional ports of entry to more-prosperous neighborhoods and suburbs like San Gabriel and Montebello. There, Mexican-Americans buy three- and four-bedroom tract houses next door to Asians. Farther east, in Hacienda Heights, Mexican-American families' yards are bigger, the driveways parked with BMWs and Jeep Cherokees.

8 *3. Barrio dwellers.* Many Mexicans move up and out, but a growing number of second- and third-generation kids are getting trapped in ghettos. Boyle Heights' housing projects are the largest west of the Mississippi; 60 gangs with 10,000 members ("homeboys") run rampant over 16 square miles of urban wasteland.

9 *4. Central Americans of Pico Union.* As tough as life may be in the Mexican barrios, it's even grimmer in Pico Union, a gang-ridden section of L.A. just east of MacArthur Park that serves as the principal U.S. port of entry for Central Americans, the fastest-growing segment of L.A.'s population. Nearby Koreatown is also now predominantly Central American. Greater L.A. is home to half of all the Salvadorans and Guatemalans who live in the United States.

10   Even though 97 percent of U.S. Central Americans are working, incomes in Pico Union commonly range from $5,000 to $10,000. Everyone works, kids and parents. Most parents have less than a sixth-grade education; their children who work full time risk remaining at society's lower rungs. Still, two thirds of the families manage to stay above the poverty line, running little markets and shops along Eighth Street.

Tejanos

11   Texas Mexicans argue with their California brethren over whose culture is more authentically Mexican-American. What's certain is the two groups couldn't be more different. In contrast to the majority of "Californios" who are recent arrivals, many Tejanos have been here for generations. They've brewed a cowboy culture that's equal parts Texas and Mexico. Tejano music, a widely popular blend of country and *ranchera,* epitomizes the hybrid. Tex-Mex conservatism on issues from abortion to immigration shocks California Mexicans.

12   *5. South Texans.*   The most Mexican part of the United States is the lower Rio Grande Valley. In Laredo and Brownsville, Mexicans form 80 to 95 percent of the population. Their roots go back to the 1700s, giving them a strong sense of belonging. Hidalgo County, one of the nation's poorest, is also a cradle of Mexican culture and scholarship. Like California, Texas was the scene of bitter battles over job and school discrimination in the 1970s, but anti-immigrant sentiment is far less virulent here. Many Anglos speak Spanish, and intermarriage is common.

13   *6. Houston Mexicans.*   In Houston, Latinos are still a minority. Anglos make up 41 percent of the population and hold most positions of political and economic power. But Hispanics—mostly Mexicans, but also a growing number of Central Americans—have grown from 18 to 28 percent since 1980. (The remaining 31 percent of Houston is mostly African-American and Asian.) Houston's Mexican-Americans are mostly working-class residents of ethnic enclaves even though 56 percent of them are U.S.-born. "South Texans who go to see their relatives in Houston feel sorry for the barrio dwellers' quality of life," says Joel Huerta of the University of Texas's Center for Mexican American Studies.

14   *7. Texas Guatemalans.*   Houston's urban sprawl could not be more foreign to the Mayan Indians of Guatemala, who grew up in the rural highlands speaking their native Indian language. Because they have little chance of upward mobility in their own highly race- and class-conscious country, the Mayas have joined Houston's Central American working class. These short, full-blooded Indians tend to keep to themselves in their southwest Houston enclave—they have their own soccer leagues and Pentecostal churches—but they did join with African-American residents of one area they colonized, Stella Link, to form crime-watch groups and youth programs. In his new

book, *Strangers Among Us: How Latino Immigration Is Transforming America,* journalist Roberto Suro recounts the trail of Guatemalans to Randall's, an upscale supermarket chain that ended up hiring 1,000 Mayas.

Chicago Latinos

15 Latinos followed Irish, Polish, and other European immigrants to this city of ethnic neighborhoods. Only Los Angeles and New York have larger Hispanic populations than Chicago, which is projected to be 27 percent Hispanic in the year 2000. And Chicago's mix of Hispanic subgroups is more diverse than that of L.A. or New York. Among U.S. cities, Chicago ranks second in the number of Puerto Ricans, fourth in the number of Mexicans, and third in the number of Ecuadorians. Guatemalans and Cubans are also here in force.

16 *8. Chicago Mexicans.*   The first of Chicago's nearly 600,000 Mexicans arrived to work on the railroad just after the turn of the century; more came to man steel mills during World War II. "Chicago's weather is so harsh that the only reason Latinos come here is jobs," says Rob Paral, research director of the Latino Institute. Chicago has absorbed the steady influx fairly well: Its manufacturing base remains strong and unemployment is low. Its Latinos mirror the national profile in that 60 percent are native-born and two thirds lack high school diplomas. But only one fourth are poor. (The national rate is 31 percent.) The commercial heart of Mexican Chicago, 26th Street, generates more tax revenue than any other retail strip except tony Michigan Avenue. It's lined with hundreds of stores like La Villita Dry Cleaner, a piñata shop, Nuevo León restaurant—but has just one Walgreen's.

17 *9. Chicago Puerto Ricans.*   Two giant, steel Puerto Rican flags fly over Division Avenue by Roberto Clemente High School. They were erected to stake out the turf of Paseo Boricua, a strip of 80 mom and pop businesses, and the Puerto Rican-owned Banco Popular, the largest Hispanic-owned bank in the United States. Sitting in his sister's bakery across from the AIDS education center he founded, community leader Jose Lopez says that urban renewal plans are pushing Puerto Ricans into suburban ghettos instead of helping them prosper. He launched the flag project as part of his drive to bolster Puerto Rican pride and identity. One of the great paradoxes of *puertorriqueños* is that while they have the benefit of being born U.S. citizens, they have fared worse economically than any other Hispanic group. They have the highest rates of poverty (38 percent), unemployment (11.2 percent), and households headed by single females (41 percent).

Miamians

18 Miami is the one major city in the United States where Hispanics dominate numerically, politically, and economically. They make up about 60 percent of the population, a meteoric rise from only 5 percent in 1960. Miami is seen as

a Cuban city, but other immigrants who have poured in since 1980 now make up 40 percent of Hispanics living here.

19 *10. Cubans.* Success stories are not hard to find among Miami's 1 million Cubans. Of the 80 Latinos in the United States worth $25 million or more (according to a recent survey in *Hispanic Business* magazine), 32 are of Cuban origin. Singer Gloria Estefan, the late exile leader Jorge Mas Canosa, and a handful of Miami builders made last year's list. Roberto Goizueta, the late head of Coca-Cola, topped it. U.S.-born Cubans have the highest incomes of any Hispanic subgroup, and over two thirds of them live in Florida.

20 For this influx of talented and successful immigrants, America has Fidel Castro to thank. The first wage of Cuban immigrants in the 1960s, following Castro's Communist takeover of Cuba, doubled their incomes in three years: Four thousand were doctors, and most had good educations. They started restaurants; clothing, furniture, and cigar businesses; and drive-up storefronts dispensing strong, sweet *café cubano*. They built subdivisions sprawling into the Everglades and provided jobs for tens of thousands of later, poorer Cuban immigrants. Alone among Hispanic subgroups, Cubans were warmly welcomed by the U.S. government throughout the cold war: They received financial assistance and, until 1995, automatic legal residency. As of 1990, 55 percent of Cubans had graduated from high school, and 20 percent held white-collar jobs. But one third do not speak English well or at all; many of them are older Cubans with little incentive to learn the language in a Spanish-speaking city.

21 *11. Nicaraguans.* During the 1980s, U.S.-backed rebel leaders plotted to overthrow Nicaragua's Communist government from offices near Miami's airport. As the war dragged on, young Nicaraguans came here to evade the military draft. After the Communists finally lost power in 1990, some 75,000 Nicaraguans remained in the United States. Congress recently granted them the right to stay, so many may eventually become U.S. citizens. Nicaraguan exiles were embraced by Cubans who sympathized with their flight from communism; they settled in Cuban areas like Hialeah and East Little Havana and found work in Cuban-owned businesses. Unlike Miami's Cubans, though, the Nicaraguan immigrants are mostly poor, rural folk, averaging 26 years of age and nine years of schooling. More than half don't speak English well or at all, and their median income of $9,000 in 1990 was the second lowest of all ethnic groups in Miami. (The lowest-ranked group was the 20,000 Hondurans who moved to Miami when the Nicaraguan war unsettled their country.)

22 *12. South Americans.* Miami's Hispanic upper crust is not just Cuban; it also includes Colombians, Peruvians, and other South Americans. These wealthy immigrants began coming to Miami when their countries' economies plunged into crisis in the 1980s. Business and professional people fled with their money, buying houses in Kendall, a Miami suburb, and condos in waterfront high-rises. They number well over 100,000.

Neoyorquinos

23   Puerto Ricans used to represent the vast majority of New York's Hispanics; now they are roughly half. Immigrants from the Dominican Republic, Colombia, and Cuba have swelled the metropolitan area's multiethnic mix to 3.6 million Latinos.

24   *13. Puerto Ricans.*   During the 1950s, the decade when *West Side Story* came to Broadway, New York was home to 80 percent of all Puerto Ricans in the United States. Cheap, frequent flights ferried the islanders back and forth. One million immigrated to New York after World War II, forming the backbone of the city's manufacturing work force. By the 1960s, Puerto Ricans also owned some 4,000 businesses. Many were in Spanish Harlem, which was dotted with restaurants serving chicken *asopao* and *pasteles,* the Puerto Rican version of tamales made with green bananas. In the 1970s Puerto Ricans' American experience turned sour: Newer immigrants began displacing them, and then the industrial base of New York withered away. Unemployed Puerto Ricans headed back home, only to return to New York when they couldn't find jobs there either. In New York, they saw their median family income drop below that of African-Americans, which was rising. "Compared to the black community, our resources are so much weaker," says Angelo Falcón, director of the Institute for Puerto Rican Policy. "We don't have their church leaders or their colleges. We don't have a solid middle class."

25   *14. Dominicans.*   Washington Heights is the expatriate capital of Dominicans, who now represent almost 10 percent of all Latinos in the New York area. They came to this rundown tip of upper Manhattan, named it Quisqueya—the Native American name for the Dominican Republic—and immediately went into business. They opened neighborhood stores called bodegas all over the city, and drove cabs that competed with yellow taxis. Some Dominicans also tapped their location by the George Washington Bridge to set up a huge drug distribution network serving the Atlantic Coast. Despite all this entrepreneurial activity and Dominicans' comparatively high median income ($10,000 to $15,000), their unemployment rate is 53 percent; 14 percent are on welfare; and 42 percent don't speak English well. New York's Dominicans have fared nearly as badly as Puerto Ricans, in part because they are overwhelmingly first-generation immigrants without high school degrees. They too suffer from a revolving-door syndrome that has kept them from putting down roots. Community leaders have yet to solve Quisqueya's many problems: discrimination against the mostly black and mulatto Dominicans, poor police relations (the 1992 killing of a Dominican immigrant sparked riots), drug-fueled crime, and high rents.

26   *15. Colombians.*   Colombians have won the economic success that has eluded most Hispanics, but they're dogged by a stereotype that all Colombians are drug traffickers. Most are in fact legitimate businesspeople and successful

professionals; yet to avoid stigma, some say they are from another country. New York is their principal U.S. destination, followed by Miami. Only 40 percent are U.S. citizens, although the number is increasing because Colombia now allows dual citizenship. Two thirds of Colombians have jobs, and their median income is close to that of non-Hispanic whites. One fifth of Colombian families earn $50,000 or more, in keeping with their reputation as South America's best entrepreneurs. But arrests of major Colombian traffickers and grisly murders in their Queens enclave of Jackson Heights have cemented a negative image in the public's mind.

Elsewhere in the U.S.

27   *16. New Mexico's Hispanos.*   Northern New Mexico is home to the nation's most unusual and least-known group of Hispanics. They are descendants of the original Spanish conquistadors and as such belong to the oldest European culture within U.S. borders. In the valleys of Rio Arriba they farm ribbonlike plots bequeathed to their ancestors by the Spanish crown; live in ancient adobe homes; and cook pork in red *chile* sauce in outdoor ovens. A proud, poor people, they call themselves Hispanos to emphasize that they are not immigrants from Latin America. The Spanish they speak is a dialect from the time of Coronado, and the holidays they celebrate are Spanish ones commemorating events like the 1692 reconquest of New Mexico and the conquest of the Moors. A dwindling Catholic sect called the Penitentes practices self-flagellation in their ancestors' *moradas,* or temples. Another subgroup are descendants of *marranos,* Spanish Jews who fled the Inquisition and continued to observe Jewish rites secretly. Centuries of subdividing their farmland have forced young Hispanos to seek seasonal work elsewhere or to move away entirely. Unemployment hovers around 20 percent and welfare dependence is high.

28   *17. Migrant workers.*   For decades, the demand for temporary farmhands has sent Hispanics all over the United States. The migrant farmhands still travel from crop to crop, living in camps straight out of a Steinbeck novel, but farm mechanization has reduced their numbers to about 70,000 for the Midwest harvest. Meanwhile, a second stream of Mexicans is being drawn to work in chicken- and beef-packing plants in places like Dodge City, Kan., where 4,000 Hispanics have arrived since 1990. In Maine, hundreds of Mexicans work on egg farms in Turner (pop. 5,000), which now has a bilingual school program. Siler City, N.C., had 200 Hispanics in 1990. Today, half its 6,000 residents are Hispanic, and the town has three churches offering services in Spanish and four Latin American grocery stores.

READING QUESTIONS

1. Robinson notes that "other Americans often have no clear idea of just who these 29 million [Hispanics] are" (paragraph 1). According to

Robinson, why do non-Hispanic Americans know so little about this group?

2. Although there are a large number of Hispanics in the United States, Robinson notes that the group does not have much "political clout" (paragraph 2). Why not?

3. List the 4 groups of Hispanics that live in California. What characteristics does Robinson use to distinguish each group from the others?

4. How do the Texas Mexicans (or Tejanos) differ from Californians of Mexican descent?

5. Why did the Texas Guatemalans come to Texas? How have they interacted with other groups in Houston?

6. What advantage do Puerto Rican Americans enjoy over other Hispanic groups? How have Puerto Ricans in Chicago fared in comparison with other Hispanic groups?

7. How is Miami different from the other major cities in the U.S. where Hispanics live?

8. Why does Miami have such a large Cuban population?

9. Why did Nicaraguans settle in Miami?

10. What difficulties have the Puerto Ricans and Dominicans in New York shared?

11. Why do Colombians have difficulty even though they have great economic success?

12. How are the Hispanics of New Mexico different from other Hispanic groups?

13. How has migrant work changed because of increased use of farm machinery?

14. Which of the 17 Hispanic groups is the largest? Which is the most successful economically? Which is the least successful? What numbers or statistics does the author use to show these characteristics?

WRITING TOPICS

1. Write an essay in which you describe the subgroups that make up another group that is generally considered homogenous.

2. Is it important to understand the subgroups that make up a larger group? Why or why not?

GROUP ACTIVITIES

1. As a group, characterize subgroups of one of the following: students, teachers, bosses, shoppers. What are the defining characteristics of each subgroup? How would you recognize members of each subgroup? (Consider appearance, manner of speech, attitude, or other characteristics.)

2. List stereotypes of Hispanic people that you have heard or seen in the media. Using Robinson's article, determine how valid these stereotypes are.

RESEARCH TOPICS

1. Choose a religious, ethnic, or cultural group you know little about. Research what the subgroups are. What makes the subgroups similar? What makes them different from each other?

2. Describe the Hispanic community in your local area.

3. Research the reaction of Miami's Cuban community to the U.S. Supreme Court's decision to return Elian Gonzalez to his father in Cuba. How do you account for the strong emotion of this reaction?

PREREADING SUGGESTION

Make a list of adults you grew up around. Who were they? What did you learn about potential adult roles from them?

The Men We Carry in Our Minds

by Scott Russell Sanders

Scott Russell Sanders, a creative writing instructor at Indiana University, writes both fiction and nonfiction. In this article, he tries to come to some understanding of the relationship between power and gender. This selection is from his book, The Paradise of Bombs *(1984).*

1   "This must be a hard time for women," I say to my friend Anneke. "They have so many paths to choose from, and so many voices calling them."

2   "I think it's a lot harder for men," she replies.

3   "How do you figure that?"

4   "The women I know feel excited, innocent, like crusaders in a just cause. The men I know are eaten up with guilt."

5   We are sitting at the kitchen table drinking sassafras tea, our hands wrapped around the mugs because this April morning is cool and drizzly. "Like a Dutch morning," Anneke told me earlier. She is Dutch herself, a writer and midwife and peacemaker, with the round face and sad eyes of a woman in a Vermeer painting who might be waiting for the rain to stop, for a door to open. She leans over to sniff a sprig of lilac, pale lavender, that rises from a vase of cobalt blue.

6   "Women feel such pressure to be everything, do everything," I say. "Career, kids, art, politics. Have their babies and get back to the office a week later. It's as if they're trying to overcome a million years' worth of evolution in one lifetime."

7   "But we help one another. We don't try to lumber on alone, like so many wounded grizzly bears, the way men do." Anneke sips her tea. I gave her the

mug with owls on it, for wisdom. "And we have this deep-down sense that we're in the *right*—we've been held back, passed over, used—while men feel they're in the wrong. Men are the ones who've been discredited, who have to search their souls."

8   I search my soul. I discover guilty feelings aplenty—toward the poor, the Vietnamese, Native Americans, the whales, an endless list of debts—a guilt in each case that is as bright and unambiguous as a neon sign. But toward women I feel something more confused, a snarl of shame, envy, wary tenderness, and amazement. This muddle troubles me. To hide my unease I say, "You're right, it's tough being a man these days."

9   "Don't laugh." Anneke frowns at me, mournful-eyed, through the sassafras steam. "I wouldn't be a man for anything. It's much easier being the victim. All the victim has to do is break free. The persecutor has to live with his past."

10   How deep is that past? I find myself wondering after Anneke has left. How much of an inheritance do I have to throw off? Is it just the beliefs I breathed in as a child? Do I have to scour memory back through father and grandfather? Through St. Paul? Beyond Stonehenge and into the twilit caves? I'm convinced the past we must contend with is deeper even than speech. When I think back on my childhood, on how I learned to see men and women, I have a sense of ancient, dizzying depths. The back roads of Tennessee and Ohio where I grew up were probably closer, in their sexual patterns, to the campsites of Stone Age hunters than to the genderless cities of the future into which we are rushing.

11   The first men, besides my father, I remember seeing were black convicts and white guards, in the cottonfield across the road from our farm on the outskirts of Memphis. I must have been three or four. The prisoners wore dingy gray-and-black zebra suits, heavy as canvas, sodden with sweat. Hatless, stooped, they chopped weeds in the fierce heat, row after row, breathing the acrid dust of boll-weevil poison. The overseers wore dazzling white shirts and broad shadowy hats. The oiled barrels of their shotguns flashed in the sunlight. Their faces in memory are utterly blank. Of course those men, white and black, have become for me an emblem of racial hatred. But they have also come to stand for the twin poles of my early vision of manhood—the brute toiling animal and the boss.

12   When I was a boy, the men I knew labored with their bodies. They were marginal farmers, just scraping by, or welders, steel-workers, carpenters; they swept floors, dug ditches, mined coal, or drove trucks, their forearms ropy with muscle; they trained horses, stoked furnaces, built tires, stood on assembly lines wrestling parts onto cars and refrigerators. They got up before light, worked all day long whatever the weather, and when they came home at night they looked as though somebody had been whipping them. In the evenings and on weekends they worked on their own places, tilling gardens that were lumpy with clay, fixing broken-down cars, hammering on houses that were always too drafty, too leaky, too small.

13   The bodies of the men I knew were twisted and maimed in ways visible and invisible. The nails of their hands were black and split, the hands tattooed with scars. Some had lost fingers. Heavy lifting had given many of them

finicky backs and guts weak from hernias. Racing against conveyor belts had given them ulcers. Their ankles and knees ached from years of standing on concrete. Anyone who had worked for long around machines was hard of hearing. They squinted, and the skin of their faces was creased like the leather of old work gloves. There were times, studying them, when I dreaded growing up. Most of them coughed, from dust or cigarettes, and most of them drank cheap wine or whiskey, so their eyes looked bloodshot and bruised. The fathers of my friends always seemed older than the mothers. Men wore out sooner. Only women lived into old age.

14   As a boy I also knew another sort of men, who did not sweat and break down like mules. They were soldiers, and so far as I could tell they scarcely worked at all. During my early school years we lived on a military base, an arsenal in Ohio, and every day I saw GIs in the guardshacks, on the stoops of barracks, at the wheels of olive drab Chevrolets. The chief fact of their lives was boredom. Long after I left the Arsenal I came to recognize the sour smell the soldiers gave off as that of souls in limbo. They were all waiting—for wars, for transfers, for leaves, for promotions, for the end of their hitch—like so many braves waiting for the hunt to begin. Unlike the warriors of older tribes, however, they would have no say about when the battle would start or how it would be waged. Their waiting was broken only when they practiced for war. They fired guns at targets, drove tanks across the churned-up fields of the military reservation, set off bombs in the wrecks of old fighter planes. I knew this was all play. But I also felt certain that when the hour for killing arrived, they would kill. When the real shooting started, many of them would die. This was what soldiers were *for*, just as a hammer was for driving nails.

15   Warriors and toilers: those seemed, in my boyhood vision, to be the chief destinies for men. They weren't the only destinies, as I learned from having a few male teachers, from reading books, and from watching television. But the men on television—the politicians, the astronauts, the generals, the savvy lawyers, the philosophical doctors, the bosses who gave orders to both soldiers and laborers—seemed as removed and unreal to me as the figures in tapestries. I could no more imagine growing up to become one of these cool, potent creatures than I could imagine becoming a prince.

16   A nearer and more hopeful example was that of my father, who had escaped from a red-dirt farm to a tire factory, and from the assembly line to the front office. Eventually he dressed in a white shirt and tie. He carried himself as if he had been born to work with his mind. But his body, remembering the earlier years of slogging work, began to give out on him in his fifties, and it quit on him entirely before he turned sixty-five. Even such a partial escape from man's fate as he had accomplished did not seem possible for most of the boys I knew. They joined the Army, stood in line for jobs in the smoky plants, helped build highways. They were bound to work as their fathers had worked, killing themselves or preparing to kill others.

17   A scholarship enabled me not only to attend college, a rare enough feat in my circle, but even to study in a university meant for the children of the rich. Here I met for the first time young men who had assumed from birth that they would lead lives of comfort and power. And for the first time I met

women who told me that men were guilty of having kept all the joys and privileges of the earth for themselves. I was baffled. What privileges? What joys? I
thought about the maimed, dismal lives of most of the men back home. What
had they stolen from their wives and daughters? The right to go five days a
week, twelve months a year, for thirty or forty years to a steel mill or a coal
mine? The right to drop bombs and die in war? The right to feel every leak in
the roof, every gap in the fence, every cough in the engine, as a wound they
must mend? The right to feel, when the lay-off comes or the plant shuts down,
not only afraid but ashamed?

18   I was slow to understand the deep grievances of women. This was because,
as a boy, I had envied them. Before college, the only people I had ever known
who were interested in art or music or literature, the only ones who read
books, the only ones who ever seemed to enjoy a sense of ease and grace were
the mothers and daughters. Like the menfolk, they fretted about money, they
scrimped and made-do. But, when the pay stopped coming in, they were not
the ones who had failed. Nor did they have to go to war, and that seemed to me
a blessed fact. By comparison with the narrow, ironclad days of fathers, there
was an expansiveness, I thought, in the days of mothers. They went to see
neighbors, to shop in town, to run errands at school, at the library, at church.
No doubt, had I looked harder at their lives, I would have envied them less. It
was not my fate to become a woman, so it was easier for me to see the graces.
Few of them held jobs outside the home, and those who did filled thankless
roles as clerks and waitresses. I didn't see, then, what a prison a house could
be, since houses seemed to me brighter, handsomer places than any factory. I
did not realize—because such things were never spoken of—how often women
suffered from men's bullying. I did learn about the wretchedness of abandoned
wives, single mothers, widows; but I also learned about the wretchedness of
lone men. Even then I could see how exhausting it was for a mother to cater
all day to the needs of young children. But if I had been asked, as a boy, to
choose between tending a baby and tending a machine, I think I would have
chosen the baby. (Having now tended both, I know I would choose the baby.)

19   So I was baffled when the women at college accused me and my sex of
having cornered the world's pleasures. I think something like my bafflement
has been felt by other boys (and by girls as well) who grew up in dirt-poor
farm country, in mining country, in black ghettos, in Hispanic barrios, in the
shadows of factories, in Third World nations—any place where the fate of
men is as grim and bleak as the fate of women. Toilers and warriors. I realize
now how ancient these identities are, how deep the tug they exert on men, the
undertow of a thousand generations. The miseries I saw, as a boy, in the lives
of nearly all men I continue to see in the lives of many—the body-breaking
toil, the tedium, the call to be tough, the humiliating powerlessness, the battle
for a living and for territory.

20   When the women I met at college thought about the joys and privileges of
men, they did not carry in their minds the sort of men I had known in my
childhood. They thought of their fathers, who were bankers, physicians, ar-
chitects, stockbrokers, the big wheels of the big cities. These fathers rode the
train to work or drove cars that cost more than any of my childhood houses.

They were attended from morning to night by female helpers, wives and nurses and secretaries. They were never laid off, never short of cash at month's end, never lined up for welfare. These fathers made decisions that mattered. They ran the world.

21   The daughters of such men wanted to share in this power, this glory. So did I. They yearned for a say over their future, for jobs worthy of their abilities, for the right to live at peace, unmolested, whole. Yes, I thought, yes yes. The difference between me and these daughters was that they saw me, because of my sex, as destined from birth to become like their fathers, and therefore as an enemy to their desires. But I knew better. I wasn't an enemy, in fact or in feeling. I was an ally. If I had known, then, how to tell them so, would they have believed me? Would they now?

READING QUESTIONS

1. Why does Sanders feel it is harder to be a woman? Why does his friend Anneke think it is harder to be a man?

2. What men did Sanders see growing up? How did this affect his view of his own possibilities?

3. What did Sanders envy about the women he grew up around?

4. Why was Sanders surprised when young women told him "that men were guilty of having kept all the joys and privileges of the earth for themselves" (paragraph 17)?

5. What do these women want? What does Sanders want?

WRITING TOPICS

1. Is this a harder time in history for women or for men?

2. What type of adult did you expect to grow up to be? Who were your models? What view did they give you of your future?

GROUP ACTIVITIES

1. Share with the members of your group a description of the adults you grew up around. How did they affect your view of your own future and potential?

2. Share with the members of your group your expectations of what it means to be a man and to be a woman. Compare these expectations. Where did you get these expectations? Can you account for the differences in your group (as Sanders accounted for his differing views)?

RESEARCH TOPICS

1. Sanders discusses two kinds of men: those he knew growing up and the fathers of the women he met in college. These men are different in education and in social class. Research to find relationships be-

tween education and social class: do people who make more money have higher levels of education? Is the same true for women and for men? Do people with high positions in companies have high levels of education?

2. Sanders discusses men who work in mines, farms, and factories. Research the working conditions in those occupations.

3. When Sanders goes to college, he meets people who are very different from those he knew growing up. Interview students to discover whether it is common to meet new kinds of people at college.

Genetic Research

Exploring the Theme

■ What choices do human beings have about their bodies and minds that they did not have a century ago?

■ Who should be able to make the choices? What kinds of preparation or understanding do those people need before they choose?

■ Should laws govern the kind of scientific work that can be done? How could such laws cause harm?

■ What might be some consequences of unregulated genetic and reproductive engineering?

■ What kinds of things cannot be controlled by genetic engineering?

PREREADING SUGGESTIONS

1. What do you know about how medical conditions can be inherited?

2. Do you think it's necessary to have medical insurance? Why or why not?

Flunk the Gene Test and Lose Your Insurance: Genetic Discrimination

by Geoffrey Cowley

Often we think that genetic testing will provide many benefits for future generations. This article warns that genetic testing may also cause problems for patients with inherited conditions. This article was first published in 1996 in Newsweek.

1   DNA probes may offer dazzling insights. But they have helped foster a pernicious new form of discrimination.

2   Jamie Stephenson has seen firsthand what modern genetic science can do for a family. When her son David was two years old, a pediatrician noticed developmental delays and suspected fragile X syndrome, a hereditary form of mental retardation. A lab test confirmed the diagnosis, and the Stephensons spent several years learning to live with it. When David was six, he visited a neurologist, who scribbled "fragile X" on an insurance-company claim form. The company responded promptly—by canceling coverage for the entire family of six. There is no medical treatment for fragile X, and none of David's siblings had been diagnosed with the condition. "The company didn't care," Stephenson says. "They just saw a positive genetic test and said, 'You're out'."

3   From the dawn of the DNA era, critics have worried that genetic testing would create a "biological underclass"—a population of people whose genes brand them as poor risks for employment, insurance, even marriage. The future is arriving fast. Medical labs can now test human cells for hundreds of anomalous genes. Besides tracking rare conditions, such as Huntington's disease and cystic fibrosis, some firms now gauge people's susceptibility to more common scourges. By masking inherited mutations in p53 and other genes, the new tests can signal increased risk of everything from breast, colon and prostate tumors to lymphoma and leukemia. Many of the tests are still too costly for mass marketing, but that will change. And as the Stephensons' story suggests, the consequences won't all be benign. "This is bigger than race or sexual orientation," says Martha Volner, health-policy director for the Alliance of Genetic Support Groups. "Genetic discrimination is the civil-rights issue of the 21st century."

4   No one would argue that genetic tests are worthless. Used properly, they can give people unprecedented power over their lives. Prospective parents who discover they're silent carriers of the gene for a disease like Tay-Sachs, which causes death by the age of 3, can make better-informed decisions about whether and how to have kids. Some genetic maladies can be managed through medication and lifestyle changes once they're identified. And while knowing that you're at special risk for cancer may be an emotional burden, it can also alert you to the need for intensive monitoring. Jane Gorrell knows her family is prone to colon cancer. Her father developed hundreds of precancerous polyps back in the 1960s, and both she and her sister had the same experience during the '70s. Their condition, known as familial adenomatous polyposis, has since been linked to a mutation in the p58 gene—and Gorrell has learned that one of her two children inherited it. Though the child has suffered no symptoms, she gets frequent colon exams and is helping researchers test a drug that could help save lives.

5   The catch is that no one can guarantee the privacy of genetic information. Outside of large group plans, insurance companies often scour people's medical records before extending coverage. And though employers face some restrictions, virtually any company with a benefits program can get access to workers' health data. So can schools, adoption agencies and the military. Em-

ployees of Lawrence Berkeley Laboratory (LBL), a large research institution owned by the Department of Energy and operated by the University of California, recently discovered that the organization had for three decades been quietly testing new hires' blood and urine samples for evidence of various conditions. They claim blacks were screened for sickle-cell trait, Latinos for syphilis and women for pregnancy. "I can't say the information was put to some incredibly harmful use, because we don't know what happened," says Vicki Laden, a San Francisco lawyer who has tried unsuccessfully to sue the lab for civil-rights violations. LBL recently stopped the testing.

6   How often is genetic information used against people? No one knows, but there are signs that discrimination is fairly common—even in the absence of sophisticated tests. In one recent study, researchers led by Georgetown University sociologist Virginia Lapham surveyed 482 families belonging to genetic-disease support groups; 22 percent of the respondents said they'd been refused health insurance, and 18 percent claimed their perceived risks had cost them jobs.

7   In another 1996 study, a team led by Lisa Geller of Harvard Medical School documented more than 200 instances in which healthy people experienced genetic discrimination. As in Lapham's study, many participants told of losing their health and life insurance. But that wasn't their only problem. One respondent was denied a job selling insurance after he disclosed that he had hemachromatosis, a hereditary iron-storage problem that can be treated for about $81,200 a year. A social worker who had excelled during her first year at a Wisconsin healthcare company was quickly forced out after mentioning that her uncle had Huntington's, a degenerative brain disease that victims' offspring have a 50 percent chance of developing. Carol Isaacson Barash, the bioethics consultant who administered the Geller study, recalls another case in which a woman in the early stages of Huntington's disease was unable to place her child with a private adoption agency. A public agency took the child, eventually matching her with a couple who had previously been rejected themselves—because one partner carried the Huntington's gene. "It's a stark commentary on how society regards people at risk," says Barash.

8   Not surprisingly, people from high-risk families have come to fear tests almost as much as disease. Lori Andrews, a Chicago law professor and former head of a federal task force on the social implications of genetic research, notes that only 15 percent of people with a Huntington's afflicted parent choose to learn their own status. Discrimination isn't their only concern; virtually everyone testing positive for the Huntington's gene develops debilitating symptoms during middle age, and doctors can do nothing to help. But people who might benefit from genetic tests are almost as leery. When researchers at the Georgetown University Medical Center surveyed 279 people from families plagued by breast and ovarian cancer, only 43 percent wanted to be tested for hereditary mutations in BRCA1, a recently discovered gene that is often implicated in those diseases. Many said the prospect of discrimination scared them off. Kendra McCarthy, a 47-year-old administrator at the Virginia Department of Mental Health, saw her mother die of breast cancer at

34, her father of esophageal cancer at 41. When scientists developed tests that might have gauged her own susceptibility, she always declined to take one. McCarthy doesn't regret that decision. She has developed breast cancer, but she still has her health coverage, and a life-insurance plan to protect her two sons.

9   Besides depriving people of potentially useful information, the fear of discrimination can hamper scientific progress. Barbara Weber, a geneticist with the University of Pennsylvania Cancer Center, often asks women who learn they have BRCA1 mutations to take part in confidential follow-up studies. She wants to know which strategies are most effective for preserving their health. "We have the tools to answer these questions," she says. "All they have to do is tell us how they're doing every six months." Yet three fourths of the women she approaches say no.

10   The federal government is now taking steps to make genetic information less threatening. The recently enacted Health Insurance Portability and Accountability Act (better known as Kennedy-Kassebaum) bars insurers from treating genetic mutations as "pre-existing conditions" unless they're causing illness. The insurance act also guarantees coverage to anyone leaving one group plan for another, whatever his pre-existing conditions. That will make switching jobs easier for many people, but ethicists say the act is only a first step. Because it covers only group plans and doesn't deal with disability insurance, it won't do much for folks like Theresa Morelli, an Ohio lawyer who applied for independent coverage several years ago. Morelli was 28 and in perfect health when she met with an insurance agent and paid her first premium. A month later, she got her check back, along with a letter saying her application had been denied because her father had Huntington's disease. Morelli's dad had in fact received that diagnosis—erroneously, it turned out—and her doctor had made a note of it in her chart.

11   The restrictions on employers are as porous as those on insurers. The 1990 Americans with Disabilities Act bars companies from discriminating against people with disabilities—and it defines that term broadly enough to include genetic mutations that have yet to cause symptoms. But the act does nothing to keep employers from gathering medical information. "As long as employers have access to genetic information," says Lewis Maltby of the ACLU, "they'll have an irresistible incentive to use it."

12   Lawmakers are now racing to strengthen the protections. At least 15 states have recently placed restrictions on insurers or employers, and Congress will consider several bills in the new session. The insurance industry argues that it should be free to charge people rates that reflect their risks, at least when dealing with individuals and small companies. That way, says Richard Coorsh of the Health Insurance Association of America, each applicant pays the fairest possible price. But most ethicists contend that where health coverage is concerned, people shouldn't be penalized for risks they can't modify.

13   Discrimination isn't the only potential downside to genetic testing. Some of the new susceptibility tests are only vaguely predictive of illness—and no one forces the companies that offer them to counsel patients about what the

results actually mean. Even when the tests are sound and the results secure, the knowledge they create can dash hopes and divide families. Unfortunately, principled ignorance doesn't always make life easier.

READING QUESTIONS

1. According to this article, what are the benefits of genetic tests?
2. What does the article say are the disadvantages of genetic tests?
3. Why is privacy a concern with genetic testing?
4. What is "genetic discrimination"?
5. What is the Health Insurance Portability and Accountability Act? What other protections against discrimination can be found?

WRITING TOPICS

1. Cowley warns that genetic testing could be misused. Use the information in this article to write an essay that is an appeal to lawmakers to pass stronger legislation to protect people who are found to have genetic disorders.
2. Cowley points out some of the problems and benefits of genetic testing. Are the problems so great that testing should not be allowed? Write an essay that argues for your position.
3. Would you want a member of your family to undergo genetic testing? Write an essay explaining the choice you would make and your reasons for that choice.

GROUP ACTIVITIES

1. Make a chart listing the disadvantages and advantages of genetic testing.
2. Brainstorm to list at least five inherited conditions most parents would hope their children could avoid.

RESEARCH TOPICS

1. What else besides genetic problems can cause insurance to be canceled or denied? Look for newspaper or magazine articles that give information.
2. What are the diseases and medical conditions listed in the article? Look on the Internet to find more information about the symptoms and treatment for one of these diseases or conditions.

PREREADING SUGGESTIONS

1. Would you like to be able to make a duplicate of yourself? Why or why not?
2. What would be some of the problems of allowing any living creature to be cloned?

The Case for Cloning

by J. Madeleine Nash

J. Madeleine Nash, a native of Greensboro, North Carolina, is a senior corre-
spondent for Time *magazine, which published this article in 1998. Nash writes*
primarily on science and technology, although she was not originally trained as
a scientist. She believes that she can help readers understand difficult technical
subjects through her own process of learning to understand them.

1 An elderly man develops macular degeneration, a disease that destroys vision.
To bolster his failing eyesight, he receives a transplant of healthy retinal tissue—cloned from his own cells and cultivated in a lab dish.

2   A baby girl is born free of the gene that causes Tay-Sachs disease, even
though both her parents are carriers. The reason? In the embryonic cell from
which she was cloned, the flawed gene was replaced with normal DNA.

3   These futuristic scenarios are not now part of the debate over human
cloning, but they should be. Spurred by the fear that maverick physicist
Richard Seed, or someone like him, will open a cloning clinic, lawmakers are
rushing to enact broad restrictions against human cloning. To date, 19 European nations have signed an anticloning treaty. The Clinton Administration
backs a proposal that would impose a five-year moratorium. House majority
leader Dick Armey has thrown his weight behind a bill that would ban human
cloning permanently, and at least 18 states are contemplating legislative action of their own. "This is the right thing to do, at the right time, for the sake
of human dignity," said Armey last week. "How can you put a statute of limitations on right and wrong?"

4   But hasty legislation could easily be too restrictive. Last year, for instance,
Florida considered a law that would have barred the cloning of human DNA,
a routine procedure in biomedical research. California passed badly worded
legislation that temporarily bans not just human cloning but also a procedure
that shows promise as a new treatment for infertility.

5   Most lawmakers are focused on a nightmarish vision in which billionaires
and celebrities flood the world with genetic copies of themselves. But scientists say it's unlikely that anyone is going to be churning out limited editions
of Michael Jordan or Madeleine Albright. "Oh, it can be done," says Dr. Mark
Sauer, chief of reproductive endocrinology at Columbia University's College
of Physicians and Surgeons. "It's just that the best people, who could do it,
aren't going to be doing it."

6   Cloning individual human cells, however, is another matter. Biologists are
already talking about harnessing for medical purposes the technique that produced the sheep called Dolly. They might, for example, obtain healthy cells
from a patient with leukemia or a burn victim and then transfer the nucleus
of each cell into an unfertilized egg from which the nucleus has been removed. Coddled in culture dishes, these embryonic clones—each genetically
identical to the patient from which the nuclei came—would begin to divide.

7   The cells would not have to grow into a fetus, however. The addition of powerful growth factors could ensure that the clones develop only into specialized cells and tissue. For the leukemia patient, for example, the cloned cells could provide infusion of fresh bone marrow, and for the burn victim, grafts or brand-new skin. Unlike cells from an unrelated donor, these cloned cells would incur no danger of rejection; patients would be spared the need to take powerful drugs to suppress the immune system. "Given its potential benefit," says Dr. Robert Winston, a fertility expert at London's Hammersmith Hospital, "I would argue that it would be unethical not to continue this line of research."

8   There are dangers, but not the ones everyone's talking about, according to Princeton University molecular biologist Lee Silver, author of *Remaking Eden* (Avon Books). Silver believes that cloning is the technology that will finally make it possible to apply genetic engineering to humans. First, parents will want to banish inherited diseases like Tay-Sachs. Then they will try to eliminate predispositions to alcoholism and obesity. In the end, says Silver, they will attempt to augment normal traits like intelligence and athletic prowess.

9   Cloning could be vital to that process. At present, introducing genes into chromosomes is very much a hit-or-miss proposition. Scientists might achieve the result they intend once in 20 times, making the procedure far too risky to perform on a human embryo. Through cloning, however, scientists could make 20 copies of the embryo they wished to modify, greatly boosting their chance of success.

10   Perhaps now would be a good time to ask ourselves which we fear more: that cloning will produce multiple copies of crazed despots, as in the film *The Boys from Brazil;* or that it will lead to the society portrayed in *Gattaca,* the recent science-fiction thriller in which genetic enhancement of a privileged few creates a rigid caste structure. By acting sensibly, we might avoid both traps.

READING QUESTIONS

1. What position have most nations taken on human cloning?
2. What are the dangers of human cloning?
3. What are the medical benefits of cloning?
4. What parts of a person or animal can be cloned to help that person or others?
5. What is Nash's position on cloning?

WRITING TOPICS

1. Nash offers several possible benefits of cloning. Is it important for a person like yourself to understand those benefits? Write an essay explaining why you should or should not make the effort to be informed about this issue.
2. Lee Silver is quoted as saying that cloning will lead to parents' attempts to create "perfect" children. Would you want to be able to choose your child's inherited features? Write an essay arguing for or against this possibility.

GROUP ACTIVITIES

1. Where does Nash report ideas by other people? Locate at least five places where she refers to someone else's ideas. How does she let you know that those ideas are not her own? How does she let you know whether she agrees or disagrees with their statements?

2. Make a list of medical terms used in the article. Which terms does Nash explain? Which does she expect her readers to understand? What guesses can you make about those terms using context clues or word parts (roots, suffixes, prefixes)?

RESEARCH TOPICS

1. Look up the terms located by your group in Group Activity 2. Were your guesses correct?

2. What does *cloning* mean? What new animals or plants have been cloned since this article was written?

3. Watch a videotape of the science fiction movie *Gattaca*. What problems of cloning does this movie show?

PREREADING SUGGESTIONS

1. What would be some benefits of knowing exactly what conditions your child has inherited?

2. What about your current physical condition did you inherit? What did you acquire from the environment you live in?

Genetic Testing Set for Takeoff

by Rachel Nowak

Would it help most people or hurt them if they knew what diseases might eventually attack their bodies? Looking for a cure for our problems can also possibly lead to problems, as shown in this article. This article was first published in 1994 in Science.

1   If your mother had died of Huntington's disease, would you want to be tested to see whether you had inherited the flawed gene that causes this fatal condition? Before answering, you'd want to balance costs and benefits of testing. A negative result would give you tremendous peace of mind, allowing you to lead an ordinary life. A positive result, on the other hand, would cause you to live the rest of your life knowing your ultimate fate would be the intellectual

deterioration and involuntary movements that characterize Huntington's disease. Some studies indicate that as many as one in 10 patients who test positive for the mutation never make a full emotional recovery—not surprising, given that there's currently no cure for the disease.

2 Despite the risk of psychological devastation, and in full knowledge that there's no cure, in March medical geneticist and psychologist Richard Myers of Boston University School of Medicine began offering fee-for-service testing for the Huntington's gene. Myers acknowledges that the benefits of testing for Huntington's are ambiguous. But he offers the service, along with full psychological counseling, he says, because he believes a person has an inalienable right to know his or her genetic destiny. And Huntington's is only one of several heritable diseases for which a test can pick up the genetic defect long before any symptoms appear.

3 Like prenatal testing in the 1980s, "predictive" presymptomatic genetic testing for diseases that hit later in life is destined to become a medical boom industry. Presymptomatic testing is already available for certain uncommon disorders, but the driving force for explosive growth will be the development of genetic tests for susceptibility to two very common cancers. The past 8 months has seen the identification of MSH2 and MLH1, genes that can predispose people to hereditary nonpolyposis colon cancer when they contain specific defects. Nonpolyposis colon cancer strikes one in 20 people, and as many as 18% of these cancers may result from mutations in MSH2 and MLH1.

4 Commercial genetics labs are already staking their claims on this huge potential market. No fewer than 10 companies have already purchased the rights to develop MSH2 and MLH1 tests. And if BRCA1—the putative gene that when damaged dramatically increases the risk of breast and ovarian cancer—is "cloned by Christmas" as some researchers have predicted, it will undoubtedly spawn a second presymptomatic gene test with a huge market waiting for it.

5 But as predictive gene testing gets set to take off, it trails in its wake a swarm of tough questions, some of which are hinted at by the case of Huntington's disease. Is it ethical to test for diseases for which there are no known cures? How reliable are the available tests? What are the psychological consequences for healthy patients of learning their destiny? Is the regulation of laboratories that offer genetic testing stringent enough to ensure that life-shattering errors are not made? How can perfectly healthy people who may carry a defective gene be protected from discrimination by health and life insurance companies and potential employers?

6 Those uncertainties have the research, clinical, and patient communities in turmoil about where to go from here. Some favor taking the research high road. "Genetic testing should be considered in the same way as a new drug. It can have efficacy, and it can have toxicity," argues Francis Collins, head of the National Center for Human Genome Research in Bethesda, Maryland. The National Advisory Council for Human Genome Research (NACHGR), which Collins chairs, currently recommends against testing for BRCA1 (which, in

some cases, can already be done, not by DNA testing but by more cumbersome linkage analysis), MSH2, or MLH1, except in research settings.

7   Fran Visco, president of the National Breast Cancer Coalition in Washington, D.C., shares some of NACHGR's worries. "We're very concerned about how good the tests will be," she says. She adds, however, that "the demand will be high," and she says her organization is asking that the test "be made widely available," albeit only through peer-reviewed research protocols.

8   Others argue that confining testing to the research arena is unethical, precisely because it would limit its availability. Medical geneticist David Rimoin of Cedars-Sinai Medical Center in Los Angeles calls the NACHGR's stance "far too restrictive." Rimoin, president of the newly formed American College of Medical Genetics, argues that presymptomatic genetic testing for colon and breast cancer should be available to any individual judged to be at risk by a doctor trained in medical genetics. To "ensure that false diagnoses and false reassurances are not made," he says, tests should not be made available through general practitioners.

Is Knowledge Power?

9   In the face of these widely varying opinions, what are the real pros and cons of presymptomatic genetic testing? One key issue is whether the knowledge provided by gene testing will actually save lives. For Huntington's disease, the answer is clearly no. For hereditary nonpolyposis colon cancer and breast and ovarian cancer, however, the answer is far from clear. In general, early detection of these cancers is associated with improved survival. But "the question everyone is asking," says Collins, is whether interventions that work for the general population "are going to apply to these individuals who have a very strong genetic risk."

10   For instance, mammograms, which have been shown to save lives among women 50 and over by detecting breast cancer early, won't necessarily help when BRCA1 mutations trigger breast cancer. In fact, says Collins, it is conceivable that "these may be the people who are most sensitive to very low doses of radiation and therefore should avoid mammograms." Nonetheless, Mary-Claire King of the University of California at Berkeley, a leader in the hunt for BRCA1, points out, a woman who tests positive might choose to be more rigorous about breast self-examinations. Some women who test positive opt for prophylactic mastectomy.

11   But even in the absence of any clear-cut treatment strategy for people who carry cancer susceptibility genes, presymptomatic gene testing still has something important to offer a fortunate group of testees: a negative result. If a patient gets that result, the physician is able to "say—go in peace. Do whatever you plan to do with your life," says Frederick Li of the Dana-Farber Cancer Institute in Boston, who is studying the pros and cons of testing members of high-risk families for the mutations that may trigger the multiple early-onset cancers that constitute Li-Fraumeni syndrome. A negative test also saves patients discomfort, disfigurement, and dollars, clinicians say, as they avoid

screening procedures such as colonoscopies and prophylactic therapies such as mastectomy.

Bearing False Witness

12   In spite of those potential advantages, widespread testing now would be a mistake, says Collins, because we don't yet "understand what type of false positives and false negatives are going to occur." Such errors are easier to avoid when testing is conducted in a meticulous research environment and is restricted to members of large high-risk families in which the specific mutation afflicting them can be identified.

13   But such families include only a tiny minority of all potential testees, and when testing moves beyond these families, it enters a much more complex arena. To reliably test individuals for hereditary susceptibility to cancer without reference to affected family members, it's necessary to be able to identify a whole range of possible mutations (each gene has room for hundreds); the risk of cancer associated with each mutation; and the difference between a dangerous mutation and a polymorphism, a harmless genetic variant. Richard Fishel of the University of Vermont School of Medicine, who with Richard Kolodner of the Dana-Farber led one of the teams that pinpointed MSH2 and MLH1, says "the very first mutation we identified may turn out to be a polymorphism—a potential false positive that needs to be rigorously examined."

14   The assays currently available "aren't guaranteed to find a mutation. They are prone to false negatives," says Kenneth Kinzler of the Johns Hopkins University Medical School, who, with Hopkins' Bert Vogelstein and Albert de la Chapelle of the University of Helsinki in Finland, led another team that identified MLH1 and MSH2. One problem is that, even with automated sequencers, it takes days, even weeks, to reliably sequence each gene. By necessity, the assays concentrate on the gene's protein-coding regions rather than on their regulatory regions or their introns (the pieces of the code that are chopped out after the DNA is converted into RNA). Yet mutations in these regions may also trigger cancer.

15   "Everyone sees some grand potential," says molecular geneticist Raymond Fenwick of Dianon Systems Inc., a Stratford, Connecticut, diagnostics company that offers gene testing for Huntington's, "but until someone comes up with some dynamo technology to search through the whole gene, it's going to be too expensive" to do widespread testing for all possible mutations in MSH2, MLH1, and, once it's been tracked down, BRCA1.

16   Fishel thinks it's too early even for testing in high-risk families. "I'm very uncomfortable with identifying a mutation and saying this is responsible for disease," he says, because in all but the largest families it is impossible to conclude definitively that a mutation present only in family members that have cancer is actually causing the cancer rather than simply being a chance association.

17   Rather than relying solely on mutation testing, Fishel says, "we need to develop functional assays in order to assess what a mutation means." Functional

assays, which monitor the action of the gene's protein product, can more easily pick out defective genes. Fishel's lab is in the process of developing such a test for MSH2 and MLH1.

18   Even when the whole spectrum of mutations is bagged and functional assays are available, problems will remain, as geneticists need to tighten up their estimates of the actual risk of cancer—or "penetrance"—associated with each mutation. Geneticists usually give the penetrance for mutations in MSH2, MLH1, and BRCA1 as about 85%. But those estimates are derived from studies designed to pin down the genetic basis for cancer by homing in on families with extremely high incidence of early-onset cancers.

19   The degree of penetrance, however, is likely to be different for each of the hundreds of different mutations that are floating around in the population. Those high-risk families may suffer peculiarly damaging mutations, or may be unusually vulnerable to a given mutation, so using them to calculate cancer risk associated with the mutated gene is likely to lead to a huge overestimation. "When you are not picking those glorious pedigrees that allow you to identify genes, there's remarkably less penetrance," says Stephen Friend of Harvard Medical School in Boston, a cancer-gene expert.

20   Such complexities, says breast-cancer gene prospector Bruce Ponder of Cambridge University's Addenbrooke's Hospital in Cambridge, England, mean that "we are going to have to do a lot of genetic epidemiology, correlating mutations and risk in different families," before widespread gene testing for cancer risk will be a reliable proposition.

21   Yet despite the current weaknesses in testing methods, Ponder says he would be hard pressed to deny members of a high-risk breast cancer family the right to take a presymptomatic gene test. "We are dealing with adults," he says, "and if people ask, you have a duty to inform them of what's available and what the potential advantages and disadvantages are."

Testing Testing

22   Like others involved in this field, which is poised to take off before it's fully explored, Ponder is of two minds about testing. Although he doesn't think it should be denied to adults, he recognizes there's a risk the tests might actually increase cancer mortality. Specifically, he and others are concerned that positive tests, by triggering depression, could actually worsen a patient's chances of survival. For example, "do they become so frightened that they stop [breast] self-examination?" asks genetic counselor Barbara Biesecker of the National Center for Human Genome Research.

23   The answer to her question isn't known, but with the medical axiom "first do no harm" firmly in mind, teams of geneticists, oncologists, and psychologists around the world are gearing up to find out. The studies they are planning will test the impact of testing for susceptibility to Li-Fraumeni, breast, and colon cancer. Most studies will provide intensive pre- and post-test counseling similar to what is given in Huntington's gene testing.

24   Six months ago, Ponder and his co-workers started a pilot study to test testing in members of families who have an increased incidence of breast cancer. "One or two [women] have been fairly cracked up about [a positive result], despite our best attempts at counseling," he says.

25   Similarly, positive Huntington's results have led to depressions so severe that a few patients have had to be hospitalized. One longer term Huntington's study did, however, suggest positive benefits of testing. According to a 1992 study by the Canadian Collaborative Study of Predictive Testing, one year after testing, 37 patients who tested positive and 58 who tested negative for Huntington's scored higher on standard psychological tests of well-being and lower on tests for depression than the 40 whose test results were ambiguous. That result suggests that for patients who know they are at risk (because they come from families in which some members have already fallen prey to Huntington's), testing for a genetic defect can have benefits based on the relief of uncertainty.

26   But studies like these are conducted under excellent conditions by researchers at topflight medical centers, who provide plenty of reliable information to their patients. Many medical geneticists worry about what will happen when gene testing leaves the setting of the university hospital and enters the doctor's office. Counseling is essential to educate patients about genetics, about probabilities, and about false negatives and false positives, as well as to prepare them to handle the impact of their results. But there are currently only a handful of genetic counselors—a mere 1000 in the United States—and "most doctors, let alone most members of the general public, have only the foggiest idea of the implications of a result," says Ponder.

III Without Symptoms

27   Even if a patient receives an accurate result and thorough counseling to go with it, their problems are not over. Myers points out that "all the time, people are turned down for life and health insurance" on the basis of test results of the Huntington mutation. In a 1992 article in the *American Journal of Human Genetics,* a team led by Paul Billings of the California Pacific Medical Center in San Francisco reported 41 cases of discrimination against healthy people based solely on their genetic risk. In most cases, the victims were refused health or life insurance. Some were refused jobs. Others were banned from adopting children. Billings calls these people the "asymptomatic ill."

28   But moves are afoot to stamp out this new form of discrimination. A draft version of a treaty released in June by the 32-nation Council of Europe proposes banning gene testing for insurance and employment purposes (*Science,* 8 July, p. 175). A National Academy of Sciences report called "Assessing Genetic Risks: Implications for Health and Social Policy," released in November, recommends a legal ban on discrimination based on genetic risks; that option is being pursued by some states.

29   It seems clear that, at the moment, the dangers of genetic testing are substantial, and the benefits, though they may one day be much larger, are small

for some who test positive. Yet public demand is likely to lead to widespread testing long before all the glitches have been ironed out. *Time*/CNN pollsters recently asked 500 Americans whether they would take an imaginary genetic test that would tell them which diseases they would suffer later in life; half said yes.

30   Since Myers started offering his Huntington's gene testing service, he's had two inquiries a day, which he calls an "unbelievable number" for a rare disease. One breast cancer activist says she understands that response. Patients at risk of inheriting an incurable disease want every weapon they can get. And for many patients, in the absence of a cure or an effective form of preventive therapy, all that's available is a mental weapon: the knowledge offered by testing.

Gene Tests: Who's Minding the Store?

31   When it comes to testing for disease-causing genes, it's important to get the results right, because they can have life-shattering consequences, determining whether a patient refrains from having children, becomes uninsurable, or is plunged into depression. Given the importance of accuracy, a panel of the National Academy of Sciences (NAS) came up with a disturbing conclusion last year: Federal oversight of gene testing is in dire need of an overhaul. In theory, the Health Care Financing Administration (HCFA) and Food and Drug Administration (FDA) are responsible for ensuring high-quality testing in commercial and academic labs. In practice, however, such authority "is not being applied to genetic testing at all," the NAS panel said last November in a report called "Assessing Genetic Risks: Implications for Health and Social Policy." And "without regulatory backup," says Patricia Murphy of OncorMed Inc. in Gaithersburg, Maryland, who set up the genetic testing regulations for the New York State Department of Health, "nightmares occur, mistakes are made, and you don't get equivalency between labs."

32   The problem is that HCFA has no standards specific to labs that analyze DNA. Moreover, says geneticist and health policy expert Neil Holtzman of Johns Hopkins University in Baltimore, a member of the NAS panel, "HCFA inspectors are not trained to recognize how to run a genetic test—for susceptibility to cancer, for example—and to ensure its quality."

33   The FDA isn't doing much better. The agency requires that manufacturers win marketing approval for test kits and that labs offering experimental genetic tests obtain an Investigational Device Exemption or conduct the tests under Institutional Review Board-approved protocols and mark the results "for investigational use only." Few do. "We've had a paucity of genetic tests that have actually been cleared or approved," says Steven Gutman, acting director of the FDA's division of clinical laboratory devices, the unit that oversees genetic testing. Gutman admits that part of the problem is that the FDA prefers to leave oversight of genetic testing to HCFA.

34   But there may be some hope for improvement on the horizon. The American College of Medical Genetics, the College of American Pathologists, and the human genome project's Ethical, Legal, and Social Implications branch in Bethesda, Maryland, are working with FDA and HCFA to tighten up their

methods for oversight of gene testing. It remains to be seen, however, whether any improvements will come before the explosion of genetic testing that is expected soon.

READING QUESTIONS

1. What is a "presymptomatic gene test"?
2. What are the pros and cons of presymptomatic genetic testing?
3. What concerns have been raised about widespread genetic testing?
4. How does the medical axiom "first, do no harm" relate to the concerns about genetic testing raised in this article?
5. Who are the "asymptomatic ill"?
6. How does the regulation of genetic laboratories affect the reliability of genetic testing?

WRITING TOPICS

1. Based on the arguments presented in this article, what law do you think would be important to pass? Write an essay explaining why that law is needed.
2. Would you want your children to be tested? Write an essay explaining what benefits or harm you would expect from genetic testing.
3. Who should make decisions about genetic testing: doctors, patients, or lawmakers? Write an essay defending your choice.

GROUP ACTIVITIES

1. Form groups to debate on benefits and dangers of genetic testing. Assign half of the group to each side. Use the information in the article as the basis of your argument.
2. The article is divided into sections with headings. Write a 2 to 3 sentence summary of the main idea of each section. Work as a group to check the accuracy of each summary and to revise them if necessary.

RESEARCH TOPICS

1. Find recent news stories about preventive mastectomies. How many women have had this procedure?
2. Find information on one of the scientists or institutions named in the article. Is this person or place still an important resource for genetic testing?
3. Are there any laws governing genetic research in your state?

PREREADING SUGGESTIONS

1. At what point do you believe a fetus becomes a person?
2. What would you do to be able to have a baby of your own?

Human in the Age of Mechanical Reproduction

by Karen Wright and Sarah Richardson

Up until a few decades ago, couples who could not conceive a baby could turn only to adoption. Modern techniques of improving fertility have made giving birth an option for many, but have also created some moral dilemmas. Karen Wright and Sarah Richardson examine some ethical problems raised by new techniques of assisted reproduction. This article was first published in 1998 in Discover.

1 "Mommy, where do babies come from?"

2   Parents have dreaded this question since the stork made its first delivery. But today's mommies and daddies have more explaining to do than their own parents could possibly have imagined. Though the birds and the bees discussion was never easy, its elements were fairly straightforward: the fireworks exploding, the train chugging through the tunnel, the waves pounding the shore, the occasional reference to anatomy. Once upon a time, baby-making was synonymous with whoopee-making, and frozen eggs were for pastry dough, and seven was how many times you should let the phone ring before you hang up, not how many fetuses you could fit in a womb.

3   These days, though, the facts of life can sound a lot like science fiction, as late-twentieth-century humanity grapples with the rise of noncoital conception. There are now more than a dozen ways to make a baby, the vast majority of which bypass the antiquated act of sexual congress. The last three decades have seen the advent of such high-tech interventions as fertility drugs, in vitro fertilization, donor eggs, donor sperm, donor embryos, and surrogate mothering. In the works are still more advanced technologies, such as the transfer of cell nuclei, embryo splitting, and even, if at least one man has his way, the cloning of human adults.

4   These techniques generally are gathered under the heading of "assisted reproduction." All the ones in use today were pioneered for and are usually employed by infertile couples of childbearing age. But they are also used by people with less conventional notions of parenting—singles, postmenopausal women, and gay partners. In the near future, assisted reproduction may become standard procedure for anyone who wants to conceive, and who can afford it. The allure, of course, is control: control over the timing of parenthood, control over "embryo quality," control over genetic disease, control over less pernicious characteristics, such as gender, that are also determined by genes.

5   So far, owing to federal policy and societal preference, the practice of assisted reproduction is largely unregulated. One specialist has even called it the Wild West of medicine. It's also expensive, bothersome, inefficient, and fraught with ethical complications—but none of those considerations has slowed its growth. Since 1978, when the first test-tube baby was born, the

number of fertility clinics in the United States has gone from less than 30 to more than 300. The multibillion-dollar fertility industry has created tens of thousands of babies. Assisted reproduction has relieved the anguish of men and women, who, just decades ago, would have had to abandon their hopes of having children. It's also created a world where a dead man can impregnate a stranger, where a woman can rent out her uterus, and where a child can have five parents—and still end up an orphan. It's not at all clear how this new world will change the meaning of family. But it has already transformed what used to be known as the miracle of birth.

6   Last November an Iowa couple made history, national television, and the covers of *Time* and *Newsweek* when their seven babies were born alive. "We're trusting in God," the McCaugheys told reporters when asked how they would cope with the sudden surfeit of offspring. But to conceive for the second time, Bobbi McCaughey had trusted in Metrodin, a fertility drug that stimulates the ripening of eggs in the ovaries. A woman on Metrodin can produce dozens of eggs in a month instead of just one.

7   Metrodin belongs to a suite of hormones that are used to increase egg development and release, or ovulation. Fertility drugs go by many brand names, like Clomid, Pergonal, Humegon, Fertinex, Follistim, and some have been around for decades. Women who have problems ovulating regularly can often conceive by the time-honored method once fertility drugs have improved their chances of success.

8   Even so, taking fertility drugs is not like taking aspirin. Most are administered by daily injections that couples are trained to perform. The drugs themselves aren't cheap—a single dose of Fertinex, for example, is about $60—and most doctors monitor the progress of egg ripening with ultrasound scans and blood tests that add to the overall cost. Ultimately, a cycle of treatment with fertility drugs may cost more than $1,500.

9   And there are risks. The most common is multiple pregnancy: the simultaneous conception of two or (many) more fetuses, like the McCaugheys'. Despite the celebratory atmosphere that greeted the Iowa septuplets, such pregnancies are in fact a grave predicament for would-be parents. Multiple pregnancies increase the odds of maternal complications such as high blood pressure and diabetes. And they pose even greater risks for the unborn. The fetuses gestating in a multiple pregnancy are far more susceptible than their singlet peers to miscarriage, birth defects, low birth weight, and premature birth, as well as lifelong problems that can result from prematurity—including cerebral palsy, blindness, kidney failure, and mental retardation.

10   There are ways to get around the problem of multiple pregnancy. One is to abstain from sex if ultrasound scans reveal that a plethora of eggs is poised for release. Statistics suggest, however, that many couples choose not to exercise this option. Whereas in the general population the rate of multiple pregnancy is 1 to 2 percent, the rate among women treated with fertility drugs can be as high as 25 percent.

11   Another way to deal with the risks of multiple pregnancy is to eliminate some fetuses before they are born. Infertility specialists call this technique

selective reduction. It is performed before the third month of pregnancy by injecting selected fetuses with potassium chloride, which stops the heart. A doctor inserts a needle through the abdomen or vagina of the mother-to-be to deliver the injection.

12   Like most techniques of assisted reproduction, selective reduction introduces ethical problems as it solves medical ones. For many couples, the decision of whether and how much to reduce is traumatic. Some, including the McCaugheys, simply refuse to do it. Others accept the agony—and irony—of destroying surplus fetuses as an unfortunate consequence of their condition. Yet still other people feel comfortable enough with the techniques to use it for practical, rather than medical, reasons. "There are patients that will push very hard to reduce from three fetuses to two," says Benjamin Younger, executive director of the American Society for Reproductive Medicine. "They'll say, 'Doctor, I can't cope with triplets.'"

13   If an infertile couple chooses to pursue the more advanced procedures of assisted reproduction, selective reduction is only one of several trials they may face. "I don't think I've ever done anything as difficult," admits a Boston woman who became pregnant after two years of ever-escalating interventions. "You have to really want it."

14   Kathryn Graven and her husband decided to start a family when Graven was 34. After nine months of trying by the usual route, they went to an area clinic for a fertility workup. There are various causes for infertility, including hormonal imbalance in women, low sperm count in men, and blockages in the reproductive tract of either partner. But tests failed to identify a specific cause for the Gravens', so their doctor recommended conservative treatment. In each of three months, Graven tried the fertility drug, Clomid, which is taken orally, to stimulate egg production, followed by artificial insemination with her husband's sperm. When that didn't work, Graven switched to Fertinex, which is injected beneath the skin. After two rounds of Fertinex and artificial insemination also failed, the couple decided to try in vitro fertilization.

15   IVF is the cornerstone of assisted reproductive technology. The procedure—in which ripe eggs are removed from the ovaries and incubated with sperm—greatly improves the haphazard gambit of traditional in vivo fertilization. It also introduces another level of complexity and expense. In addition to egg-ripening hormones, a woman undergoing IVF will usually take a protean cocktail of drugs designed to suppress and then trigger the release of mature eggs. Egg retrieval, done by guiding a hollow needle through the wall of the vagina and into the nearby ovaries, is characterized as a minor surgical procedure. ("The next day I felt like a Roto-Rooter had gone through my insides," says Graven.) And then the fertilized embryos have to be transferred back to the uterus.

16   When Graven's IVF attempt failed as well, her doctor recommended a more advanced technique: gamete intrafallopian transfer, or GIFT. In this procedure, eggs are harvested, mixed with sperm, then returned to the fallopian tubes—where egg and sperm normally meet—to fertilize. GIFT requires a longer and more complicated operation, with three incisions in the patient's

abdomen, and about two days' recovery. But the success rates are 5 to 10 percent higher than those of IVF. It worked for Graven: she is due to give birth in July, at the age of 37.

17 GIFT is one of several variations of the IVF theme that were introduced in the 1980s as infertility specialists sought to expand their skills in assisted reproduction. Even with these innovations, however, the efficacy of assisted reproduction is sobering. Graven's experience was typical of what many infertile couples might undergo, except in one respect: Graven got pregnant. Success rates for IVF depend on a patient's age and vary from clinic to clinic and from procedure to procedure. But the ballpark figure—the so-called take-home baby rate—is one live birth for every five IVF cycles. Infertility specialists point out that the success rates for these procedures increase every year and that in any given month a fertile couple's chance of conceiving by traditional means is also one in five. According to the American Society for Reproductive Medicine, more than half of all infertile couples could attain pregnancy if they persisted long enough with treatments for assisted reproduction.

18 But that also means that about half will never have a baby, no matter how much therapy they get. And one thing about making babies by usual means is that it's free. If at first you don't succeed, you can try, try again, without taking out a second mortgage. A single cycle of IVF, on the other hand, costs between $8,000 and $10,000. Special options like GIFT may cost more. Graven didn't have to pay for most of her treatment, because Massachusetts is one of ten states that mandate insurance coverage for infertility treatment. The bill for her pregnancy would have been well over $25,000.

19 Is it worth it? The market says yes. Although rates of infertility have remained constant, demand for infertility services has risen steadily in the past two decades. Today about 6 million couples in the United States have fertility problems; half of them go to their doctors for help, and about a quarter end up trying assisted reproduction. Whether those couples view these attempts as a blessing or a curse "depends on the outcome," says Margaret Hollister, director of the help line at RESOLVE, a national infertility support group based in Somerville, Massachusetts. "The treatments are stressful, expensive, and require a big time commitment."

20 Of course, the same could be said of parenting. The stress associated with infertility, however, may be especially pernicious. Alice Domar, director of the behavioral-medicine program for infertility at Beth Israel Deaconess Medical Center in Boston, has found that women who have been trying to get pregnant via assisted reproduction for two years or more have rates of depression as high as those of patients with cancer, heart disease, and AIDS. She also finds that conception rates in severely depressed patients improve when the depression is treated.

21 Domar has used her results to argue that infertility should be regarded as a serious medical condition and that more research needs to be done on the connection between mind and reproductive machinery. Trouble is, Domar's studies don't ascertain whether her subjects' depression is caused by the trials of infertility per se or by the tribulations of infertility treatments. Infertility

patients describing their encounters with assisted reproduction use words like roller-coaster ride, addiction, and obsession. Fertility drugs are renowned for causing moodiness, as well as cramping, weight gain, and bloating. And the demands of tracking ovulation can turn a person's world upside down. During some parts of the cycle, a patient might visit her IVF clinic once or even twice a day for blood tests, ultrasound scans, and injections. "Your life starts revolving around the beginning, middle, and end of your cycle," says Graven. "Monitoring your body becomes a full-time job."

22   Moreover, pursuing parenthood via assisted reproduction means being confronted with ethical decisions well outside the range of most people's moral radars. Because IVF techniques often give rise to multiple pregnancies, selective reduction is an issue here as well. Couples undergoing IVF must also decide how many eggs to fertilize and transfer at one time (which bears on the question of multiple pregnancy), whether they want to create and freeze embryos for future use, and what the eventual disposition of any unused frozen embryos should be. Former spouses have waged custody battles over frozen embryos, and in at least one case the attending IVF clinic claimed the embryo as its lawful property. Legally, human embryos occupy a gray area all their own, somewhere between human life and some rarefied form of property.

23   Assisted reproduction also invites the preselection of embryos based on genetic traits, and all the moral dilemmas that may accrue thereto. Screening is done by removing a single cell from an eight-cell embryo and analyzing the chromosomes or DNA in the cell nucleus. Already some clinics offer to screen in vitro embryos for genes related to cystic fibrosis, hemophilia, and muscular dystrophy. Couples can decide which of the embryos they've created meet their specifications; the rejected embryos can be discarded or donated to research.

24   Finally, assisted reproduction has opened the door to all manner of gamete swapping and surrogacy, from the simplest and oldest method—artificial insemination with a donor's sperm—to more complex scenarios in which any combination of donor eggs, donor sperm, and donor embryos may be used. In addition to biological surrogate motherhood (the method that created the celebrated Baby M), "gestational surrogates" will agree to carry and give birth to a baby to whom they bear no genetic relation whatsoever. It is now possible for a person to "have" a baby by procuring eggs and sperm from donors and hiring a "birth mother" to do the rest (this has been done). It is possible for a woman to use a birth mother for cosmetic reasons or convenience alone (this has also been done). It is possible for the sperm of dead men to be retrieved and used to impregnate their widows (likewise). It is possible for women long past the age of menopause to give birth (this, too, has already happened).

25   Another exceptional birth captured headlines last October, when a woman whose ovaries were nonfunctional delivered two healthy boys courtesy of Reproductive Biology Associates in Atlanta. RBA had engineered the twins' conception using donor eggs frozen for more than two years. Because the sheer size and complexity of the human egg make it more susceptible than sperm to damage during freezing, protocols for the cryopreservation of eggs have been

difficult to perfect. Until recently, in fact, most attempts at egg freezing have failed. The twins are the first of their kind to be born in the United States.

26   Though RBA's achievement was quickly overshadowed by the arrival of the Iowa septuplets, the egg-freezing feat has more significant ramifications. Once it becomes widely available, cryopreservation will offer a unique opportunity to women: the chance to store their young eggs for use at a later date. Defects in aging eggs are thought to be responsible for the declining fertility of older women; indeed, donor-egg technology has demonstrated that the rest of the female reproductive apparatus withstands the test of time. By assuring women a lifetime of viable gametes, egg freezing could let them beat the biological clock.

27   Of course, women would then be using assisted reproduction for their own convenience rather than for treatment of an existing medical condition. In this respect, egg freezing echoes a common theme in assisted reproduction. Current techniques were developed to help patients with specific medical problems—egg freezing, for example, will allow cancer patients whose eggs would be destroyed by radiation to set aside some gametes prior to therapy. Yet inevitably, the fruits of infertility research expand reproductive options for all men and women. And these choices are not always easy to live with, for individuals or for society.

28   A striking example comes from the laboratory of reproductive endocrinologist Jamie Grifo at New York University Medical Center. In another effort to beat the biological clock, Grifo is transferring the nuclei from older women's eggs into younger eggs from which the nuclei have been removed—that is, enucleated eggs. When these hybrid cells are artificially stimulated to divide, the transferred nuclei don't show the chromosomal abnormalities typical of vintage eggs. Grifo's work is still in the research stage, but he hopes eventually to fertilize such eggs and implant them in his patients.

29   Grifo is not cloning humans, but his experiments draw on established mammalian cloning technology. Lamb 6LL3, better known as Dolly, was created by nuclear transfer from an adult cell to an enucleated egg. Grifo emphasizes that he's concerned only with transfers between egg cells for the purpose of treating infertility; he says he is strongly opposed to human cloning, and that in any case it will take years for researchers to figure out how to do it. "But the fact is, it's possible," he says. "I just can't think of any clinical indications for it."

30   If Grifo can't, someone else can. Richard Seed, a physicist turned infertility entrepreneur, made headlines in January when he announced that he was seeking funds to establish a laboratory for the cloning of adult human beings.

31   The National Bioethics Advisory Commission recommended a ban on human cloning back when Dolly first saw daylight. More recently, President Clinton reiterated his call for a five-year moratorium on human cloning research. But the American Society for Reproductive Medicine, which issues ethical guidelines for the use of assisted-reproduction technologies, has taken the middle ground. "We do not support the cloning of an existing—or previously existing—individual," says Younger. "But that is not to say that cloning technology

is bad." Cultures of cloned nerve cells, for example, could be used to treat spinal-cord injuries, he says. "We would not like to see research curtailed."

32   The society has also come out in favor of continuing research on embryo "twinning"—a procedure, done so far only in animals, in which a single embryo is divided to create two genetically identical individuals. The society's rationale is that the technique of embryo twinning could provide infertile couples with twice as many embryos to implant. But the distinction between cloning and twinning grows obscure if, say, one of the twinned embryos is frozen until its sibling has grown to adulthood.

33   Critics of assisted reproduction fear that today's innovations will become tomorrow's imperatives. Already some infertile couples feel entrapped by the catalog of choices. "All these technologies, by providing more and more options, make it very difficult to say, 'No, we've tried enough,'" says R. Alta Charo, a law professor at the University of Wisconsin and member of the National Bioethics Advisory Commission. "Choice is not a bad thing—but neither is it an unalloyed good."

34   And lack of regulation only exacerbates the problems surrounding assisted reproduction. "This field is screaming for regulation, oversight, and control," says Arthur Caplan, a noted bioethicist at the University of Pennsylvania. "What keeps us from doing so is the notion that individuals should have procreative freedom."

35   Rancor over abortion has also impeded the regulation of technologies for assisted reproduction. Since the 1970s, the United States has outlawed federal funding of research on human embryos or fetal tissue in response to concerns that such research would encourage trafficking in embryos and fetuses. The ban has not been applied to privately funded efforts, however; consequently, most research on assisted reproduction has been conducted beyond the reach of federal regulation and oversight.

36   Specialists in assisted reproduction, including Grifo, say this is just as well—that regulators wouldn't appreciate the technical and moral complexities of the work. But with the bulk of experimentation going on in private clinics, patients—and their children—can become guinea pigs. Even when couples are not directly involved in experimental procedures, they may be confronted with uncomfortable choices, such as financial incentives to donate their gametes or embryos.

37   "People often feel compelled by the circumstances—'What else could we do?'" says Barbara Katz Rothman, professor of sociology at Baruch College. "I'm not sure how we should make these decisions, but I'm pretty sure they shouldn't be made by the market."

38   And market forces affect more than just infertile couples. Although eggs are far more scarce and difficult to obtain than sperm, young women donors are typically given minimal compensation for their time and trouble. But in February the *New York Times* reported that St. Barnabas Medical Center, a fertility clinic in Livingston, New Jersey, has begun offering young women $5,000 to donate eggs—a price reported to be twice that of competitors. Unlike payment for organs, which is illegal, limited payment for eggs is legal.

The professional guidelines of the American Society for Reproductive Medicine deem them "body products," not "body parts."

39 Many observers fear that it is not the participants in assisted reproduction but their children who may suffer most from the imprudent use of these new technologies. For example, with the rising popularity of assisted reproduction, more and more children are being exposed to the risks of premature birth: since 1971 the annual number of multiple births in the United States has more than quadrupled. Scientists and ethicists alike have spoken out against helping single, postmenopausal mothers conceive, arguing that it is morally reprehensible to create children who may well be orphaned. Some question the wisdom of arrangements—like surrogacy or gamete donation—that could diffuse the responsibility of parenthood. And some researchers are concerned with the safety of the procedures themselves for assisted reproduction. A recent—and controversial—Australian study of 420 children suggests that babies produced with the aid of intracytoplasmic sperm injection, in which a single sperm is injected into an incubating egg cell, are twice as likely to suffer major birth defects of the heart, genitals, and digestive tract.

40 "Everything we do in vitro to a mammalian embryo causes it stress," says Robert Edwards, the specialist who presided over the first test-tube baby 20 years ago. "But there's immense responsibility in the scientific community" to evaluate and eliminate any adverse consequences of new procedures, he says.

41 Other commentators note that the rights of participants and progeny in assisted reproduction are still undefined. Laws vary widely from state to state on whether a child conceived by donor insemination has the right to know the identity of her biological father. "We never resolved the issues surrounding artificial insemination," says George Annas, a professor of law, medicine, and public health at Boston University. "We just act like we did. And then we import these issues into the new technology."

42 With the rapid advances in assisted-reproduction techniques, the ethical and legal issues can only become more complicated, and the task of resolving them will fall to future generations. But that may be fitting, if it's the children of assisted reproduction who pass judgment on the technology that helped create them.

READING QUESTIONS

1. What is "assisted reproduction"? When did this technique first lead to the birth of a baby? How has the field grown since then?

2. What are the problems of multiple pregnancy? How can they be avoided?

3. What is selective reduction? Why might it be necessary? Why is it a problem?

4. What is IVF? How successful is it? What ethical issues does this procedure raise?

5. What are some of the pressures on prospective parents or other people created by the availability of many different methods of assisted reproduction? How are these methods regulated by law?

WRITING TOPICS

1. Of all the various choices for assisted reproduction described by Wright and Richardson, which one would you be least willing to attempt? Why? Write an essay explaining the ethical problems you see in this method.

2. Should laws regulate assisted reproduction? Why or why not? Write an essay arguing for or against such laws.

GROUP ACTIVITIES

1. Assign each member of the group a technical term. Explain the meaning of this term in language the rest of the class can easily understand. Let the group review the explanations for correctness and clarity.

2. Prepare for an imaginary presentation by a fertility specialist and a couple who have used assisted reproduction. List some questions you would like to ask them, and explain why those questions are important.

RESEARCH TOPICS

1. Are there any facilities for assisted reproduction in your community? Find the location of the nearest one.

2. Read a newspaper or magazine article about a famous multiple birth or other case of assisted reproduction. How does the procedure affect family life?

Answers for Chapters 23 and 24

BAS EXERCISE 1 The story of the Heike is a very sad story from Japanese history. The emperor (whose family was called the Heike) was fighting his enemies, who chased him until finally he boarded a ship with his family and followers. A nurse carried the baby, the son of the emperor. When the enemies captured the ship, she took the baby emperor to the prow of the ship and jumped into the water where she and the baby drowned, but escaped their enemy in death. All the family and soldiers of the Heike were killed and their bodies were lost at sea. Now the crabs who are caught in that part of the ocean have strange markings on their shells. Local people call them the faces of the Heike.

BAS EXERCISE 2 A very old story from the Middle East is called *Gilgamesh*. Gilgamesh was the ruler of his country, and he was very strong and handsome. Another man in that country was called Enkidu. Enkidu lived in the forest and had only animals for friends. Gilgamesh sent a woman to Enkidu, and when the animals saw him with another human, they became afraid of him. Enkidu left the forest. He and Gilgamesh fought each other, but finally became good friends. The importance of friendship is a theme of the story.

BAS EXERCISE 3 From an ancient African county in Mali comes the story of Son-Jara who was born a prince. His mother was one of the king's wives, but another of the king's wives hated her. (Being jealous) was a common problem among the king's wives in those days. This woman cursed Son-Jara so that he was unable to walk when he was a child. (To be) a king's mother was his mother's ambition, so she wanted him (to be) stronger than other men, but instead he was weaker. His mother's hopes for her son seemed impossible, but she went (to ask) help from a Djinn, a supernatural creature. (Following) the Djinn's instructions was difficult, but she obeyed. She sent her son on a Haj, which is a pilgrimage to Mecca. Finally the curse was destroyed, and Son-Jara became a great king.

BAS EXERCISE 4 Do all people have the same idea about how the world was created? People in different parts of the world can sometimes have very different ideas. Many cultures have asked these questions: Where do we come from? How were we made? The question is often answered by a story. The Mayan people of ancient Guatemala long ago told the story of creation, which, according to the stories they told, had been accomplished by a group of gods. These gods were called Bearer, Begetter, Maker, and Modeler (also called Plumed Serpent). They used many grains, fruits, and vegetables to create the first people.

BAS EXERCISE 5 Many (of the stories) we find (in one country) are also found (in the tales) (from other countries.) (For example,) the story (of a great flood) that destroys the earth is found (in many stories) (from all over the world). (In ancient China,) (in Babylon,) (in Israel,) (in South America,) and probably (in many other lands) as well, we can read or hear (of one man) who survives the flood (with his family and starts the world again.) The story (of the flood) appears (in the Bible) and (in the Koran.) One man suggested a theory (about these universal stories.) (In his book *Man and His Symbols*,) Carl Jung called these stories *archetypes*, and reminded us that people (in all parts) (of the world) tell similar stories, and also dream similar dreams.

BND EXERCISE 1   A writer of many plays and poems. William Shakespeare is considered to be one of the greatest writers in the English language. We usually think of Shakespeare as the writer of tragic plays. Plays about murder and unfortunate deaths. However, Shakespeare also wrote plays referred to as the histories and the romances. Also, twelve plays which are called the comedies. His plays were very popular in his own time. Performed at the Old Globe theater. Today, his plays are perhaps most often seen in movie theaters. Some film directors will update the play and set it in modern times. Rewriting the play's original language so it is more accessible for today's audiences. These directors may also film the play outdoors. Instead of indoors on the stage.

Revision for BND 1: (answers may vary, but all sentences should be complete):
A writer of many plays and poems, **W**illiam Shakespeare is considered to be one of the greatest writers in the English language. We usually think of Shakespeare as the writer of tragic plays, **p**lays about murder and unfortunate deaths. However, Shakespeare also wrote plays referred to as the histories and the romances, **as well as** twelve plays which are called the comedies. His plays were very popular in his own time **and were p**erformed at the Old Globe theater. Today, his plays are perhaps most often seen in movie theaters. Some film directors will update the play and set it in modern times, **r**ewriting the plays original language so it is more accessible for today's audiences. These directors may also film the play outdoors, **i**nstead of indoors on the stage.

BND EXERCISE 2   William Shakespeare, who wrote the play *Hamlet*. Was born in England in 1564. The town of his birth was Stratford-on-Avon, and after his death, he was buried there. Little is known about his father, who some biographers say was a merchant. However, Shakespeare's father may also have been a mayor. Although it is not known for certain. It is believed that Shakespeare attended grammar school where he learned to read and write. At the age of 18 he became a husband. When he married Anne Hathaway. We think of Shakespeare as a playwright, but he was also known for his acting. While most people have heard of *Hamlet* and *Romeo and Juliet*. Many of us don't realize that he wrote more than 30 other plays. In addition, he was an accomplished poet. Who wrote some of the greatest sonnets in the English language. Because he wrote plays that are still popular today and wrote poems that are still models for aspiring poets. He is considered one of the greatest writers who ever lived.

Revision for BND 2 (answers may vary, but all sentences should be complete):
William Shakespeare, who wrote the play *Hamlet*, **w**as born in England in 1564. The town of his birth was Stratford-on-Avon, and after his death, he was

buried there. Little is known about his father, who some biographers say was a merchant. However, Shakespeare's father may also have been a mayor **a**lthough it is not known for certain. It is believed that Shakespeare attended grammar school where he learned to read and write. At the age of 18 he became a husband **w**hen he married Anne Hathaway. We think of Shakespeare as a playwright, but he was also known for his acting. While most people have heard of Hamlet and Romeo and Juliet, **m**any of us don't realize that he wrote more than 30 other plays. In addition, he was an accomplished poet**, who** wrote some of the greatest sonnets in the English language. Because he wrote plays that are still popular today and wrote poems that are still models for aspiring poets, **h**e is considered one of the greatest writers who ever lived.

BND EXERCISE 3   One of Shakespeare's outstanding works is *Hamlet*. <u>Which is about a young prince trying to avenge his father's death.</u> The play begins with the ghost of Hamlet's father appearing to Horatio and the sentries on duty. They tell Hamlet about their experience. That night, Hamlet also sees the ghost of his father. <u>Who was the former king of Denmark.</u> The experience that young Hamlet has. <u>Deeply disturbs him.</u> Hamlet discovers that his father was murdered by Hamlet's uncle, Claudius. <u>Who is now the King of Denmark and who has married Hamlet's widowed mother.</u> Hamlet is commanded by his father's ghost to kill Claudius. Although Hamlet seems to know that he must take revenge, he delays. <u>Which leads to the deaths of other characters in the play.</u> It can even be argued that Hamlet's inability to carry out the act of revenge leads to the death of Ophelia. <u>Who was Hamlet's true love.</u> That the play ends on a tragic note. Is a vast understatement. In the final scene, there are four dead bodies sprawled across the stage.

Revision for BND 3 (answers may vary, but all sentences should be complete):

One of Shakespeare's outstanding works is Hamlet, **w**hich is about a young prince trying to avenge his father's death. The play begins with the ghost of Hamlet's father appearing to Horatio and the sentries on duty. They tell Hamlet about their experience. That night, Hamlet also sees the apparition, **w**hich leaves him with a question. Who is the ghost? It could be a demon or could be his father, **w**ho was the former king of Denmark. The experience that young Hamlet has **d**eeply disturbs him. Hamlet discovers that his father was murdered by Hamlet's uncle, Claudius, who is now the King of Denmark and who has married Hamlet's widowed mother. Hamlet is commanded by his father's ghost to kill Claudius. Although Hamlet seems to know that he must take revenge, he delays, **w**hich leads to the deaths of other characters in the play. It can even be argued that Hamlet's inability to carry out the act of revenge leads to the death of Ophelia, **w**ho was Hamlet's true love. That the play ends on a tragic note **i**s a vast understatement. In the final scene, there are four dead bodies sprawled across the stage.

BND EXERCISE 4   <u>Because this play has so many problems.</u> Readers have always argued about Hamlet's character. They can decide whether he is a brave and cautious man.

<u>Or just can't make up his mind. A really indecisive character!</u> Why should we care about a fictional character? Some readers see themselves reflected in characters like Hamlet. <u>Who may seem to have unusual problems, but is very human all the same.</u>

Revision for BND 4 (answers may vary, but all sentences should be complete):

Because this play has so many problems, **r**eaders have always argued about Hamlet's character. They can decide whether he is a brave and cautious man **or** just can't make up his mind. He is a really indecisive character! Why should we care about a fictional character? Some readers see themselves reflected in characters like Hamlet**, w**ho may seem to have unusual problems, but is very human all the same.

BND EXERCISE 5   One of the most interesting characters in the play *Hamlet* is Ophelia, who is Hamlet's love interest. She is often portrayed as a weak-willed person \ she is dominated by her father Polonius. In the beginning of the play, Ophelia tells her father that Prince Hamlet has been expressing his love to her. Polonius tells her that she should ignore Hamlet's vows of love, \ Ophelia obeys him \ she doesn't even protest. Even though she loves Hamlet and wants to see him, she follows her father's orders. Later in the play when Polonius and the king want to spy on Hamlet, she allows herself to be used \ she talks to Hamlet while Polonius and the king hide behind the curtains and listen. After this scene, Hamlet never sees her alive again, \ she is later found dead in a stream. It is said that Hamlet couldn't decide what to do \ Ophelia couldn't stand up for what she wanted.

BND EXERCISE 6   An often overlooked character in the play *Hamlet* is Fortinbras, \ however, he is very important. Hamlet and Fortinbras are in the same situation, \ they have both lost their fathers. At the beginning of the play, we learn that Fortinbras has raised an army and is demanding that Denmark return the lands his father lost. This is Fortinbras' way of avenging his father's death \ Fortinbras is a man of action. Hamlet, like Fortinbras, formulates plans to take revenge for his father's murder \ he delays \ he doesn't act. In the middle of the play, Fortinbras' army is allowed to cross Denmark on its way to do battle with the Poles. Again we see that Fortinbras craves action \ Hamlet, at this point in the play, is being shipped off to England \ he still hasn't taken action against Claudius, his father's murderer. Fortinbras only appears in the play once. In the very last scene, Fortinbras arrives at the castle \ he finds Hamlet dead. The man of action has survived, \ the man of thought has perished.

Revision for BND 6 (answers may vary, but all should be correct sentences):

An often overlooked character in the play *Hamlet* is Fortinbras**;** however, he is very important. Hamlet and Fortinbras are in the same situation **since** they have both lost their fathers. At the beginning of the play, we learn that Fortinbras has raised an army and is demanding that Denmark return the lands his father lost. This is Fortinbras' way of avenging his father's death**. F**ortinbras is a man of action. Hamlet, like Fortinbras, formulates plans to take revenge for his father's murder, **but** he delays **and** he doesn't act. In the middle of the play, Fortinbras' army is allowed to cross Denmark on its way to do battle with the Poles. Again we see that Fortinbras craves action. Hamlet, at this point in the play, is being shipped off to England **although** he still hasn't taken action against Claudius, his father's murderer. Fortinbras only appears in the play once. In the very last scene, **when** Fortinbras arrives at the castle, he finds Hamlet dead. The man of action has survived; the man of thought has perished.

BND EXERCISE 7　Hamlet believes that his mother, Gertrude, has betrayed his father's memory. After the death of King Hamlet, Gertrude marries Claudius. Who is King Hamlet's brother this infuriates Hamlet. Hamlet sees his father as a god, he sees Claudius as a satyr, a creature half goat. Hamlet cannot understand how his mother could so quickly forget his godlike father, therefore he concludes that women are faithless. In addition to feeling betrayed by his mother, Hamlet also feels that Ophelia has betrayed him. At her father's command, Ophelia rejects Hamlet and she returns the letters and gifts he has given her. This sends Hamlet into a rage, it confirms his belief that women are weak and unfaithful.

Revision for BND 7 (answers may vary , but all sentences should be correctly punctuated):

Hamlet believes that his mother, Gertrude, has betrayed his father's memory. After the death of King Hamlet, Gertrude marries Claudius, **w**ho is King Hamlet's brother. This infuriates Hamlet. Hamlet sees his father as a god, **but** he sees Claudius as a satyr, a creature that is half goat. Hamlet cannot understand how his mother could so quickly forget his god-like father; therefore, he concludes that women are faithless. In addition to feeling betrayed by his mother, Hamlet also feels that Ophelia has betrayed him. At her father's command, Ophelia rejects Hamlet and she returns the letters and gifts he has given her. This sends Hamlet into a rage. **I**t confirms his belief that women are weak and unfaithful.

BND EXERCISE 8　Although *Hamlet* is one of Shakespeare's tragedies, it has moments of humor. One of the most humorous scenes takes place in a graveyard, Hamlet has a dialogue with a gravedigger who won't give Hamlet a straight answer. When Hamlet and his friend Horatio enter, they find the gravedigger in the act of digging a grave. Hamlet asks to whom the grave belongs, the gravedigger responds that it is his own grave. Hamlet wants to know who will be buried in the grave, however, the gravedigger's logic is that the one who makes the grave owns the grave. This gravedigger is fond of wordplay he is also fond of riddles. Prior to the arrival of Hamlet and Horatio, the gravedigger has asked his fellow worker who builds stronger than a mason, a shipwright, or a carpenter. His co-worker's answer is good he says a gallows-maker. After all, the man who makes the gallows lives longer than those who find themselves on the gallows. The gravedigger, however, has a better answer. Which he gives to his co-worker. The gravedigger says that a grave maker builds stronger than a mason, a shipwright, or a carpenter, his logic is twisted but sound. The grave you are buried in lasts longer than the house a mason might <u>build, therefore, the grave</u> maker builds the strongest.

Revision for Exercise 8 (answers may vary, but all should be correct sentences):

Although <u>Hamlet</u> is one of Shakespeare's tragedies, it has moments of humor. One of the most humorous scenes takes place in a graveyard **where** Hamlet has a dialogue with a gravedigger who won't give Hamlet a straight answer. When Hamlet and his friend Horatio enter, they find the gravedigger in the act of digging a grave. **When** Hamlet asks to whom the grave belongs, the gravedigger responds that it is his own grave. Hamlet wants to know who will be buried in the grave; however, the gravedigger's logic is that the one who makes the grave owns the grave. This gravedigger is fond of wordplay, **and** he is also fond of riddles. Prior to the arrival of Hamlet and Horatio, the gravedigger has asked his fellow worker who builds stronger than a mason, a shipwright, or a carpenter. His co-worker's answer is good; he says a gallows-maker. After all, the man who makes the gallows lives longer than those who find themselves on the gallows. The gravedigger, however, has a better answer, **w**hich he gives to his co-worker. The gravedigger says that a grave maker builds stronger than a mason, a shipwright, or a carpenter. **H**is logic is twisted but sound. The grave you are buried in lasts longer than the house a mason might build; therefore, the grave maker builds the strongest.

BND EXERCISE 9   Hamlet's negative view of life is in part the result of the betrayals he has <u>experienced. Which</u> leave him with few people to trust. His mother betrayed both King Hamlet and Hamlet <u>by quickly marrying Claudius Ophelia betrayed Hamlet</u> by rejecting his affections. In addition to these betrayals, Hamlet is also betrayed by Rosencrantz and <u>Guildenstern. Who</u> are friends of Hamlet's. Although Hamlet doesn't know it, his two friends are really <u>spying</u> on him for Claudius. Hamlet finds out they are spying <u>on him, therefore, he decides</u> to toy with them. He asks Guildenstern to play <u>a recorder. Which is a wooden</u> flute. Guildenstern says that he doesn't <u>know how to play the instrument, then Hamlet tells</u> his two friends what he thinks of them. Hamlet says that they think they can play him more easily than one can play a flute. This is not however the end of their betrayal. The King has Hamlet sent to England so he can have Hamlet executed. Rosencrantz and Guildenstern <u>accompany Hamlet they are carrying</u> a letter which requests that Hamlet be killed immediately upon his arrival in England. Hamlet <u>changes the letter now it says that Rosencrantz and Guildenstern</u> should be killed immediately. Rosencrantz and Guildenstern pay dearly for the betrayal of their friend.

Revision for Exercise 9 (answers may vary, but all sentences should be correctly punctuated):

Hamlet's negative view of life is in part the result of the betrayals he has experienced **w**hich leave him with few people to trust. His mother betrayed both King Hamlet and Hamlet by quickly marrying Claudius, **and** Ophelia betrayed Hamlet by rejecting his affections. In addition to these betrayals, Hamlet is also betrayed by Rosencrantz and Guildenstern, **w**ho are friends of Hamlet's. Although Hamlet doesn't know it, his two friends are really spying on him for Claudius. Hamlet finds out they are spying on him; therefore, he decides to toy with them. He asks Guildenstern to play a recorder, **w**hich is a wooden flute. Guildenstern says that he doesn't know how to play the instrument. **T**hen Hamlet tells his two friends what he thinks of them. Hamlet says that they think they can play him more easily than one can play a flute. This is not however the end of their betrayal. The King has Hamlet sent to England so he can have Hamlet executed. Rosencrantz and Guildenstern accompany Hamlet. **T**hey are carrying a letter which requests that Hamlet be killed immediately upon his arrival in England. Hamlet changes the letter **so that** now it says that Rosencrantz and Guildenstern should be killed immediately. Rosencrantz and Guildenstern pay dearly for the betrayal of their friend.

END EXERCISE 1   Many single <u>mothers</u> who work have too many <u>responsibilit**ies**</u>—they can't find enough <u>hours</u> in one day to do all the <u>jobs</u> that must be done. Their children need lunch for school, the <u>dish**es**</u> need washing, the car needs gas—all at the same time. No magic will give those <u>mothers</u> the five extra <u>minutes</u> in each hour, but some <u>tricks</u> will help them. <u>Mothers</u> with too many <u>chores</u> can try this: set a timer for fifteen <u>minutes</u> after each meal, and each member of the family must spend those <u>minutes</u> putting away <u>objects</u> that are out of place. Keep a table or a shelf by the door, and put on it all the <u>books</u>, <u>coats</u>, <u>lunchs</u>, keys, and other <u>things</u> that need to be taken when the family leaves.

END EXERCISE 2   Another problem for single mothers' families is keeping the children's rooms neat. When a child's toys are scattered everywhere, children fight about them more often. Is the truck in the living room Renita's or Robert's truck? Is that Lara's paintbrush or her brother's? If the children know each toy's place, they will be more likely to put their toys away.

END EXERCISE 3   Keeping <u>children</u>**'s** clothes clean is yet another problem for single <u>mothers</u>' families. If the laundry is just the <u>mother</u>**'s** job, then she will be washing her <u>family</u>**'s** clothes all day. Each child must learn to be responsible for clothes. If <u>Tara</u>**'s** shirt is dirty, or if her <u>brother</u>**'s** sheets need washing, the children themselves must be sure to put them in the hamper. Each <u>child</u>**'s** room should have a hamper, and it should also be the <u>children</u>**'s** job to put towels in the bathroom hamper.

END EXERCISE 4   What are the most important foods to eat? Whether it's dieters' waistlines or <u>athletes</u>' muscles, many people are trying to change their bodies, but they need to know their <u>bodies</u>' needs. Everybody should eat some foods with protein, some with carbohydrates, some with fats. Your <u>muscles</u>' strength comes from protein—it's found in meats, soybeans, and dairy products. Carbohydrates give us quick energy for the <u>day</u>**'s** work. Carbohydrates are found in bread, candy, alcohol, potatoes, rice, and cereal. Fats store energy to meet your <u>body</u>**'s** needs at any time. Be sure to give your body enough to meet (its) needs. Without any fats, (we'd) be like bunnies without batteries, but we only need a few batteries at a time.

END EXERCISE 5   A student's future may not totally depend on her grad**es**, but grades will help when she looks for jo**bs**, so a course in study skill**s** might make a difference in a student's life. Studen**ts** sometimes don't want to take these cours**es**, because the credits aren't required for degree**s**, but they don't realize that what's most important is having a good GPA. When cred**its** are analyzed at graduation time, a course's grade might be just as important as its credi**ts**.

END EXERCISE 6   When Lisa <u>plants</u> a garden, she always <u>uses</u> lots of fertilizer, just as her mother <u>did</u> when she <u>was</u> a little girl. Her mother <u>told</u> her how to plant, and now Lisa <u>follows</u> that advice. Lisa sometimes <u>buys</u> fertilizer at a discount store but she also <u>gets</u> compost from the city. Last fall the city <u>took</u> all the leaves people <u>had</u> <u>raked</u> and <u>ground</u> them up. Now the compost <u>is</u> ready to use. Each weekend, Lisa <u>spreads</u> the compost on her garden and <u>digs</u> it in. Then she <u>rakes</u> it smooth.

END EXERCISE 7   Sean always <u>takes</u> care of his car. He <u>cleans</u> it every weekend, he <u>changes</u> the oil every three thousand miles, and he <u>takes</u> it for a tune-up every thirty thousand miles. The tires <u>take</u> some of his attention, too, because they <u>need</u> to be rotated often so that they <u>wear</u> evenly. Sean's brother Charles <u>takes</u> care of the tires for him, but he <u>charges</u> Sean a small amount. Rotating the tires <u>takes</u> time and tools, Charles <u>says</u>. Time and tools <u>cost</u> him money, so he <u>wants</u> Sean to pay.

END EXERCISE 8   Computers <u>do</u> exactly what we <u>tell</u> them to do. If we <u>tell</u> a computer to type a letter, the computer <u>types</u> a letter. If we <u>tell</u> a computer to sing a song, it <u>will sing</u> a song. Sometimes when I <u>write</u>, I <u>look</u> back and <u>see</u> that what I <u>have written</u> <u>looks</u> really strange. It <u>looks</u> strange because I <u>told</u> the computer to write in capital letters or italics. Of course the computer <u>did</u> exactly what I <u>told</u> it to do. Sometimes my hands <u>write</u> words that my brain <u>knows</u>, and other times my hands <u>seem</u> to write on their own. It <u>takes</u> time to go back and correct these mistakes, but it <u>saves</u> more time since I just <u>type</u> the corrections, not the whole paper.

END EXERCISE 9   Trying to lose weight <u>has</u> <u>been</u> really confusing. (It also <u>takes</u> a lot of will power, of course.) Some experts <u>were</u> <u>saying</u> that bread <u>makes</u> you fat and others <u>have</u> <u>said</u> that butter and cheese <u>make</u> you fat. My friend <u>was</u> <u>reading</u> a book that <u>says</u> exercise <u>works</u> best. My friends Marla and Rene <u>were</u> <u>trying</u> to run a mile every day, and Mike <u>went</u> with them. Mike <u>has been</u> <u>losing</u> weight by not eating any dessert, because he <u>had</u> <u>heard</u> that sugar <u>makes</u> you fat.

END EXERCISE 10 We sometimes wonder what would have happened if things in history had been different. For example, things might have been safer for everyone if the nuclear bomb had never been invented. Maybe scientists should think more carefully about what will happen to their inventions. An inventor who make**s** a new way to run cars may think she will help the world, but she may really fin**d** that the new invention can kill many people.

END EXERCISE 11 We'd like to think that the invention of medicine was one way to impro**ve** the world. It is certainly better that no child has to catch polio and that no one even has to get a smallpox vaccination any more. But now that fewer people die from infectious diseases, there is not enough room for all of us to liv**e** well. We are going to become even more crowded every year. So even the miraculous inventions of a vaccine to cure a terrible disease can turn out to be a problem no one knows how to sol**ve**.

END EXERCISE 12 Sometimes a <u>person</u> <u>wants</u> (to go) on a trip but do<u>es</u>n't know how (to get) to her destination. Now there <u>is</u> a <u>site</u> on the Internet that <u>tells</u> you how (to get) from one place to another. The <u>traveler</u> <u>has</u> (to type) in the city <u>she</u> <u>is</u> leaving from and the place where <u>she</u> <u>wants</u> (to go). Then the <u>computer</u> <u>tells</u> her what route (to take) and also <u>warns</u> her (to avoid) any delays.

END EXERCISE 13 Yesterday Alicia <u>want**ed**</u> some ice cream, so she <u>borrow**ed**</u> her sister's car. Then she <u>remember**ed**</u> that she also <u>need**ed**</u> some money, so she <u>ask**ed**</u> her sister for money. Her sister <u>laugh**ed**</u>. She <u>want**ed**</u> some ice cream, too, so she <u>call**ed**</u> to Alicia: "When you get to the store, please buy two cones! I want chocolate!" Alicia <u>us**ed**</u> the money for the cones of ice cream. She and her sister <u>lick**ed**</u> the cones while they <u>watch**ed**</u> TV yesterday evening.

END EXERCISE 14 If you <u>have</u> ever <u>us**ed**</u> a car with a manual shift, you must <u>have</u> <u>notic**ed**</u> the clutch. In most cars, clutches <u>are</u> <u>locat**ed**</u> on the floor to the left of the brake pedal. When the clutch <u>is</u> <u>push**ed**</u> in, the driver <u>is</u> able to change gears with the right hand, using a gearshift on the floor. Drivers who <u>are</u> <u>us**ed**</u> to this arrangement <u>are</u> sometimes <u>confus**ed**</u> when they <u>change</u> to an automatic transmission. In these cars, there <u>is</u> no clutch, and the gears <u>are</u> <u>chang**ed**</u> by a gear shift that <u>is</u> <u>locat**ed**</u> on the steering column.

END EXERCISE 15 <u>Did</u> the weather <u>seem</u> warmer this year? <u>Has</u> it <u>rain**ed**</u> as much as it usually <u>does</u>? If you <u>are</u>n't <u>worr**ied**</u> about the icebergs <u>melting</u>, maybe you <u>don't</u> <u>worry</u> about the ocean <u>rising</u> near the beach, either. When the temperature of the water <u>has been</u> <u>raised</u> only a few degrees, the level of the water <u>will have been</u> <u>raised</u> by a few feet. That's not much, but it <u>doesn't</u> <u>take</u> much to make a difference if you <u>live</u> in Miami or Charleston or Boston.

END EXERCISE 16 Have you ever <u>been</u> <u>charg**ed**</u> a lot for medicine? People who (would) <u>pay</u> $50 to see a basketball game <u>will</u> not <u>pay</u> $50 for medicine, <u>will</u> they? Most people <u>say</u> they (would) <u>think</u> about whether they (could) <u>find</u> cheaper medicine, and then they (might) <u>try</u> to wait a few days. If they <u>had</u> <u>learn**ed**</u> about another medicine that they (could) buy, they (would) buy it. If they hadn't asked their doctor for cheaper medicine, they (might) call the office and ask the nurse.

END EXERCISE 17   Why do athletes receive so much money? When a major league pitcher has ~~brung~~ **brought** in as much money as Greg Maddux, the fans have ~~gave~~ **given** him their respect. But other athletes haven't ~~came~~ **come** as far as he has, and they don't deserve the salary he makes.

AGR EXERCISE 1   One ~~of the biggest problems for students~~ **is** finding time to keep ~~in shape. In the morning~~, a student could get up early to run if it is the time ~~of year~~ when mornings are lighted, but ~~in the winter~~ the light ~~of the sun~~ **does**n't appear ~~until almost seven~~. A woman ~~by herself in the darkness~~ has to be a little more careful than usual. ~~After school~~, a student could go ~~to the gym~~, but a student ~~with expenses~~ must work. ~~At night~~, a student ~~with a family~~ make**s** dinner for them, and a student ~~without a family~~ tr**ies** to have a little time to be ~~with her friends~~. Nevertheless, most ~~of the students~~ I know have found some time to get the exercise they nee**d**.

AGR EXERCISE 2   If you want to be healthy, eating and exercising **are** very important subjects to understand. Being a healthy vegetarian requires a little knowledge about the foods your body and your health nee**d**. Protein and iron **are** nutrients you must be sure to have. A milk product and a bean dish usually provid**e** enough protein, but iron is more difficult. A vegetarian often must take an iron supplement.

AGR EXERCISE 3   My friends thin**k** that getting in shape mean**s** getting smaller, period. They don't realize that muscles are healthy and also attractive, even on a woman. Diets and pills **are** a bad way to lose weight, but eating well and exercising are good ways. Even weightlifting can be healthy for a woman. If she **does**n't want big muscles, small weights hel**p** her to be strong. Muscles and bones benefi**t** from weightlifting, because the pressure of the weights makes bones tougher.

AGR EXERCISE 4   Traveling in the summer can be very unpleasant. It can make you want to stay at home forever. Travelers sometimes forget their manners. You have to expect the worst from an airline trip. They can take twice as long as scheduled. When the traveler comes home, he calls the airline to complain, but they don't offer him a refund.

Revision for AGR Exercise 4: Traveling in the summer can be very unpleasant. That experience can make travelers want to stay at home forever. Travelers sometimes forget their manners. They have to expect the worst from an airline trip. It can take twice as long as scheduled. When travelers come home, they call the airline to complain, but the airline doesn't offer them a refund.

CLR EXERCISE 1   Mathabane was embarrassed because his father insisted on wearing tribal ~~cloths~~ **clothes** and his friends referred to him as Tarzan. He wanted to live a modern life like his friends did instead of the traditional ~~weigh~~ **way** of life his father ~~wonted~~ **wanted** him ~~too~~ **to**. My parents always ~~wonted~~ **wanted** me to dress like a nice young man but the ~~cloths~~ **clothes** that were in style when I was a teenager were those jeans with ~~wholes~~ **holes** in the knees. Even though I ~~new~~ **knew** that my parents thought that I looked like a hood in those pants, I would change into my favorite jeans the minute I left the house so I would be dressed the way my friends ~~where~~ **were** when I got to school.

CLR EXERCISE 2 When my brother and I would play basketball, I would always ~~loose~~ **lose** because I was shorter ~~then~~ **than** him and he used to block every shot I tried to make. In fact, he would tease me ~~sense~~ **since** he could just stand ~~their~~ **there** and still reach higher than me even when I jumped as high as I could. But now that I'm taller ~~then~~ **than** he is, I'm the one ~~whose~~ **who's** winning every game. ~~Its~~ **It's** nice to get him back for all those games I ~~loss~~ **lost**.

CLR EXERCISE 3
               S   V
1. (By me working very hard) was able to pull up my grade in math.
   By working very hard, I was able to pull up my grade in math.
               S   V
2. (With them taking care of my children) helped me to have time to study.
   Their taking care of my children helped me to have time to study.
                           S   V
3. (In the textbook for my math class) says that calculators are sometimes necessary.
   The textbook for my math class says that calculators are sometimes necessary.
                          S   V
4. (With two children at home,) I can't always have time for myself.
                     S   V
5. (By knowing about my problems) helped my teacher understand how to help me.
   Knowing about my problems helped my teacher understand how to help me.

CLR EXERCISE 4 Gus said that he'd like to go to the mountains. (answers may vary)

CLR EXERCISE 5 Lara asked Gus when he would be ready to go.

CLR EXERCISE 6 Pollution is everywhere: <u>out in the country,</u> <u>in the city,</u> and <u>also found in our homes.</u> Pollution is caused <u>by manufacturing processeses</u> and <u>we also drive cars,</u> as well as <u>to waste many products.</u> For example, when consumers buy broccoli at the store, the vegetable <u>has a wire around it</u> and <u>in a plastic bag, then puts it in a bigger bag with other vegetables.</u> This makes three different wrappings for the broccoli when one would be enough.

Revision for CLR Exercise 6: Pollution is everywhere: out in the country, in the city, and in our homes. Pollution is caused by manufacturing processes, driving cars, and wasting many products. For example, when consumers buy broccoli at the store, the vegetable has a wire around it, is in a plastic bag, and is also in a bigger bag with other vegetables. This makes three different wrappings for the broccoli when one would be enough.

PUNC EXERCISE 1   On my way home, I passed a group of older women. Since I could see that they were walking slowly, I felt that I should ask if they needed any assistance. One of them thanked me and said she was able to walk but just not very quickly. Although I worried about them, I felt that I needed to get to my destination. When I came back, I saw the same ladies. They had walked just one more block while I had walked five.

PUNC EXERCISE 2   When a single parent is a man, he may have more problems, however, than a woman. My brother, the parent of a three year old, has to work and arrange for child care. With these problems, he's just a like a single mother. In the evening, though, it's hard for him to find another single father to share child care or to trade babysitting jobs. Surprisingly, he doesn't know any other single fathers. He knows single women who have children, but they live far away from him.

PUNC EXERCISE 3   The best rituals in my family were those around holidays, birthdays, and vacations. Those were the times when we cooked special food, visited family, and went on trips. We might visit our cousins, they might visit us, or we might all go to the beach together. When we went to the beach with my older cousin, her favorite rituals were singing silly songs in the car, telling ghost stories, and playing card games in the middle of the night.

PUNC EXERCISE 4   We all react differently to feelings of guilt. Orwell and the prison officials may have felt guilty about hanging the man, but they denied their feelings and hid from them by drinking and joking. Other people may use these same ways to hide from guilt, or they may get angry at the person they have hurt. Admitting that you feel guilty is a difficult thing to do, and many people never can take that step. Thinking about your feelings and your reactions is difficult but necessary.

PUNC EXERCISE 5   The interview with the new governor was really boring, wasn't it? First a reporter asked him if he planned any changes in the next year. He said that he would wait and see what happened. Then another reporter asked, "Will you approve a bill to raise taxes?" The governor replied, "Didn't I just answer that?" Would you listen to an interview as boring as that? Why do the sponsors want to pay for boring news? I just don't get it.

PUNC EXERCISE 6   I found a number of good sources for my paper. I'm going to use a novel called The Scarlet Letter, a story entitled "Where I'm Calling From," and a poem called "My Papa's Waltz." The best book I read was The Firm, but I don't think I'll use that. I might also discuss the movie How Green Was My Valley, or another movie, American Beauty. My little sister used the movie Beauty and The Beast for her project.

PUNC EXERCISE 7   Marla went to visit her **a**unt in Buffalo, New **Y**ork. Aunt Mary told her, "**D**on't expect it to be as warm here as it is in California, but **M**arla thought it would be warm anywhere by **E**aster. She took her **t**ee shirts and plenty of Levis. Her **c**ousins laughed at her idea of warm clothes, and told her, "**Y**ou need to go to the **m**all to get some **really warm c**lothes."

PUNC EXERCISE 8   The capital of the United States is Washington, D.C., and the capital of China is Beijing (Sims 156). Beijing is like Washington is some ways and different in others. Beijing once had emperors who **"**lived in the center of Beijing in a great palace called the Forbidden City**" (Sims 156)**. Washington has the White House and our president lives there now, but the leader of China does not live in the Forbidden City which is now open to all of the people of China (Sims 156). Washington and Beijing both have many museums and restaurants, and in both you might find exotic ethnic foods, elegant cuisine, and streets where **"**Pizza Hut competes with McDonald's**"** (Sims 157).

PUNC EXERCISE 9   (Answers will vary. Students should use quotations and paraphrases from the selection and should punctuate them correctly.)

PUNC EXERCISE 10   A natural disaster in the US occurred recently when "Mt. St. Helens erupted with ashes." We don't expect volcanoes to erupt so suddenly, because they look so peaceful, "like kindly white-haired grandparents." However, we should be afraid of volcanoes which can "spew tons of suffocating ashes."

PUNC EXERCISE 11   1. Some results of volcano eruptions include "suffocating ashes, . . . hot mud, or . . . rivers of lava."

2. Three volcanoes that have erupted recently are "Mt. St. Helens . . . in the United States; Mt. Pinatubo in the Phillipines and Mt. Fako in Cameroon. . . ."

PUNC EXERCISE 12   1. People who live near a volcano should be concerned because the "eruptions [could] destroy all life in the path of the outpouring."

2. Anyone who was climbing a volcano and thought that it was peaceful should have realized that "this [was] deceptive."

ESL EXERCISE 1   Even though **the** United States is one country with **an** official language which is called English, many people speak **a** dialect which means that they use language differently from people in other parts of **the** country. **A** person who lives in **the** North Carolina mountains might not understand **a** person who lives in **a** northern city like New York. Sometimes **the** misunderstanding is funny, but sometimes **a** big problem can result .

ESL EXERCISE 2   When Adam first arrived **at** this college, he insisted **on** buy**ing** new books. He worried **about** having the books because he hoped **for** a good grade in his classes. When he went **to** the bookstore, he looked **at** many books. He didn't want to leave out any of his courses. He listened **to** the salesman explain

about new books and used books, and finally Adam decided **on** the ones he needed to buy. While he stood in line, he met a friend who introduced him **to** another student who wanted to sell his used books.

ESL EXERCISE 3   Many people have difficulty living **in** a climate that is different from their home. They may complain **about** the cold or the heat. If they become ill, they blame their illnesses **on** the climate. They fool **with** the thermostat in their homes. After living in a new climate for several years, they may get used **to** the new climate, and may no longer ask **for** changes in the temperature **of** the office.

ESL EXERCISE 4   Tomorrow we will **be** going to our new apartment. We **own** too much furniture, so we **will hire** a van to help us move. We will **have** worked all day packing things when the van arrives. Last time we were moving, we **tried** to do all the work ourselves. We **have** better judgment this time, even though it **will cost** us more money. However, we **will save** money if the dishes are not **broken** and the chairs **are** not **lost**.

ESL EXERCISE 5   Lee **must hope** to make a high salary, because he will **be** majoring in computer science. He thinks he **ought to** (or **should**) **start** at a salary as high as many people make with several year's experience because he **is going to study** many new aspects of computers. He will be very disappointed if he **receives** a lower salary. He **can** (or **could**) make more than his friends who study art, but they **might enjoy** their work, even if their salaries **are** low.

ESL EXERCISE 6   I **own** a car now, and it **can be** a big responsibility. I **must worry** about gasoline, repairs, and insurance. Because my car **is painted** white, it **gets** dirty very easily. My brother **is teaching** me how to take care of the car. He **drives** to work every day, and he **must park** in a garage, which also **costs** him more money. One day I was driving my car and I **could** hear a terrible sound. I was very worried, but then I saw that the door was open and the seat belt **was dragging** on the road.

The answers for the exercises in Chapter 24 will show all editing corrections, but will not show revisions because those answers vary. Instead, comments will be inserted at appropriate places in each essay that will explain the problem and the type of revision needed.

EXERCISE 24.1   Revision Problem: Relating support paragraphs to thesis

Editing Problem: Sentence Boundaries—fragments

Be Fair to Teens

"Teenagers set off bomb!" "Fifteen-year-old held in shooting!" Headlines such as these appear every day, **s**uggesting that teenagers are violent, angry people. Newspapers make similar judgments about AIDS patients, according to Michael Bronski. In his essay "Magic and AIDS: Presumed Innocent," Bronski shows how media increase prejudice by portraying some victims of AIDS as innocent **and o**thers as guilty. He says that the media's unfair judgment creates problems for everyone, and I agree. I believe that the media is not accurate in many cases.

Sometimes the media make innocent people appear guilty **b**y presenting stereotypes of groups. Bronski shows how the media make it seem that some people deserve AIDS: "Sympathy for people with AIDS has *always* been predicated upon an understanding of how they contracted the virus." TV news also stereotypes teenagers as violent **p**eople who are always involved in crimes. If it's a young person who commits a crime**, t**hat person's age is part of the headline**, w**hether it's a bomb threat or a drive-by shooting. We never see headlines saying, "middle-aged man holds up bank," or "40-year-old woman held in husband's murder." Why is age always mentioned when teenagers are the suspects? To stereotype teens as the media often do is a way of distorting the truth.

But sometimes the media are accurate and fair. **[Revision note: Beginning with this topic sentence, this paragraph covers a topic not mentioned or implied in the thesis, which states clearly that the essay will discuss the media's inaccuracy. The revision should be a new paragraph that shows another aspect of media inaccuracy.]** For example, natural disasters **are reported fairly**. When a hurricane or flood comes, we need the media to tell us about the problem. If we know that a hurricane will come to our city, we can prepare **by s**toring water, buying batteries, and putting up shutters. Even in the case of diseases, Bronski shows how media could help prevent the spread of AIDS **by d**escribing real safety precautions like abstinence, use of condoms, and regular testing**, w**hich is one way that media can be helpful and accurate.

With fair reporting, media can be an asset to the community. Media should focus on being helpful to readers and viewers **b**y giving us real information that we can use to live safer lives. **[Revision note: The conclusion is also not related to the idea of how the media is inaccurate. The revised conclusion should relate to that thesis, even if it also includes these sentences as a final statement.]**

EXERCISE 24.2	Revision Problem: Relating support paragraphs to thesis

Editing Problem: Sentence boundaries: run-ons

Sports and the Media

Once there was a time when children looked at Michael Jordan as a real hero**. E**very kid wanted to "be like Mike!" Athletes like Michael Jordan and Magic Johnson get special treatment from the media, suggests Michael Bronski in "Magic and AIDS: Presumed Innocent." **When** Bronski focuses on athletes like Magic Johnson, he misses the media's unfavorable pictures of other athletes like Mike Tyson and Charles Barkley, who are shown to be as violent as anyone. I don't think the media always distorts when it describes athletes**. I**t actually shows us many views of athletes, both good and bad.

The media may sometimes give extra credit to a well-known athlete as they did when Michael Jordan left baseball and returned to basketball**.** Fans and media alike were so happy for his return that there was no criticism**;** they only praised him. Also, Bronski shows how media immediately began to portray Magic as an innocent victim of bad women with AIDS. **T**hey didn't focus on Magic's own irresponsible actions of having unsafe, promiscuous sex. However, other athletes are shown as bad by the media. Mike Tyson and Pete Rose both committed crimes. Few papers sympathized with Tyson against the charge of rape**. M**any sportscasters criticized Rose for gambling. **[Revision note: This paragraph fits the thesis, which states that the essay will show how the media portray athletes realistically. Linking the final example to that thesis will help the reader to follow the argument more easily.]**

But why should we expect sports heroes to be wonderful people? **[Revision note: This topic sentence shows that this paragraph is not going to focus on the thesis idea of the media's accuracy, but will begin a new topic, unrealistic expectations for athletes' morality. The revision should show another aspect of the media's portraying athletes accurately rather than idealizing them.]** Michael Jordan was hired because he was a good basketball player, not because he was such a good person. Many people live moral, honest lives**;** for example, my father always worked hard and defended his country in the Vietnam War**, b**ut my father isn't famous because he can't help a team win the NBA championship. Charles Barkley was another famous basketball player **who** was often criticized for rough playing. He asked why we expect basketball players to be good role models just because they are good at sports. Bronski says that "media declared Johnson...the new hero of the AIDS epidemic.**" D**oes it make sense to call him a hero and a role model just because he's a good ball player?

So the media isn't really unfair to athletes, **because** we see descriptions of both good and bad people as athletes, not just a distorted picture of one kind of person. The media does not stereotype athletes.

EXERCISE 24.3

Revision Problem: Relating support paragraphs to thesis

Editing Problem: Sentence boundaries—fragments and run-ons

Be Fair

Do the media distort the truth? Bronski, in "Magic and AIDS: Presumed Innocent," says that the media are unfair to AIDS victims **b**y classifying them as "innocent" and "guilty." He shows how some famous people were considered "innocent" while others were "guilty**.**" I agree that the media often makes unfair judgments.

The media do judge AIDS victims unfairly. Bronski describes how gays and drug users are blamed for contracting AIDS, **while** other people with the disease, like Kimberly Bergalis, are seen as being innocent victims. Bronski says that media "distinguish between those people with AIDS who are morally culpable for their illness and those who 'truly' deserve sympathy and compassion." This is an accurate statement**.** I've seen this happen in my own family **w**hen my cousin contracted AIDS. Because he might have gotten the disease from drug use, some people in my family thought he was a bad person**. T**hey never visited him or helped him in any way. But we didn't really know how he got AIDS, so they weren't being fair **t**o treat him as a guilty person.

If we don't know about a person's life, we shouldn't judge them for being sick. **[Revision note: This topic sentence indicates that this paragraph will not be related to the idea in the thesis which states that the essay will show how the media makes unfair judgments. The revision should offer a new paragraph, focusing on another aspect of the media's unfair judgments.]** There are many ways to get AIDS, **i**ncluding blood transfusions and other things. Maybe my cousin had not gotten AIDS from drug use. We should not have blamed him when he needed our help**.** **I**nstead we should have brought him food, medicine, and moral support **a**s some members of the family tried to do. As Bronski says, we shouldn't put AIDS patients into categories, **e**specially if we don't know how they got the disease.

So I do agree that the media is unfair **i**n the way that it stereotypes and categorizes AIDS patients. I hope everyone will realize that AIDS patients need all the sympathy and support we can give them, **w**ithout worrying about how they got the disease. "All people with AIDS Are Innocent" is a good slogan from ACT UP, according to Bronski**.** **W**e should all accept it.

EXERCISE 24.4

<u>Revision Problem:</u> Paragraph unity and difference

<u>Editing Problem:</u> Verbs ending: *–s*

All Alone?

You're nineteen, you've just graduated from high school, and you're not married. Now you discover that you're pregnant. Will you be able to raise your child on your own? "No," says Teresa McCrary, author of "Getting Off the Welfare Carousel." She believe**s** that an uneducated parent must have government assistance. I agree that welfare is necessary for single parents who **are** young and alone.

First of all, a young, single parent who is uneducated will need to continue their education to be able to get a good job in the future. This mean**s** attending college, and while the parent is in class, who will car**e** for the child? The parent also ha**s** to do homework, because college is much more difficult than high school. **[Revision note: At this point, the paragraph changes focus. The topic sentences leads the reader to expect a paragraph about problems encountered when trying to be a student and a parent at the same time. From this point on, the paragraph begins to focus on the difficulty of college alone. The revision should clearly link these ideas to the problems of being a parent while being a student.]** You really nee**d** to be dedicated and give your whole attention to college, because instructors expec**t** you to do work for every class. You may have to read several chapters of economics, work ten hard math problems, and write an English paper in one evening.

Also, a single parent ha**s** many expenses, and often can't afford to do everything without some assistance from welfare. But welfare ha**s** too many rules and really tr**ies** to hold people back. Welfare expects the parent to report any gifts or family assistance, including money from the child's father, according to McCrary. Welfare need**s** to be more realistic, because children nee**d** both parents to grow up happy and healthy. **[At this point, the paragraph leaves**

the idea expressed in the topic sentence, which focuses on financial problems of being a single parent. The rest of this paragraph changes to the idea of demands on the parent's time. The revision should continue to discuss financial problems of being a single parent.] A mother has to be both mother and father, and that's not easy. She has to do a lot of schoolwork and still have time to play with the children and help them with their homework. That is not easy.

Last of all, minimum wage jobs don't pay enough to live. As McCrary says, when people make minimum wage, "the whole paycheck would go to housing and job expenses," and it is very hard not to be able to buy your baby all the things she needs and also not to buy the things you need for yourself. My advice is to wait until you are married or have a well-paying job before you have children. **[Revision note: Here the paragraph moves away from the idea of not being able to live on a minimum wage salary. Instead, it begins to discuss ways to avoid becoming a single parent. The revision should continue to discuss the problems of living on the salary from a minimum wage job.]** You should not get involved with boys if you are not ready to be a parent. It is hard for a young woman because there is a lot of peer pressure to be popular, but she has to be strong and respect herself. She can't let her boyfriend talk her into having sex if she doesn't feel ready.

In conclusion, single mothers can't raise children without welfare. It's too hard to work, go to school, and be a parent, so some government assistance is necessary.

EXERCISE 24.5	Revision Problem: Paragraph unity and difference
	Editing Problem: Verb endings: *-ed*

You Can Do It!

Raising a child is very difficult for a parent, especially one who must work or attend school. It's even more difficult for parents who are unmarried. Teresa McCrary, in " Getting Off the Welfare Carousel," says that government assistance is required for young single mothers to be good parents. Perhaps this is true, but I believe that it is possible to be a good single parent without relying on welfare.

The first requirement for survival as a single parent is a stable income. McCrary says that single parents "could hold down a minimum wage job, inarguably the hardest work for the least amount of money," with no medical benefits, but not all jobs have these problems. When I graduated from high school, I already had been working for the same company for a year in retail sales, and I was promoted to supervisor, which gave me higher pay, regular working hours, and medical benefits. When I realized that I was pregnant, I was afraid I would lose my job, but I only missed six weeks at work. Fortunately my aunt and my grandmother helped me financially, so I was able to survive without welfare until I returned to work. **[Revision note: This paragraph concerns the topic of avoiding welfare by having and keeping a job that pays well. With this sentence, the paragraph begins to include an idea that will be the topic of the next paragraph: family assistance instead of governmental aid. In the revision,**

this paragraph should focus only on relying on a job rather than welfare.] With a good job and family support, I did not nee**d** government assistance.

A single parent does need assistance, but it can come from family instead of the government. McCrary points out that "those of us who do not have a man in our lives do the job of both mother and father." **[Revision note: The beginning and end of this paragraph suggest a focus on financial support from family instead of government, but this sentence and the ones following are related to emotional support. The revision should maintain the focus on financial support.]** The government cannot give emotional assistance but your family can. When I was feeling lonely and sad because I want**ed** to go out and buy nice clothes, my aunt help**ed** by giving me some money to buy a new coat. I was really worr**ied** about being able to meet all my expenses, but my grandmother also helped. She cover**ed** the rent after the baby was born. My family was always ready to help me when I needed them. I will never forget how they all assist**ed** me, and it seem**ed** much better to me because it didn't come from the government.

So McCrary was wrong when she claim**ed** that single parents must rel**y** on government assistance. If a parent has good family support, they will not requir**e** welfare to be able to suppor**t** the child and raise it well.

Revision Problem: Paragraph unity

Editing Problem: Word endings: –'s and –s

Welfare and Single Parents

Can single parent**s** raise a child well without the government**'s** assistance? In my experience, that**'s** a very hard thing to do. In Teresa McCrary**'s** essay, "Getting Off the Welfare Carousel," she explains why single parents may need welfare to be good parent**s**. This is true. Single parent**s** must have some assistance to be able to raise a child well, and many times it**'s** the government that must provide assistance.

A single parent who is young and alone will have a very hard time. **[Revision note: This paragraph begins with an unclear focus, so the rest of the paragraph seems to wander without making a clear point related to the thesis, which led the reader to expect body paragraphs supporting the idea that government assistance is necessary. The revision should develop a clearly focused topic sentence that is related to the need for governmental assistance.]** There are so many problem**s** to face. McCrary says that a minimum wage job "will not pay for housing costs, health care, child care, transportation, and work clothes that an untrained, uneducated woman needs to support even one child." My friend**'s** situation was similar to McCrary**'s**. Anna was a young single mother and at first she didn't want to tell her parents that she was pregnant. Anna**'s** parent**s** had always expected her to be a good student. She was in the church choir and she knew that her parent**s** would be disappointed with her. When she heard about Anna**'s** pregnancy, her mother cried, but then her mother and father told her that she could bring the baby to live at the parents' house. She had a very hard time with the baby**'s** birth and almost died, but the doctor**s** did a C-section. When we found out that she'd be all right, we were so happy. We loved the baby when we saw it**s** face. It**'s** times like this that let you know who your friends are. But then the next problem was that the baby**'s** father wouldn't give her any money, because he wasn't sure that it was his baby. So then my friend had to apply for welfare, but then her baby's father changed his mind.

Also single parents have many lonely feelings. **[Revision note: The problems in this paragraph are the same as those in the previous one. The revision of this paragraph should have a clear focus on one aspect of the need for governmental assistance.]** My friend was used to going out with her friends every weekend. Of course she should have been more careful and used birth control, so she wouldn't have gotten pregnant. However, some teenager**s** use birth control and get pregnant anyway. That**'s** why some people think teenagers should not have sex, and I agree. You can't tell when you might become pregnant. McCrary says that a single parent has to be both mother and father and I agree that government assistance is necessary.

So there are very many problem**s** for young single parents, including money and emotions. For these reasons, the government**'s** assistance is necessary, especially for young mothers who can't raise a child alone. The child**'s** welfare is the most important thing.

EXERCISE 24.7	<u>Revision Problem:</u> Paragraph unity and difference
	<u>Editing Problem:</u> Word endings

The Successful Single Parent

Diaper**s**, babysitter**s**, doctor**s**, clothe**s**—there are so many expense**s** for a parent. If the parents **are** young and single, they may not believ**e** that they can manage these expense**s** all alone. Teresa McCrary, in "Getting Off the Welfare Carousel," says, "Any mother, married or single, will tell you that motherhood is a career in itself." I agree that raising a child alone is difficult, but it**'s** not necessary for every single parent to ha**ve** government assistance. If the parent**s** use all the resources available to them, then they won't need to depen**d** on welfare.

Many necessit**ies** of life are expensive, but if a parent tr**ies**, she can often choose a cheaper alternative. Using baby formula is a very costly way to fee**d** a baby, but breastfeeding is free, and it**'s** better for the baby**'s** health. For older children**'s** dinner**s**, a dinner at McDonald**'s** cost**s** $5.00 per child, and a frozen dinner cost**s** $3.00, but vegetable soup can be prepare**d** at home for about $1.00 per child, especially if big pots **are** cook**ed** and frozen for later use. Clothes can be bought on sale, pass**ed** down from friend**s**, or bought at second-hand store**s**—sometimes these are just as good as new one**s**. The library**'s** books **are** free, and the child will remember an hour spent with the parent reading *The Cat in the Hat* long after he forget**s** the latest Pokemon or computer game. McCrary say**s** that a single parent can't meet all the expense**s**, but a parent who**'s** careful can tak**e** care of a child on very little money.

It**'s** also difficult to manage the responsibility of raising a child if a parent**'s** alone. As McCrary say**s**, sick children **are** a real problem for a working parent, because most day care**s** and schools don't wan**t** sick children. All parents can pla**n** ahead for their children**'s** normal childhood diseases and use family, friends, church, and community as back-up childcare. Parent**s** can get to know other single parents who**se** working hours are different so that they can trade babysitting for emergencies. The parent will know that the child ha**s** received good care and met many different kind**s** of people. The paren**t** also feels less lonely and isolate**d**. **[Revision note: This paragraph focuses on both emotional and financial aspects of managing a sick child without relying on welfare. A concluding sentence in the paragraph would make clear how the two are related.]**

The worst proble**m** for single parents is facing the future. A young parent can become discourage**d** if she work**s** at a low-paying job and comes home to face a parent's responsibilities alone. Life seem**s** to be a trap or a cycle without an end. It'**s** true that with the government's assistance, a parent can go to college full time to prepare for a new career and improve her children'**s** future. McCrary's essay describe**s** how she uses her time to be a good parent; she go**es** to college to be educate**d** so she eventually won't need to be on welfare. But many parent**s** also tak**e** one or two courses at a time when the children **are** in school. Many college**s** now offers courses on the Internet or on videotape, so parents actually tak**e** the whole course at home. Babysitting can be easier to arrange if a parent takes a class that meet**s** only once a week, and some colleges offer cheap daycare for student'**s** children. **[In this paragraph also, the focus on being independent of governmental assistance while getting an education needs to be emphasized by a clear concluding sentence.]**

Not every single parent **is** ready for working hard and making sacrifice**s**. Just being a responsible parent is a big enough challenge for some young parents. However, for those who really want independence, it'**s** possible to be a good parent without governmental assistance. Parent**s** who aren't assist**ed** by the government ha**ve** to plan carefully, but they can succeed.

EXERCISE 24.8

Revision Problem: Paragraph development

Editing Problem: Pronoun and verb agreement

My Successful Career

Success—what do**es** it mean? In "Measuring Success," Renee Loth says that "fame and money" is what success mean**s** to her, but I think **success is** having a good career. **[Revision note: This introduction has the elements of a good introduction, but each is mentioned briefly. A good revision will offer a more intriguing lead-in, a clearer summary of the author's ideas, and a fuller statement of the thesis.]**

First a good career is one that's meaningful, not just a job. **A job** is just a way to make money, but a career really means something to you. **[Revision note: The writer's ideas are stated, but not developed with explanation or examples and details. No connection to the reading is offered, although the idea is also discussed in Loth's essay. A good revision would develop this point fully.]**

Second, a good career is secure. You know you can feel sure about it. Loth says you change and things change. I don't want a bad change to happen, like losing my career. One of the things I want to accomplish **is** having security. **[Revision note: In this paragraph also, the writer's ideas are not developed** with explanation or examples and details, nor is the reference to the read-ing explained and illustrated. In the revision, examples, details, quota-tions, and explanations should be included to support the main ideas.]

Third, a good career is suited to me. I want a job that's right for me, and I'm willing to wait and look for **it**. I don't want to settle for a job that's not the best one for my abilities. **[Revision note: Once more, the paragraph should be revised to develop the writer's ideas and include material from the read-ing, if appropriate.]**

So success to me means having employment that is really a meaningful ca-reer, not just a job. Having a career that's meaningful, secure, and suited to me **is** my idea of success. **[Revision note: The conclusion is also very brief, and needs more complete development by summarizing or other technique.]**

EXERCISE 24.9	Revision Problem: Paragraph development
	Editing Problem: Confused words

Success is a Family

According to Loth, "success.... means different things to different peo-ple." I have a clear idea of success. To me, success would be having a loving family. . **[Revision note: This introduction has some of the elements of a good introduction, but only briefly, and the lead-in is missing, while con-nections and explanations of the ideas needed to be made clear. A good re-vision will offer a more intriguing lead-in, a clearer summary of the au-thor's ideas, and a fuller statement of the thesis.]**

Whatever job I may have, even if I'm a star basketball player like Michael Jordan or a rich computer genius like Bill Gates, I ~~want~~ **won't** feel successful if I'm lonely. I'd need my wife ~~too~~ **to** share my success if I make money or become well known. If I'm poor and unknown, a loving wife would change failure to success. My wife can laugh at my jokes, eat the ~~hole~~ **whole** ~~diner~~ **dinner** that I cook, and somehow ~~no~~ know when I'm tired or sick. I don't know what I would ~~of~~ have done without her, but life would be ~~to~~ **too** hard. There are times also when she shares her own success with me, so when she gets a raise or gets pro-moted, I feel good, too. She and I do things together, like collecting food for a church project or going to the mountains for a walk. We ~~where~~ **were** meant ~~too~~ **to** be together. My wife is the first ~~peace~~ **piece** of my success. **[Revision note: This paragraph does a good job of developing the idea using the writer's ex-perience. However, since the idea of the paragraph, that love is more im-portant than financial success, is one that Loth also discusses, the revision should add development that quotes, summarizes, or paraphrases Loth's ideas on the topic.]**

We ~~all ready~~ **already** have one son and plan to have another child soon. If my children grow up healthy and happy, I'll have another big part of my suc-cess. If ~~your~~ **you're** like me, you'll know that children can make you a ~~knew~~ **new** person. I've really changed myself since my son was born so that I'll be ready to help him as he grows up. Whenever I feel like being lazy at work or going to a party instead of studying for an exam at school, I think about the things I want to do for my son and I'm ready to work hard. Thanks to him, I ~~past~~ **passed** all my ~~coarses~~ **courses** this semester. I want to be able to send my children to college and I want to ~~here~~ **hear** them say they admire me. If I can do these things for them, I'll be a real success. . **[Revision note: This paragraph also does a good job of developing the idea using the writer's experience, but again does not include discussing of Loth's use of the same ideas. Since the idea of the paragraph, that love and health are more important than financial success, is one that Loth also discusses, the revision should add development that quotes, summarizes, or paraphrases Loth's ideas on the topic.]**

So money, fame, and other things may make some people feel successful, but for me, success is my family. Everything I do is for them. ~~There~~ **They're** my ~~hole~~ **whole** life. . **[Revision note: This conclusion also does not refer to any of the ideas that Loth also discusses. The revision should add development that summarizes or paraphrases Loth's ideas on the topic as well as the author's response to her ideas, and should give her credit.]**

EXERCISE 24.10   Revision Problem: Paragraph development

Editing Problem: Punctuating titles and quotations

Make Mine Money

Some people may think of success as being famou**s** for their accomplishments, and others may think that it's being an important executive or politician. Renee Loth, in "Measuring **S**uccess," says that her own ideas of success have changed. As I grow older, my ideas may also change, but right now I know what success means to me. It's money. I'll feel successful when I'm really rich.

Loth says "success is defined differently by different people." She also says that wealth is superfluous if it goes beyond being able to take care of your family and "hav**[ing]** something left over for airfare to someplace sub-tropical in January." She obviously has a different idea about being wealthy. She doesn't really feel the need to be rich. **[Revision note: This paragraph gives a good report of Loth's ideas, but it does not tell us anything about the writer's ideas. The revision should include examples, details, and explanations about the writer's need to be rich.]**

According to Loth, "The trouble with struggling and searching is that it keeps us in a permanent state of wanting—always reaching for more." I don't see what's wrong with wanting more. **[Revision note: Again, the writer has not given any explanations or details about his own desire to be rich. The revision should develop his ideas fully.]** As Loth says, "The drive to succeed keeps us focused on the future. Wanting to have more in the future is important, and my desire to be wealthy causes me to put forth effort in the present." **[Revision note: The use of the reading is not very effective either. The unexplained and unconnected quotations need to be revised and presented with some comment from the writer. Summary or paraphrase can be as helpful as quotations.]**

Loth tells how she "disliked fame when **[she]** finally achieved it. It was downright scary." She doesn't tell how the money she earned affected her, but

I don't think I'll be disappointed. I believe I'd know how to use my money if I ever became rich. **[Revision note: The writer still has not given any explanations or details about his plans for using his money when he becomes rich. The revision should develop his ideas fully.]**

I realize that I may change in many ways as I grow older, but I don't expect to lose sight of my most important goal. I hope I'll be healthy and happy, but I won't really feel that I'm a success until I'm really wealthy. For me, there are no real qualities of success that live outside of wealth. . **[Revision note: The writer should refer to Loth's ideas as well as his own in the conclusion since he has used her so extensively.]**

EXERCISE 24.11

Killing is Wrong

I have never ~~saw~~ **seen** a person die. I hope I never will. But when I read George Orwell**'s** description of an execution in "A Hanging," I realized that I also never ~~won't~~ **want** to be responsible for another person**'s** death**, e**ven if that person ha**s** commit**ted** a terrible crime. Though Orwell never state**s** his position on the death penalty, his story leaves little doubt that he would oppose it**.** I too believe that we have ~~know~~ **no** right to take a life **f**or any reason.

Many people argue for the death penalty on the ground**s** that it will prevent murders of other people. Yet is there any logical reason to think that this would be true**?** If the death penalty really deterred criminals, ~~they're~~ **there** should be no murders in states with the death penalty **l**ike South **C**arolina and Texas. Yet hardly a week go**es** by without a murder being report**ed** in the newspaper. Just this morning while I drove to school, I heard of a woman**'s** body being found in an abandon**ed** trailer in South Carolina and a gunman shooting several people at an office in Texas**. C**learly these murderer**s** did not car**e** about the death penalty.

However, Orwell do**es** not discuss execution as a possible deterrent ~~too~~ **to** crime. He is more concern**ed** with the effect that the execution ha**s** on the executioners. He tell**s** how he went to drink and laugh with the guards after the execution**, e**ven though he had earlier "realized the mystery, the unspeakable wrongness, of cutting a life short when it is in full tide." Reading this passage made me think that I too am often doing the same thing. **I am e**njoying myself at the same time that a person is being execute**d** ~~hear~~ **here** in my state. I care nothing for the person**'s** life. As a citizen of the state, I ~~two~~ **too** am really a ~~peace~~ **piece** of the execution. So I am like Orwell, **b**linding myself to the realitie**s** of what I am doing. Like Orwell, I **don't** have the power to stop the execution, but now I think that I should have been more aware of what**'s** happening and what the government do**es** in my name. Now I think I should pa**y** attention when my government class discuss**es** constitutional right**s and t**ry to listen when the news report on trials, so that I**'m** not jus**t** acting like the guards at the end of Orwell's essay.

We could find many arguments in favor of **capital punishment**, but one of the strongest argument**s** against it seem**s** to be the one that Orwell makes. He show**s** us that execution may not stop a crime, **but** it is a crime.

EXERCISE 24.12

The Right Thing to Do

When we read an essay like "A Hanging" by George Orwell, our first reaction is sympathy with the prisoner**.** **W**e se**e** many reasons to care for him because Orwell show**s** him as powerless and pathetic. **S**howing only the appealing side of the prisoner makes the reader believe that killing him is wrong. But perhaps if we ~~new~~ **knew** the whole story**,** **we'd** know that~~,~~ the execution was the right punishment for this criminal. I understan**d** Orwell**'s** reaction to the execution, but I **can't** agree with him. I believe that some crime**s** should be punish**ed** **b**y deat**h.**

Orwell make**s** the prisoner appealing by showing that he prays when he know**s** that death is near. **Orwell tells us that** "when the noose was fixed, the prisoner began crying out to his god." His belief cause**d** him to call for help, but my belief say**s** that crimes should be punish**ed.** "An eye for an eye," says the Bible**. A** criminal should be willing to suffer in the same way that he makes other people suffer. We don't know what crime the **prisoner** in Orwell's essay commit**ted**, but in this country, it would ~~of~~ **have** been murder. **If he** ~~He~~ ha**s** taken a life, he should pay by giving his life.

We ha**ve** ~~too~~ **to** think about the victim. Orwell makes us think about the prisoner when he tells detail**s** such as the fact that ~~his~~ **the prisoner's** cell is "like a small animal cage," and that he has "a shaven head and vague liquid eyes." He seems very real. Orwell's horror at the man**'s** death is easy to see. "He and we were a party of men walking together, seeing, hearing, feeling, understanding the same world; and in two minutes, with a sudden snap, one of us would be gone—one mind less, one world less." But Orwell do**es** not give us any information about the victim of the crime. If this man is a murderer, **h**is victim also use**d** to be a live person with a mind and feeling, like him—did **the prisoner** sto**p** ~~too~~ **to** think about the victim**'s** feelings when he committed the murder? Maybe his victim was a child, who had big brown eyes **and** liked to play with his kitten. Maybe his victim**'s** parents where poor and lonely. I'd like to ask if we might **have** react**ed** differently if we knew about the victim as well as the prisoner.

Finally, we ha**ve** ~~too~~ **to** think about the purpose of execution**. It's** intended to prevent crime. Orwell ha**s** not told us much about the time or place, so we can't know what crimes were common ~~than~~ **then**. But if we look at our present time, with **s**choolyard shooting**s** and airplane bombings**, w**e know that many of **the perpetrators don't** care what happens to them. That's why we ha**ve** to make it impossible for them ever to commit another crime. If we just pu**t** them in jail**, t**hey could eventually be free to continue their crimes. Just last week I read of a man who return**ed** home to kill his wife only a month after being release**d** from prison for beating her**. E**xecution is the only certain way to make sure these criminals never kil**l** again.

Orwell is a good writer, but his one-sided description of this event could mak**e** a person agree that execution is wrong. **I've** thought about the things Orwell ha**s** told us and the things he ha**s**n't told us and I've decide**d** that I do not share his reaction**. I** believe that execution is sometimes necessary and right.

Glossary

Abstract—referring to something that can not be seen, touched, or directly experienced. The opposite is **concrete.** For example, *bicycle* is concrete; *transportation* is abstract.

Academic reading/writing—work done for college classes or other scholarly purposes.

Action words—words in a prompt that indicates what the student has to do to successfully complete the assignment. Also called key action word.

Active reading—reading in which the reader pays close attention to the ideas, evidence, tone, and strategies an author uses as well as to his or her own thoughts and emotional reactions to the written piece.

Active voice—verb in which the subject does the action of the verb. For example, in the sentence *I broke the window,* the verb *broke* is active voice since the subject *I* did the action.

Annotation—notes made in the margin of a reading.

APA—documentation style issued by the American Psychological Association, used primarily in the social sciences such as psychology, sociology, and linguistics.

Argument—reasons and evidence presented to support a position, but without intending the audience to change its actions or attitudes. Similar to persuasion.

Argumentative writing—writing which presents reasons and evidence to support a position, but without intending the audience to change its actions or attitudes. Similar to persuasion.

Article—word used to specify a noun (*a, an, the*).

Audience—the readers of a piece of writing.

Auxiliary verb—the word in a verb phrase that may affect tense, aspect, or voice. For example, in the verb *will learn,* the auxiliary verb is *will.* Also called a helping verb.

Body—the middle portion of an essay, between the **introduction** and **conclusion,** that contains the main ideas and support for the thesis.

Body paragraph—a paragraph in an essay which contains a main idea and development (examples and explanations) that supports the thesis.

Cause and Effect—organization in which the writer discusses the reasons for or the results of an event.

Chronological organization—organization in which the order is based on a time sequence.

Citation—information about a source used in a piece of writing, giving the source of words or ideas. This information allows others to find it or judge its reliability.

Classification—organizing information into groups and categories in order to show the relationships, differences, connections, and associations among them.

Cluster map—a visual depiction of ideas in which related ideas are joined by circles or lines.

Clustering—making a cluster map.

Collaboration—working with others.

Collocations—words that are customarily used with other words; synonyms for the words can not be substituted into the phrase. For example, *pay the bill* can not be changed to *spend the bill* even though *pay* and *spend* have the very similar meanings.

Colloquial communication—communication intended for an audience the speaker or writer knows well and who does not expect formality or correctness in the communication. An example of colloquial communication is a letter to a friend.

Collusion—accepting or providing help on a piece of writing that incorporates the ideas or words of the helper without proper documentation.

Comma splice—grammatical error in which two complete sentences are joined by a comma.

Compare and contrast—to explore the similarities and differences among related items.

Comprehension—understanding what one is reading.

Conclusion—the last section of an essay which typically summarizes the main idea of the essay.

Concrete—refers to a thing or event that can be directly experienced (seen or touched). The opposite of concrete is **abstract.**

Connecting word—coordinating conjunction or word that connects the previous part of the sentence to the next part of the sentence (*and*, *but*, *or*, *nor*, *for*, *yet*). For example, in the sentence *I told you when I left*, the word *when* is a connecting word.

Connotation—the emotional meaning of a word that goes beyond the dictionary definition; ideas or feelings associated with a word. For example, the dictionary may list *strong-willed* and *stubborn* as having the same definitions, but *stubborn* has the connotation of being negative, while *strong-willed* is positive.

Context—the parts of a reading that surround a word, phrase, or sentence and can make the meaning of that word, phrase or sentence clearer.

Count noun—name of things that can be counted.

Critical reading—reading analytically. This type of reading includes separating emotional reactions from intellectual ones, understanding ideas presented in a reading, applying these ideas to other situations, recognizing the techniques used by the writer, and evaluating the writer's logic.

Critical thinking—thinking analytically. This type of thinking includes separating emotional reactions from intellectual ones, understanding new ideas, applying ideas to different situations, recognizing the techniques used to present the ideas, and evaluating logic.

Critique—(v) to discuss what a writer attempts to do and how well he or she does it; (n) discussion of what a writer attempts to do and how well he or she does it.

Definite article—the article *the*; it specifies the noun that follows. For example, *the dog* means only one specific dog.

Denotation—the dictionary definition of a word.

Descriptive writing—writing that puts into words how something looks, appears, or acts.

Determiner—like an article; specifies a particular noun or a general one.

Development—clarifying ideas with examples and explanations.

Direct quote—repeated words spoken or written by another exactly as they were originally used.

Documentation—the identification of words or ideas used by a writer or speaker and the source where the words or ideas were found.

Draft—version of a written document.

Drafting—step in the writing process in which the writer produces the first version of a written document.

Editing—a step in the writing process in which the writer makes the writing correct, ensuring that it follows the rules of written English. Editing usually includes making changes in grammar and usage, punctuation, and spelling.

Editing log—a written record of grammar, punctuation, and spelling errors kept by a writer to help him or her learn to recognize, correct, and prevent the errors he or she most commonly makes.

End notes—notes published at the end of a piece of writing to identify a source of information or provide additional information.

ESL—English as a Second Language.

Essay—a format for writing characterized by an introduction which contains a thesis (or point the writer is trying to make) supported by main ideas presented in separate paragraphs and a conclusion.

Evocative description—description which emphasizes the emotional aspects of the subject to create a vivid impression.

Example—a specific thing presented to demonstrate what is true about other similar things.

Exemplification—writing that uses extended examples as its major form of development.

Explanation—information given to make an idea or example clear and understandable.

Flowchart—a diagram that shows steps that should be taken to complete a process.

Focus words—words in a prompt that point you to specific ideas or issues you are to write about; also called key focus words.

Focused freewriting—type of prewriting in which the writer focuses on one idea and records whatever comes to mind about that idea without regard for correctness.

Footnote—notes published at the bottom of a page to identify a source or provide additional information.

Formal writing/communication—writing intended for an audience who expects standard forms and correctness. Job resumes and research papers are examples.

Format—the placement and presentation of an essay on paper. Format may include line spacing, margins, page numbering, and running headers.

Fragment—part of a sentence punctuated as if it were a whole sentence; also called a sentence fragment.

Fragment word—word used to join two sentences which causes a sentence fragment if the two sentences are not joined. These words are also called subordinating conjunctions or relative pronouns.

Freewriting—type of prewriting in which the writer records whatever comes to mind without regard for relevance or correctness.

Fused sentence—grammar error in which two sentences are written as though they are one with no punctuation mark separating them. Also known as a **run-on sentence.**

Grammar—the rules that govern how sentences can correctly be constructed.

Grammar checker—program in a word processor that indicates possible grammar problems and suggests corrections.

Hanging indent—a group of lines of text in which the first line is flush with the margin and each additional line is indented. (The entries in this glossary are all formatted with hanging indents.).

Helping verb—the word in a verb that may show tense, aspect, or voice, but that does not carry the meaning of the verb. For example, in the verb *will learn*, the helping verb is *will*. Also called an auxiliary verb.

Hypothetical example—example that is made up by the author and clearly presented as fiction.

Idea tree—a diagram that shows a hierarchy of ideas (like an outline).

Idiom—combinations of words which have meanings that are different from the meaning of the individual words. For example, the phrase "to throw light on" means to make the meaning clearer, not to physically toss light.

Indefinite article—*a* or *an*; this type of article does not refer to a specific person, place, or thing. For example, *a dog* could be any dog.

Indirect quote—quote that paraphrases or uses some of the original words but paraphrases other words.

Infinitive—the word "to" followed by a verb; for example, *to learn.* It does not have tense.

Informal communication—communication intended for an audience that expects standard form and some amount of correctness but not formality. An example is a newsletter.

Introduction—the first section of an essay in which the writer makes clear the subject of the essay as well as the ideas he or she will address.

Justification—spacing words of type so that the ends of printed lines are even. Left justification means lining up the left sides of lines of print; full justification means spacing words so the left and right sides of each line are even. In academic essays, left justification is preferable.

Key action words—words in a prompt that indicate what the student has to do to successfully complete the assignment. Also called action words.

Key focus words—words in a **prompt** that point you to specific ideas or issues you are to write about; also called focus words.

Keyword—an identifying word or phrase used in indexes or to tell **a search engine** what to look for.

Ladder of abstraction—metaphor describing the relationship of increasingly general or increasingly specific ideas.

Lead-in—the first part of an essay which introduces the topic of the essay and captures the readers' interest.

Listing—**prewriting** method in which the writer jots down words and phrases quickly to generate as many ideas as possible.

Main verb—the word that carries the meaning of a verb that consists of more than one word. For example, if the verb is *will learn,* the main verb is *learn.*

Map—a diagram or drawing that lets you visualize the connections between ideas, either in a reading or as a prewriting exercise.

Mapping—type of prewriting in which the writer diagrams the connections between ideas.

Mechanics—refers to spelling, apostrophes, capitalization, underlining and italics, abbreviations, and other details.

MLA—**documentation** style issued by the Modern Language Association, used primarily in the discipline of English.

Mode—a standard way of organizing written material.

Model—(n) an example you try to imitate; (v) to use an example for imitation.

Narration/Narrative writing—writing that describes a series of events or actions.

Non-count noun—a noun that cannot be counted. For example, *dirt* is a non-count noun; it cannot be counted.

Noun—a word that refers to a person, place, thing, or idea.

Organization—the order in which a writer presents his or her ideas.

Outline—list of ideas found in a piece of writing which shows how smaller, more specific ideas and details are related to larger, more general ones.

Overview—summary; a brief statement that repeats the major ideas included in a longer work.

Paragraph—a group of sentences which are closely related to each other and address a common idea.

Paraphrase—(v) to repeat an author's ideas using different words. (n) The author's ideas restated in different words.

Passive voice—verb in which the subject is acted upon. For example, in the sentence, *the window is broken*, the verb *is broken* is passive voice, since the subject *window* did not do the action of the verb.

Peer editing—process in which people who are equals (such as fellow students) help each other improve their writing.

Personal writing—writing produced only for the writer. Examples are journals, prewriting, shopping lists.

Persuade/Persuasion—to convince someone through your writing to believe in a certain way or take a certain action.

Plagiarism—using someone else's ideas, facts, or words as if they were your own.

Plan of development—list of ideas sometimes included in a thesis to indicate what will be covered in the **body** of an essay.

Point—idea a writer is trying to get across to an audience.

Point of view—perspective from which a narrative is told. This perspective can be first-person (using I) or third-person (using he or she).

Portfolio—collection of writing that represents a writer's work.

Prefix—syllable added to the beginning of a word that changes the meaning of the original word. For example, adding the prefix *anti-* to the word *inflammatory* creates a different word, *anti-inflammatory*, which has a different meaning.

Preposition—a word that connects a noun or pronoun to a noun or pronoun that appears earlier in the sentence. Most prepositions will make sense when inserted into the blank in the following sentence: *The airplane flew _____ the cloud.*

Prepositional phrase—a group of words which includes a preposition, the noun or pronoun after the preposition and any words that come in between the preposition and noun or pronoun.

Prewriting—writing used to generate ideas, may include **freewriting, listing, mapping,** and **questioning** as well as research.

Primary research—research in which the researcher collects data and interprets it; also called field research—for example, the experiment a scientist conducts is primary research.

Primary source—information that is studied directly by a researcher. For example, if a student is analyzing an essay by Mark Mathabane, this essay is the primary source since the student is reading and studying it.

Professional reading—reading done to keep up with new developments in a career field.

Prompt—a statement or question that directs you to write an essay.

Pronoun—a word that takes the place of a noun.

Proofreading—the final step in the writing process in which the writer corrects misspelled words, omitted words, punctuation errors or typographical errors.

Purpose—reason for producing a piece of writing.

Question word—word used to indicate the beginning of a question. For example, in the sentence *When did you leave?*, the question word is *when.*

Questioning—type of prewriting in which the writer asks and answers questions about the topic in an attempt to find deeper and more complicated meanings.

Quote—(v) to use words that someone else has already spoken or written. (n) the use of words that someone else has already spoken or written.

Revision—step in the writing process in which the writer makes big changes to improve thesis, ideas, organization, examples, or explanations.

Rhetorical analysis—an analysis in which the writer identifies and explains the strategies or techniques used in a piece of writing to get a point across or create an effect in a reader.

Rogerian argument—method of structuring an argument in which the writer states the audience's position, shows where he or she finds the position to be valid, explains where the position is not valid, presents his or her own position, and describes the advantages of this position.

Root—the central part of a word that contains the basic meaning.

Rough draft—a version of an essay that is not ready to be submitted.

Run-on sentence—two or more sentences joined together without the correct punctuation. Also called a **comma splice** or **fused sentence.**

Search engine—computerized research tool that finds resources related to specified words or fitting specified criteria.

Secondary research—research in which the researcher uses someone else's primary research and analyses it. For example, the newspaper reporter who summarizes the data a scientist collected in an experiment is conducting secondary research.

Secondary source—source which contains a report and analysis of someone else's primary research. For example, if you were writing about Mark Mathabane's essay "My Father's Tribal Rule", this essay would be your primary source and J.P. Myers' essay analyzing Mathabane's essay would be a secondary source.

Sentence boundaries—the beginning and end of a sentence.

Sentence fragment—part of a sentence punctuated as if it is a sentence. Also called a fragment.

Sentence-level editing—editing that focuses on the correctness of sentences, including fragments, comma splices, fused sentences, word choice, spelling, subject verb agreement, etc.

Skim—to read very quickly, not attempting to read every word but to pick up important words, main ideas, and the organization of a reading.

Simple verb—a one-word verb.

Source—place or person where information and ideas used in a piece of writing originated.

Spatial organization—organization which is based on physical or geographical layout. For example, a paragraph describing a room could be organized from left to right or ceiling to floor.

Spell checker—program within a word processor that indicates words which may be misspelled and suggests alternatives.

Standard English—dialect of English most commonly accepted in workplace and school settings.

Standard written English—dialect of written English most commonly accepted in workplace and school settings.

Story line—the events presented in a **narrative,** usually in chronological order (that is, the order in which the events happened).

Subject—the word that tells who or what performed the action of the verb.

Subject-verb agreement—the match of number (singular or plural) between a subject and verb.

Subordinating word—word used to join two sentences which causes a sentence fragment if the two sentences are not joined. These words are also called fragment words or relative pronouns.

Suffix—a syllable added to the end of a word that changes the meaning or part of speech of a word. For example, adding the suffix *-less* to the word *home* creates a new word, *homeless*, which has a different meaning.

Summary—a short statement that contains the main ideas of the original.

Support—information offered as proof of an idea. Support may be an example, an explanation, a fact, or a quote.

Survey—to look at the overall content, organization, and form of a reading.

Technical description—description which provides pictorial data in an orderly manner that reveals the purpose, function, or appearance of the subject. This type of description is most often found in instructional materials and manuals.

Tense—form or part of a verb that indicates the time of an action or condition.

Thesis—main idea of a piece of writing.

Tone—the attitude of the writer toward the subject and reader as revealed in a piece of writing.

Topic sentence—sentence in a paragraph that announces the specific subject and focus of a paragraph; also called a main idea.

Transition—word, phrase, sentence, or paragraph that connects new information that follows to old information that has already been presented.

Transitional word—word that provides information about the relationship between the ideas that come before and after it.

Usage—the way a word is used; *good usage* refers to using words in generally accepted ways.

Verb—a word that shows action or state of being. Verbs are the part of the sentence that changes when the time of the sentence is changed.

Verb phrase—a verb containing more than one word (the main verb and at least one helping or auxiliary verb). For example, in the sentence "I would have ridden my bicycle yesterday", the verb phrase is "would have ridden".

Works Cited page—list of articles, essays, and books used in an essay; included at the end of the essay.

Text and Photo Credits

"The Sanctuary of School" by Lynda Barry from *The New York Times*, January 5, 1992, "Educational Life" section. Copyright © 1992 by the New York Times Co. Reprinted by permission.

Elizabeth Wong, "The Struggle to Be an All-American Girl," *Los Angeles Times*, September 7, 1980. Copyright 1980 the Los Angeles Times. Reprinted by permission.

Lynell Hancock, "The Have and Have-Nots," *Newsweek*, February 27, 1995. Copyright 1995. All Rights Reserved. Reprinted by permission.

Jon D. Hull, "Slow Descent Into Hell," *Time*, February 2, 1987. © 1987 Time, Inc. Reprinted by permission.

Ernest L. Wiggins, "Experiencing Poverty Might Do Us All Good," *The State*, September 21, 1998. Copyright 1998. Reprinted by permission. Mr. Wiggins is an associate professor at the University of South Carolina College of Journalism and Mass Communication.

Cindi Ross Scoppe, "Every Choice Has its Consequences, Or Should Have," *The State*, March 18, 1995. Coyright 1995. Reprinted by permission of the author.

"Money for Morality" by Mary Arguelles. Reprinted by permission of the author.

Amitai Etzioni, "Restoring the Moral Voice: Virtue and Community Pressure," *Current*, September 1994. Copyright 1994. Reprinted by permission of the author.

All pages from THE PERIL OF OBEDIENCE ABRIDGED AND ADAPTED FROM OBEDIENCE TO AUTHORITY by STANLEY MILGRAM. Published in *Harper's Magazine*. Copyright © 1974 by Stanley Milgram. Reprinted by permission of HarperCollins Publishers, Inc.

"On Being Cripple," from *Plaintext*, by Nancy Mairs. Copyright © 1986 The Arizona Board of Regents. Reprinted by permission of the University of Arizona Press.

Linda Robinson, "Hispanics Don't Exist," *US News & World Report*. May 11, 1998. Copyright 1998 **US News & World Report**. Reprinted by permission.

Scott Russell Sanders, "The Men We Carry in Our Minds," copyright © 1984 by Scott Russell Sanders; first appeared in Milkweed Chronicle from THE PARADISE OF BOMBS; reprinted by permission of the author and the Virginia Kidd Agency, Inc.

Geoffrey Cowley, "Flunk the Gene Test and Lose Your Insurance: Genetic Discrimination," *Newsweek*, December 23, 1996. Copyright 1996. All Rights Reserved. Reprinted by permission.

Madeleine J. Nash, "The Case For Cloning," *Time*, February 9, 1998. © 1998 Time, Inc. Reprinted by permission.

"Genetic Testing Set for Takeoff" by Rachel Nowak from *Science*, July 22, 1994, Vol. 265, Number 5171, pp. 464–467. Copyright © 1994 by American Association for the Advancement of Science. Reprinted with permission.

Karen Wright, "Human in the Age of Mechanical Reproduction," *Discover*, May 1998. Karen Wright/© 1998. Reprinted with permission of Discover Magazine.

Photos

page 1: © Bob Krist/CORBIS; 39: *The Boston Globe*; 40: Courtesy of Simon & Schuster; 44: Photo by Joshua Oppenheimer; 54: © Bettmann/CORBIS; 59: Bob Daemmrich/Stock Boston; 225: B.W. Hoffmann/Unicorn Stock Photos; 253, 347, 433: The Image Works

Index